T0235396

Lecture Notes in Computer Science   12145

More information about this series at http://www.springer.com/series/7407

Ying Tan · Yuhui Shi · Milan Tuba (Eds.)

Advances in Swarm Intelligence

11th International Conference, ICSI 2020
Belgrade, Serbia, July 14–20, 2020
Proceedings

 Springer

Editors
Ying Tan (iD)
Peking University
Beijing, China

Milan Tuba
Singidunum University
Belgrade, Serbia

Yuhui Shi
Southern University of Science
and Technology
Shenzhen, China

ISSN 0302-9743   ISSN 1611-3349   (electronic)
Lecture Notes in Computer Science
ISBN 978-3-030-53955-9   ISBN 978-3-030-53956-6   (eBook)
https://doi.org/10.1007/978-3-030-53956-6

LNCS Sublibrary: SL1 – Theoretical Computer Science and General Issues

This Springer imprint is published by the registered company Springer Nature Switzerland AG
The registered company address is: Gewerbestrasse 11, 6330 Cham, Switzerland

Preface

This book, LNCS vol. 12145, constitutes the proceedings of the 11th International Conference on Swarm Intelligence (ICSI 2020) held virtually online during July 14–20, 2020, due to the pandemic of COVID-19.

The theme of ICSI 2020 was "Serving Life with Swarm Intelligence." ICSI 2020 provided an excellent opportunity and/or an academic forum for academics and practitioners to present and discuss the latest scientific results and methods, innovative ideas, and advantages in theories, technologies, and applications in swarm intelligence. The technical program covered a number of aspects of swarm intelligence and its related areas.

ICSI 2020 was the eleventh international gathering in the world for researchers working on most aspects of swarm intelligence, following successful events in Chiang Mai (ICSI 2019), Shanghai (ICSI 2018), Fukuoka (ICSI 2017), Bali (ICSI 2016), Beijing (ICSI-CCI 2015), Hefei (ICSI 2014), Harbin (ICSI 2013), Shenzhen (ICSI 2012), Chongqing (ICSI 2011), and Beijing (ICSI 2010), which provided a high-level academic forum for participants to disseminate their new research findings and discuss emerging areas of research. It also created a stimulating environment for participants to interact and exchange information on future challenges and opportunities in the field of swarm intelligence research. ICSI 2020 was held in conjunction with the 5th International Conference on Data Mining and Big Data (DMBD 2020) in Belgrade, Serbia, sharing common mutual ideas, promoting transverse fusion, and stimulating innovation.

ICSI 2020 was originally planned to be held at Singidunum University, Serbia, but after carefully evaluating most announcements and guidance regarding COVID-19, as well as restrictions on overseas travel released by relevant national departments, the ICSI 2020 Organizing Committee made the decision to host ICSI 2020 as a virtual conference, keeping the scheduled dates of July 14–19, 2020. The ICSI 2020 technical team provided the ability for the authors of accepted papers to present their work through an interactive online platform or video replay. The presentations by accepted authors will be made available to all registered attendees online.

ICSI 2020 received 127 submissions and invited submissions from about 291 authors in 24 countries and regions (Brazil, Bulgaria, Cameroon, Canada, China, Colombia, Ecuador, Germany, Greece, India, Iran, Italy, Japan, Mexico, Peru, Russia, Serbia, Slovakia, Taiwan (SAR China), Thailand, Turkey, the UK, the USA, and Venezuela) across 6 continents (Asia, Europe, North America, South America, Africa, and Oceania). Each submission was reviewed by at least 2 reviewers, and on average 2.4 reviewers. Based on rigorous reviews by the Program Committee members and reviewers, 63 high-quality papers were selected for publication in this proceedings volume with an acceptance rate of 49.6%. The papers are organized into 12 cohesive sections covering major topics of swarm intelligence research and its development and applications.

On behalf of the Organizing Committee of ICSI 2020, we would like to express our sincere thanks to the International Association of Swarm and Evolutionary Intelligence (IASEI)(iasei.org), which is the premier international scholarly society devoted to advancing the theories, algorithms, real-world applications, and developments of swarm intelligence and evolutionary intelligence. We would also like to thank Peking University, Southern University of Science and Technology, and Singidunum University for their cosponsorship, and to Computational Intelligence Laboratory of Peking University and IEEE Beijing Chapter for its technical co-sponsorship, as well as to our supporters of International Neural Network Society, World Federation on Soft Computing, Beijing Xinghui Hi-Tech Co., and Springer Nature.

We would also like to thank the members of the Advisory Committee for their guidance, the members of the International Program Committee and additional reviewers for reviewing the papers, and the members of the Publication Committee for checking the accepted papers in a short period of time. We are particularly grateful to the proceedings publisher Springer for publishing the proceedings in the prestigious series of *Lecture Notes in Computer Science*. Moreover, we wish to express our heartfelt appreciation to the plenary speakers, session chairs, and student helpers. In addition, there are still many more colleagues, associates, friends, and supporters who helped us in immeasurable ways; we express our sincere gratitude to them all. Last but not the least, we would like to thank all the speakers, authors, and participants for their great contributions that made ICSI 2020 successful and all the hard work worthwhile.

June 2020

Ying Tan
Yuhui Shi
Milan Tuba

Organization

General Co-chairs

Ying Tan	Peking University, China
Milan Tuba	Singidunum University, Serbia

Program Committee Chair

Yuhui Shi	Southern University of Science and Technology, China

Advisory Committee Chairs

Milovan Stanisic	Singidunum University, Serbia
Russell C. Eberhart	IUPUI, USA
Gary G. Yen	Oklahoma State University, USA

Technical Committee Co-chairs

Haibo He	University of Rhode Island, USA
Kay Chen Tan	City University of Hong Kong, China
Nikola Kasabov	Aukland University of Technology, New Zealand
Ponnuthurai Nagaratnam Suganthan	Nanyang Technological University, Singapore
Xiaodong Li	RMIT University, Australia
Hideyuki Takagi	Kyushu University, Japan
M. Middendorf	University of Leipzig, Germany
Mengjie Zhang	Victoria University of Wellington, New Zealand

Plenary Session Co-chairs

Andreas Engelbrecht	University of Pretoria, South Africa
Chaoming Luo	University of Mississippi, USA

Invited Session Co-chairs

Andres Iglesias	University of Cantabria, Spain
Haibin Duan	Beihang University, China
Junfeng Chen	Hohai University, China

Special Sessions Chairs

Ben Niu   Shenzhen University, China
Yan Pei   University of Aizu, Japan
Qirong Tang   Tongji University, China

Tutorial Co-chairs

Junqi Zhang   Tongji University, China
Shi Cheng   Shanxi Normal University, China
Yinan Guo   China University of Mining and Technology, China

Publications Co-chairs

Swagatam Das   Indian Statistical Institute, India
Radu-Emil Precup   Politehnica University of Timisoara, Romania

Publicity Co-chairs

Yew-Soon Ong   Nanyang Technological University, Singapore
Carlos Coello   CINVESTAV-IPN, Mexico
Yaochu Jin   University of Surrey, UK
Rossi Kamal   GERIOT, Bangladesh
Dongbin Zhao   Institute of Automation, Chinese Academy of Sciences,
                             China

Finance and Registration Chairs

Andreas Janecek   University of Vienna, Austria
Suicheng Gu   Google Corporation, USA

Local Arrangement Chairs

Mladen Veinovic   Singidunum University, Serbia
Nebojsa Bacanin   Singidunum University, Serbia
Eva Tuba   Singidunum University, Serbia

Conference Secretariat

Renlong Chen   Peking University, China

Program Committee

Ashik Ahmed   Islamic University of Technology, Bangladesh
Abdelmalek Amine   GeCoDe Laboratory, Tahar Moulay University
                             of Saida, Algeria

Esther Andrés	INTA, USA
Sabri Arik	Istanbul University, Turkey
Nebojsa Bacanin	Singidunum University, Serbia
Carmelo J. A. Bastos Filho	University of Pernambuco, Brazil
Sandeep Bhongade	G.S. Institute of Technology, India
Sujin Bureerat	Khon Kaen University, Thailand
David Camacho	Universidad Politécnica de Madrid, Spain
Bin Cao	Tsinghua University, China
Abdelghani Chahmi	Universite des Sciences et Technologie d'Oran, Algeria
Mu-Song Chen	Dayeh University, Taiwan
Walter Chen	National Taipei University of Technology, Taiwan
Long Cheng	Institute of Automation, Chinese Academy of Sciences, China
Prithviraj Dasgupta	U. S. Naval Research Laboratory, USA
Haibin Duan	Beijing University of Aeronautics and Astronautics, China
Andries Engelbrecht	University of Stellenbosch, South Africa
Amir H. Gandomi	University of Technology Sydney, Australia
Hongyuan Gao	Harbin Engineering University, China
Shangce Gao	University of Toyama, Japan
Ping Guo	Beijing Normal University, China
Ahmed Hafaifa	University of Djelfa, Algeria
Guosheng Hao	Jiangsu Normal University, China
Weiwei Hu	Peking University, China
Changan Jiang	Ritsumeikan University, Japan
Mingyan Jiang	Shandong University, China
Colin Johnson	University of Nottingham, UK
Yasushi Kambayashi	Nippon Institute of Technology, Japan
Vivek Kumar	Università degli Studi di Cagliari, Italy
Xiujuan Lei	Shaanxi Normal University, China
Bin Li	University of Science and Technology of China, China
Jing Liang	Zhengzhou University, China
Ju Liu	Shandong University, China
Wenlian Lu	Fudan University, China
Chaomin Luo	Mississippi State University, USA
Wenjian Luo	Harbin Institute of Technology (Shenzhen), China
Chengying Mao	Jiangxi University of Finance and Economics, China
Sreeja N. K.	PSG College of Technology, India
Endre Pap	Singidunum University, Serbia
Yan Pei	University of Aizu, Japan
Thomas Potok	ORNL, USA
Radu-Emil Precup	Politehnica University of Timisoara, Romania
Boyang Qu	Zhongyuan University, China
Ivana Strumberger	Singidunum University, Serbia
Ponnuthurai Suganthan	Nanyang Technological University, Singapore
Ying Tan	Peking University, China

Akash Tayal	IGDTUW, India
Eva Tuba	University of Belgrade, Serbia
Mladen Veinović	Singidunum University, Serbia
Guoyin Wang	Chongqing University of Posts and Telecommunications, China
Yan Wang	The Ohio State University, USA
Benlian Xu	Changshu Institute of Technology, China
Yu Xue	Nanjing University of Information Science and Technology, China
Yingjie Yang	De Montfort University, UK
Peng-Yeng Yin	National Chi Nan University, Taiwan
Jun Yu	Kyushu University, Japan
Ling Yu	Jinan University, China
Jie Zhang	Newcastle University, UK
Junqi Zhang	Tongji University, China
Qieshi Zhang	Shenzhen Institutes of Advanced Technology, Chinese Academy of Sciences, China
Xinchao Zhao	Beijing University of Posts and Telecommunications, China
Dejan Zivkovic	Singidunum University, Serbia
Miodrag Zivkovic	Singidunum University, Serbia

Additional Reviewers

Araújo, Danilo
Macedo, Mariana
Oliveira, Marcos
Siqueira, Hugo
Thomas, Kent

Contents

Particle Swarm Optimization

Ant Colony Optimization

Brain Storm Optimization Algorithm

Bacterial Foraging Optimization

Genetic Algorithm and Evolutionary Computation

Multi-objective Optimization

Machine Learning

Data Mining

Swarm Intelligence and Nature-Inspired Computing

Swarm Intelligence in Data Science: Applications, Opportunities and Challenges

Jian Yang[1], Liang Qu[1], Yang Shen[1], Yuhui Shi[1(✉)], Shi Cheng[2],
Junfeng Zhao[3], and Xiaolong Shen[3]

[1] Department of Computer Science and Engineering,
Southern University of Science and Technology, Shenzhen 518055, China
shiyh@sustech.edu.cn
[2] School of Computer Science, Shaanxi Normal University, Xi'an 710119, China
[3] 2012 Laboratories, Huawei Technologies Co., Ltd., Shenzhen 518129, China

Abstract. The Swarm Intelligence (SI) algorithms have been proved
to be a comprehensive method to solve complex optimization problems
by simulating the emergence behaviors of biological swarms. Nowadays,
data science is getting more and more attention, which needs quick management and analysis of massive data. Most traditional methods can
only be applied to continuous and differentiable functions. As a set of
population-based approaches, it is proven by some recent research works
that the SI algorithms have great potential for relevant tasks in this field.
In order to gather better insight into the utilization of these methods in
data science and to provide a further reference for future researches, this
paper focuses on the relationship between data science and swarm intelligence. After introducing the mainstream swarm intelligence algorithms
and their common characteristics, both the theoretical and real-world
applications in the literature which utilize the swarm intelligence to the
related domains of data analytics are reviewed. Based on the summary of
the existing works, this paper also analyzes the opportunities and challenges in this field, which attempts to shed some light on designing more
effective algorithms to solve the problems in data science for real-world
applications.

Keywords: Swarm Intelligence · Data science · Evolutionary
computation · Unified Swarm Intelligence

This work is partially supported by National Key R&D Program of China under the
Grant No. 2017YFC0804003, National Science Foundation of China under grant
number 61761136008, 61806119, Shenzhen Peacock Plan under Grant No. KQTD2016
112514355531, Program for Guangdong Introducing Innovative and Entrepreneurial
Teams under grant number 2017ZT07X386, the Science and Technology Innovation
Committee Foundation of Shenzhen under the Grant No. ZDSYS201703031748284,
Natural Science Basic Research Plan In Shaanxi Province of China under grant No.
2019JM-320, Huawei HIRP Open Project under grant No. HO2019040806003P118,
Guangdong Provincial Key Laboratory under Grant No. 2020B121201001, and
SUSTech Artificial Intelligence Institute (SAINT).

Y. Tan et al. (Eds.): ICSI 2020, LNCS 12145, pp. 3–14, 2020.
https://doi.org/10.1007/978-3-030-53956-6_1

1   Introduction

Data science has been widely concerned in recent years. One of the most important aspects of data science is data analytics, which aims to automatic extraction of knowledge from massive data. Traditional model-based methods are mainly on fitting the collected data to some predefined mathematical models. However, these models may fail when encountering problem varieties such as the volume, the dynamical changes, noise, and so forth. With the increase of the above varieties, traditional data processing approaches will become inefficient or even ineffective. Because of the above difficulties, new and efficient methods should be developed to deal with data analysis tasks [11]. Now the mainstream methods are shifting from traditional model-driven to data-driven paradigms. Many applications in data science can be transferred to optimization problems. Thus it requires the algorithms to have the ability to search the solution space and find the optimums [9]. Traditional model-based methods need the problems that can be written into the form of continuous and differentiable functions. However, in the face of a large amount of data and complex tasks, it is often difficult to achieve.

The population-based meta-heuristic algorithms are good at solving those problems, which the traditional methods can not deal with or, at least, be challenging to solve [10]. Swarm Intelligence (SI), a kind of meta-heuristic algorithms, is attracting more and more attention and has been proven to be sufficient to handle the large scale, dynamic, multi-objective problems in data analytics. As shown in Fig. 1, there are mainly two categories of approaches that utilize SI algorithms in data science [41]. The first approach uses swarm intelligence as a parameter tuning/optimizing method of data mining technologies may including machine learning, statistics, and others. The second category directly applies the SI algorithms on data organization, i.e., move data instances place on a low-dimensional feature space to reach a suitable clustering or reduce the dimensionality of the data.

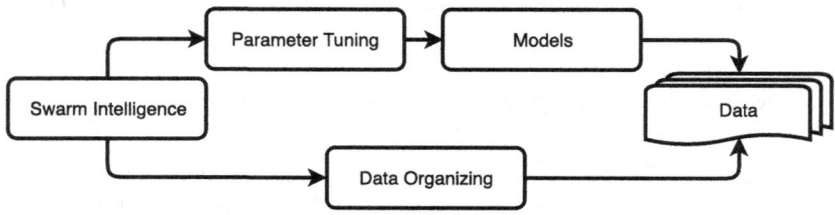

Fig. 1. Two approaches of Swarm Intelligence for data science

Swarm Intelligence is a group of nature-inspired searching and optimization techniques that studies collective intelligence in a population of low complexity individuals [32]. The SI algorithms are inspired by the interactions among individuals within a group or several groups, which involves the patterns of competition and cooperation [16]. SI algorithms use a population of individuals to search in a problem domain. Each individual represents a potential solution for the problem being optimized. During a guided search process, SI algorithms maintain and improve a collection of potential solutions successively until some predefined stopping condition is met, i.e., either the result is acceptable, or the number of iterations is reached [26].

In order to gather better insight into the utilization of these methods in data science and to provide a further reference for future researches, this paper focuses on the data science related works that utilizing swarm intelligence in the past few years. After introducing the mainstream swarm intelligence algorithms and their common characteristics, both the theoretical and real-world applications in the literature which utilize the swarm intelligence to the related domains of data analytics are reviewed. Based on the summary of the existing works, this paper also analyzes the opportunities and challenges in this field, which attempts to shed some light on designing more effective algorithms to solve the problems in data science for real-world applications. The remaining of the paper is organized as follows. Section 2 briefly reviews the development of swarm intelligence and some major algorithms in this field. Section 3 introduces some theoretical applications in the literature that adopt swarm intelligence algorithms in data science. Section 4 gives a set of real-world applications. The opportunities and challenges of applying SI algorithms to data science are discussed in Sect. 5, followed by the conclusions reached in Sect. 6.

2 Swarm Intelligence Algorithms

2.1 General Procedure of SI Algorithms

SI Algorithms is a set of artificial intelligence techniques inspired by biological swarm behaviors at both macro and micro levels. They generally have self-organizing and decentralizing paradigms with the characteristics of scalability, adaptability, robustness, and individual simplicity. In SI algorithms, a population of individuals, which indicates potential candidate solutions, cooperating among themselves and statistically becoming better and better over iterations, then eventually finding good enough solutions [45]. In recent years, a large number of swarm intelligence methods have been proposed. These methods have different inspiration sources and various operations. In general, these different operations are trying to balance the convergence and diversity of the search process, i.e., the balance between exploration and exploitation.

The general procedure of swarm intelligence algorithms can be summarized in Algorithm 1. Starting from the random initialization of a population of individuals in solution space, followed by the corresponding evaluation process and new solution generation process, after a certain number of iterations, swarm intelligence algorithms can eventually find acceptable solutions.

As a general principle, the expected fitness value of a solution should improve as more computational resources in time and/or space are given. More desirable,

Algorithm 1. General procedure of swarm intelligence algorithms

1 Population Initialization: Generate random solutions for an optimized problem, repair solutions if solutions violate any of the constraints;
2 Evaluate all initialized individuals;
3 **while** *not terminated* **do**
4 | Reproduce individuals to form a new population;
5 | Evaluate the fitness of each solution;
6 | Select solutions with better fitness values;
7 |_ Update solutions in the archive;

Result: Relatively good solution(s)

the quality of the solution should improve monotonically over iterations, i.e., the fitness value of the solution at time $t+1$ should be no worse than the fitness at time t.

2.2 Developments

In the past 30 years, a large number of swarm intelligence algorithms have emerged. They get inspiration from different phenomena, and design corresponding new solution generation operations with the considerations of balancing convergence and diversity of the swarm. As shown in Table 1, the source of inspirations are varying from human society (BSO, TLBO), animals (BA, GWO, MA, LOA), insects and birds (PSO, ACO, ABC, FA, CS, GSO), bacterias (BFO), and also some human-made phenomenon (FWA).

With the increasing prominence of NP-hard problems, it is almost impossible to find the optimal solutions in real-time. The number of potential solutions to these problems is often infinite. In this case, it is essential to find a feasible solution within the time limit. SI algorithms have found its practicability in the practical application of solving nonlinear problems in almost all fields of science, engineering, and industrial fields: From data mining to optimization, computational intelligence, business planning, bioinformatics, as well as industrial applications. Now is the era of big data, those mentioned above scientific and engineering problems, more or less, are related to data issues. Swarm intelligence has made a lot of successful applications in data relevant applications. Meanwhile, with the increasing dynamics, noises, and complexity of tasks, there still are many opportunities along with challenges in the applications of swarm intelligence with data sciences.

3 Theoretical Applications

For decades, data mining has been a hot academic topic in the field of computer science statistics. As mentioned, the SI algorithm is mainly used in data mining tasks in two forms: parameter tuning or data organizing. Main applications, including dimensionality reduction, classification, and clustering, as well as automated machine learning.

Table 1. Some Swarm Intelligence algorithms with source of inspiration

Algorithms	Source of inspiration	
Brain Storm Opt., BSO [49]	Brainstorming process of human	Human society
Teaching-learning-based Opt., TLBO [48]	How teachers influence learners	
Particle Swarm Opt., PSO [31]	Bird flocking and foraging	Insects, birds, etc.
Ant Colony Opt., ACO [15]	Ants foraging mechanisms	
Artificial Bee Colony, ABC [29]	Foraging behavior of honey bees	
Firefly Algorithms, FA [66]	Bioluminescence of fireflies	
Glowworm Swarm Opt., GSO [36]	Luciferin induced glow of a glowworm	
Cuckoo Search, CS [67]	Obligate brood parasitism in cuckoos	
Bat Algorithm, BA [68]	Echolocation behaviors of micro-bats	Animals
Grey Wolf Opt., GWO [42]	Leadership and hunting of grey wolves	
Monkey Algorithm, MA [73]	Climbing techniques used by monkeys	
Lion Opt. Algorithm, LOA [69]	Cooperation characteristics of lions	
Bacterial Foraging Opt, BFO [13]	Group foraging behavior of bacteria	Microscopic
Fireworks Algorithm, FWA [57]	Fireworks explosion	Other

3.1   Dimensionality Reduction

Dimensionality reduction is the process of reducing the number of random variables or attributes in a dataset under consideration. It plays a vital role in data preprocessing for data mining. There are generally two operations for dimensionality reduction: feature selection and feature extraction. Feature selection is a process of selecting an optimal subset of relevant features for use in model construction. While feature extraction is a process of project original data in a high dimensional space onto a smaller space. The accuracy of a model will be enhanced by using wisely selected/projected features rather than all available features in a large amount of data.

Since feature selection is an NP-hard combinatorial optimization problem, SI algorithms are found to be a promise option to solve those kinds of problems. A lot of related works has emerged recently, the following are some examples: Gu et al. proposed a feature selection method for high dimensional classification based on a very recent PSO variant, known as Competitive Swarm Optimizer (CSO) [23]. Hang et al. designed an FA based method for feature selection, which has the ability to prevent premature convergence [72]. Pourpanah et al. combine the Fuzzy ARTMAP (FAM) model with the BSO algorithm for feature selection tasks [47], etc. A more detailed survey about SI powered feature selection can be found in [44].

3.2   Classification and Clustering

Classification and clustering are essential aspects of data science. They have been studied widely in the domain of statistics, neural networks, machine learning, and knowledgeable systems over the decades. In general, classification is to predict the target class by analyzing the training dataset, while clustering is to group the similar kind of targets by considering the most satisfying condition.

The SI applications in those two aspects are mainly related to parameter tuning. For classification, works can be found in literature that combine SI algorithms with regression model [53], support vector machine [7,14,60], k-nearest neighbor classifiers [58,65], Decision trees [3,35], as well as the neural networks [30,62]. For clustering, some recent works are related to utilizing SI with k-means [28,59,61], c-means [21], and other linear or non-linear clustering algorithms [19,27].

3.3 Automated Machine Learning

In the past decade, the research and application of machine learning have seen explosive growth, especially the Deep neural networks (DNNs) [37] has made great progress in many application fields. However, the performance of many machine learning methods is very sensitive to too many design decisions. In particular, the architecture designing of DNNs is very complex and highly rely on the experts' prior knowledge. To address this problem, many SI based methods are proposed to automatically design DNNs [54].

Wang *et al.* [64] propose an efficient particle swarm optimisation (EPSOCNN) approach to automatically design the architectures of convolutional neural networks (CNNs). Specifically, in order to reduce the computation cost, EPSOCNN minimises the hyperparameter space of CNNs to a single block and evaluates the candidate CNNs with the small subset of the training set. Wang *et al.* [63] propose a multi-objective evolutionary CNNs (MOCNN) to search the non-dominant CNN architectures at the Pareto front in terms of the classification accuracy objective and the computational cost objective. It introduces a novel encoding strategy to encode CNNs and utilizes a multi-objective particle swarm optimization (OMOPSO) to optimize the candidate CNNs architectures.

4   Real-World Applications

Social Community Network Analysis. Social network analysis plays an important role in many real-world problems, such as the community detection techniques [20,46] which aims to mine the implicit community structures in the networks. Recently, many SI methods have shown a promising potential in many community detection problems. Lyu *et al.* [40] propose a novel local community detection method called evolutionary-based local community detection (ECLD), which utilizes the entire obtained information and PSO algorithm to find the local community structures in the complex networks. Sun *et al.* [55] introduce a Parallel Self-organizing Overlapping Community Detection (PSOCD) method inspired by the swarm intelligence system to detect the overlapping communities in the large scale dynamic complex networks. It treats the complex networks as a decentralized, self-organized, and self-evolving system. They can iteratively find the community structures. Other releavant works can be refer to [6,22,25].

Scheduling and Routing. Scheduling and routing problems are very common in real world, as long as there are resources to manage. For example, the PSO algorithm was used in power systems for demand response management [17], consumer demand management [38], etc.

Internet of Things. Internet of Things (IoT) is another real-world application in which SI algorithms have been widely used [5]. For example, in IoT-based systems, the SI algorithm has been used for task scheduling [4]. In IoT-based smart cities, SI algorithms have been used due to its population-based feature to make the system flexible and scalable [70].

Bioinformatics is an interdisciplinary field that develops algorithms and software tools for processing biological data samples. Various biological problems could be represented as an optimization problem and solved by SI algorithms. For example, the protein design problem could be represented as a combinatorial optimization problem [24]. More information is summarized in [56].

Resource Allocation. Resource allocation is the process of allocating and managing assets in an optimized way to support the strategic objectives of an organization. SI algorithms have been used in many related applications such as Cloud service resource allocation [8], wireless network planning [2], etc.

Others. Apart from the real-world applications discussed above, SI algorithms have also been applied to many other real-world systems that are data related. For example, the wind farm decision system [74] to reduce the cost of wind farms, autonomous DDoS attack detection [33], anomaly intrusion detection [18], image analysis [34,51], facial recognition [43], Medical Image Segmentation [52], and natural language processing [1,39], etc.

5   Opportunities and Challenges

Unified Swarm Intelligence. Unified Swarm Intelligence Are there any universal rules behind this growing field? What are the fundamental components of a good swarm intelligence algorithm to have? There are dozens of SI algorithms proposed so far and sharing similar operations on solving problems. Is there a unified framework for SI algorithms that has the ability to develop its learning capacity that can better solve an optimization problem which is unknown at the algorithms design or implementation time [50]. How to correctly identify and extract the fundamental components of SI algorithms, so that they can form new algorithms automatically according to the character of the problem on hand, is a challenge. Some efforts are trying to solve this problem [12,50,71], but more work is needed to make it a reality.

Handling High Dimensional and Dynamical Data. The "curse of dimensionality" happens on high-dimensional data mining problems when the dimension of the data space increases. For example, the nearest neighbor approaches are instrumental in categorization. However, for high dimensional data, it is complicated to solve the similarity search problem due to the computational complexity, which was caused by the increase of dimensionality. Furthermore, when the problems are in non-stationary environments, or uncertain environments, i.e., the conditions of data dynamically change over time, additional measures must be taken, so that swarm intelligence algorithms are still able to solve satisfactorily dynamic problems.

SI Based AutoML. As mentioned before, swarm intelligence algorithms can not only be used for automatic optimization of hyper-parameters of the machine learning model, but also the automated design of the model structure. With the development of AutoML, the swarm intelligence algorithm has great potential in this field. However, in addition to hyper-parameter optimization, the representation of learning model and the mechanism of model evaluation are also come with challenges.

6   Conclusion

This paper has reviewed related works that applying swarm intelligence algorithms in data science. The fundamentals and developments of swarm intelligence are briefly summarized. The theoretical applications such as SI based dimensionality reduction, classification, clustering, as well as automated machine learning are also introduced. A short review of real-world applications, including social community network analysis, scheduling and routing, internet of things, bioinformatics, and resource allocation, are also given, then followed by the opportunities and challenges in this field. Generally speaking, the swarm intelligence algorithm has been widely used in the field of data science in the past decades, including theoretical and practical applications. Moreover, with the development of artificial intelligence technology and data science, swarm intelligence algorithms have great opportunities in different aspects of data science. Nevertheless, it also faces a series of challenges, which need more in-depth research.

References

1. Abualigah, L.M., Khader, A.T., Hanandeh, E.S.: A new feature selection method to improve the document clustering using particle swarm optimization algorithm. J. Comput. Sci. **25**, 456–466 (2018)
2. Ari, A.A.A., Gueroui, A., Titouna, C., Thiare, O., Aliouat, Z.: Resource allocation scheme for 5G C-RAN: a swarm intelligence based approach. Comput. Netw. **165**, 106957 (2019)
3. Bida, I., Aouat, S.: A new approach based on bat algorithm for inducing optimal decision trees classifiers. In: Rocha, Á., Serrhini, M. (eds.) EMENA-ISTL 2018. SIST, vol. 111, pp. 631–640. Springer, Cham (2019). https://doi.org/10.1007/978-3-030-03577-8_69

4. Boveiri, H.R., Khayami, R., Elhoseny, M., Gunasekaran, M.: An efficient swarm-intelligence approach for task scheduling in cloud-based internet of things applications. J. Ambient Intell. Humaniz. Comput. **10**(9), 3469–3479 (2019)
5. Chakraborty, T., Datta, S.K.: Application of swarm intelligence in internet of things. In: 2017 IEEE International Symposium on Consumer Electronics (ISCE), pp. 67–68. IEEE (2017)
6. Honghao, C., Zuren, F., Zhigang, R.: Community detection using ant colony optimization. In: 2013 IEEE Congress on Evolutionary Computation, Cancun, Mexico, pp. 3072–3078. IEEE (2013)
7. Chen, H.L., Yang, B., Wang, G., Wang, S.J., Liu, J., Liu, D.Y.: Support vector machine based diagnostic system for breast cancer using swarm intelligence. J. Med. Syst. **36**(4), 2505–2519 (2012)
8. Cheng, S., et al.: Cloud service resource allocation with particle swarm optimization algorithm. In: He, C., Mo, H., Pan, L., Zhao, Y. (eds.) BIC-TA 2017. CCIS, vol. 791, pp. 523–532. Springer, Singapore (2017). https://doi.org/10.1007/978-981-10-7179-9_41
9. Cheng, S., Liu, B., Shi, Y., Jin, Y., Li, B.: Evolutionary computation and big data: key challenges and future directions. In: Tan, Y., Shi, Y. (eds.) DMBD 2016. LNCS, vol. 9714, pp. 3–14. Springer, Cham (2016). https://doi.org/10.1007/978-3-319-40973-3_1
10. Cheng, S., Liu, B., Ting, T., Qin, Q., Shi, Y., Huang, K.: Survey on data science with population-based algorithms. Big Data Anal. **1**(1), 3 (2016)
11. Cheng, S., Shi, Y., Qin, Q., Bai, R.: Swarm intelligence in big data analytics. In: Yin, H., et al. (eds.) IDEAL 2013. LNCS, vol. 8206, pp. 417–426. Springer, Heidelberg (2013). https://doi.org/10.1007/978-3-642-41278-3_51
12. Chu, X., Wu, T., Weir, J.D., Shi, Y., Niu, B., Li, L.: Learning-interaction-diversification framework for swarm intelligence optimizers: a unified perspective. Neural Comput. Appl. **32**, 1–21 (2018). https://doi.org/10.1007/s00521-018-3657-0
13. Das, S., Biswas, A., Dasgupta, S., Abraham, A.: Bacterial foraging optimization algorithm: theoretical foundations, analysis, and applications. In: Abraham, A., Hassanien, A.E., Siarry, P., Engelbrecht, A. (eds.) Foundations of Computational Intelligence, vol. 3, pp. 23–55. Springer, Heidelberg (2009). https://doi.org/10.1007/978-3-642-01085-9_2
14. Ding, S., An, Y., Zhang, X., Wu, F., Xue, Y.: Wavelet twin support vector machines based on glowworm swarm optimization. Neurocomputing **225**, 157–163 (2017)
15. Dorigo, M., Birattari, M., Stutzle, T.: Ant colony optimization. IEEE Comput. Intell. Mag. **1**(4), 28–39 (2006)
16. Eberhart, R.C., Shi, Y., Kennedy, J.: Swarm Intelligence. Elsevier, London (2001)
17. Faria, P., Vale, Z., Soares, J., Ferreira, J.: Demand response management in power systems using particle swarm optimization. IEEE Intell. Syst. **28**(4), 43–51 (2011)
18. Feng, Y., Wu, Z.F., Wu, K.G., Xiong, Z.Y., Zhou, Y.: An unsupervised anomaly intrusion detection algorithm based on swarm intelligence. In: 2005 International Conference on Machine Learning and Cybernetics, vol. 7, pp. 3965–3969. IEEE (2005)
19. Figueiredo, E., Macedo, M., Siqueira, H.V., Santana Jr., C.J., Gokhale, A., Bastos-Filho, C.J.: Swarm intelligence for clustering-a systematic review with new perspectives on data mining. Eng. Appl. Artif. Intell. **82**, 313–329 (2019)
20. Fortunato, S.: Community detection in graphs. Phys. Rep. **486**(3–5), 75–174 (2010). arXiv:0906.0612

21. Fuchs, C., Spolaor, S., Nobile, M.S., Kaymak, U.: A swarm intelligence approach to avoid local optima in fuzzy c-means clustering. In: 2019 IEEE International Conference on Fuzzy Systems (FUZZ-IEEE), pp. 1–6. IEEE (2019)
22. Ghasabeh, A., Abadeh, M.S.: Community detection in social networks using a hybrid swarm intelligence approach. Int. J. Knowl. Based Intell. Eng. Syst. **19**(4), 255–267 (2015). IOS Press
23. Gu, S., Cheng, R., Jin, Y.: Feature selection for high-dimensional classification using a competitive swarm optimizer. Soft. Comput. **22**(3), 811–822 (2018)
24. Hallen, M.A., Donald, B.R.: Protein design by provable algorithms. Commun. ACM **62**(10), 76–84 (2019)
25. Hassan, E.A., Hafez, A.I., Hassanien, A.E., Fahmy, A.A.: Community detection algorithm based on artificial fish swarm optimization. In: Filev, D., et al. (eds.) Intelligent Systems'2014. AISC, vol. 323, pp. 509–521. Springer, Cham (2015). https://doi.org/10.1007/978-3-319-11310-4_44
26. Hussain, K., Salleh, M.N.M., Cheng, S., Shi, Y.: Metaheuristic research: a comprehensive survey. Artif. Intell. Rev. **52**(4), 2191–2233 (2019)
27. Inkaya, T., Kayalıgil, S., Özdemirel, N.E.: Swarm intelligence-based clustering algorithms: a survey. In: Celebi, M., Aydin, K. (eds.) Unsupervised Learning Algorithms, pp. 303–341. Springer, Cham (2016). https://doi.org/10.1007/978-3-319-24211-8_12
28. Kang, Q., Liu, S., Zhou, M., Li, S.: A weight-incorporated similarity-based clustering ensemble method based on swarm intelligence. Knowl. Based Syst. **104**, 156–164 (2016)
29. Karaboga, D., Basturk, B.: A powerful and efficient algorithm for numerical function optimization: artificial bee colony (ABC) algorithm. J. Global Optim. **39**(3), 459–471 (2007). https://doi.org/10.1007/s10898-007-9149-x
30. Karpat, Y., Ozel, T.: Hard Turning Optimization Using Neural Network Modeling and Swarm Intelligence. Society of Manufacturing Engineers, Dearborn (2000)
31. Kennedy, J., Eberhart, R.: Particle swarm optimization. In: Proceedings of ICNN 1995-International Conference on Neural Networks, vol. 4, pp. 1942–1948. IEEE (1995)
32. Kennedy, J., Eberhart, R., Shi, Y.: Swarm Intelligence. Morgan Kaufmann Publisher, San Francisco (2001)
33. Kesavamoorthy, R., Soundar, K.R.: Swarm intelligence based autonomous DDOS attack detection and defense using multi agent system. Cluster Comput. **22**(4), 9469–9476 (2019). https://doi.org/10.1007/s10586-018-2365-y
34. Khadhraoui, T., Ktata, S., Benzarti, F., Amiri, H.: Features selection based on modified PSO algorithm for 2D face recognition. In: 2016 13th International Conference on Computer Graphics, Imaging and Visualization (CGiV), pp. 99–104. IEEE (2016)
35. Kozak, J., Boryczka, U.: Collective data mining in the ant colony decision tree approach. Inf. Sci. **372**, 126–147 (2016)
36. Krishnanand, K., Ghose, D.: Glowworm swarm optimization for simultaneous capture of multiple local optima of multimodal functions. Swarm Intell. **3**(2), 87–124 (2009)
37. LeCun, Y., Bengio, Y., Hinton, G.: Deep learning. Nature **521**(7553), 436–444 (2015)
38. Lin, Y.H., Hu, Y.C.: Residential consumer-centric demand-side management based on energy disaggregation-piloting constrained swarm intelligence: towards edge computing. Sensors **18**(5), 1365 (2018)

39. Lu, Y., Liang, M., Ye, Z., Cao, L.: Improved particle swarm optimization algorithm and its application in text feature selection. Appl. Soft Comput. **35**, 629–636 (2015)
40. Lyu, C., Shi, Y., Sun, L.: A novel local community detection method using evolutionary computation. IEEE Trans. Cybern., 1–13 (2019). https://doi.org/10.1109/TCYB.2019.2933041
41. Martens, D., Baesens, B., Fawcett, T.: Editorial survey: swarm intelligence for data mining. Mach. Learn. **82**(1), 1–42 (2011). https://doi.org/10.1007/s10994-010-5216-5
42. Mirjalili, S., Mirjalili, S.M., Lewis, A.: Grey wolf optimizer. Adv. Eng. Softw. **69**, 46–61 (2014)
43. Nebti, S., Boukerram, A.: Swarm intelligence inspired classifiers for facial recognition. Swarm Evol. Comput. **32**, 150–166 (2017)
44. Nguyen, B.H., Xue, B., Zhang, M.: A survey on swarm intelligence approaches to feature selection in data mining. Swarm Evol. Comput. **54**, 100663 (2020)
45. Panigrahi, B.K., Shi, Y., Lim, M.H.: Handbook of Swarm Intelligence: Concepts, Principles and Applications, vol. 8. Springer, Heidelberg (2011). https://doi.org/10.1007/978-3-642-17390-5
46. Pizzuti, C.: Evolutionary computation for community detection in networks: a review. IEEE Trans. Evol. Comput. **22**(3), 464–483 (2018)
47. Pourpanah, F., Shi, Y., Lim, C.P., Hao, Q., Tan, C.J.: Feature selection based on brain storm optimization for data classification. Appl. Soft Comput. **80**, 761–775 (2019)
48. Rao, R.V., Savsani, V.J., Vakharia, D.: Teaching-learning-based optimization: a novel method for constrained mechanical design optimization problems. Comput. Aided Des. **43**(3), 303–315 (2011)
49. Shi, Y.: Brain storm optimization algorithm. In: Tan, Y., Shi, Y., Chai, Y., Wang, G. (eds.) ICSI 2011. LNCS, vol. 6728, pp. 303–309. Springer, Heidelberg (2011). https://doi.org/10.1007/978-3-642-21515-5_36
50. Shi, Y.: Unified swarm intelligence algorithms. In: Shi, Y. (ed.) Critical Developments and Applications of Swarm Intelligence, pp. 1–26. IGI Global, Hershey (2018)
51. Silva, P.H., Luz, E., Zanlorensi, L.A., Menotti, D., Moreira, G.: Multimodal feature level fusion based on particle swarm optimization with deep transfer learning. In: 2018 IEEE Congress on Evolutionary Computation (CEC), pp. 1–8. IEEE (2018)
52. Singh, T.I., Laishram, R., Roy, S.: Comparative study of combination of swarm intelligence and fuzzy C means clustering for medical image segmentation. In: Luhach, A., Hawari, K., Mihai, I., Hsiung, P.A., Mishra, R. (eds.) Smart Computational Strategies: Theoretical and Practical Aspects, pp. 69–80. Springer, Singapore (2019). https://doi.org/10.1007/978-981-13-6295-8_7
53. Soltani, M., Chaari, A., Hmida, F.B.: A novel fuzzy C-regression model algorithm using a new error measure and particle swarm optimization. Int. J. Appl. Math. Comput. Sci. **22**(3), 617–628 (2012)
54. Stanley, K.O., Clune, J., Lehman, J., Miikkulainen, R.: Designing neural networks through neuroevolution. Nat. Mach. Intell. **1**(1), 24–35 (2019)
55. Sun, H., et al.: A parallel self-organizing overlapping community detection algorithm based on swarm intelligence for large scale complex networks. Future Gener. Comput. Syst. **89**, 265–285 (2018)
56. Tan, Y., Shi, Y.: Special section on swarm-based algorithms and applications in computational biology and bioinformatics. IEEE/ACM Trans. Comput. Biol. Bioinf. **15**(6), 1863–1864 (2018)

57. Tan, Y., Zhu, Y.: Fireworks algorithm for optimization. In: Tan, Y., Shi, Y., Tan, K.C. (eds.) ICSI 2010. LNCS, vol. 6145, pp. 355–364. Springer, Heidelberg (2010). https://doi.org/10.1007/978-3-642-13495-1_44
58. Tang, H., et al.: Predicting green consumption behaviors of students using efficient firefly grey wolf-assisted k-nearest neighbor classifiers. IEEE Access (2020)
59. Tarkhaneh, O., Isazadeh, A., Khamnei, H.J.: A new hybrid strategy for data clustering using cuckoo search based on mantegna levy distribution, PSO and k-means. Int. J. Comput. Appl. Technol. **58**(2), 137–149 (2018)
60. Tuba, E., Mrkela, L., Tuba, M.: Support vector machine parameter tuning using firefly algorithm. In: 2016 26th International Conference Radioelektronika (RADIOELEKTRONIKA), pp. 413–418. IEEE (2016)
61. Tuba, E., Strumberger, I., Bacanin, N., Zivkovic, D., Tuba, M.: Cooperative clustering algorithm based on brain storm optimization and k-means. In: 2018 28th International Conference Radioelektronika (RADIOELEKTRONIKA), pp. 1–5. IEEE (2018)
62. Vrbančič, G., Fister Jr., I., Podgorelec, V.: Swarm intelligence approaches for parameter setting of deep learning neural network: case study on phishing websites classification. In: Proceedings of the 8th International Conference on Web Intelligence, Mining and Semantics, pp. 1–8 (2018)
63. Wang, B., Sun, Y., Xue, B., Zhang, M.: Evolving deep neural networks by multi-objective particle swarm optimization for image classification. arXiv:1904.09035 (2019)
64. Wang, B., Xue, B., Zhang, M.: Particle swarm optimisation for evolving deep neural networks for image classification by evolving and stacking transferable blocks. arXiv:1907.12659 (2019)
65. Wu, Q., Liu, H., Yan, X.: Multi-label classification algorithm research based on swarm intelligence. Cluster Comput. **19**(4), 2075–2085 (2016)
66. Yang, X.-S.: Firefly algorithms for multimodal optimization. In: Watanabe, O., Zeugmann, T. (eds.) SAGA 2009. LNCS, vol. 5792, pp. 169–178. Springer, Heidelberg (2009). https://doi.org/10.1007/978-3-642-04944-6_14
67. Yang, X.S., Deb, S.: Cuckoo search via lévy flights. In: 2009 World Congress on Nature & Biologically Inspired Computing (NaBIC), pp. 210–214. IEEE (2009)
68. Yang, X.S., Gandomi, A.H.: Bat algorithm: a novel approach for global engineering optimization. Eng. Comput. **29**(5), 464–483 (2012)
69. Yazdani, M., Jolai, F.: Lion optimization algorithm (LOA): a nature-inspired meta-heuristic algorithm. J. Comput. Des. Eng. **3**(1), 24–36 (2016)
70. Zedadra, O., Guerrieri, A., Jouandeau, N., Spezzano, G., Seridi, H., Fortino, G.: Swarm intelligence and IoT-based smart cities: a review. In: Cicirelli, F., Guerrieri, A., Mastroianni, C., Spezzano, G., Vinci, A. (eds.) The Internet of Things for Smart Urban Ecosystems. IT, pp. 177–200. Springer, Cham (2019). https://doi.org/10.1007/978-3-319-96550-5_8
71. Zhang, S., Lee, C.K., Yu, K., Lau, H.C.: Design and development of a unified framework towards swarm intelligence. Artif. Intell. Rev. **47**(2), 253–277 (2017). https://doi.org/10.1007/s10462-016-9481-y
72. Zhang, Y., Song, X.F., Gong, D.W.: A return-cost-based binary firefly algorithm for feature selection. Inf. Sci. **418**, 561–574 (2017)
73. Zhao, R.Q., Tang, W.S.: Monkey algorithm for global numerical optimization. J. Uncertain Syst. **2**(3), 165–176 (2008)
74. Zhao, X., Wang, C., Su, J., Wang, J.: Research and application based on the swarm intelligence algorithm and artificial intelligence for wind farm decision system. Renew. Energy **134**, 681–697 (2019)

Synchronized Swarm Operation

Eugene Larkin[1]([✉]), Tatyana Akimenko[1], and Aleksandr Privalov[2]

[1] Tula State University, Tula 300012, Russia
elarkin@mail.ru
[2] Tula State Lev Tolstoy Pedagogical University, Tula 300026, Russia
privalov.61@mail.ru

Abstract. Physical swarm system, including number of units, operated in physical time according to corporative algorithm, is considered. It is shown, that for proper corporative algorithm interpretation it is necessary to synchronize computational processes in units. Structural-parametric model of synchronized swarm operation, based on Petri-Markov nets apparatus, is worked out. In the Petri-Markov net transitions are abstract analogues of synchronization procedure, while places simulate corporative algorithm parts interpretation by swarm units. Primary Petri-Markov model is transformed into complex semi-Markov process. Formulae for calculation of stochastic and time characteristics of the process are obtained. It is shown, that after transformation all methods of ordinary semi-Markov processes investigation may be used for synchronized systems. With use the concept of distributed forfeit effectiveness of synchronization is evaluated.

Keywords: Swarm · Unit · Corporative algorithm · Semi-Markov process · Petri-Markov net · Time characteristics · Stochastic characteristics · Distributed forfeit effectiveness

1 Introduction

Physical swarms, which solve corporative task, are widely used in different branches of human activity, industrial and mobile robotics, concurrent computation, control systems, etc. [1–5]. Such systems include number of units, each of which operates accordingly to its own algorithm realized on Von Neumann type controllers. Due to consecutive interpretation of algorithm operators and accidental character of data processed, runtime of controller is a random value, and outcome of program operation is stochastic [6]. So for proper operation, when solving a corporative task, swarm should be tuned in such a way, that corporative algorithm should be divided on pieces, which are realized on swarm units, and interpretation of algorithm pieces should be carried out in the proper sequence [7]. Such alignment is called synchronization. For optimal synchronization adequate model of parallel process should be worked out. Below approach to simulation, based on Petri-Markov nets [8], which from one side permits to evaluate random time intervals characteristics, and from other side take into account interaction of parallel processes, is used. Also for optimal synchronization it is necessary to have criterion, which permits to evaluate effectiveness of corporative algorithm division. Below universal criterion,

© Springer Nature Switzerland AG 2020
Y. Tan et al. (Eds.): ICSI 2020, LNCS 12145, pp. 15–24, 2020.
https://doi.org/10.1007/978-3-030-53956-6_2

called distributed forfeit, is proposed, and formulae for effectiveness estimation with use proposed criterion are obtained.

Approaches to simulation of synchronized operation of swarm are currently known insufficiently, that explains necessity and relevance of the investigations in this domain.

2 Petri-Markov Model of Synchronized Operation

Operation of swarm, which includes M units and solves some corporative task, may be described with use Petri-Markov net (PMN) apparatus [8]. Swarm operation model is as follows (Fig. 1).

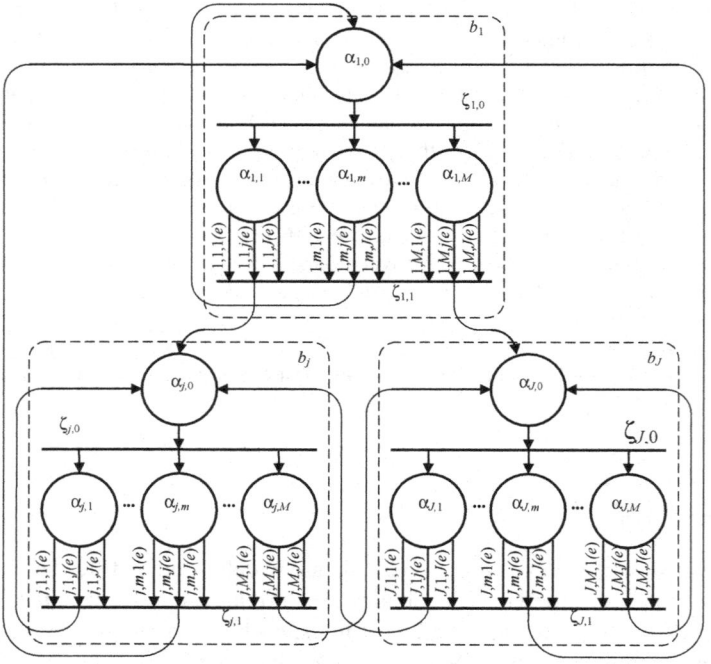

Fig. 1. Petri-Markov network describing the synchronous operation of equipment.

$$\Pi = \{A, Z, \iota(Z), o(Z)\}, \tag{1}$$

where $A = \{A_1, \ldots, A_j, \ldots, A_J\}$ is the set op places, which describes operation of M swarm units; $Z = \{Z_1, \ldots, Z_j, \ldots, Z_J\}$ is the set of transitions, which describes synchronization procedures; $\iota(Z)$ $o(Z)$ are input and output functions of transitions, correspondingly; J number of operators in corporative algorithm of swarm behavior when solving corporative task;

$$A_j = \{\alpha_{j,0}, \alpha_{j,1}, \ldots, \alpha_{j,m}, \ldots, \alpha_{j,M}\}, \quad 1 \le j \le J; \tag{2}$$

$$Z_j = \{\zeta_{j,0}, \zeta_{j,1}\}, \quad 1 \le j \le J; \tag{3}$$

$$\begin{cases} \iota(Z) == \{\iota(Z_1), \ldots, \iota(Z_j), \ldots, \iota(Z_J)\}; \\ \iota(Z_j) = \{\iota(\zeta_{j,0}), \iota(\zeta_{j,1})\}, 1 \le j \le J; \\ \iota(\zeta_{j,0}) = \alpha_{j,0}; \\ \iota(\zeta_{j,1}) = \{\alpha_{j,1}, \ldots, \alpha_{j,m}, \ldots, \alpha_{j,M}\}; \end{cases} \tag{4}$$

$$\begin{cases} o(Z) == \{o(Z_1), \ldots, o(Z_j), \ldots, o(Z_J)\}; \\ o(Z_j) = \{o(\zeta_{j,0}), o(\zeta_{j,1})\}, 1 \le j \le J; \\ o(\zeta_{j,0}) = \{\alpha_{j,1}, \ldots, \alpha_{j,m}, \ldots, \alpha_{j,M}\}; \\ o(\zeta_{j,1}) = \{\alpha_{1,0}, \ldots, \alpha_{j,0}, \ldots, \alpha_{J,0}\}. \end{cases} \tag{5}$$

PMN operation may be considered as sequence semi-steps, which may be done either from places to transitions, $(\alpha_{j,0}, \zeta_{j,0})$, $(\alpha_{j,m,j(e)}, \zeta_{j,1})$, $1 \le j \le J, 1 \le m \le M$, $1 \le j(e) \le J(e)$, or from transitions to places, $(\zeta_{j,0}, \alpha_{j,m})$, $1 \le m \le M, 1 \le j \le J$; $(\zeta_{j,1}, \alpha_{1,0})$, ..., $(\zeta_{j,1}, \alpha_{l,0})$, ..., $(\zeta_{j,1}, \alpha_{J,0})$, $1 \le j \le J$. For semi-step execution from places $\alpha_{j,0}, \alpha_{j,1}, \ldots, \alpha_{j,m}, \ldots, \alpha_{j,M}$ into corresponding transitions random time interval t should be spent, which begins from the moment, when semi-step was done into this place. Time intervals are determined with an accuracy to time densities $f_{j,0}(t), f_{j,m,j(e)}(t)$, $1 \le j \le J, 1 \le m \le M, 1 \le j(e) \le J(e)$. For semi-step execution from transition $\zeta_{j,0}$ simultaneously to all places $\alpha_{j,1}, \ldots, \alpha_{j,m}, \ldots, \alpha_{j,M}$, constituting its output function $o(\zeta_{j,0})$ only semi-step $(\alpha_{j,0}, \zeta_{j,0})$ should be done. For execution of one of semi-step from the transition $\zeta_{j,1}$, the proper $(\alpha_{j,m,j(e)}, \zeta_{j,1})$ semi-steps combination to named transition must be done, due to only one direction of the set $\{1(e), \ldots, j(e), \ldots, J(e)\}$ may be choose for doing semi-step (Fig. 1).

In such a way, transitions $\zeta_{j,0}$, and $\zeta_{j,1}$, are the synchronized one: transition $\zeta_{j,0}$ in the sense that all semi-steps, included into its output function $o(\zeta_{j,0})$, are executed simultaneously (synchronous start), but transition $\zeta_{j,1}$ in the sense, that semi-step from it would not be done until all semi-steps from places of $\iota(\zeta_{j,1})$ will be done.

PMN timing elements are places. Time of residence PMN at places $\alpha_{1,0}, \ldots, \alpha_{j,0}, \ldots, \alpha_{J,0}$ is as follows

$$f_{j,0}(t) = \delta(t), \tag{6}$$

where $\delta(t)$ is the Dirac δ-function.

Time of residence PMN at places $\alpha_{1,1}, \ldots, \alpha_{1,m}, \ldots, \alpha_{1,M}$, ..., $\alpha_{j,1}, \ldots, \alpha_{j,m}, \ldots, \alpha_{j,M}$, ..., $\alpha_{J,1}, \ldots, \alpha_{J,m}, \ldots, \alpha_{J,M}$ is defined as the time of wandering through semi-Markov processes [9, 10] $\mu_{j,m}(t)$, $1 \le j \le J, 1 \le m \le M$, which are abstract analogues of swarm unit onboard computers operation, and are defined as follows (Fig. 2):

$$\mu_{j,m} = \{A_{j,m}, r_{j,m}, h_{j,m}(t)\}, \tag{7}$$

where $A_{j,m}$, $|A_{j,m}| = J(a) + 1$, is the set of states, which are abstract analogues of swarm unit onboard computer algorithm operators; $r_{j,m}$ is the $[J(a) + 1] \times [J(a) + 1]$ adjacency

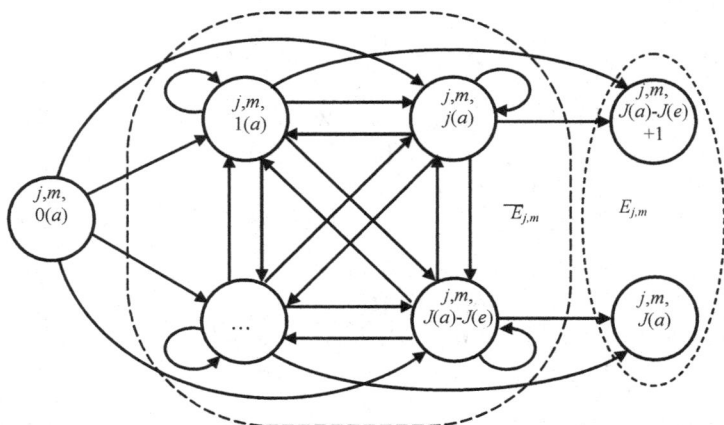

Fig. 2. Semi-Markov process $\mu_{j,m}(t)$

matrix, which describes links between operators; $\boldsymbol{h}_{j,m}(t)$ is the $[J(a)+1] \times [J(a)+1]$ semi-Markov matrix, which define time intervals of operators interpretation;

$$A_{j,m} = \left\{ a_{j,m,0(a)}, a_{j,m,1(a)}, \ldots, a_{j,m,J(a)-J(e)}, \ldots, a_{j,m,J(a)-J(e)} \right\}; \tag{8}$$

$$\boldsymbol{r}_{j,m} = \left[r_{j,m,j(a),n(a)} \right]; \tag{9}$$

$$\boldsymbol{h}_{j,m}(t) = \left[h_{j,m,j(a),n(a)}(t) \right]. \tag{10}$$

The set $A_{j,m}$ is divided onto two disjoint subsets, subset of non-absorbing states

$$\bar{E}_{j,m} = \left\{ a_{j,m,0(a)}, a_{j,m,1(a)}, \ldots, a_{j,m,j(a)}, \ldots, a_{j,m,J(a)-J(e)} \right\}, \tag{11}$$

and subset of absorbing states $E_{j,m}$.

$$\bar{E}_{j,m} = \left\{ a_{j,m,J(a)-J(e)+1}, \ldots, a_{j,m,j(e)}, \ldots, a_{j,m,J(a)} \right\}. \tag{12}$$

Wandering through states of semi-Markov process $\boldsymbol{h}_{j,m}(t)$ start at the state $a_{j,m,0(a)}$, which is the abstract analogue of "begin" operator. States $a_{j,m,j(e)} \in \bar{E}_{j,m}$ are the abstract analogues of "end" operators for different outcomes of algorithm operation.

Element $h_{j,m,j(a),n(a)}(t) \in \boldsymbol{h}_{j,m}(t)$ performs weighted time density of m-th swarm unit residence in the state $a_{j,m,j(a)}$ when decision was made about next switch into the state $a_{j,m,n(a)}$.

Weighted time density of the semi-Markov process $\mu_{j,m}$ wandering from the state $a_{j,m,0(a)}$ till the state $a_{j,m,J(a)-J(e)+j(e)} \in E$ is as follows:

$$h_{j,m,j(e)}(t) = {}^{r}\boldsymbol{I}_{0(a)} \cdot L^{-1} \left[\sum_{k=1}^{\infty} \left\{ L[\boldsymbol{h}_{j,m}(t)] \right\}^{k} \right] \cdot {}^{c}\boldsymbol{I}_{J(a)-J(e)+j(e)}, \tag{13}$$

where ${}^R I_{0(a)}$ is the row vector of size $[J(a) + 1]$, whose $0(a)$-th element is equal to one, and all other elements are equal to zeros; ${}^c I_{J(a)-J(e)+j(e)}$ is column vector, whose $[J(a) - J(e) + j(e)]$-th element is equal to one, and all other elements are equal to zeros; $L[\ldots]$ и $L^{-1}[\ldots]$ are correspondingly direct and inverse Laplace transforms.

When $J(e) = 1$ the algorithm simulated has the only outcome, and consequently $h_{j,m,J(e)}(t) = f_{j,m,J(e)}(t)$. When $J(e) > 1$, then semi-Markov process $\mu_{j,m}$ gets subset E, veraciously, but the state $a_{j,m,J(a)-J(e)+j(e)}$ it gets with probability [12]

$$p_{j,m,j(e)} = \int_0^\infty h_{j,m,j(e)}(t)dt. \qquad (14)$$

Pure (non-weighted) time density, expectation and dispersion are equal, correspondingly [13]

$$f_{j,m,j(e)}(t) = \frac{h_{j,m,j(e)}(t)}{p_{j,m,j(e)}}. \qquad (15)$$

$$T_{j,m,j(e)} = \int_0^\infty t \cdot f_{j,m,j(e)}(t)dt; \qquad (16)$$

$$D_{j,m,j(e)} = \int_0^\infty \left(t - T_{m(\Sigma),n(\Sigma)}\right)^2 \cdot f_{j,m,j(e)}(t)dt. \qquad (17)$$

Due to $\mu_{j,m}$ gets subset E, veraciously,

$$\sum_{j(e)=1(e)}^{J(e)} p_{j,m,j(e)} = 1. \qquad (18)$$

3 Transformation PMN to Complex Semi-Markov Process

With use formulae (13), (14), (15) obtained, Petri-Markov sublet, circled on the Fig. 2 with dashed line, may be replaced with the single state, and so the PMN Π may be replaced with complex semi-Markov process, which describes behavior of the swarm as a whole. Circled with dashed line subset is as follows

$$\Pi_j = \left\{A_j, Z_j, \iota(Z_j), o(Z_j)\right\}, \qquad (19)$$

$$A_j = \left\{\alpha_{j,0}, \alpha_{j,1}, \ldots, \alpha_{j,m}, \ldots, \alpha_{j,M}\right\}, \qquad (20)$$

$$\begin{cases} Z_j = \{\zeta_{j,0}, \zeta_{j,1}\}; \\ \iota(\zeta_{j,0}) = \alpha_{j,0}; \\ \iota(\zeta_{j,1}) = \{\alpha_{j,1}, \ldots, \alpha_{j,m}, \ldots, \alpha_{j,M}\}; \end{cases} \qquad (21)$$

$$\begin{cases} o\big(Z_j\big) = \big\{o\big(\zeta_{j,0}\big), o\big(\zeta_{j,1}\big)\big\}; \\ o\big(\zeta_{j,0}\big) = \big\{\alpha_{j,1}, \ldots, \alpha_{j,m}, \ldots, \alpha_{j,M}\big\}; , \\ o\big(\zeta_{j,1}\big) = \big\{\alpha_{1,0}, \ldots, \alpha_{j,0}, \ldots, \alpha_{J,0}\big\} \end{cases} \quad (22)$$

Semi-Markov process is as follows

$$\mu = \{B, \boldsymbol{r}, \boldsymbol{h}(t)\}, \quad (23)$$

where $B = \big\{b_1, \ldots, b_j, \ldots, b_J\big\}$ is the set of states, which are abstract analogues of execution by swarm the complex operation due to algorithm of swarm behavior; $\boldsymbol{r} = \big[r_{j,n}\big]$ is the $J \times J$ adjacency matrix; $\boldsymbol{h}_{j,m}(t) = \big[h_{j,n}(t)\big]$ is the $J \times J$ semi-Markov matrix.

Let us define probabilities and time densities of switch from the complex state $b_j \in B$ to the complex state $b_n \in B$. Semi-steps $\big(\alpha_{j,0}, \zeta_{j,0}\big)$ and $\big(\zeta_{j,0}, \alpha_{j,m}\big)$, $1 \leq m \leq M$ are executed during the time which is defined with Dirac δ-function. Semi-steps $\big(\zeta_{j,1}, \alpha_{0,n}\big)$, $1 \leq n \leq J$ are executed after logical conditions fulfillment also during defied with Dirac δ-function time. So time of residence the complex semi-Markov process in the state b_j till switch to the complex state b_n may be defined as result of competition between ordinary semi-Markov processes $\mu_{j,m}$, with taking into account outcomes of getting subsets $E_{j,m}$ states.

For definition of all possible outcomes, from indexes trios $\big[j, m, j(e)\big]$, $1 \leq m \leq M$, following set may be constructed

$$\tilde{J}_{j,m} = \big\{[j, m, 1(e)], \ldots, [j, m, j(e)], \ldots, [j, m, J(e)]\big\}, \quad 1 \leq m \leq M. \quad (24)$$

Cartesian product of sets $\tilde{J}_{j,m}$ gives all possible combinations of outcomes of swarm units operation:

$$\tilde{J}_j = \coprod_{m=1}^{M} \tilde{J}_{j,m} = \{([j, 1, 1(e)], \ldots, [j, m, 1(e)], \ldots, [j, M, 1(e)]), \ldots,$$

$$([j, 1, j(e)], \ldots, [j, m, j(e)], \ldots, [j, M, j(e)]), \ldots, ([j, 1, J(e)], \ldots, [j, m, J(e)], \ldots, [j, M, J(e)])\}; \quad (25)$$

From (25) may be selected those vectors, combination of trios of which permit to do emi-step $\big(\zeta_{j,1}, \alpha_{n,0}\big)$:

$$\tilde{J}_j \supseteq \tilde{J}_{j(n)} = \big\{([j, 1, i(e, n)], \ldots, [j, m, j(e, n)], \ldots, [j, M, k(e, n)]),$$

$$\ldots, ([j, 1, l(e, n)], \ldots, [j, m, q(e, n)], \ldots, [j, M, s(e, n)])\big\}; \quad (26)$$

$$\big|\tilde{J}_{j(n)}\big| = \mathrm{K}(n) \quad (27)$$

Probability of $\kappa(n)$-th combination emergence is as follows:

$$p_{j,\kappa(n)} = \prod_{m=1}^{M} p_{j,m,j[e,\kappa(n)]}, \quad 1 \leq \kappa(n) \leq \mathrm{K}(n). \quad (28)$$

So, probability $p_{j,n}$ of switch the complex semi-Markov process μ from b_j to b_n is equal to the sum

$$p_{j,n} = \sum_{\kappa(n)=1}^{K(n)} p_{j(n),\kappa(n)}. \tag{29}$$

For calculation of time density $f_{j,n}(t)$ one should consider the competition [9, 14] on the transition $\zeta_{j,1}$ between ordinary semi-Markov processes $\mu_{j,m}$. Residence at the state b_j is considered as completed, when last ordinary semi-Markov process reaches its $E_{j,m}$ state according the combination (25). This is why semi-Markov processes compete for not being the last in the competition. Time of reaching subset $E_{j,m}$ by all M may be described with the following formula:

$$f_{j,j[e,\kappa(n)]}(t) = \frac{d \prod_{m=1}^{M} F_{j,m,j[e,\kappa(n)]}(t)}{dt}$$

$$= \sum_{m=1}^{M} f_{j,m,j[e,\kappa(n)]}(t) \prod_{\substack{i=1, \\ i \neq m}}^{M} F_{j,i,j[e,\kappa(n)]}(t). \tag{30}$$

where $f_{j,m,j[e,\kappa(n)]}(t)$ is the time density of reaching the transition $\zeta_{j,1}$ by m-th semi-Markov process due to $\kappa(n)$-th combination; $F_{...}(t) = \int_0^t f_{...}(\tau)d\tau$ if the function of distribution of probabilities.

With taking into account combination of outcomes, weighted and pure time densities of switch from the state b_j to the state b_n are as follows:

$$h_{j,n}(t) = \sum_{\kappa(n)=1}^{K(n)} p_{j,\kappa(n)} f_{j,j[e,\kappa(n)]}(t). \tag{31}$$

$$f_{j,n}(t) = \frac{h_{j,n}(t)}{p_{j,n}}. \tag{32}$$

After transformation for investigation of swarm behavior investigation and calculation of wandering time intervals all possible methods of semi-Markov process analysis may be used [9–12].

4   Effectiveness of Synchronization

One of the important aspects of swarm operation organization is elimination of unproductive units downtime when corporative task is solved. Parameter, which defines effectiveness, may be any, but when investigation of relay-races, distributed forfeit is of widely used. Let us considered competition of m-th и l-th swarm units, first of which gets the transition $\zeta_{j,1}$ during time $f_{j,m,j[e,\kappa(n)]}(t)$, but second - during the time $f_{j,l,j[e,\kappa(n)]}(t)$. In the case of winning in competition the first swarm unit he waits until l-th swarm unit gets $\zeta_{j,1}$. Waiting time is calculated as follows [15]:

$$f_{j,m\to l,j[e,\kappa(n)]}(t) = \frac{\eta(t)\int_0^\infty f_{j,m,j[e,\kappa(n)]}(\tau)f_{j,l,j[e,\kappa(n)]}(t+\tau)d\tau}{\int_0^\infty F_{j,m,j[e,\kappa(n)]}(t)dF_{j,l,j[e,\kappa(n)]}(t)}, \tag{33}$$

where τ is an auxiliary argument; $\eta(t)$ is the Heaviside function.

Probability of such event, expectation and dispersion of waiting time are as follows

$$p_{j,m\to l,j[e,\kappa(n)]} = \int_0^\infty F_{j,m,j[e,\kappa(n)]}(t)dF_{j,l,j[e,\kappa(n)]}(t); \tag{34}$$

$$T_{j,m\to l,j[e,\kappa(n)]} = \int_0^\infty t\cdot f_{j,m\to l,j[e,\kappa(n)]}(t)dt; \tag{35}$$

$$D_{j,m\to l,j[e,\kappa(n)]} = \int_0^\infty \left[t - T_{j,m\to l,j[e,\kappa(n)]}\right]^2 f_{j,m\to l,j[e,\kappa(n)]}(t)dt. \tag{36}$$

Every of value (34), (35), (36) may characterized those or that effectiveness aspect, but more universal is the criterion, which is defined as distributed forfeit [15] $c_{j,m\to l,j[e,\kappa(n)]}(t)$. Forfeit, receives m-th swarm unit from the l-th swarm unit if it gets the transition $\zeta_{j,1}$ earlier. Latecomer pays forfeit during whole the time until he m-th swarm unit waits him. In this case weighted forfeit sum is equal to

$$C_{j,m\to l,j[e,\kappa(n)]} = p_{j,m\to l,j[e,\kappa(n)]} \int_o^\infty c_{j,m\to l,j[e,\kappa(n)]}(t)f_{j,m\to l,j[e,\kappa(n)]}(t)dt; \tag{37}$$

Common forfeit sum, which m-th swarm unit receives from all other units by $\kappa(n)$-th combination variant is as follows:

$$C_{j,m,j[e,\kappa(n)]} = \sum_{\substack{l=1,\\ l\neq m}}^M C_{j,m\to l,j[e,\kappa(n)]}. \tag{38}$$

Common forfeit sum, which m-th swarm unit receives from all other units in the case of further switch into state b_n is equal to

$$C_{j,m,n} = \sum_{\kappa(n)=1}^{K(n)} p_{j,m,j[e,\kappa(n)]} \cdot C_{j,m,j[e,\kappa(n)]}. \tag{39}$$

Sum $C_{j(b),m}$ depends on parameters of ordinary semi-Markov processes (7), and forfeit discipline. Such sum may be used as optimization criterion in the task of producing optimal swarm behavior.

5   Conclusion

Working out the model of swarm synchronized operation opens new page in parallel systems theory because it permits to link real physical parameters of hardware with structure and logics of operation oh corporative algorithm, distributed among swarm units. Algorithm splitting may be done with those or that way, but with use approach proposed, swarm program designer for every mode of splitting may evaluate main characteristics both corporative algorithm as a whole, and parts of it, realized on swarm units.

Further investigation in this area should be directed to working out an algorithm splitting optimization method, based on proposed approach to parallelization modeling and evaluation of effectiveness.

The research was supported by the Foundation for Basic Research under the project 19-47-710004 r_a.

References

1. Tzafestas, S.G.: Introduction to Mobile Robot Control, p. 750. Elsevier (2014)
2. Siciliano, B.: Springer Handbook of Robotics, p. 1611. Springer, Heidelberg (2008). https://doi.org/10.1007/978-3-540-30301-5
3. Squillante, M.S.: Stochastic analysis and optimization of multiserver systems. In: Ardagna, D., Zhang, L. (eds.) Run-time Models for Self-managing Systems and Applications, pp. 1–24. Springer, Basel (2010). https://doi.org/10.1007/978-3-0346-0433-8_1
4. Landau, I.D., Zito, G.: Digital Control Systems, Design, Identification and Implementation, p. 484. Springer, Heidelberg (2006). https://doi.org/10.1007/978-1-84628-056-6
5. Aström, J., Wittenmark, B.: Computer Controlled Systems: Theory and Design, p. 557. Tsinghua University Press. Prentice Hall (2002)
6. Larkin, E.V., Ivutin, A.N.: Estimation of latency in embedded real-time systems. In: 3rd Meditteranean Conference on Embedded Computing (MECO 2014), Budva, Montenegro, 15–19 June 2014, pp. 236–239 (2014). https://doi.org/10.1109/MECO.2014.6862704
7. Pacheco, P.S.: An Introduction to Parallel Programming, p. 361. Elsevier (2011)
8. Larkin, E.V., Malikov, A.A., Ivutin, A.N.: Petri-Markov model of fault-tolerant computer systems. In: 4th International Conference on Control, Decision and Information Technologies (CoDIT), Barcelona, Spain, pp. 416–420. IEEE (2017)
9. Du, R., Ai, S., Hu, O.: Competition and cooperation between brands in a segment: an analysis based on a semi-Markov model. Int. J. Serv. Sci. 2(1), 70–82 (2009)
10. Janssen, J., Manca, R.: Applied Semi-Markov Processes, p. 310. Springer, Boston (2006). https://doi.org/10.1007/0-387-29548-8
11. Jiang, Q., Xi, H.-S., Yin, B.-Q.: Event-driven semi-Markov switching state-space control processes. IET Control Theory Appl. 6(12), 1861–1869 (2012)
12. Larkin, E., Ivutin, A., Kotov, V., Privalov, A.: Semi-Markov modelling of commands execution by mobile robot. In: Ronzhin, A., Rigoll, G., Meshcheryakov, R. (eds.) ICR 2016. LNCS (LNAI), vol. 9812, pp. 189–198. Springer, Cham (2016). https://doi.org/10.1007/978-3-319-43955-6_23
13. Kobayashi, H., Marl, B.L., Turin, W.: Probability, Random Processes and Statistical Analysis, p. 812. Cambridge University Press, Cambridge (2012)

14. Eisentraut, C., Hermanns, H., Zhang, L.: Concurrency and composition in a stochastic world. In: Gastin, P., Laroussinie, F. (eds.) CONCUR 2010. LNCS, vol. 6269, pp. 21–39. Springer, Heidelberg (2010). https://doi.org/10.1007/978-3-642-15375-4_3
15. Larkin, E.V., Ivutin, A.N., Kotov, V.V., Privalov, A.N.: Simulation of Relay-races. Bull. South Ural State Univ. Math. Model. Program. Comput. Softw. **9**(4), 117–128 (2016)

Prediction of Photovoltaic Power Using Nature-Inspired Computing

Miroslav Sumega$^{(\boxtimes)}$, Anna Bou Ezzeddine, Gabriela Grmanová,
and Viera Rozinajová

Faculty of Informatics and Information Technologies,
Slovak University of Technology in Bratislava,
Ilkovičova 2, 842 16 Bratislava, Slovakia
miro.sumega@gmail.com
{anna.bou.ezzeddine,gabriela.grmanova,viera.rozinajova}@stuba.sk

Abstract. Prediction of photovoltaic (PV) energy is an important task. It allows grid operators to plan production of energy in order to secure stability of electrical grid. In this work we focus on improving prediction of PV energy using nature-inspired algorithms for optimization of Support Vector Regression (SVR) models. We propose method, which uses different models optimized for various types of weather in order to achieve higher overall accuracy compared to single optimized model. Each sample is classified by Multi-Layer Perceptron (MLP) into some weather class and then model is trained for each weather class. Our method achieved slightly better results compared to single optimized model.

Keywords: Firefly Algorithm · Optimization · Support Vector Regression

1 Introduction

Renewable sources of energy are increasingly involved in total energy production. One of the most important sources of renewable energy is solar radiation. PV panels are used in order to obtain energy from solar radiation. However this type of energy can be unstable, resulting in large fluctuations of energy production which might cause instability of electrical grid. Therefore, it is necessary to predict the output of these power plants so that grid operators can plan power generation or effectively regulate the grid to ensure its stability.

Various approaches to prediction of PV energy are used. According to [1] there are 3 types of approaches: physical, statistical and hybrid. Physical approaches use technical parameters of PV power plants and weather forecasts. Statistical approaches use only data from the past, which contains information about weather and production of PV power plant. Statistical methods are further subdivided into regression and artificial intelligence methods, which are able to use these data to create prediction models. Hybrid approaches combine previous approaches to the ensembles to improve prediction.

© Springer Nature Switzerland AG 2020
Y. Tan et al. (Eds.): ICSI 2020, LNCS 12145, pp. 25–36, 2020.
https://doi.org/10.1007/978-3-030-53956-6_3

Artificial intelligence methods are powerful in predicting PV power production, but their accuracy is highly dependent on their hyperparameter setting. The hyperparameter setting can be done in various ways, either manually or by using algorithms capable of finding and evaluating different hyperparameter settings. A group of algorithms used for hyperparameter setting is called nature-inspired algorithms. These algorithms are able to avoid local minima and find global minimum. Many of these algorithms use large amounts of agents representing specific solutions. Firefly algorithm (FA), particle swarm optimization (PSO) and genetic algorithm (GA) are some of nature-inspired algorithms.

In this paper artificial intelligence approach is used. We are using SVR for predictions. In order to increase prediction accuracy we are using FA to optimize SVR hyperparameters. We also classify each sample with MLP and we train multiple SVR models, one for each weather type.

2   Related Work

There are many different approaches to prediction of PV power in the literature.

Multiple SVR models were used for different weather types, which were obtained with SOM and LVQ, were used in [16]. In [9] comparison of ANN, kNN, SVM and MLR was done. Simple parameter optimization was performed for each algorithm. Multiple weather types were also used in [12]. In [6] ten different optimized machine learning algorithms were used for predicting. Various algorithms were also used in [14], specifically FFNN, SVR and RT. Parameter optimization was done for each algorithm. Classifying weather into weather types with SOM was used in [2]. For each weather type one model of RBF network was trained. SVR and ensemble of NN were used in [11]. They also used CFS for feature selection. In [10] they compared accuracy of SVR to accuracy of physical model. In [13] they used GBDT with Taylor formula for predictions and compared it to original data and prediction of optimized SVM with RBF kernel. Different approach was used in [3]. They used v-SVR with parameter optimization. In order to achieve best results, model was retrained each night. MARS was used for predictions in [8], where it was compared to multiple different algorithms. In [7] ELM, ANN and SVR were used. MLP, LSTM, DBN and Auto-LSTM neural networks along with physical P-PVFM model were used in [5] for prediction of PV power production of 21 power plants. In [15] multiple physical and SVR models were used for various time intervals for 921 power plants. SVR was optimized using GridSearch to obtain higher accuracy.

3   Firefly Algorithm

Firefly algorithm [17] is a metaheuristic inspired by firefly behaviour in nature. Idea of this algorithm is that each firefly represents one solution of optimized problem. All fireflies move towards other fireflies they see according to movement equation. Since fireflies represent solutions, change of position of firefly also means change of solution.

We use firefly algorithm to optimize SVR models. In our case firefly represents model hyperparameters which change when firefly moves. SVR hyperparameters we optimized using FA are C, ϵ, γ and tolerance for stopping criterion.

We chose FA because its parameters α, β_0 and γ, which are described in following subsection, allow great control over optimization process. Several experiments were performed to find the best setting of those parameters.

3.1 Movement Equation

In our implementation, each firefly moves according to following equation:

$$x_i^{t+1} = x_i^t + \beta_0 e^{-\gamma r_{ij}^2}(x_j^t - x_i^t) + \alpha \epsilon_i^t \delta^t \tag{1}$$

where x_i^{t+1} is new position of a firefly, x_i^t is actual position of a firefly. Attractivity coefficient β_0 determines how fast fireflies move towards each other. Visibility coefficient γ is used to change perceived attractivity of fireflies. α is random movement coefficient, which decreases with every generation, ϵ_i^t is vector of random numbers representing random movement of firefly and δ^t is vector of coefficients used for changing range from which random movement is generated.

4   Methods of Prediction

We are using two methods of prediction. Both of our methods are based on SVR [4], which is regression method based on an idea of Support Vector Machine. SVR utilizes hyperplane that maximizes margins of tolerance for data points while tolerating some error. In case data are not linear, SVR also uses kernel functions to transform them to linear feature space.

First method is single SVR model optimized on entire training data set. Second method (Fig. 1) is based on multiple models of SVR with each model optimized on specific weather class. Weather class is a numerical representation of weather type (sunny, cloudy, etc.). We use combination of clustering and classification to obtain weather classes.

4.1 Weather Classes Discovery

First step to discover weather classes is obtaining of initial weather class labels from training data set. We are using agglomerative clustering to obtain labels. Each cluster that agglomerative clustering discovers is considered a unique weather class. Before clustering is started, we specify the number of initial classes it should discover. Initial classes represent the first division of samples according to weather. After initial weather classes are discovered, we train MLP classifier so we can use it to classify new samples.

With weather classes discovered, we use FA to optimize one SVR model for each class. Then accuracy of SVR for each weather class is compared to accuracy of the first method on that class. After accuracy of models of all weather classes

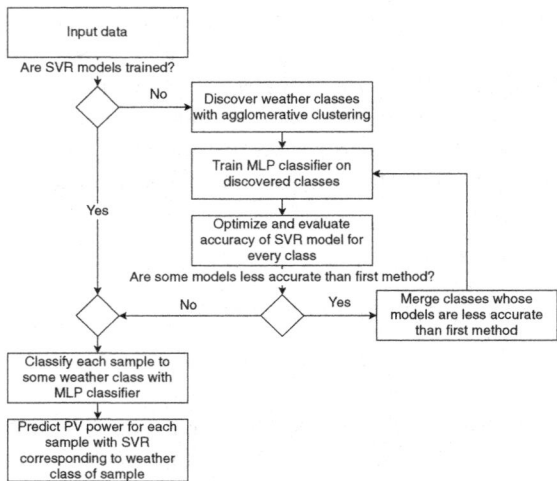

Fig. 1. Diagram showing how method based on weather classes works.

is checked, all classes whose SVR performed worse compared to the first method are merged. Obtained weather class should be more similar to the whole training data set than any of the classes that were merged together, therefore model optimized for this new class should perform more similarly to the first method.

After merging, SVR model is optimized for new weather class and MLP classifier is retrained. Then accuracy of prediction on all classes is checked again. Because of merging of classes and retraining of classifier, some samples might be classified into different classes than before. This might cause that models of some classes, which were better before merging, are now worse that the first method. Then merging of classes and optimization will happen again. This process of optimization, accuracy evaluation and merging of classes repeats in a cycle while there are at least two weather classes to merge. When cycle ends, we have final weather classes and SVR models, which we can now use for prediction.

4.2   Use of Multiple Weather Classes for Prediction

We use MLP classifier to obtain weather classes. This classifier can predict probability that sample belongs to a specific weather class. We use these probabilities to improve accuracy of a prediction according to the following equation:

$$X = \sum_{i=0}^{n} p_i x_i \qquad (2)$$

where X is final prediction, x_i is prediction if sample belongs to weather class i, p_i is probability of sample belonging to weather class i and n is a number of weather classes. When predicting, we first obtain probabilities of sample belonging to specific weather classes. Then for each weather class we make prediction with its SVR model and multiply it by probability of sample belonging to that weather class. Sum of all augmented predictions is considered as the final prediction.

4.3 Bias Correction

Since machine learning models might be slightly biased if not trained perfectly, we decided to use simple bias correction for all models in order to decrease prediction error. To perform bias correction, we first evaluate Mean Bias Error according to Eq. 8 on validation data set. Then from simple equation:

$$coef = 1 - \frac{MBE}{R} \tag{3}$$

where MBE and R are described in Sect. 6.1, we obtain bias coefficient which we use to correct bias of prediction. This correction is performed by multiplicating predicted values with obtained bias coefficient.

5 Data

In our experiments we used data set from University of Queensland[1]. This data set has one minute resolution, but we aggregated it to higher resolution depending on what series of experiments we were performing. Data sets contain following attributes: air temperature, humidity, wind speed and direction, insolation, power production in watts (W) and timestamp.

For the first and second series of experiments we used data from UQ Centre from 1.1.2014 to 31.12.2017 and aggregated it to hourly resolution. Time interval of data we used was 5 am to 7 pm. Data from years 2014 and 2015 were used for training, data from year 2016 were used for validation and data from year 2017 were used for testing.

In order to compare our results to [11], we used the same subset of data, therefore data were only from years 2013 and 2014 from 7 am to 5 pm and we aggregated it to 5 min resolution. In case of insolation and power we used addition to aggregate them. Other attributes were aggregated as mean hourly values. Training data were from year 2013. As validation data we chose every other day from year 2014 starting with 2nd January. Test data were chosen in the same way as validation data, however it started with 1st January.

In all experiments training and validation data were used in optimization process and test data were used to evaluate accuracy of optimized models.

5.1 Data Preprocessing

We transformed production to kilowatts (kW) and we also extracted minute (for third series of experiments), hour, day, month and year for each sample

---

[1] https://solar-energy.uq.edu.au/research/open-access-data.

from timestamp. We also derived weather changes in last hour for the first and second series of experiments and in last 55 min for third series of experiments. We also scaled power production and all attributes used for prediction.

For each sample we also used hourly production from last 3 h for the first and second series of experiments and last 6 h for third series of experiments. In some experiments we used also production from the most similar sample in entire data set if the first method was used or only in specific weather class if second method was used. We checked for similar production only in samples where absolute hour difference between original and similar sample is not larger than 1. This difference in case of months was set to 2. We decided to use those limits because production difference between those limits is not too large.

6   Experiments

We made three series of experiments. In the first series we focused on finding a good setting of FA. In the second series we used our methods of prediction to predict hour ahead PV production and in the third series we compared our approach with existing approach.

6.1   Evaluation Metrics

To evaluate accuracy of both of our methods of prediction, we use Root Mean Squared Error (RMSE), Mean Absolute Error (MAE) and their percentage transformations: normalized RMSE (nRMSE) and Mean Relative Error (MRE). Because we are using simple bias correction, we also use Mean Bias Error (MBE) to obtain bias. Following are formulas used for calculation of errors:

$$MAE = \frac{1}{N} * \sum_{i=1}^{N} |x_i - y_i| \qquad (4)$$

$$MRE = 100\% * \frac{MAE}{R} \qquad (5)$$

$$RMSE = \sqrt{\frac{1}{N} * \sum_{i=1}^{N} (x_i - y_i)^2} \qquad (6)$$

$$nRMSE = 100\% * \frac{RMSE}{R} \qquad (7)$$

$$MBE = \frac{1}{N} * \sum_{i=1}^{N} (x_i - y_i) \qquad (8)$$

where x_i is predicted value, y_i is real value, N is number of samples and R is computed as a difference between maximal and minimal power production in training data set. In case of predictions for one hour ahead we used largest value in training data set where $R = 21856.645$ kW and in case of predictions

Table 1. Experiments to find good settings of FA.

α	β_0	γ	RMSE	MAE	Best generation	Scattering
0	0.2	0	2229.0	1258.8	1	None
0	0.2	1	2579.3	2230.5	0	Very small
0	0.2	2	1983.5	1382.0	0	Very small
1	0	0	2043.7	1397.7	18	Medium
1	**1**	**0**	**1920.5**	**1221.7**	**19**	**Very small**
1	2	0	1972.1	1258.8	6	Small
1	1	1	1921.9	1223.5	30	Very small
1	1	2	1958.3	1316.8	29	Big
1	2	1	1931.4	1230.5	15	Small
1	2	2	2061.5	1451.5	27	Big

for 55–60 min ahead interval we used largest value in entire dataset (training, validation and test) $R = 1150.27$ kW because same approach was used in solution with which we compare our methods.

In all experiments metrics RMSE and MAE are in kW and metrics nRMSE and MRE are in %.

6.2 Experiments with Settings of Firefly Algorithm

In this series of experiments we tried various settings of FA to find the most suitable setting we could use in further experiments. We investigated the impact of parameters α, β and γ described in Subsect. 3.1 on the speed of finding the best solution in that run (column *Best generation*) and how scattered were fireflies after last generation. This series of experiments were performed on first method of prediction which used only current weather to forecast hour ahead production. For each experiment we used 15 fireflies and 30 generations.

We must note that data used in these experiments were later slightly changed and therefore model performances are slightly different compared to other experiments. However we did not run these experiments again because we could use the results to decide which setting is most suitable for further experiments.

We can see in Table 1 that when $\alpha = 0$ firefly algorithm was not able to find good hyperparameter settings of SVR model, but very small scattering was achieved. We assume that this is because there was no random movement, therefore fireflies moved directly towards each other. We can also see that scattering is smaller when value of γ is smaller. This happens because smaller values of γ mean better visibility. When $\beta_0 = 0$ movement is completely random because β_0 controls attractivity of fireflies. Otherwise there does not seem to be any significant influence of β_0 on optimization.

We chose settings where $\alpha = 1$, $\beta_0 = 1$ and $\gamma = 0$ for further use because of the small spread after last generation and also because best solution was not found too late nor too early.

Table 2. Results of experiments with first method. In column *Used attributes* value 1 represents only current weather, value 2 represents weather change in last hour, value 3 represents measured production in 3 previous hours and value 4 represents measured production from most similar sample. Last row (in italic) is SVR with default parameters and best attributes.

Used attributes	Single model		Single model with bias correction	
	RMSE (nRMSE)	MAE (MRE)	RMSE (nRMSE)	MAE (MRE)
1	1968.2 (9.01)	1256.7 (5.75)	1954.2 (8.94)	1267.7 (5.80)
1, 2	2043.5 (9.35)	1354.0 (6.19)	2037.9 (9.32)	1379.9 (6.31)
1, 3	1511.1 (6.91)	948.1 (4.34)	1510.1 (6.91)	947.7 (4.34)
1, 4	1916.3 (8.77)	1220.6 (5.58)	1906.6 (8.72)	1237.1 (5.66)
1, 2, 3	1477.2 (6.76)	932.9 (4.27)	1475.0 (6.75)	934.8 (4.28)
1, 2, 4	1959.5 (8.97)	1380.5 (6.31)	1967.6 (9.00)	1403.3 (6.42)
1, 2, 3, 4	**1464.0 (6.70)**	**888.7 (4.07)**	**1461.9 (6.69)**	**890.2 (4.07)**
1, 2, 3, 4	*1498.3 (6.86)*	*952.9 (4.36)*	*1496.1 (6.84)*	*956.9 (4.38)*

6.3   Experiments with Hour Ahead Prediction

In this series of experiments we used various features for prediction of hour ahead production of PV power. We grouped those features into four sets: current weather, weather change in last hour, power production for last three hours, power production from most similar sample in the past.

Single Model Experiments. In order to decide which attributes are most suitable for second method, we evaluated accuracy of the first method on multiple combinations of attributes. We include prediction with and without bias correction for comparison. For each experiment we used 15 fireflies and 50 generations.

Best results in Table 2 were obtained when previous power production was used. Using weather changes also improved results when it was used along with current weather and previous production. However, when used only with current weather, trained model was less accurate. Similar production improved accuracy in most cases except one, where MAE of trained model was higher compared to model trained on same attributes but without similar production.

In case of bias correction, we evaluated every model with and without bias correction. We noticed that when using bias correction, RMSE tends to be smaller compared to RMSE without bias correction, however MAE tends to increase slightly. We think this happened because bias correction flattened high errors, but increased overall error.

We have added SVR with default hyperparameters and best attributes to show that optimization helped us to improve results. It is best seen when comparing the best model (in bold) with default SVR on MAE metric. Other models were less accurate than default, but it is because of attributes.

Table 3. The attributes current weather and previous production were used. Initial number of weather classes was 2. No classes merged.

Method variations	RMSE (nRMSE)	MAE (MRE)
Basic	1500.8 (6.87)	914.7 (4.19)
Bias correction	1497.1 (6.85)	918.9 (4.20)
Multiclass	1498.9 (6.86)	914.1 (4.18)
Multiclass with bias correction	1495.3 (6.84)	918.3 (4.20)

Table 4. The attributes current weather, weather change and previous production were used. Initial number of weather classes was 5 and after merging 3.

Method variations	RMSE (nRMSE)	MAE (MRE)
Basic	1486.0 (6.80)	896.2 (4.10)
Bias correction	1484.6 (6.79)	900.1 (4.12)
Multiclass	1480.5 (6.77)	892.1 (4.08)
Multiclass with bias correction	1479.1 (6.77)	896.0 (4.10)

Multiple Model Experiments. In Tables 3, 4 and 5 are the best results of the experiments with the second method for each attribute combination. We used three best attribute combinations from experiments with first method. For each used combination of attributes we evaluated accuracy without any improvements, with bias correction, with multiclass prediction (Subsect. 4.2) and with combination of bias correction and multiclass prediction. For each experiment we used 10 fireflies and 20 generations.

We can see in Tables 4 and 5 that RMSE slightly increased compared to the single model experiments (Table 2) and in Table 3 that RMSE decreased. However in all cases MAE decreased.

Increase of RMSE means that some deviations from real values are larger compared to the first method and decrease of MAE means that overall deviations are smaller. Increase of RMSE might have happened because optimization of models for specific weather class did not achieve global optimum. Other reason might be that model could not be more accurate on given class because samples in a class were too different due to merging of classes.

Regarding improvement of accuracy of second method, we noticed that both bias correction and usage of multiple classes for prediction decreased RMSE. However bias correction increases MAE. Best results for MAE were achieved with usage of multiple classes, however combination of bias correction and multiple classes achieved smallest RMSE.

Bias correction has probably flattened high errors, but increased overall error as in single model experiments. We think multiclass predictions improved accuracy because it took into consideration that samples might be misclassified.

Table 5. The attributes current weather, weather change, previous and similar production were used. Initial number of weather classes was 25 and after merging 8.

Method variations	RMSE (nRMSE)	MAE (MRE)
Basic	1474.4 (6.75)	874.3 (4.00)
Bias correction	1473.1 (6.74)	878.7 (4.02)
Multiclass	1471.5 (6.73)	872.3 (3.99)
Multiclass with bias correction	1470.2 (6.73)	876.5 (4.01)

Table 6. Comparison of our solution with solution from [11]. Values of MAE and MRE for NN ensemble and SVR are taken from compared article. Single model represents first method and Multiclass with bias correction represents second method.

Method of prediction	MAE	MRE
NN ensemble	100.2	8.71
SVR	107.4	9.34
Single model	100.4	8.73
Multiclass with bias correction	102.0	8.87

6.4   Comparison with Existing Solution

In this series of experiments, we compared the best solutions of both our methods to the best solution from [11]. They also used data from University of Queensland, but from years 2013 and 2014 and from multiple buildings.

In order to obtain most accurate results, we tried to replicate data used in the mentioned solution. However we were not able to fully reproduce data they used and therefore results might have been slightly different as if data were identical.

They made predictions for every 5-min interval for next hour. We compared our solutions to theirs only on the last interval (55–60 min ahead). For experiments we used feature sets combinations for both methods where highest accuracy was acquired when predicting for one hour ahead. For both methods the best combination was current weather, weather changes, previous and similar production. In both experiments we used 10 fireflies and 20 generations.

In Table 6 we can see that first method has performance similar to ensemble of neural networks, but outperformed their SVR. Difference is that in our method SVR is optimized using FA and SVR from [11] does not seem to be optimized. Also we did not use same features. That might have caused better performance.

We can see that second method performed worse than first method. This probably happened because we had to change the application of second method due to high computational complexity of SVR. Instead of optimizing for various numbers of weather classes, models were only trained with optimal parameters obtained from the first method on the same data. Then we optimized models for best number of weather classes. As a result the optimal number of weather classes might not have been used. Another reason might be that models were not optimized enough to perform better.

7 Conclusion

In this paper, we proposed approach to prediction of PV power based on classifying samples into different weather classes and using FA to optimize model for each weather class.

We compared this approach to single SVR model optimized on entire training data set. Experiments show that our approach tends to decrease MAE compared to single model. We also compared our methods with [11]. We achieved similar accuracy with both of our methods, however the second method performed worse than expected. This is probably caused by the fact that we did not utilize FA optimization fully when comparing with [11]. From this and comparison of optimized and unoptimized single SVR model we conclude that optimization has visible impact on accuracy of predictions and we recommend using it.

Our approach has proven to have potential, however it still needs improvements. It might be improved by changing merging of weather classes from one large class into several smaller classes to avoid the problem of merging of two too different classes. Also optimization of classifier could result in more accurate assignment to classes and therefore better performance.

In the future we might also try different optimization algorithms to compare them with FA, however we do not expect any significant improvements from using different optimization algorithm.

Acknowledgements. This work was supported by the project "Knowledge-based Approach to Intelligent Big Data Analysis" - Slovak Research and Development Agency under the contract No. APVV-16-0213 and by the project "International Centre of Excellence for Research of Intelligent and Secure Information-Communication Technologies and Systems - phase II", No. ITMS: 313021W404, cofinanced by the European Regional Development Fund.

References

1. Antonanzas, J., Osorio, N., Escobar, R., Urraca, R., Martinez-de Pison, F., Antonanzas-Torres, F.: Review of photovoltaic power forecasting. Solar Energy **136**, 78–111 (2016). https://doi.org/10.1016/J.SOLENER.2016.06.069
2. Chen, C., Duan, S., Cai, T., Liu, B.: Online 24-h solar power forecasting based on weather type classification using artificial neural network. Solar Energy **85**(11), 2856–2870 (2011). https://doi.org/10.1016/J.SOLENER.2011.08.027
3. De Leone, R., Pietrini, M., Giovannelli, A.: Photovoltaic energy production forecast using support vector regression. Neural Comput. Appl. **26**(8), 1955–1962 (2015). https://doi.org/10.1007/s00521-015-1842-y
4. Drucker, H., Burges, C.J., Kaufman, L., Smola, A.J., Vapnik, V.: Support vector regression machines. In: Advances in Neural Information Processing Systems, pp. 155–161 (1997)
5. Gensler, A., Henze, J., Sick, B., Raabe, N.: Deep learning for solar power forecasting - an approach using AutoEncoder and LSTM neural networks. In: 2016 IEEE International Conference on Systems, Man, and Cybernetics SMC 2016 - Conference Proceedings, pp. 2858–2865. IEEE, October 2017. https://doi.org/10.1109/SMC.2016.7844673

6. Hossain, M.R., Oo, A.M.T., Ali, A.B.M.S.: Hybrid prediction method for solar power using different computational intelligence algorithms. Smart Grid Renew. Energy **04**(01), 76–87 (2013). https://doi.org/10.4236/sgre.2013.41011
7. Hossain, M., Mekhilef, S., Danesh, M., Olatomiwa, L., Shamshirband, S.: Application of extreme learning machine for short term output power forecasting of three grid-connected PV systems. J. Clean. Prod. **167**, 395–405 (2018). https://doi.org/10.1016/j.jclepro.2017.08.081
8. Li, Y., He, Y., Su, Y., Shu, L.: Forecasting the daily power output of a grid-connected photovoltaic system based on multivariate adaptive regression splines. Appl. Energy **180**, 392–401 (2016). https://doi.org/10.1016/j.apenergy.2016.07.052
9. Long, H., Zhang, Z., Su, Y.: Analysis of daily solar power prediction with data-driven approaches. Appl. Energy **126**, 29–37 (2014). https://doi.org/10.1016/j.apenergy.2014.03.084
10. Nageem, R., Jayabarathi, R.: Predicting the power output of a grid-connected solar panel using multi-input support vector regression. Procedia Comput. Sci. **115**, 723–730 (2017). https://doi.org/10.1016/j.procs.2017.09.143
11. Rana, M., Koprinska, I., Agelidis, V.G.: Univariate and multivariate methods for very short-term solar photovoltaic power forecasting. Energy Convers. Manag. **121**, 380–390 (2016). https://doi.org/10.1016/J.ENCONMAN.2016.05.025
12. Shi, J., Lee, W.J., Liu, Y., Yang, Y., Wang, P.: Forecasting power output of photovoltaic systems based on weather classification and support vector machines. In: IEEE Transactions on Industry Applications, vol. 48, pp. 1064–1069, October 2012. https://doi.org/10.1109/TIA.2012.2190816
13. Sun, X., Zhang, T.: Solar power prediction in smart grid based on NWP data and an improved boosting method. In: 2017 IEEE International Conference on Energy Internet (ICEI), pp. 89–94. IEEE, April 2017. https://doi.org/10.1109/ICEI.2017.23
14. Theocharides, S., Makrides, G., Georghiou, G.E., Kyprianou, A.: Machine learning algorithms for photovoltaic system power output prediction. In: 2018 IEEE International Energy Conference (ENERGYCON), pp. 1–6. IEEE, June 2018. https://doi.org/10.1109/ENERGYCON.2018.8398737
15. Wolff, B., Kühnert, J., Lorenz, E., Kramer, O., Heinemann, D.: Comparing support vector regression for PV power forecasting to a physical modeling approach using measurement, numerical weather prediction, and cloud motion data. Solar Energy **135**, 197–208 (2016). https://doi.org/10.1016/j.solener.2016.05.051
16. Yang, H.T., Huang, C.M., Huang, Y.C., Pai, Y.S.: A weather-based hybrid method for 1-day ahead hourly forecasting of PV power output. IEEE Trans. Sustain. Energy **5**(3), 917–926 (2014). https://doi.org/10.1109/TSTE.2014.2313600
17. Yang, X.: Firefly algorithm, stochastic test functions and design optimisation. Int. J. Bio-Inspired Comput. **2**(2), 78–84 (2010)

A Two-Step Approach to the Search of Minimum Energy Designs via Swarm Intelligence

Frederick Kin Hing Phoa[✉] and Tzu-Chieh Tsai

Institute of Statistical Science, Academia Sinica, Taipei, Taiwan
fredphoa@stat.sinica.edu.tw

Abstract. Recently, Swarm Intelligence Based (SIB) method, a nature-inspired metaheuristic optimization method, has been widely used in many problems that their solutions fall in discrete and continuous domains. SIB 1.0 is efficient to converge to optimal solution but its particle size is fixed and pre-defined, while SIB 2.0 allows particle size changes during the procedure but it takes longer time to converge. This paper introduces a two-step SIB method that combines the advantages of two SIB methods. The first step via SIB 2.0 serves as a preliminary study to determine the optimal particle size and the second step via SIB 1.0 serves as a follow-up study to obtain the optimal solution. This method is applied to the search of optimal minimum energy design and the result outperforms the results from both SIB 1.0 and SIB 2.0.

Keywords: Swarm intelligence · Nature-inspired metaheuristic method · Optimization · Two-step method · Minimum Energy Design

1 Introduction

Optimization problems in the real world are sometimes too complex and very challenging to solve within a reasonable amount of time. In order to obtain adequately good results, metaheuristics becomes a powerful method for this manner. Nature-inspired metaheuristic algorithms have been derived from the behavior of biological systems, physical or chemistry systems in nature [1]. A major class of metaheuristic is swarm intelligence (SI) [2], which is the collective intelligence behavior of self-organized and decentralized systems, including Genetic Algorithms (GA) [3], Artificial Bee Colony [4], Particle Swarm Optimization (PSO) [5] and many others listed in [6]. Among them, PSO is commonly used in solving many different types of high-dimensional optimization problems due to its simple form for implementation, its relatively small number of tuning parameters and a fast convergence towards optimum. However, the standard PSO method was not suitable for problems with the solutions in discrete domains.

Supported by Ministry of Science and Technology (MOST) of Taiwan (107-2118-M-001-011-MY3 and 108-2321-B-001-016) and Thematic Project of Academia Sinica, Taiwan (AS-TP-109-M07).

© Springer Nature Switzerland AG 2020
Y. Tan et al. (Eds.): ICSI 2020, LNCS 12145, pp. 37–45, 2020.
https://doi.org/10.1007/978-3-030-53956-6_4

[7] proposed a new nature-inspired metaheuristic optimization method called the Swarm Intelligence Based (SIB) method. This algorithm works well in a wide range of discrete optimization problems, such as searching for circulant partial Hadamard matrices with maximum number of columns [8], $E(s^2)$-optimal super-saturated designs [9], and optimal designs of computer experiments under multiple objectives [10]. In addition, SIB also performed well in optimization problems for continuous domains, like efficient construction of confidence sets and the confidence bands for target localization [11]. Besides, the computational efficiency of the SIB method can be improved via a smart initialization procedure [12]. Recently, [14] modified the standard framework of the SIB method by allowing the particle size to be changed during the search. The details of this augmented framework will be briefly reviewed in the next section.

Notice that the standard framework of the SIB method is limited to be applied due to the pre-defined particle sizes, but when the particle size is allowed to be changed, the SIB 2.0 suffers from high algorithmic complexity. The purpose of this paper is to provide a two-step approach that combines the standard framework and the augmented version of the SIB method, so that the particle size is allowed to be changed while the algorithm can be executed efficiently. We demonstrate our proposed method in the search of optimal Minimum Energy Design. The rest of the paper is organized as follows. We reviewed the essential components of the SIB method and the basic knowledge of the Minimum Energy Design in the second section. We introduce the proposed two-step method in the third section. In Sect. 4, we show a performance check via simulation studies, and we summarize the contribution and concluded remarks in the last section.

2   The Swarm Intelligence Based Method: A Review

2.1   The Swarm Intelligence Based (SIB) Method

A pseudo-code of the SIB method is given below.

S0: Randomly generate a set of initial particles, each with different number of entries.
S1: Evaluate objective function values of all particles.
S2: Initialize the local best (LB) for each particle and the global best (GB).
S3: For each particle, perform the MIX and MOVE operation.
S4: If NO UPDATE in the previous MOVE operation: Perform the VARY and MOVE operation.
S5: If NO UPDATE in the previous MOVE operation: Perform the random jump.
S6: Update the LB for each particle and the GB among all particles.
S7: If NOT CONVERGE or the stopping criterion is NOT REACHED, repeat (S3) to (S6).

The SIB method starts with a set of initialization steps. It includes the initialization of a user-defined (N) number of particles (S0), the evaluation of these particles under an objective function of interest (S1), the definition of the LB for each particle, and the selection of the GB among all particles (S2). Additional parameters are being set before the end of the initialization, including the number of components being exchanged with the LB (q_{LB}), the number of components being exchanged with the GB (q_{GB}), and the maximum number of iteration allowed. The details on the setting of these parameters are referred to [7]. After the initialization steps, it enters the iteration steps for optimization.

The standard framework of the SIB method, abbreviated as SIB 1.0 thereafter, consists of all above step except S4. For each particle in S3, every iteration step starts with an exchange procedure called the MIX operation. It is an exchange procedure between the current particle and the best particles, both the particle's LB and the GB. In brief, q (q_{LB} when exchanged with the particle's LB and q_{GB} when exchanged with the GB) components are first selected in the best particle and add to the current particle, then q components among all components in the current particles are deleted. After the MIX operation, two new particles, namely *mixwLB* and *mixwGB*, are formed and they are compared to the current particle under the objective function in the MOVE operation. If one of the new particles has the best objective function value, the current particle will be updated to that new particle, otherwise, the random jump procedure that some components in the current particle are exchanged to the randomly selected components is performed in S5. When the exchange procedures of all particles are completed, the updates of the LBs of all particles are performed followed by the update of the GB among all LBs (S6). If the GB does not converge to the optimal value of the objective function (if known), or the number of iteration has not reached its maximum number yet, the iteration will repeat. Readers who were interested in the details of the SIB 1.0 are referred to [7].

The wide use of the SIB 1.0 is hindered by its limitation of the fixed particle size. Note that the MIX operation adds and deletes exactly q number of components in the current particle, so the size is always fixed. It is sometimes a requirement in some applications, like the application in experimental designs [9], but in most cases, it becomes inefficient when one applies the SIB 1.0 multiple times for different particle sizes. Thus, it is desired to develop an enhanced framework of the SIB method, abbreviated as SIB 2.0, for problems with flexible run sizes during the optimization.

The key addition of the SIB 2.0 (S4) appears after the MIX and MOVE operations in S3. If the current particle is still the best among all three particles in MOVE operation in S3, or in other words, both best particles cannot further improve the current particle in this iteration, we make the size change on the current particle in S4 via the VARY operation first before considering the random jump. The VARY operation consists of unit shortening and unit expansion, and it results in a particle with reduced number of component and a particle with additional number of component respectively. Then we perform the MOVE operation to compare the objective function values among the current particle, the shortened particle and the expanded particle. Similar judgement is used to determine whether particle is updated or the random jump is performed. Readers who were interested in the details of the SIB 2.0 are referred to [14].

3   The Two-Step Swarm Intelligence Based Method

As discussed in [14], the goal of developing SIB 2.0 is to avoid a multiple implementation of the SIB 1.0 for various particle sizes when the optimal particle size is unknown in prior. This greatly reduces the computational time as only one SIB algorithm is required to search for optimal solution together with the particle's optimal size. However, it is also true that if the optimal particle size is known in prior, SIB 1.0 performs better than SIB 2.0 under the same amount of searching time because of the much larger particle choices in SIB 2.0. Therefore, an ideal strategy of efficient use of the SIB method is to find the optimal particle size followed by the application of SIB 1.0 at that specific particle size. Thus, we propose our two-step SIB method as follows.

> Input user-defined parameters: number of seeds N, number of iterations L, numbers of unit exchanges, and other parameters for specific problems.
> Step 1: Perform SIB 2.0 to detect optimal particle size (L iterations).
> Result: A suggested value of particle size k.
> Part 2: Perform SIB 1.0 at particle size k to obtain the optimal solution ($0.2L$ iterations).
> Result: GB particle as the optimal particle suggested in this method.

Here are some details on this two-step SIB method. The first step is basically a standard SIB 2.0 with a slightly different goal. Instead of finding the optimal solution via the objective function, it simply needs to detect the best choice of particle size that leads to good objective function values. Therefore, even though it is known that the solution of SIB 2.0 may not be as good as SIB 1.0 (known particle size in prior) at the same computational time, it is still good enough to detect a good particle size only. Next, the second step is a standard SIB 1.0 that the particle size is obtained from the first step. We suggest to use only 1/5 number of iterations because we have inserted the best particle obtained from the first step into the initial particle set. This implies that the GB in the very first step has already been as good as all searches in the first step, so it is reasonable to save some iterations in the second step.

In fact, the idea of the second step in our proposed method is equivalent to the follow-up procedure in many industrial experiments. Thus, when compared to the SIB 2.0, our proposed method spends slightly more resources (20% more) to efficiently optimize the results based on the findings of the SIB 2.0 (the first step). On the other hands, our proposed method still saves a tremendous amount of computational time when compared to multiple implementation of SIB 1.0 at various particle sizes.

4 Demonstration: A Search of Minimum Energy Designs

4.1 A Brief Introduction to Minimum Energy Design (MED)

Computer experiment has become a new trend for many industrial experiments and scientific testings, especially for those with astronomical costs or infeasible procedures. Traditionally, Latin hypercube designs and uniform designs are two classical types of designs for computer experiments. The former design, constructed systematically via algebra, is particularly useful in grid-type domain while the latter design, obtained via computer search, enjoys an uniform distribution of particles over continuous domain. However, both designs are desired under an important assumption that there is its domain gradient is a uniform function, meaning that every single position in the domain is evenly important.

It is obvious that most domains do not have a uniform gradient in the real world, because some parts are more important than others when prior knowledge from experts are given. [13] proposed the minimum energy design (MED) for the computer experiments when the domain gradient follows a given function known in prior. When a defined number of particles are assigned to the domain, they suggest to put more particles in more important regions instead of evenly distributed all particles. This suggestion is reasonable because an important domain region deserves to spend extra particles to detect its value of interest.

[13] provides examples that the MEDs are obtained via computer searches. When the domain is in grid forms and the grid size is not large, it is certainly desired to search over all possible combinations to obtain the best particle orientation. However, when the grid size is too large that becomes infeasible to search over all possible combinations, or the grid size is continuous in nature, we need an efficient approach to obtain the adequately good MED, even if it is not optimal. Thus, we suggest to use our proposed two-step SIB method.

We recall some basic terminologies in MED below. Based on an analogy of the physical system, MED treated every design points as charged particles. The key idea (objective function) was to minimize the total potential energy of the system. In specific, an MED with its design points $\{x_1, ..., x_n\}$ was optimal if it satisfied the criterion $\max_D \min_{i,j} \frac{d(x_i, x_j)}{q(x_i) q(x_j)}$ and the charge function was defined as $q(x) = \frac{1}{f(x)^{1/(2p)}}$, where p is the dimension and $f(x)$ is a desired density. In general, a good MED tried to place its design points as apart as possible under a modified distance weighted by the charge function $f(x)$.

4.2 Implementation of the Two-Step SIB Method

Instead of the computer search in [13], a recent work by [12] applied the SIB 1.0 method to obtain an improved result on the search of MEDs, and the search efficiency is also improved. Their results are under an assumption that the particle size is given, and they argued that it was normal because the experimental budget was usually fixed in prior. However, this argument fails to consider the possibility that less amount of resources sometimes can achieve similar performance, or in other words, it is still able to save experimental resources by conducting an expriment via MED below the maximum possible budget.

In specific, our experimental domain is a three-dimensional cube that different locations (points) have different temperatures shown in Fig. 1. This temperature gradient is arbitrary for demonstration purpose. Each pair of points is apart from 0.2 units, so there were 4096 points in the cube. Our goal is to create a MED with unknown number of points in this experimental region. Notice that a evenly-distributed point allocation will obviously not satisfy the minimum energy criterion. For the initialization, we set the number of iteration in the first step as $L = 500$, the number of iteration in the second step as 100 ($0.2L$), and the number of MED sets $N = 204$ (about 5% of maximum number of points). We also initialize these particles with different sizes ranging from 3 to 20 (about 10% of N), and all exchange parameters are set as $q_{LB} = q_{GB} = q_s = q_e = 1$.

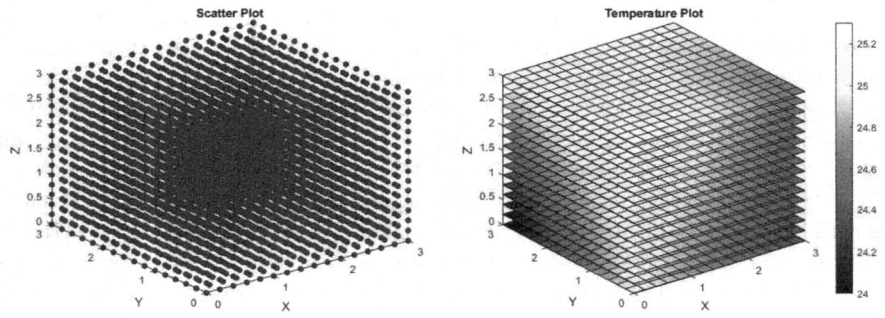

Fig. 1. Experimental region

4.3 Result

After 500 iterations of 204 particles, the GB particle resulted in the first step suggests that the optimal particle size is 7 and this particle has energy -11.831543. Then we set $k = 7$ in the second step and an extra 100 iterations are run. Table 1 lists the coordinates of the seven points in the domain and the dots in Fig. 2 visually shows their locations in the domain. This GB particle has the minimum energy -12.856852. The whole procedure can be done within 5 min using a standard personal computer.

In order to check if the MED suggested in this method is good, we conduct 18 SIB 1.0, each with different particle size ranging from 3 to 20 and the maximum number of iteration is 500. The energies of their GB particles are shown in Fig. 3. Although this figure suggests that $k = 8$ may have the lowest energy among all 18 k, the difference between the results of $k = 7$ (-12.33198) and $k = 8$ (-12.38761) is very small. Notice that an additional point may imply an increase in the experimental cost, the marginal improvement by adding one point

Table 1. Coordinates of positions with temperatures

	Node1	Node2	Node3	Node4	Node5	Node6	Node7
X	2.8	0.2	3.0	0.4	3.0	0.2	0.4
Y	2.6	0.4	2.8	3.0	0.0	2.8	0.2
Z	2.8	0.2	0.2	0.0	0.0	2.6	3.0
Temperature	24.9267	24.8709	24.6702	24.34	25.3	24.2576	24.1448

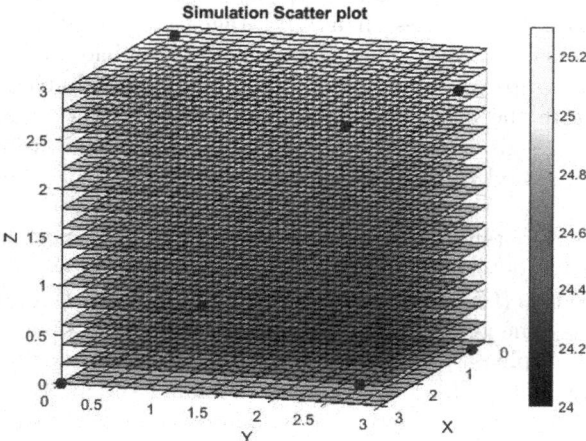

Fig. 2. SIB 2.0 simulation scatter plot

from $k = 7$ and $k = 8$ is small. In addition, our result is better than all results in Fig. 3 including those of $k = 7$ and $k = 8$. It is the advantage of inserting the best particle from the first step to the initial stage of the second step.

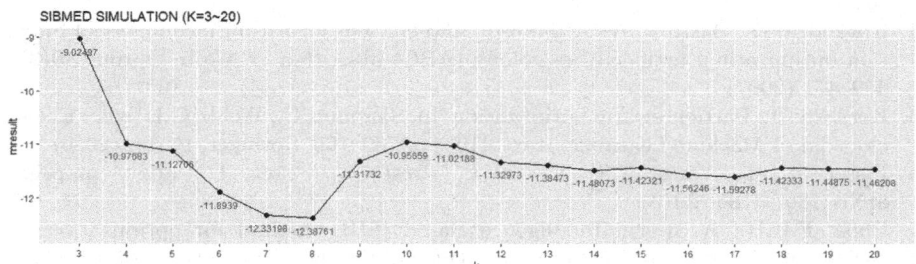

Fig. 3. SIB 1.0 simulation result plot

5   Discussion and Conclusion

SIB 1.0 is widely known as an efficient nature-inspired metaheuristic method for optimization problems in discrete and continuous domain, but its use is hindered by its pre-defined particle size. SIB 2.0 allows particle size to be changed during the optimization procedure, but it also greatly expands the number of possible outcomes. Thus it needs to spend longer time to obtain the results as good as the results obtained by SIB 1.0 when the particle size is known. Therefore, the main contribution of this paper is to propose a two-step method that combines SIB 1.0 and SIB 2.0 and takes their advantages into account. We treat SIB 2.0 as a preliminary study to obtain the optimal particle size, then we treat SIB 1.0 as a follow-up experiment and conduct it under that optimal particle size. We deonstrate the use of this two-step method in the search of optimal minimum energy design. The result outperforms both results from SIB 1.0 and SIB 2.0 and the method is comparably efficient to conducting multiple SIB 1.0 at various sizes.

There are many potential applications to this two-step methods. For example, it can be used to determine the sensor allocations in a given space to monitor environmental factors (temperature, humidity, gas concentration, etc.). It is better to achieve the same performance by using small number of sensors to reduce costs. Another example is to determine a set of biomarkers that have significant impact to the response. The exact number of biomarker in this significant set is not known in prior, but the fewer the biomarkers, the lower the experimental costs to detect the quantities of these biomarkers from the instruments.

References

1. Mirjalili, S.: The art lion optimizer. Adv. Eng. Softw. **83**, 80–98 (2015)
2. Ab Wahab, M.N., Nefti-Meziani, S., Atyabi, A.: A comprehensive review of swarm optimization algorithms. PLoS ONE **10**(5), e0122827 (2015)
3. Goldberg, D.: Genetic Algorithms in Optimization. Search and Machine Learning. Addison Wesley, New York (2003)
4. Karaboga, D., Basturk, B.: A powerful and efficient algorithm for numerical function optimization: artificial bee colony (ABC) algorithm. J. Glob. Optim. **39**(3), 459–471 (2007)
5. Kennedy, J.: Particle swarm optimization. In: Sammut, C., Webb, G.I. (eds.) Encyclopedia of Machine Learning, /textbf10, pp. 760–766. Springer, Berlin (2010)
6. Fister Jr., I., Yang, X.S., Fister, I., Brest, J., Fister, D.: arXiv preprint arXiv:1307.4186 (2013)
7. Phoa, F.K.H.: A Swarm Intelligence Based (SIB) method for optimization in designs of experiments. Nat. Comput. **16**(4), 597–605 (2016). https://doi.org/10.1007/s11047-016-9555-4
8. Phoa, F.K.H., Lin, Y.-L., Wang, T.-C.: Using swarm intelligence to search for circulant partial Hadamard matrices. In: Tan, Y., Shi, Y., Coello, C.A.C. (eds.) ICSI 2014. LNCS, vol. 8794, pp. 158–164. Springer, Cham (2014). https://doi.org/10.1007/978-3-319-11857-4_18

9. Phoa, F.K.H., Chen, R.B., Wang, W.C., Wong, W.K.: Optimizing two-level super-saturated designs using swarm intelligence techniques. Technometrics **58**(1), 43–49 (2016)
10. Phoa, F.K.H., Chang, L.L.N.: A multi-objective implementation in swarm intelligence and its applications in designs of computer experiments. In: Proceedings of 12th International Conference on Natural Computation, Fuzzy Systems and Knowledge Discovery (ICNC-FSKD) 2016, pp. 253–258. IEEE (2016)
11. Lin, F.P.C., Phoa, F.K.H.: An efficient construction of confidence regions via swarm intelligence and its application in target localization. IEEE Access **6**, 8610–8618 (2017)
12. Hsu, T.-C., Phoa, F.K.H.: A smart initialization on the swarm intelligence based method for efficient search of optimal minimum energy design. In: Tan, Y., Shi, Y., Tang, Q. (eds.) ICSI 2018. LNCS, vol. 10941, pp. 78–87. Springer, Cham (2018). https://doi.org/10.1007/978-3-319-93815-8_9
13. Joseph, V.R., Dasgupta, T., Tuo, R., Wu, C.F.J.: Sequential exploration of complex surfaces using minimum energy designs. Technometrics **57**(1), 64–74 (2015)
14. Phoa, F.K.H., Wang, T.C., Chang, L.L.N.: An enhanced version of the swarm intelligence based method (SIB 2.0). In Review

On Assessing the Temporal Characteristics of Reaching the Milestone by a Swarm

Eugene Larkin and Maxim Antonov[✉]

Tula State University, Tula 300012, Russia
elarkin@mail.ru, max0594@yandex.ru

Abstract. The physical swarm operation is investigated. Swarm units are considered as three-wheeled mobile robots, moving through rough terrain. For the longitudinal movement of such type vehicle the dynamic model is obtained. The article discusses the issue of forecasting the time a physical swarm reaches a milestone and proposes a hypothesis on the form of the law of the distribution of time during which a swarm unit reaches a milestone. Obtaining this time distribution is carried out with use the Petri-Markov net fundamental apparatus. With use Petri-Markov nets time densities of reaching the milestone both one unit and swarm as a whole are obtained. More common formula of distribution of time of milestone reaching by l units of K is obtained too. To confirm the hypothesis about the type of theoretical time distribution a computer experiment was carried out using the Monte Carlo method.

Keywords: Swarm · Swarm unit · Longitudinal movement · Milestone temporal characteristics · Petri-Markov net · Monte Carlo method

1 Introduction

At the present time, the physical swarm is widely used in various fields of human activity, such as industry, defense, ecology [1], as well as to perform tasks of locating objects on the ground, reconnaissance, counter-terrorism, mine clearance operations, etc.

The study of a physical swarm and modeling of its behavior is a field of active scientific research, popular for more than two decades. After the work of Reynolds [2], devoted to the study of the behavior of a flock of birds in flight, extensive studies were carried out to model and analyze the behavior of the swarm, as well as to develop algorithms for controlling and coordinating the swarm [3].

Of greatest interest are the tasks of swarm coordination, requiring that the milestone be reached by all units of the physical swarm at the same time or with a minimum time spread. Such a need arises, for example when it is necessary to surround the target and not miss it. In real conditions, each unit of a physical swarm moves along its own unique trajectory, determined by the relief and micro-relief of the terrain, weather conditions, etc.

Therefore, the achievement of a milestone by each unit of a physical swarm occurs with random time, which in turn, is determined by robot design and properties of terrain.

© Springer Nature Switzerland AG 2020
Y. Tan et al. (Eds.): ICSI 2020, LNCS 12145, pp. 46–55, 2020.
https://doi.org/10.1007/978-3-030-53956-6_5

Known methods for modeling the behavior of the swarm [4, 5], as well as algorithms for coordinating the swarm on the ground [6, 7] have a significant drawback, which at the stage of designing a physical swarm, not allow to evaluate the temporal and probabilistic characteristics of its functioning in real conditions, therefore, they do not allow to solve the problem of reaching the milestone with all units of the physical swarm with a minimum time spread. Therefore, the investigation, carried out below are relevant, and important for the practice of swarm design.

2 Dynamics of Swarm Unit Longitudinal Movement

Structure of swarm unit, as a transport vehicle, is shown on the Fig. 1.

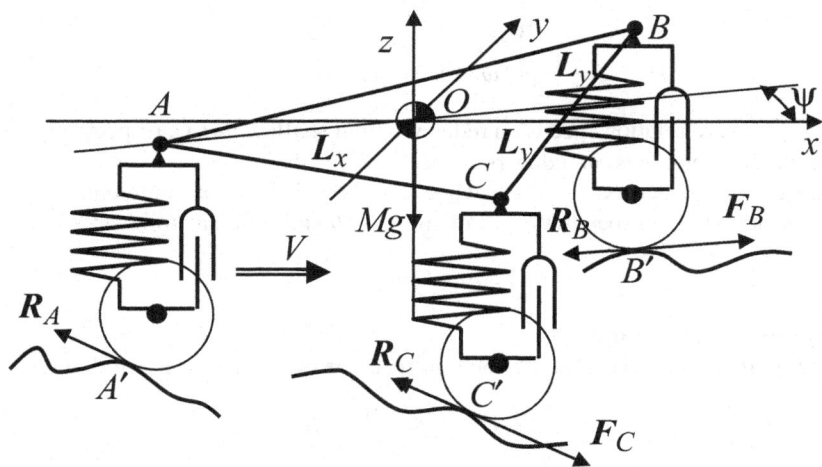

Fig. 1. Kinematics of swarm unit.

Unit is considered as the absolutely rigid trunk, based on viscose/elastic supports, placed at isosceles triangle vertices A, B, C. Swarm unit moves on the rugged terrain and every wheel is in its individual road conditions. Wheels B and C are active [8]. The combined moment of these wheels provides the longitudinal movement of the unit, and the differential moment provides maneuvering on a terrain. Wheel A is strongly passive. It provides third fulcrum only, and is installed on the support, which in turn, rotates at hinge. Axis of rotation is perpendicular to the ABC-plane. The trunk has no longitudinal not transverse mobility degree relatively to supports, in such a way centers of wheels may move the straights line perpendicular ABC-plane only. Lengths of supports counterbalance the weight of trunk Mg, where M is the trunk mass; g is the gravity acceleration. Wheels touch the terrain at points A', B', C'. In points of touch forces tangential component provides both resistance R_A, R_B, R_C, and driving forces F_B, F_C.

To describe the influence of terrain relief on the time of getting by swarm unit milestone one should work out the differential equation, describing robot longitudinal movement. Differential equation, which describes angle velocity of B and C electric engines shafts are as follows:

$$\begin{cases} T\dot{\omega}_B + \omega_B + K_\mu\mu_B + K_\nu\nu_B = K_U U_B; \\ T\dot{\omega}_C + \omega_C + K_\mu\mu_C + K_\nu\nu_C = K_U U_C, \end{cases} \tag{1}$$

where ω_B, ω_C are rotation speeds of B and C motor shafts; T is the time constant of motors; μ_B, μ_C are payload moments on B and C motor shafts; ν_B, ν_C are moments of dry friction in the bears of engine; U_B, U_C are control actions applied to B and C motors; K_μ, K_ν, K_U are proportionality factors.

If necessary, motors are equipped with reduction gears with transmitting coefficient i (when motor have no reducer, then $i = 1$). So moments and rotation speeds at reduction gear output shafts are as follows:

$$\begin{cases} \frac{{}^r\mu_{B,C}}{i} = \mu_{B,C}; \\ {}^r\omega_{B,C}i = \omega_{B,C}, \end{cases} \tag{2}$$

where ${}^r\omega_B\,{}^r\omega_C$ are rotation speeds on reducer output shafts B and C, respectively; ${}^r\mu_B$, ${}^r\mu_C$ are payload moments on reducers B and C output shafts.

Reducers are loaded on the drive wheels, so wheel drive circumferential speeds, which coincide with the speeds V_B, V_c of supports B and C, are as follows:

$$V_{B,C} = {}^r\omega_{B,C}q, \tag{3}$$

where q is the wheel radius.

Longitudinal speed and azimuth rotation speed of swarm unit are as follows:

$$\begin{cases} V = \dfrac{V_B + V_c}{2}; \\ \dot{\psi} = \dfrac{V_B - V_c}{2L_y}, \end{cases} \tag{4}$$

where $2L_y$ is width between supports B and C; $\dot{\psi} = \frac{d\psi}{dt}$.

Swarm unit moves forward and rotates around z axis under the action of driving and resistance forces. Center of rotation is situated on the straight line, passing through points B and C.

Differential equation system, which describes dynamic of longitudinal movement and azimuth angle rotation of unit, is as follows:

$$\begin{cases} M\dot{V} + \eta_V V = (F_B - R_B)\cos\alpha_B + (F_C - R_C)\cos\alpha_C - R_A\cos\alpha_A; \\ J\ddot{\psi} + \eta_\psi\dot{\psi} = [(F_B - R_B)\cos\alpha_B - (F_C - R_C)\cos\alpha_C]L_y - R_A L_x \cos\alpha_A \sin\phi, \end{cases} \tag{5}$$

where M is the unit mass; J is the moment of inertia of swarm unit relative to center of rotation; η_V and η_ψ are coefficients, describing dissipative forces, affected on the unit (f.e. viscous friction); F_B, F_C are driving forces; R_A, R_B, R_C are resistance forces; α_A, α_B, α_C are angles between horizontal plane and tangential force in points A', B', C' respectively; φ is angle of the passive wheel A rotation.

Joint solution of Eqs. (3)–(5) gives following system, describing longitudinal movement and azimuth angle maneuvering of three wheels swarm unit:

$$\delta_V(\kappa) \cdot D_{VV}(\kappa) + \delta_{\dot\psi}(\kappa) \cdot D_{V\dot\psi}(\kappa) = \delta_{FV}(\kappa);$$ (6)

$$\delta_V(\kappa) \cdot D_{\dot\psi V}(\kappa) + \delta_{\dot\psi}(\kappa) \cdot D_{\dot\psi\dot\psi}(\kappa) = \delta_{F\dot\psi}(\kappa),$$

where κ is the Laplace variable; $\delta_V(\kappa)$ - is increment of longitudinal speed; $\delta_{\dot\psi}(\kappa)$ - is increment of azimuth rotation speed; δ_{FV} is deviation of driving force, that provides longitudinal speed; $\delta_{F\dot\psi}$ is deviation of azimuth rotation force, that provides azimuth rotation speed.

$$D_{VV}(\kappa) = D_{\dot\psi V}(\kappa) = \kappa\left(M + \frac{2Ti^2}{K_\mu q^2}\right) + \left(\eta_V + \frac{2i^2}{K_\mu q^2}\right);$$

$$D_{V\dot\psi}(\kappa) = -D_{\dot\psi\dot\psi}(\kappa) = \kappa\left(\frac{J_z}{L_y} + \frac{2TL_y i^2}{K_\mu q^2}\right) + \left(\frac{\eta_\psi}{L_y} + \frac{2L_y i^2}{K_\mu q^2}\right).$$

Solving the system (6) gives

$$\delta_V(\kappa) = \frac{k_U \delta_{UB}}{T_{SU}\kappa + 1} + \frac{k_U \delta_{UC}}{T_{SU}\kappa + 1} - \frac{k_{\alpha A}\delta_{\alpha A}}{T_{SU}\kappa + 1} - \frac{k_{\alpha BC}\delta_{\alpha B}}{T_{SU}\kappa + 1} - \frac{k_{\alpha BC}\delta_{\alpha C}}{T_{SU}\kappa + 1},$$ (7)

where k_U, $k_{\alpha A}$, $k_{\alpha BC}$ are coefficients of proportionality; T_{SU} is the speedup time constant of swarm unit; $\delta_{\alpha A}$, $\delta_{\alpha B}$, $\delta_{\alpha C}$ is deviations of angles α_A, α_B, α_C between horizontal plane and tangential forces.

It is necessary to admit, that (7) is valid, when wheels does not lose mechanical contact with a road and transverse slip of the wheels on the surface is absent. Expressions (7) shows, that dynamics of longitudinal movement of 3-wheel swarm unit depends on characteristics of motors, gear ratio, design of chassis etc. Current swarm unit speed depends on deviations δ_{UB}, δ_{UC} of control actions U_B, U_C, applied to B and C motors, and deviations $\delta_{\alpha A}$, $\delta_{\alpha B}$, $\delta_{\alpha C}$. So, deviations of angles cause the deviation of swarm unit velocity from pre-determined level, and slowing down reaching the milestone by the unit. If such parameter of road, as profile correlation function, is known, time density of milestone achievement may be obtained.

3 Reaching the Milestone by the Swarm Unit

Let the swarm unit move to the milestone located at a distance S from it. When unit runs on the perfect flat surface, without hollows and/or hedges, the milestone may be reached at the time T, value of which is determined by the maximum speed developed by unit. At the same time, as it follows from (7), every obstacle on the movement trace increases this time. For a simulation of passing the distance by vehicle approach, based on Petri-Markov net (PMN) [9–12] conception may be proposed. Structure of PMN is shown on the Fig. 2. To obtain such structure the distance S from starting point till the milestone is divided onto elementary pieces s. After passing every piece swarm unit immediately starts to pass next piece. Petri-Markov net is described with the following set:

$$\Pi = \{\{a_1, a_1, a_2, \ldots, a_j, \ldots\}, \{z_1, z_2, \ldots, z_j, \ldots\},$$
$$\{I(z_1) = \emptyset, I(z_j) = a_{i-1}, i = 0, \ldots j, \ldots\}, \{O(z_j) = a_j, i = 0, \ldots j, \ldots\}\}, \quad (8)$$

where a_j are places; z_j are transitions; $I(\ldots)$ are transition input functions $O(\ldots)$ are transition output functions; $\emptyset$ is the zero set.

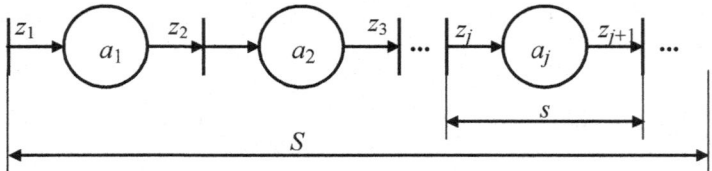

Fig. 2. PMN modeling the process of achieving the milestone.

Transition z_1 is the starting one, and simulates beginning swarm unit movement. Transition z_j simulates achievement the end of stage s. When $j \to \infty$ it simulates the end of the distance S. Places simulate generation of time intervals when swarm unit passes the stages.

Every stage may be passed by swarm unit with current velocity $V(t)$. Time, during of which unit passes the stage, is occasional and equal to

$$t_s = \frac{s}{V(t)} = T_s + \Delta(t), \qquad T_s = \frac{s}{V + \delta_V} = \bar{T}_s + \delta_{T_S} \quad (9)$$

where V is mean swarm unit velocity, caused by control actions U_B, U_C, applied to B and C motors according to Eq. (7); δ_V is a deviation of velocity from mean value, caused by roughness of terrain under wheels A, B, C; $\bar{T}_s$ is the mean time of passing the stage by swarm unit; δ_s is a deviation of time from mean value.

When deviation δ_V is occasional value, then deviation δ_{T_S} is occasional value too. It would be considered, that δ_{T_S} has zero mean value. So density of time of passing the stage is as follows:

$$f_s(t) = \delta(t - T_s) * f_\Delta(t), f_s(t) = \delta(t - \bar{T}_s) * \bar{f}_s(t) \quad (10)$$

where $\delta(t - \bar{T}_s)$ is the Dirac δ-function; $\bar{f}_s(t)$ is the time deviation density from mean value.

Accordingly to [13]

$$f_S(t) = \lim_{\substack{J \to \infty, \\ s \to 0}} L^{-1} \left[\prod_{j=1}^{J} L[\delta(t - \bar{T}_s) * \bar{f}_s(t)] \right] = \delta(t - \bar{T}_s) * \lim_{\substack{J \to \infty, \\ s \to 0}} L^{-1} \left[\prod_{j=1}^{J} L[\bar{f}_s(t)] \right]$$
$$(11)$$

where $L[\ldots]$ and $L^{-1}[\ldots]$ are direct and inverse Laplace transforms; $\bar{T}_S$ is the mean time spent by swarm unit for passing the whole distance S with pre-determined velocity V;

$$\bar{T}_S = \frac{S}{V}. \tag{12}$$

It is necessary to admit, that

$$\bar{f}_S(t) = \lim_{\substack{J \to \infty, \\ s \to 0}} L^{-1}\left[\prod_{j=1}^{J} L[\bar{f}_s(t)]\right] \tag{13}$$

is the convolution, describing sum of great number of small random values, which equally contribute to resulting random value. Accordingly to central limit theorem [14, 15] $\bar{f}_S(t)$ is normally distributed. Also swarm unit cannot reach the milestone earlier than at the time τ when driving the whole distance with maximal velocity $V_{\max}$;

$$\tau = \frac{S}{V_{\max}} \tag{14}$$

Taking into account the above circumstances, finally the time density of reaching the milestone by swarm unit takes the following form:

$$f_S(t) = \begin{cases} \dfrac{exp\left[-\frac{(t-T_S)^2}{2D_\Delta}\right] \cdot \eta(t-\tau)}{\int\limits_{\tau}^{\infty} exp\left[-\frac{(t-T_S)^2}{2D_\Delta}\right] dt}, & when\ t \geq \tau; \\ 0\ otherwise \end{cases} \tag{15}$$

where T_S is expectation of unclipped normal distribution; D_S is dispersion of density $\bar{f}_S(t)$; $\eta(t-\tau)$ is Heaviside function.

4 Reaching the Milestone by a Swarm

Let there is a swarm of mobile robots moving towards the milestone. The process of functioning of the swarm when reaching milestone can be described by the PMN [14–16], shown on the Fig. 3:

$$\begin{aligned} \Pi = \{&\{a_1, \ldots, a_k, \ldots, a_K\}, \{z_b, z_e\}, \\ &\{O(z_b) = \{a_1, \ldots, a_k, \ldots, a_K\}, O(z_e) = \emptyset\}, \\ &\{I(z_b) = \emptyset; I(z_e) = \{a_1, \ldots, a_k, \ldots, a_K\}\}\}. \end{aligned} \tag{16}$$

On the Fig. 3, transition z_b simulates the start of swarm movement; transition z_e simulates the reaching the milestone by the swarm units and the swarm as a whole; places $a_1,\ldots,$ $a_k,\ldots, a_K$ simulate process of movement units toward the milestone.

There is the competition between units for not to be last when passing the distance [17]. Time density of event of gathering the whole swarm at the milestone is as follows:

$$f_g(t) = \frac{d \prod\limits_{k=1}^{K} F_k(t)}{dt} = \sum_{k=1}^{K} f_k(t) \prod_{\substack{i=1, \\ i \neq k}}^{K} F_i(t), \tag{17}$$

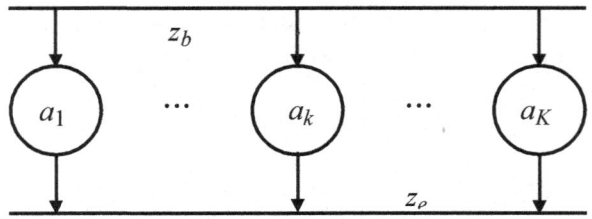

Fig. 3. PMN, that simulates the swarm functioning.

where $f_k(t)$ is the time density of reaching the milestone by k-th swarm unit, described with formula (15); $F_k(t) = \int_0^t f_k(\theta)d\theta$; θ is auxiliary variable.

When $f_k(t)$ is described with formula (15), then

$$F_S(t) = \begin{cases} \dfrac{\int_\tau^t exp\left[-\frac{(\theta-T_S)^2}{2D_\Delta}\right]d\theta}{\int_\tau^\infty exp\left[-\frac{(t-T_S)^2}{2D_\Delta}\right]dt} & when \ t \geq \tau; \\ 0 \ otherwise. \end{cases} \tag{18}$$

Probability and pure time density, that namely k-th unit of swarm finishes the distance the last is as follows [13]:

$$\tilde{p}_k = \int_0^\infty f_k(t) \prod_{\substack{i=1, \\ i \neq k}}^K F_i(t)dt; \tag{19}$$

$$\tilde{f}_k(t) = \frac{f_k(t) \displaystyle\prod_{\substack{i=1, \\ i \neq k}}^K F_i(t)dt}{\tilde{p}_k}. \tag{20}$$

Probability and pure time density, that namely k-th unit of swarm finishes the distance the first is as follows [13]:

$$\hat{p}_k = \int_0^\infty f_k(t) \prod_{\substack{i=1, \\ i \neq k}}^K [1 - F_i(t)]dt; \tag{21}$$

$$\hat{f}_k(t) = \frac{f_k(t) \displaystyle\prod_{\substack{i=1, \\ i \neq k}}^K [1 - F_i(t)]dt}{\hat{p}_k}. \tag{22}$$

Let us introduce K-digit binary number $N(K) = \langle n_1, \ldots, n_k, \ldots, n_K \rangle$ and select from N^K those numbers, which contain l zeros and $K - l$ ones. Quantity of such combinations is

$$C(K, l) = \frac{K!}{(K - l)! \cdot l!}. \tag{23}$$

Let us introduce function

$$\Phi_k[t, c(K, l)] = \begin{cases} F_k(t), & when \ n_k[c(K, l)] = 0; \\ 1 - F_k(t), & when \ n_k[c(K, l)] = 0, \end{cases} \tag{24}$$

where $c(K, l)$ is number of combination of binary number, which contain l zeros and $K - l$ ones; $n_k[c(K, l)]$ is k-th binary digit in $c(K, l)$-th combination.

Then time density of the event, that l drom K swarm units get the milestone is as follow

$$\tilde{f}_{K,l}(t) = \sum_{c(K,l)=1}^{C(K,l)} \sum_{k \in c(K,l)} f_k(t) \prod_{\substack{i=1, \\ i \neq k}}^{K} \Phi_i[t, c(K, L)], \tag{25}$$

where $k \in c(K, l)$ means, that summation should be executed only on all k's, which are in combination of $\langle n_1, \ldots, n_k, \ldots, n_K \rangle$, containing l zeros.

5 Computer Experiment

The direct computer experiment was performed to verify the proposed method. It was performed for swarm unit, which moves over rough terrain with random velocity $V + \delta_V$, where $V = 5$ m/s, δ_V is a random value, which is uniformly distributed at the domain $-0.5 \leq \delta_V \leq 0.5$ m/s. Distance 1 km is divided onto 100 stages of length 10 m. Histogram of reaching the milestone by swarm unit, obtained with use the Monte-Carlo method, is shown on the Fig. 4. Error evaluation of time expectation (200 s) is equal to 1,3%, error of standard deviation evaluation (0,9 s) is equal to 3,4%.

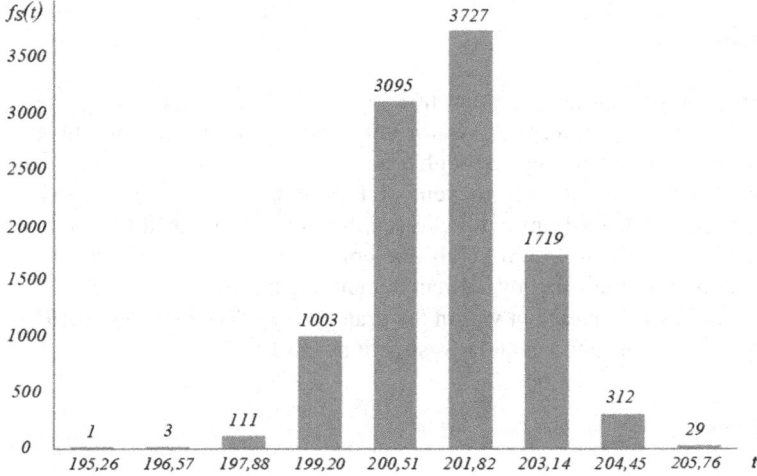

Fig. 4. Histograms of reaching the milestone by swarm unit

Histogram of reaching the milestone by swarm, consisting of 5 units, is shown on the Fig. 5. This histogram illustrates (17). As it follows from named formula, moda of histogram is shifted in comparison with histogram, sown on the Fig. 4. This fact one should took into account when planning operations, executed by swarm.

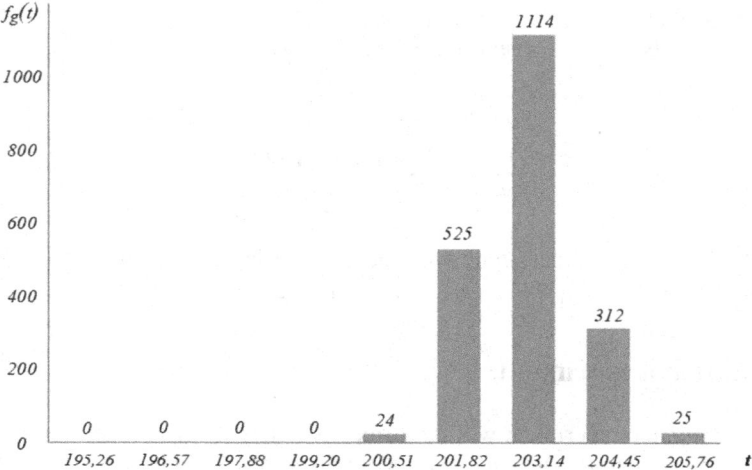

Fig. 5. Histograms of reaching the milestone by swarm as a whole

The result of computer experiment, shown on the Fig. 4 and the Fig. 5, confirms the validity of the hypothesis of the time density of a milestone achievement by the swarm unit.

6   Conclusion

So, the article notes that an important task of swarm operation planning is evaluation of milestone achieving time, both swarm unit, and swarm as a whole. In the case of physical swarm, moving through a rough terrain, it may be done by means of analytical simulation of vehicle longitudinal movement. Proposed approach permits to link design and physical parameters of unit with characteristics of terrain as a road and with time density of reaching the milestone both one unit and l units of K. The fidelity of the proposed method is confirmed by a direct computer experiment.

The research was carried out within the grant (19-38-90058\19 (Ц61019ГРФа)) of Russian foundation of fundamental investigations (RFFI).

References

1. Brambilla, M., Ferrante, E., Birattari, M., Dorigo, M.: Swarm robotics: a review from the swarm engineering perspective. Swarm Intell. **7**(1), 1–41 (2013)

2. Reynolds, C.W.: Flocks, herds, and schools: a distributed behavioral model. Comput. Graph. **21**(4), 25–34 (1987)
3. Kececi, E.F., Ceccarelli, M.: Robot Swarms: Dynamics and Control, 1st edn. ASME Press, New York (2015)
4. Balch, T., Arkin, R.C.: Behavior-based formation control for multirobot teams. IEEE Trans. Robot. Autom. **14**(6), 926–939 (1998)
5. Beard, R.W., Lawton, J., Hadaegh, F.Y.: A coordination architecture for spacecraft formation control. IEEE Trans. Control Syst. Technol. **9**(6), 777–790 (2001)
6. Saaj, C.M., Lappas, V., Gazi, V.: Spacecraft swarm navigation and control using artificial potential field and sliding mode control. In: IEEE International Conference on Industrial Technology, Mumbai, pp. 2646–2652. IEEE (2006)
7. Akat, S.B., Gazi, V., Marques, L.: Asynchronous particle swarm optimization based search with a multi-robot system: simulation and implementation on a real robotic system. Turk. J. Electr. Eng. Comput. Sci. **18**(5), 749–764 (2010)
8. Morin, P., Samson, C.: Motion Control of Wheeled Mobile Robots. In: Siciliano, B., Khatib, O. (eds.) Springer Handbook of Robotics, pp. 799–826. Springer, Heidelberg (2008)
9. Ivutin, A., Larkin, E., Kotov, V.: Established routine of swarm monitoring systems functioning. In: Tan, Y., Shi, Y., Buarque, F., Gelbukh, A., Das, S., Engelbrecht, A. (eds.) ICSI 2015. LNCS, vol. 9141, pp. 415–422. Springer, Cham (2015). https://doi.org/10.1007/978-3-319-20472-7_45
10. Larkin, E.V., Ivutin, A.N.: Estimation of latency in embedded real-time systems. In: 3-rd Meditteranean Conference on Embedded Computing (MECO-2014), Budva, pp. 236–239. IEEE (2014)
11. Larkin, E., Ivutin, A., Kotov, V., Privalov, A.: Semi-Markov modelling of commands execution by mobile robot. In: Ronzhin, A., Rigoll, G., Meshcheryakov, R. (eds.) ICR 2016. LNCS (LNAI), vol. 9812, pp. 189–198. Springer, Cham (2016). https://doi.org/10.1007/978-3-319-43955-6_23
12. Korolyuk, V., Swishchuk, A.: Semi-Markov Random Evolutions, 1st edn. Springer Science+Business Media, Dordrecht (1995)
13. Shiryaev, A.N.: Probability-2, 2nd edn. Springer Science+Business Media, New York (2019)
14. Dinov, I.D., Christou, N., Sanchez, J.: Central limit theorem: new SOCR applet and demonstration activity. J. Stat. Educ. **16**(2), 1–5 (2008)
15. Bárány, I., Van, V.: Central limit theorems for Gaussian polytopes. Ann. Prob. **35**(4), 1593–1621 (2007)
16. Limnios, N., Swishchuk, A.: Discrete-time semi-Markov random evolutions and their applications. Adv. Appl. Probab. **45**(1), 214–240 (2013)
17. Bielecki, T.R., Jakubowski, J., Niewęgłowski, M.: Conditional Markov chains: properties, construction and structured dependence. Stochast. Process. Appl. **127**(4), 1125–1170 (2017)

Swarm-Based Computing Algorithms
for Optimization

Learning Automata-Based Fireworks Algorithm on Adaptive Assigning Sparks

Junqi Zhang[1,2(✉)], Lei Che[1,2(✉)], and Jianqing Chen[1,2(✉)]

[1] Department of Computer Science and Technology, Tongji University,
Shanghai, China
zhangjunqi@tongji.edu.cn, 623685281@qq.com, 2096536579@qq.com
[2] Key Laboratory of Embedded System and Service Computing,
Ministry of Education, Shanghai, China

Abstract. Fireworks algorithm (FWA) is an emerging swarm intelligence inspired by the phenomenon of fireworks explosion. The numbers of sparks generated by fireworks have a great impact on the algorithm performance. It is widely accepted that promising fireworks should generate more sparks. However, in many researches, the quality of a firework is judged only on its current fitness value. This work proposes a Learning Automata-based Fireworks Algorithm (LA-FWA) introduced Learning automata (LA) to assign sparks for a better algorithm performance. Sparks are assigned to fireworks according to a state probability vector, which is updated constantly based on feedbacks from an environment so that it accumulates historical information. The probability vector converges as the search proceeds so that the local search ability of the LAFWA turns strong in the late search stage. Experimental results performed on CEC2013 benchmark functions show that the LAFWA outperforms several pioneering FWA variants.

Keywords: Evolutionary algorithms · Fireworks algorithm · Learning automata · Swarm intelligence

1 Introduction

Fireworks algorithm (FWA) is inspired by the phenomenon of fireworks explosion and proposed by Tan [1,2]. Fireworks are initialized in solution space randomly in FWA and sparks are generated by the explosion process of fireworks. All fireworks and sparks are regarded as candidate solutions, and the explosion process is considered to be a stochastic search around the fireworks. The original FWA works as follows: N fireworks are initialized randomly in a search space, and their quality (the fitness value is used to represent the quality of fireworks in the original FWA) is evaluated to determine the number of sparks and explosion amplitude for all fireworks. Afterwards, the fireworks explode and generate sparks within their local space. Finally, N candidate fireworks are selected from all the fireworks and sparks as new fireworks of the next generation. The workflow continues until the termination criterion is reached.

Y. Tan et al. (Eds.): ICSI 2020, LNCS 12145, pp. 59–70, 2020.
https://doi.org/10.1007/978-3-030-53956-6_6

Since FWA is raised in [1], it arouses lots of interests from researchers. The FWA has been applied to many real word optimization problems, including optimizing anti-spam model [3], solving the network reconfiguration [4], solving the path problem of vehicle congestion [5], swarm robotics [6,7] modern web information retrieval [8], single-row facility layout problem [9], etc.

At the same time, there has been many researches attempting improving the performance of FWA. Zheng proposes the Enhanced Fireworks Algorithm (EFWA) [10], five modifications combined with conventional FWA eliminate some disadvantages of the original algorithm among it. Li proposes GFWA which puts forward a simple and efficient mutation operator called guiding vector. The Adaptive Fireworks Algorithm (AFWA) [11] uses a new adaptive amplitude calculated according to the fitness value instead of the amplitude operator in EFWA. Based on EFWA, Zheng proposes the Dynamic Search in Fireworks Algorithm (dynFWA) [12] as an improvement. In dynFWA, the firework with the smallest fitness value uses the dynamic explosion amplitude strategy. Variants mentioned above optimize the performance by adjusting the explosion amplitude adaptively. [13] proposes a fireworks algorithm based on a loser-out tournament, which also uses an independent selection operators to select fireworks for the next generation.

Learning automata (LA) [14] is a kind of machine learning algorithm which can be used as a general-purpose stochastic optimization tool. An learning automaton maintains a state probability vector where each component represents a reward probability of an action. The vector is updated through interactions with a stochastic unknown environment. LA tries to find the optimal action from a finite number of actions by applying actions to environment constantly. Environment returns a reinforcement signal which shows the relative quality of a selected action. An learning automaton receives signals and updates the vector according to its own strategy. When the termination criterion is satisfied, the optimal action is found out. So far, several PSO algorithms combined with LA have been proposed. Hashemi [15] proposes a PSO variant using LA to adaptively select parameters of PSO. A PSO variant that integrates with LA in a noisy environment is proposed by Zhang [16]. It uses LA through its unique selection mechanism to allocate re-evaluations in an adaptive manner and reduce computing resources.

Since the state probability vector of LA is updated constantly, it accumulates historical information and evaluates the quality of each action. It is more reasonable to apply learning automata to determine the number of sparks of each firework than the use of current fitness value only. On the other side, the probability vector converges gradually as the search proceeds, which leads to a strong local search ability in the late search stage.

In this paper, a Learning Automata-based Fireworks Algorithm (LAFWA) is proposed. Fireworks obtain reasonable numbers of sparks by applying LA to FWA, which leads to a competitive performance, as sparks will only be assigned to promising fireworks which brings a strong local search ability.

The rest of this paper is organized as follows. Section 2 reviews the related works of FWA and Learning Automata. Section 3 proposes the LAFWA. Experimental results based on the CEC 2013 benchmark suite are given in Sect. 4 and compared with its peers. Conclusions are drawn in Sect. 5.

2   Related Work

2.1   Fireworks Algorithm

This paper is based on GFWA [17]. In this section, GFWA will be introduced first. Without loss of generality, a minimization problem is considered as the optimization problem in this paper:

$$min \quad f(x) \tag{1}$$

where x is a vector in the solution space.

Explosion Strategy. GFWA follows the explosion strategy of dynFWA. In GFWA, the number of explosion sparks of each firework is calculated as following:

$$\lambda_i = \hat{\lambda} \cdot \frac{\max_{j}(f(X_j)) - f(X_i)}{\sum_{j}(\max_{k}(f(X_k)) - f(X_j))}, \tag{2}$$

where λ is a parameter to control the number of explosion sparks. A firework with smaller fitness value generates more sparks according to this formula. Secondly, GFWA adopts a dynamic explosion amplitude update strategy for each firework from dynFWA. The explosion amplitude of each firework is calculated as follows:

$$A_i(t) = \begin{cases} A_i(t-1) \cdot \rho^+ & \text{if } f(X_i(t)) - f(X_i(t-1)) < 0 \\ A_i(t-1) \cdot \rho^- & \text{otherwise} \end{cases} \tag{3}$$

where $A_i(t)$ and $X_i(t)$ represent the explosion amplitude and the position of i-th firework at generation t. $\rho^- \in (0,1)$ is the reduction coefficient while $\rho^+ \in (1,+\infty)$ is the amplification coefficient. Sparks are generated uniformly within a hypercube. The explosion amplitude is the radius of the hypercube and the center of the hypercube is the firework. Algorithm 1 shows the process of sparks generated by a firework where D is the dimension, B_U and B_L are the upper and lower bounds of the search space, respectively.

Algorithm 1. Generating explosion sparks for the i-th firework

---
1: **for** $j = 1$ to λ_i **do**
2:    **for** $d = 1, 2, ..., D$ **do**
3:        $s_{i,j}^d = X_i^d + A_i \cdot rand(-1, 1)$
4:        **if** $s_{i,j}^d < B_L$ or $s_{i,j}^d > B_U$ **then**
5:            $s_{i,j}^d = B_L + rand(0, 1) \cdot (B_U - B_L)$
6:        **end if**
7:    **end for**
8: **end for**
9: **return** all the $s_{i,j}$

Guiding Vector. A mechanism called guiding vector (GV) is proposed in GFWA. A group of sparks with good quality and another group of sparks with bad quality are utilized to build a guiding vector. The GV guides a firework to move farther. Note that each firework only generates one guiding vector. The GV of i-th firework named Δ_i is calculated from its explosion sparks $s_{i,j}(1 \leq j \leq \lambda_i)$ as follows:

$$\Delta_i = \frac{1}{\sigma\lambda_i} \sum_{j=1}^{\sigma\lambda_i}(s_{i,j} - s_{i,\lambda_i-j+1}) \tag{4}$$

where σ is a parameter to control the proportion of adopted explosion sparks and $s_{i,j}$ means the spark of i-th firework with j-th smallest fitness value. A guiding spark (GS_i) is generated by add a GV to the i-th firework as shown in (5).

$$GS_i = X_i + \Delta_i \tag{5}$$

The main process of GFWA is described in Algorithm 2.

Algorithm 2. GFWA

1: Initialize n fireworks and evaluate their fitness
2: **while** (the stopping criterion not met) **do**
3:    **for** $i = 1$ to n **do**
4:        Calculate the number of sparks by (2)
5:        Calculate the explosion amplitude by (3)
6:        Generate explosion sparks with the explosion amplitude
7:        Generate the guiding spark by (4) and (5)
8:        Evaluate all the sparks
9:        Select the best individual among the sparks, guiding spark, and the firework as a new firework for the next generation
10:    **end for**
11: **end while**
12: **return** the position and the fitness value of the best individual

---

2.2   Learning Automata

LA with a variable structure can be represented as a quadruple $\{\alpha, \beta, P, T\}$, where $\alpha = \{\alpha_1, \alpha_2, \ldots, \alpha_r\}$ is a set of actions; $\beta = \{\beta_1, \beta_2, \ldots, \beta_s\}$ is a set of inputs; $P = \{p_1, p_2, \ldots, p_r\}$ is a state probability vector of actions and T is a pursuit scheme to update the state probability vector, $P(t+1) = T(\alpha(t), \beta(t), P(t))$. The most popular pursuit scheme DP$_{RI}$ is proposed in [18,19] which increases the state probability of the estimated optimal action and decreases others. The pursuit scheme can be described as follows:

$$p_w(t+1) = max(0, p_w(t) - \Delta) \qquad w \neq i \tag{6}$$

$$p_i(t+1) = \sum p_w(t) - p_w(t+1) + p_i(t) \tag{7}$$

where the optimal action is the i-th action. Another famous pursuit scheme DGPA is proposed in [20], it increases the state probability of the actions with higher reward estimates than the current chosen action and decreases others. It can be described as follows:

$$p_w(t+1) = max(0, p_w(t) - \Delta) \qquad p_w < p_i \tag{8}$$

$$p_w(t+1) = \frac{\sum p_i(t) - p_i(t+1)}{k} + p_w(t) \qquad p_w \geq p_i \tag{9}$$

where i represents i-th action selected this time and k is the number of the actions whose probability is not less than the i-th action. And Zhang [21] proposes a new pursuit scheme Last-position Elimination-based Learning Automata (LELA) inspired by a reverse philosophy. $Z(t)$ is the set of actions whose probability is not zero at time t. LELA decreases the state probability of the estimated worst action in $Z(t)$, and increases others in $Z(t)$. It can be described as follows:

$$p_w(t+1) = max(0, p_w(t) - \Delta) \tag{10}$$

$$p_i(t+1) = \frac{p_w(t) - p_w(t+1)}{||Z(t)||} + p_w(t) \qquad \forall i \neq w, i \epsilon Z(t) \tag{11}$$

3   Learning Automata-Based Fireworks Algorithm

3.1   m-DP$_{RI}$

In this paper, we modify DP$_{RI}$ to make it more suitable for our algorithm. In the classic DP$_{RI}$, it rewards the estimated optimal action and punishes others. However, the pursuit scheme leads to a fast convergence of the state probability vector which is harmful for the global search ability in the early search stage. In the m-DP$_{RI}$, the best m actions will be rewarded besides the best one. And m decreases linearly as the search progresses to enhance the local search ability gradually. The update strategy can be expressed as follows:

$$p_w(t+1) = max(0, p_w(t) - \Delta) \qquad w \in [m+1, n] \tag{12}$$

$$p_w(t+1) = \frac{\sum_{m+1}^{n} p_i(t) - p_i(t+1)}{m} + p_w(t) \qquad w \in [1, m] \tag{13}$$

$$m = m - 1 \quad if \quad g\%\frac{MG}{M} = 0 \tag{14}$$

where Δ is the step size, g is the generation number now, MG is maximum number of generation allowed and M is the initial number of m. The state probability vector will be sorted after the update to decide the m actions to be rewarded again.

3.2 Assigning Sparks

LA is applied to assigning sparks to fireworks according to the state probability vector in this paper. The firework with larger probability will generate more sparks. The probability vector converges as the search proceeds, the promising fireworks generates most sparks in the late search stage so that the algorithm has a strong local search ability. n probability intervals P are calculated to assign sparks by (15) based on the state probability vector p. Algorithm 3 shows how the LAFWA assigns sparks by the probability intervals P.

$$P_i = \left[\sum_{1}^{i-1} p_j, \sum_{1}^{i-1} p_j + p_i\right] \tag{15}$$

Algorithm 3. Assign SPARKS

1: **for** $i = 1$ to λ **do**
2:     Randomly generate a number $Rand$ in $(0, 1)$
3:     Find the probability interval i where $Rand$ in
4:     $\lambda_i = \lambda_i + 1$
5: **end for**

3.3 Learning Automata-Based Fireworks Algorithm

The procedure of LAFWA is given as the pseudo code shown in Algorithm 4 and explained as follows:

Step 1 *Initialization*: Generate the positions and velocities of n fireworks randomly. Initialize the state probability vector of assigning the sparks p evenly and step size Δ, where p represents the probability that the spark assigned to the firework and Δ represents the step size that p decreases or increases.
Step 2 *Assign Sparks*: Each one of the λ sparks will be assigned to n fireworks according to Algorithm 3, the firework with greater probability will generate more sparks.

Step 3 *Perform Explosion*: For each firework, the explosion amplitude is calculated by (3). Sparks generated uniformly within a hypercube. The explosion amplitude is the radius of the hypercube and the center of the hypercube is the firework. Generate sparks by Algorithm 1

Step 4 *Generate Guiding Sparks*: Generate the guiding spark by (4) and (5).

Step 5 *Select Fireworks*: Evaluate the fitness value of sparks and guiding vector. Select the best individual among the sparks, guiding spark, and the firework as a new firework for each firework.

Step 6 *Update Probability*: Update p according to (12) and (13) and sort p.

Step 7 *Decrease Linearly*: Complete linear decrement of m by performing (14).

Step 8 *Terminal Condition Check*: If any of pre-defined termination criteria is satisfied, the algorithm terminates. Otherwise, repeat from Step 2.

Algorithm 4. LAFWA

1: **BEGIN**
2: Initialize n fireworks, the initial state probability vector $p=(1/n,...,1/n)$, step size Δ
3: Evaluate the fitness value of the n fireworks
4: **while** stopping criterion not met **do**
5:    Assign sparks according to Algorithm 3
6:    i=1
7:    **for** i<n **do**
8:       Calculate the explosion amplitude according to (3).
9:       Generate the sparks by Algorithm 1
10:      Generate the guiding spark by (4) and (5)
11:      Evaluate the fitness value of sparks and guiding vector. Select the optimal one as the new firework
12:      i=i+1
13:   **end for**
14:   Update p according to (12) and (13) and sort p
15:   Perform linear decrement of m by (14).
16: **end while**
17: Output the optimal firework.
18: **END**

Table 1. 28 test functions

	Function notation	Optimum (f_i^*)	Function name
Unimodal	f_1	−1400	Sphere function
	f_2	−1300	Rotated high conditioned elliptic function
	f_3	−1200	Rotated Bent Cigar function
	f_4	−1100	Rotated discus function
	f_5	−1000	Different powers function
Basic multimodal	f_6	−900	Rotated Rosenbrock's function
	f_7	−800	Rotated Schaffers F7 function
	f_8	−700	Rotated Ackley's function
	f_9	−600	Rotated Weierstrass function
	f_{10}	−500	Rotated Griewank's function
	f_{11}	−400	Rastrigin's function
	f_{12}	−300	Rotated Rastrigin's function
	f_{13}	−200	Non-continuous rotated Rastrigin's function
	f_{14}	−100	Schwefel's function
	f_{15}	100	Rotated Schwefel's function
	f_{16}	200	Rotated Katsuura function
	f_{17}	300	Lunacek Bi_Rastrigin function
	f_{18}	400	Rotated Lunacek Bi_Rastrigin function
	f_{19}	500	Expanded Griewank's plus Rosenbrock's function
	f_{20}	600	Expanded Scaffer's F6 function
Composition	f_{21}	700	Composition function 1
	f_{22}	800	Composition function 2
	f_{23}	900	Composition function 3
	f_{24}	1000	Composition function 4
	f_{25}	1100	Composition function 5
	f_{26}	1200	Composition function 6
	f_{27}	1300	Composition function 7
	f_{28}	1400	Composition function 8

*All test functions are described in [23]. Please refer to [23] and also the website http://www.ntu.edu.sg/home/EPNSugan/index_files/CEC2013/CEC2013.htm

4 Experimental Results and Comparisons

In this section, experiments are carried out to illustrate the advantages of LAFWA in comparison with four pioneering FWA variants.

4.1 Benchmark and Experimental Settings

Parameter setting in LAFWA is given in the following. The main parameters include:

- n: The number of fireworks.
- λ: The total number of sparks.
- ρ^- and ρ^+: The reduction and amplification factors.
- Δ: The step size of LA.
- M: The initial number of m.

For each firework, a larger n can explore more but generate less sparks. In the proposed LAFWA, we set $n = 10$ to get a good global search ability in the early stage. The reduction and amplification factors ρ^- and ρ^+ are two important parameters for dynamic search. We set the two coefficients to 0.9 and 1.2 respectively according to [12]. Δ and M is set to 0.01 and 4 according our experiments.

The experimental results are evaluated on the CEC 2013 single objective optimization benchmark suite [22], including 5 single-mode functions and 23 multi-mode functions (shown in Table 2). Standard settings are adopted for the range of parameters, such as dimensions, maximum functional evaluation numbers, and have been widely used for testing algorithms. The search ranges of all the 28 test functions are set to $[-100, 100]^D$ and D is set to 30. According to the suggestions of this benchmark suite, all the algorithms repeated for 51 times for each function and the maximal number of function evaluations in each run is $1000*D$. All the experiments are carried out using MATLAB R2016a on a PC with Intel(R) Core(TM) i5-8400 running at 2.80 GHz with 8G RAM.

4.2   Experimental Results and Comparison

To validate the effectiveness of LAFWA, we compare it with four pioneering FWA variants, including AFWA, dynFWA, COFFWA [24], GFWA. Parameters for these four algorithms are set to the suggested values according to their published papers. The results of the performance on the solution accuracy are listed in Table 2. Boldface indicates the best results from all listed algorithms, "Mean" is the mean results of 51 independent runs, "AR" is the average ranking of an algorithm, calculated by the sum of ranking on the 28 functions divided by the number of functions. The less AR, the better performance. LAFWA shows its outstanding convergence accuracy among all the listed FWA variants. In the unimodal part of Table 3, LAFWA performs well, achieves first 3 times among 5 functions. For the challenging multimodal and composition functions, the global optimal value is more difficult to locate. LAFWA shows its superiority and get first 15 times and second 6 times among 23 functions. The A.R. of LAFWA is 1.5 in general, which ranks the first compared with other competitors.

Table 2. LAFWA accuracy compared with other FWAs.

Func		AFWA	dynFWA	COFFWA	GFWA	LAFWA
f_1	Mean	0.00E+00	0.00E+00	0.00E+00	0.00E+00	0.00E+00
	Rank	1	1	1	1	1
f_2	Mean	8.92E+05	7.87E+05	8.80E+05	6.96E+05	**5.63E+05**
	Rank	5	3	4	2	1
f_3	Mean	1.26E+08	1.57E+08	8.04E+07	3.74E+07	**1.91E+07**
	Rank	4	5	3	2	1
f_4	Mean	1.14E+01	1.28E+01	2.01E+03	**5.00E−05**	1.70E+00
	Rank	3	4	5	1	2
f_5	Mean	6.04E−04	**5.42E−04**	7.41E−04	1.55E−03	1.43E−03
	Rank	2	1	3	5	4
f_6	Mean	2.99E+01	3.15E+01	2.47E+01	3.49E+01	**9.84E+00**
	Rank	3	4	2	5	1
f_7	Mean	9.19E+01	1.03E+02	8.99E+01	**7.58E+01**	7.64E+01
	Rank	4	5	1	1	2
f_8	Mean	**2.09E+01**	**2.09E+01**	**2.09E+01**	**2.09E+01**	**2.09E+01**
	Rank	1	1	1	1	1
f_9	Mean	2.48E+01	2.56E+01	2.40E+01	1.83E+01	**1.74E+01**
	Rank	4	5	3	2	1
f_{10}	Mean	4.73E−02	4.20E−02	4.10E−02	6.08E−02	**5.42E−03**
	Rank	4	3	2	5	1
f_{11}	Mean	1.05E+02	1.07E+02	9.90E+01	**7.50E+01**	8.88E+01
	Rank	4	5	3	1	2
f_{12}	Mean	1.52E+02	1.56E+02	1.40E+02	9.41E+01	**8.64E+01**
	Rank	4	5	3	2	1
f_{13}	Mean	2.36E+02	2.44E+02	2.50E+02	**1.61E+02**	1.98E+02
	Rank	3	4	5	1	2
f_{14}	Mean	2.97E+03	2.95E+03	2.70E+03	3.49E+03	**2.66E+03**
	Rank	4	3	2	5	1
f_{15}	Mean	3.81E+03	3.71E+03	3.37E+03	3.67E+03	**3.08E+03**
	Rank	5	4	2	3	1
f_{16}	Mean	4.97E−01	4.77E−01	4.56E−01	1.00E−01	**9.56E−02**
	Rank	5	4	3	2	1
f_{17}	Mean	1.45E+02	1.48E+02	1.10E+02	**8.49E+01**	1.06E+02
	Rank	4	5	3	1	2
f_{18}	Mean	1.75E+02	1.89E+02	1.80E+02	**8.60E+01**	1.12E+02
	Rank	3	5	4	1	2
f_{19}	Mean	6.92E+00	6.87E+00	6.51E+00	5.08E+00	**4.58E+00**
	Rank	5	4	3	2	1
f_{20}	Mean	**1.30E+01**	**1.30E+01**	1.32E+01	1.31E+01	1.33E+01
	Rank	1	1	4	3	5
f_{21}	Mean	3.16E+02	2.92E+02	2.06E+02	2.59E+02	**2.00E+02**
	Rank	5	4	2	3	1
f_{22}	Mean	3.45E+03	3.41E+03	**3.32E+03**	4.27E+03	3.41E+03
	Rank	4	2	1	5	2
f_{23}	Mean	4.70E+03	4.55E+03	4.47E+03	4.32E+03	**3.59E+03**
	Rank	5	4	3	2	1
f_{24}	Mean	2.70E+02	2.72E+02	2.68E+02	2.56E+02	**2.55E+02**
	Rank	5	4	3	2	1
f_{25}	Mean	2.99E+02	2.97E+02	2.94E+02	2.89E+02	**2.83E+02**
	Rank	5	4	3	2	1
f_{26}	Mean	2.73E+02	2.62E+02	2.13E+02	2.05E+02	**2.00E+02**
	Rank	5	4	3	2	1
f_{27}	Mean	9.72E+02	9.92E+02	8.71E+02	8.15E+02	**8.08E+02**
	Rank	4	5	3	2	1
f_{28}	Mean	4.37E+02	3.40E+02	2.84E+02	3.60E+02	**2.20E+02**
	Rank	5	3	2	4	1
Overall	A_R	3.82	3.64	2.75	2.43	**1.50**

5 Conclusion

In this work, Learning Automata-based Fireworks Algorithm (LAFWA) is proposed to assign sparks to the fireworks more reasonable by using LA. The state probability vector is average so that the global search ability is well at the early search stage. As the search proceeds, the probability vector converges which leads to a strong local search ability in the late search stage. Experimental results performed on CEC2013 benchmark functions show that the LAFWA outperforms several pioneering FWA variants. Future work focuses on improving the update strategy of the state probability vector of LA.

References

1. Tan, Y., Zhu, Y.: Fireworks algorithm for optimization. In: Proceedings of the International Conference on Swarm Intelligence, Beijing, China, pp. 355–364, June 2010
2. Li, J., Tan, Y.: A comprehensive review of the fireworks algorithm. ACM Comput. Surv. 52(6), 1–28 (2019)
3. He, W., Mi, G., Tan, Y.: Parameter optimization of local-concentration model for spam detection by using fireworks algorithm. In: Tan, Y., Shi, Y., Mo, H. (eds.) ICSI 2013. LNCS, vol. 7928, pp. 439–450. Springer, Heidelberg (2013). https://doi.org/10.1007/978-3-642-38703-6_52
4. Imran, A.M., Kowsalya, M.: A new power system reconfiguration scheme for power loss minimization and voltage profile enhancement using fireworks algorithm. Int. J. Electr. Power Energ. Syst. 62, 312–322 (2014)
5. Abdelaziz, M.M., Elghareeb, H.A., Ksasy, M.S.M.: Hybrid heuristic algorithm for solving capacitated vehicle routing problem. Int. J. Comput. Technol. 12(9), 3845–3851 (2014)
6. Zheng, Z., Ying, T.: Group explosion strategy for searching multiple targets using swarm robotic. In: IEEE Congress on Evolutionary Computation (CEC) (2013)
7. Zheng, Z., Li, J., Jie, L., Ying, T.: Avoiding decoys in multiple targets searching problems using swarm robotics. In: 2014 IEEE Congress on Evolutionary Computation (CEC) (2014)
8. Hamou, H.A., Rahmani, A., Bouarara, H.A., Amine, A.: A fireworks algorithm for modern web information retrieval with visual results mining. Int. J. Swarm Intell. Res. 6(3), 1–23 (2015)
9. Liu, S., Zhang, Z., Guan, C., Zhu, L., Zhang, M., Guo, P.: An improved fireworks algorithm for the constrained single-row facility layout problem. Int. J. Prod. Res. 1–19 (2020)
10. Zheng, S., Janecek, A., Tan, Y.: Enhanced fireworks algorithm. In: IEEE Congress on Evolutionary Computation (CEC), pp. 2069–2077, June 2013
11. Li, J., Zheng, S., Tan, Y.: Adaptive fireworks algorithm. In: IEEE Congress on Evolutionary Computation (CEC), pp. 3214–3221, July 2014
12. Zheng, S., Janecek, A., Li, J., Tan, Y.: Dynamic search in fireworks algorithm. In: IEEE Congress on Evolutionary Computation (CEC), pp. 3222–3229, July 2014
13. Li, J., Tan, Y.: Loser-out tournament-based fireworks algorithm for multimodal function optimization. IEEE Trans. Evol. Comput. 22(5), 679–691 (2017)
14. Narendra, K.S., Thathachar, M.A.L.: Learning automata - a survey. IEEE Trans. Syst. Man Cybern. SMC–4(4), 323–334 (1974)

15. Hashemi, A.B., Meybodi, M.R.: A note on the learning automata based algorithms for adaptive parameter selection in PSO. Appl. Soft Comput. J. **11**(1), 689–705 (2009)
16. Zhang, J., Xu, L., Li, J., Kang, Q., Zhou, M.: Integrating particle swarm optimization with learning automata to solve optimization problems in noisy environment. In: Proceeding IEEE International Conference on Systems, Man, and Cybernetics, pp. 1432–1437, October 2014
17. Li, J., Zheng, S., Tan, Y.: The effect of information utilization: introducing a novel guiding spark in the fireworks algorithm. IEEE Trans. Evol. Comput. **21**(1), 153–166 (2017)
18. Oommen, B.J., Lanctot, J.K.: Discretized pursuit learning automata. IEEE Trans. Syst. Man Cybern. **20**(4), 931–938 (1990)
19. Oommen, B.J., Agache, M.: Continuous and discretized pursuit learning schemes: various algorithms and their comparison. IEEE Trans. Syst. Man Cybern. **31**(3), 277–287 (2001)
20. Agache, M., Oommen, B.J.: Generalized pursuit learning schemes: new families of continuous and discretized learning automata. IEEE Trans. Syst. Man Cybern. Part B Cybern. **32**(6), 738–749 (2002)
21. Zhang, J., Cheng, W., Zhou, M.: Last-position elimination-based learning automata. IEEE Trans. Cybern. **44**(12), 2484–2492 (2014)
22. Zambrano, H., Felipe, R.M.R.: Standard particle swarm optimization 2011 at CEC-2013: a baseline for future PSO improvements. In: IEEE Congress on Evolutionary Computation (CEC) (2013)
23. Liang, J.J., Qu, B.Y., Suganthan, P.N., Hernández-Díaz, A.G.: Problem definitions and evaluation criteria for the CEC 2013 special session on real-parameter optimization, Zhengzhou University, China and Nanyang Technological University, Singapore, 201212, January 2013
24. Zheng, S., Li, J., Janecek, A., Tan, Y.: A cooperative framework for fireworks algorithm. IEEE/ACM Trans. Comput. Biol. Bioinf. **14**(1), 27–41 (2017)

Binary Pigeon-Inspired Optimization for Quadrotor Swarm Formation Control

Zhiqiang Zheng[1], Haibin Duan[1,2($\boxtimes$)], and Chen Wei[1]

[1] School of Automation Science and Electrical Engineering,
Beihang University, Beijing 100083, China
hbduan@buaa.edu.cn
[2] Peng Cheng Laboratory, Shenzhen 518000, China

Abstract. This paper proposes a binary pigeon-inspired optimization (BPIO) algorithm, for the quadrotor swarm formation control problem. The expected position is provided by the BPIO. Quadrotor moves to the position with control strategy, and the strategy is based on the proportional integral derivative (PID) control method. The BPIO algorithm which is based on pigeon-inspired optimization (PIO) algorithm can effectively solve the combination problem in the binary solution space. The BPIO keeps the fast convergence of the PIO, and can explore the space effectively at the same time. The parameters to be optimized are encoded with binary bits. A special fitness function is designed to avoid the happening of crash. The simulation experiment shows how the BPIO works. The results of simulation verify the feasibility and effectiveness of the BPIO to solve the swarm formation problem.

Keywords: Binary pigeon-inspired optimization (BPIO) · Quadrotor · Swarm formation

1 Introduction

The quadrotor has small size, light weight and the ability to Vertically Take-Off and Land (VTOL) [1]. For a single quadcopter, many effective control strategies are proposed, like PID control strategy [2]. On the other hand, Unmanned Aircraft System (UAS) has been applied in military and other fields, which brings many problems of swarm formation. The swarm formation requests the agents in the swarm complete a task together, and the agents usually have to form a given formation. The quadcopter swarm formation problem is one of the research focuses. However, the swarm formation control has strong coupling and nonlinearity [3]. Some kinds of methods to solve it are proposed, like artificial potential function-based [3], observer-based, leader-follower [4] and so on. The problem is how to find the best way to form the formation accurately and quickly. In this case, intelligence optimization algorithms can solve this problem efficiently because of their irreplaceable feature [3].

The PIO algorithm is presented in 2014, which is based on the natural characteristics of pigeons [5]. The homing ability of pigeons used by PIO is based on the sun, the

© Springer Nature Switzerland AG 2020
Y. Tan et al. (Eds.): ICSI 2020, LNCS 12145, pp. 71–82, 2020.
https://doi.org/10.1007/978-3-030-53956-6_7

Earth's magnetic field and landmarks. However, the basic PIO algorithm is easy to fall into the local optimal solution [3]. It is necessary to try to strengthen PIO's global search capability [6, 7]. The binary particle swarm optimization (BPSO) is developed by Kennedy and Eberhart [8] and used to optimize combinational problems. Over the years, many kinds of novel BPSO algorithms have been developed, like sticky binary PSO [9], chaotic BPSO [10] and so on.

In this paper, the model of quadrotor and how to control a quadrotor with PID control method are introduced firstly. Then the BPIO is developed and use it to solve the quadrotor swarm formation control problem. At last, the BPIO is compared with other binary algorithms to confirm its rapid convergence.

2   Dynamics Modeling and Control of a Quadrotor

2.1   Coordinate System

Two coordinate systems are defined and shown in Fig. 1. The coordinate system Σ_e is defined as an earth-fixed coordinate system, and also as an inertial coordinate system. The o_e is the take-off position. The x_e axis points to an arbitrary direction in the horizontal plane. The z_e axis is perpendicular and points downward, and y_e is defined by the right-hand rule. The coordinate system Σ_b is defined as the body-fixed coordinate system. The o_b is the center of gravity (COG) of the quadrotor. The x_b axis is in the symmetry plane and points to the nose direction. The z_b axis is also in the symmetry plane, and perpendicular to x_b axis, and the y_b is also defined by right-hand rule. The rotation angles around x_b, y_b and z_b axes are defined as roll angle, pitch angle and yaw angle and denoted as ϕ, θ and ψ, respectively [2].

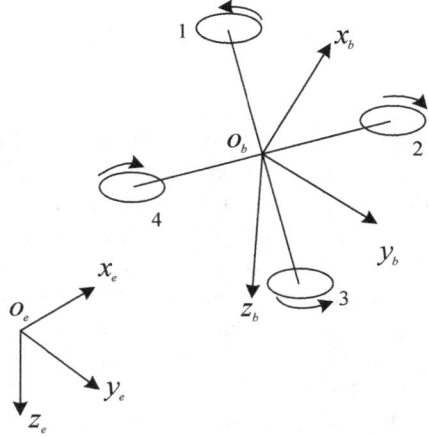

Fig. 1. The coordinate systems

2.2 Dynamics Modeling

To simplify the problem, the quadrotor is simplified as a rigid body and the deformation of the blade is ignored. The equations are expressed as follows [2]:

$$
\begin{cases}
{}^e\dot{\mathbf{p}} = {}^e\mathbf{v} \\
m\,{}^e\dot{\mathbf{v}} = m\mathbf{g} + \mathbf{R} \cdot ({}^b\mathbf{f} + {}^b\mathbf{D}) \\
\dot{\boldsymbol{\Theta}} = \mathbf{W} \cdot {}^b\boldsymbol{\omega} \\
\mathbf{J} \cdot {}^b\dot{\boldsymbol{\omega}} = -{}^b\boldsymbol{\omega} \times (\mathbf{J} \cdot {}^b\boldsymbol{\omega}) + \mathbf{G}_a + \boldsymbol{\tau}
\end{cases}
\tag{1}
$$

where e means the vector is defined in Σ_e, and b means in Σ_b. And m is the total mass of a quadrotor. Other symbols are listed in Table 1.

Table 1. The symbols in Eq. (1)

	Explain		Explain
$\mathbf{p}$	The vector of position	$\mathbf{D}$	The vector of drag
$\mathbf{v}$	The vector of velocity	$\boldsymbol{\Theta}$	The vector of Euler angle[a]
$\mathbf{g}$	Acceleration of gravity	$\boldsymbol{\omega}$	The vector of angle velocity
$\mathbf{R}$	Rotation matrix from Σ_b to Σ_e	$\mathbf{W}$	See Eq. (2)
$\mathbf{f}$	The force from propellers	$\mathbf{G}_a$	The gyroscopic moments
$\mathbf{J}$	Rotational inertia	$\boldsymbol{\tau}$	The moments from propellers

[a] $\boldsymbol{\Theta} = [\phi, \theta, \psi]^T$

$$
\mathbf{W} = \begin{bmatrix}
1 & \tan\theta\sin\phi & \tan\theta\cos\phi \\
0 & \cos\phi & -\sin\phi \\
0 & \sin\phi/\cos\theta & \cos\phi/\cos\theta
\end{bmatrix}
\tag{2}
$$

2.3 The Strategy of Control Design

To control the quadrotor effectively, PID control method is used in this paper [1, 2]. The designed control system is shown in Fig. 2.

For position controller and attitude controller, the control variables, $\mathbf{f}_d$ and $\boldsymbol{\tau}_d$, are generated by the PID control rules based on $\mathbf{v}$, $\boldsymbol{\omega}$ and the rates of errors. The rates of errors are generated by P control rules based on the error of input variables, $\mathbf{p}$ and $\mathbf{p}_d$, $\boldsymbol{\Theta}$ and $\boldsymbol{\Theta}_d$. Noting that $\boldsymbol{\Theta}_d = [\phi_d, \theta_d, \psi_d]^T$. ψ_d is usually set to zero, and ϕ_d and θ_d are generated by position controller. And the rates of errors are looked as $\mathbf{v}_d$ and $\boldsymbol{\omega}_d$. The control distributor can generate the desired angular speeds of rotors based on the control variables. Then, based on Eq. (1), the state of quadrotor can be calculated and the state values can be used for the next iteration [1, 2].

The main data of leader and followers is given in the Table 2, where d is the distance between COG and the motor, c_T is the thrust constant and c_M is the torque constant [2].

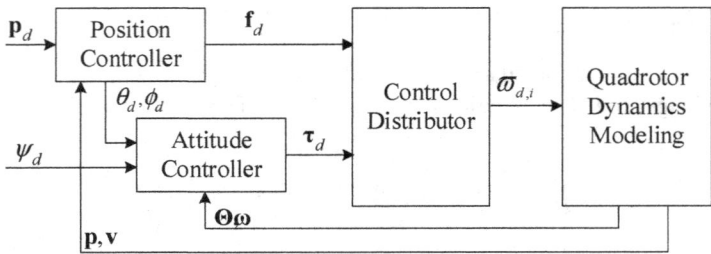

Fig. 2. The control strategy

Table 2. Data of the leader and followers

	Leader	Follower 1&3	Follower 2&4
m/kg	1.0230	1.5230	1.0830
$J/kg \cdot m^2$	$diag(0.0095,$ $0.0095, 0.0186)$	$diag(0.0105,$ $0.0105, 0.0186)$	$diag(0.0088,$ $0.0088, 0.0176)$
d/m	0.2223	0.2323	0.2023
$c_T/kg \cdot m$	1.4865×10^{-7}	1.6865×10^{-7}	1.1865×10^{-7}
$c_M/kg \cdot m^2$	2.9250×10^{-9}	3.0250×10^{-9}	2.4250×10^{-9}

3   The BPIO Algorithm

3.1   Pigeon-Inspired Optimization

The PIO algorithm includes the map and compass operator and the landmark operator [5–7]. In PIO, each pigeon individual represents a feasible solution. The pigeon individual i has its position X_i and velocity V_i. The positions and velocities are in the D-dimension solution space, and the value of dimension is based on the problem under study. Every pigeon is evaluated by its fitness value. The fitness value is calculated by the fitness function. A brief presentation of basic PIO is given as follow.

Map and Compass Operator
The map and compass operator is used at the beginning of the calculation. When this operator is working, every pigeon's position and velocity are updated in every iteration as follows [5]:

$$V_i(t) = V_i(t-1) \cdot e^{-Rt} + rand \cdot (X_{gbest} - X_i(t-1)) \tag{3}$$

$$X_i(t) = X_i(t-1) + V_i(t) \tag{4}$$

where t is current iteration number, R is defined as the map and compass factor, X_{gbest} denotes the global best position among all individual in current iteration, $rand$ means a random number in [0, 1].

In every iteration, the individual fitness value is calculated using the new position, and the X_{gbest} is updated only if a smaller fitness value appears under the condition that the cost function is a minimization problem.

Landmark Operator
When the landmark operator is working, the number of pigeons reduces by half in every iteration, and the positions of pigeons are updated by the strategy as follows [5].

$$N_p(t) = \frac{N_p(t-1)}{2} \tag{5}$$

$$X_c(t) = \frac{\sum X_i(t) \cdot \text{fitness}(X_i(t))}{N_p \sum \text{fitness}(X_i(t))} \tag{6}$$

$$X_i(t) = X_i(t-1) + rand \cdot (X_c(t) - X_i(t-1)) \tag{7}$$

where N_p is the population size of pigeons, X_c is the center of the current pigeons, and fitness() is the fitness function. Noting that the minimum of N_p is 1, and for the minimum problems, usually, fitness $(X_i(t)) = \frac{1}{\text{fitness}_{\min}(X_i(t))+\varepsilon}$, where ε is a constant.

According to Eq. (5), half of the pigeons are ignored in every iteration because these pigeons are far away from the destination, the center of the left individuals, and the pigeons near the destination will fly to the destination very quickly.

3.2 Binary Pigeon-Inspired Optimization

It is obvious that the original PIO algorithm is a kind of continuous algorithm, like the PSO. To solve combinational problems, the Binary PSO (BPSO) and improved algorithms are developed [8–10]. In the same way, the Binary PIO (BPIO) is developed.

In BPIO, the velocity entries are used to indicate the probability that the corresponding position entries flip either from 1 to 0 or from 0 to 1. The position entries are either 1 or 0, as defined in BPSO [9].

When the map and compass operator works, to make the pigeon have cognitive ability, $X_{pbest,i}$ is taken into consideration where $X_{pbest,i}$ is the best position of the pigeon i. The velocity is updated when map and compass operator works as follow:

$$V_i(t) = V_i(t-1)e^{-Rt} + (1-s) \cdot r_1(X_{gbest} - X_i(t-1)) + s \cdot r_2(X_{pbest,i} - X_i(t-1)) \tag{8}$$

where r_1 and r_2 are random number in [0, 1] and s is the cognitive factor that declines as the map and compass operator works.

To make the pigeon have stronger global search ability in the beginning and stronger convergence as the iteration goes on, the value of s is dynamically updated as follow [9]:

$$s = s_{\max} - (s_{\max} - s_{\min}) \cdot \frac{t}{N_1} \tag{9}$$

where $s_{\max}$ and $s_{\min}$ represent the maximum and minimum value of the cognitive factor s. N_1 is the maximum number of iterations of the map and compass operator.

The strategy of how to flip the position of the individual is given now. Because the velocity entries indicate the probability, its value should be limited in the range [0, 1]. Hence, like BPSO, the sigmoid function is also used to meet the requirement [9, 10]. The sigmoid function is given as follow.

$$\text{sigmoid}(V_i(t)) = \frac{2}{1 + e^{-|V_i(t)|}} - 1 \tag{10}$$

The position entries can be updated by the equation as follow.

$$X_i(t+1) = \begin{cases} 1 & r_3 < \text{sigmoid}(V_i(t)) \\ 0 & other \end{cases} \tag{11}$$

where r_3 is a random number uniformly distributed between 0 and 1.

When the landmark operator works, the population size reduces by half and the positions and velocities are updated in every iteration. To avoid the value being smaller than 1, the population size is updated as follow.

$$N_p(t) = \left\lceil \frac{N_p(t-1)}{2} \right\rceil \tag{12}$$

where $\lceil \bullet \rceil$ means the ceiling operation.

The pigeons left will fly to the destination X_{gbest}. At the beginning of the iteration, to make the pigeons have stronger ability to search the solution space near the destination, the velocity is redefined as follow.

$$V_i(N_1) = rand \cdot V_i(N_1) \tag{13}$$

Then the velocity is updated as follow and the position is updated in the same way as Eq. (11).

$$V_i(t) = w \cdot V_i(t-1) + rand \cdot (X_{gbest} - X_i(t-1)) \tag{14}$$

where w is the inertia factor.

Steps of the BPIO algorithm are given as follows.

Step 1: Initialize parameters of BPIO algorithm. Set the population size N_p, solution space dimension D, the map and compass factor R, the number of iterations N_1 and N_2 for two operators and the ranges of velocity for each dimensions. Encode the possible solutions of the problem with binary bits.

Step 2: Initialize the positions and velocities of pigeons with random numbers. Decode the position, calculate the fitness and record as $X_{pbest,i}$ for every pigeon. Then find the X_{gbest}.

Step 3: Map and compass operator works. Update velocity according to Eq. (8) and position according to Eq. (11) for every pigeon. Decode the position and calculate the fitness for every pigeon. Then update the $X_{pbest,i}$ and X_{gbest} if necessary.

Step 4: If $k > N_1$, update the latest velocity entries according to Eq. (13) and change to landmark operator. Otherwise, go to step 3.

Step 5: Landmark operator works. Rank pigeons according to fitness values, and ignore half of the individuals far away from the destination. Then update the other pigeons' velocities according to Eq. (14) and positions according to Eq. (11). Decode the position and calculate the fitness for every pigeon. Then find the X_{gbest}.

Step 6: If $k > N_1 + N_2$, stop the landmark operator and output the result. If not, go to step 5.

4   BPIO for the Quadrotor Swarm Formation Control

4.1   Encoding the Parameters to be Optimized

In this problem, there are three parameters to be optimized, as shown in Table 3. The definitions of these parameters are shown in Fig. 3. Noting that the coordinate system $o_b x'_e y'_e z'_e$ is produced by translating the $o_e x_e y_e z_e$ until o_e is coincident with o_b.

Table 3. Encoding of the parameters

Parameter	Range	Binary bits
λ/rad	$\frac{\pi}{3}, \frac{\pi}{2}, \frac{2\pi}{3}, \frac{5\pi}{6}, \frac{7\pi}{6}, \frac{4\pi}{3}, \frac{3\pi}{2}, \frac{5\pi}{3}$	000, 001, 010, 011, 100, 101, 110, 111
ρ/m	2, 3, 3.5, 4	00, 01, 10, 11
h/m	$-3, -1.5, 1.5, 3$	00, 01, 10, 11

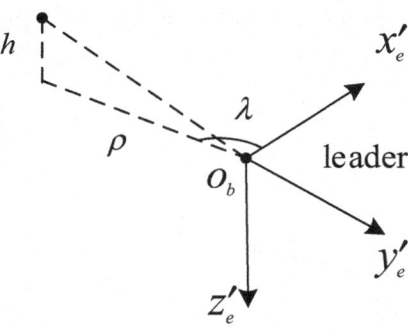

Fig. 3. The definitions of the parameters

From the Table 3, the dimension number is seven which means that every pigeon represents seven binary bits in the binary solution space. The meaning of every bit and the map of bits and parameters' values are also shown in Table 3.

For a follower, when the combination of three parameters' values is selected by the BPIO, the desired position of the follower is selected.

4.2 The Fitness Function

When selecting a suitable fitness function for the quadcopter swarm formation problem, there are two basic parts that must be included. Firstly, the fitness function should include the information of the expected position and the current position of the followers. Secondly, the crash of the followers must be avoided. To satisfy these requests, the fitness function of $i\text{-}th$ follower is defined as follow:

$$\text{fitness}_i = \begin{cases} \left\| \mathbf{p}_{i,cur} - \mathbf{p}_{i,exp} \right\|^2 & \left\| \mathbf{p}_{i,cur} - \mathbf{p}_{j,cur} \right\|_{\min} > 1 \\ f_{\max} & \left\| \mathbf{p}_{i,cur} - \mathbf{p}_{j,cur} \right\|_{\min} < 1 \end{cases} \tag{15}$$

where $\mathbf{p}_{i,cur}$ is the current position, $\mathbf{p}_{i,exp}$ is the desired position, and $f_{\max}$ is a large number which is always larger than $\left\| \mathbf{p}_{i,cur} - \mathbf{p}_{i,exp} \right\|^2$. Also, i is not equal to j. The minimum distance of followers is set to 1 m. If the distance between $i\text{-}th$ follower and another follower is smaller than 1 m, $f_{\max}$ will be assigned to fitness_i.

4.3 Simulation Results and Analysis

In the simulation, there are five quadrotors including a leader and four followers. Figures 4, 5, 6 and 7 show the result when the BPIO is used to optimize the flight path. The leader starts at the position $[0, 0, -3]^T$, and then flies to the position $[10, 10, -13]^T$. After hovering for 3 s, the leader flies to the position $[20, 10, -13]^T$ and arrives at 22 s. After that, the leader flies to the position $[45, 10, -18]^T$ and arrives at 45 s and lastly, it hovers at there until the simulation stops (at 52 s). The followers take off at the same time, and their desired positions are given by BPIO for every a second. The step of simulation is 0.01 s. The followers then update their desired position according to the results of optimization and the real time location of the leader for each iteration. Then, followers can flight to the desired position by the control strategy shown in Fig. 2.

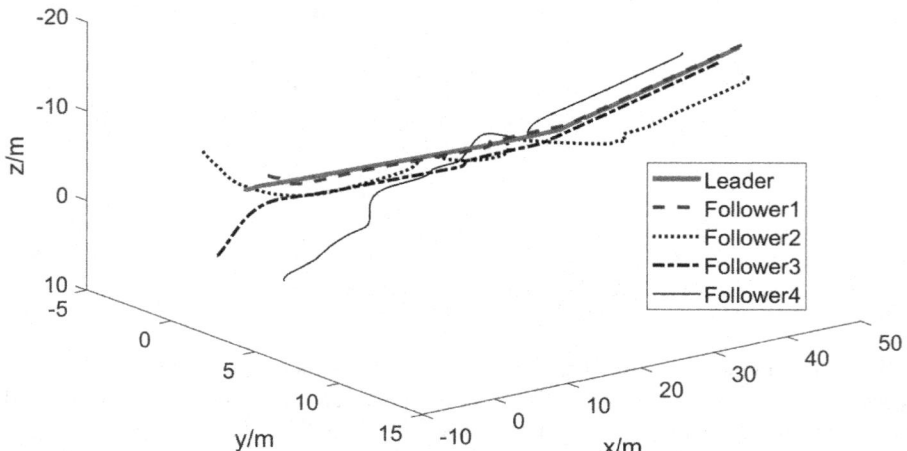

Fig. 4. Simulation result in a 3-D view

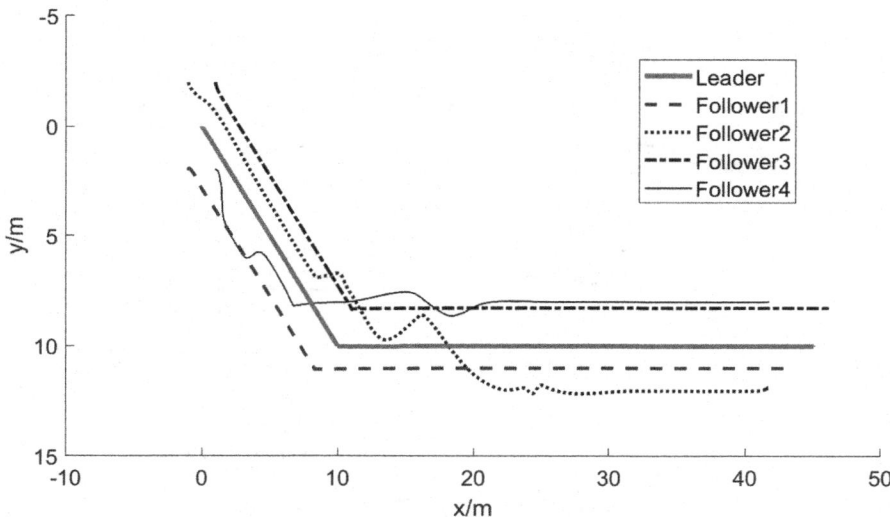

Fig. 5. Simulation result in a top-down view

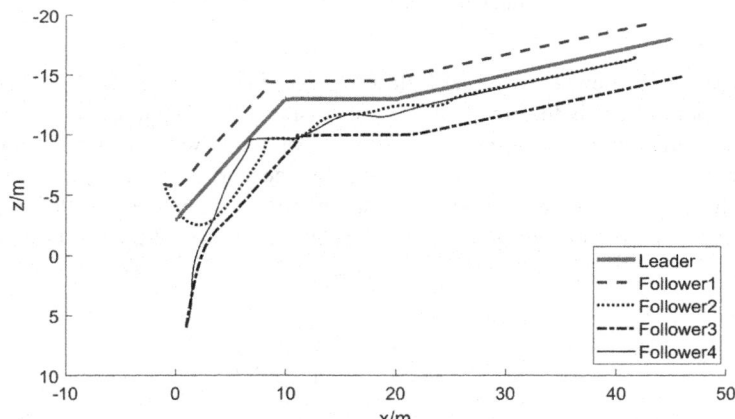

Fig. 6. Simulation result in a side view

From Figs. 4, 5 and 6, it is obvious that BPIO algorithm can form a feasible swarm. Because responding to the position signals, the velocity of leader almost always changes with time. On the other hand, the followers have their own mobility. Thus the followers sometimes may be unable to response to the current desired position quickly and need to get a new expect position. The BPIO algorithm can optimize a new desired position for the followers immediately. Specially, the follower 2 and 4 have more complex flight path. Because follower 2 and 4 optimize their path later than follower 1 and 3, follower 2

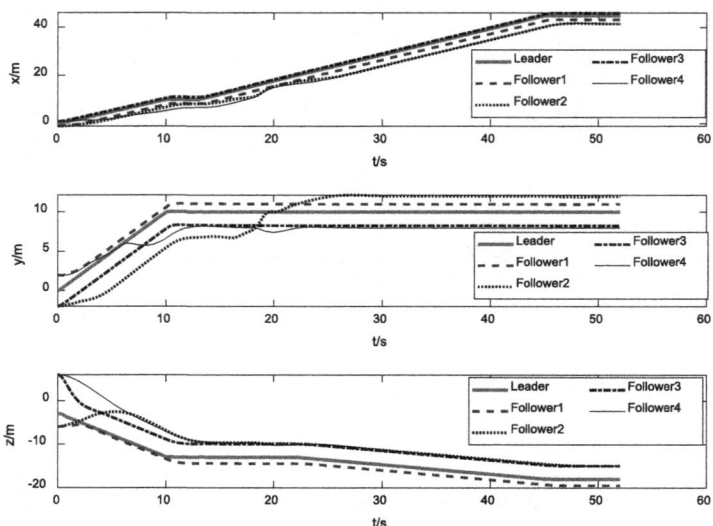

Fig. 7. Simulation result in position-time figure

and 4 must respond when near to other followers. The simulation result also verifies that the fitness function (15) is feasible to avoid the crash even if the equation is so simple.

To confirm the rapid convergence, the BPIO is compared with the novel binary PSO in [11] and the binary PSO in [12]. The range of the particles (or pigeons) is set to $[-50, 50]$, the population size is 100 and the number of iteration is set to 1000 as in [11]. For BPIO, N_1 is set to 600, and N_2 is set to 400. The expression of the test function is as follow:

$$f(x) = \frac{1}{4000} \sum_{i=1}^{3} x_i^2 - \prod_{i=1}^{3} \cos \frac{x_i}{\sqrt{i}} + 1 \qquad (16)$$

Figure 8 shows that the BPIO can converge more quickly. Table 4 shows the optimization results after running the algorithms for 20 times.

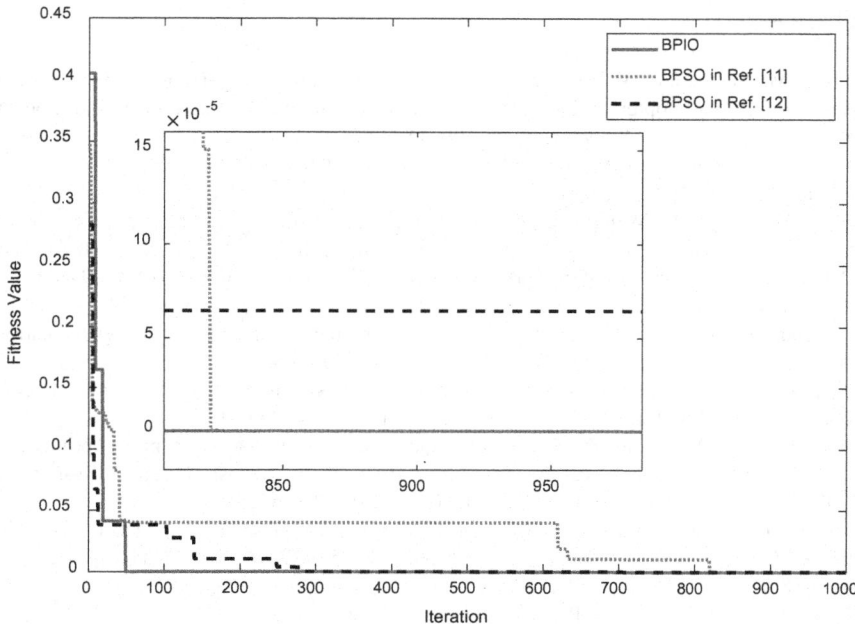

Fig. 8. Iterative curve of the algorithms

Table 4. The results after running the algorithms 20 times

	BPIO	BPSO as in [11]	BPSO as in [12]
Best optimization result	2.085968×10^{-9}	2.085968×10^{-9}	7.354714×10^{-6}
The cost time of the best result	1.949235 s	2.155005 s	2.770884 s
Mean of the optimization results	0.000110	0.014247	0.007056
Mean of the cost time	2.087806 s	2.382623 s	2.904913 s

5   Conclusion

The swarm formation is a challenging problem. In this paper, the rigid body model of quadrotor is used for simulation. The BPIO algorithm is used to optimize the expected position for the followers, and then the followers move to the expected position based on the PID control method. At the same time, the method to avoid the crash is applied when selecting the fitness function. The simulation verifies that the BPIO algorithm can effectively produce the expected position, avoid the crash and converge quickly. From the comparison of BPIO algorithm and other two kinds of BPSO algorithm, the high performance of BPIO algorithm is confirmed.

References

1. Qasim, M., Susanto, E., Wibowo, A.S.: PID control for attitude stabilization of an unmanned aerial vehicle quad-copter. In: 2017 5th International Conference on Instrumentation, Control, and Automation (ICA), Yogyakarta, pp. 109–114 (2017)
2. Quan, Q.: Introduction to Multicopter Design and Control. Springer, Singapore (2017). https://doi.org/10.1007/978-981-10-3382-7
3. Duan, H., Tong, B., Wang, Y., Wei, C.: Mixed game pigeon-inspired optimization for unmanned aircraft system swarm formation. In: Tan, Y., Shi, Y., Niu, B. (eds.) ICSI 2019. LNCS, vol. 11655, pp. 429–438. Springer, Cham (2019). https://doi.org/10.1007/978-3-030-26369-0_40
4. Panagou, D., Kumar, V.: Cooperative visibility maintenance for leader–follower formations in obstacle environments. IEEE Trans. Robot. **30**(4), 831–844 (2014)
5. Duan, H., Qiao, P.: Pigeon-inspired optimization: a new swarm intelligence optimizer for air robot path planning. Int. J. Intell. Comput. Cybern. **7**(1), 24–37 (2014)
6. Duan, H., Huo, M., Yang, Z., Shi, Y., Luo, Q.: Predator-prey pigeon-inspired optimization for UAV ALS longitudinal parameters tuning. IEEE Trans. Aerosp. Electron. Syst. **55**(5), 2347–2358 (2019). https://doi.org/10.1109/TAES.2018.2886612
7. Qiu, H., Duan, H.: A multi-objective pigeon-inspired optimization approach to UAV distributed flocking among obstacles. Inf. Sci. **509**, 515–529 (2020). https://doi.org/10.1016/j.ins.2018.06.061
8. Kennedy, J., Eberhart, R.: Particle swarm optimization. In: Proceedings of the IEEE International Conference of Neural Networks, vol. 4, no. 2, pp. 1942–1948 (1995)
9. Nguyen, B.H., Xue, B., Zhang, M.: A new binary particle swarm optimization approach: momentum and dynamic balance between exploration and exploitation. IEEE Trans. Cybern. 1–15 (2019). https://doi.org/10.1109/TCYB.2019.2944141
10. Li, P., Xu, D., Zhou, Z., Lee, W., Zhao, B.: Stochastic optimal operation of microgrid based on chaotic binary particle swarm optimization. IEEE Trans. Smart Grid **7**(1), 66–73 (2016)
11. Khanesar, M.A., Teshnehlab, M., Shoorehdeli, M.A.: A novel binary particle swarm optimization. In: Mediterranean Conference on Control & Automation 2007, MED 2007, pp. 1–6 (2007)
12. Kennedy, J., Eberhart, R.C.: A discrete binary version of the particle swarm algorithm. In: 1997 IEEE International Conference on Systems, Man, and Cybernetics. Computational Cybernetics and Simulation, vol. 5, pp. 4104–4108 (1997)

A Novel Biogeography-Based Optimization Algorithm with Momentum Migration and Taxonomic Mutation

Xinchao Zhao[1]([✉]), Yisheng Ji[1], and Junling Hao[2]

[1] School of Science, Beijing University of Post and Telecommunications, Beijing 100876, China
zhaoxc@bupt.edu.cn
[2] School of Statistics, University of International Business and Economics, Beijing 10029, China

Abstract. Biogeography-based optimization (BBO) algorithm is not good at dealing with regions where function values change dramatically or barely. A novel biogeography-based optimization algorithm is proposed in this paper based on Momentum migration and taxonomic mutation. The momentum item is added to the original migration operation of BBO. It makes the algorithm more advantageous in dealing with regions where function values change dramatically or barely. At the same time, taxonomic mutation strategy divides the solutions into three categories: promising class, middle class and inferior class. Promising solutions do not take part in this mutation operation. Solutions of middle class use balanced differential mutation, and inferior solutions adopt exploration-biased random mutation. This strategy further increases the diversity of population. The simulation experiments are carried out with different types of CEC2014 benchmark functions. The proposed algorithm is compared with other algorithms and shows stronger global search ability, faster convergence speed and higher convergence accuracy.

Keywords: Biogeography-based optimization · BBO · Momentum · Differential mutation · Random mutation

1 Introduction

Biogeography-based optimization (BBO) algorithm was proposed by Dan Simon in 2008 [1], which is used to study the geographic distribution mathematical algorithm of organisms in the optimization problem.

BBO algorithm attracts widely attention from theory, development and application. Ma and Simon [2] proposed blended biogeography-based optimization for constrained optimization. Cai et al. [3] introduced a biogeography-based algorithm based on evolutionary programming. Ma [4] found that cosine migration curve provides the best performance among six different models. Bhattacharya et al. [5] proposed biogeography-based optimization for different economic Load dispatch problems. Some more BBO variants are also appeared [6–9]. Bhattacharya and Chattopadhyay [11] applied biogeography-based optimization to solve different optimal power flow problems. BBO algorithm

© Springer Nature Switzerland AG 2020
Y. Tan et al. (Eds.): ICSI 2020, LNCS 12145, pp. 83–93, 2020.
https://doi.org/10.1007/978-3-030-53956-6_8

is also used to classification problems [12] and task scheduling scheme [13, 14] and Estimation of landslide susceptibility [10].

However, BBO algorithm still doesn't work very well for some functions whose values change drastically or barely. Later stage of BBO algorithm is prone to lose population diversity. Aiming at these problems, this paper proposes a novel BBO algorithm based on momentum migration and taxonomic mutation.

The remainder of the paper is organized as follows. Section 2 reviews BBO algorithm. Section 3 describes the proposed algorithm MTBBO with momentum migration and taxonomic mutation. Simulation results and analysis are elaborated in Sect. 4. The work is concluded in Sect. 5.

2   Biogeography-Based Optimization (BBO) Algorithm

BBO is a population-based optimization algorithm, which sets each solution as a habitat, fitness of solution as Habitat Suitability Index (*HSI*), and component of each solution as Suitable Index Variable (*SIV*). There are many factors that affect SIVs in natural solutions, such as rainfall, land area, plant diversity, address diversity, and climate. A good habitat has a high HSI, while a poor habitat has a low *HSI*. The algorithm simulates the searching process of species searching for the best adaptive islands. BBO mainly consists of migration operation and mutation operation. The main operations of BBO algorithm are as follows.

2.1   Migration Operation

Each habitat H_i has corresponding immigration rate λ_i and emigration rate μ_i. Both two parameters are closely related to *HSI*. In general, high HSI habitat has more species, and species tend to saturation. For high *HSI* habitat, there will be a high trend of outward migration. At this time, the emigration rate is high and the immigration rate is low due to the pressure of species competition. For low HSI habitat population, it tends to have low emigration rate and high immigration rate.

Assuming habitat H_i currently accommodates S_i species. S_{max} is maximum number of species. λ_i and μ_i are immigration rate and emigration rate of H_i, respectively, which are adjusted as Eq. (1).

$$\begin{cases} \lambda_i = I \times \left(1 - \frac{S_i}{S_{max}}\right) \\ \mu_i = E \times \frac{S_i}{S_{max}} \end{cases} \tag{1}$$

Where I is the maximum immigration rate and E is maximum emigration rate. Migration operation is described as Algorithm 1.

Algorithm 1: Migration Operation
1: For i=1 to N do
2:    For d=1 to D do
3:        If habitat H_i is selected with λ_i
4:            If habitat H_j is selected with μ_j
5:                $H_i(d) \leftarrow H_j(d)$;
6:            End if
7:        End if
8:    End for
9: End for

2.2 Mutation Operation

Some unexpected events cause some properties of the habitat change, such as HSI and the number of species. Mutation rate is determined by species probability. According to biogeography, when number of species in habitat is too large or too small, species probability is low. When the number of species in habitat is moderate, species probability is high. Equation (2) gives the relationship of Mutation rate m_i and species probability P_i. Species probability P_i is decided by number of species S_i [1] (In this paper, $S_{max} = N$ and $S_i = S_{max} - i$).

$$m_i = m_{max} \times \left(1 - \frac{P_i}{P_{max}}\right) \qquad (2)$$

where m_{max} is the maximum mutation rate and P_{max} is maximum species probability. Mutation operation is described as Algorithm 2.

Algorithm 2: Mutation Operation
1: For i=1 to N do
2:    For d=1 to D do
3:        If $H_i(d)$ is selected with probability m_i;
4:            Replace $H_i(d)$ with a randomly generated SIV;
5:        End if
6:    End for
7: End for

3 Proposed Algorithm: MTBBO

It is known that randomness of migration operation may make probability of migrating to better solution is not very large. The simple mutation operation also leads to the fact that mutation is not so ideal. In view of these problems, momentum idea in migration operation and taxonomic mutation idea in mutation operation are introduced in this paper. Then a novel biogeography-based optimization algorithm with momentum migration and taxonomic mutation is proposed.

3.1 Momentum Migration

3.1.1 Cosine Migration Model

The relationship between migration rate and the number of species in the original BBO is linear as Eq. (1). But this is not in accordance with the situation in nature, and cosine function is more in line with actual relationship in nature. When number of habitat species is large or small, the change of emigration rate and immigration rate is a little slow. When number of species in habitat is moderate, the change of emigration rate and immigration rate is a little fast. Some migration models are discussed in the literature [4], and they concluded that the cosine model performs best. So it is a better way to choose cosine migration model, which is indicated as Eq. (3).

$$\begin{cases} \lambda_i = \frac{I}{2} \times \left[\cos\left(\pi \times \frac{S_i}{S_{max}} \right) + 1 \right] \\ \mu_i = \frac{E}{2} \times \left[-\cos\left(\pi \times \frac{S_i}{S_{max}} \right) + 1 \right] \end{cases} \tag{3}$$

Where I is the maximum immigration rate and E is maximum emigration rate.

3.1.2 Momentum Migration Operation

The migration operation in original BBO is not so ideal. So the concept of momentum item of deep learning is introduced to make migration more ideal [15]. First of all, the concept of "gradient" is extended so that it can be applied to swarm intelligence algorithms. For the migration result of H_i is H_i', the "gradient" of H_i is defined as Eq. (4).

$$\widetilde{\nabla} f(H_i) = \frac{H_i' - H_i}{\left\| H_i' - H_i \right\|_2} \tag{4}$$

Momentum migration operator is described as Algorithm 3.

Algorithm 3: Momentum Migration Operation

1: Initialization: momentum coefficient α, learning rate η, step v=0.
2: While FE≤maxFE do
3:    Follow algorithm 1 and get the pre-migration result H_i' for each solution H_i.
4:    Calculate the gradient $\widetilde{\nabla}$f(Hi) for each H_i, and select 10 gradients randomly to calculate their average gradients g_t;
5:    Step update: v=α*v+η*g_t;
6:    Solution update: H_i=H_i+v;
7: End while

3.2 Taxonomic Mutation

Taxonomic mutation operation is adopted for individual dependent mutation scale in this paper. Solutions are divided into three classes: optimal class, middle class and poor class. Solutions of promising class are not executed mutation operation. Mutation is only for middle and inferior class, but mutation operations of middle class and poor class are different. For the solutions of middle class, their own information is somewhat beneficial. So these solutions are modified with differential mutation. The crossover rate P_C is introduced to judge whether it is cross or not. For the solutions of inferior class, they are normally far away from global optimal solution, so mutations are implemented on them which are independent of their own information.

3.2.1 Differential Mutation Operation

For the solutions of middle class, their information has good pattern, which are hoped to incorporated into the mutation process. There are many mutations strategies in differential evolution algorithm. The operator with the randomly selected solution and the best solution is chosen. To enhance the performance, another different search behaver is also adopted for these solutions with crossover rate P_C. Differential mutation operation is described as Algorithm 4.

Algorithm 4: Differential Mutation operation

1: For i=1 to N do
2:      Select 3 solutions (H_{i1}, H_{i2}, H_{i3}) and a dimension (d_rand) randomly;
3 :   For d=1 to D do
4 :   If rand<mi
5 :   If (rand<=P_C) or (d==d_rand)
6 : $H_i(d)=H_{i1}(d)+F*(H_{i2}(d)-H_{i3}(d))$;
7 :   Else
8 : $H_i(d)= H_{min}(d)+rand*(H_{max}(d)-H_{min}(d))$;
9 :   End if
10 :   Else
11 :   If (rand<=P_C) or (d=d_rand)
12 : $H_i(d)=H_{i1}(d)$;
13 :   Else
14 : $H_i(d)=H_{best}(d)+F*(H_{i2}(d)-H_{i3}(d))$;
15 :   End if
16:         End if
17:     End for
18:End for

---

where $H_{best}(d)$ is the d-th component of the best solution, $H_{max}(d)$ and $H_{min}(d)$ are the maximum and the minimum of the d-th component of all solutions.

3.2.2 Random Mutation Operation

For inferior class, their beneficial information is few. So random mutation with a self-adaptive interval enclosed by the current population is adopted here. Mutates between the maximum and the minimum of the one dimension is randomly chosen from the current population which is described as Algorithm 5.

Algorithm 5:   Random Mutation
1: For i=1 to N do
2:     For d=1 to D do
3:         If $H_i(d)$ is selected with probability m_i;
4:             $H_i(d)=H_{min}(d)+rand*(H_{max}(d)-H_{min}(d))$;
5:         End if
6:     End for
7: End for

3.3 Elitism Strategy

To preserve the current best solution, elitism strategy is adopted. Two best solutions are chosen for elitism strategy and not to participate in the migration operation.

3.4 MTBBO Optimization Process

Based on the above operations, MTBBO algorithm with momentum migration operation and taxonomic mutation is as follows:

(1) Initialize N habitats randomly and the necessary parameters;
(2) Sort and calculate the relevant parameters: N habitats are sorted according to *HSI*. Calculating the indicators for each habitat, number of species, emigration rate, immigration rate, species probability and mutation rate. The best quarter solutions are classified into promising class, the worst quarter are classified into inferior class and the rest belongs the middle class;
(3) Migration operation: Elitist strategy and the rests habitats take part in migration operation according to Algorithm 3;
(4) Mutation operation: Middle class carries on differential mutation according to Algorithm 4, inferior class carries on random mutation according to Algorithm 5;
(5) Selection operation based on HSI;
(6) Determine whether the termination criterion is satisfied.

4 Numerical Experiment and Analysis

To verify the performance of MTBBO, MTBBO is compared with classical BBO [1] and BBO-EP [3] based on CEC2014 benchmark functions [16].

4.1 Benchmark Functions and Parameter Settings

All functions are selected from CEC2014 benchmark suite [16] as follows. f1 and f3 are unimodal functions. f14 and f15 are simple multimodal functions. f17, f19, f20 and f21 are hybrid functions. f26 and f30 are composition functions. For convenience, these functions are relabeled as F1–F10. In this paper, population size N = 50, dimension D = 50, search ranges are all $[-100, 100]^D$, 30 independent runs conducted in MATLAB 2017b, momentum coefficient $\alpha = 0.99$, learning rate $\eta = 0.001$, crossover rate $P_C = 0.5$, difference coefficient F = 0.6.

4.2 Numerical Experiment

Results of BBO, BBO-EP and MTBBO are statistically shown in Table 1. "Min", "Mean", "Median" and "STD" indicate the minimum function error, the mean function error, the median function error and the standard deviation, respectively. The numbers achieving the best Mean of three algorithms are listed in the last row.

Table 1. Experimental Results of BBO, BBO-EP and MTBBO on CEC2014 Benchmark.

Fun	Item	BBO	BBO-EP	MTBBO
F1	Min	6.2770E+06	2.0654E+06	**2.7712E+05**
	Mean	1.3915E+07	5.2787E+06	**9.5158E+05**
	Median	1.2998E+07	4.5628E+06	**7.5741E+05**
	STD	5.6907E+06	2.4820E+06	**6.0452E+05**
F2	Min	4.3809E+03	3.4642E+03	**3.4908E+02**
	Mean	1.4757E+04	1.1885E+04	**3.2182E+03**
	Median	1.4349E+04	1.1369E+04	**1.8839E+03**
	STD	6.8686E+03	4.1480E+03	**3.0363E+03**
F3	Min	1.4003E+03	1.4003E+03	**1.4002E+03**
	Mean	1.4005E+03	1.4004E+03	**1.4003E+03**
	Median	1.4004E+03	1.4004E+03	**1.4003E+03**
	STD	2.4567E−01	1.8716E−01	**3.8149E−02**
F4	Min	1.5143E+03	1.5151E+03	**1.5078E+03**
	Mean	1.5256E+03	1.5260E+03	**1.5168E+03**
	Median	1.5244E+03	1.5241E+03	**1.5160E+03**
	STD	6.7787E+00	7.6171E+00	**5.3862E+00**
F5	Min	1.6847E+06	3.3400E+05	**2.4812E+04**
	Mean	4.4889E+06	1.5499E+06	**3.4019E+05**
	Median	4.1148E+06	1.4566E+06	**2.1782E+05**
	STD	2.3226E+06	8.3385E+05	**3.2738E+05**
F6	Min	1.9221E+03	1.9174E+03	**1.9108E+03**
	Mean	1.9507E+03	1.9195E+03	**1.9155E+03**
	Median	1.9465E+03	1.9192E+03	**1.9156E+03**
	STD	1.4230E+01	**1.4798E+00**	2.5134E+00
F7	Min	5.5132E+03	4.5715E+03	**2.2905E+03**
	Mean	1.7698E+04	1.4706E+04	**6.7526E+03**
	Median	1.5233E+04	1.2871E+04	**4.6224E+03**
	STD	7.6960E+03	8.2104E+03	**6.4113E+03**
F8	Min	1.0547E+06	4.0301E+05	**2.5053E+04**
	Mean	4.7210E+06	2.1493E+06	**2.1726E+05**
	Median	3.6827E+06	2.1358E+06	**1.5151E+05**
	STD	2.9399E+06	9.5448E+05	**2.8995E+05**

(continued)

Table 1. (*continued*)

Fun	Item	BBO	BBO-EP	MTBBO
F9	Min	2.7004E+03	**2.7003E+03**	**2.7003E+03**
	Mean	2.7472E+03	2.7327E+03	**2.7005E+03**
	Median	2.7007E+03	2.7006E+03	**2.7005E+03**
	STD	5.7614E+01	6.0570E+01	**1.1179E−01**
F10	Min	1.2787E+04	1.2688E+04	**1.1365E+04**
	Mean	1.8686E+04	1.6709E+04	**1.5014E+04**
	Median	1.8453E+04	1.6804E+04	**1.4848E+04**
	STD	3.5709E+03	2.2759E+03	**2.1685E+03**
Number of best Mean		0	0	10

Generally speaking, it can be observed from Table 1 that MTBBO achieves best results from all the functions when comparing with its competitors. For unimodal function and simple multimodal function, MTBBO is significantly better than BBO and BBO-EP. For hybrid function and composition function, MTBBO is slightly superior to BBO and BBO-EP.

4.3 Converging Curves of the Average Best Fitness

To visually examine the evolutionary trends of three algorithms, eight converging curves of the average best fitness are illustrated in Fig. 1.

In Fig. 1, x-axis shows the number of calculated function values and y-axis shows average function values. It can be seen that MTBBO has best searching ability, especially for unimodal function and hybrid function. The evolutionary trend curves in Fig. 1 and the experimental in Table 1 are cooperative and support each other.

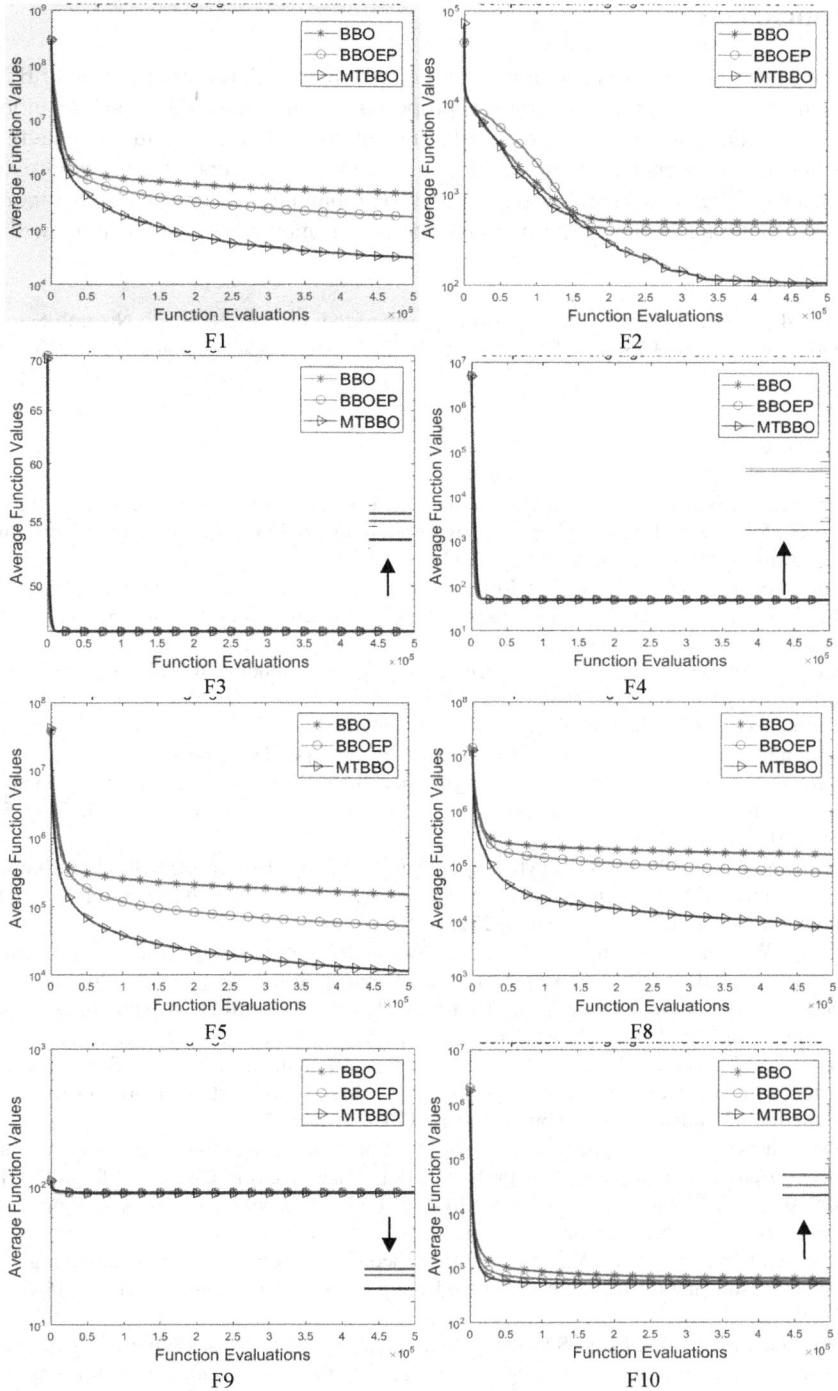

Fig. 1. Converging curves of the average best fitness.

5 Conclusion

Inspired by the momentum idea, momentum is introduced migration operation of BBO, and the momentum migration operator is proposed. An individual depended taxonomic mutation operation is implemented to different solutions. It divides solutions into three categories and difference individuals adopt different mutation operations, respectively. Finally, a novel BBO variant is proposed based on momentum migration and taxonomic mutation. In future, more properties and combining methods of momentum will be considered.

Acknowledgement. This research is partially supported by the National Natural Science Foundation of China (61973042, 71772060) and Beijing Natural Science Foundation (1202020).

References

1. Simon, D.: Biogeography-based optimization. IEEE Trans. Evol. Comput. **12**, 702–713 (2008)
2. Ma, H., Simon, D.: Blended biogeography-based optimization for constrained optimization. Eng. Appl. Artif. Intell. **24**, 517–525 (2011)
3. Cai, Z., Gong, W., Ling, C.-X.: Research on a novel biogeography-based optimization algorithm based on evolutionary programming. Syst. Eng. Theory Pract. **30**, 1106–1112 (2010)
4. Ma, H.: An analysis of the equilibrium of migration models for biogeography-based optimization. Inf. Sci. **180**, 3444–3464 (2010)
5. Bhattacharya, A., Chattopadhyay, P.K.: Biogeography-based optimization for different economic load dispatch problems. IEEE Trans. Power Syst. **25**, 1064–1077 (2010)
6. Reihanian, A., Feizi-Derakhshi, M.-R., Aghdasi, H.S.: NBBO: a new variant of biogeography-based optimization with a novel framework and a two-phase migration operator. Inf. Sci. **504**, 178–201 (2019)
7. Zhang, S., Xu, S., Zhang, W.: A hybrid approach combining an extended BBO algorithm with an intuitionistic fuzzy entropy weight method for QoS-aware manufacturing service supply chain optimization. Neurocomputing **272**, 439–452 (2018)
8. Zhang, W., Liu, T., Zhang, Y., Jiang, Z.: Research on biogeography-based optimization algorithm based on self-adaptive performance. Comput. Simul. **35**, 277–282 (2018)
9. Saremi, S., Mirjalili, S., Lewis, A.: Biogeography-based optimisation with chaos. Neural Comput. Appl. **25**, 1077–1097 (2014)
10. Jaafari, A., Panahi, M., Pham, B.T.: Meta optimization of an adaptive neuro-fuzzy inference system with grey wolf optimizer and biogeography-based optimization algorithms for spatial prediction of landslide susceptibility. Catena **175**, 430–445 (2019)
11. Bhattacharya, A., Chattopadhyay, P.K.: Application of biogeography-based optimisation to solve different optimal power flow problems. IET Gener. Transm. Distrib. **5**, 70–80 (2011)
12. Alweshah, M.: Construction biogeography-based optimization algorithm for solving classification problems. Neural Comput. Appl. **31**, 5679–5688 (2019)
13. Tong, Z., Chen, H., Deng, X.: A novel task scheduling scheme in a cloud computing environment using hybrid biogeography-based optimization. Soft. Comput. **23**, 11035–11054 (2019)
14. Xiao, J., Zhang, W., Zhang, S.: Game theory-based multi-task scheduling in cloud manufacturing using an extended biogeography-based optimization algorithm. Concurr. Eng. Res. Appl. **27**, 314–330 (2019)

15. Sutskever, I., Martens, J., Dahl, G., Hinton, G.: On the importance of initialization and momentum in deep learning. In: Proceedings of the 30th International Conference on International Conference on Machine Learning, (ICML 2013), USA, vol. 28 (2013)
16. Liang, J.J., Qu, B.Y., Suganthan, P.N.: Problem definitions and evaluation criteria for CEC2014 special session and competition on single objective real-parameter numerical optimization, Nanyang Technological University (Singapore) and Zhengzhou University, China (2013)

A Modified Artificial Bee Colony Algorithm for Scheduling Optimization of Multi-aisle AS/RS System

Xiaohui Yan[1,2]([✉]), Felix T. S. Chan[2], Zhicong Zhang[1], Cixing Lv[1], and Shuai Li[1]

[1] School of Mechanical Engineering,
Dongguan University of Technology, Dongguan 523808, China
Yxhsunshine@gmail.com
[2] Department of Industrial and Systems Engineering, The Hong Kong Polytechnic University,
Hong Hum, Kowloon, Hong Kong

Abstract. A modified artificial bee colony algorithm is proposed for solving the scheduling optimization problem of multi-aisle automatic storage/retrieval system. The optimization model of the problem is analyzed and founded, in which the sequence constraint of tasks and calculation of the number of aisles are more realistic. According to the features of the problem, the encoding and decoding strategies for solutions to MABC algorithm are redesigned. Probability selection-based updating method is also introduced to enhance the neighborhood search and preserve the good fragments. The experimental results show that MABC can obtain better results than PSO and GA algorithm, and is a competitive approach for AS/RS scheduling optimization.

Keywords: Automatic storage retrieval system · Modified artificial bee colony · Scheduling optimization

1 Introduction

Automatic Storage/Retrieval System (AS/RS) is an indispensable part of modern logistics. It has been widely used in manufacturing and logistics enterprises due to its advantages of high efficiency, economic space occupation and labor saving. In an AS/RS warehouse, S/R (storage/retrieval) machine is used instead of manual picking, which the saving labor cost usually accounts for 60–70% of the total warehouse operation cost [1]. Therefore, the scheduling optimization of S/R machine is the key point to AS/RS warehouse optimization. Many scholars have studied on it these years. Shiau et al. pointed out that picking scheduling optimization was a special case of Traveling Salesman Problem (TSP), and proposed a three-stage heuristic algorithm to optimize the order of the products to be picked [2]. Lerher et al. established travel time models for aisle transfer systems and shuttle-based systems for AS/RS warehouse [3, 4]. Ma et al. founded a multi-objective automated warehouse scheduling model and proposed an ensemble multi-objective biogeography-based optimization algorithm to solve it [5]. Cinar et al.

© Springer Nature Switzerland AG 2020
Y. Tan et al. (Eds.): ICSI 2020, LNCS 12145, pp. 94–103, 2020.
https://doi.org/10.1007/978-3-030-53956-6_9

investigated the scheduling of truck load operations in AS/RS, and proposed a priority based genetic algorithm to sequence the retrieving pallets [6].

However, there are also some shortcomings in existing studies. For example, in the multi-aisle AS/RS warehouse, one aisle corresponds to two storage racks on its both sides. Even if two products are on two different storage racks, the S/R machine can complete these two tasks without switching aisles if they are adjacent and located on two sides of the same aisle separately. Besides, S/R machines usually have more than one carrier and can hold several products at one time. However, it needs unoccupied carrier to pick up outbound products, which has certain requirements on the order of inbound and outbound tasks.

In this paper, the scheduling optimization model of multi-aisles AS/RS with multi-carrier S/R machine is established, and a modified artificial bee colony (MABC) algorithm is proposed to solve it. The new algorithm keeps the advantage of neighborhood searching of ABC algorithm and is also redesigned to adapt the AS/RS scheduling problem. Experimental results show that the proposed MABC algorithm has better performance than the particle swarm optimization (PSO) and genetic algorithm (GA) in solving this problem.

The rest of the paper is organized as follows. In Sect. 2, the multi-aisle AS/RS scheduling problem is introduced and its model is established. In Sect. 3, the MABC algorithm is proposed and described in detail. The experiment and discussion are given in Sect. 4 and conclusions are drawn in Sect. 5.

2 Scheduling Model of Multi-aisle AS/RS System

In this paper, we consider a multi-aisle AS/RS warehouse system which has been used in many enterprises. In this kind of warehouse, there are several rows of storage racks [7]. Usually, the two edges of the warehouse are one side rack, close to the wall, while the middle storage racks are two side racks back-to-back. There are passable aisles between the storage racks for S/R machines to travel, store and retrieve products. And the S/R machines can enter and exit freely at both ends of the storage racks. Each rack has a number of layers and columns, each of them has its own coordinates, corresponding to a storage unit which used to storage products. We use triples $[X, Y, Z]$ to represent the location of a storage unit, and Z, X, Y represent the serial number of the rack and the serial numbers of column and layer of the location in the rack respectively.

There is an I/O location for inbound and outbound operation. It is located at one side of the warehouse and denoted by the triple $[0, 0, 1]$. Most of the existing S/R machines have multiple carriers (such as forks) in order to improve efficiency, which can load more than one product at a time. We assume that the number of carriers is N. On one travel, the S/R machine picks up a maximum of N inbound products from the I/O location and places them in the designated location, then it picks up a maximum of N outbound products from the designated location and returns to the I/O point. In this paper, we mainly concern the total operation time for S/R machine to complete all tasks.

Generally, in order to maximize the efficiency of S/R machine, reduce the operation time, it is better to carry as many as possible products at the same time. In each route, the S/R machine should carry N storage products, complete N inbound tasks, and take out

N outbound products, complete N outbound tasks if the number of rest task is no less than N. Suppose there are m inbound tasks, n outbound tasks, $r = \max(\text{ceil}(m/N), \text{ceil}(n/N))$, where ceil($x$) stands for rounding the elements of x to the nearest integers towards infinity. It needs r routes to complete all inbound and outbound tasks. For situation that $m \neq n$, we can add $|m - n|$ virtual inbound or outbound tasks to make them be equal, which is more convenient for coding and calculation. The locations of virtual tasks are set as [0, 0, 0]. These tasks will be ignored when calculating the operation time.

As it has mentioned above, the AS/RS scheduling optimization problem can be regarded as a special case of TSP problem, we can construct its 0–1 integer programming model.

Define $e_{jk} = 1$, if the S/R machine travels from storage unit j (corresponding to task j) to storage unit k, otherwise, $e_{jk} = 0$. Define $a_{ji} = 1$, if the task j is executed in route i, otherwise, $a_{ji} = 0$. Define $b_{gi} = 1$, $c_{gi} = 0$, if the gth task in route i is an inbound task, else if it is an outbound task, $b_{gi} = 0$, $c_{gi} = 1$.

The goal is to minimize the total operation time.

$$min f = \sum_{i=1}^{r} \left(\sum_{j=1}^{m+n} \sum_{k=1}^{m+n} t_{jk} e_{jk} a_{ji} a_{ki} \right). \tag{1}$$

Among that, t_{jk} is the time for S/R machines moves from storage unit j to storage unit k.

The constraints are listed as below.

$$\sum_{i=1}^{r} a_{ji} = 1, \ \forall j \in 1, 2, 3 \ldots m + n, \tag{2}$$

$$\sum_{j=1}^{m} a_{ji} \leq N, \ \forall i \in 1, 2, 3 \ldots r, \tag{3}$$

$$\sum_{j=m+1}^{m+n} a_{ji} \leq N, \ \forall i \in 1, 2, 3 \ldots r, \tag{4}$$

$$\sum_{i=1}^{r} \sum_{j=1}^{m+n} a_{ji} = m + n, \tag{5}$$

$$\sum_{g=1}^{h} b_{gi} - \sum_{g=1}^{h} c_{gi} \geq 0, \ \forall i \in 1, 2, 3 \ldots r, \ \forall h \in 1, 2, 3 \ldots 2N. \tag{6}$$

Formulation (2) indicates that each task is executed only once. Formulations (3) and (4) are the load capacity constraint. It indicates that there can be no more than N inbound tasks and N outbound tasks are executed in each route. Formulation (5) grantees that all tasks are executed. Formulation (6) grantees that the S/R machine can pick up outbound products only when it has unoccupied carrier.

Suppose the storage racks are numbered start from 1, as it has mentioned in Sect. 1, the first rack is close to the wall. The first and second racks are separated by an aisle. The second and third racks are back to back close to each other. The third and fourth racks are separated by an aisle, and so on.

The time for S/R machine moves from storage unit j to storage unit k is calculated as follow.

$$t_{jk} = \begin{cases} max(W \times |X_j - X_k|/V_x, H \times |Y_j - Y_k|/V_y), & \text{if it doesn't need to swith aisles} \\ max((W \times min(|X_j - X_k|, 2C - X_j - X_k) + L \times \theta(Z_j, Z_k))/V_x, H \times |Y_j - Y_k|/V_y), & \text{else} \end{cases} \tag{7}$$

where W is the width for each storage unit, H is the height of each storage unit, L is the width of each aisle. $\theta(Z_j, Z_k)$ is a function to calculate the number of aisles between the location of the jth and kth tasks. C is the number of columns for each storage rack. If the locations of task j and k are at the same storage rack or at the adjacent storage but are distributed on two sides of the same roadway (this condition can be expressed as $Z_j = Z_k$ or $(|Z_j - Z_k| = 1$ && $mod(min(Z_i, Z_i), 2) \neq 0)$), the S/R machine can move from location j to k without switching aisles. Otherwise, the S/R machine needs to switch aisles. Since the S/R machine can move from both ends of the aisles, it is necessary to consider from which end the distance is shorter. In addition, it is also necessary to consider the time required on switching aisles.

$\theta(Z_j, Z_k)$ is calculated as follows.

$$\theta(Z_j, Z_k) =$$
$$\begin{cases} |Z_j - Z_k|/2 & if\ mod(|Z_j - Z_k|, 2) = 0 \\ |Z_j - Z_k|/2 - 0.5, & if\ mod(|Z_j - Z_k|, 2) \neq 0\ \&\&\ mod(min(Z_j, Z_k), 2) \neq 0 \\ |Z_j - Z_k|/2 + 0.5, & if\ mod(|Z_j - Z_k|, 2) \neq 0\ \&\&\ mod(min(Z_j, Z_k), 2) = 0 \end{cases} \tag{8}$$

3 Modified Artificial Bee Colony Algorithm

3.1 Artificial Bee Colony Algorithm

Artificial bee colony algorithm is proposed by Karaboga in 2005, which inspired by the behaviors of the bee colony searching food sources [8]. In ABC algorithm, it regards the searching space as the natural environment, and each solution of the problem represents a food sources to be exploited. The amount of nectar of the food sources corresponds to the fitness of the solution. There are three kinds of bees in ABC algorithm, employed bees, onlooker bees and scout bees. In ABC algorithm, half of the colony is employed bees the other half is onlooker bees. The number of scout bees is set to 1.

The process of ABC algorithm is also divided into the stage of employed bees, the stage of onlooker bees and the stage of the scout bee.

At the initialization stage, a set of food sources is randomly generated in the search space. The number of food sources equals half of the number of bees. The dimension of the food sources is the same with the problem to be solving. For each food source, there is a counter used to record the cumulative iterations for which it has not been improved.

At the employed bees' stage, each employed bee looks for a new food source near the original one according to formula (9).

$$v_{i,j} = x_{i,j} + \phi(x_{i,j} - x_{k,j}). \tag{9}$$

Among that, x_i is the original food source, x_k is a randomly selected neighbor, v_i is the candidate food source newly produced, j is a randomly selected dimension. ϕ is a random number according to uniform distribution between $[-1, 1]$. If the new food source is better than the original one, then the employed bee turns to the new one and the original one is abandoned. Otherwise, the original one is kept and the corresponding counter is increased by 1.

At the onlooker bees' stage, the onlooker bee chooses a food sources to exploit depending on a probability related to the fitness of the food sources, seen as formula (10). The food source with higher fitness has larger probability to be chosen and may be chosen more than once.

$$P_i = \frac{fitness_i}{\sum_{j=1}^{SN} fitness_j}. \tag{10}$$

After the food source is chosen, the onlooker bee will exploit a new food source nearby, just like it does at the employed bees' stage. Greedy selection and un-improved counter are also used.

At the scout bee's stage, if a bee's un-improved counter is larger than a predetermined parameter "*limit*", it indicates that the food source has been exploited out, the bee becomes scout bee, and will find a random food source in the searching area. At the same time, the counter is reset to 0.

Compared with PSO and other algorithm, ABC algorithm pays more attention to neighborhood search and obtains good results in many numerical and engineering optimization problems [9]. The optimal solution of scheduling optimization is usually obtained by neighborhood transformation of the suboptimal solution. Therefore, ABC algorithm may have better optimization potential in the AS/RS scheduling problem. However, we also need to redesign the encoding, decoding and updating methods of solutions to make the algorithm suitable for discrete AS/RS scheduling optimization problem.

3.2 Modified Artificial Bee Colony Algorithm

3.2.1 Encoding and Decoding Strategies

As mentioned above, the solution to the multi-aisle AS/RS warehouse scheduling problem is a sequence of inbound and outbound tasks. For the convenience of programming and solving, we use real number coding in MABC algorithm. The solution of the problem is a random sequence of the task numbers without repetition. However, according to the above constraints, the feasible solution also has certain requirements. The S/R machine must have an empty carrier to carry outbound tasks. As a result, in each route, the number of inbound tasks (including virtual task) must be larger than or equal to the number of outbound tasks from the first task to the end of the route. A repair mechanism is designed to ensure the feasibility of the solution.

a) Divide the solution into inbound task sequence and outbound task sequence according to the serial number.

b) Each time select N inbound tasks and N outbound tasks in sequence to form a route (including virtual tasks, and the number of tasks may be less than N at the last time due to the number of tasks may be not a multiple of $2N$ exactly). And then remove them from the task sequences.
c) In each route, the first task must be the inbound task. From the second one, compare the order of the first remaining inbound and first remaining outbound tasks in the original solution. If it is not against the rule following the order, then add the first task in order to the route. Otherwise, add the inbound task to the route.

Through this mechanism, all randomly generated solutions can be converted to the corresponding feasible solutions. This repair mechanism is not only used in MABC algorithm, but also used in the other comparison algorithms. Each time a new solution is produced, it needs to use this repair mechanism to convert it to a feasible solution before calculating its fitness.

3.2.2 Probability Selection-Based Solution Updating Strategy

The solution updating strategy of the original ABC algorithm is designed for continuous optimization problem. It learns from a random neighbor on a randomly selected dimension. The AS/RS scheduling optimization problem is a discrete optimization problem. We must redesign the solution updating strategy so that it can adapt to and solve the problem better. The neighborhood searching of ABC is modified as follows.

a) Select a neighbor solution randomly.
b) The values on dimensions which their values are the same with the neighbor solution are inherited into the same location of the new solution.
c) For the dimensions which their values are not the same, they are selected with a probability of 0.5.
d) For the selected dimensions, the values of the original food source on these dimensions are directly inherited into the same location of the new solution.
e) For the dimensions which are not selected, find the positions of their values in the neighbor solution, and insert them into the vacant positions of the new solution in order.

This solution updating strategy can guarantee that the solution newly produced is a non-repetitive task sequence, which can be transformed to a feasible solution of the AS/RS scheduling problem. On another hand, the solution is produced using neighborhood searching on the basis of the original solution. It keeps the advantage of original ABC algorithm. Both the neighborhood searching in employed bees and onlooker bees' phases use this strategy. In the scout bees' phase, a random solution is generated to keep diversity.

4 Experiments and Results

In this section, we tested the optimization ability of MABC algorithm on AS/RS scheduling problem and compared it with GA and PSO algorithm.

4.1 Test Instances

The width of each storage unit $W = 0.5$ m, The height of each storage unit $H = 0.8$ m, the width of each aisle $L = 3.0$ m, The numbers of the storage racks is 14. The numbers of columns and layers of each rack are 15 and 6. Accordingly, location X, Y and Z for the inbound and outbound tasks are distributed randomly from [1, 15], [1, 6] and [1, 14] separately. The movement velocity on the horizontal direction is 1.2 m/s. The movement velocity on the vertical direction is 0.4 m/s, which is close to the actual value. In this experiment, we generated three instances. In the first instance, the total number of tasks is 30, the number of inbound tasks m equals 14, number of outbound tasks n equals 16. In the second instance, m equals 22, n equals 18. In the third instance, m equals 26, n equals 24. The numbers of carriers of the S/R machine N of all instances are 2.

4.2 Parameters Setting

In this experiment, the population sizes of all algorithms are 50. Maximum number of function evaluations (FEs) is used as the terminated criterion [10, 11], and its value is 10000. In MABC algorithm, $limit = 50$. In PSO, learning factor $C1 = C2 = 2$, inertia weight ω decreases linearly from 0.9 to 0.4 [12]. The continuous version is used. The boundaries of all dimensions are [0, 1], and the maximum and velocity is 0.1 and minimum velocity is -0.1, the solutions are converted to desecrate solutions of AS/RS problem by rank of order (ROV) after each updating. In GA algorithm, crossover probability $p_c = 0.95$, mutation probability $p_m = 0.1$ [13]. In the crossover stage, some tasks may appear twice, and some others may be missing in the offspring solutions. These solutions will be checked and repaired to the sequence of tasks numbers without repetition. Greedy selection is also used in this stage. In the mutation stage, swap operator is used. The values of two randomly selected dimensions will be swapped with each other.

For all the three algorithms, the repair mechanism mentioned in Sect. 3.2.1 is used to make the solutions feasible and won't break the requirements of orders of inbound and outbound. All solutions will use this mechanism before being evaluated.

4.3 Results and Analysis

The results obtained by MABC, PSO and GA are listed in Table 1. It is intuitive that we can obtain an acceptable feasible solution if we sort all the tasks according to the serial numbers of racks (Z), and then repaired it according to the above repair mechanism. Therefore, we define this solution as the base solution and the time it takes as the base time. In the initialization phase of the three algorithms, all the solutions in the initial populations are generated by applying a swap operator on the base solution.

Each algorithm will run for 20 times independently on the instances. The best mean and standard are marked as bold. The mean convergence plots and boxplots of the final results are also given in Fig. 1.

It is clear that MABC obtained the best results on all the three instances. Its convergence speed and accuracy are all the best from Fig. 1. The mean results obtained by MABC are reduced more than 20% compared with base time. PSO algorithm converges fast at the beginning but hardly improves after $FEs = 5000$, and obtained the worst results

Table 1. Results obtained by MABC, PSO and GA on the three instances (unit: second)

Instances	Base time	MABC		PSO		GA	
		Mean	Std	Mean	Std	Mean	Std
1	371.00	**286.3750**	6.7432	300.7750	9.0619	293.4000	**6.0188**
2	465.00	**371.5750**	**6.9609**	411.4750	10.4874	383.4750	10.3942
3	652.00	**508.7000**	**4.4290**	555.1750	10.2396	524.9750	8.0761

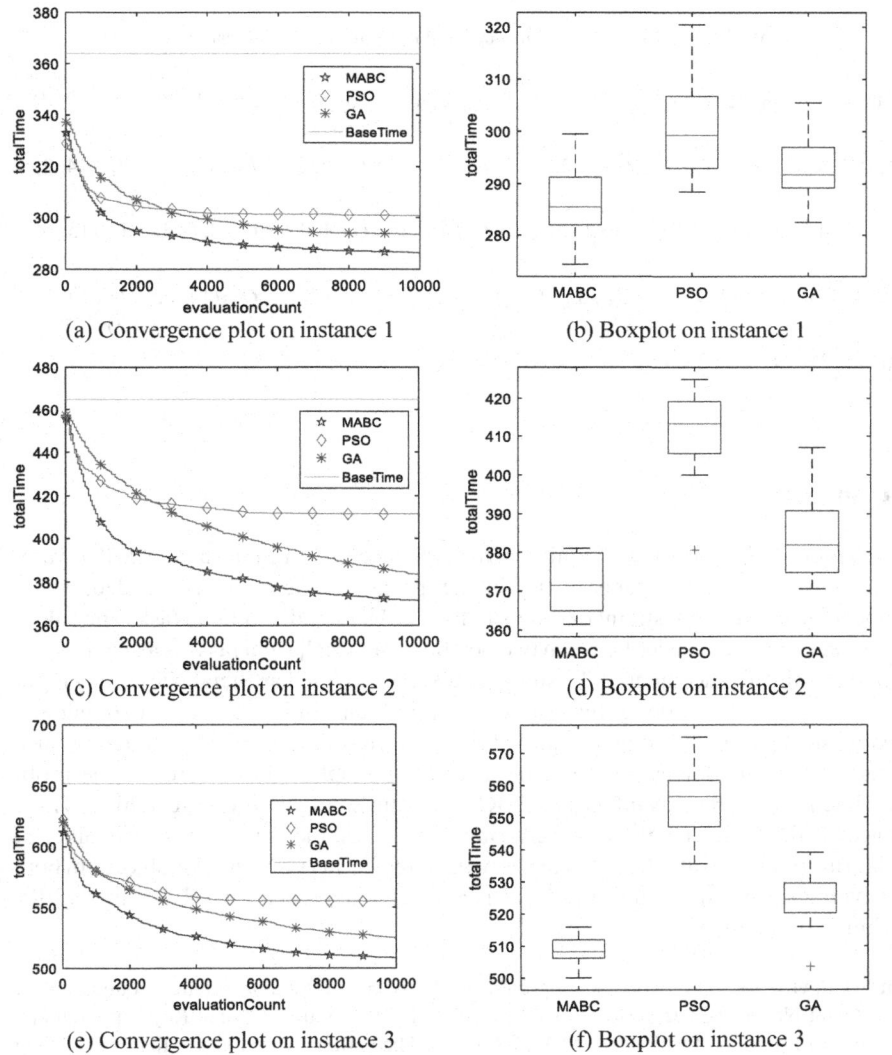

(a) Convergence plot on instance 1   (b) Boxplot on instance 1

(c) Convergence plot on instance 2   (d) Boxplot on instance 2

(e) Convergence plot on instance 3   (f) Boxplot on instance 3

Fig. 1. Convergence plots and boxplots obtained by MABC, PSO and GA on the instances

among the three algorithms. The standard deviations of MABC are also the smallest on instance 2 and instance 3. On instance1, its standard deviation is only a little worse than GA, which can also be seen from the boxplots in Fig. 1. The results show that MABC is superior to PSO and GA and is suitable for solving AS/RS scheduling problem.

The locations of inbound and outbound tasks in instance 1are listed in Table 2. The best solution obtained by ABC algorithm on this instance is $(I_5\text{-}O_{11}\text{-}I_9\text{-}O_{16})$, $(O_3\text{-}O_{12})$, $(I_{11}\text{-}I_7\text{-}O_{15}\text{-}O_6)$, $(I_4\text{-}O_{14}\text{-}I_2\text{-}O_4)$, $(I_{10}\text{-}I_3\text{-}O_{13}\text{-}O_7)$, $(I_{12}\text{-}I_1\text{-}O_8\text{-}O_9)$, $(I_8\text{-}I_{14}\text{-}O_{10}\text{-}O_1)$, $(I_{13}\text{-}I_6\text{-}O_2\text{-}O_5)$, each bracket represents a route. And there are two virtual inbound tasks in the second route when calculating. The total operation time of this solution is 274.5 s.

Table 2. The locations of inbound and outbound tasks in instance 1

$I_1(11, 3, 9)$	$I_2(12, 2, 5)$	$I_3(9, 6, 10)$	$I_4(3, 2, 4)$	$I_5(15, 4, 1)$	$I_6(4, 4, 14)$	$I_7(1, 3, 4)$
$I_8(15, 2, 9)$	$I_9(10, 5, 2)$	$I_{10}(5, 2, 8)$	$I_{11}(1, 2, 3)$	$I_{12}(7, 2, 10)$	$I_{13}(3, 3, 11)$	$I_{14}(14, 2, 11)$
$O_1(3, 1, 14)$	$O_2(7, 3, 13)$	$O_3(2, 1, 3)$	$O_4(10, 1, 6)$	$O_5(1, 1, 12)$	$O_6(8, 6, 4)$	$O_7(15, 6, 9)$
$O_8(9, 4, 10)$	$O_9(13, 4, 6)$	$O_{10}(11, 2, 13)$	$O_{11}(15, 3, 1)$	$O_{12}(2, 2, 2)$	$O_{13}(14, 6, 9)$	$O_{14}(9, 1, 3)$
$O_{15}(4, 5, 3)$	$O_{16}(5, 3, 1)$					

5 Conclusions

The scheduling optimization of multi carrier S/R machine in multi-aisle AS/RS warehouse is introduced in this paper. A 0–1 integer programming model is founded, which considers the realistic constraint of orders to inbound task and outbound task. The calculation of the number of aisles between two positions of the adjacent tasks is also redefined due to the realistic placement of the storage racks. A modified artificial bee colony algorithm is proposed for solving this optimization problem. In MABC, the encoding and decoding strategy are redesigned, a probability selection-based updating strategy is also introduced. The modifications make the algorithm adapt to the features of the problem, while keeping the advantages of ABC algorithm's neighborhood searching. Three instances with 30, 40 and 50 tasks were employed to test the optimization capability of the algorithm. The results show that the MABC outperforms PSO and GA algorithm both on convergence speed and accuracy, and is a suitable approach for solving the AS/RS scheduling problem.

Acknowledgements. This work is supported by the National Natural Science Foundation of China (Grant No. 61703102, 71971143, 71801045, 71801046), the National Key Research and Development Program of China (2018YFB1004004). The authors would like to thank The Hong Kong Polytechnic University Research Committee for financial and technical support.

References

1. Chen, T.L., Cheng, C.Y., Chen, Y.Y., et al.: An efficient hybrid algorithm for integrated order batching, sequencing and routing problem. Int. J. Prod. Econ. **159**, 158–167 (2015)
2. Shiau, J.Y., Lee, C.M.: A warehouse management system with sequential picking for multi-container deliveries. Comput. Ind. Eng. **58**(3), 382–392 (2010)
3. Lerher, T., Potrc, I., Sraml, M., Tollazzi, T.: Travel time models for automated warehouses with aisle transferring storage and retrieval machine. Eur. J. Oper. Res. **205**(3), 571–583 (2010)
4. Lerher, T., Ekren, B.Y., Dukic, G., Rosi, B.: Travel time model for shuttle-based storage and retrieval systems. Int. J. Adv. Manuf. Technol. **40**(3), 101–121 (2015)
5. Ma, H., Su, S., Simon, D., Fei, M.: Ensemble multi-objective biogeography-based optimization with application to automated warehouse scheduling. Eng. Appl. Artif. Intell. **44**, 79–90 (2015)
6. Cinar, D., Oliveira, J.A., Topcu, Y.I., Pardalos, P.M.: Scheduling the truckload operations in automated warehouses with alternative aisles for pallets. Appl. Soft Comput. **52**, 566–574 (2017)
7. Dornberger, R., Hanne, T., Ryter, R., Stauffer, M.: Optimization of the picking sequence of an automated storage and retrieval system (AS/RS). In: 2014 IEEE Congress on Evolutionary Computation (CEC), Beijing, pp. 2817–2824 (2014)
8. Karaboga, D.: An idea based on honey bee swarm for numerical optimization. Technical Report-TR06, Erciyes University, Engineering Faculty, Computer Engineering Department (2005)
9. Li, J.Q., Pan, Q.K., Duan, P.Y.: An improved artificial bee colony algorithm for solving hybrid flexible flowshop with dynamic operation skipping. IEEE Trans. Cybern. **46**(6), 1311–1324 (2017)
10. Ma, L., Wang, X., Huang, M., Lin, Z., Tian, L., Chen, H.: Two-level master-slave RFID networks planning via hybrid multiobjective artificial bee colony optimizer. IEEE Trans. Syst. Man Cybern. Syst. **49**(5), 861–880 (2019)
11. Liang, J., Xu, W., Yue, C., et al.: Multimodal multiobjective optimization with differential evolution. Swarm Evol. Comput. **44**, 1028–1059 (2019)
12. Bonyadi, M.R., Michalewicz, Z.: Particle swarm optimization for single objective continuous space problems: a review. Evol. Comput. **25**(1), 1–54 (2017)
13. Kerh, T., Su, Y.H., Mosallam, A.: Incorporating global search capability of a genetic algorithm into neural computing to model seismic records and soil test data. Neural Comput. Appl. **28**(3), 437–448 (2017)

The Research of Flexible Scheduling of Workshop Based on Artificial Fish Swarm Algorithm and Knowledge Mining

Jieyang Peng[1], Jiahai Wang[1(✉)], Dongkun Wang[2], Andreas Kimmig[3], and Jivka Ovtcharova[3]

[1] College of Mechanical Engineering, Tongji University, Siping Road, Shanghai 200083, China
jhwang@tongji.edu.cn
[2] Universität Stuttgart, Keplerstr. 7, 70174 Stuttgart, Germany
[3] Karlsruhe Institute of Technology, 76133 Karlsruhe, Germany

Abstract. The Job Shop Scheduling problem is critical in the manufacturing industry. At present, the decision tree reasoning technique and data mining are often used in multi-objective optimization research to solve flexible job shop scheduling issues. Unfortunately, when job shop scheduling problems involve complex logic, it becomes difficult to implement data-driven automatic scheduling without human intervention. Based on the analysis of mass data and specialized knowledge in the scheduling domain, an ontology-based scheduling knowledge model and a method of knowledge representation can be established. Considering the relationship between data mining and knowledge, this paper illustrates the acquisition process of scheduling rules. These scheduling rules were applied to improve the initialization process of the artificial fish algorithm. Then, a scheduling experiment was designed, the results of which show that the efficiency and accuracy of the algorithm has been improved. The desired uncertain information analysis, decision-making support for production planning and scheduling on the shop floor are provided and an adaptive scheduling algorithm for complex manufacturing systems is established by building a knowledge-based system.

Keywords: Data-driven · Ontology · Knowledge mining · Production scheduling · Artificial fish swarm algorithm

1 Introduction

Massive production data contains abundant knowledge of production scheduling. Through the data mining technology, valuable rules can be obtained, which contribute to decision-making in the field of production scheduling. Under such urgent demand, how to analyze scheduling data has become a key issue.

For the optimal dispatching of the production workshop, the establishment of a multi-objective optimization model is currently an effective solution. There are many achievements in the study of job shop scheduling problems [1–3]. However, the following issues remain to be resolved: (1) The calculation accuracy is relatively low,

© Springer Nature Switzerland AG 2020
Y. Tan et al. (Eds.): ICSI 2020, LNCS 12145, pp. 104–116, 2020.
https://doi.org/10.1007/978-3-030-53956-6_10

which brings certain difficulties to the implementation; (2) The solution procedure is inefficient. (3) Lack of knowledge-based guidance leads to limitations in the selection of scheduling optimization goals and rules. Therefore, it is necessary to study how to discover scheduling knowledge from the results of the scheduling algorithm [4], which aims at forming new scheduling rules, and apply them to the further optimization of the scheduling solution.

In recent years, the knowledge-based production scheduling method [5–9] has gradually become a research hotspot. However, due to the bottlenecks of knowledge acquisition, the knowledge-based scheduling method cannot be directly applied to the production scheduling field. To solve the above problems, an ontological knowledge representation method and a multi-objective optimization method for job shop scheduling based on knowledge mining is proposed, which improves on traditional knowledge representation and has become widely applied in the field of knowledge engineering.

2 Ontology-Based Scheduling Knowledge Representation

The representation of scheduling knowledge is key to realize knowledge mining of production scheduling. The purpose of establishing a scheduling ontology is to abstract the knowledge and describe the relationships between the entities.

2.1 Ontology Modeling of Scheduling Knowledge

To analyze the information in the field of shop scheduling, semantically label the knowledge on the basis of ontology, we sort out the basic relationship between the knowledge in the scheduling field, so that the scheduling knowledge can be understood and used by the controller.

Triplet $C = <D, W, K>$ can be adopted to formalize the concept ontology, where C represents the set of elements in the domain, W represents the state set of related transactions in the domain, and K represents the conceptual relationship set in the domain space $<D, W>$. According to the meta-language proposed by Perez et al., including classes or concepts, relationships, functions, axioms, and examples, the core concepts selected from the field include: tasks, indicators, goals, constraints, rules, resources, and solutions. The attributes of the concept ontology include decomposition, satisfaction, guidance, implementation, distribution, and execution. Other relationships include subclass-of, has, and attribute-of.

Based on the above theory, the domain ontology of the JSSP (Job Shop Scheduling Problem) scheduling problem can be defined with a six-tuple:

$$JSSP\_Ontology = <C, A^C, R, A^R, H, X>$$

In the formula, C represents a concept set, A^C denotes sets of attributes, R represents set of conceptual relationships, A^R represents relational attribute set, H represents set of Conceptual dependency, and X denotes axiom set.

The Knowledge Ontology in the field of real-time scheduling described by core concepts and well-defined attributes is shown in Fig. 1. Based on the production tasks and the Job Shop production scheduling theory, the task is often divided into several sub-tasks and assigned on different assembly-line in parallel to realize production allocation optimization. The scheduling rules are applied to guide the scheduling process under the constraint's conditions, and then the production resources are allocated according to the optimal scheduling scheme so that the task running cycle can be reduced.

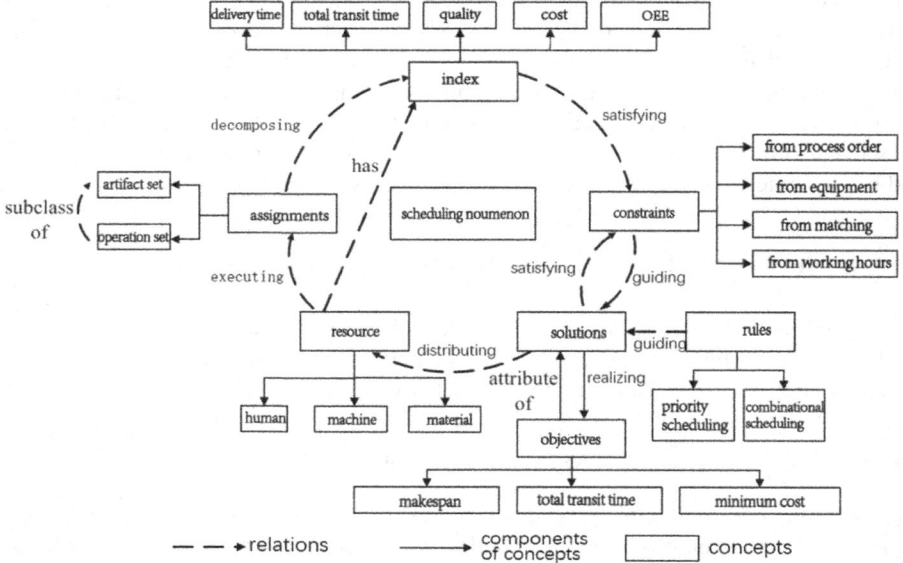

Fig. 1. Relational model of scheduling noumenon

2.2 Conception-Ontology and Attribute Representation in the Field of Scheduling

The ontology relationship diagram can directly represent the scheduling ontology model. However, in order to further investigate the constructing method of knowledge ontology, it is necessary to define its core concepts, essential attributes, and relational attributes. The ontology can be described by the following formula:

$$JSSP\_ConceptOntology = <N, P, \rho^n>$$

In the formula, N denotes the name of the concept; P denotes the attribute of the concept; ρ^n denotes the concept relation. The production scheduling task includes all machining tasks and its subtasks. The subtasks set should contain the corresponding process flow. The concept ontology of the task can be expressed as:

$$JSSP\_TaskConcept = <Task\_Details, Task\_Attribute, Task\_Relation>$$

In the formula, Task_Details includes the task's name, type (workpiece set/working procedure set), target number, and other specific information; Task_Attribute represents attribute decomposition, which means the work piece set can be decomposed into process sets, and the process sets can be decomposed into work steps; Task_Relation represents the subordinate relationship between tasks, such as, working steps subset to the process.

In terms of production scheduling problems, there are many performance indicators, such as time metrics, production cost index, quality index, and OEE (Overall Equipment Effectiveness). When solving the multi-objective optimization problem, the weight balance between different indicators needs to be considered. Based on principles above, the target ontology can be defined as:

$$JSSP\_TargetConcept = <Target\_Sett, Target\_Attribute, Target\_Functions>$$

In the formula, Target_Sett represents the set of indicators; Target_Attribute represents the attribute such as coefficient and attribution function; Target_Functions denotes the relationship between different goals, that is, weight information of different indicators.

Based on the above indicators, production tasks are allocated to production resources according to the constraints and different scheduling rules, for example, rules based on the shortest machining cycle, rules based on the earliest delivery date, rules based on optimal shop condition etc. These scheduling rules can be defined as:

$$JSSP\_RuleConcept = <Rule\_Name, Rule\_Attribute, Rule\_Relation>$$

In the formula, Rule_Name represents the name and unique identifier of the scheduling rule; Rule_Attribute represents the content of the scheduling rule, that is, by comparing processing time, number of tasks, delivery time, and other factors to determine the product task priority list; Rule_Relation represents that the relationships between various scheduling rules, such as inclusion, combination, and confliction.

In the field of scheduling, the core concepts of resource ontology include workers, machines, materials, etc. The formal definition of the core concept is determined by the specific resource type. The concept of scheduling resource ontology can be defined with five tuples:

$$JSSPResourceOntology = <C(man, machines, materials),$$
$$A^C(Person\_Attribute, Machine\_Attribute, Material\_Attribute),$$
$$R(attribute, hierarchy, instance relations, etc.), H(parallel scheduling),$$
$$X(matching constraint, mutual exclusion constraint)>.$$

3 Association Rules Mining Based on Decision Tree

In data mining field, traditional approaches, for instance, machine learning techniques can be applied to mine implicit and explicit knowledge behind scheduling data [12, 13]. This paper applies the multivariate decision tree to extract the knowledge of the scheduling rules from the scheduling data sets, and assign a value to its attribute based on information theory. Different attribute values form decision tree branches, and the decision trees can be constructed recursively. Then, a certain kind of knowledge and rules can be obtained from the decision tree.

3.1 The Framework of Scheduling Knowledge Acquisition

Data-driven production scheduling optimization focuses on how to let the integration of data and knowledge play an important role. As is shown in Fig. 2, the scheduling knowledge mining system performs data conversion and pre-processing on the collected sample data. The generated rules are stored in the fuzzy rule base and updated on-line by a self-organizing procedure, which improves the knowledge base, and implementing knowledge-driven automation decisions at decision points, so that better results can be achieved.

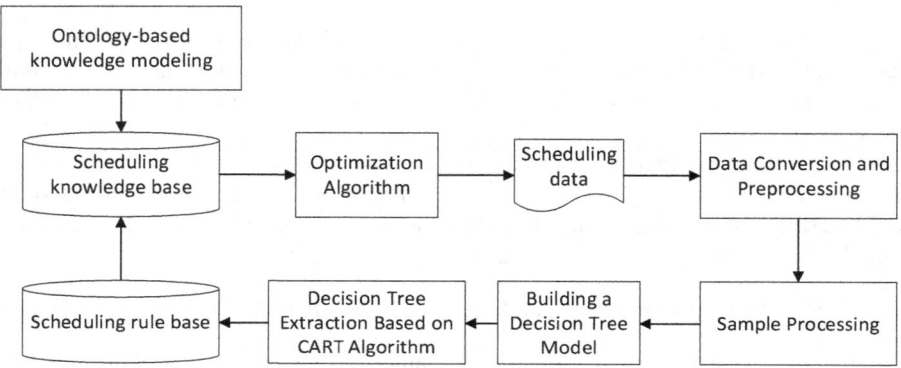

Fig. 2. Scheduling knowledge mining framework based on data mining

3.2 Rules Extraction of Decision Tree Based on CART Algorithm

Attribute is the branch point of the decision tree, and its selection strategy becomes the core of the decision tree construction. The most common attribute selection rules are the entropy-based information gain and the Gini Impurity Index. The CART algorithm determines the attributes of each node based on the Gini purity minimization classification criteria. The definition of the Gini Impurity Index is as follows:

If a schedule data set D has k classes, its Gini index is:

$$G(D) = 1 - \sum\nolimits_{k=1}^{k} [f(k|D)]^2 \qquad (1)$$

Where: D denotes the scheduling data set and $f(k|D)$ denotes the probability of the k-class in the data set D. When the probability of the category of the node attribute is the same, the maximum value of $1 - 1/n$ is taken, and the minimum value of 0 means that there is only one category at the node.

The parent node of the decision tree selects the sample t. If the CART selects the attribute x into two sub-nodes, the corresponding sets are t_{v_1} and t_{v_2}. The split Gini Impurity Index is:

$$G(t, x) = \frac{|t_{v_1}|}{|t|} Gt_{v_1} + \frac{|t_{v_2}|}{|t|} Gt_{v_2} \qquad (2)$$

$|\cdot|$ represents the number of records in the corresponding collection, and v_i represents different values of the attribute x.

At each node, calculate the Gini index of the attribute and select the attribute with the largest amount of reduction in impurity. The definition of impurity reduction is as follows:

$$\Delta = G(\text{parent}) - \sum_{v \in V} f_{\text{parent},v} G(\text{child}|v) \qquad (3)$$

In the above formula, V is a set of all attribute values corresponding to the attribute. $f_{\text{parent},v}$ represents the probability that the instance satisfied by the parent node attribute value v accounts for the entire data set, and $G(\text{child}|v)$ indicates that the child node attribute value satisfies Gini Impurity Index of v.

The specific steps of the algorithm are as follows:

Step 1: Convert and pre-process the scheduling data set to determine the attributes, attribute values, and category values.

Step 2: Select the training set and test set that contain all classes from the sample set;

Step 3: The parent node corresponds to the sample set t, and the attribute with the least Gini impurity is taken as the root node of the branch.

Step 4: In each subset, select the attribute with the greatest amount of reduction in impurity as the root node of the branch. Build the decision tree recursively. If the subset contains only one category, the split ends.

Step 5: The test set can be used to determine the error in the decision tree in step 4. If there is an over-fitting, then use the post-prune to optimize the decision tree.

Taking the JSSP scheduling problem of 6×6 scale as an example, 300 groups of scheduling data are selected obtained by the optimization algorithm to constitute the scheduling data set, among which 250 groups of data are used to train the classifier, and the remaining 50 are used to test the decision tree. The premise of the CART algorithm is the discreteness of the data, and it is necessary to discretize the continuous data in the samples. For 6×6 scheduling problems, the goal is to meet the earliest delivery data and shortest processing time. Select the indicator related to the target as the input attribute of the decision tree, take the data of each sample's corresponding indicator as the attribute value, use the sorting status of the work piece waiting for processing on the same machine tool as a category, and the numerical data can be used to represent the sorting and serve as the category value. The structure of the processed scheduling data set is shown in Table 1.

The CART algorithm uses post-pruning method to prevent over-fitting of the decision tree. After removing the leaf node of the same parent node, the impurity error is smaller, so starting from the leaf node, remove the leaf nodes and re-starting the cycle calculation from the parent node, as shown in Fig. 3. The decision tree as shown in Fig. 3 can be represented as the "if-then" rule combination as in Table 2.

Table 1. Data structure of MOO data set (CR = (Time of Delivery − current time)/processing time)

Attributes	Attributes value	Type value
RPT (remaining process time)	H (high)	0 (executed first)
ROPN (remaining operation process number)	L (low)	1 (executed later)
DT (delivery time)	H (high)	0 (executed first)
CR (critical ratio)	H (high)	0 (executed first)

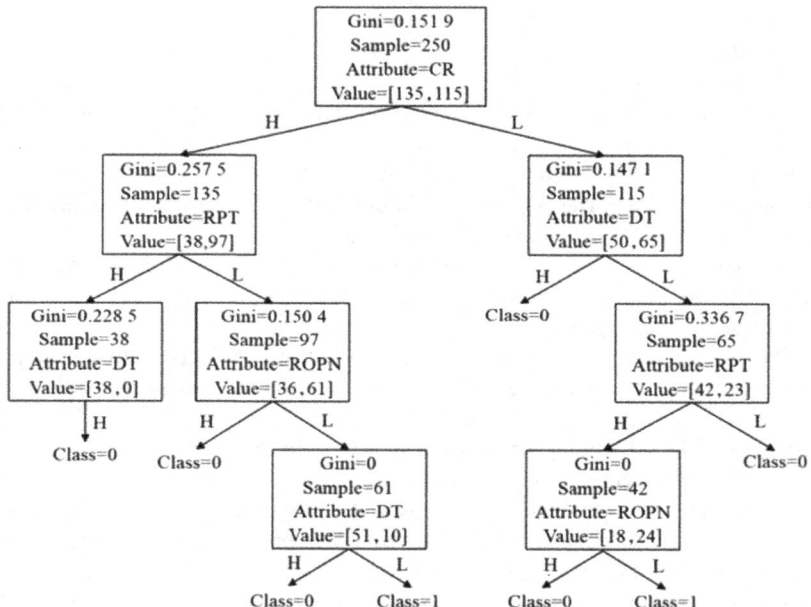

Fig. 3. CART tree diagram with the lowest impurity classification

4   Knowledge-Driven Production Scheduling Optimization

In this chapter, a method of improving initialization process of artificial fish swarm algorithm is proposed based on the data-based scheduling rules mining and scheduling knowledge representation.

4.1   Target Model

The target model of knowledge-driven Production Scheduling Optimization problem can be summarized as follows. If a job shop has n work pieces to be processed, the work piece set is N = {1, 2, ..., n}; there are m sets of machining equipment, and the equipment set is M = {1, 2, ..., m}; each work piece contains a variety of processes

Table 2. If-Then decision tree rules

No.	If	Then
1	CR=L, DT=H	result=0
2	CR=L, DT=L, RPT=L	result=0
3	CR=L, DT=L, RPT=H, ROPN=L	result=1
4	CR=H, RPT=L, ROPN=H	result=0
5	CR=H, RPT=H, DT=H	result=0
6	CR=H, RPT=L, ROPN=L, DT=L	result=1

j, $1 \leq j \leq m$. $O_{ijk} = 1$ represents that the jth process of the work piece i should be processed on the kth machine, the process starting time is S_{ijk}, the processing time is T_{ijk}, time of completion is E_{ijk}. The machine start time of the last process of the workpiece is LS_{ijk}, and the processing time is LT_{ijk}. The set of processes waiting for the machine at the same time on device k is combined as $[O_{ijk}, O_{nmk}]$, and the priority of the process is expressed as a binary value. $[O_{ijk}, O_{nmk}] = [1, 0]$ means that O_{ijk} is processed on device k first.

Based on the above features, the scheduling objective function can be defined as:

$$F = min\left[\max_{1 \leq i \leq n} \left(LS_{ijk} + LT_{ijk}\right)\right] \quad (4)$$

During the processing, some process constraints must be satisfied:

(1) One device can only operate one process at a time:

$$\sum_{i=1}^{n} O_{ijk} = 1 \ (k = 1, 2, 3, \ldots, m) \quad (5)$$

(2) One work piece can only be processed on one device at the same time;

$$\sum_{k=1}^{m} O_{ijk} = 1 \ (i = 1, 2, 3, \ldots, n) \quad (6)$$

(3) The completion time is equal to the start time plus the processing time:

$$E_{ijk} = S_{ijk} + T_{ijk} \quad (7)$$

(4) Only after the previous procedure of the same workpiece is completed can the next procedure be started:

$$S_{i(j+1)} > E_{ij} \quad (8)$$

Besides, the processes between different work pieces are independent of each other, the process of a work piece is determined and cannot be changed;

4.2 Artificial Fish Swarm Algorithm with Improved Initial Population

In the traditional artificial fish swarm algorithm, artificial fish populations are initialized randomly [14], resulting in a slow initial search speed and a slow convergence in the later period of the algorithm, which reduces the convergence speed of the algorithm. For the JSSP scheduling problem, combined with the application of decision tree scheduling rule, the scheduling knowledge can be used to initialize the process sequencing at each decision point. Then, the IF-THEN rules generated by the decision tree are used to compare the attribute value of different processes so as to determine the execution sequence of the processes.

The knowledge-driven initial population optimization method for artificial fish swarm algorithm is used to minimize the total processing time. The algorithm flowchart is shown in Fig. 4.

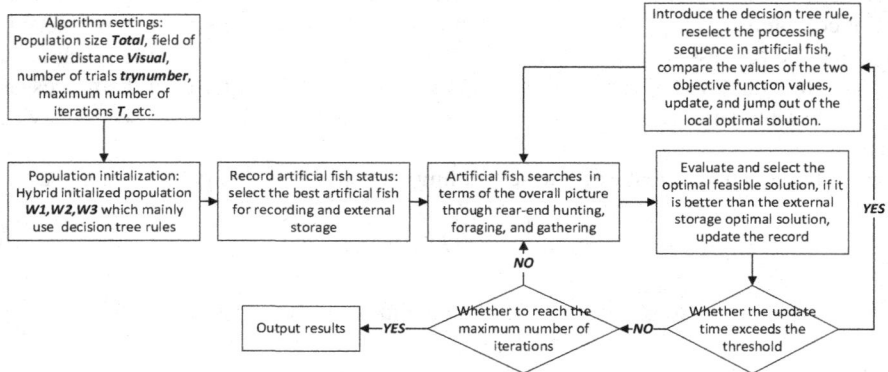

Fig. 4. Improved artificial fish swarm algorithm based on scheduling knowledge

5 Experiment Analysis

In order to verify the validity of the decision tree rules and the improvement of the decision tree rules on the artificial fish swarm algorithm in solution to the scheduling problem, the 6 × 6 and 8 × 8 JSSP scheduling problem is taken as an example.

The object model of 6 × 6 JSSP and constraint conditions are described in Sect. 4.1, while the model of 8 × 8 JSSP is derived from real workshop data in reference [15]. The scheduling data of 6 × 6 JSSP is shown in Table 3, in which 5 (130) indicates that the fifth process of the workpiece 1 is processed on the equipment M1, and the processing time is 130.

The algorithm parameters are set as follows: population size Total = 40, visual distance Visual = 6×6 = 36, crowd factor δ = 9, maximum number of iteration T = 20, tentative number try number = 30.

Table 3. 6 × 6 Scheduling data

Work piece	Machines					
	M1	M2	M3	M4	M5	M6
1	5(130)	3(240)	6(180)	4(270)	1(90)	2(180)
2	1(200)	4(160)	3(300)	5(240)	2(190)	6(100)
3	3(250)	5(80)	6(120)	2(110)	1(90)	4(280)
4	1(130)	3(240)	5(120)	4(270)	6(150)	2(90)
5	2(90)	4(140)	3(190)	5(140)	1(230)	6(100)
6	1(150)	6(190)	5(180)	2(190)	3(190)	4(90)

We perform 10 repeated simulations of the above two cases, and compare them with other scheduling rules, as showed in Table 4 and Table 5. It turned out that compared with other algorithms, the improved artificial fish swarm algorithm has a smaller variance, a better stability and robustness, and the optimal objective function value can be obtained in a relatively short time, which means the new algorithm has a higher efficiency.

Table 4. Comparison of results of algorithms (6 × 6 Scheduling data)

Optimization method	Total processing time/s	Variance	Average running time/s	Frequency of simulation
Traditional Artificial Fish Swarm-Algorithm	1660	1.53	5.42	10
Improved Artificial Fish-Swarm Algorithm	1560	0.38	4.10	10
Genetic algorithm	1690	1.46	4.76	10
Priority scheduling rules	1710	0	7.22	10

Table 5. Comparison of results of algorithms (8 × 8 Scheduling data)

Objective function	Genetic algorithm	Ant colony algorithm	Traditional Artificial Fish Swarm-Algorithm	Improved Artificial Fish-Swarm Algorithm
Minimum completion time	16	15	16	14

Figure 5 and Fig. 6 show the optimal scheduling sequence of the two algorithms through the Gantt chart. The Gantt chart reveals that due to the reduction of waiting time, the operation sequence obtained by knowledge-driven artificial fish swarm algorithm has higher equipment utilization and the make span is minimizing. Thus, it's a better scheduling solution.

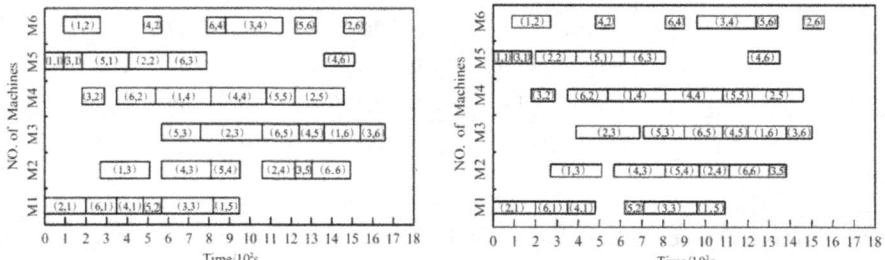

Fig. 5. Gantt-chart of traditional and improved Artificial Fish Swarm Algorithm (6 × 6 Scheduling data)

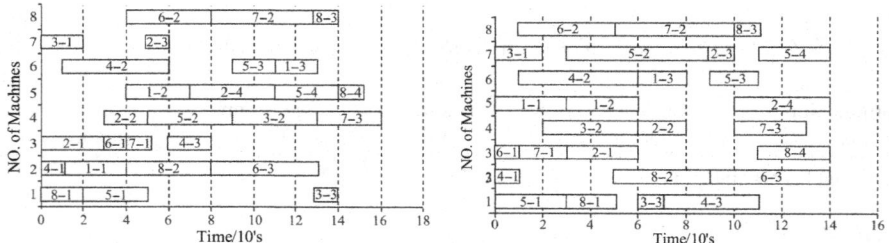

Fig. 6. Gantt-chart of traditional and improved Artificial Fish Swarm Algorithm (8 × 8 Scheduling data)

The above experiment re-processes the optimization problem by using the decision tree rule as algorithm constraint conditions. The optimized results are taken as new samples to rebuild the initial decision tree classifier so that the improved decision tree classification with higher accuracy rate is better performing. The rules of the decision tree after training are shown in Table 6.

Table 6. Decision tree rules after training

No.	If	Then
1	CR=L, DT=H	result=0
2	CR=L, DT=L, RPT=L	result=0
3	CR=H, RPT=L, ROPN=H	result=1
4	CR=H, RPT=H	result=0
6	CR=H, RPT=L, ROPN=L, DT=L	result=1

6 Conclusion

Aiming at the limitation of knowledge acquisition and application of a manufacturing system, this paper summarizes the professional experience and knowledge in the field of scheduling. From the aspect of knowledge representation, we adopt an ontology-based method. This is to represent the scheduling knowledge in the form of conception and formalization, to advance the cooperation of heterogeneous systems and prompt the communion of the scheduling knowledge. Secondly, it integrates CART-based learning algorithms to extract a decision tree classification rule set and a class association rule set respectively so that the dynamic scheduling rules Library can be built. Based on this, we study the effective combination of decision tree rules and artificial fish swarm algorithm to realize the acquisition of scheduling knowledge, and then use the knowledge to realize the optimization of production scheduling. Finally, a computer simulation experiment is designed to test the effectiveness and practicability of the solution. The simulation results show that knowledge-driven artificial fish-swarm algorithm can significantly improve the solution of the Job-Shop Scheduling Problem. The results also have some reference value to develop the scheduling system and improve the productivity and resource utilization of workshop in practical application.

References

1. Xu, B., Fei, X., Zhang, X.: Batch division and parallel scheduling optimization of flexible job shop. Comput. Integr. Manuf. Syst. **22**(8), 1953–1964 (2016)
2. Meeran, S., Morshed, M.S.: A hybrid genetic tabu search algorithm for solving job shop scheduling problems: a case study. J. Intell. Manuf. **23**(4), 1063–1078 (2012)
3. Cupek, R., Ziebinski, A., Huczala, L., et al.: Agent-based manufacturing execution systems for short-series production scheduling. Comput. Ind. **82**, 245–258 (2016)
4. Yan, H., Liu, F.: Knowledgeable manufacturing system-a new kind of advanced manufacturing system. Comput. Integr. Manuf. Syst. **7**(8), 7–11 (2001)
5. Yao, L., Wang, Z., Mu, H.: Knowledge-based optimization of manufacturing system and implementation under ASP.net. Comput. Technol. Dev. **21**(11), 1–3 (2011)
6. Wang, H., Yan, H.: Interoperable dynamic adaptive scheduling strategy in knowledgeable manufacturing based on multi-agent. Control Decis. **28**(2), 161–168 (2013)
7. Vegetti, M., Roldán, L., Gonnet, S., et al.: A framework to represent, capture, and trace ontology development processes. Eng. Appl. Artif. Intell. **56**, 230–249 (2016)

8. Zhang, X., Qiu, J.: Research on knowledge fusion framework in big data environment. Libr. Sci. Res. (8), 66–70 (2016)
9. Wu, Q.: Ontology-based domain knowledge representation and acquirement. Comput. Eng. Appl. **41**(31), 23–25 (2005)
10. Bandaru, S., Ng, A.H.C., Deb, K.: Data mining methods for knowledge discovery in multi-objective optimization: Part A - Survey. Expert Syst. Appl. **70**, 139–159 (2017)
11. Bandaru, S., Ng, A.H.C., Deb, K.: Data mining methods for knowledge discovery in multi-objective optimization: Part B - New developments and applications. Expert Syst. Appl. **70**, 119–138 (2017)
12. Zhao, M., Yin, H., Sun, D., et al.: Flexible job shop scheduling problem based on modified artificial fish swarm alogorithm. China Mech. Eng. **27**(8), 1059–1065 (2016)
13. Chen, X.: Research of Flexible Job Shop Scheduling Problem based on Artificial Fish Swarm Algorithm. Dalian University of Technology (2015)
14. Sun, F., Zhang, J.: Research on modified artificial fish swarm algorithm under framework of cultural algorithm. Comput. Simul. **31**(4), 407–411 (2014)
15. Kacem, I., Hammadi, S., Borne, P.: Approach by localization and multi-objective evolutionary optimization for flexible job-shop scheduling problems. IEEE Trans. Syst. Cybern. Part C **32**(1), 408–419 (2002)

A Novel Image Segmentation Based on Clustering and Population-Based Optimisation

Seyed Jalaleddin Mousavirad[1], Gerald Schaefer[2],
Hossein Ebrahimpour-Komleh[3], and Iakov Korovin[4]

[1] Faculty of Engineering, Sabzevar University of New Technology, Sabzevar, Iran
[2] Department of Computer Science, Loughborough University, Loughborough, UK
[3] Computer Engineering Department, University of Kashan, Kashan, Iran
[4] Southern Federal University, Taganrog, Russia

Abstract. Image segmentation is an essential step in image processing and computer vision with many image segmentation algorithms having been proposed in the literature. Among these, clustering is one of the prominent approaches to achieve segmentation. Traditional clustering algorithms have been used extensively for this purpose, although they have disadvantages such as dependence on initialisation conditions and a tendency to find only local optima. To overcome these disadvantages, population-based metaheuristic algorithms can be applied.

In this paper, we propose a novel clustering algorithm based on human mental search (HMS) for image segmentation. HMS is a relatively new population-based metaheuristic inspired from the manner of searching in online auctions. HMS comprises three operators: mental search, which explores the neighbourhood of candidate solutions using Levy flight; grouping, which clusters candidate solutions; and moving candidate solutions towards a promising area. To verify the efficacy of the proposed algorithm, we conduct several experiments based on different criteria including mean cost function value, statistical analysis and image segmentation criteria. The obtained results confirm superior performance of our proposed algorithm compared to competitors.

Keywords: Image segmentation · Clustering · Optimisation · Population-based algorithms · Human mental search

1 Introduction

Image segmentation is a critical task in computer vision. It partitions an image in terms of pixel-based features into several homogeneous and disjoint regions so that the members within the same region share the same characteristics. Image segmentation is employed as a pre-processing step in many applications such as medical image processing [4,15] or modelling of microstructures [16].

© Springer Nature Switzerland AG 2020
Y. Tan et al. (Eds.): ICSI 2020, LNCS 12145, pp. 117–129, 2020.
https://doi.org/10.1007/978-3-030-53956-6_11

Clustering is one of the most commonly employed approaches for image segmentation. It divides an image into clusters (groups) so that the members located in the same cluster have more resemblance to each other than to those in others clusters. The k-means algorithm is the most popular clustering algorithm. It initialises k cluster centres randomly and each pattern is then assigned to the closest cluster centre. In the next step, the location of each cluster centre is recomputed and the process continues until a stopping criterion is met. However, k-means suffers from some drawbacks such as dependence on initialisation and getting stuck in local optima.

Population-based metaheuristics are problem-independent optimisation algorithms with stochastic characteristics and can be used to overcome these drawbacks. They typically create a random population of candidate solutions which are then iteratively updated based on operations that are stochastic and share information within the population.

Popular population-based metaheuristics that have been used for clustering-based image segmentation include particle swarm optimisation (PSO) [12,17], differential evolution (DE) [2,7], artificial bee colony (ABC) [13] and harmony search (HS) [20] among others.

Human mental search (HMS) [11] is a relatively new population-based metaheuristic that has shown competitive performance in solving optimisation problems [11]. HMS has three main operators: mental search, grouping, and movement. Mental search seeks around a candidate solution based on Levy flight, grouping clusters the population to find a promising region, and movement steers candidate solutions towards the promising area.

In this paper, we propose a novel image segmentation based on clustering and HMS. To this end, our encoding strategy is an array to define the cluster centres and we employ an objective function based on the mean squared error. An extensive set of experiments demonstrates very good segmentation performance and superiority over other methods.

The remainder of the paper is organised as follows. Section 2 summarises the human mental search algorithm, while Sect. 3 details our proposed image segmentation algorithm. Section 4 presents experimental results, and Sect. 5 concludes the paper.

2   Human Mental Search

Human mental search (HMS) [11] is a recent population-based metaheuristic algorithm where candidate solutions are bids in the space of online auctions.

The workings of HMS are detailed in Algorithm 1 in terms of pseudo-code. Like other population-based algorithms, HMS starts with a set of random candidate solutions. Candidate solutions try to move towards the optimum using mental search (to explore the vicinity of bids), grouping (to find the promising area), and movement (to steer bids toward the promising area) operators. In the following, we briefly explain these three operators.

Algorithm 1. HMS algorithm pseudo code

1: // L, U: lower, upper bound; M_l, M_h: minimum, maximum number of mental processes; N_{pop}: number of bids; K: number of clusters; NFE, NFE_{max}: current, maximum number of objective function evaluations
2:
3: X = initialise population of N_{pop} bids
4: Calculate objective function values (OFVs) of bids
5: x^* = find best bid in initial population
6: **for** i from 1 to N_{pop} **do**
7:     β_i = generate random number in $[L; U]$
8: **end for**
9: **while** $NFE < NFE_{max}$ **do**
10:     // Mental Search
11:     **for** i from 1 to N_{pop} **do**
12:         q_i = generate random integer number in $[M_l; M_h]$
13:     **end for**
14:     **for** i from 1 to N_{pop} **do**
15:         **for** j from 1 to q_i **do**
16:             $S = (2 - NFE(2/NFE_{max}))0.01\frac{u}{v^{1/\beta_i}}(x^i - x^*)$
17:             $NS_j = x^i + s$
18:         **end for**
19:         t = find NS with lowest OFV
20:         **if** $cost(t) < cost(x^i)$ **then**
21:             $x^i = t$
22:         **end if**
23:     **end for**
24:     // Clustering
25:     Cluster N_{pop} bids into K clusters
26:     Calculate mean OFV of each cluster
27:     Winner cluster = cluster with lowest mean OBV
28:     $winner$ = best bid in winner cluster
29:     // Movement
30:     **for** i from 1 to N_{pop} **do**
31:         **for** n from 1 to N_{var} **do**
32:             $x_n^i = x_n^i + C(r \times winner_n - x_n^i)$
33:         **end for**
34:     **end for**
35:     **for** i from 1 to N_{pop} **do**
36:         β_i = generate random number in $[L; U]$
37:     **end for**
38:     x^+ = find best bid in current bids
39:     **if** $cost(x^+) < cost(x^*)$ **then**
40:         $x^* = x^+$
41:     **end if**
42: **end while**

2.1   Mental Search

Here, each bid explores its vicinity based on a Levy flight distribution, resulting in both small and long jumps to enhance both exploration and exploitation ability of the algorithm simultaneously.

A bid x^i is updated as

$$x^i = x^i + S, \tag{1}$$

with S calculated as

$$S = (2 - NFE(2/NFE_{\max}))0.01\frac{u}{v^{1/\beta}}(x^i - x^*), \tag{2}$$

where NFE is the number of objective function evaluations so far, $NFE_{\max}$ is the maximum number of function evaluations, x^* is the best bid found so far, and u and v are two random numbers calculated as

$$u \sim N(0, \sigma_u^2), \ v \sim N(0, \sigma_v^2), \tag{3}$$

with

$$\sigma_u = \left\{ \frac{\Gamma(1+\beta)\sin(\frac{\pi\beta}{2})}{\Gamma[(\frac{1+\beta}{2})]\beta 2^{(\beta-1)/2}} \right\}^{1/\beta}, \ \sigma_v = 1, \tag{4}$$

where Γ is a standard gamma function.

2.2   Grouping

A clustering approach is used to group the current population of bids. After clustering, which is performed using the k-means algorithm, similar bids are located in the same group. Then, the mean objective function value is calculated for each group, and the group with the lowest value selected as the winner group.

2.3   Movement

Here, bids move towards the best bid in the winner cluster as

$$x_n^{t+1} = x_n^t + C(r \times winner_n^t - x_n^t), \tag{5}$$

where x_n^{t+1} is the n-th bid element at iteration $t+1$, $winner_n^t$ is the n-th element of the best bid in the winner group, t is the current iteration, C is a constant, and r is a number in $[0; 1]$ taken from a normal distribution.

3   Proposed Segmentation Algorithm

This paper introduces a novel clustering-based image segmentation algorithm based on clustering and HMS.

Assume that a dataset has N objects, $O_1, O_2, ..., O_N$. A clustering algorithm tries to find K cluster centres, $C_1, C_2, ..., C_K$ with the following conditions:

Fig. 1. Test image dataset.

1. Each cluster contains at least one object.
2. Distinct clusters have no objects in common.
3. The total number of cluster members is equal to the total number of objects in the dataset.

For our application of HMS, two issues need to be taken into account: encoding strategy and objective function. The encoding strategy determines the structure of each bid in HMS. We use an array to encode the cluster centres, and the length of the array is thus the number of cluster centres. Also, the upper and lower bound of the array is set to the maximum and minimum of pixel values in the image. As objective function, we use the mean squared error (MSE) defined as

$$MSE = \frac{\sum_{j=1}^{K} \sum_{P_i \in C_j} d(P_i, C_j)}{n}, \tag{6}$$

where $d(P_i, c_j)$ is the Euclidean distance between pixel P_i and its cluster centre C_j, and n is the total number of pixels in the image.

Our image segmentation algorithm proceeds in the following steps:

Step 1: Parameter initialisation: population size N_{pop}, minimum M_l and maximum M_h number of mental searches, number of clusters for bid grouping N, number of objective function evaluations NFE, and number of clusters for image segmentation K.

Step 2: Generate an initial random set of bids.

Step 3: Calculate the objective function value for each bid using Eq. (6).

Step 4: Create a random integer number for each bid in $[M_l; M_h]$ indicating the number of mental searches for the bid.

Step 5: Mental search: generate new bids based on Levy flight distribution in the vicinity of each bid.

Step 6: Replacement: in case a newly produced bid is better than the old one, it will replace the latter.

Step 7: Bid grouping: all bids in the search space are clustered using the k-means algorithm.

Table 1. Parameter settings for all algorithms.

Algorithm	Parameter	Value
GA	Crossover probability	0.8
	Mutation probability	1/(number of thresholds)
DE [18]	Scaling factor	0.5
	Crossover probability	0.1
PSO [19]	Cognitive constant	2
	Social constant	2
	Inertia constant	1 to 0
ABC [5]	Limit	n_e × dimensionality of problem
HS [3]	Harmony memory considering rate	0.9
	Pitch adjusting rate	0.1
HMS	Number of clusters	5
	C	2

Step 8: Calculate the mean objective function value for each cluster.

Step 9: The cluster with the minimum mean objective function value is selected as the winner cluster.

Step 10: Other bids move towards the best bid in the winner cluster based on Eq. (5).

Step 11: Find the best bid in the current population and if it is better than the previous best bid, substitute the latter with it.

Step 12: If the stopping condition is not met, go back to Step 3.

4   Experimental Results

In our experiments, we select 10 images, shown in Fig. 1, which are commonly used in the literature: Lenna, House, Airplane, Peppers, and MRI, and five images from Berkeley image segmentation dataset [9], namely 12003, 42049, 181079, 198054, and 385028. We compare our algorithm with other population-based algorithms that have been previously used for image segmentation.

The population size and the number of objective function evaluations for all algorithms are set to 50 and 6000, respectively, and all results are run for $K = 5$. For HMS, we set the number of clusters used during grouping to 5 and C to 2, while $M_l = 2$, $M_h = 10$, $L = 0.3$, and $U = 1.99$. For the other algorithms, we adapt default values previously employed in this context, listed in Table 1. Since the algorithms are stochastic, we run each algorithm 25 times on each image, and report the average over these runs. We also rank the algorithms for each image and calculate Friedmann ranks which are obtained by averaging the ranks over the image set.

Table 2. Objective function value results.

Image	HMS	ABC	HS	PSO	DE	GA
Lenna	0.0453	0.0481	0.0464	0.0457	0.0475	0.0458
	1	6	4	2	5	3
Airplane	0.0335	0.0493	0.0351	0.0370	0.0336	0.0372
	1	6	3	4	2	5
House	0.0801	0.0873	0.0847	0.0796	0.0821	0.0803
	2	6	5	1	4	3
Peppers	0.1025	0.1084	0.1039	0.1024	0.1031	0.2538
	2	5	4	1	3	6
MRI	0.0217	0.0446	0.0234	0.0226	0.0218	0.0263
	1	6	4	3	2	5
42049	0.0578	0.0793	0.0574	0.0665	0.0586	0.0593
	2	6	1	5	3	4
12003	0.0606	0.0720	0.0618	0.0609	0.0606	0.0614
	2	6	5	3	1	4
81079	0.0661	0.0812	0.0668	0.0745	0.0673	0.0677
	1	6	2	5	3	4
198054	0.0738	0.0785	0.0745	0.0745	0.0739	0.0749
	1	6	4	3	2	5
385028	0.0690	0.0752	0.0697	0.0693	0.0680	0.0699
	2	6	4	3	1	5
Average rank	1.5	5.9	3.6	3.0	2.6	4.4
Overall rank	1	6	4	3	2	5

Table 2 compares the results in terms of objective function values. As we can see, HMS is ranked first for 5 of the 10 images, and second for the other ones, leading to a clear best overall rank, followed by DE and PSO.

We also perform a statistical analysis, using the Wilcoxon signed rank test to compare our HMS-based algorithm with the other techniques. The null hypothesis H_0 here indicates no statistical difference between two algorithms, while the alternative hypothesis H_1 points to a statistically significant difference. The obtained p-values are 0.0020 for ABC, 0.0039 for HS, 0.0273 for PSO, 0.0488 for DE, and 0.0020 for GA and are thus all below 0.05 demonstrating statistical superiority of HMS.

We further assess our proposed algorithm using several image segmentation criteria, in particular:

– Borsotti criterion (BOR) [1]: an unsupervised criterion based on the number, the variance, and the area of segmented image regions. A lower BOR indicates a better segmentation performance.

Table 3. BOR results.

Image	HMS	ABC	HS	PSO	DE	GA
Lenna	0.0187	0.0279	0.0201	0.0285	0.0193	0.0245
	1	5	3	6	2	4
Airplane	0.0412	0.2650	0.3185	0.0609	0.2945	0.0778
	1	4	6	2	5	3
House	0.0220	0.0238	0.0236	0.0231	0.0230	0.0242
	1	5	4	3	2	6
Peppers	0.0761	0.1072	0.1067	0.0924	0.1097	0.0894
	1	5	4	3	6	2
MRI	0.0538	0.1028	0.1063	0.1022	0.1002	0.0870
	1	5	6	4	3	2
42049	0.1289	0.2387	0.3460	0.2175	0.2587	0.1669
	1	4	6	3	5	2
12003	0.0375	0.1308	0.4101	0.0420	0.2839	0.0602
	1	4	6	2	5	3
181079	0.1798	0.2870	0.3008	0.2840	0.3194	0.2678
	1	4	5	3	6	2
198054	0.2449	0.4620	0.6141	0.1916	0.6244	0.3020
	2	4	5	1	6	3
385028	0.1107	0.2108	0.2187	0.2060	0.2353	0.2136
	1	3	5	2	6	4
Average rank	1.1	4.3	5.0	2.9	4.6	3.1
Overall rank	1	4	6	2	5	3

- Levine and Nazif interclass contrast (LNIC) [8]: an unsupervised criterion based on the sum of region contrasts weighted by their areas. A higher LNIC indicates a better segmentation performance.
- Levine and Nazif intra-class uniformity (LNIU) [8]: an unsupervised criterion based on the sum of normalised standard deviations of image areas. A higher LNIU indicates a better segmentation performance.
- Variation of information (VoI) [10]: a supervised criterion that calculates the information shared between a ground truth and a segmented image. A lower VoI indicates better segmentation performance.
- Probabilistic Rand index (PRI) [14]: a supervised criterion that computes the fraction of pairs of pixels whose labels are consistent between computed and ground truth segmentations. A higher PRI indicates better segmentation performance.

Since the latter two require a ground truth, we can only evaluate these measures on the images of the Berkeley dataset.

Table 4. LNIC results.

Image	HMS	ABC	HS	PSO	DE	GA
Lenna	0.2342	0.2321	0.2330	0.2364	0.2322	0.2307
	2	5	3	1	4	6
Airplane	0.1177	0.1070	0.1057	0.1084	0.1178	0.1160
	2	5	6	4	1	3
House	0.1760	0.1727	0.1737	0.1743	0.1732	0.1720
	1	5	3	2	4	6
Peppers	0.2326	0.2043	0.2232	0.2308	0.2302	0.2057
	1	6	4	2	3	5
MRI	0.7145	0.5265	0.7119	0.7007	0.7061	0.5849
	1	6	2	4	3	5
42049	0.3976	0.2719	0.3429	0.3870	0.3421	0.3100
	1	6	3	2	4	5
12003	0.2024	0.1957	0.1213	0.2018	0.1604	0.2192
	2	4	6	3	5	1
181079	0.3095	0.2541	0.3225	0.3079	0.3008	0.3021
	2	6	1	3	5	4
198054	0.6791	0.4541	0.6773	0.5106	0.6159	0.5612
	1	6	2	5	3	4
385028	0.2638	0.2165	0.2657	0.2772	0.2573	0.2507
	3	6	2	1	4	5
Average rank	1.6	5.5	3.2	2.7	3.6	4.4
Overall rank	1	6	3	2	4	5

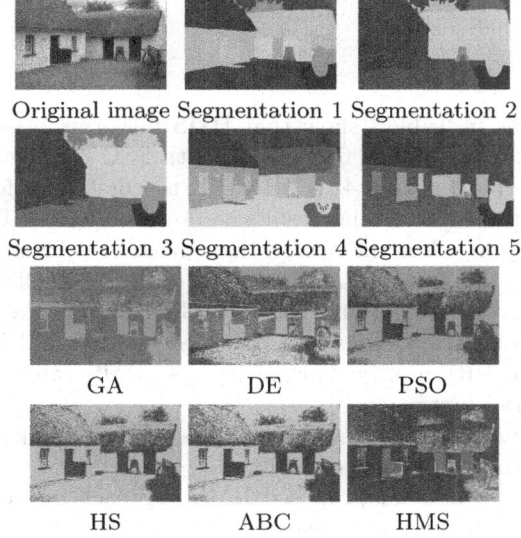

Original image Segmentation 1 Segmentation 2

Segmentation 3 Segmentation 4 Segmentation 5

GA   DE   PSO

HS   ABC   HMS

Fig. 2. Segmented images for image 385028.

Table 5. LNIU results.

Image	HMS	ABC	HS	PSO	DE	GA
Lenna	0.0304	0.0301	0.0307	0.0302	0.0305	0.0303
	3	6	1	5	2	4
Airplane	0.1251	0.0620	0.1044	0.0698	0.1160	0.1733
	2	6	4	5	3	1
House	0.0283	0.0278	0.0280	0.0281	0.0280	0.0288
	2	6	4	3	5	1
Peppers	0.0740	0.0626	0.0741	0.0689	0.0755	0.0658
	3	6	2	4	1	5
MRI	0.0648	0.0623	0.0646	0.0642	0.0643	0.0634
	1	6	2	4	3	5
42049	0.1216	0.1166	0.1063	0.1163	0.1068	0.1048
	1	2	5	3	4	6
12003	0.1055	0.1042	0.1006	0.1022	0.1006	0.0793
	1	2	4	3	5	6
181079	0.1350	0.1190	0.1313	0.1317	0.1302	0.1304
	1	6	3	2	5	4
198054	0.2123	0.1653	0.2004	0.1351	0.2422	0.1812
	2	5	3	6	1	4
385028	0.1196	0.1878	0.1076	0.1165	0.1112	0.1144
	2	1	6	3	5	4
Average rank	1.8	4.6	3.4	3.8	3.4	4
Overall rank	1	6	2.5	4	2.5	5

The BOR results in Table 3 show that HMS performs best for all but one image and is thus clearly ranked first overall with PSO coming second.

For LNIC, reported in Table 4, HMS yields the first rank for 5 images and second for a further 4, while similar results can be seen for LNIU in Table 5. For both criteria, our approach is the overall top-ranked algorithm.

Table 6 indicates the VoI results. Here, HMS obtained the first rank for 2 and second rank for the remaining 3 images, while GA, HS, and PSO rank first each for one image. Overall, HMS ranks first, followed by PSO and DE.

Table 7 lists the PRI results. For all images, HMS ranks first or second, resulting in an overall first rank.

Last not least, we show an example of the obtained results in Fig. 2 which also demonstrates the superiority of HMS.

Overall, it is clear that our proposed HMS approach outperforms all other algorithms based on all employed measures.

Table 6. VoI results.

Image	HMS	ABC	HS	PSO	DE	GA
42049	3.2839	3.3877	3.5316	3.2966	3.3127	3.2037
	2	5	6	3	4	1
12003	3.1758	3.6519	2.7900	3.2028	3.2215	3.4100
	2	6	1	3	4	5
181079	3.0395	3.4102	3.1569	3.1781	3.0423	3.0594
	1	6	4	5	2	3
198054	2.2528	2.5951	2.2880	2.2952	2.2729	2.3517
	1	6	3	4	2	5
385028	3.8173	3.9470	3.8233	3.7099	3.8688	3.8769
	2	6	3	1	4	5
Average rank	1.6	5.8	3.4	3.2	3.2	3.8
Overall rank	1	6	4	2.5	2.5	5

Table 7. PRI results.

Image	HMS	ABC	HS	PSO	DE	GA
42049	0.6110	0.6092	0.4331	0.6088	0.4836	0.6002
	1	2	6	3	5	4
12003	0.4658	0.4032	0.3894	0.4017	0.4461	0.5692
	2	4	6	5	3	1
181079	0.4885	0.4653	0.4800	0.4767	0.470	0.4889
	2	6	3	4	5	1
198054	0.4824	0.6426	0.3498	0.4730	0.3434	0.4015
	2	1	5	3	6	4
385028	0.5386	0.5059	0.5267	0.5333	0.4907	0.5240
	1	5	3	2	6	4
Average rank	1.6	3.6	4.6	3.4	5	2.8
Overall rank	1	4	5	3	6	2

5   Conclusions

This paper proposes a novel clustering-based image segmentation based on human mental search (HMS). Our proposed algorithm encodes cluster centres as the candidate solutions, uses the mean squared error as objective function and employs HMS for optimisation of the latter. The proposed algorithm is compared with five other metaheuristic algorithms and the obtained experimental results verify the efficacy of the proposed algorithm for image segmentation and show it to outperform the other approaches. In future, we plan to extend our approach to find the number of optimal clusters automatically, while integrating a local search mechanism is also being investigated. We also currently explore our algorithm in the context of video analysis [6].

Acknowledgements. This paper is published due to the financial support of the Federal Target Programme of the Ministry of Science and Higher Education of the Russian Federation, project unique identifier RFMEFI60819X0281.

References

1. Borsotti, M., Campadelli, P., Schettini, R.: Quantitative evaluation of color image segmentation results. Pattern Recogn. Lett. **19**(8), 741–747 (1998)
2. Das, S., Konar, A.: Automatic image pixel clustering with an improved differential evolution. Appl. Soft Comput. **9**(1), 226–236 (2009)
3. Geem, Z.W., Kim, J.H., Loganathan, G.V.: A new heuristic optimization algorithm: harmony search. Simulation **76**(2), 60–68 (2001)
4. Jamil, U., Sajid, A., Hussain, M., Aldabbas, O., Alam, A., Shafiq, M.U.: Melanoma segmentation using bio-medical image analysis for smarter mobile healthcare. J. Ambient Intell. Hum. Comput. **10**, 1–22 (2019)
5. Karaboga, D., Akay, B.: A comparative study of artificial bee colony algorithm. Appl. Math. Comput. **214**(1), 108–132 (2009)
6. Korovin, I.S., Khisamutdinov, M.V.: Obtaining a noise-free image based on an analysis of an unstabilized video sequence under conditions of a probable optical flow failure. In: 12th International Conference on Machine Vision (2019)
7. Kwedlo, W.: A clustering method combining differential evolution with the k-means algorithm. Pattern Recogn. Lett. **32**(12), 1613–1621 (2011)
8. Levine, M.D., Nazif, A.M.: Dynamic measurement of computer generated image segmentations. IEEE Trans. Pattern Anal. Mach. Intell. **7**(2), 155–164 (1985)
9. Martin, D., Fowlkes, C., Tal, D., Malik, J.: A database of human segmented natural images and its application to evaluating segmentation algorithms and measuring ecological statistics. In: 8th International Conference on Computer Vision, vol. 2, pp. 416–423 (2001)
10. Meilă, M.: Comparing clusterings: an axiomatic view. In: 22nd International Conference on Machine Learning, pp. 577–584 (2005)
11. Mousavirad, S.J., Ebrahimpour-Komleh, H.: Human mental search: a new population-based metaheuristic optimization algorithm. Appl. Intell. **47**(3), 850–887 (2017). https://doi.org/10.1007/s10489-017-0903-6
12. Omran, M.G., Engelbrecht, A.P., Salman, A.: Image classification using particle swarm optimization. In: Recent Advances in Simulated Evolution and Learning, pp. 347–365. World Scientific (2004)
13. Ozturk, C., Hancer, E., Karaboga, D.: Improved clustering criterion for image clustering with artificial bee colony algorithm. Pattern Anal. Appl. **18**(3), 587–599 (2014). https://doi.org/10.1007/s10044-014-0365-y
14. Pantofaru, C., Hebert, M.: A comparison of image segmentation algorithms. Technical report, Robotics Institute (2005)
15. Rose, R.A., Annadhason, A.: GHT based automatic kidney image segmentation using modified AAM and GBDT. Health Technol. **10**, 1–10 (2019)
16. Sanei, S.H.R., Fertig III, R.S.: Uncorrelated volume element for stochastic modeling of microstructures based on local fiber volume fraction variation. Compos. Sci. Technol. **117**, 191–198 (2015)

17. Shi, Y., Eberhart, R.: A modified particle swarm optimizer. In: IEEE International Conference on Evolutionary Computation, pp. 69–73 (1998)
18. Storn, R., Price, K.: Differential evolution–a simple and efficient heuristic for global optimization over continuous spaces. J. Global Optim. **11**(4), 341–359 (1997)
19. Suganthan, P.N., et al.: Problem definitions and evaluation criteria for the CEC 2005 special session on real-parameter optimization. Technical report, Nanyang Technological University Singapore (2005)
20. Wang, L., Yufeng, Y., Liu, J.: Clustering with a novel global harmony search algorithm for image segmentation. Int. J. Hybrid Inf. Technol. **9**(2), 183–194 (2016)

Colour Quantisation by Human Mental Search

Seyed Jalaleddin Mousavirad[1], Gerald Schaefer[2], Hui Fang[2], Xiyao Liu[3], and Iakov Korovin[4]

[1] Faculty of Engineering, Sabzevar University of New Technology, Sabzevar, Iran
[2] Department of Computer Science, Loughborough University, Loughborough, UK
[3] Computer Science and Engineering, Central South University, Changsha, China
[4] Southern Federal University, Taganrog, Russia

Abstract. Colour quantisation is a common image processing technique to reduce the number of distinct colours in an image which are then represented by a colour palette. The selection of appropriate entries in this palette is a challenging issue while the quality of the quantised image is directly related to the colour palette. In this paper, we propose a novel colour quantisation algorithm based on the human mental search (HMS) algorithm. HMS is a recent population-based metaheuristic algorithm with three main operators: mental search to explore the vicinity of candidate solutions based on Levy flight, grouping to determine a promising region based on a clustering algorithm, and movement towards the best strategy. The performance of our proposed algorithm is evaluated on a set of benchmark images and in comparison to four conventional algorithms and seven soft computing-based colour quantisation algorithms. The obtained experimental results convincingly show that our proposed algorithm is capable of outperforming these approaches.

Keywords: Colour quantisation · Colour palette · Image quality · Human mental search · Metaheuristic

1 Introduction

Colour images usually use 24 bits per pixel, which results in 2^{24} distinct colours. However, humans can recognise only up to a thousand different colours. Therefore, reducing the number of colours may not affect perception while leading to reduced complexity and resources. Colour quantisation is a process to reduce the number of distinct colours in an image and represent image colours by a colour palette comprising a small number of colours (often between 8 and 256) [1]. Colour quantisation is essential in some applications such as video conferencing and transmission through limited bandwidth channels [13,14], while also providing a compression method that simplifies the feature space [5].

© Springer Nature Switzerland AG 2020
Y. Tan et al. (Eds.): ICSI 2020, LNCS 12145, pp. 130–141, 2020.
https://doi.org/10.1007/978-3-030-53956-6_12

The primary goal of colour quantisation algorithms is to yield a good palette. If the values of the palette are not properly selected, the resulting image will show more discrepancies compared to the original image and thus lower image quality. Therefore, choosing appropriate entries in the palette is important, it is however also known as an NP-hard problem, making colour quantisation a challenging task.

In the literature, various colour quantisation algorithms have been proposed. A relatively simple method is the popularity algorithm [4] which chooses the colours that are represented most often in the image. In median cut quantisation [4], the colour space is divided into sub-spaces in an iterative process, while in [3], the colour space is represented as an octree whose sub-branches combine to form the pallete. Self-organising Kohonen neural networks have also been proposed [2], as have a number of soft computing methods [8] such as simulated annealing [10], fuzzy c-means [11], rough c-means [12], and fuzzy-rough c-means [9].

Human mental search (HMS) [7] is a recent population-based metaheuristic algorithm inspired by the exploration strategies in the bid space of online auctions. HMS has three main operators: (1) mental search, which explores the vicinity of each solution based on Levy flight, (2) grouping, which partitions the search space using a clustering algorithm, and (3) moving bids towards promising regions.

In this paper, we propose a novel method for colour quantisation based on the HMS algorithm. We formulate the colour quantisation problem as an optimisation problem and employ HMS to identify an optimal colour palette. Experimental results obtained on a benchmark image set show that our proposed approach is capable of outperforming both conventional and other soft computing-based colour quantisation methods.

The remainder of this paper is organised as follows. Section 2 introduces the HMS algorithm, while our proposed algorithm is presented in Sect. 3. Section 4 gives experimental results and discusses the performance of the proposed algorithm against other approaches. Finally, Sect. 5 concludes the paper.

2   Human Mental Search

Human mental search (HMS) is a recent population-based metaheuristic algorithm inspired by exploring strategies in the bid space of online auctions. Each candidate solution in HMS is called a bid, and the algorithm is based on three main operators, mental search, grouping, and movement towards a promising region. In the following, these operators are described in more detail, while Algorithm 1 lists the pseudo-code of the HMS algorithm.

2.1   Mental Search

Mental search explores the vicinity of a candidate solution using Levy flight. Levy flight is a type of random walk that generates random movements based

Algorithm 1. HMS algorithm

1: **procedure** HMS ALGORITHM
2:    // Variables: L: lower bound; U: upper bound,
3:    // M_l: minimum, M_h: maximum number of mental processes.
4:    // N_{pop}: number of bids, N_{var}: number of variables, K: number of clusters,
5:    // $iter$: current iteration, $MaxIter$: maximum number of iterations
6:
7:    X = initialise population of N_{pop} bids
8:    Calculate the objective function values of bids
9:    x^* = find the best bid in the initial population
10:   **for** i from 1 to N_{pop} **do**
11:       β_i = generate random number between L and U
12:   **end for**
13:   **for** $iter$ from 1 to $MaxIter$ **do**
14:       // Mental Search
15:       **for** i from 1 to N_{pop} **do**
16:          q_i = generate random integer number between M_l and M_h
17:       **end for**
18:       **for** i from 1 to N_{pop} **do**
19:          **for** j from 1 to q_i **do**
20:             $s = (2 - iter(2/MaxIter))0.01\frac{u}{v^{1/\beta_i}}(x^i - x^*)$
21:             $NS_j = X^i + s$
22:          **end for**
23:          t = find NS with the lowest objective function value
24:          **if** $cost(t) < cost(x^i)$ **then**
25:             $x^i = t$
26:          **end if**
27:       **end for**
28:       // Clustering
29:       Cluster N_{pop} bids into K clusters
30:       Calculate the mean objective function value of each cluster
31:       Select cluster with lowest mean objective function value as the winner cluster
32:       $winner$ = select the best bid in the winner cluster
33:       // Move bids towards best strategy
34:       **for** i from 1 to N_{pop} **do**
35:          **for** n from 1 to N_{var} **do**
36:             $x_n^i = x_n^i + C(r \times winner_n - x_n^i)$
37:          **end for**
38:       **end for**
39:       **for** i from 1 to N_{pop} **do**
40:          β_i = generate random number between L and U
41:       **end for**
42:       x^+ = find best bid in current bids
43:       **if** $cost(x^+) < cost(x^*)$ **then**
44:          $x^* = x^+$
45:       **end if**
46:    **end for**
47: **end procedure**

---

on a Levy distribution. In Levy flight, there are some small movements and then a long jump which increases both exploration (due to the long jumps) and exploitation (due to the small movements) simultaneously. Mental search generates some new solutions according to

$$NS = bid + S, \tag{1}$$

with

$$S = (2 - iter(2/MaxIter))0.01\frac{u}{v^{1/\beta}}(x^i - x^*), \tag{2}$$

where x^* is the best position found so far, u and v are two random numbers with normal distributions, $MaxIter$ is the maximum number of iterations, $iter$ shows the current iteration, and β is a random number, while $\oplus$ denotes element-wise multiplication. $(2 - iter(2/MaxIter))$ is a descending factor, starting at a point near 2 and ending towards 0, and thus considers a larger vicinity of a solution at the beginning (exploration) and smaller vicinities at the end of the algorithm (exploitation).

2.2 Grouping

In this step, the solutions are grouped using a clustering algorithm. For this, we use the k-means algorithm to cluster the population. Then, the mean cost of each cluster is calculated and the cluster with the lowest mean cost value selected as a promising region.

2.3 Movement Towards Promising Region

In this step, candidate solutions move towards the best solution in the promising region, governed by

$$x_n^{t+1} = x_n^t + C(r \times winner_n^t - x_n^t), \tag{3}$$

where x_n^{t+1} is the n-th bid element at iteration $t+1$, $winner_n^t$ is the n-th element of the best bid in the winner group, t is the current iteration, C is a constant, and r is in is a random number drawn from a uniform distribution between 0 and 1.

3 Human Mental Search for Colour Quantisation

In this paper, we apply an improved HMS algorithm to the colour quantisation problem. For this, two issues need to be determined: (1) representation and (2) objective function.

In our approach, the representation is an array which encodes the colours of the colour palette. The length of the array is to $N_{var} = 3k$ where k is the number of colours in the palette and we store the RGB values of each colour. The objective function is chosen to minimise the mean squared error (MSE) between the original and quanitsed image

$$f(I_o, I_q) = \frac{1}{3nm} \left(\sum_{i=1}^{n} \sum_{j=1}^{m} [(R_o(i,j) - R_q(i,j))^2] \right.$$

$$+ \sum_{i=1}^{n} \sum_{j=1}^{m} [(G_o(i,j) - G_q(i,j))^2]$$

$$\left. + \sum_{i=1}^{n} \sum_{j=1}^{m} [(B_o(i,j) - B_q(i,j))^2] \right), \tag{4}$$

where m and n are the dimensions of the image, and $R(i,j)$, $G(i,j)$, and $B(i,j)$ are the red, green, and blue pixel values at location (i,j) while the subscripts o and q denote the original and quantised image.

In our approach, we improve the human mental search based on the personal experience of each candidate solution. To this end, the update equation, Eq. (3), is changed to

$$x_n^{t+1} = bid_n^t + C_1 r(winner_n^t - x_n^t) + C_2 r(pbest_n^t - x_n^t), \tag{5}$$

where $pbest$ is the position of the best solution found so far by the n-th candidate, and C_1 and C_2 are constants.

4   Experimental Results

To verify the performance of the proposed method, we have used six commonly employed benchmark images shown in Fig. 1, namely Lenna, Peppers, Mandrill, Sailboat, Airplane, and Pool. In all experiments, the number of colours in the palette is set to 16 [8] and we set $M_l = 2$, $M_h = 10$, K (the number of clusters during grouping) to 5, $L = 0.3$, $U = 1.99$, and $c_1 = c_2 = 1.5$. HMS is run with a population size of 50 for 500 iterations.

We compare our proposed algorithm to four conventional quantisation algorithms namely popularity algorithm [4], median cut [4], octree quantisation [3], and Neuquant [2], and seven soft computing-based approaches including SWASA [10], fuzzy c-means (FCM) [11], random sampling FCM (RSFCM) [11], Enhanced FCM (EnFCM) [11], anisotropic mean shift based FCM (AMS-FCM) [11], rough c-means (RCM) [12], and fuzzy-rough c-means (FRCM) [9].

As evaluation measure we use the peak signal-to-noise-ratio (PSNR), which is the most commonly employed metric to evaluate colour quantisation algorithms and is defined as

$$PSNR(I_o, I_q) = 10 \log_{10} \frac{255^2}{MSE(I_o, I_q)}, \tag{6}$$

where MSE is the mean squared error calculated as in Eq. (4).

Fig. 1. Test images: Lenna, Peppers, Mandrill, Sailboat, Pool, and Airplane.

Table 1 compares the results obtained for our proposed algorithm against the other evaluated techniques. It can be observed that the octree and Neuquant algorithms outperform the popularity and median cut approaches. Furthermore, it is clear that the soft computing-based colour quantisation algorithms outperform octree and Neuquant confirming that methods based on soft computing techniques are effective tools for colour quantisation [8].

Table 1. Comparison of proposed algorithm with other colour quantisation algorithms. Results are given in terms of PSNR [dB].

	Lenna	Pepper	Mandrill	Sailboat	Pool	Airplane
Popularity [4]	22.4 0	18.56	18.00	8.73	19.87	15.91
Median cut [4]	23.79	24.10	21.52	22.01	24.57	24.32
Octree [3]	27.45	25.80	24.21	26.04	29.39	28.77
Neuquant [2]	27.82	26.04	24.59	26.81	27.08	28.24
SWASA [10]	27.79	26.16	24.46	26.69	29.84	29.43
FCM [11]	28.81	26.77	25.03	27.25	31.03	30.23
RSFCM [11]	28.70	26.70	24.98	27.32	30.81	30.73
EnFCM [11]	28.61	26.74	24.87	27.22	31.11	29.92
AMSFCM [11]	28.63	26.71	24.66	27.24	30.87	29.96
RCM [12]	28.63	26.67	25.02	27.62	29.40	30.50
FRCM [9]	28.44	26.80	25.03	27.47	**31.20**	31.24
HMS	**29.68**	**27.13**	**25.36**	**27.89**	31.04	**31.70**

Table 2. Algorithm ranking

	Lenna	Pepper	Mandrill	Sailboat	Pool	Airplane	Avg. rank	Overall rank
Popularity [4]	12	12	12	12	12	12	12.00	12
Median cut [4]	11	11	11	11	11	11	11.00	11
Octree [3]	10	10	10	10	9	9	9.67	10
Neuquant [2]	8	9	8	8	10	10	8.83	9
SWASA [10]	9	8	9	9	7	8	8.33	8
FCM [11]	2	3	2.5	5	4	5	3.58	3
RSFCM [11]	3	6	5	4	6	3	4.50	4
EnFCM [11]	6	4	6	7	2	7	5.33	6
AMSFCM [11]	4.5	5	7	6	5	6	5.58	7
RCM [12]	4.5	7	4	2	8	4	4.92	5
FRCM [9]	7	2	2.5	3	1	2	2.92	2
HMS	1	1	1	1	3	1	1.33	1

Also apparent from Table 1 is that our proposed HMS colour quantisation algorithm yields excellent results and is convincingly shown to outperform all other algorithms giving the best image quality for all images except Pool, for which FRCM and EnFCM perform slightly better.

We also perform a ranking analysis where, as shown in Table 2, we rank all algorithms on each image based on the PSNR results. We then average the ranks for each algorithm to identify an overall ranking. From Table 2, it is clear not only that our proposed algorithm ranks first but also that it yields a significantly lower average rank of 1.33 compared to all other algorithms with FRCM second with an average rank of 2.92. FCM ranks third while, as expected, the conventional quantisation algorithms are the lowest ranked techniques.

In Figs. 2, 3 and 4, we show, as examples, the quantisation results from several algorithms on three of the images, namely Sailboat, Pool and Airplane. For each quantised image, we also show an error image [15] obtained by calculating the difference between the original image and its quantised counterpart[1]. The shown examples further illustrate the excellent colour quantisation results we obtain using our proposed technique and that it yields improved image quality to the other techniques.

---

[1] In particular, we calculate the squared error between pixel values, while for better visualisation we invert the resulting image and apply an image gamma of 5.

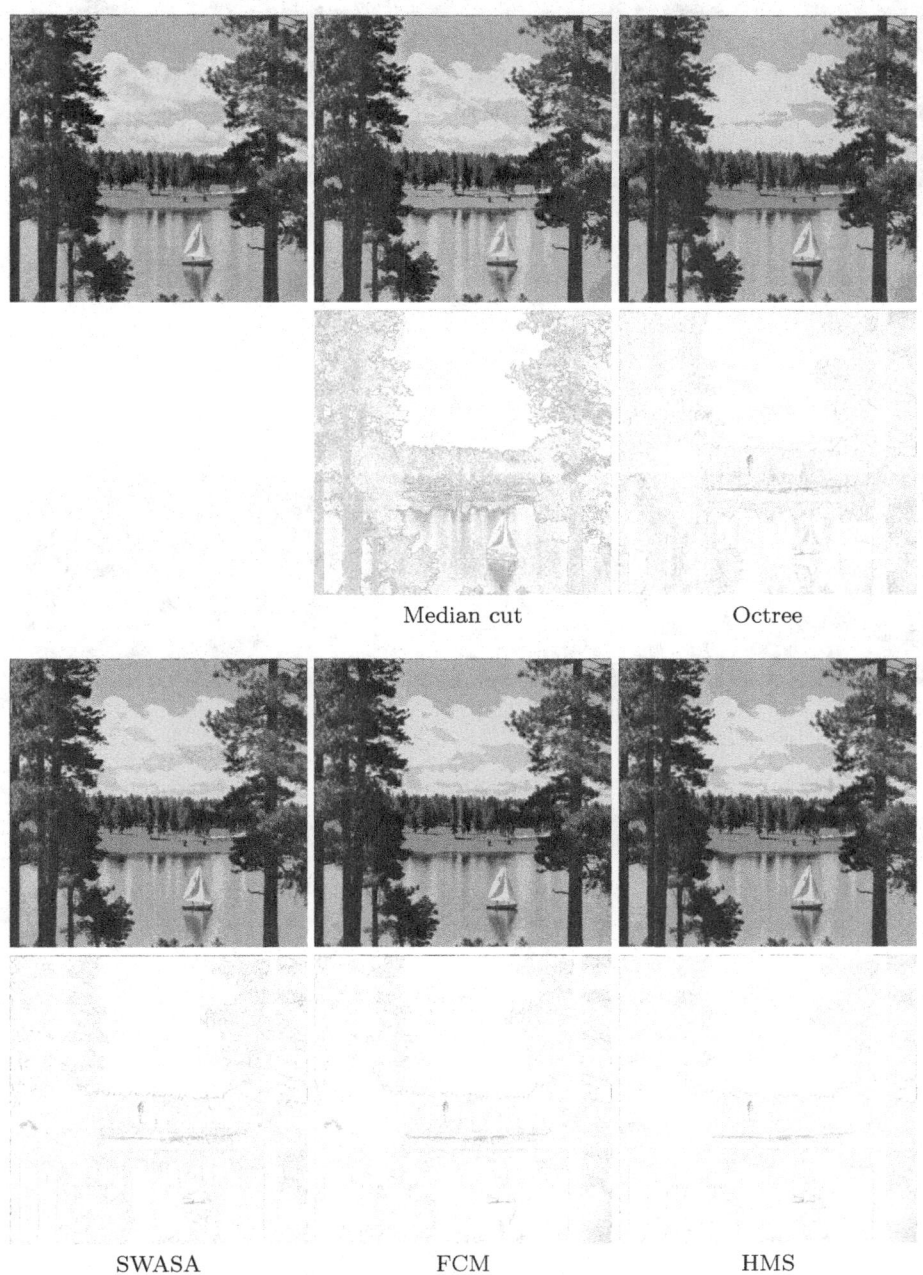

Median cut   Octree

SWASA   FCM   HMS

Fig. 2. Quantisation results for Sailboat image.

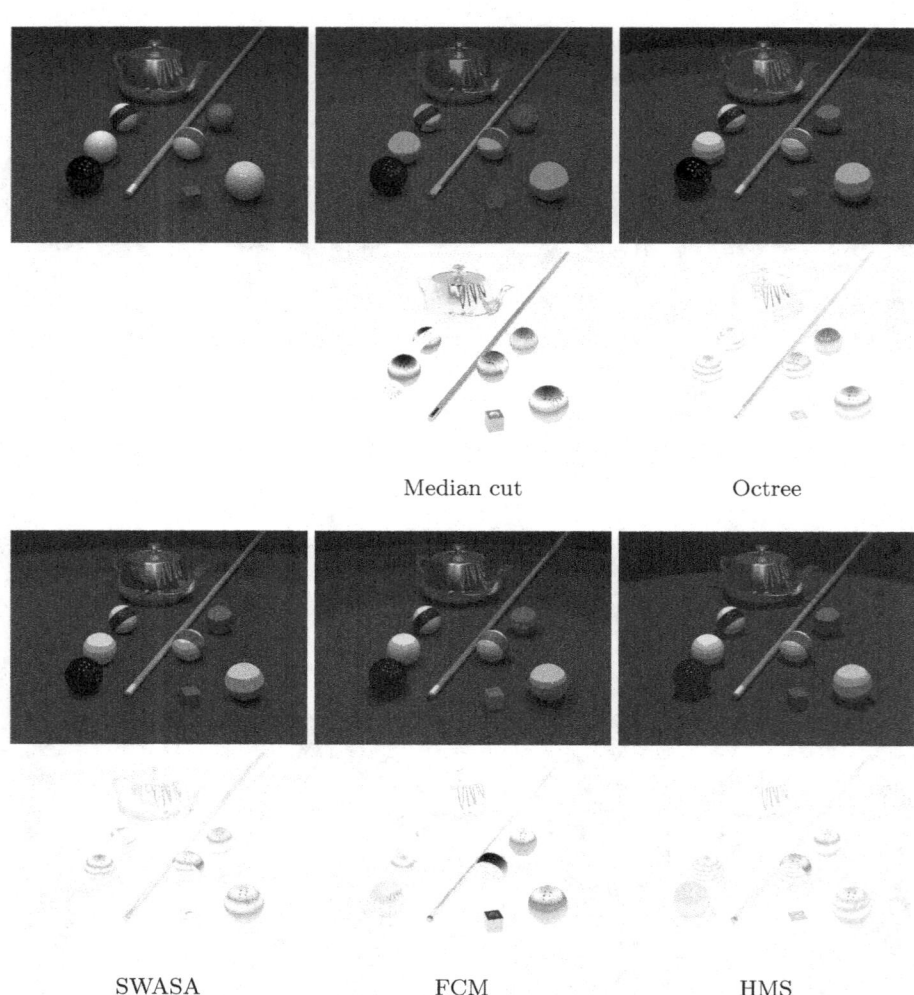

Median cut   Octree

SWASA   FCM   HMS

Fig. 3. Quantisation results for Pool image.

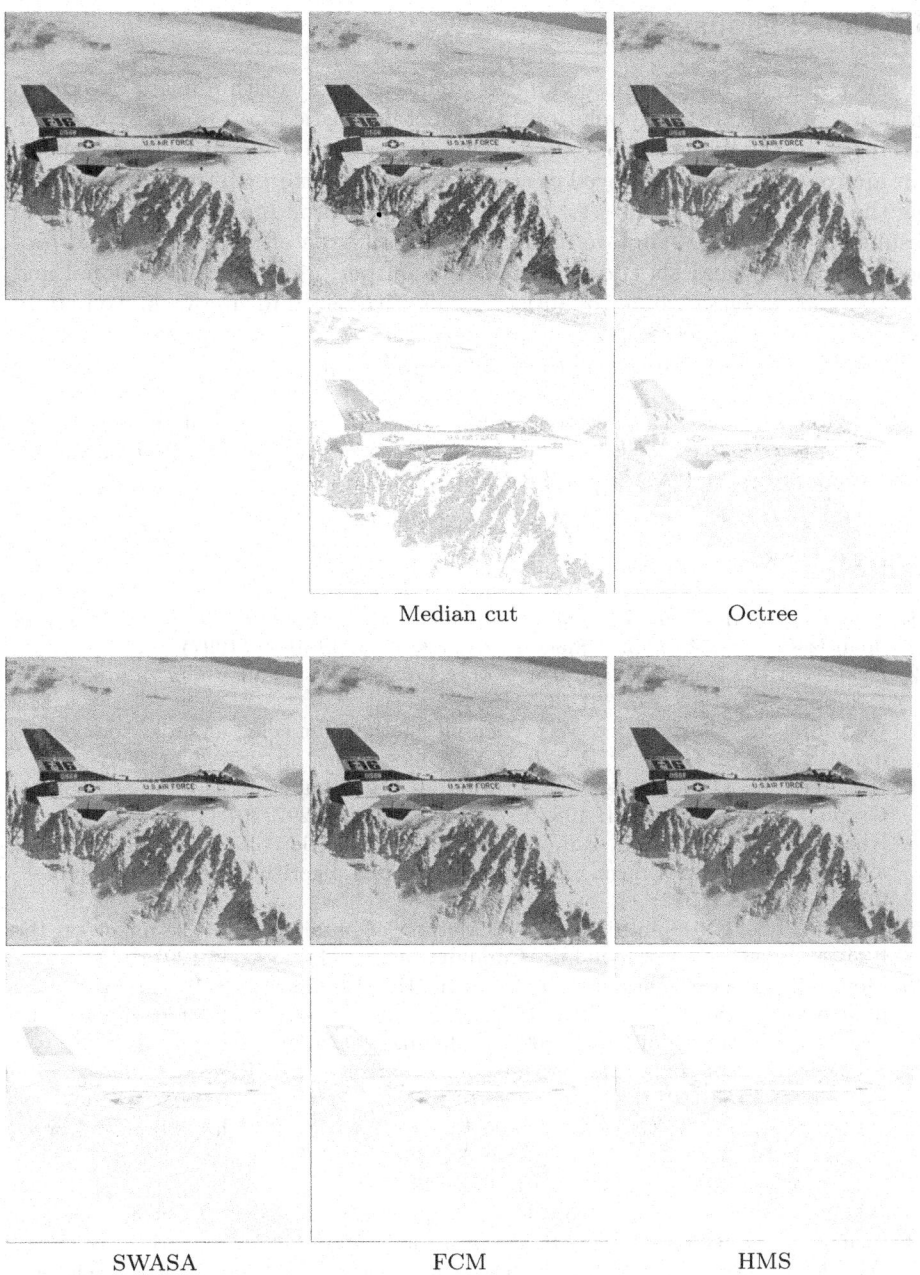

Median cut   Octree

SWASA   FCM   HMS

Fig. 4. Quantisation results for Airplane image.

5 Conclusions

In this paper, we have proposed a novel quantisation algorithm based on human mental search (HMS), a population-based metaheuristic that mimics exploration strategies in the bid space of online auctions to solve optimisation problems. In our approach, HMS is employed to create a colour palette with the aim of obtaining the highest image quality for the colour quantisation problem. Experimental results on commonly employed test images verify the effectiveness of the proposed algorithm and show our approach to outperform both conventional and soft computing-based colour quantisation algorithms. In future work, we plan to integrate the proposed algorithm with k-means for further improvement, while we also investigate its use in video analysis tasks [6].

Acknowledgements. This paper is published due to the financial support of the Federal Target Programme of the Ministry of Science and Higher Education of Russian Federation, project unique identifier RFMEFI60819X0281.

References

1. Braquelaire, J.P., Brun, L.: Comparison and optimization of methods of color image quantization. IEEE Trans. Image Process. **6**(7), 1048–1052 (1997)
2. Dekker, A.H.: Kohonen neural networks for optimal colour quantization. Netw. Comput. Neural Syst. **5**, 351–367 (1994)
3. Gervautz, M., Purgathofer, W.: A simple method for color quantization: octree quantization. In: Glassner, A.S. (ed.) Graphics Gems, pp. 287–293 (1990)
4. Heckbert, P.S.: Color image quantization for frame buffer display. ACM Comput. Graph. (ACM SIGGRAPH 1982 Proceedings) **16**(3), 297–307 (1982)
5. Khaled, A., Abdel-Kader, R.F., Yasein, M.S.: A hybrid color image quantization algorithm based on k-means and harmony search algorithms. Appl. Artif. Intell. **30**(4), 331–351 (2016)
6. Korovin, I.S., Khisamutdinov, M.V.: Method of obtaining unnoise image on the basis of video sequence handling. Comput. Opt. **38**(1), 112–117 (2014)
7. Mousavirad, S.J., Ebrahimpour-Komleh, H.: Human mental search: a new population-based metaheuristic optimization algorithm. Appl. Intell. **47**(3), 850–887 (2017). https://doi.org/10.1007/s10489-017-0903-6
8. Schaefer, G.: Soft computing based colour quantisation. EURASIP J. Image Video Process. **2014**, 8 (2014)
9. Schaefer, G., Hu, G., Zhou, H., Peters, J., Hassanien, A.: Rough c-means and fuzzy rough c-means for colour quantisation. Fundamenta Informaticae **119**(1), 113–120 (2012). https://doi.org/10.3233/FI-2012-729
10. Schaefer, G., Nolle, L.: A hybrid colour quantisation algorithm incorporating a human visual perception model. Comput. Intell. **31**(4), 684–698 (2015)
11. Schaefer, G., Zhou, H.: Fuzzy clustering for colour reduction in images. Telecommun. Syst. **40**(1–2), 17–25 (2009). https://doi.org/10.1007/s11235-008-9143-8
12. Schaefer, G., Zhou, H., Celebi, M., Hassanien, A.: Rough colour quantisation. Int. J. Hybrid Inf. Syst. **8**(1), 25–30 (2011). https://doi.org/10.3233/HIS-2011-0128
13. Scheunders, P.: A comparison of clustering algorithms applied to color image quantization. Pattern Recogn. Lett. **18**(11–13), 1379–1384 (1997)

14. Scheunders, P.: A genetic c-means clustering algorithm applied to color image quantization. Pattern Recogn. **30**(6), 859–866 (1997)
15. Zhang, X.M., Wandell, B.A.: Color image fidelity metrics evaluated using image distortion maps. Sig. Process. **70**(3), 201–214 (1998)

Canine Algorithm for Node Disjoint Paths

R. Ananthalakshmi Ammal[1]([✉]), P. C. Sajimon[1], and Vinod Chandra S S[2]

[1] Cyber Security Group, Centre for Development of Advanced Computing,
Thiruvananthapuram, India
{lakshmi,pcsaji}@cdac.in
[2] Computer Centre, University of Kerala, Thiruvananthapuram, India
vinod@keralauniversity.ac.in

Abstract. Node Disjoint Paths (NDP) is one of the extensively studied Graph Theory problem. In this problem, the input is a directed n vertex graph and the set of source destination pair of vertices. The goal is to find the maximum number of paths connecting each such pair, so that such discovered paths are node-disjoint. In this paper, a novel Canine Inspired Algorithm is proposed which is a bio-inspired one, based on the olfactory capabilities of canines in tracing and reaching a destination. Currently many of the existing algorithms try to identify disjoint paths in a linear manner, whereas the Canine algorithm can be executed in a concurrent manner, depending on the number of canines deployed to find the disjoint paths. The time complexity of the algorithm is estimated to be $O(n \log n)$. We hope that this algorithm finds many applications in problems related to various fields such as communication networks, scheduling and transportation and provides better results.

Keywords: Node Disjoint Paths · Canine Algorithm · Bio-inspired

1 Introduction

Disjoint path is an extensively studied fundamental routing problem of Graph Theory.Disjoint paths can be Edge Disjoint Paths (EDP) or Node Disjoint Paths (NDP) for directed or undirected graphs. EDP share no common edges or links and NDP share no common nodes or vertices. Finding NDP is more limited than EDP and if two paths are node disjoint, they are edge disjoint as well. Disjoint path finds many applications in various fields such as communication networks, design of Very Large Scale Integrated (VLSI) circuits, transportation problems and scheduling problems. Many algorithms have been published and the problem is seen as an extension of the shortest path problem.

The disjoint path problem has been shown to be NP-Complete by Karp [1], Lynch [2] and others for many variants of planar graphs and grids. We studied the problem of NDP in graphs and we propose a simple bio-inspired algorithm based on the behavior of canines to solve the problem. As part of the solution multiple paths between a source and destination are computed that do not share nodes or links.

© Springer Nature Switzerland AG 2020
Y. Tan et al. (Eds.): ICSI 2020, LNCS 12145, pp. 142–148, 2020.
https://doi.org/10.1007/978-3-030-53956-6_13

2 Preliminaries

Let G = (V, E) be a simple directed graph where V is the set of nodes and E is the set of edges. Assume that the graph G has *n* nodes and *m* edges. The source-destination vertices are denoted as $\{v_i, v_j\}$ and V(P) denotes the set of nodes and E(P) denotes the set of edges on the path P respectively.

For the same source destination pair $\{v_1, v_j\}$, let $P_1, P_2, P_3, \ldots., P_k$ be the set of k node disjoint paths such that $E(P_i) \cap E(P_j) = \emptyset$ and $V(P_i) \cap V(P_j) = \{v_1, v_j\}$ for different $i, j \in \{1, 2, 3 \ldots k\}$. An example of NDP topology is shown in Fig. 1.

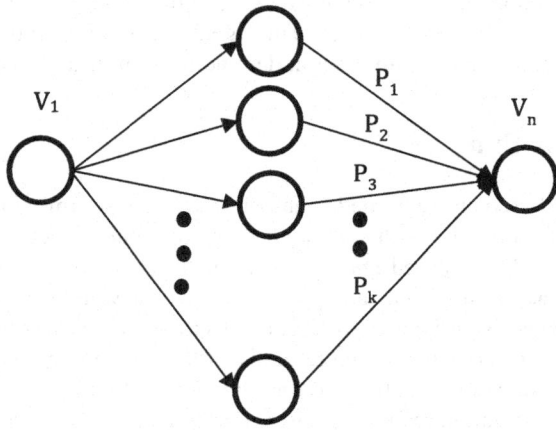

Fig. 1. k Node disjoint source destination paths

In a directed graph, each node can be considered to be split up into two nodes v_{in} and v_{out} and the undirected edges (s, t) can be replaced with directed edges (s_{out}, t_{in}) and (s_{in}, t_{out}). All then incoming edges of v will be connected to node v_{in} and all the outgoing edges will be connected to node v_{out}.

The degree of a node $d_G(v)$ in graph G is the number of edges incident on v, each loop counting as two edges. This can be considered as the sum of indegree and outdegree of the node in a directed graph.

The goal of this paper is to find for every node $v_1 \neq v_n$, a set P_1 of disjoint paths from source node v_1 to destination node v_n in the graph G in which the paths of the set P_1 are node disjoint.

3 Related Works

One of the extensively studied problem in Graph Theory is the Shortest Path problem, which is the problem of finding the path between two nodes in a graph so that the sum of the link cost is minimal. The most widely used shortest path algorithms include Dijkstra's algorithm [3] and Bellman – Ford algorithm [4, 5]. Bio inspired algorithms for optimal path computations are also in use for quite some time. The famous AntNet algorithm based on Ant Colony Optimisation [6] is used in many telecommunication Networks for routing purposes. Smell Detection Agent (SDA) [7] based algorithm is a novel bio-inspired optimisation algorithm. The authors of this paper have also published a SDA based algorithm [8] for the shortest path problem. The disjoint path problem can be seen as an extension of the shortest path problem.

One of the earlier published algorithms for finding disjoint paths in a network was from Suurballe [9] and subsequently from Bhandari [10]. Many variants of disjoint paths algorithms such as availability based disjoint [11], maximally disjoint [12] and region based disjoint paths [13] are published. Several other constraints including the weights of the constituent edges of the paths are also added such as min-sum and min-max.

The proposed Canine algorithm is an extension of the Smell Detection Agent based algorithm published by the same authors. This agent-based algorithm can be used for finding all NDP from one node to all other nodes and is a simple and easy to implement.

4   Canine Algorithm

Canine algorithm is based on the trained behavior of the canine family in detecting smell trails. The method for identifying disjoint paths from the source node to the destination node is based on the bio-inspired analogy of trained behaviour of dogs in detecting smell trails. The olfactory mechanism of dogs can detect as well as memorize different smell signatures. Dogs also urinate in different spots to mark their territory as occupied. These two properties of dogs have been used to mark the path they undertake to reach the destination. Multiple dogs can be used for the identification of disjoint paths from a source node to the destination node using the property that one dog's territory shall not be traversed by the other dog.

Each node in the graph is considered as a smell spot, which is visited by the canine. Each smell spot is characterized by the signature related to the canine which visited the spot and the other the smell trail which is a function of the outdegree of the node. Each canine is also characterized by its unique signature value to mark the smell spots and its olfactory capability. The olfactory capability of the canine can be earmarked as the smell radius for the canine to traverse and is assumed to be proportional to the domain of the given graph which is the set of nodes and edges. The whole algorithm is based on the given graph with the set of nodes and edges. The number of canines deployed for the algorithm is equal to the maximum outdegree of the source node in the given graph. The canines deployed from each node determine the disjoint paths by traversing the unvisited highest smell trail smell spots until the destination node. This is repeated for all the nodes with their roles changing as source and destination to find all the node disjoint paths among all nodes within a given graph. The symbolic representation is given in Fig. 2.

Canine Algorithm for finding all Node Disjoint Paths in a Graph for all the nodes

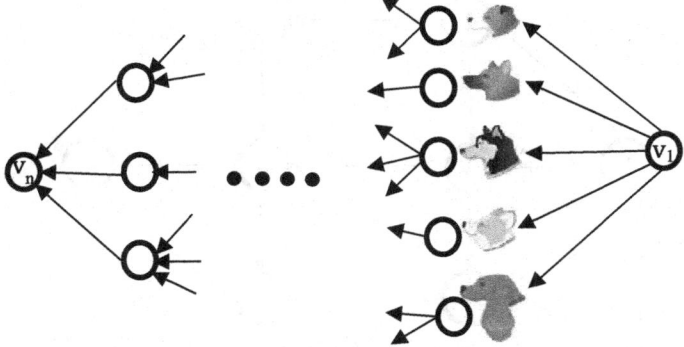

Fig. 2. Symbolic representation of Canine deployment from source node

---

Input: Graph - G(V,E); Number of nodes - n; Maximum outdegree of node - $\Delta_{Gout}(v)$; Degree of each node - $d_G(v)$

Output: P -Set of all Node Disjoint Paths from each node to every other node in the graph G(V,E)

1. Initialise:
   a. Number of smell spots = n
   b. Maximum number of canines = $\Delta_{Gout}(v)$
   c. For each $v_i \in V$ smell value = $d_G(v_i)$
2. For each $v_i \in V$, do
   a. Reset all smell spots as not visited
   b. For each $v_j \in V$, do
      i. Set the number of canines as $\delta_{Gout}(v_i)$
      ii. Set signature value of each canine
      iii. For each canine, do

      o Identify path by canine traversal through unvisited highest value smell spot until v_j
      o Populate the path set P_i for the canine which reached destination node v_j

---

5 Algorithm Analysis

The algorithm is inspired from the smell detection capability of the canine to reach the destination. The objective of the algorithm is to find all the NDP from each node to every other node in the graph. So, the major input to the algorithm is the graph with its set of nodes G(V) and the set of edges G(E) connecting the nodes. Consider the problem of finding the node disjoint paths from node 1 to 8, in graph of 8 nodes and 13 edges as shown in Fig. 3.

With node v_1 having an outdegree $\delta_{Gout}(v_1)$ of 3, three canine agents are to be deployed to traverse the graph and identify the disjoint paths to node v_8. Initially all

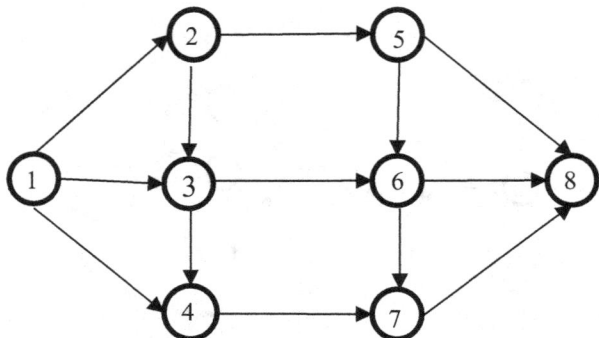

Fig. 3. Illustrative example of an 8 node directed graph

nodes are marked as unvisited. The canine agents traverse from the outbound edges of the node through the neighbouring smell spots which are unvisited and having the highest smell trail until they reach the destination. The smell spot is marked as visited by the unique signature of the canine. The smell trail of a smell spot is proportional to the degree of the node. This process results in discovery of all disjoint paths from the source to the destination. Thus, the identified paths include P1 = {1-3-6-8, 1-2-5-8, 1-4-7-8} as shown in Fig. 4. As another example, the set of disjoint paths from node v_2 to node v_8 can be identified as P2 = {2-3-6-8, 2-5-8}. In a directed graph, all the node disjoint paths can be iteratively identified from one node to all the other nodes. The neighboring nodes may be excluded from destination nodes.

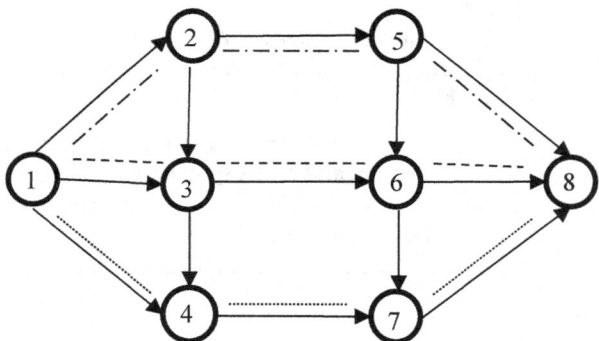

Fig. 4. The three identified disjoint paths from node 1 to node 8

It has been found that the number of disjoint paths identified conforms to the Menger's theorem [14] which states that the maximum number of vertex-disjoint (s, t) paths is equal to the minimum size of an (s, t) disconnecting vertex set. In other words, the maximum number of vertex-disjoint paths from node v_1 to node v_8 is equal to the minimal number of vertices to be removed which disconnects node v_1 from node v_8. In the example taken, the (s, t) cut disconnects the three nodes v_5, v_6 and v_7 resulting in node v_1 in one partition and the node v_8 in the other partition. Thus, as per the theorem, the number of disjoint paths identified is also equal to three.

In the illustrated example, the path from v_8 to other nodes seems to be non-existent, as there are no directed edges available. In the case of communication networks, duplex communication over the network links exists and, in such cases, the paths can be computed. Present day communication networks are configured in such a way that no loops or cycles exist as part of the network topology.

5.1 Comparison

Many of the algorithms for identifying NDPs use Depth First Search and Breadth First Search techniques to arrive at the results. Bhandari's algorithm [10] use the min-sum disjoint path algorithm and the split node technique for directed graphs. Broder et al. [15] has used the flow techniques by eliminating the vertices. They identified that in a random graph with n nodes, we can connect at most O(n log d/log n) pairs. The proposed Canine algorithm is simple, easy to implement and the time complexity is estimated as O($n \log n$) for a graph with n nodes.

6 Discussions

The NDP finds application in many real-life problems. One of the applications where this algorithm was tested was in a simulated communication network setup with 18 nodes corresponding to 18 core routers connected with multiple links among them. The knowledge of all existing NDP were essential to configure a resilient network.

Swarm Intelligence algorithms such as Ant Colony Optimization and Bee Colony optimization, are among the commonly used bio-inspired algorithms for the identification of shortest paths and disjoint paths. In such swarm intelligent algorithms, the stigmergic aspects of pheromone in the case of ants and waggle dance in the case of bees are made use of in the optimization problems. Prior to the start of the optimal path identification, many of the Swarm Intelligent algorithms requires an initial random walk or search to be performed. For example, in Ant Colony Optimization, this leaves a trail of the chemical for the other ants to follow. In the Bee Colony Optimization, the scout bees do the initial survey of the food sources. In the Canine Algorithm, the intelligent behavior of canines with their olfactory capability is applied. No prior random search is envisaged in the algorithm. This is specifically useful in cases where the network topology details are either not discovered or the network link states change dynamically.

7 Conclusions

The Canine Algorithm is an algorithm derived from the rather curious and efficient mechanisms used by canines; which could be used to solve many computational problems. The advantage is that multiple canine agents can be used concurrently to obtain a faster and better solution. This provides a better performance of the algorithm compared to the existing algorithms. As part of the future works, identification of NDP with constraints can be done, by suitably modifying the Canine Algorithm to handle the constraints.

References

1. Karp, R.M.: On the computational complexity of combinatorial problems. Networks **5**, 45–68 (1975)
2. Lynch, J.F.: The equivalence of theorem proving and the interconnection problem. SIGDA Newsl. **5**, 31–36 (1975)
3. Dijkstra, E.W.: A note on two problems in connection with graphs. Numer. Math. **1** (1959). https://doi.org/10.1007/BF01386390
4. Bellman, R.: On a routing problem. Q. Appl. Math. **16**, 87–90 (1958). https://doi.org/10.1090/qam/102435
5. Ford, L., Fulkerson, D.R.: Flows in Networks. Princeton Princeton University Press, Princeton (1962)
6. Ducatelle, F., Di Caro, G.A., Gambardella, L.M.: Principles and applications of swarm intelligence for adaptive routing in telecommunications networks. Swarm Intell. 4 (2010). https://doi.org/10.1007/s11721-010-0040-x
7. VinodChandra, S.S.: Smell detection agent based optimization algorithm. J. Inst. Eng. India Ser. B. **97**, 431–436 (2016)
8. Ananthalakshmi Ammal, R., Sajimon, P.C., Vinodchandra, S.S.: Application of smell detection agent based algorithm for optimal path identification by sdn controllers. In: Tan, Y., Takagi, H., Shi, Y., Niu, B. (eds.) ICSI 2017. LNCS, vol. 10386, pp. 502–510. Springer, Cham (2017). https://doi.org/10.1007/978-3-319-61833-3_53
9. Suurballe, J.W.: Disjoint paths in a network. Networks **4** (1974). https://doi.org/10.1002/net.3230040204
10. Bhandari, R.: Optimal physical diversity algorithms and survivable networks. In: IEEE Symposium on Computers and Communications – Proceedings, pp. 433–441. IEEE (1997). https://doi.org/10.1109/iscc.1997.616037
11. Yang, S., Trajanovski, S., Kuipers, F.A.: Availability based path selection. In: Proceedings of International Workshop on Reliable Networks Design and Modeling (RNDM) (2014)
12. Omran, M.T., Sack, J.-R., Zarrabi-Zadeh, H.: Finding paths with minimum shared edges. J. Comb. Optim. **26**(4), 709–722 (2012). https://doi.org/10.1007/s10878-012-9462-2
13. Trajanovski, S., Kuipers, F.A., Ilic, A., Crowcroft, J., Van Mieghem, P.: Finding critical regions and region-disjoint paths in a network. IEEE/ACM Trans. Netw. **23**, 908–921 (2015). https://doi.org/10.1109/TNET.2014.2309253
14. Menger, K.: Zur allgemeinen Kurventheorie. Fundam. Math. **10**, 96–115 (1927)
15. Broder, A.Z., Frieze, A.M., Suen, S., Upfal, E.: An efficient algorithm for the vertex-disjoint paths problem in random graphs. In: Proceedings of the Annual ACM-SIAM Symposium on Discrete Algorithms, pp. 261–268 (1996)

Particle Swarm Optimization

Optimizing Hydrography Ontology Alignment Through Compact Particle Swarm Optimization Algorithm

Yifeng Wang[1], Hanguang Yao[1], Liangpeng Wan[1], Hua Li[1], Junjun Jiang[2],
Yun Zhang[2], Fangmin Wu[2], Junfeng Chen[3], Xingsi Xue[4,5(✉)], and Cai Dai[6]

[1] China Three Gorges Corporation, Beijing 100038, China
{wang_yifeng1,li_hua5}@ctgpc.com.cn,
{yao_hanguang,wan_liangpeng}@ctg.com.cn
[2] Hangzhou HuaNeng Engineering Safety Technology Co., Ltd.,
Hangzhou 311121, China
67692059@qq.com, 441079379@qq.com, 329537060@qq.com
[3] College of IOT Engineering, Hohai University, Changzhou 213022, Jiangsu, China
chen-1997@163.com
[4] Fujian Key Lab for Automotive Electronics and Electric Drive,
Fujian University of Technology, Fuzhou 350118, Fujian, China
[5] Guangxi Key Laboratory of Automatic Detecting Technology and Instruments,
Guilin University of Electronic Technology, Guilin 541004, Guangxi, China
jack8375@gmail.com
[6] School of Computer Science, Shaanxi Normal University, Xi'an 710119, China
cdai0320@snnu.edu.cn

Abstract. With the explosive growth in generating data in the hydrographical domain, many hydrography ontologies have been developed and maintained to describe hydrographical features and the relationships between them. However, the existing hydrography ontologies are developed with varying project perspectives and objectives, which inevitably results in the differences in terms of knowledge representation. Determining various relationships between two entities in different ontologies offers the opportunity to link hydrographical data for multiple purposes, though the research on this topic is in its infancy. Different from the traditional ontology alignment whose cardinality is 1:1, i.e. one source ontology entity is mapping with one target ontology entity and vice versa, and the relationship is the equivalence, matching hydrography ontologies is a more complex task, whose cardinality could be 1:1, 1:n or m:n and the relationships could be equivalence or subsumption. To efficiently optimize the ontology alignment, in this paper, a discrete optimal model is first constructed for the ontology matching problem, and then a Compact Particle Swarm Optimization algorithm (CPSO) based matching technique is proposed to efficiently solve it. CPSO utilizes the compact real-value encoding and decoding mechanism and the objective-decomposing strategy to approximate the PSO's evolving process, which can dramatically reduce PSO's memory consumption and runtime while at the same time ensure the solution's quality. The experiment exploits the Hydrography dataset in Complex track provided by the Ontology

© Springer Nature Switzerland AG 2020
Y. Tan et al. (Eds.): ICSI 2020, LNCS 12145, pp. 151–162, 2020.
https://doi.org/10.1007/978-3-030-53956-6_14

Alignment Evaluation Initiative (OAEI) to test our proposal's performance. The experimental results show that CPSO-based approach can effectively reduce PSO's runtime and memory consumption, and determine high-quality hydrography ontology alignments.

Keywords: Hydrography ontology · Complex alignment · Compact Particle Swarm Optimization Algorithm

1 Introduction

To solve water features's heterogeneity problem, many hydrography ontologies, such as the United States Geological Survey's Surface Water Ontology (SWO) [9], Spanish National Geographic Institute (IGN)'s hydrOntology [14], the Hydro3 module from the University of Maine's HydroGazetteer [13] and the Cree surface water ontology [15], have been developed and maintained to describe hydrographic features and the relationships between them. However, these ontologies are independently developed with varying project perspectives and objectives, and therefore, they might use the same terminology for different concepts, they may be at different levels of abstraction, they may not include all of the same concepts, and they may not even be in the same language [2]. For example, SWO describes surface water features from the perspective of the earth's terrain, the water bodies and flows between them, while Cree surface water ontology presents the surface water features based on the people's utility for transportation via canoe, which largely focuses on water bodies' locations relative to one another. Matching ontologies aims at determining various relationships between two entities in different ontologies, which offers the opportunity to link hydrographical data for multiple purposes.

The traditional ontology matching techniques [3,16–18] dedicate to find the simple alignment whose cardinality is 1:1, i.e. one source ontology entity is mapping with one target ontology entity and vice versa, and the relationship is the equivalence, e.g. a "Wetlands" in one ontology is equivalent to a "Swamp Or Marsh" in another ontology. However, matching hydrography ontologies is a more complex task, whose cardinality could be 1:1, 1:n or m:n and the relationships could be equivalence or subsumption [19]. Therefore, the traditional ontology matchers is not able to determine the high-quality ontology alignment, and the complex ontology matching problem is one of the challenges in the ontology matching domain [11], e.g. a "Watershed" in one ontology is a subclass of the union of the "Lake Or Pond" and "Swamp Or Marsh" in another. Being inspired by the success of Particle Swarm Optimization algorithm (PSO) based ontology matcher [1] in the ontology matching domain, we propose to use it to optimize the ontology alignment's quality. To this end, we propose a Compact PSO (CPSO), which uses the compact real-value encoding and decoding mechanism and the objective-decomposing strategy to execute the evolving process.

The rest of the paper is organized as follows: Sect. 2 defines the hydrography ontology matching problem and proposes a hybrid similarity measure for calculating the similarity values between two hydrographical entities; Sect. 3 presents the CPSO in details, which includes the compact encoding mechanism, the Probability Vector (PV) and the crossover operator; Sect. 4 presents the experimental configuration and results; finally, Sect. 5 draws the conclusion.

2 Preliminaries

2.1 Hydrography Ontology Matching Problem

To evaluate the quality of an ontology alignment and the effectiveness of a matching approach, it is necessary to determine whether all correct correspondences have been discovered (completeness) and whether all discovered correspondences are correct (soundness). Normally, the alignment is assessed in terms of two measures, commonly known as precision and recall. Precision (or soundness) measures the fraction of the selected correspondences that are actually correct. Recall (or completeness) measures the fraction of the number of correct mappings discovered against the total number of existing correct alignments. Maximum precision (no false positive) and maximum recall (no false negative) refer to the absence of type I and type II errors respectively. Although a precision of 1 means that all correspondences found are correct, it does not imply that all correct ones have been found. Analogously, a recall of 1 means that all the correct correspondences have been discovered, but it does not provide the information about the number of falsely identified ones. Therefore, precision and recall are often balanced against each other by the so-called f-measure, which is the uniformly weighted harmonic meaning of recall and precision. Since f-measure can better balance the precision and recall, it is the most popular indicator that is utilized to measure the quality of an ontology alignment. Given a Reference Alignment (RA) R, which is the golden ontology alignment provided by the expert, and an alignment A, recall, precision and f-measure are respectively defined as follows [12]:

$$precision = \frac{|R \cap A|}{|A|} \tag{1}$$

$$recall = \frac{|R \cap A|}{|R|} \tag{2}$$

$$f - measure = \frac{recall \times precision}{\alpha \times recall + (1 - \alpha) \times precision} \tag{3}$$

where α is the weight to tradeoff recall and precision. Although recall, precision and f-measure can reflect the quality of the resulting alignment, they require domain experts to provide the reference alignment in advance, which is generally unknown for difficult real-life matching problems. Based on the observations that the more correspondences found and the higher mean similarity values of the correspondences are, the better the alignment quality is [1], we utilize the following two metrics to approximate the f-measure:

$$f(A) = \frac{\phi(A) \times \frac{\sum_{i=1}^{|A|} \delta_i}{|A|}}{\alpha \times \phi(A) + (1 - \alpha) \times \frac{\sum_{i=1}^{|A|} \delta_i}{|A|}} \tag{4}$$

where $|A|$ is the number of correspondences in A, ϕ is a function of normalization in $[0,1]$, δ_i is the similarity value of the ith correspondence in A, $\phi(A)$ and $\frac{\sum_{i=1}^{|A|} \delta_i}{|A|}$ respectively approximate recall and precision.

On this basis, the optimal model for the ontology matching problem is defined as follows:

$$\begin{cases} max & f(X) \\ s.t. & X = (x_1, x_2, \cdots, x_{|O_1|})^T \\ & x_i \in \{1, 2, \cdots, |O_2|\}, i = 1, 2, \cdots, |O_1| \end{cases} \tag{5}$$

where O_1 and O_2 are two ontologies, $|O_1|$ and $|O_2|$ are respectively the entity number of O_1 and O_2; x_i means the ith entity correspondences, i.e. ith source entity is related with x_i target entities; and the objective function is maximize the alignment's $f()$.

2.2   Similarity Measure on Hydrographical Class

This work utilizes a hybrid similarity measure to calculate the similarity value between two hydrographical classes. Given two hydrographical classes, we first extract their label and comments from the corresponding ontologies. Before calculating their similarity value, we utilize the natural language processing technique and Babelnet Translate which covers 271 different languages and becomes an appropriate machine translation tool in cross-lingual ontology matching domain, to process their labels l_1 and l_2 and comments c_1 and c_2. In particular, this process consists in the following successive steps:

- remove the numbers, punctuations and stop-words;
- split the strings into words;
- translate the words into English, and convert them into lower-case;
- lemmatizing and stemming the English words;

Then, four similarity values, i.e. $sim(l_1, l_2)$, $sim(c_1, c_2)$, $sim(l_1, c_2)$ and $sim(c_1, l_2)$, are calculated with soft TF-IDF [7] where two words are identical when they are the same literally or they are synonymous in the English Wordnet [6], and the maximum one is selected as two classes' similarity value.

3   Compact Particle Swarm Optimization Algorithm

In the next, CPSO for solving the ontology matching problem is presented in details, which approximates the population-based PSO's evolving process through a PV [5]. In the next, we first describe the encoding mechanism and PV, and then present the crossover operator and CPSO's pseudo-code.

3.1   Encoding and Decoding Mechanism

We utilize the real-number encoding mechanism. Since we need to encode a alignment in a solution whose kernel elements are two mapped concepts, we can simply make use of their indices in the ontologies. In an individual, each gene bit encode a positive integer that encoding the information that a source class with the same index as it are mapped with several target classes. In an alignment, if the ith source class is mapped with the target classes with index $j_1, j_2, \cdots, j_n, j_n < O_2$ the ith gene bit's value will be $(2, 3, 5, \cdots, primeNumber_{O_2}) \otimes (j_1, j_2, \cdots, j_n, 0, 0, \cdots) = 2^{j_1} \times 3^{j_2} \times 5^{j_3} \times \cdots \times primeNumber_m^{j_n} \times primeNumber_{m+1}^0 \times \cdots$. An example of the encoding mechanism is shown in the Fig. 1. As can be seen from the figure, the source concept "exocrine pancreas" with index 1 is mapped to target concepts "Exocrine_Pancreas" with index 1 and "Oropharynx_Epithelium" with index 4, and therefore, the first gene bit's value is $2^1 \times 3^4 \times 5^0 \times 7^0 = 162$.

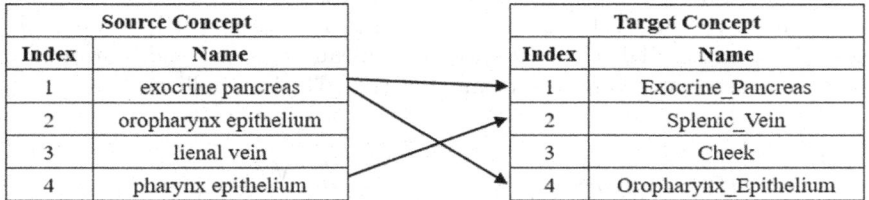

	Source Concept			Target Concept	
Index	**Name**		**Index**	**Name**	
1	exocrine pancreas		1	Exocrine_Pancreas	
2	oropharynx epithelium		2	Splenic_Vein	
3	lienal vein		3	Cheek	
4	pharynx epithelium		4	Oropharynx_Epithelium	

The individual's chromosome

Value	$2^1 \times 3^4 \times 5^0 \times 7^0$	$2^0 \times 3^0 \times 5^0 \times 7^0$	$2^0 \times 3^0 \times 5^0 \times 7^0$	$2^2 \times 3^0 \times 5^0 \times 7^0$
Index	1	2	3	4

Fig. 1. An example of encoding mechanism.

The decoding process is show in Algorithm 1.

In the obtain alignment, we utilize two thresholds, i.e. the upper threshold and lower threshold, to filter the class correspondences. When the class pair's similarity value is bigger than upper threshold, its correspondence's relationship is "equivalent"; when the class pair's similarity value is between upper threshold and lower threshold, its correspondence's relationship is "subsumption"; when the class pair's similarity value is lower than lower threshold, this correspondence will be removed. Next, for each object class, we utilize the approach proposed by D. Oliveira et al. [8] to further determine the relationships of "union" and "intersection" among its subsumed target classes.

3.2   Probability Vector

In CPSO, the Probability Vector (PV) [5] is used to represent the entire population. PV is defined as a $n \times 2$ matrix $[\mu^t, \delta^t]$ where t indicates the generation, μ

Algorithm 1. Decoding Mechanism

Input: an individual *ind*, a positive prime number list *pNum*
Output: an alignment *align*

1: **for** int $i = 1$; $i <= |O_1|$, $i{+}{+}$ **do**
2:     int *count* = 0;
3:     **while** ind_i mod $pNum_i = 0$ **do**
4:         *count* = *count* + 1;
5:     **end while**
6:     $align_i.add(count)$
7: **end for**
8: return *align*;

---

and δ are, respectively, vectors containing, for each gene value, mean and standard deviation values of a Gaussian Probability Distribution Function (PDF) truncated within the interval $[-1,1]$. In particular, for a gene bit indexed by i, a truncated Gaussian PDF characterized by a mean value μ_i, and a standard deviations δ_i is associated, and the formula of the PDF is as follows:

$$PDF(truncNorm(x)) = \frac{e^{-\frac{(x-\mu_i)^2}{2\delta_i^2}}\sqrt{\frac{2}{\pi}}}{\delta_i(erf(\frac{\mu_i+1}{\sqrt{2}\delta_i}) - erf(\frac{\mu_i-1}{\sqrt{2}\delta_i}))} \qquad (6)$$

where erf is the error function [10]. From the PDF, the corresponding Cumulative Distribution Function (CDF) is constructed by means of Chebyshev polynomials [4], whose codomain of CDF is $[0,1]$. In order to sample the design variable x_i from PV a random number $rand(0,1)$ is sampled from a uniform distribution. The inverse function of CDF, in correspondence of $rand(0,1)$, is then calculated, whose round value is x_i.

In each generation, PV is updated to moved to the elite so that the newly generated solutions could be closer to the elite. In particular, the update rules for each element of μ and δ are respectively given as follows:

$$\mu_i^{t+1} = \mu_i^t + \frac{1}{N_p}(winner_i - loser_i) \qquad (7)$$

$$(\delta_i^{t+1})^2 = (\delta_i^t)^2 + (\mu_i^t)^2 - (\mu_i^{t+1})^2 + \frac{1}{N_p}(winner_i^2 - loser_i^2) \qquad (8)$$

where N_p represents the population scale.

3.3   Crossover Operator

Given two individuals (called parents), the crossover operator generates one children, which are obtained by mixing the genes of the parents. Crossover is applied with a certain probability, a parameter of the PSO. Here, we use the widely used

Algorithm 2. Crossover Operator

Input: two individuals ind_1 and ind_2, crossover probability p_{cr}
Output: a new individual ind_{new}

1: **for** int $i = 1$; $i <= |O_1|$, $i++$ **do**
2:   **if** $rand(0,1) < p_{cr}$ **then**
3:     $align_1 = decode(ind_{1,i})$;
4:     $align_2 = decode(ind_{2,i})$;
5:     int $cutPoint$ = a random number in $\{1, 2, \cdots, ind.length\}$;
6:     **for** int $j = 1$; $i <= cutPoint$, $i++$ **do**
7:       $align_{new,i,j} = align_{1,i,j}$;
8:     **end for**
9:     **for** int $j = cutPoint$; $j <= |O_1|$, $j++$ **do**
10:       $align_{new,i,j} = align_{2,i,j}$;
11:     **end for**
12:   **end if**
13: **end for**
14: $ind_{new} = encode(align_{new})$;
15: **return** ind_{new};

one-cut-point crossover operator. First, two individuals are decoded to obtain the corresponding alignments, and a cut position in two parent alignments is randomly determined and this position is a cut point which cuts each parent alignment into two parts: the left part and the right part. Then, the left part of one parent and the right part of the other are combined to form the children. For the sake of clarity, the pseudo-code of crossover operator is shown in Algorithm 2.

3.4 The Pseudo-code of Compact Particle Swarm Optimization Algorithm

The pseudo-code of CPSO is presented in Algorithm 3. CPSO first divides the problem into three sub-problems that respectively maximizes $f_{\alpha=0}$, $f_{\alpha=0.5}$ and $f_{\alpha=1}$. We initialize three PVs and local best individuals for three sub-problems, and then initialize the global best individual by selecting the one with best $f_{0.5}$ from them. In each generation, CPSO tries to solve each sub-problem by approximating PSO's position updating strategy, i.e. crossover an individual with the local best individual and global best individual to obtain a new individual, and then use the new one to update the local best individual and PV. After solving each sub-problem, we try to update the global individual with three new local best individuals.

Algorithm 3. Compact Particle Swarm Optimization Algorithm

Input: maximum generation $maxGen$, crossover rate p_{cr}, virtual population N_p
Output: global best individual ind_{elite}

1: ** Initialization **
2: generation $t = 0$;
3: initialize $PV_{\alpha=0}$, $PV_{\alpha=0.5}$ and $PV_{\alpha=1}$ by setting $\mu_i^t = 0$ and $\delta_i^t = 10$;
4: generate three individuals through $PV_{\alpha=0}$, $PV_{\alpha=0.5}$ and $PV_{\alpha=1}$ to respectively initialize three local best individuals $ind_{\alpha=0,elite}$, $ind_{\alpha=0.5,elite}$ and $ind_{\alpha=0,elite}$;
5: initialize $ind_{elite} = opti\{ind_{\alpha=0,elite}, ind_{\alpha=0.5,elite}, ind_{\alpha=0,elite}\}$;
6: ** Evolving Process **
7: **while** $t < maxGen$ **do**
8:     ** Updating $ind_{\alpha=0,elite}$ **
9:     generate an individual $ind_{\alpha=0,new}$ through $PV_{\alpha=0}$;
10:    $ind_{\alpha=0,new} = crossover(ind_{\alpha=0,new}, ind_{\alpha=0,elite})$;
11:    $ind_{\alpha=0,new} = crossover(ind_{\alpha=0,new}, ind_{elite})$;
12:    $[winner, loser] = compete(ind_{\alpha=0,new}, ind_{\alpha=0,elite})$;
13:    $updatePV(winner, loser)$;
14:    **if** $winner == ind_{\alpha=0,new}$ **then**
15:        $ind_{\alpha=0,elite} = ind_{\alpha=0,new}$;
16:    **end if**
17:    ** Updating $ind_{\alpha=0.5,elite}$ **
18:    generate an individual $ind_{\alpha=0.5,new}$ through $PV_{\alpha=0.5}$;
19:    $ind_{\alpha=0.5,new} = crossover(ind_{\alpha=0.5,new}, ind_{\alpha=0.5,elite})$;
20:    $ind_{\alpha=0.5,new} = crossover(ind_{\alpha=0.5,new}, ind_{elite})$;
21:    $[winner, loser] = compete(ind_{\alpha=0.5,new}, ind_{\alpha=0.5,elite})$;
22:    $updatePV(winner, loser)$;
23:    **if** $winner == ind_{\alpha=0.5,new}$ **then**
24:        $ind_{\alpha=0.5,elite} = ind_{\alpha=0.5,new}$;
25:    **end if**
26:    ** Updating $ind_{\alpha=1,elite}$ **
27:    generate an individual $ind_{\alpha=1,new}$ through $PV_{\alpha=1}$;
28:    $ind_{\alpha=1,new} = crossover(ind_{\alpha=1,new}, ind_{\alpha=1,elite})$;
29:    $ind_{\alpha=1,new} = crossover(ind_{\alpha=1,new}, ind_{elite})$;
30:    $[winner, loser] = compete(ind_{\alpha=1,new}, ind_{\alpha=1,elite})$;
31:    $updatePV(winner, loser)$;
32:    **if** $winner == ind_{\alpha=1,new}$ **then**
33:        $ind_{\alpha=1,elite} = ind_{\alpha=1,new}$;
34:    **end if**
35:    ** Updating ind_{elite} **
36:    $ind_{current} = opti\{ind_{\alpha=0,elite}, ind_{\alpha=0.5,elite}, ind_{\alpha=0,elite}\}$;
37:    $[winner, loser] = compete(ind_{current}, ind_{elite})$;
38:    **if** $winner == ind_{current}$ **then**
39:        $ind_{elite} = ind_{current}$;
40:    **end if**
41:    $t = t + 1$;
42: **end while**
43: **return** ind_{elite};

4 Experiment

In order to test the performance of CPSO, the experiment exploits Hydrography dataset in Complex track provided by the Ontology Alignment Evaluation Initiative (OAEI). The hydrography dataset is composed of 4 source ontologies (Hydro3, hydrOntology_ native, hydrOntology_translated and Cree) that each should be aligned to a single target Surface Water Ontology (SWO). The source ontologies vary in their similarity to the target ontology C Hydro3 is similar in both language and structure, hydrOntology_native and hydrOntology_translated are similar in structure but hydrOntology_translated is in Spanish rather than English, and Cree is very different in terms of both language and structure. We compare the alignment's quality among PSO-based matcher [1] and OAEI's participants in Table 1, and we also compare the runtime and memory consumption between PSO-based matcher and CPSO-based matcher in Table 2. PSO and CPSO's results are the mean values of thirty independent executions. PSO's configuration is referred to its literature, and CPSO uses the following parameters which represent a trade-off setting obtained in an empirical way to achieve the highest average alignment quality on all testing cases.

- Maximum generation: $maxGen = 3000$;
- Crossover probability: $p_{cr} = 0.6$;
- Virtual population: $N_p = 20$;
- Upper threshold: $threshold_{up} = 0.8$;
- Lower threshold: $threshold_{lo} = 0.5$;

As can be seen from Table 1, CPSO can determine better alignments than PSO-based matcher and OAEI's participants in terms of both precision and recall. In Table 2, CPSO can significantly improve the converging speed and reduce the memory consumption, which shows the effectiveness of the compact encoding mechanism and the compact evolutionary operators. CPSO combines the mechanisms of a classic PSO with a competitive learning, and the results achieved by CPSO are better and are attained faster than classic PSO. The gains in solution quality and algorithm's performance are achieved respectively due to CPSO's particular competitive learning, which is effective to lead the algorithm to determine the optimal solution, and the simplicity of CPSO, which does not require all the mechanisms of a PSO, rather the few steps in the algorithm are small and simple.

Table 1. Comparisons on the alignment's quality.

Matcher	Precision	Recall	F-measure
Hydro3-SWO			
ABC	0.47	0.28	0.36
ALOD2Vec	1.00	0.13	0.23
DOME	1.00	0.13	0.23
FMapX	0.83	0.23	0.36
KEPLER	1.00	0.15	0.27
LogMap	1.00	0.15	0.27
POMAP++	1.00	0.13	0.23
XMap	0.83	0.23	0.36
PSO	0.79	0.21	0.33
CPSO	0.93	0.32	0.47
HydrOntology_translated-SWO			
ABC	0.17	0.05	0.09
DOME	0.26	0.02	0.04
LogMap	0.77	0.03	0.06
POMAP++	0.66	0.01	0.02
PSO	0.75	0.13	0.22
CPSO	0.82	0.23	0.35
HydrOntology_native-SWO			
ABC	0.25	0.005	0.01
PSO	0.21	0.13	0.16
CPSO	0.28	0.20	0.23
Cree-SWO			
ABC	0.83	0.13	0.24
ALOD2Vec	1.00	0.06	0.12
DOME	0.11	0.06	0.08
FMapX	1.00	0.04	0.08
KEPLER	1.00	0.04	0.08
PSO	0.80	0.12	0.20
CPSO	0.84	0.26	0.39

Table 2. Comparison on the runtime and memory consumption.

Testing case	PSO	CPSO	PSO	CPSO
	Runtime (second)	Runtime (second)	Memory (byte)	Memory(byte)
Hydro3-SWO	92	34	12,124,407	1,570,205
HydrOntology_translated-SWO	154	67	51,124,173	6,117,447
HydrOntology_native-SWO	142	64	49,143,746	5,219,357
Cree-SWO	64	28	34,109,561	2,749,235
Average	113	48	36,625,471	3,914,061

5   Conclusion

To efficiently optimize the hydrography ontology alignment's quality, in this paper, a discrete optimal model is constructed for the ontology matching problem, and a CPSO-based ontology matching technique is presented to solve it. CPSO utilizes the compact real-value encoding mechanism to approximate PSO's evolving process, which can dramatically reduce PSO's runtime and memory consumption while at the same time ensure the solution's quality. The experimental results show the effectiveness of our proposal.

Acknowledgements. This work is supported by the National Key Research and Development Project (No. 2016YFC0401607), the National Natural Science Foundation of China (No. 61503082), the Natural Science Foundation of Fujian Province (No. 2016J05145), the Guangxi Key Laboratory of Automatic Detecting Technology and Instruments (No. YQ20206), the Program for New Century Excellent Talents in Fujian Province University (No. GY-Z18155), the Program for Outstanding Young Scientific Researcher in Fujian Province University (No. GY-Z160149), the Scientific Research Foundation of Fujian University of Technology (Nos. GY-Z17162 and GY-Z15007),the Fundamental Research Funds for the Central Universities (No. 2019B22314), the National Key R&D Program of China (No. 2018YFC0407101), the Science and Technology Planning Project in Fuzhou City (No. 2019-G-40) and the Foreign Cooperation Project in Fujian Province (No. 2019I0019).

References

1. Bock, J., Hettenhausen, J.: Discrete particle swarm optimisation for ontology alignment. Inf. Sci. **192**, 152–173 (2012)
2. Cheatham, M., Varanka, D., Arauz, F., Zhou, L.: Alignment of surface water ontologies: a comparison of manual and automated approaches. J. Geograph. Syst. **22**, 1–23 (2019)
3. Chu, S.C., Xue, X., Pan, J.S., Wu, X.: Optimizing ontology alignment in vector space. J. Internet Technol. **21**(1), 15–22 (2020)
4. Cody, W.J.: Rational Chebyshev approximations for the error function. Math. Comput. **23**(107), 631–637 (1969)
5. Harik, G.R., Lobo, F.G., Goldberg, D.E.: The compact genetic algorithm. IEEE Trans. Evol. Comput. **3**(4), 287–297 (1999)
6. Miller, G.A.: WordNet: a lexical database for english. Commun. ACM **38**(11), 39–41 (1995)

7. Ngo, D.H., Bellahsene, Z., Todorov, K.: Extended Tversky similarity for resolving terminological heterogeneities across ontologies. In: Meersman, R., et al. (eds.) OTM 2013. LNCS, vol. 8185, pp. 711–718. Springer, Heidelberg (2013). https://doi.org/10.1007/978-3-642-41030-7_52
8. Oliveira, D., Pesquita, C.: Improving the interoperability of biomedical ontologies with compound alignments. J. Biomed. Semant. **9**(1), 1–13 (2018)
9. Sinha, G., et al.: An ontology design pattern for surface water features. In: Duckham, M., Pebesma, E., Stewart, K., Frank, A.U. (eds.) GIScience 2014. LNCS, vol. 8728, pp. 187–203. Springer, Cham (2014). https://doi.org/10.1007/978-3-319-11593-1_13
10. Temme, N.: Error functions, Dawsons and Fresnel integrals. In: NIST Handbook of Mathematical Functions, pp. 159–171 (2010)
11. Thiéblin, E., Haemmerlé, O., Hernandez, N., Trojahn, C.: Survey on complex ontology matching. In: Semantic Web (Preprint), pp. 1–39 (2019)
12. Van Rijsbergen, C.J.: Foundation of evaluation. J. Doc. **30**(4), 365–373 (1974)
13. Vijayasankaran, N.: Enhanced place name search using semantic gazetteers (2015)
14. Vilches-Blázquez, L., Ramos, J., López-Pellicer, F.J., Corcho, O., Nogueras-Iso, J.: An approach to comparing different ontologies in the context of hydrographical information. In: Popovich, V.V., Claramunt, C., Schrenk, M., Korolenko, K.V. (eds.) Information fusion and geographic information systems, pp. 193–207. Springer, Heidelberg (2009). https://doi.org/10.1007/978-3-642-00304-2_13
15. Wellen, C.C., Sieber, R.E.: Toward an inclusive semantic interoperability: the case of cree hydrographic features. Int. J. Geogr. Inf. Sci. **27**(1), 168–191 (2013)
16. Xue, X., Chen, J., Yao, X.: Efficient user involvement in semiautomatic ontology matching. IEEE Trans. Emerg. Top. Comput. Intell. 1–11 (2018)
17. Xue, X., Wang, Y.: Optimizing ontology alignments through a memetic algorithm using both matchfmeasure and unanimous improvement ratio. Artif. Intell. **223**, 65–81 (2015)
18. Xue, X., Wang, Y.: Using memetic algorithm for instance coreference resolution. IEEE Trans. Knowl. Data Eng. **28**(2), 580–591 (2015)
19. Zhou, L., Cheatham, M., Krisnadhi, A., Hitzler, P.: A complex alignment benchmark: GeoLink dataset. In: Vrandečić, D., et al. (eds.) ISWC 2018. LNCS, vol. 11137, pp. 273–288. Springer, Cham (2018). https://doi.org/10.1007/978-3-030-00668-6_17

Map Generation and Balance in the Terra Mystica Board Game Using Particle Swarm and Local Search

Luiz Jonatã Pires de Araújo[1]([✉]), Alexandr Grichshenko[1],
Rodrigo Lankaites Pinheiro[2], Rommel D. Saraiva[3], and Susanna Gimaeva[1]

[1] Innopolis University, Innopolis 420500, Russia
l.araujo@innopolis.university
[2] Webroster, Peterborough, UK
[3] University of Fortaleza, Fortaleza, Brazil

Abstract. Modern board games offer an interesting opportunity for automatically generating content and models for ensuring balance among players. This paper tackles the problem of generating balanced maps for a popular and sophisticated board game called Terra Mystica. The complexity of the involved requirements coupled with a large search space makes of this a complex combinatorial optimisation problem which has not been investigated in the literature, to the best of the authors' knowledge. This paper investigates the use of particle swarm optimisation and steepest ascent hill climbing with a random restart for generating maps in accordance with a designed subset of requirements. The results of applying these methods are very encouraging, fully showcasing the potential of search-based metaheuristics in procedural content generation.

Keywords: Combinatorial optimisation · Particle swarm · Procedural content generation · Steepest ascent hill climbing with random restart · Terra Mystica

1 Introduction

Procedural content generation (PCG) occupies an essential role in the development of modern video games and tabletop games [21]. Computation techniques such as optimisation algorithms and machine learning have been used, for example, to generate new maps conveying features such as a balanced distribution of resources and conditions among players [10]. However, there has been limited work assessing different metaheuristics for generating maps in games in the various media. One of the reasons is the complexity and nonlinearity of constraints involved in such games [15]. Moreover, there is a need for quick and online map generation, which prevents the use of computationally expensive approaches [20].

Terra Mystica (TM) has been one of the most popular and complex tabletop Euro game in the market for years. In TM, players from different factions should evolve an economy building engine which is profoundly affected by the initial

© Springer Nature Switzerland AG 2020
Y. Tan et al. (Eds.): ICSI 2020, LNCS 12145, pp. 163–175, 2020.
https://doi.org/10.1007/978-3-030-53956-6_15

distribution of resources in the map, notably the proximity of favourable types of terrain. One of the core elements in TM is, therefore, terraforming, which is an action that converts a different type into another. Players use spades (from 1 to 3 based on the terrain types) to terraform regions. The greater number of required spades corresponds to the greater complexity of the action. The difficulties in achieving map balance for different factions and a long and complicated list of requirements for the map contribute to the limited number (only three) of available maps.

The complexity of the search space of the described problem suggests the use of artificial intelligence techniques. The aim of the paper is to assess population-based metaheuristics applied to the task of generating maps for TM, which also convey balanced features. The compared algorithms are particle swarm optimisation (PSO) and steepest ascent hill climbing with random restart (SAHC). Applications of PSO and SAHC to PCG in such a scale have not been reported to the best of authors' knowledge.

The remaining part of the paper is organised according to the following structure: Sect. 2 presents a survey of the state-of-the-art of map generation using evolutionary techniques and approaches to ensure map balance. In Sect. 3, we describe a mathematical model for the requirements which the generated maps must meet as well as implementation details of selected algorithms. Subsequently, Sect. 4 provides an overview of the obtained results and the performance analysis of PSO and SAHC. To conclude, the contributions of the paper are evaluated, and suggestions for future research are outlined in Sect. 6.

2   Related Work

2.1   Map Generation Approaches

Map generation is an essential part of PCG that has attracted attention, especially in recent years, with search-based algorithms emerging as the dominant approach [10]. Togelius et al. [21] categorise the algorithms for map generation in two main approaches: *constructive methods*, which incrementally build complete solutions from a partial solution; and *generate-and-test methods*, which iteratively examine candidate solutions [20].

One of the first examples of a generate-and-test algorithm applied for map generation was reported in [18] for the *Almansur Battlegrounds*, a turn-based game. A similar method was also employed to *Dune 2*, which is a real-time strategy game in which the terrain affects the performance of the player [14]. Both studies succeeded in producing playable maps, although the authors recognise that map balance issues were not completely resolved. Studies applying genetic algorithms and genetic programming for *Siphon* [17] and *Planet Wars* [12] achieved slightly better results. However, these studies operated in a relatively small search space, which is not the case for more realistic maps. More recent examples of PCG approaches in map generation include applications of reinforcement learning for *Zelda* and *Sokoban* games [9] and quality-diversity algorithms for *Mario* [8]. Interestingly, there has not been much work demonstrating the use of computation techniques for generating maps in tabletop games. The example of generate-and-test approach with Tabu search have shown the relevance of such methods for balanced map creation in Terra Mystica board game [2].

2.2 Achieving Map Balance

One prerequisite for a balanced map is that it must provide equal chances of winning to players of equal skills and that no starting position can guarantee the victory [22]. According to [21], map balance is often achieved by evaluation functions consisting of features and corresponding weights inferred by the game designer. Another method involves the use of artificial agents to playtest several maps, which is a time-consuming process. Examples of evaluation function-based methods for map balance include studies on *StarCraft* [19], *Civilization* [5] and *Ms PacMan* [16] games. A similar methodology was proposed by Ashlock et.al using dynamic programming to design more suitable fitness functions [4].

3 Methodology

This section presents the employed evaluation functions and search space of maps in TM. Moreover, it shows the implementation details of the PSO and SAHC metaheuristics for this particular domain.

3.1 Mathematical Formalisation for TM Map

Maps in TM must conform several requirements regarding the distribution of types of terrains. For this study, the following requirements have been implemented: no land (or non-river) hexagon has a neighbour of the same terrain type (REQ1); each river hexagon has between one and three river neighbours to prevent the occurrences of lakes (REQ2); the number of disconnected river components should be one (REQ3); each land hexagon has at least one neighbour which can be terraformed using only one spade (REQ4). While REQ2 and REQ3 promote the generation of maps that resemble the original map shown in Fig. 1, the remaining requirements (REQ1 and REQ4) promote map balance among the factions.

Equation 1 gives the number of times in which REQ1 is violated (f_1). Let h_i be the ith hexagon in the list of 113 hexagons in the map; $isRiver(h_i)$ is 1 if h_i is a river hexagon, and 0 otherwise; n_j is an element of $nbs(h_i)$, which is the set of hexagons which are neighbours of h_i.

$$f_1 = \sum_{i=0}^{112}((1 - isRiver(h_i)) \sum_{j=0}^{|nbs(h_i)|} equal(h_i, n_j)) \qquad (1)$$

Fig. 1. Original map of Terra Mystica.

Equation 2 calculates the number of river hexagons that does not meet the requirement REQ2.

$$f_2 = \sum_{i=0}^{112}(isRiver(a_i)(1 - min(1, \sum_{j=0}^{|nbs(a_i)|} isRiver(n_j)))) \qquad (2)$$

Next, let *connected*(R) be the number of river components in the map, which is preferably one (REQ3). A simple graph search algorithm like breadth first search can be used for calculating the number of river components. The number of violations of REQ3 is given in Eq. 3, shown as follows.

$$f_3 = connected(R) - 1 \qquad (3)$$

Terraforming, i.e. casting one type terrain into another, is one of the most important actions in the game and has an important role for reaching map balance between different factions. Each faction has a "home terrain" where it can build. In Fig. 2, the Nomads faction has as home terrain desert (yellow) and it would need to spend two spades (indicated in the figure) to convert mountains (grey) into desert. We refer to the number of spades to terraform a terrain into another as the spade-distance between them.

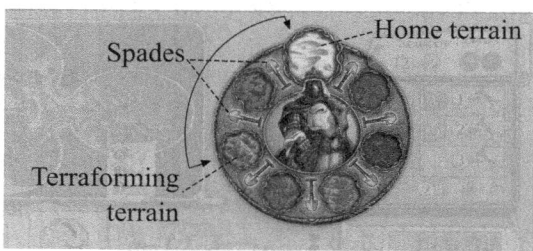

Fig. 2. A player board indicating the terraforming circle. (Color figure online)

Let $isOneSpade(h_i, n_j)$ be a function that determines whether it is possible to terraform a hexagon n_j which is neighbour of the hexagon h_i using only one spade (i.e. the spade-distance between n_j and h_j equals to 1). Equation 4 calculates the number of hexagons that does not conform to the requirement (REQ4).

$$f_4 = \sum_{i=0}^{112}((1 - isRiver(h_i))(1 - min(1, \sum_{j=0}^{|nbs(h_i)|} isOneSpade(h_i, n_j))))) \qquad (4)$$

Lastly, the minimisation objective function for a map in TM (F_{total}) is given by Eq. 5. The generated map has not violated requirements REQ1 - REQ4 has F_{tot} equal to 0.

$$F_{tot} = f_1 + f_2 + f_3 + f_4 \qquad (5)$$

In a TM map, there are 36 river tiles and 11 hexagons of each of the 7 type terrains. This gives rise to a search space S of approximately $3.7 * 10^{89}$ candidate solutions, which is significantly larger that several other problem domains explored in the PCG literature.

3.2   Particle Swarm Optimisation

Particle swarm optimisation (PSO) is a paradigm for optimising non-linear functions, inspired by the evident collective intelligence in several natural systems such as bird flock, bee swarm, among others [1]. For example, several studies confirm that different kinds of animals often avoid predators more effectively when in a group than individually [11]. PSO starts initialising the population of particles with random position and velocities. Each particle tracks its best position (pbest) according to the evaluation function. In addition, the best position across all particles (gbest) is tracked. The positions of the particles are updated at each step, as well as their velocities based on random variables and predefined parameters [7].

The PSO was implemented as follows. Because a feasible solution must have a fixed number of each type of tiles, we first created a list Γ containing the correct amount of each type of tiles, e.g. 11 tiles of each colour and 36 river tiles. We represented the solution as the vector Δ, the same size as Γ, where each position Δ_i can be an integer number between 0 and $|\Gamma|$ corresponding to an element of Γ_{Δ_i} and a coordinate of a TM map. Thus, the content of an element of the solution vector is a number which maps to an element of Γ.

However, that representation would not allow repeated entries in Δ, creating regions of infeasibility for the algorithm. In order to eliminate repeated entries (and limit the search to the feasible solution space), before converting Δ to a TM map and evaluating its fitness, for every Δ_i, starting from Δ_1, if Γ_{Δ_i} is not marked, then mark Γ_{Δ_i}. Now, while Γ_{Δ_i} is already marked, $\Delta_i = \{\Delta_i + 1$ if $\Delta_i < |\Gamma|$ or 0 otherwise$\}$. Because $|\Delta| = |\Gamma|$, there is always a non-marked index for Δ_i.

As for the PSO, we utilise a standard implementation where each particle's position is represented by a vector of real numbers. The numbers are truncated to integer numbers when converting to a valid solution.

3.3 Steepest Ascent Hill Climbing with Random Restart

Steepest ascent hill climbing with random restart (SAHC) is a greedy search-based metaheuristic that, unlike traditional hill climbing (HC), is capable of escaping from areas of local optimum and provides a better chance of locating the best global solution [13]. SAHC has several applications in both industry and academia, such as 3D printing and packing [3] and protein structure prediction [6]. The key distinction between HC and SAHC is how both of them handle situations when candidate solutions fail to produce better fitness value. Such case is the stopping condition for HC, and thus the final solution is equivalent to the first encountered local optimum. On the contrary, the stopping condition for SAHC is the run time, and upon encountering the local optimum, the algorithm randomises the current solution and starts again in hopes of locating a better local or even global solution.

Taking into account the design of TM map, the SAHC was implemented as follows. At the very beginning, the initial map is obtained by randomly assigning terrains to each hexagon. Subsequently, at each iteration, the algorithm generates candidate solutions by choosing a random hexagon and swapping its terrain with a terrain of one of the neighbours. The above procedure is done for each of the neighbours of the chosen hexagon. Thus the range of candidate solutions to evaluate is [2; 6]. Furthermore, the important input parameter to specify is the maximum possible run time of SAHC. The initial test has pointed out that the average time of convergence is 270 s. In the subsequent tests, the fitness value is captured every second.

4 Results

4.1 Results of Particle Swarm Optimisation

First, a hyperparameter optimisation was performed considering three of the main PSO parameters: *inertia weight*, which is the key feature in balancing exploration and exploitation, determining the contribution of particle's previous velocity to its current one; *cognitive* and *social scaling*, which are also weights used in computing particle's velocity at current step. The values that were assigned to each of these parameters are 0.01, 0.33, 0.66, 0.99. For each hyperparameter, PSO was executed 30 times using a timeout limit of five minutes as the stopping criterion. Figure 5 presents the mean score and the mean time to find the solution with the best score of each hyperparameter.

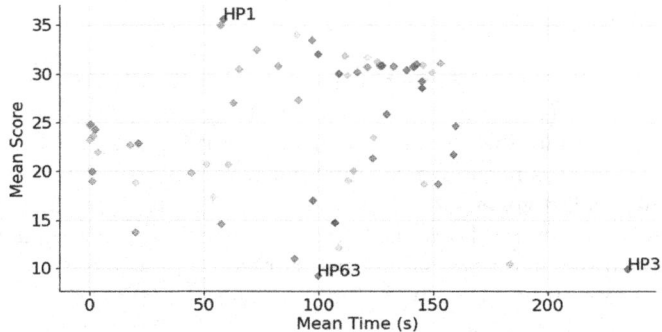

Fig. 3. Mean score and time for PSO hyperparameters. HP1: cognitive = 0.01, social = 0.01, inertia = 0.01. HP63: cognitive = 0.99, social = 0.99, inertia = 0.66.

Figure 5 presents the comparative performance of the hyperparameters, which were evaluated with respect to the mean score of the proposed minimization function and the mean time to converge to a solution. It should be clarified that since we use timeout as stopping criterion, the horizontal axis in Fig. 5 refers to the elapsed time until the algorithm stopped improving the score. Two hyperparameters can be easily distinguished in Fig. 5: HP1, which results in the worst mean score, and HP63, which has the best mean score. The mean scores for each hyperparameter are detailed in the appendix. Although other hyperparameters result in comparable mean scores, they require higher mean time to find the best solution (Fig. 3).

Another noteworthy and probably more relevant observation concerns the scores of the best map obtained by each hyperparameter in PSO, shown in Fig. 4. In addition to the best mean score, hyperparameter HP3 also found the map (see Appendix) with the best overall score 3.0. The observation of the hyperparameters sorted in ascending order of score (from the best to the worst) provides the insight that some parameter values seem to favour better results like, for example, all eight highest results have *inertia weight* value set to 0.66.

4.2 Results of Steepest Ascent Hill Climbing with Random Restart

Figure 5 illustrates how the mean score of the maps found by the SAHC consistently improves through the run time, stabilising after 270 s. The mean score from the SAHC after 30 executions was 24.9 with a standard deviation of 2.05. The best overall score was 21 (see Appendix).

5 Discussion

Some PSO hyperparameters present a mean score which is comparable to the best hyperparameter (HP63), as shown in Fig. 4. Those hyperparameters, however, present a considerably higher mean time for finding the best solution. However, the same does not occur for different media like in video-games which require the on-demand generation of content. The findings are shown in Sect. 4 suggest that local search methods like SAHC are more suitable to generate good-enough configurations in a reasonable time. For example, while PSO using HP63 reached mean score 10 in mean time of approximately 100 s (Fig. 4), SAHC can reach the score of 22 in half of the time (Fig. 5) with a trade-off of resulting in worst scores over a long period of time.

Runtime is usually a critical performance indicator considering in hyperparameter optimisation and algorithm selection. However, in procedural content generation for tabletop games, this indicator becomes less important as the execution of the algorithms occurs in early design stages, prior to the manufacturing. In an offline tabletop game manufacturing pipeline, the relevance of algorithm runtime can be often ignored. The comparison of the results of the

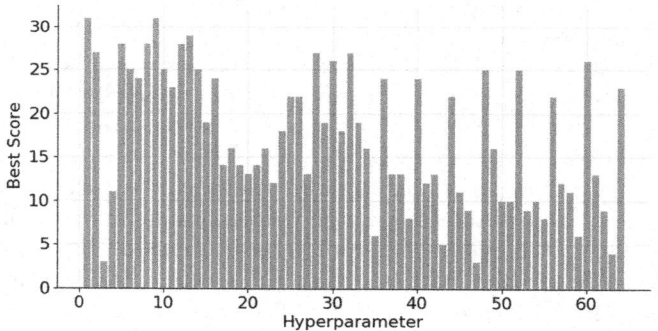

Fig. 4. Best fitness for each PSO parameter set.

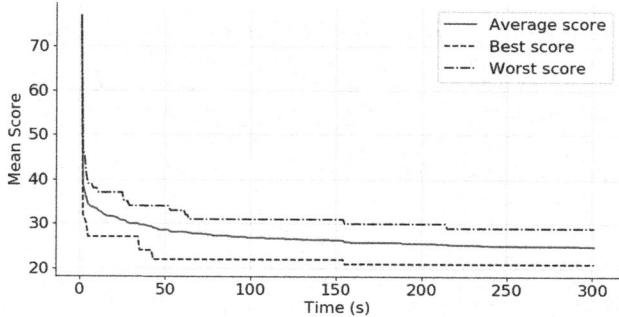

Fig. 5. Mean score and time for SAHC.

PSO and SAHC metaheuristics demonstrates that PSO is consistently more efficient in finding maps with the best scores. In other words, PSO can find maps
that violate the smallest number of requirements (Eqs. 1–5). Interestingly, some
requirements are often more disregarded than others, as shown in Table 1.

Table 1. Number of times each requirement is violated.

Map	Score (F_{tot})	REQ1	REQ2	REQ3	REQ4
PSO HP3	3	0	0	0	3
SAHC	21	4	8	3	6
Original map	9	0	3	0	6
Fire and ice	12	0	3	0	9
Fjords	9	0	0	0	9

As shown in Table 1, the number of violated requirements of the best map
obtained by SAHC suggest that this metaheuristic is not the most suitable algorithm to be used in early stages of offline manufacturing. Interestingly, the existing maps and the best map obtained by PSO present no violations of requirements REQ1 and REQ3. The reasons for such seem to have root on the nature
of the perturb operator of the tested metaheuristics, which randomly select a
hexagon and swap by one of its neighbours. More complex operators designed to
address REQ4 requirement can contribute to the generation of more balanced
maps.

PCG using metaheuristics can answer the demand from the gaming community for new maps in TM that satisfy complex requirements that, if attended,
contribute to more balanced and enjoyable games. A user could play with generated maps in online platforms like 'TM AI'[1]. Moreover, the algorithms offer new
material that can be commercialised in future expansions. Only one expansion
containing two maps has been released to the date.

6 Conclusion

This paper demonstrates how PSO and SAHC metaheuristics can be used for
generating new maps for the popular game Terra Mystica. Such maps address
the need from a large gaming community eager for new maps. Moreover, the
generated maps comply with requirements for map balance, supporting equal
initial conditions for players. These features provide the opportunity for com-
mercialising expansions with new material and maps.

One interesting research direction to be addressed is to expand the set of
requirements contributing to balance with the use of integer programming. It is
also essential to interact with the gaming community as well as the creators of

---

[1] https://lodev.org/tmai/.

Terra Mystica in order to receive play-testing feedback. Moreover, it is necessary to consider more sophisticated and refined evolutionary algorithms for this combinatorial optimisation problem that are able to produce balanced maps according to the expanded set of rules.

Appendix

(See Fig. 6 and Table 2).

(a) Best map by PSO (score 3.0).

(b) Best map by SAHC (21.0).

Fig. 6. Maps generated by PSO and SAHC (Color figure online)

Table 2. Best and mean score for each PSO hyperparameter after 30 executions.

Hyperparameter	Cognitive	Social	Inertia	Best score	Mean score	Standard deviation
3	0.01	0.01	0.66	3.0	10.0	3.710
47	0.66	0.99	0.66	3.0	10.5	3.947
63	0.99	0.99	0.66	4.0	9.3	2.620
43	0.66	0.66	0.66	5.0	12.1	4.080
59	0.99	0.66	0.66	6.0	11.0	3.337
35	0.66	0.01	0.66	6.0	20.0	5.089
55	0.99	0.33	0.66	8.0	13.7	3.386
39	0.66	0.33	0.66	8.0	14.6	3.746
62	0.99	0.99	0.33	9.0	14.7	3.119
46	0.66	0.99	0.33	9.0	18.7	4.532
53	0.99	0.33	0.01	9.0	22.8	5.011
54	0.99	0.33	0.33	10.0	18.9	3.850
51	0.99	0.01	0.66	10.0	19.0	5.174
50	0.99	0.01	0.33	10.0	23.3	5.738
58	0.99	0.66	0.33	11.0	17.4	4.224
4	0.01	0.01	0.99	11.0	21.4	4.483
45	0.66	0.99	0.01	11.0	21.8	4.387
23	0.33	0.33	0.66	12.0	18.7	4.748
57	0.99	0.66	0.01	12.0	19.9	3.191
41	0.66	0.66	0.01	12.0	20.1	3.609
61	0.99	0.99	0.01	13.0	17.1	2.792
42	0.66	0.66	0.33	13.0	19.1	3.794
38	0.66	0.33	0.33	13.0	20.7	3.752
37	0.66	0.33	0.01	13.0	20.7	4.123
27	0.33	0.66	0.66	13.0	24.7	5.014
20	0.33	0.01	0.99	13.0	28.6	4.773
19	0.33	0.01	0.66	14.0	22.0	3.573
17	0.33	0.01	0.01	14.0	22.9	4.230
21	0.33	0.33	0.01	14.0	25.9	4.654
22	0.33	0.33	0.33	16.0	23.5	4.544
34	0.66	0.01	0.33	16.0	23.7	4.036
18	0.33	0.01	0.33	16.0	24.4	4.579
49	0.99	0.01	0.01	16.0	24.8	4.377
31	0.33	0.99	0.66	18.0	27.4	3.535
24	0.33	0.33	0.99	18.0	29.3	3.216
33	0.66	0.01	0.01	19.0	24.9	3.509
15	0.01	0.99	0.66	19.0	27.1	3.130
29	0.33	0.99	0.01	19.0	31.1	2.741
26	0.33	0.66	0.33	22.0	30.2	3.184
56	0.99	0.33	0.99	22.0	30.2	3.059
44	0.66	0.66	0.99	22.0	30.8	2.565
25	0.33	0.66	0.01	22.0	32.0	2.633
11	0.01	0.66	0.66	23.0	30.0	2.345
64	0.99	0.99	0.99	23.0	30.8	2.565
36	0.66	0.01	0.99	24.0	30.4	3.029
7	0.01	0.33	0.66	24.0	30.5	2.680
40	0.66	0.33	0.99	24.0	30.8	2.522
16	0.01	0.99	0.99	24.0	31.0	2.066

(continued)

Table 2. (*continued*)

Hyperparameter	Cognitive	Social	Inertia	Best score	Mean score	Standard deviation
14	0.01	0.99	0.33	25.0	30.8	2.891
48	0.66	0.99	0.99	25.0	30.8	2.315
52	0.99	0.01	0.99	25.0	31.7	3.226
10	0.01	0.66	0.33	25.0	31.9	3.304
6	0.01	0.33	0.33	25.0	32.5	3.159
30	0.33	0.99	0.33	26.0	29.9	2.077
60	0.99	0.66	0.99	26.0	31.1	2.294
32	0.33	0.99	0.99	27.0	30.8	1.621
28	0.33	0.66	0.99	27.0	31.3	1.750
2	0.01	0.01	0.33	27.0	33.5	2.540
12	0.01	0.66	0.99	28.0	30.9	1.746
8	0.01	0.33	0.99	28.0	31.0	1.449
5	0.01	0.33	0.01	28.0	34.6	2.246
13	0.01	0.99	0.01	29.0	34.0	2.543
9	0.01	0.66	0.01	31.0	35.0	2.137
1	0.01	0.01	0.01	31.0	35.6	2.057

References

1. Alam, M.N.: Particle swarm optimization: algorithm and its codes in MATLAB, pp. 1–10. ResearchGate (2016)
2. Grichshenko, A., Jonatã, L., de Araújo, P., Gimaeva, S., Brown, J.A.: Using Tabu search algorithm for map generation in the Terra Mystica tabletop game (2020)
3. Araújo, L.J., Özcan, E., Atkin, J.A., Baumers, M.: A part complexity measurement method supporting 3D printing. In: NIP and Digital Fabrication Conference, vol. 2016, pp. 329–334. Society for Imaging Science and Technology (2016)
4. Ashlock, D., Lee, C., McGuinness, C.: Search-based procedural generation of maze-like levels. IEEE Trans. Comput. Intell. AI Games **3**(3), 260–273 (2011)
5. Barros, G.A., Togelius, J.: Balanced civilization map generation based on open data. In: 2015 IEEE Congress on Evolutionary Computation (CEC), pp. 1482–1489. IEEE (2015)
6. Chira, C., Horvath, D., Dumitrescu, D.: An evolutionary model based on hill-climbing search operators for protein structure prediction. In: Pizzuti, C., Ritchie, M.D., Giacobini, M. (eds.) EvoBIO 2010. LNCS, vol. 6023, pp. 38–49. Springer, Heidelberg (2010). https://doi.org/10.1007/978-3-642-12211-8_4
7. Eberhart, R., Kennedy, J.: Particle swarm optimization. In: Proceedings of the IEEE International Conference on Neural Networks, vol. 4, pp. 1942–1948. Citeseer (1995)
8. Gravina, D., Khalifa, A., Liapis, A., Togelius, J., Yannakakis, G.N.: Procedural content generation through quality diversity. In: 2019 IEEE Conference on Games (CoG), pp. 1–8. IEEE (2019)
9. Khalifa, A., Bontrager, P., Earle, S., Togelius, J.: PCGRL: procedural content generation via reinforcement learning. arXiv preprint arXiv:2001.09212 (2020)
10. Khalifa, A., Fayek, M.: Literature review of procedural content generation in puzzle games (2015)
11. Krause, J., Ruxton, G.D., Ruxton, G.D., Ruxton, I.G., et al.: Living in Groups. Oxford University Press, Oxford (2002)

12. Lara-Cabrera, R., Cotta, C., Fernández-Leiva, A.J.: A procedural balanced map generator with self-adaptive complexity for the real-time strategy game planet wars. In: Esparcia-Alcázar, A.I. (ed.) EvoApplications 2013. LNCS, vol. 7835, pp. 274–283. Springer, Heidelberg (2013). https://doi.org/10.1007/978-3-642-37192-9_28

13. Lin, S.W., Ying, K.C., Lu, C.C., Gupta, J.N.: Applying multi-start simulated annealing to schedule a flowline manufacturing cell with sequence dependent family setup times. Int. J. Prod. Econ. **130**(2), 246–254 (2011)

14. Mahlmann, T., Togelius, J., Yannakakis, G.N.: Spicing up map generation. In: Di Chio, C., et al. (eds.) EvoApplications 2012. LNCS, vol. 7248, pp. 224–233. Springer, Heidelberg (2012). https://doi.org/10.1007/978-3-642-29178-4_23

15. de Mesentier Silva, F., Lee, S., Togelius, J., Nealen, A.: Ai-based playtesting of contemporary board games. In: Proceedings of the 12th International Conference on the Foundations of Digital Games, p. 13. ACM (2017)

16. Morosan, M., Poli, R.: Automated game balancing in MS PacMan and StarCraft using evolutionary algorithms. In: Squillero, G., Sim, K. (eds.) EvoApplications 2017. LNCS, vol. 10199, pp. 377–392. Springer, Cham (2017). https://doi.org/10.1007/978-3-319-55849-3_25

17. Nielsen, J.J., Scirea, M.: Balanced map generation using genetic algorithms in the siphon board-game. In: Ciancarini, P., Mazzara, M., Messina, A., Sillitti, A., Succi, G. (eds.) SEDA 2018. AISC, vol. 925, pp. 221–231. Springer, Cham (2020). https://doi.org/10.1007/978-3-030-14687-0_20

18. Pereira, G., Santos, P.A., Prada, R.: Self-adapting dynamically generated maps for turn-based strategic multiplayer browser games. In: Proceedings of the International Conference on Advances in Computer Entertainment Technology, pp. 353–356. ACM (2009)

19. Togelius, J., Preuss, M., Beume, N., Wessing, S., Hagelbäck, J., Yannakakis, G.N.: Multiobjective exploration of the StarCraft map space. In: Proceedings of the 2010 IEEE Conference on Computational Intelligence and Games, pp. 265–272. IEEE (2010)

20. Togelius, J., Yannakakis, G.N., Stanley, K.O., Browne, C.: Search-based procedural content generation. In: Di Chio, C., et al. (eds.) EvoApplications 2010. LNCS, vol. 6024, pp. 141–150. Springer, Heidelberg (2010). https://doi.org/10.1007/978-3-642-12239-2_15

21. Togelius, J., Yannakakis, G.N., Stanley, K.O., Browne, C.: Search-based procedural content generation: a taxonomy and survey. IEEE Trans. Comput. Intell. AI Games **3**(3), 172–186 (2011)

22. Uriarte, A., Ontanón, S.: PSMAGE: balanced map generation for StarCraft. In: 2013 IEEE Conference on Computational Intelligence in Games (CIG), pp. 1–8. IEEE (2013)

A Performance Class-Based Particle Swarm Optimizer

Chia Emmanuel Tungom[1], Maja Gulan[2(✉)], and Ben Niu[1(✉)]

[1] College of Management, Shenzhen University, Shenzhen 518060, China
chemago99@yahoo.com, drniuben@gmail.com
[2] Faculty of Technical Sciences, University of Novi Sad, Novi Sad, Serbia
majica.gulan@gmail.com

Abstract. One of the main concerns with Particle Swarm Optimization (PSO) is to increase or maintain diversity during search in order to avoid premature convergence. In this study, a Performance Class-Based learning PSO (PCB-PSO) algorithm is proposed, that not only increases and maintains swarm diversity but also improves exploration and exploitation while speeding up convergence simultaneously. In the PCB-PSO algorithm, each particle belongs to a class based on its fitness value and particles might change classes at evolutionary stages or search step based on their updated position. The particles are divided into an upper, middle and lower. In the upper class are particles with top fitness values, the middle are those with average while particles in the bottom class are the worst performing in the swarm. The number of particles in each group is predetermined. Each class has a unique learning strategy designed specifically for a given task. The upper class is designed to converge towards the best solution found, Middle class particles exploit the search space while lower class particles explore. The algorithm's strength is its flexibility and robustness as the population of each class allows us to prioritize a desired swarm behavior. The Algorithm is tested on a set of 8 benchmark functions which have generally proven to be difficult to optimize. The algorithm is able to be on par with some cutting edge PSO variants and outperforms other swarm and evolutionary algorithms on a number of functions. On complex multimodal functions, it is able to outperform other PSO variants showing its ability to escape local optima solutions.

Keywords: Particle Swarm Optimization · Learning strategy · Swarm intelligence

1 Introduction

Optimization is one of the key features in obtaining good performance in systems. In fact optimization problems can be found everywhere in real life from transportation to even dieting. PSO is an intelligent optimization algorithm designed

Y. Tan et al. (Eds.): ICSI 2020, LNCS 12145, pp. 176–188, 2020.
https://doi.org/10.1007/978-3-030-53956-6_16

in the mid 1990's by Eberth and Shi [1,2]. The algorithm's working principle is based off-of simulating the collective behavior of bird flock and fish school.

The original PSO algorithm has a topology fully connected network where all particles learn from their personal best historical search position and the global best particle in the swarm. This learning structure is the main reason why the original PSO algorithm is inefficient and ca easily be trapped into a local minima as all particles are guided by one global leader. Several other topological structures have been introduce to enhanced performance e.g. the ring topology, the von Neumann topology, the pyramid topology [3]. These topologies use different ways to update the velocity and position of particles in the swarm. Fully Informed PSO (FIPS) determines the velocity of a particle by looking at its neighborhood topology [4]. Comprehensive learning PSO (CLPSO) tries to solve the problem of premature convergence by using different learning topologies on different dimensions to ensure diversity is maintained [5].

Exploration, the ability of the swarm to search its entire environment (global search) and exploitation, the ability for particles to thoroughly search their neighborhood (local search) are two important features of any PSO or search algorithm. To ensure swarm stability, stability based adaptive inertia weight (SAIW) uses a performance based approach to determine each particles inertia weight [6]. Mixed Swarm Cooperative PSO (MCPSO) achieves exploration and exploitation by dividing particles into exploration and exploitation groups [7]. By leveraging comprehensive learning strategy, Heterogeneous Comprehensive Learning PSO (HCLPSO) enhances its exploration and exploitation [8]. There are several other balanced Algorithms that are specifically designed to ensure both exploration and exploitation [8–10].

In this study, a novel PSO algorithm called PCB-PSO is proposed, with a new learning topology to ensure exploration and exploitation while also ensuring a high convergence speed therefore avoiding premature convergence. In PCB-PSO, particles are divided into three groups, upper class, middle class and lower class based on their fitness values, and a particles' group might change from iteration to iteration. The upper class consist of particles with superior performance while the lower class consist of the poorest performing members. The middle class is made-up of members considered not to be performing poorly and not having superior performance. Particles in the same group have a common learning strategy or topology, which is different from those in the other groups. Lower class particles are designed to enhance exploration while the middle class particles are designed for exploitation. Upper class particles are designed for fast convergence. The intuition here is that if a particle is performing poorly, it has to do more exploration and if its performance is good, it focuses on converging faster, and if its performing neither poorly nor well, then it should exploit its neighborhood. The main contributions of this study can be listed as follows:

1. Introduces a new paradigm of PSO learning that enhances exploration, exploitation and convergence speed simultaneously.
2. Deals with the problem of premature convergence by making some particles continue exploration and exploitation while others converge to a given minima or optima.
3. The problem of swarm diversity is dealt with by continuous exploration of the search space by lower class particles.
4. Introduces flexibility by allowing a given behavior to be prioritized by simply assigning more or all particles to a given class.

The rest of the paper is organized as follows: The original PSO algorithm and some learning topologies are reviewed in Sect. 2. The proposed PCB-PSO algorithm is discussed in Sect. 3 and in Sect. 4, analysis and comparison of the results with other PSO variants on several benchmark functions is discussed. Finally, in Sect. 5 we draw our conclusion from this paper and propose future research directions.

2   Basic PSO Algorithm

PSO is a population based stochastic swarm and evolutionary computational algorithm. In PSO, a population of particles, with each having a position and velocity component, is use to find the solution to an optimization problem. Each particle is a solution and the search space is the set of all solutions to the given problem. The particles or solutions are evolved by updating the velocity and position after every iteration. A particles update is done using its personal best experience and the best experience of the entire swarm. This update is designed to guide the particles towards the global best solution and eventually and eventually towards the optimal solution. The update of velocity and position of each particle are done using Eqs. 1 and 2 respectively. The particles continue to evolve until a termination criterion is met usually the maximum iteration pre-determined before start of search.

$$V_i^{t+1} = wV_i^t + c_1r_1(X_{Pb}^t - X_i^t) + c_2r_2(X_{Gb}^t - X_i^t) \tag{1}$$

$$X_i^{t+1)} = X_i^t + V_i^{t+1} \tag{2}$$

where w is the inertia weight and wV_i^t the Inertia or momentum component. The inertia component directs a particles' trajectory in the search space for both exploration and exploitation towards unvisited search areas, its choice of value usually depend on the search dimension and varies in the range $[0, 1]$. Particles trajectories are maintained by the inertia component, which forces particles to navigate through areas independent of previously successful searches. For a given particle in the swarm, X_i is its current positon, X_i^t its personal best solution at a given iteration time is X_{Pb}^t and the best position X_{Gb}^t of the entire swarm referred to as global best. The social component $c_2 r_2 (X_{Gb}^t - X_i^t)$ and cognitive component $c_1 r_1 (X_{Pb}^t - X_i^t)$ guide the particles towards the swarms best solution and a particles personal best solution respectively.

c_1 and c_2 are cognitive and social acceleration coefficients respectively usually set to 2 by default in the basic PSO algorithm. r1 and r2 are uniform random numbers generated between 0 and 1. w, c_1 and c_2 play an influential role in determining the swarm's behavior. A choice of each value is problem dependent and determines the convergence speed, exploitation and exploration ability of the swarm. Therefore, the choice of values should be harmonious. In a simple PSO algorithm, w can be between 0.4 and 0.9 and c_1 and c_2 can be set to 2.

3   Proposed PSO Algorithm

In this section, an efficient variant of PSO called PCB-PSO is proposed to simultaneously tackle the problems of premature convergence, exploration, exploitation and diversity while also converging faster to the global minima. The algorithm introduces a new learning topology and the major difference from the base PSO is as follows (1) Particles in the swarm belong to one of three groups based of their fitness value. (2) Each group has a learning strategy or update mechanism unique to it. In PCB-PSO, The best or top performing particles fall in the Upper Class (UC), average performing in the Middle Class (MC) and poorly performing particles fall in the Lower Class (LC). The population size of each class is predetermined and will be discussed in the later section. The intuition here is that, classifying particles into three groups can allow us to design a learning strategy for each group of the swarm to simultaneously explore, exploit and converge while maintaining diversity throughout the search. This is opposed to the base PSO where all the particles learn from a global leader making them to move towards one region of the search space. UC particles, which, have good performance and are most likely to find the optimal solution are designed to enhance convergence speed. LC particles, which are poorly performing in the swarm, roam the search area exploring new solutions and maintaining diversity of the swarm. MC particles, which are performing neither poorly nor well, are designed for exploitation since they move in areas between UC and MC particles (Fig. 1).

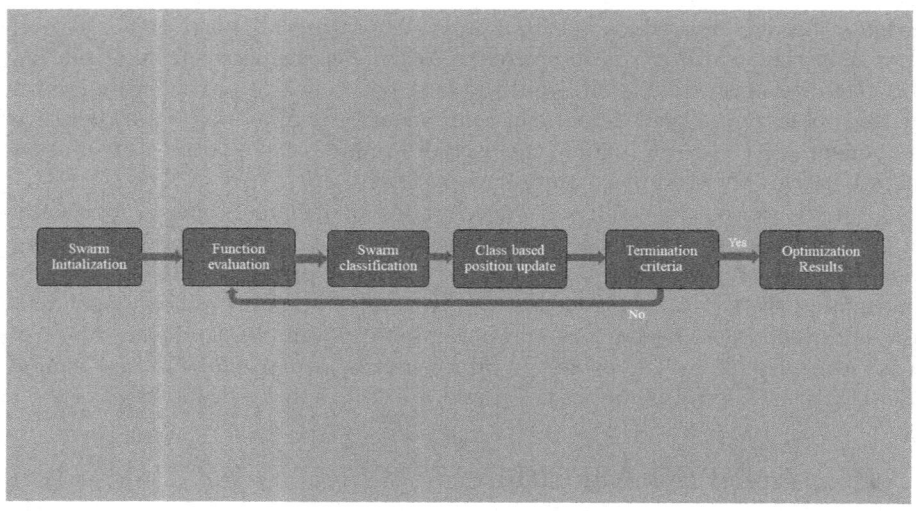

Fig. 1. Shows the sequential search process of the PCB-PSO.

3.1 Swarm Classes

We want to sort the particles into three classes UC, MC and LC with population sizes N_{uc}, N_{mc} and N_{lc} respectively. The population of each class is determined in three simple steps. First, a class is chosen and the proportion of the total population N to belong to that class is assigned to determine the population of the given class. Secondly, the remaining population is used and a proportion of it is determined to fall in to the next class. Finally, the last remainder of the population falls into the last class. Note that we can start with any class. For convenience sake, in this paper, we will be starting with UC, MC and then LC in that order. Let us say the proportion of particles we want in UC is 1/3 of N then $S_{uc} = 3$ and Let's assume the proportion of the remaining particles we want for MC is 1/2, then $S_{mc} = 2$. N is used to determine N_{uc} while $N - N_{uc}$ is use to determine N_{mc} as shown in Eqs. 3 and 4 respectively. The remaining particles after selecting N_{uc} and N_{mc} make up N_{lc} (Fig. 2).

$$N_{uc} = \frac{N}{S_{uc}} \tag{3}$$

$$N_{mc} = \frac{(N - N_{uc})}{S_{mc}} \tag{4}$$

$$N_{lc} = |N_{uc} - N_{mc}| \tag{5}$$

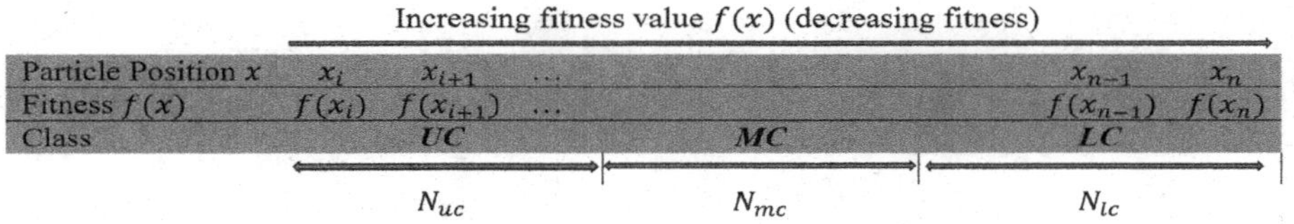

Increasing fitness value $f(x)$ (decreasing fitness)

Particle Position x	x_i	x_{i+1}	$\cdots$				x_{n-1}	x_n
Fitness $f(x)$	$f(x_i)$	$f(x_{i+1})$	$\cdots$				$f(x_{n-1})$	$f(x_n)$
Class		*UC*		*MC*		*LC*		

N_{uc} N_{mc} N_{lc}

Fig. 2. Illustrates the classification of particles based on fitness with their corresponding classes and population sizes search process of the PCB-PSO.

UC and LC particles have probabilities associated to them. This associated probability is a measure of how likely a particle is chosen to be learned from by another particle in the learning strategy of a given class, which will be discussed later. For UC particles, the probability is proportional to the fitness value meaning the higher the value, the higher the probability while for LC particles; the probability is inversely proportional to the fitness value. MC particles learn from both UC and LC members and so we want the best particles in UC to be less likely to learn from and the best particles in LC to be more likely to learn from so as to keep them exploiting regions between MC and LC. The probability of a UC particle is calculated using Eq. 6 while that of LC is calculated using Eq. 7.

$$P_{UC_i} = \frac{f(X_{UC_i})}{\sum_{j=1}^{n} f(X_{UC_j})} \tag{6}$$

$$P_{LC_i} = \frac{\tilde{f}(X_{LC_i})}{\sum_{j=1}^{n} \tilde{f}(X_{LC_j})} \tag{7}$$

where UC_i is the ith particle of UC and P_{UC_i} is the probability of that particle. LC_i is the ith particle of LC and P_{LC_i} is the probability of that particle. $\tilde{f}$ is calculated such that the appropriate probabilities are derived for LC particles i.e. the lowest fitness values are flipped for all members with the poorest fit particle becoming the fittest and vice versa.

3.2   Update Mechanism

In PSO particles are updated by directing them towards the global best solution of the swarm and the personal best solution of the given particle with a velocity. This might be problematic if the solution found is not actually the best solution in the search space then particles will fail to explore other search regions missing other potentially better solutions. This problem has been solved by introducing different learning strategies and parameter modification. The simplest way is to vary the inertia weight and acceleration coefficients throughout the search to enhance exploration in the early stages and exploitation in the late stages. We leverage this idea but ensure both exploration and exploitation are carried-out throughout the search by introducing a new topology structure. This ensures a thorough search of the solution space making it less likely to miss a global

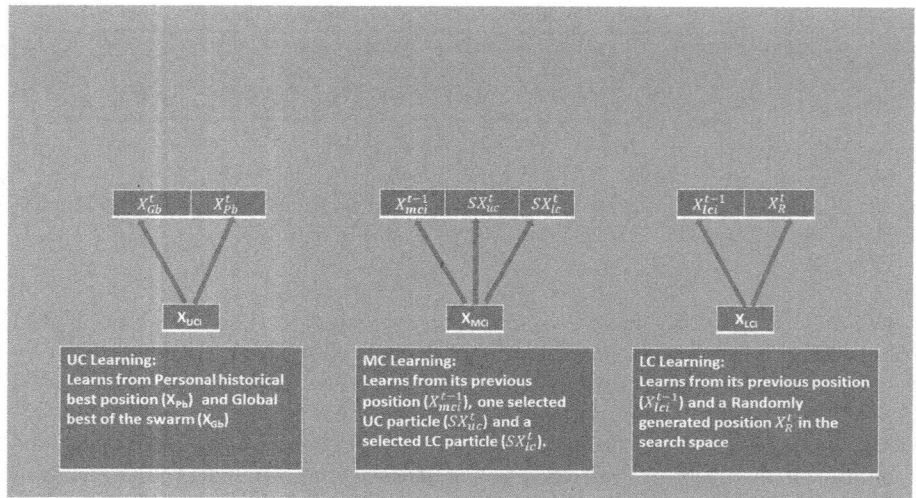

Fig. 3. Illustrates the learning mechanisms of each class with their source of information indicated by arrows.

best solution. The velocity component is not used in this algorithm because in higher dimensions, the inertia weight is required to be less than 0.1 to achieve reasonable results. Instead of using the recommended small value of the inertia weight, we focus on tuning acceleration of the social and cognitive component, which further simplifies the position update equation by eliminating the inertia weight and velocity. Hence, in this algorithm, we do not need to calculate the velocity component of a particle. In PCB-PSO, the update mechanism of each class is design for a given property of exploration, exploitation and convergence of the particles. Three different update mechanisms are designed for the three classes. Each update strategy is unique to a given class.

UC Update Mechanism. These are the best performing particles in the swarm and so are close to the best solution found at any period during the search. The update equation for UC is as shown in Eq. 8

$$X_i^{t+1} = X_i^t + c_1 r_1 (X_{Pb}^t - X_i^t) + c_2 r_2 (X_{Gb}^t - X_i^t) \tag{8}$$

The parameters are same as discussed in Sect. 2 (Fig. 3).

MC Update Mechanism. Particles in this class are designed to exploit the region outside the best solution found which ensures diversity and thorough exploitation of the space. The position update of this class is as shown in Eq. 9.

$$X_i^{t+1} = wV_i^t + c_3r_3(X_i^{t-1} - X_i^t) + c_4r_4(SX_{uc}^t - SX_{lc}^t) \tag{9}$$

where SX_{uc}^t and SX_{lc}^t are stochastically selected UC and LC particles at time t respectively. Taking the difference between a UC and LC particle allows the particle to fall somewhere outside the best solution already found and using the particles previous position instead of the personal best boosts the stochasticity of the search.

LC Update Mechanism. The update mechanism here is designed so that particles will explore the entire search region. The movement of particles in this class is chaotic which helps them to roam the swarm looking for better solutions. The position update is as shown in Eq. 10.

$$X_i^{t+1} = X_i^t + c_5r_5(X_i^{t-1} - X_i^t) + c_6r_6(X_R^{t-1} - X_i^t) \tag{10}$$

where X_R^t is a randomly generated position in the search space at iteration t aiding with the chaotic movement of particles in this group across the search space.

To further speed up convergence, at certain short intervals during the search, the population of the entire swarm is set to N_{uc} for UC learning as shown in Algorithm 1.

3.3   Parameter Setting

There are two groups of parameters to be set in this algorithm. The first is the class populations and the second is the acceleration coefficients for each class. The recommended settings for the proposed algorithm is outlined in Table 1. Note that the population size of any group cannot be greater than the entire swarm and the sum of all class population must be equal to the population of the entire swarm. At shown in Algorithm one, Such can be varied to push for quicker convergence at certain periods of the search. A higher swarm population will always enhance better results as opposed to other algorithms where increasing the swarm size after a certain threshold is reached might not help the performance of the algorithm which is because of the classification and behavioral setting of the particles. In PCB-PSO, the threshold is very high especially for problems with higher complexity.

Table 1. Parameters for proposed algorithm with desired and recommended settings.

Parameter	Name	Recommended value	Desired range
N	Population of swarm	[D*5, D*10]	[D*5, D*10]
N_{uc}	UC Population	>N/4	[1, N]
N_{mc}	MC Population	>N/4	[1, N]
N_{lc}	LC Population	>N/4	[1, N]
t	Iteration number	>D*3	>0
c_1	UC social acceleration coefficient	2.5	[0.0, 4.0]
c_2	UC cognitive acceleration coefficient	0.5	[0.0, 4.0]
c_3	MC social acceleration coefficient	1.5	[0.0, 4.0]
c_4	MC cognitive acceleration coefficient	1.5	[0.0, 4.0]
c_5	LC cognitive acceleration coefficient	1	[0.0, 4.0]
c_6	LC random acceleration coefficient	2	[0.0, 4.0]

4   Experiment Simulation and Results

To evaluate and ascertain the capability of the proposed algorithm, it is compared with other existing swarm and evolutionary algorithms on a set of benchmark functions. The PSO variants we compare with have been adopted for real world engineering applications and so can be regarded as state of the art. The algorithms used for this comparison include PSO, Harmony Search (HS), GA, Artificial Bee Colony (ABC), Cultural Algorithm (CA) and other advanced PSO variants.

Table 2. Outline of parameter settings for algorithms used for comparison.

Algorithm	Parameters
PSO	maximum velocity = 0.6, inertia weight=0.9, acceleration constants $c_1 = c_2 = 2$
HS	bandwidth = 0.2, harmony memory accepting rate = 0.95, pitch-adjusting rate = 0.3
GA	crossover probability = 0.7, mutation probability = 0.3
ABC	limit = 0.6×dimension×population
CA	Probability of the knowledge source = 0.35, number of accepted individuals = probability of the knowledge source × population
BBPSO	No parameter setting required
BBPSOV	Logistic map used as the search parameter
Proposed PSO	$N_{uc} = N_{mc} = N_{lc}$, $c_1 = 2.5$, $c_2 = 0.5$, $c_3 = c_4 = 1.5$, c_5 and c_6 are set to 1.0 and 2.0 respectively

4.1 Benchmark Functions

The benchmark functions used for evaluation have widely been used to evaluate swarm intelligence and evolutionary algorithms [11–13]. They include a set of 8 benchmark unimodal and multimodal functions as shown in Table 3. These functions have varied difficulty and have proven to be difficult to find optima solutions in high dimensions (>30). The unimodal functions (F1-F5) have single optimal solutions while the multimodal functions (F6-F8) have multiple. These functions are challenging and are often used to evaluate local exploitation and global exploration ability of a search algorithm.

Table 3. Shows benchmark functions used for performance testing.

Function	Range	Global minima
F1 Dixon-Price	$[-10, 10]$	0
F2 Sphere	$[-5.12, 5.12]$	0
F3 Rotated hyper-ellipsoid	$[-65.536, 65.536]$	0
F4 Sum squares	$[-5.12, 5.12]$	0
F5 Sum of different powers	$[-1, 1]$	0
F6 Ackley	$[-32, 32]$	0
F7 Griewank	$[-600, 600]$	0
F8 Powell	$[-4, 5]$	0

4.2 Experiment Setup and Results

For each of the Algorithms, swarm size is set to 50 and the search Dimension for each optimization function is set to 50. The maximum number of iteration is 1000 and each algorithm undertakes 30 independent runs. The parameter settings for each of the algorithms to be used is as shown in Table 2.

The proposed Algorithm shows superior performance in comparison to the other variants on the multimodal functions F6–F8. This shows the agility of the algorithms and its ability to escape the local optima while still managing to push for faster convergence. On unimodal functions, F1–F5 the performance is on par with other PSO variants but outperforms the other swarm and evolutionary algorithms. In unimodal functions, there is only one minima but our algorithm was still set to continuously explore and exploit other regions. If we set the whole population to UC, the algorithm will work towards faster convergence and we will expect achieve better quality results. In all we can see the flexibility and robustness of the algorithm given its built characteristics and swarm behavior in mind (Table 4).

Table 4. Results of algorithms on benchmark functions.

Function	Algorithm	Mean	Std	Min	Max
F1	PSO	2.30E+06	7.71E+05	1.28E+06	5.13E+06
	HS	7.91E+01	1.87E+01	4.54E+01	1.19E+02
	GA	4.12E+05	2.49E+05	1.02E+05	1.01E+06
	ABC	3.19E+06	8.10E+05	1.67E+06	4.97E+06
	CA	4.96E+03	4.51E+03	5.91E+02	1.86E+04
	BBPSO	2.63E+05	3.53E+05	7.86E+01	1.41E+06
	BBPSOV	4.77E+00	3.16E+00	6.70E−01	9.82E+00
	Proposed PSO	3.15E−06	4.96E−06	3.59E−08	2.05E−05
F2	PSO	1.47E+02	2.59E+01	8.46E+01	1.80E+02
	HS	3.91E−01	4.28E−02	3.09E−01	4.61E−01
	GA	4.12E+05	2.49E+05	1.02E+05	8.40E+01
	ABC	1.54E+02	2.35E+01	1.06E+02	1.94E+02
	CA	1.01E+00	1.25E+00	7.09E−02	6.42E+00
	BBPSO	2.35E+01	2.57E+01	1.29E−02	1.05E+02
	BBPSOV	5.21E−08	1.03E−07	9.30E−10	3.22E−07
	Proposed PSO	2.21E−06	7.45E−06	4.11E−09	4.00E−05
F3	PSO	6.03E+05	1.29E+05	3.96E+05	8.79E+05
	HS	1.68E+03	4.51E+02	7.65E+02	2.73E+03
	GA	2.40E+05	4.88E+04	1.53E+05	3.87E+05
	ABC	5.05E+05	7.24E+04	3.88E+05	6.54E+05
	CA	4.85E+03	4.89E+03	5.01E+02	2.33E+04
	BBPSO	1.21E+05	1.13E+05	4.46E+03	3.48E+05
	BBPSOV	1.88E−04	3.94E−04	3.84E−06	1.74E−03
	Proposed PSO	1.24E−03,	1.90E−05	4.19E−06	8.40E−04
F4	PSO	1.48E+04	3.97E+03	7.65E+03	2.47E+04
	HS	1.52E+01	2.16E+00	1.21E+01	2.27E+01
	GA	4.09E+03	1.25E+03	2.44E+03	7.34E+03
	ABC	1.18E+04	1.62E+03	8.60E+03	1.43E+04
	CA	1.46E+02	1.91E+02	5.08E+00	1.01E+03
	BBPSO	2.32E+03	1.53E+03	3.02E+02	5.71E+03
	BBPSOV	4.78E−06	8.15E−06	1.41E−07	3.11E−05
	Proposed PSO	1.50E−06	2.52E−06	1.12E−05	1.12E−05
F5	PSO	3.43E−01	2.60E−01	2.36E−02	9.53E−01
	HS	4.78E−07	6.68E−07	1.08E−08	3.45E−06
	GA	2.39E−02	2.15E−02	2.92E−03	8.04E−02
	ABC	7.59E−01	3.00E−01	1.87E−01	1.50E+00
	CA	6.15E−05	1.38E−04	1.86E−07	6.89E−04
	BBPSO	7.92E−10	3.68E−09	1.27E−15	2.01E−08
	BBPSOV	3.28E−18	1.01E−17	1.20E−22	5.33E−17
	Proposed PSO	9.25E−08	3.23E−07	1.27E−10	1.78E−06

(*continued*)

Table 4. (*continued*)

Function	Algorithm	Mean	Std	Min	Max
F6	PSO	1.95E+01	5.71E−01	1.82E+01	2.05E+01
	HS	3.09E+01	3.97E−01	3.02E+01	4.08E+01
	GA	1.61E+01	8.56E−01	1.44E+01	1.81E+01
	ABC	2.03E+01	2.54E−01	1.98E+01	2.08E+01
	CA	1.10E+01	2.36E+00	5.46E+00	1.74E+01
	BBPSO	1.85E+01	1.41E+00	1.42E+01	2.01E+01
	BBPSOV	3.27E+00	8.23E−01	2.08E+00	5.68E+00
	Proposed PSO	6.94E−05	1.17E−05	3.31E−07	5.31E−05
F7	PSO	5.28E+02	9.93E+01	3.09E+02	6.91E+02
	HS	3.06E+00	4.47E−01	2.08E+00	3.78E+00
	GA	2.56E+02	7.11E+01	1.45E+02	4.39E+02
	ABC	5.59E+02	7.47E+01	3.73E+02	7.23E+02
	CA	5.77E+00	5.48E+00	1.15E+00	2.83E+01
	BBPSO	7.27E+01	8.93E+01	1.04E+00	3.62E+02
	BBPSOV	1.78E−02	2.43E−02	1.14E−06	8.50E−02
	Proposed PSO	3.27E−04	4.37E−04	2.93E−05	1.70E−03
F8	PSO	1.40E+04	4.03E+03	6.44E+03	2.24E+04
	HS	2.25E+01	8.61E+00	8.69E+00	4.77E+01
	GA	2.35E+03	1.10E+03	1.02E+03	6.55E+03
	ABC	1.56E+04	3.57E+03	1.10E+04	2.35E+04
	CA	1.49E+02	1.14E+02	1.99E+01	4.62E+02
	BBPSO	2.67E+03	1.97E+03	1.79E+02	6.93E+03
	BBPSOV	5.79E−02	4.07E−02	1.85E−02	1.76E−01
	Proposed PSO	8.24E−07	9.19E−07	2.35E−08	3.08E−06

5 Conclusion and Future Work

In this study, a novel learning paradigm for PSO is introduce to balance exploration, exploitation and convergence while maintaining diversity of the swarm. The algorithm uses only the social and cognitive components of PSO for learning which further simplifies the algorithm. Particles Learn according to the class they fall in and these gives flexibility and robustness to the algorithm as different learning methods are in cooperated at the same time. The algorithm further introduces dynamism by varying class population at given intervals during the search. The algorithm is tested on a number of benchmark functions, compared with other swarm and evolutionary optimization algorithms including other advance PSO techniques, and see the superiority of the proposed algorithm. In future work, this algorithm will be tested on more functions like the 2013 or 2017 CEC suit. It will also be used to solve a real world problem.

Acknowledgement. This work is partially supported by Shenzhen Philosophy and Social Sciences Plan Project (SZ2019D018), Guangdong Provincial Soft Science Project (2019A101002075)

References

1. Kennedy, J., Eberhart, R.: Particle swarm optimization. In: Proceedings of IEEE International Conference on Neural Networks, vol. 4, pp. 1942–1948 (1995)
2. Eberhart, R.C., Kennedy, J.: A new optimizer using particle swarm theory. In: Proceedings of 6th International Symposium on Micro Machine and Human Science, pp. 39–43 (1995)
3. Kennedy, J., Mendes, R.: Population structure and particle swarm performance. In: Proceedings of the Congress on Evolutionary Computation, vol. 2, pp. 1671–1676 (2002)
4. Mendes, R., Kennedy, J., Neves, J.: The fully informed particle swarm: simpler, maybe better. IEEE Trans. Evol. Comput. **8**(3), 204–210 (2004)
5. Liang, J.J., Qin, A.K., Suganthan, P.N., Baska, S.: Comprehensive learning particleswarm optimizer for global optimization of multimodal functions. IEEE Trans. Evol. Comput. **10**(3), 281–295 (2006)
6. Taherkhani, M., Safabakhsh, R.: A novel stability-based adaptive inertia weight for particle swarm optimization. Appl. Soft Comput. **38**, 281–295 (2016)
7. Jie, J., Zang, J., Zheng, H., Hou, B.: Formalized model and analysis of mixed swarm based cooperative particle swarm optimization. Neurocomputing **174**, 542–552 (2016)
8. Zhao, X., Lin, W., Hao, J., Zuo, X., Yuan, J.: Clustering and pattern search for enhancing particle swarm optimization with Euclidean spatial neighborhood search. Neurocomputing **171**, 966–981 (2016)
9. Meng, A., Li, Z., Yin, H., Chen, S., Guo, Z.: Accelerating particle swarm optimization using crisscross search. Inf. Sci. **329**, 52–72 (2016)
10. Yu, K., Wang, X., Wang, Z.: Multiple learning particle swarm optimization with space transformation perturbation and its application in ethylene cracking furnace optimization. Knowl.-Based Syst. **96**, 156–170 (2016)
11. Zhang, L., Srisukkham, W., Neoh, S.C., Lim, C.P., Pandit, D.: Classifier ensemble reduction using a modified firefly algorithm: an empirical evaluation. Expert Syst. Appl. **93**, 395–422 (2018)
12. Mirjalili, S.: Dragonfly algorithm: a new meta-heuristic optimization technique for solving single-objective, discrete, and multi-objective problems. Neural Comput. Appl. **27**(4), 1053–1073 (2015). https://doi.org/10.1007/s00521-015-1920-1
13. Mirjalili, S.: Moth-flame optimization algorithm: a novel nature-inspired heuristic paradigm. Knowl.-Based Syst. **89**, 228–249 (2015)

Research on Crowd-Sensing Task Assignment Based on Fuzzy Inference PSO Algorithm

Jianjun Li[1,2(✉)], Jia Fu[1,2], Yu Yang[1,2], Xiaoling Wang[1,2], and Xin Rong[1,2]

[1] School of Computer and Information Engineering,
Harbin University of Commerce, Harbin 150028, China
854616040@qq.com
[2] Heilongjiang Provincial Key Laboratory of Electronic Commerce
and Information Processing, Harbin 150028, China

Abstract. To solve the problem of load unbalance in the case of few users and multi-task, a fuzzy inference PSO algorithm (FPSO) crowd sensing single objective task assignment method is proposed. With task completion time, user load balancing and perceived cost as the optimization goals, the fuzzy learning algorithm dynamically adjusts the learning factor in the PSO algorithm, so that the PSO algorithm can perform global search in the scope of the task space, thus obtaining the optimal task assignment solution set. Finally, the FPSO algorithm is compared with the PSO, GA and ABC algorithms on the optimization objectives, such as the algorithm convergence, task completion time, perceived cost and load balance. The experimental results show that the FPSO algorithm not only has faster convergence rate than the other algorithms, and shorten the task completion time, reduce the platform's perceived cost, improve the user's load balance, and have a good application effect in the crowd sensing task assignment.

Keywords: Fuzzy inference · Particle swarm algorithm · Crowd sensing · Task assignment · Load balancing

1 Introduction

With the widespread use of mobile users, smartphones have become an important bridge between the physical world and the online world. These advances have driven a new paradigm for collecting data and sharing data, namely group intelligence perception [1, 2]. At present, the application of group intelligence perception mainly includes: air quality monitoring [3], traffic information management [4], public information sharing [5] and so on. As the task assignment of the key problem of the crowd-sensing system, it is necessary to meet the optimization objectives under the constraints while completing the specified tasks, such as the shortest time to complete the task, the least perceived cost required to complete the task, the maximum benefit from completing the task, etc. Therefore, the main problem solved by the fuzzy inference PSO algorithm crowd sensing task assignment method is: how to perform task assignment for the multi-task of less user participants, which can ensure that the given number of tasks is completed in the

© Springer Nature Switzerland AG 2020
Y. Tan et al. (Eds.): ICSI 2020, LNCS 12145, pp. 189–201, 2020.
https://doi.org/10.1007/978-3-030-53956-6_17

shortest time, the perceived cost is the lowest, and user load balancing is optimal. For the problem of poor user load balance in mobile commerce, a fuzzy inference particle swarm crowd sensing task assignment method is proposed to improve the global search ability of the algorithm and avoid falling into local optimum. The main contributions of this paper include:

(1) A single objective task assignment optimization model is constructed, with task completion time, perceived cost and user load balance as the objective function.
(2) Based on the task assignment optimization model, a fuzzy inference particle swarm intelligence discernment task assignment method is proposed to solve the task assignment problem in discrete space.
(3) Through the simulation experiment, the proposed fuzzy inference particle swarm task assignment method (FPSO) is compared with PSO, GA and ABC algorithms. The experimental results show that fuzzy inference particle swarm optimization algorithm can minimize the task completion time, the lowest perceived cost and the maximum user load balance.

2 Related Works

The paper mainly reviews the literature on single target assignment and dual objective assignment.

For single-objective task assignment: Xiao et al. [6] considered the independent perceptual task scheme to minimize the task average completion time as the optimization goal, proposed the AOTA algorithm (average time-sensitive online task assignment algorithm); and considered the cooperative perception. In the task assignment scheme, the LOTA algorithm (the maximum completion time sensitive online task assignment algorithm) is proposed to minimize the maximum completion time of the task, and the important performance of the two algorithms is proved by simulation experiments. Yang et al. [7] considered the biggest problem of budget information in crowd-sensing, modeled by Gaussian process and proposed an algorithm BIM for quantifying the amount of information based on common standards based on information. The algorithm is suitable for the inability to obtain user cost. Xiao et al. [8] focused on the recruitment of users who are sensitive to deadlines for probabilistic collaboration. Mobile users perform crowd-sensing tasks within a certain probability range, and can recruit multiple user systems to perform common tasks to ensure expected the completion time does not exceed the deadline, and ag DUR (Criteria for Time-sensitive Greedy User Recruitment Algorithm) is proposed to maximize utility for recruiting users and to minimize perceived cost expenditures during the deadline. Azzam et al. [9] proposed a user group recruitment model based on genetic algorithm in order to recruit more participants to perform tasks, considering user interest points, related device perception capabilities and user basic information. By comparing with the personal recruitment model, the user group recruitment model based on genetic algorithm can improve the quality of collecting perceived data and ensure the reliability of perceived results. Yang et al. [10] designed the problem of heterogeneous sensor task assignment, and designed the heuristic algorithm to combine the genetic algorithm and the greedy algorithm to achieve the optimization goal of minimizing the total penalty caused by delay.

For dual-target assignments: Liu et al. [11] mainly studied the multi-task assignment of dual-objective optimization. For FPMT (less participants multitasking), to maximize the total number of tasks and minimize the moving distance as the optimization goal, use the MCMF (minimum cost maximum flow) theory to convert the FPMT problem, and consider the FPMT problem to build a new MCMF model. Xiong et al. [12] proposed a task assignment search algorithm based on maximizing space-time coverage and minimizing perceived cost in task assignment. Considering the perceived time and the quality of task completion. Wang et al. [13] only studied the perceptual task assignment problem to minimize the overall perceived cost and maximize the total utility of group intelligence perception, while meeting various quality of service (QoS) requirements, and proposed a new hybrid method combines the greedy algorithm with the bee colony algorithm. Messaoud et al. [14] mainly studied the participatory crowd-sensing user, and under the condition of satisfying information quality and energy constraints, to optimize the data perceptual quality and minimize the perceptual time of all participants, the appropriate task participants designed a crowd-sensing task assignment mechanism based on the tabu search algorithm combined with information quality and energy perception. Dindar Oz [15] proposed a solution to the problem of multi-objective task assignment, and designed a neighboring function that successfully solved the quadratic assignment problem for the metaheuristic algorithm, namely the maximum release of greedy allocation. Ziwen Sun et al. [16] proposed an attack location assignment (ALTA) algorithm based on multi-objective binary PSO optimization algorithm, which models the task as a multi-objective optimization model. The objective function is total task execution time, total energy consumption and load balancing. The method of nonlinearly adjusting inertia weight overcomes the shortcomings of binary particle swarm optimization (BPSO) which is easy to fall into local optimum.

In summary, for the crowd-sensing task assignment problem, most researchers only consider one or two optimization goals such as perceived cost, task completion time, and task completion quality, and there are few studies that satisfy both optimization goals. This paper considers the problem of poor user load balance encountered in the process of task problems, combines task completion time and perceived cost, establishes single objective task assignment optimization model, and proposes fuzzy inference particle swarm task assignment method to solve task assignment problem in discrete space.

3   Problem Description and Model Establishment

3.1   Description of the Problem

There are two main types of task assignments: multi-participant less tasks and fewer participants multitasking. This topic mainly studies the task assignment of multi-tasks with fewer participants. How to perform reasonable task assignment makes the user load balance more, and the user participation enthusiasm can reduce the task completion time and reduce the perceived cost. In a specific environment, after the cognitive platform publishes the task, the mobile terminal users who are interested in these tasks will confirm the tasks to indicate their intentions, and finally confirm the set of end users $U = \{u_1, u_2, \ldots, u_n\}$, and the set of the published task $R = \{r_1, r_2, \ldots, r_m\}$ (n < m). At the same time, an end user can complete one or more tasks. Reasonable task assignment enables each task target to be assigned to the appropriate user or user community to perform. Each user is also assigned to a task target that matches its own performance, using each user's maximum energy to complete the task, saving costs, improve task completion rates.

3.2 Single Objective Task Assignment Optimization Model Establishment

3.2.1 Model Assumption

In order to satisfy the establishment of the crowd-sensing task assignment model under defined conditions, the following assumptions are made:

(1) The task assignment studied in this paper is in a specific time range, and only the participating users and tasks are allocated during this time.
(2) The matching of the published tasks and the participating users within the coverage of the specified task area is not a task for all coverage areas. This narrows the scope of the task space and improves the quality of the task completion.
(3) For the tasks released by the crowd-sensing platform, users who are suitable for performing the task will be found. There is no case that the appropriate users cannot be found after the task is released.
(4) All users move from the current position to the task position at the same speed, regardless of the user's moving speed.

3.2.2 Notations

(See Table 1).

Table 1. Notations

Symbol	Notations
m	Number of tasks
n	Number of user
T	Total execution time of the tasks
t_{ij}	Time taken by the i user to perform the j task
β	Load balancing
C	Total perceived cost
c_i	Single task perceived cost
d_{ij}	Distance of user and task distance
A_i	Number of tasks performed by a single user
V_{ij}	Number of times the task was executed by the user
ω_{jk}	Tasks are only executed by one user
γ	Maximum number of tasks performed by the user

3.2.3 Model Objective Function

(1) Task completion time

The total time taken by n users to complete m tasks is T:

$$T = \sum_{i=1}^{n} \sum_{j=1}^{m} t_{ij} \tag{1}$$

Which t_{ij} represents the time taken by the i user to perform the j task.

(2) Load balance

Load balancing is measured using the ratio of task completion times. The expression is the ratio of each user's completion time to the total task completion time.

$$\beta = \frac{t_{ij}}{T}, 0 < \beta < 1 \tag{2}$$

Which t_{ij} represents the completion time of each user on behalf of each user, and T represents the total task completion time. The closer the task completion time to the total task completion time, the more balanced the load is. Therefore, the larger the β, the higher the load balance.

(3) Perceived cost

The perceived cost is related to the distance the user moves to the location of the task and is proportional to the distance traveled by the perceived user to the task location. If the position coordinate of the user 1 is (x_{u_1}, y_{u_1}), and the position coordinate of the task 1 is (x_{r_1}, y_{r_1}), the distance between the user and the task is $d_{11} = \sqrt{(x_{u_1} - x_{r_1})^2 + (y_{u_1} - y_{r_1})^2}$, if the ratio coefficient of the perceived cost and the moving distance is constant α, the perceived cost of the user to the task is $c_1 = \alpha d_{11}$. Therefore, the single objective task assignment optimization model is:

$$\begin{cases} \min T = \sum_{i=1}^{n} \sum_{j=1}^{m} t_{ij} \\ \min C = \sum_{i=1}^{n} c_i = \sum_{i=1}^{n} \sum_{j=1}^{m} \alpha d_{ij} \\ \max \beta = \frac{t_{ij}}{T} \end{cases} \tag{3}$$

The constraints are: (1) m tasks are completely assigned to n users; $\sum_{i=1}^{n} A_i = m$

(2) Each sensing task can only be executed once by a certain perceived user; $\sum_{i=1}^{n} V_{ij} = 1, \forall j \in R.$

(3) The task and the task can only be executed once by a certain user;

$$\sum_{i=1}^{m} \omega_{jk} = 1, \forall k \in R$$

$$\sum_{k=1}^{m} \omega_{jk} = 1, \forall j \in R$$

(4) The number of tasks assigned by each perceptual user is not more than γ; $1 \leq A_i \leq \gamma$

4 Fuzzy Inference Particle Swarm Intelligence Perception Task Assignment Method

4.1 Particle Swarm Optimization

Particle Swarm Optimization (PSO) is proposed to be influenced by bird predation behavior [17, 18]. The PSO algorithm is modeled as follows:

$$v_i(t) = wv_i(t) + c_1 r_1(t)(x_i^{(p)}(t) - x_i(t)) + c_2 r_2(t)(x_i^{(g)}(t) - x_i(t)) \tag{4}$$

$$x_i(t) = \begin{cases} 1, random < S(v_i(t+1)) \\ 0, others \end{cases} \tag{5}$$

Which $v_i(t)$ represents the velocity of the particle i at the iteration time t, i represents the number of particles, $i \in \{1, 2, \ldots, N\}$. w is the weight function, and c_1, c_2 are the weight acceleration coefficient; *random* is a uniformly distributed random variable in the interval (0,1); $x_i(t)$ represents the current position of the particle i at the iteration time t; $x_i^{(p)}(t)$ represents the individual optimal position of the particle i at the time of iteration t; $x_i^{(g)}(t)$ represents the global optimal position of the particle i at the time of iteration t; $Sig(x) = \frac{1}{1+\exp(-x)}$ represents the function.

4.2 PSO Algorithm Based on Fuzzy Inference Technology

In order to improve the overall performance of the swarm intelligence algorithm, fuzzy inference technology is added to the particle swarm optimization algorithm, and the learning factor in the PSO algorithm is dynamically adjusted by the fuzzy inference technology, so that the PSO algorithm can perform global search in the task space to avoid the algorithm falling into the local optimal area, so as to get the optimal task assignment solution set. In order to verify that the fuzzy inference PSO algorithm improves the performance of the original algorithm, several typical algorithms are selected for comparison. As shown in Fig. 1, the FPSO algorithm has a faster convergence rate than other algorithms.

In this paper, a fuzzy system with two inputs, two outputs and nine rules is designed. The input is the current optimal performance index (VB), the current iteration number iter; the output is c_1 and c_2; the Mamdani type [19] is blurred. The system adjusts c_1 and c_2.

(1) Fuzzy set: For the input variables V and iter, three fuzzy sets are defined: Low, Medium, High. For the output variables c_1 and c_2, five fuzzy sets are defined: Low, Medium Low, Medium, Medium High, and High, using a triangular membership function.

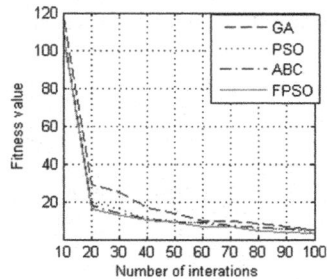

Fig. 1. Comparison of fitness values between different algorithms

(2) Variable range. In order to apply to various optimization problems, the input variables need to be converted to a normalized form, that is:

$$NV = \frac{VB - VB_{min}}{VB_{max} - VB_{min}} \tag{6}$$

$$Niter = \frac{iter}{iter_{max}} \tag{7}$$

Where VB is the current optimal estimate of the population; VB_{min} is the optimal estimate of the population; VB_{max} is the worst estimate of the population; iter is the current number of iterations; $iter_{max}$ is the maximum number of iterations of the algorithm. After normalization, the range of NV and Niter is [0, 1].

(3) Fuzzy rules: The overall idea of fuzzy rule setting is that in the early stage of algorithm iteration, when the evaluation value is poor, it needs strong global search ability, large shrinkage factor value, and the particle is the most Excellent learning ability is stronger than the ability of particles to learn from the society, that is $c_1 > c_2$; in the later stage of algorithm iteration, when the evaluation value is good, it needs less global search ability and shrinkage factor value, and the ability of particles to learn from society is stronger. The ability of a particle to learn optimally from itself, that is $c_1 < c_2$. Therefore, the following nine fuzzy rules are designed:

If NB is Low and Niter is Low, then c_1 is Medium Low and c_2 is Low.
If NB is Low and Niter is Medium, then c_1 is Medium High and c_2 is Medium.
If NB is Low and Niter is High, then c_1 is Medium High and c_2 is High.
If NB is Medium and Niter is Low, then c_1 is Medium Low and c_2 is Low.
If NB is Medium and Niter is Medium, then c_1 is Medium and c_2 is Medium.
If NB is Medium and Niter is High, then c_1 is Medium High and c_2 is High.
If NB is High and Niter is Low, then c_1 is Medium Low and c_2 is Low.
If NB is High and Niter is Medium, then c_1 is Medium Low and c_2 is Medium High.
If NB is High and Niter is High, then c_1 is Medium High and c_2 is High.

Therefore, the FPSO algorithm flow chart is shown in Fig. 2:

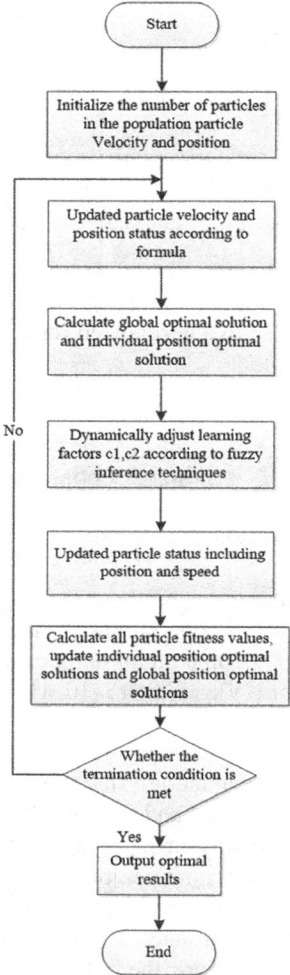

Fig. 2. FPSO algorithm flow chart

4.3 Fuzzy-Inferred Particle Swarm Crowd-Sensing Task Assignment

The particle swarm optimization algorithm in the swarm intelligence algorithm is used to map the optimal objective function and constraint conditions of the crowd-sensing task assignment problem to each element of the fuzzy inference particle swarm optimization algorithm to complete the task solving.

Task assignment process:

(1) Analyze the task assignment problem of mobile commerce group in a specific environment;
(2) Establishing a crowd-sensing single objective task assignment optimization model, and determining the task assignment constraints and optimization objective function, and transforming into the evaluation index function of the fuzzy inference particle swarm optimization algorithm;
(3) Using the FPSO algorithm to optimize the search for decision variables;
(4) Optimized search of decision variables by FPSO algorithm, and evaluate the optimization results according to the objective function;
(5) When the result satisfies the task assignment requirement, the output result ends with the FPSO algorithm.

5 Experimental Simulations

5.1 Experimental Environment and Parameter Settings

In the set environment of mobile commerce crowd-sensing, taking the Drip taxi as an example, the time spent by the passenger to release the taxi task to the vehicle owner to start executing the task within the specified time is recorded as the task completion time; The owner of the vehicle arrives at the distance that the passenger user releases the position of the ride, and the fuel cost, the loss fee, etc. consumed during the period are recorded as task-aware costs; the load balance is reflected in the number of tasks received by each vehicle owner. Therefore, the number of simulation tasks is 200, 400, 600, 800, 1000, and the maximum number of iterations of the algorithm is 200. Experiments are performed on the Matlab R2016b simulation platform. The FPSO algorithm parameter settings are shown in Table 2.

Table 2. FPSO algorithm parameter setting table

Parameter	Value
Population size	100
Learning factor c_1	2
Learning factor c_2	2
Maximum inertia factor w_{max}	0.9
Minimum inertia factor w_{min}	0.4
Maximum particle speed V_{max}	4

5.2 Experimental Process and Results Analysis

The experiment uses three optimization objectives to compare the advantages and disadvantages of several algorithms, namely task completion time, task-aware cost and load balancing. The experimental results and analysis are as follows:

(1) Analysis of task completion time

The task completion time comparison chart is shown in Fig. 3 and Fig. 4. It can be seen from Fig. 3 that PSO, ABC and GA algorithms have good convergence in the early iteration compared with the FPSO algorithm. However, with the increase of the number of iterations, PSO, ABC and GA are easy to fall into local optimum, and FPSO algorithm can achieve global optimization and enhance global search ability. Therefore, from Fig. 3 to complete the task total time and Fig. 4 to complete the task average time can be seen the superiority of the FPSO algorithm, while the task completion time is minimum.

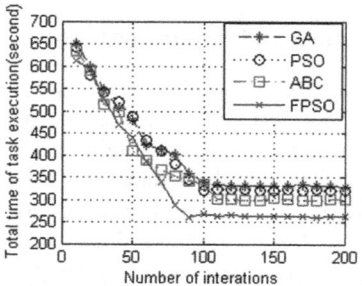

Fig. 3. Comparison of total tasks completed between different algorithms

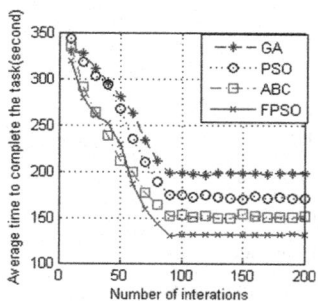

Fig. 4. Comparison of average time between tasks completed by different algorithms

(2) Perceived cost analysis

In the task assignment model, task completion time, perceived cost, and load balance are used as task optimization goals. In the experiment, we mainly consider the perceived cost of applying different algorithms to complete the comparison of the same number of tasks. The number of tasks is 200, 400, 600, 800 and 1000 respectively in FPSO, PSO, ABC and GA algorithms. It can be seen from Fig. 5, as the number of tasks increases (600, 800, 1000, respectively), the perceived cost of the FPSO algorithm is significantly lower than the PSO, ABC and GA algorithms.

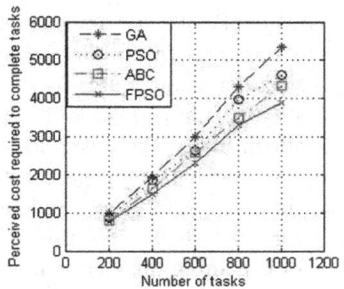

Fig. 5. Comparison of task-aware costs between different algorithms

(3) Load balance analysis

Load balancing is one of the important optimization goals in the paper. The greater the load balancing degree, the more reasonable the task assignment is, It can be seen from Fig. 6 that as the number of iterations increases, the curve of the FPSO algorithm is always above the PSO, ABC and GA algorithm curves, and finally tends to 0.92, so the FPSO algorithm is better implemented than the PSO, ABC and GA algorithms. Load balancing optimization goals make task assignments more reasonable.

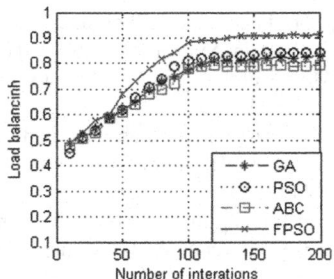

Fig. 6. Comparison of load balancing between different algorithms

Through the above experiments, we know that the FPSO algorithm can shorten the task completion time, reduce the perceived cost of the task, and balance the user's task load. Therefore, in the actual task allocation, it is possible to improve the timeliness of the task, reduce the operating cost of the platform, and improve the task completion amount of the user.

6 Conclusion

This paper proposes a crowd-sensing task assignment method based on fuzzy inference particle swarm optimization to solve the problem of load unbalance in task assignment. In the proposed method, the fuzzy inference technology can dynamically adjust the learning factor in the PSO algorithm, so that the PSO algorithm can perform global search in the task space to obtain the optimal task assignment solution set. Compared with PSO, ABC and GA algorithms, it has higher precision and better stability in solving performance. At the same time, applying FPSO algorithm for task assignment can greatly shorten task completion time, reduce platform perceived cost and improve user load balance. In the future research, not only the load balancing problem of task allocation should be considered, but also the user interest preference problem in the allocation process is also an important factor to determine whether the user performs the task. The user must not only consider the cost of executing the task, but also Considering the degree of interest in the task, a combination of various factors motivates the user to perform the task. Therefore, in the next study, the user's interest in the task can be listed as an important factor in the user's work, and the task assignment can be further studied.

Acknowledgement. This work was supported by the National Natural Science Foundation of China (60975071); Heilongjiang Province New Think Tank Research Project (No. 18ZK015); Heilongjiang Province Philosophy and Social Science Research Project (No. 17GLE298, 16EDE16); Harbin University of Commerce School-level Project(No. 18XN065); Harbin University of Commerce Ph.D. Research Foundation Fund (No. 2019DS029).

References

1. Lane, N.D., Miluzzo, E., Lu, H., Peebles, D., Choudhury, T., Campbell, A.T.: A survey of mobile phone sensing. IEEE Commun. Mag. **48**(9), 140–150 (2010)
2. Ganti, R.K., Ye, F., Lei, H.: Mobile crowd sensing: current state and future challenges. IEEE Commun. Mag. **49**(11), 32–39 (2011)
3. Zheng, Y., Liu, F., Hsieh, H.: U-Air: when urban air quality inference meets big data. In: Proceedings of the 19th ACM SIGKDD international conference on Knowledge discovery and data mining, pp. 1436–1444 (2013)
4. Coric, V., Gruteser, M.: Crowd sensing maps of on-street parking spaces. In: Proceedings of the 2013 IEEE International Conference on Distributed Computing in Sensor Systems, pp. 115–122 (2013)
5. Guo, B., Chen, H., Yu, Z., Xie, X., Huangfu, S., Zhang, D.: Flier Meet: a mobile crowd sensing system for cross-space public information reposting, tagging and sharing. IEEE Trans. Mob. Comput. **14**, 2020–2033 (2015)
6. Xiao, M., Wu, J., Huang, L., et al.: Online task assignment for crowd sensing in predictable mobile social networks. IEEE Trans. Mob. Comput. **16**(8), 2306–2320 (2017)
7. Yang, S., Wu, F., Tang, S., et al.: Selecting most informative contributors with unknown costs for budgeted crowd sensing. In: Proceeding of the 24th IEEE/ACM International Symposium on Quality of Service, pp. 1–6 (2016)
8. Xiao, M, Wu, J., Huang, H., et al.: Deadline-sensitive user recruitment for probabilistically collaborative mobile crowd sensing. In: Proceeding of the 36th International Conference on Distributed Computing Systems, pp. 721–722 (2017)

9. Azzam, R., Mizouni, R., Otrok, H., et al.: GRS: a group-based recruitment system for mobile crowd sensing. J. Netw. Comput. Appl. **72**, 38–50 (2016)
10. Yang, F., Lu, J.L., Zhu, Y., et al.: Heterogeneous task assignment in participatory sensing. In: Proceedings of IEEE Global Communications Conference, pp. 1–6 (2015)
11. Liu, Y., Guo, B., Wang, Y., et al.: Task me: multi-task assignment in mobile crowd sensing. In: Proceeding of ACM International Joint Conference on Pervasive and Ubiquitous Computing, pp. 403–414 (2016)
12. Xiong, H., Zhang, D., Chen, G., Crowd, I., et al.: Near-optimal task assignment for piggyback crowd sensing. IEEE Trans. Mob. Comput. **15**(8), 2010–2022 (2017)
13. Wang, Z., Huang, D., Wu, H., et al.: Qos-constrained sensing task assignment for mobile crowd sensing. In: Proceedings of IEEE Global Communications Conference, pp. 311–316 (2017)
14. Messaoud, R.B., Ghamri Doudane, Y.: Fair QoI and energy-aware task assignment in participatory sensing. In: Proceedings of IEEE Wireless Communications and Networking Conference, pp. 1–6 (2016)
15. Oz, D.: An improvement on the migrating birds optimization with a problem-specific neighboring function for the multi-objective task allocation problem. Expert Syst. Appl. **67**, 304–311 (2017)
16. Sun, Z., Liu, Y., Tao, L.: Attack localization task allocation in wireless sensor networks based on multi-objective binary particle swarm optimization. J. Netw. Comput. Appl. **112**, 29–40 (2018)
17. Poli, R., Kennedy, J., Blackwell, T.: Particle swarm optimization: an overview. Swarm Intell. **1**(1), 33–57 (2007)
18. Tao, X., Xu, J.: Multi-species cooperative particle swarm optimization algorithm. Control Decis. **24**(9), 1406–1411 (2009)
19. El Aziz, M.A., Hemdan, A.M., Ewees, A.A., et al.: Prediction of biochar yield using adaptive neuro-fuzzy inference system with particle swarm optimization. In: 2017 IEEE PES PowerAfrica Conference, pp. 115–120 (2017)

The Improvement of V-Shaped Transfer Function of Binary Particle Swarm Optimization

Dong-Yang Zhang[1,2], Jian-Hua Liu[1,2(✉)], Lei Jiang[1,2], Guan-Nan Bu[1,2], Ren-Yuan Hu[1,2], and Yi-Xuan Luo[1,2]

[1] School of Information Science and Engineering, Fujian University of Technology, Fuzhou, China
jhliu@fjnu.edu.cn
[2] Fujian Provicial Key Laboraty of BigData Mining and Application, Fuzhou, China

Abstract. Binary Particle Swarm Optimization (BPSO) is a swarm intelligence to optimize discrete space problems by extending the Particle Swarm Optimization. Its transfer function is the key element of BPSO. In this paper, a new V-shaped transfer function with a parameter k has been proposed. The parameter k was used to control the opening size of the transfer function. At first, the setting of the parameter k has been obtained by the experiments, and then the new V-shaped transfer with the optimal k value is compared with the other kinds of the V-shaped transfer functions by the experiment of feature selection. The results have indicated that the new V-shaped transfer function improved the performance of Binary Particle Swarm Optimization.

Keywords: Binary Particle Swarm Optimization · V-shaped transfer function · Classification accuracy · Iterative variation of distance between particles

1 Introduction

Particle Swarm Optimization (PSO) is an evolutionary computational technique proposed by J. Kennedy and R.C. Eberhart in 1995 [1] and [2]. It is inspired by the social behavior of birds and fish. It uses many particles (candidate solutions) to fly around in the search space to find the best solution. At the same time, they track the best location (best solution) in their own path. In other words, the particles will consider the best solution of their individual and the best solution of the group to get the final best solution. In 1998, Y.Shi and R.C.Eberhart added a weight to control the exploitation and exploration of the PSO algorithm [3]. Because the PSO is simple and computationally inexpensive, it is used in many fields, such as medical diagnosis [4], network scheduling [5], robot path planning [6], wavelength detection [7] and production scheduling [8] and many more.

In order to make the PSO algorithm solve the optimization problem of discrete space, J. Kennedy and R.C. Eberhart proposed a Binary Particle Swarm

Y. Tan et al. (Eds.): ICSI 2020, LNCS 12145, pp. 202–211, 2020.
https://doi.org/10.1007/978-3-030-53956-6_18

Optimization (BPSO) based on PSO algorithm [9] to solve the optimization problem of discrete space in 1997. In 2008, Yin et al. proposed a new location update formula to improve the BPSO algorithm [10]. In the same year, Wang et al. proposed a new probability mapping formula and applied it to solve the discrete combination of knapsack problems [11]. A key step in BPSO is to require a transfer function to transform the real value to a binary value of 0 or 1. The classical transfer function is an S-shaped transfer function. In 2011, Liu et al. experimentally analyzed the S-shaped transfer function and found the algorithm lack the late local search ability, a V-shaped transfer function, which enhanced the local search ability of the algorithm and effectively improved the performance of the BPSO algorithm [12]. Seyedali et al. also proposed a similar V-shaped transfer function, and compared four S-shaped transfer functions and four V-shaped transfer functions, which proved that the V-shaped transfer function has the advantage of the algorithm [13].

From the above analysis, the V-shaped transfer function is of great significance for the improvement and optimization of the BPSO algorithm. Although the V-shaped transfer function has better performance than the S-shaped transfer function, but what is the best form of the V-shaped transfer function, and how to control the V-shaped transfer function opening size and studied whether the opening size of the V-shaped transfer function has influence on the performance of the algorithm. In this paper proposes a new V-shaped transfer function, which has a parameter k to control the opening size of this V-shaped transfer function, and study the setting of the analysis parameter k algorithm. The parameter k is set to the principle method, and the optimal k-value transfer function is compared with other V-shaped transfer functions to verify that the proposed method performs better.

2   BPSO Algorithm and Its Transfer Function Principle

Each particle in the BPSO should consider the current position, the current velocity, the distance of the individual best solution *pbest*, and the distance to the global optimal solution *gbest* to updata its position. The mathematical model of PSO is shown in Eq.(1) and Eq.(2).

$$v_{id}(t+1) = \omega v_{id}(t) + c_1 \times rand \times (pbest - x_{id}(t)) + c_2 \times rand \times (gbest - x_{id}(t)) \quad (1)$$

$$x_{id}(t+1) = x_{id}(t) + v_{id}(t) \quad (2)$$

where t is the current number of iterations, c_1 and c_2 are the acceleration coefficients, $v_{id}(t)$ is the speed of the ith particle in the dth dimension at the tth generation iteration, w is the inertia weight, $rand$ is a random number between 0 and 1, $x_{id}(t)$ is the current position of the ith particle in the dth dimension at the tth generation iteration at iteration t, *pbest* is the best solution obtained by the ith particle in the dth dimension at the tth generation iteration so far, and *gbest* indicates the best solution obtained by the particle swarm so far. Equation(1) is the velocity updating formula of the particle, and Eq.(2) is the position updating formula of the particle.

In order to make the PSO algorithm optimize the problem of discrete binary space and extend the application of PSO algorithm. BPSO's speed updating formula, Eq.(1), is the same as the original PSO algorithm's. But the particle updating formula Eq.(2) is not used for BPSO. In order to make the value of the velocity convert as a probability of binary taking 0 or 1, the transfer function uses the Sigmoid function of the formula Eq.(3).

$$s(v_{id}(t)) = \frac{1}{1 + e^{-v_{id}(t)}} \tag{3}$$

The Sigmoid function image is shown a kind of S-shaped function.

After converting the velocity into a probability value, each dimension of position binary vector is updated using its velocity probability formula as Eq.(4).

$$x_{id}(t+1) = \begin{cases} 0, \ if \ rand \leq s(v_{id}(t)) \\ 1, \ if \ rand \geq s(v_{id}(t)) \end{cases} \tag{4}$$

The transfer function is the probability of changing each dimension of the position vector from 0 to 1, and vice versa. The main function of the transfer function Eq.(3) in the BPSO is to convert the position real value to the probability value between $[0, 1]$, and then use the formula Eq.(4) to make the value of the bit two values of $\{0, 1\}$. According to Rashedi et al. [14], the design of such a transfer function should consider some principles.

According to the principles proposed by Rashedi et al. it can be found that the sigmoid function is a function with monotonically increaseing and does not meet the rule that the probability of its position changing increases as the absolute value of the speed increases. According to the literature [12], the original BPSO has the too strong global search ability because of using the sigmoid function as its transfer function. Therefore, it is irrational that the BPSO algorithm uses Eq.(3) as a transfer function. Rashedi et al. proposed a kind of V-shaped transfer function with adopting different position update formula as the Eq.(5).

$$x_{id}(t+1) = \begin{cases} (x_{id}(t))^{-1}, \ if \ rand < s(v_{id}(t)) \\ x_{id}(t), \qquad if \ rand \geq s(v_{id}(t)) \end{cases} \tag{5}$$

where $(x_{id}(t))^{-1}$ is the complement operator of $x_{id}(t)$.

Comparing with Eq.(4), Eq.(5) does not force the particles to be changed with the value of 0 or 1. The transfer function uses a kind of V-shaped function that is called a "V-shaped transfer function." The original V-shaped transfer function proposed by WangLin et al. It can be found that V-shaped transfer function satisfies the principles proposed by Rashedi et al.

$$s(v_{id}(t)) = |\tanh(v_{id}(t))|. \tag{6}$$

3   A New V-Shaped Transfer Function

According to the above analysis, the V-shaped transfer function has more advantage over the S-shaped transfer function, so the BPSO's transfer function should be a kind of V-shaped function. However, what kind of V-shaped function is appropriate, so this paper does some analytical experiments.

At first, a new V-shaped transfer function is proposed as shown in Eq.(7).

$$s(v_{id}(t)) = 1 - e^{-k \cdot |v_{id}(t)|}, \tag{7}$$

where $k > 0$.

The V-shaped transfer function Eq.(7) has a parameter variable k, which can control the opening size of the V-shaped transfer function, and can be used to determine the relationship between the opening size of the V-shaped transfer function and the performance of BPSO. Figure 1 demonstrates the opening size of the transfer functions Eq.(7) with different k values. The value of the transfer function with different k is guaranteed to vary between $[0, 1]$, and satisfy the principle of the transfer function. As the transfer functions of Eq.(7), parameter k control the opening size of the transfer function as shown in Fig. 1, which can be found that the opening becomes smaller as the value of k increases.

Therefore, the transfer function Eq.(7) with parameter k can be used to analyze performace of BPSO with difference opening size of V-shaped transfer function.

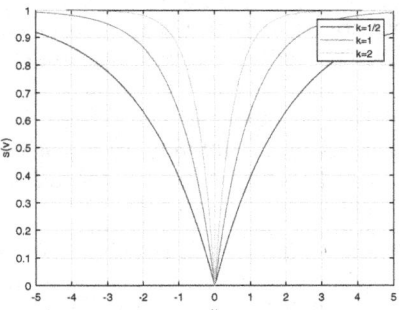

Fig. 1. k value and the size of the opening

4 k Value Analysis of the Transfer Function

4.1   The Average Distance of Particle Swarm

Definition: The average distance of particle swarm is the average of the distance between each particle in the particle swarm and the global optimal particle, which calculation formula is Eq.(8).

$$L = \frac{\sum\limits_{i=1}^{n} (\sum\limits_{d=1}^{D} g_d \bigoplus x_{id})}{n}, \tag{8}$$

where L represents the average distance of particle swarm which is the value of the average distance of all particles to the global optimal particle, $\oplus$ is the logical operator XOR, n is the number of particles, D is the dimension, and x_{id} is the current position of the ith particle in the $d$dimension Position, g_d is the position of the global optimal particle in the d dimension.

XOR operaor $\oplus$ can calculate the number of different binay value beteween two binay vectors. BPSO's particle is a binay code, so L represents the average difference of particles from the global particle. L can be used to measure the algorithm's global exploration and local exploitation capabilities. The larger L is, the stronger the global exploration is, the weaker the local exploitation is. Conversely, the smaller the L, the weaker the global exploration and the stronger the local exploitation. According to the basic principle of the swarm intelligence algorithm, the L value should constantly be smaller and smaller. By analyzing the change of the L value over iteration, the relation of the opening size of V-shaped transfer function on the performance of the algorithm can be revealled. Thus Eq.(8) can be used to analyze the principle of setting the value of k for the V-shaped transfer function Eq.(7).

4.2 The Experimental Analysis on k Value

For the sake of experimental analysis on k value of Eq.(7), BPSO with the S-shaped transfer function of Eq.(7) is appleid to feature selection.

Feature selection requires classification accuracy of supervised learner as the fitness function of BPSO. K-Nearest Neighbor(KNN) algorithm is a common supervised learner, so KNN is used as the classification algorithm for the feature selection experiment.

The algorithm parameters in the experiment are set as shown in Table 1. The test data for feature selection is six different types of data sets from the UCI machine learning database, which are shown in Table 2.

Table 1. Algorithm parameter settings

C_1,C_2	Total group number	Iterative algebra	KNN parameter k
2	20	1000	5

The k of transfer function Eq.(7) is set as two group of value, the first group's value are greater than 1 as $\{1. 2, 3, 4, 5\}$, the second group's value are less than 1 as $\{1, \frac{1}{2}, \frac{1}{3}, \frac{1}{4}, \frac{1}{5}\}$. The BPSO algorithm with V-shaped transfer function Eq.(7) using two group of k value is applied for feature selection on datasets in Table 2. During the iteration of BPSO for experimention conducting, L is calculated in each generation of iteration. Figure 2, 3, 4, 5, 6, 7, 8 and 9 show the changes of L over iteration for BPSO to do feature selction for the datasets of Table.2. Each figure of Fig. 2, 3, 4, 5, 6, 7, 8 and 9 include two subfigures which the left subfigure is about k in the first group, the right fiugre is about k in the second group.

Table 2. Dataset information

Data set	Dimension	Number of samples	Number of categories
Snoar	60	208	2
SPECTF	43	267	2
Lonosphere	34	351	2
WDBC	30	569	2
SPECT	22	267	2
Vehicle	18	846	4
Wine	13	178	13
Vowel	10	990	11

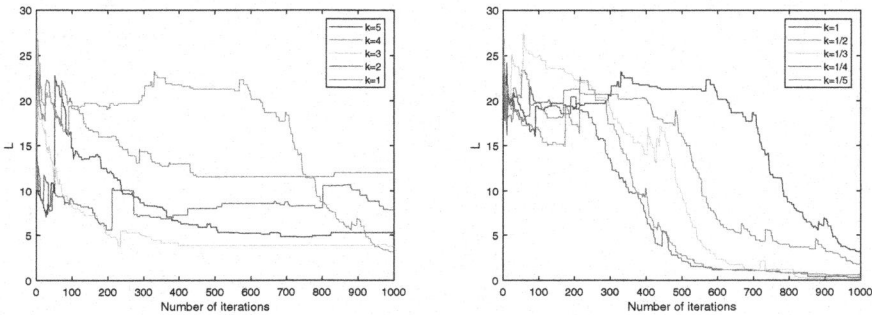

Fig. 2. L change over iteration for selection feature in dataset sonar

Investigating the left subfigures of Fig. 2, 3, 4, 5, 6, 7, 8 and 9, when $k \geq 1$ in the first group, L starts to decrease rapidly, and then tends to be stable quickly over iteration, which indicates that the algorithm are lack of the global exploration and has too strong local exploitation, so BPSO with Eq.(7) is inconsistent with the principle of heuristic random search when $k \geq 1$. Meanwhile, by observing the right subfigures of Fig. 2, 3, 4 and 5, L changes from big to small gradually over iteration when $k \leq 1$ which indicates that BPSO algorithm has the strong global exploration ability in the early stage and has strong local exploitation ability in the later stage. Therefore, BPSO with transfer function Eq.(7) satisfies the basical principle of heuristic random search when $k \leq 1$. In one word, the value range of k should be less than or equal to 1.

4.3 The Experimental Analysis on BPSO with Different k Values

In order to decide the appropriate range of k, when the experiment are conducted in Sect. 4.2, using transfer function Eq.(7) of with diferent k, BPSO do feature selection with KNN learner to classify dataset in Table 2. The classifing curracy

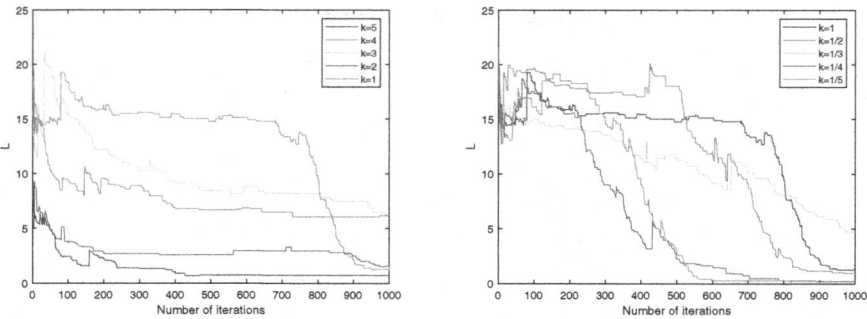

Fig. 3. L change over iteration for selection feature in dataset SPECTF

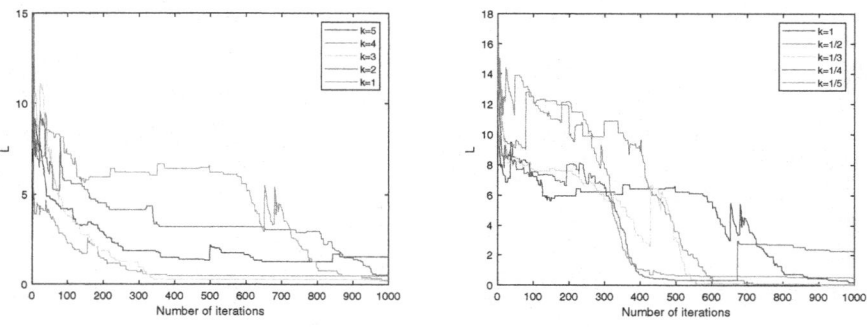

Fig. 4. L change over iteration for selection feature in dataset Ionosphere

is used to evalute the performace of BPSO with the V-shaped transfer function of different k so as to investigate which value of $k \geq 1$ is best for transfer function Eq.(7).

For comparison with different k, the k value of the transfer function Eq.(7) is set in $\{5, 4, 3, 2, 1, \frac{1}{2}, \frac{1}{3}, \frac{1}{4}, \frac{1}{5}\}$.

BPSO algorithm with each k value transfer function is iteratively run for 1000 generations and runs 5 times. The average of classifing accuracy over 5 times is calculated for each dataset in Table 2. The experimental result are shown in Table 3.

Dim denotes the dimension of dataset in Table 2. It is found from Table 3 that when the $k > 1$, the performance of the BPSO algorithm cannot access to the optimal. The larger the k value is, the worse the performance of the BPSO algorithm is, so k cannot be set as the value which is great to 1, which is in accordance with the analysis on L in subsection 4.2. However, when $k \leq 1$, k becomes smaller and smaller with dimension decreasing, which affects the change of classification accuracy. However, it can be found from Table 3 that the values

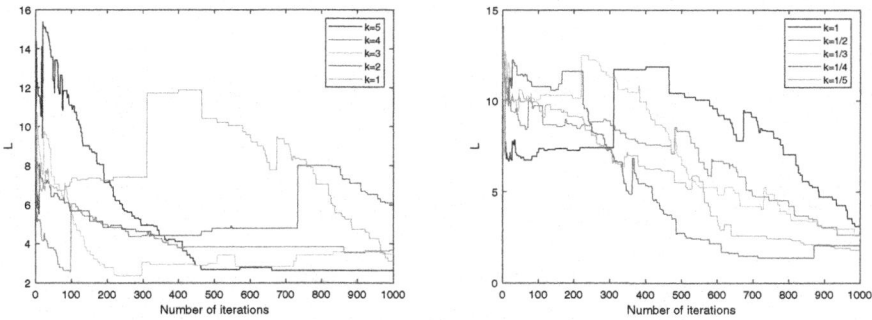

Fig. 5. L change over iteration for selection feature in dataset WDBC

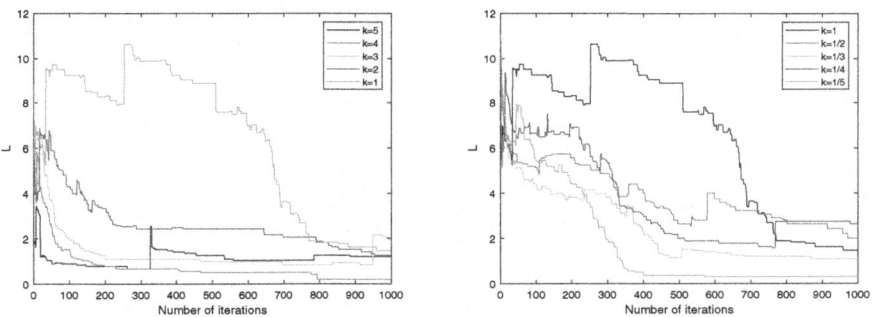

Fig. 6. L change over iteration for selection feature in dataset SPECT

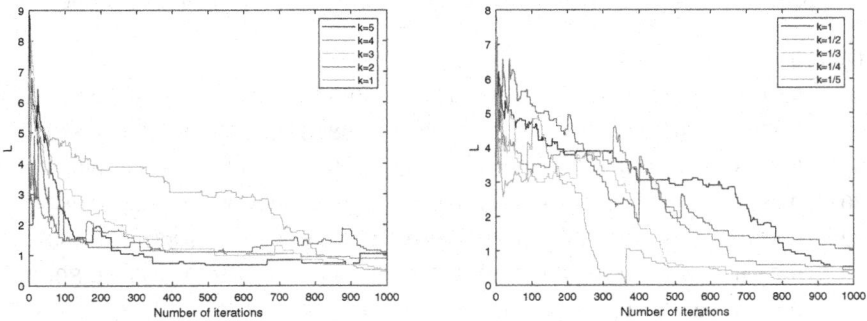

Fig. 7. L change over iteration for selection feature in dataset vehicle

obtained at $\frac{1}{2}$ are relatively high in classification accuracy, so it can be roughly concluded that the opening size of transfer function Eq.(7) will have the highest performance in the transfer function when $k = \frac{1}{2}$.

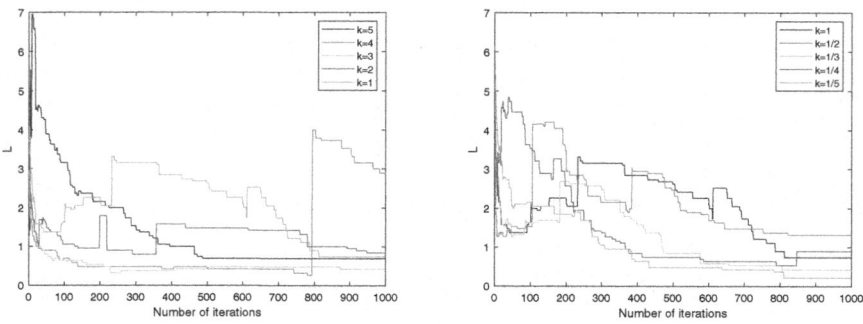

Fig. 8. L change over iteration for selection feature in dataset wine

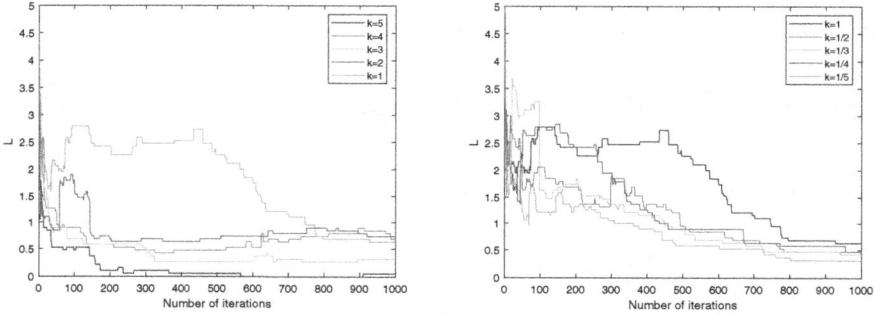

Fig. 9. L change over iteration for selection feature in dataset vowel

Table 3. Classification accuracy of feature selection for different k value

Dim	5	4	3	2	1	$\frac{1}{2}$	$\frac{1}{3}$	$\frac{1}{4}$	$\frac{1}{5}$
60	0.9178	0.9217	0.9231	0.9298	0.9399	**0.9548**	0.9442	0.9399	0.9447
43	0.8545	0.8611	0.8503	0.8623	0.8689	**0.8823**	0.8775	0.8794	0.8805
34	0.9208	0.9219	0.9253	0.9288	0.9362	0.9402	0.9425	**0.9419**	0.9385
30	0.9821	0.9845	0.9831	0.9835	0.9849	0.9852	0.9859	**0.9863**	0.9849
22	0.8734	0.8786	0.8771	0.8786	0.8809	**0.8816**	0.8816	0.8816	0.8831
18	0.7896	0.7915	0.7943	0.7950	0.7948	0.7981	0.7999	0.7995	**0.8000**
13	0.9955	0.9955	0.9966	0.9978	0.9955	**0.9989**	0.9966	0.9978	0.9978
10	0.9519	0.9485	0.9496	0.9508	0.9523	0.9508	0.9515	**0.9538**	0.9519

5   Conclusion

In this paper, the opening size of the V-shaped transfer function of the discrete binary particle swarm optimization algorithm is studied. The experimental results of the classification accuracy and the iterative variation between the particles by the V-shaped transfer function with different opening sizes indicate that the optimal point of the performance can be obtained when the parameter of the control opening size k is $\frac{1}{2}$.

References

1. Eberhart, R., Kennedy, J.: A new optimizer using particle swarm theory. In: MHS 1995 Sixth International Symposium on Micro Machine Human Science (2002)
2. Kennedy, J., Eberhart, R.: Particle swarm optimization. In: ICNN 1995-International Conference on Neural Networks (2002)
3. Shi, Y.H., Eberhart, R.C.: A modified particle swarm optimizer. In: 1998 IEEE International Conference on Evolutionary Computation Proceedings. IEEE World Congress on Computational Intelligence. IEEE (1998)
4. Chandra, S., Bhat, R., Singh, H.A.: PSO based method for detection of brain tumors from MRI. In: 2009 World Congress on Nature Biologically Inspired Computing (NABIC). IEEE (2010)
5. Martino, V.D., Mililotti, M.: Scheduling in a grid computing environment using genetic algorithms. In: IPDPS 2002 Proceedings of the International Parallel and Distributed Processing Symposium (2002)
6. Masehian, E., Sedighizadeh, D.: A multi-objective PSO-based algorithm for robot path planning. In: 2010 IEEE International Conference on Industrial Technology. IEEE (2010)
7. Liang, J.J., Suganthan, P.N., Chan, C.C., et al.: Wavelength detection in FBG sensor network using tree search DMS-PSO. IEEE Photonics Technol. Lett. **18**(12), 1305–1307 (2006)
8. Liu, J., Fan, X., Qu, Z.: An improved particle swarm optimization with mutation based on similarity. In: International Conference on Natural Computation (2007)
9. Kennedy, J., Eberhart, R.C.: A discrete binary version of the particle swarm algorithm. In: IEEE International Conference on Systems (2002)
10. Yin, P.Y.: A discrete particle swarm algorithm for optimal polygonal approximation of digital curves. J. Vis. Commun. Image Represent. **15**(2), 241–260 (2004)
11. Zhen, L., Wang, L., Huang, Z.: Probability-based binary particle swarm optimization algorithm and its application to WFGD control. In: International Conference on Computer Science Software Engineering (2008)
12. Jianhua, L., Ronghua, Y., Shuihua, S.: Analysis of discrete binary particle swarm optimization algorithm. J. Nanjing Univ. Nat. Sci. **5**, 504–514 (2011)
13. Mirjalili, S., Lewis, A.: S-shaped versus V-shaped transfer functions for binary particle swarm optimization. Swarm Evol. Comput. **9**, 1–14 (2013)
14. Rashedi, E., Nezamabadi-Pour, H., Saryazdi, S.: BGSA: binary gravitational search algorithm. Nat. Comput. **9**(3), 727–745 (2010)
15. Cover, T.M., Hart, P.: Nearest neighbor pattern classification. In: Proceeding of the IEEE Transactions Information Theory, pp. 21–27 (1967)
16. Kang, L., Minrui, F., Li, J., Irwin, G.W. (eds.): ICSEE/LSMS -2010. LNCS, vol. 6329. Springer, Heidelberg (2010). https://doi.org/10.1007/978-3-642-15597-0

Ant Colony Optimization

Hybrid Ant Colony Optimization-Based Method for Focal of a Disease Segmentation in Lung CT Images

Mingli Lu[1](✉), Benlian Xu[2], Weijian Qin[1], and Jian Shi[1,2]

[1] School of Electrical and Automatic Engineering,
Changshu Institute of Technology, Changshu 215500, China
luml@cslg.edu.cn
[2] School of Mechanical Engineering,
Changshu Institute of Technology, Changshu 215500, China

Abstract. The detection of chest CT scan images of the lung play a key role in clinical decision making for some lung disease, such as tumors, pulmonary tuberculosis, solitary pulmonary nodule, lung masses and so on. In this paper, a novel automated CT scan image segmentation algorithm based on hybrid Ant Colony algorithm and snake algorithm is proposed. Firstly, traditional snake algorithm is used to detect the possible edge points of focal of a disease. Then Ant Colony Optimization (ACO) algorithm is applied to search the possible edge points of focal of a disease repeatedly. Finally, real edges can be extracted according to the intensity of pheromones. Simulation experiment results demonstrate that the proposed algorithm is more efficient and effective than the methods we compared it to.

Keywords: Ant Colony Optimization · Snake algorithm · Image segmentation · Edge detection

1 Introduction

Lung CT scanning is used to detect: tumors in lungs, pneumonia, tuberculosis, emphysema, diffuse interstitial lung diseases, inflammation or other diseases of pleura, the membrane covering the lungs. Automatic identification of lung disorders in lung CT scan images can contribute to lung disease early diagnosis. Edge is the most important features for focal of a disease in CT images, and this feature can be used in target recognition and segmentation. In recent years, research on Segmentation of medicine images has become a hot topic and it has been widely applied in cancer metastasis, developmental biology, immunology response, etc. Conventional and manual analysis of these images is a tedious process. Accuracy Rely on experience and knowledge of observer. However, with the increasing of datasets, manual work is becoming heavy workload and inefficiency. Automated segmentation processing can extract a richness of information far beyond what a manual work can observe. For efficiency and accuracy, the development of automated segmentation methods that eliminate the bias and variability to a

© Springer Nature Switzerland AG 2020
Y. Tan et al. (Eds.): ICSI 2020, LNCS 12145, pp. 215–222, 2020.
https://doi.org/10.1007/978-3-030-53956-6_19

certain degree is of great importance, which has very broad prospects in clinical decision making.

Because medical images are complex in nature, automatic segmentation of medical images is a challenging task and medical image segmentation continues to be a difficult problem [1]. The challenges of medical image segmentation have been attracting more and more research efforts [2–9]. In [6], Elizabeth et al. proposed an approach to identify the most promising slice to diagnose lung cancer from chest CT images. In [7], an efficient cervical disease diagnosis approach using segmented images and cytology reporting is proposed. In [8], an effective liver vessel segmentation method was proposed based on two techniques, including centerline constraint and intensity model. In [9], a new adaptive approach to lung segmentation based on a non-parametric adaptive active contour method (ACM) is proposed. In summary, from the review presented above, it is found that although some of the segmentation methods mentioned above produce very good segmentation results, the overall performance of the segmentation methods still need to be improved in some situations.

ACO is a population based meta-heuristic approach proposed by Dorigo et al., which is inspired by social behavior of ant colonies and belongs to a branch of swarm intelligence [10]. In nature, ants can find the shortest route between their nest and a food source by chemical materials called pheromone that they leave when moving. Traveling salesman problem (TSP) is the first problem solved by ACO [11]. At present, it is well known that ACO is effective for many optimization problems, such as image processing problems [12], clustering problems [13], vehicle routing problems [14] and resource allocation problem [15].

In the ant colony algorithm for edge detection, searching for interest area is looked upon as an ant colony foraging process. The basic idea applying ACO to edge detection could be explained by a graph, as shown in Fig. 1.

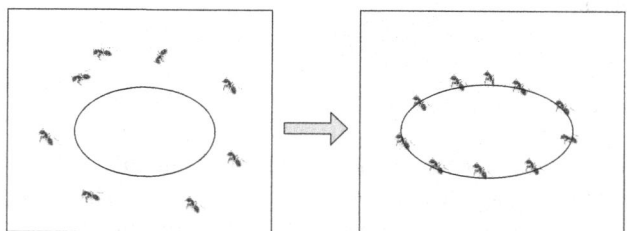

Fig. 1. The evolution process of ant searching for foods

In this paper, motivated by the self-organization ability and positive feedback mechanism of ants, we aim to develop a novel ant-based algorithm for lung CT image segmentation. The remainder of this article is structured as follows. In Sect. 2, the focal of a disease segmentation method is described in details. Section 3 presents the experimental results of the focal zone segmentation. Finally, the fourth section includes the concluding remarks.

2 Algorithm

2.1 Algorithm Description

The edge detection of focal zone in lung CT image sequence is very challenging, such as poor signal-to-noise ratios images, intensity inhomogeneity, irregular surfaces and edge branching. As the traditional approach was insufficient for overcome these challenges. So, our goal in this research is to develop a new method for automatic edge extracted in lung CT scan images based on hybrid ant colony algorithm and snake algorithm. The first step in this method is rough edge extracted from lung CT scan image by snake method. Then Ant Colony Optimization (ACO) algorithm is applied to search the possible edge points of focal of a disease, repeatedly. Finally, real edges can be extracted according to the intensity of pheromones. To visualize our proposed algorithm in a full view, we represent the flowchart of the proposed algorithm (Fig. 2).

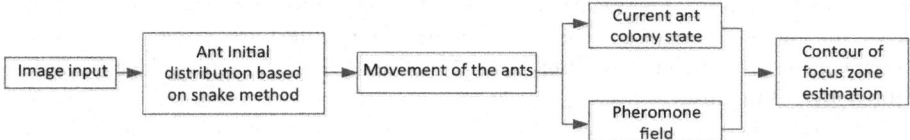

Fig. 2. The main framework of our proposed method

2.2 Edge Detection Based on Hybrid Ant Colony Algorithm and Snake Algorithm

Edge is the most important information in CT scan images. Edge characteristics are extracted to clinical decision making for some lung disease. Image edge detection based on hybrid ACO is distributing a certain number of ants on the two dimensional image to search edges by establishing the pheromone matrix, in which each element represents edge information of each pixel. The algorithm contains three steps: Initialization, movement of the ants and pheromone Update.

2.2.1 Initialization of the Algorithm

The initialization step is performed at the beginning. A number of ants are randomly assigned on image the possible edge. The initial value of each pheromone matrix component $\tau(0)$ is set to be constant. To help the ACO work faster in finding edge of focal zone, the prior information is utilized to generate initial ant colony. Considered ants are assigned on the rough outline of focal zone, which can be obtained by snake algorithm [16, 17].

Snake segmentation algorithm is used to separate the lung tissues from the CT slice by finding a suitable outline. In this method some points are required to initialize the process, the segmentation results are dependent on the choice of outline. Snake segmentation algorithm general consists of drawing curves, starting outside or inside the object of interest. The traditional approach is given as follows.

Aim to adapt an initial curve to the shape of the region of interest. The curvature occurs by the forces acting on it and evolves to the edges of the object. The deformation is guided by an energy function to be minimized:

$$B = \sum_{d=0}^{M-1} \{B_{int}[c(d)] + B_{ext}[c(d)]\} \qquad (1)$$

where c is the initial contour curve and $c(d)$ is point on the curve c, M is the total length of c. $B_{int}[c(d)]$ is the internal energy, which depends on the internal features within the segmentation curve and can be given by

$$B_{int}[c(d)] = \sigma(d)c'(d) + \upsilon(d)c''(d) \qquad (2)$$

where σ and υ are the parameters to effect the evolution of curvature at a point d of the curve, which can be adjusted according to the first and second derivatives, respectively. At the same time, $B_{ext}[c(d)]$ represents the external energy of this curve. The environment outside the curve can change this energy. The behavior of the curve, such as expansion or shrinkage is continue guided by an energy function B, until it reaching the boundaries of the object of interest.

After rough edge of focal zone is obtained by snake method, ants are assigned on the rough edge of focal zone.

2.2.2 Movement of the Ants

In contrast with classic ACO, here, nodes in the graph can be viewed as pixels of the image. During search process, an ant chooses which pixel to move to according to heuristics information and the pheromone amount of the four surrounding pixels. Assume ant a at the current position of pixel i, The probability that ant a moves from the pixel (i) to its neighboring pixel (j) is computed by

$$p_{ij}^a(t) = \begin{cases} \dfrac{[\tau_j(t)]^\gamma [\eta_j]^\beta}{\sum_{j' \in \Omega(i)} [\tau_{j'}(t)]^\gamma [\eta_j]^\beta}, & if \ \ j \in \Omega(i) \\ 0, & otherwise \end{cases} \qquad (3)$$

where p_{ij}^a is the probability with which ant a chooses to move from the pixel i to the pixel j at the t-th iteration. $\Omega(i)$ is the set of all available neighbors of pixel i, τ_j is the pheromone value on pixel j at the t-th iteration, and η_j is heuristic value, for each pixel, usually represents the attractiveness of the pixel. representing the degree of similarity between the current pixel and the target pixel. γ and β are the weights of the pheromone value and heuristic value, respectively. γ determines the relatively importance of the track, reflecting the effect of accumulated information of the ant in the course of movement. β makes up the comparative importance of heuristic information.

η_j is heuristic information of pixel j, which is estimated based on gradient information of image.

$$\eta_j = (\left| I_j^{(x+1,y)} - I_j^{(x-1,y)} \right| + \left| I_j^{(x-1,y+1)} - I_j^{(x+1,y-1)} \right|$$

$$+\left|I_j^{(x,y+1)}-I_j^{(x,y-1)}\right|+\left|I_j^{(x+1,y+1)}-I_j^{(x-1,y-1)}\right|)/I_{max} \tag{4}$$

where $I_j^{(x,y)}$ denotes intensity level on pixel j with the coordinate (x,y). I_{max} is the maximum intensity value of the image.

2.2.3 Pheromone Updating

Pheromone is another important concept in ACO algorithms. In this work, we considered two kinds of pheromone, diffusive pheromone and accumulative pheromone. Diffusive pheromone is the propagated information from the different channels of the neighbor pixels. Accumulative pheromone is the accumulative information in each step. When all ants complete a search cycle, pheromone on pixel j is updated according to the following formula:

$$\tau_j(t) \leftarrow (1-\varphi)\tau_j(t-1)+\Delta\tau_j(t-1)+h_j(t-1) \tag{5}$$

where φ is pheromone decay coefficient representing pheromone evaporation ($0<\varphi<1$). $\Delta\tau_j(t-1)=\sum_{a=1}^{N}\Delta\tau_j^a$ represents the increment of pheromones in the pixel j in this iteration, $\Delta\tau_j^a$ is the amount of pheromone left by ant a on pixel j. Term $h_j(t-1)$ models all diffusion input to pixel j.

With the increase of iteration, the search router of the ant gradually converges to the true contour, and the pheromone on the edge is significantly higher than other regions. Once the searching behavior of each ant is finished, thus edge according to the pheromone distribution can be extracted.

3 Experiments

In this section, we will discuss the implementation process in detail to verify the validity of our proposed method. All experiments were carried out in MATLAB (R2016a) on a 1.7 GHz processor computer with 4G random access memory.

Several human lung CT scans image with different disease, such as pulmonary tuberculosis (frame D0100249, D0100252, D0100263–D0100265), solitary pulmonary nodules (frame D0100151), were selected as the experimental images and the image was 512×512 pixels. The key parameters are as follows: $N_{ant}=300$ is the number of ant colony, $N_{max}=30$ is the number of iteration times, the heuristic factor γ and β are 0.5, 1 respectively. The experimental results are shown in Fig. 3 and Fig. 4. Traditional ant colony algorithm and our proposed hybrid segmentation algorithm are compared that uses the same test images.

To evaluate the performance of the proposed approach on segmentation, we would like to compare our algorithm with other techniques, such as the traditional ant colony algorithm [18]. According to Fig. 3 and Fig. 4, the results obtained in this work show that our proposed hybrid segmentation method presents promising potential and has excellent results for accuracy compared to the traditional ant colony algorithm.

In addition, average computation time (over 100 Monte-Carlo simulations) using our proposed method is not exceeding 15 s for all frames. The average time was shorter

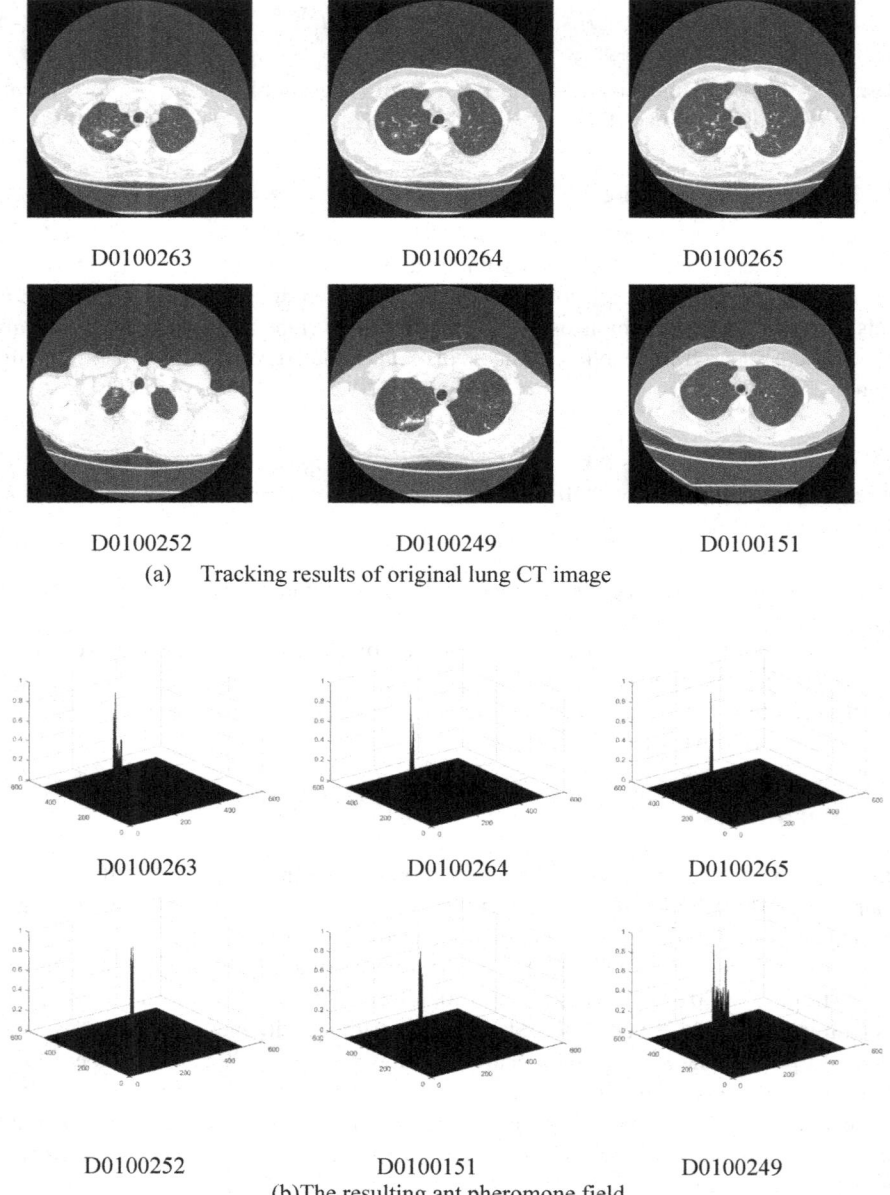

D0100263   D0100264   D0100265

D0100252   D0100249   D0100151

(a)   Tracking results of original lung CT image

D0100263   D0100264   D0100265

D0100252   D0100151   D0100249

(b)The resulting ant pheromone field

Fig. 3. Tracking results with our proposed mode

than traditional ACO. Our proposed approach can identify the region near the focal zone contour of the lung, accelerating the segmentation process.

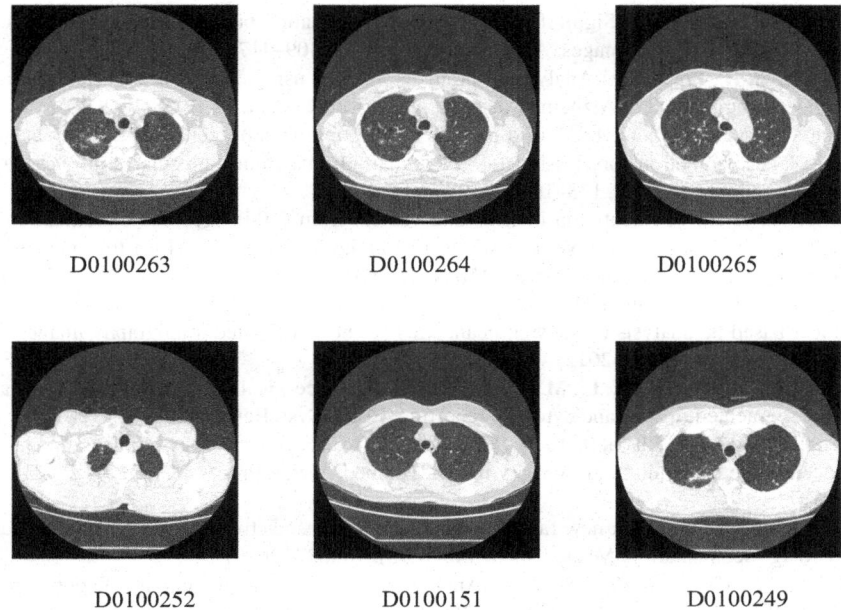

| D0100263 | D0100264 | D0100265 |
| D0100252 | D0100151 | D0100249 |

Fig. 4. Tracking results with traditional ACO

In summary, from the results, it can be clearly inferred that the proposed hybrid segmentation method has competitive potential compared to the other techniques.

4   Conclusions

Lung CT image provide lots of important information for lung-disease diagnosis and lung surgery. In this paper, a hybrid swarm intelligent approach for focal of a disease segmentation lung CT image was proposed. The lung tissues are segmented using our proposed edge detection approach. Edges are extracted from the segmented lung and from which geometrical features are extracted. Experimental results show that proposed method was robust and efficient compared with some traditional methods.

Acknowledgments. This work was supported by National Natural Science Foundation of China (No. 61876024 and No. 61673075), Project of talent peak of six industries (2017-DZXX-001), 333 Project of Jiangsu Province (No. BRA2019284), and partly supported by Jiangsu Laboratory of Lake Environment Remote Sensing Technologies Open Project Fund (JSLERS-2017-006) and The Science and Technology Development Plan Project of Chang Shu (CR0201711).

References

1. Sharma, N., Aggarwal, L.M.: Automated medical image segmentation techniques. J. Med. Phys. **35**(1), 3–14 (2010)

2. Arnay, R., Fumero, F., Sigut, J.: Ant Colony Optimization-based method for optic cup segmentation in retinal images. Appl. Soft Comput. **52**, 409–417 (2017)
3. Chitradevi, D., Prabha, S.: Analysis of brain sub regions using optimization techniques and deep learning method in Alzheimer disease. Appl. Soft Comput. **86**, 105857 (2020)
4. Bhattacharjee, K., Pant, M.: Hybrid particle swarm optimization-genetic algorithm trained multi-layer perceptron for classification of human glioma from molecular brain neoplasia data. Cogn. Syst. Res. **58**, 173–194 (2019)
5. Yang, X., et al.: Segmentation of liver and vessels from CT images and classification of liver segments for preoperative liver surgical planning in living donor liver transplantation. Comput. Methods Programs Biomed. **158**, 41–52 (2018)
6. Elizabeth, D.S., Nehemiah, H.K., Raj, C.S.R., Kannan, A.: Computer-aided diagnosis of lung cancer based on analysis of the significant slice of chest computed tomography image. IET Image Proc. **6**, 697–705 (2012)
7. Chen, H., Yang, L., Li, L., Li, M., Chen, Z.: An efficient cervical disease diagnosis approach using segmented images and cytology reporting. Cogn. Syst. Res. **58**, 265–277 (2019)
8. Zeng, Y., Zhaoa, Y., Liaoa, S., Liaoc, M., Chend, Y., Liu, X.: Liver vessel segmentation based on centerline constraint and intensity model. Biomed. Signal Process. Control **45**, 192–201 (2018)
9. Medeiros, A.G., et al.: A new fast morphological geodesic active contour method for lung CT image segmentation. Measurement **148**(1–13), 106687 (2019)
10. Dorigo, M., Maniezzo, V., Colorni, A.: Ant system: optimization by a colony of coop-erating agents. IEEE Trans. Syst. Man Cybern. **26**(1), 29–41 (1996)
11. Zhou, Y.: Runtime analysis of an ant colony optimization algorithm for TSP instances. IEEE Trans. Evol. Comput. **13**(5), 1083–1092 (2009)
12. Miria, A., Sharifianb, S., Rashidib, S., Ghodsca, M.: Medical image denoising based on 2D discrete cosine transform via ant colony optimization. Optik **156**, 938–948 (2018)
13. Abbas, F., Fan, P.: Clustering-based reliable low-latency routing scheme using ACO method for vehicular networks. Veh. Commun. **12**, 66–74 (2018)
14. Huanga, S.-H., Huangb, Y.-H., Blazquezc, C.A., Paredes Belmarda, G.: Application of the ant colony optimization in the resolution of the bridge inspection routing problem. Appl. Soft Comput. **65**, 443–461 (2018)
15. Wang, X., Choi, T.-M., Liu, H., Yue, X.: Novel ant colony optimization methods for simplifying solution construction in vehicle routing problems. IEEE Trans. Intell. Transp. Syst. **17**(11), 3132–3141 (2016)
16. Yang, S.-C., Cheng-Yi, Y., Lin, C.-J., Lin, H.-Y., Lin, C.-Y.: Reconstruction of three-dimensional breast-tumor model using multispectral gradient vector flow snake method. J. Appl. Res. Technol. **13**, 279–290 (2015)
17. Bessa, J.A., Cortez, P.C., da Silva Félix, J.H., da Rocha Neto, A.R., de Alexandria, A.R.: Radial snakes: comparison of segmentation methods in synthetic noisy images. Expert Syst. Appl. **42**, 3079–3088 (2015)
18. Li, L.: SAR image oil film detection based on ant Colony Optimization algorithm, International Congress on Image and Signal Processing. In: Bio-Medical Engineering and Informatics, pp. 619–623 (2016)

An Ant-Inspired Track-to-Track Recovery Approach for Construction of Cell Lineage Trees

Di Wu[1,3], Hui Bu[2], Benlian Xu[2(✉)], Mingli Lu[3], and Zhen Sun[1,3]

[1] School of Electrical & Automatic Engineering, Changshu Institute of Technology,
Changshu, People's Republic of China
wu_di821@163.com
[2] School of Mechanical Engineering, Changshu Institute of Technology,
Changshu, People's Republic of China
xu_benlian@cslg.edu.cn
[3] School of Electrical & Power Engineering, China University of Mining
and Technology, Xuzhou, People's Republic of China
luml@cslg.edu.cn

Abstract. Correct track-to-track association is crucial to the construction of cell lineage trees as well as the discovery of novel biological phenomenon that occur at rare frequencies. In this paper, an ant colony optimization based heuristic approach is proposed to link potential tracks through minimizing the cost function that mainly occurs on the fragmented intervals with the constraint of maximum inter-frame displacement. Specifically, both cell motion and morphology are emphasized in the defined cost function, and two decisions are made respectively to recover the mitotic and non-mitotic cases. Our method has proven to be feasible that can repair the broken tracklets caused by large migration, occlusion and mitosis missing, as well as false positives and missed detections, and can effectively help the construction of reliable cell lineage trees.

Keywords: Track recovery · Track-to-track association · Ant colony · Cell lineage

1 Introduction

The analysis of cellular behaviors is crucial for human disease diagnose and biomedical research. The existing automated cell tracking methods mainly focus on frame-by-frame association that can achieve high tracking accuracy in continuous image sequences [1,2], but it still exists some problems due to noise or segmentation error. For example, when a false negative segmentation occurs among a neighboring cell cluster, the normal tracking methods may cause a track missing. To resolve the problem, many global spatio-temporal data association approaches have been proposed to associate multiple trajectories over time of

© Springer Nature Switzerland AG 2020
Y. Tan et al. (Eds.): ICSI 2020, LNCS 12145, pp. 223–230, 2020.
https://doi.org/10.1007/978-3-030-53956-6_20

which the most well-known are the Multi-Hypothesis Tracking (MHT) [3] and Joint Probabilistic Data Association Filters (JPDAF) [4]. In [5], a batch algorithm, which utilizes information from all images in the image sequence, incorporates mitosis, apoptosis and other events into the same probabilistic framework for track linking. To reduce the computational cost, Huang *et al.* [6] first generate reliable track fragments and then stitch them by Hungarian algorithm.

In this paper, we introduce an ant colony optimization [7] based on heuristic approach linking potential tracks through minimizing the cost function that mainly occurs on the fragmented intervals with the constraint of maximum interframe displacement. In our work, each track segment is assumed to be associated with an ant colony. All ants in the colony start their foraging behaviors from the initial position of the track, and each ant makes decision via both the heuristic function and the pheromone intensity on the track. During decision, two events, namely, migration without mitosis and migration with mitosis, are considered to link the potential tracks with identical ancestry. As iterations increase, the trail pheromone field is continuously strengthened, and the trails with high pheromone intensity above a prespecified threshold are finally extracted. The rest of this paper is organized as follow: Sect. 2 details our ant-inspired track-to-track recovery method. We provide our experimental results in Sect. 3 and conclude this paper in Sect. 4.

2   Methods

Figure 1(a) illustrates an example of a set of broken cell tracks produced by an automated tracking algorithm, where cell occlusion, erratic motion and division probably cause the undetected candidates, while the presence of clutter usually generates a set of short track candidates. In order to construct correct cell lineage trees, a track recovery approach is needed to link the associated broken tracks and remove the false alarms, as shown in Fig. 1(b).

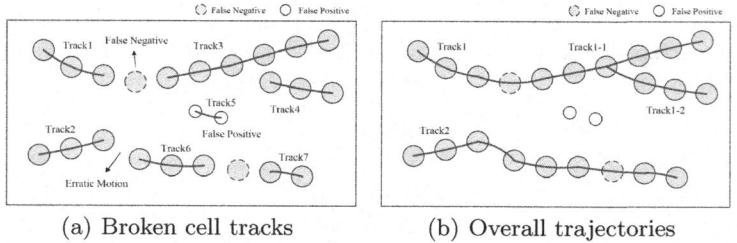

(a) Broken cell tracks   (b) Overall trajectories

Fig. 1. Examples of broken tracks and overall trajectories

Let p_u^k and p_v^{k+d}, respectively, denote the states of cell u in frame k and cell v in frame $k + d$, where d is a positive integer with the constraint of $d \leq 3$. In our work, a very small value is assigned by ant decision if an ant travels on the existing tracks while we formulate a new cost function between the cell p_u^k and the cell p_v^{k+d} that only occurs on the fragmented tracks as

$$E(p_u^k, p_v^{k+d}) = \alpha_1 E_{dis}(p_u^k, p_v^{k+d}) + (1 - \alpha_1) E_{area}(p_u^k, p_v^{k+d}), \tag{1}$$

where α_1 is a constant range in $[0, 1]$, $E_{dis}(p_u^k, p_v^{k+d})$ and $E_{area}(p_u^k, p_v^{k+d})$, respectively, represent costs of distance and overlap of area between cells p_u^k and p_v^{k+d}. The cost E_{dis} is defined as

$$E_{dis}(p_u^k, p_v^{k+d}) = \frac{d(p_u^k, p_v^{k+d})}{\sqrt{H^2 + W^2}}, \tag{2}$$

where H and W denote the height and width of an image respectively. The cost E_{area} is formulated by

$$E_{area}(p_u^k, p_v^{k+d}) = 1 - \frac{A(p_u^k) \cap A(p_v^{k+d})}{A(p_u^k) \cup A(p_v^{k+d})}, \tag{3}$$

where $A(p_u^k)$ refers to the area of the cell p_u^k, $A(p_v^{k+d})$ refers to the area of the cell p_v^{k+d}. We observe that the closer the two cells, the smaller the cost function.

An one-one mapping is defined between a track and an ant colony. With the known cell states of each track, we put a group of ant colony starting foraging from the initial position of a tracklet. Then each ant makes decision to move to the next cell in sequence with constraint of maximum inter-frame displacement.

Firstly, each ant a at the current position p_u^k finds the set of candidates N_a^{k+d} to be visited in frame $k+d$. If $|N_a^{k+d}| \geq 2$, the detection of mitotic event is carried out. Let p_m^{k+d} and p_n^{k+d} denote the states of any two cell candidates, namely cell m and cell n, in frame $k + d$, the similarity score $S(p_u^k, p_m^{k+d}, p_n^{k+d})$ is defined as

$$
\begin{aligned}
S(p_u^k, p_m^{k+d}, p_n^{k+d}) &= \beta_1 S_{area}(p_u^k, p_m^{k+d}, p_n^{k+d}) \\
&+ \beta_2 S_{dis}(p_u^k, p_m^{k+d}, p_n^{k+d}) + \beta_3 S_{def}(p_m^{k+1}, p_n^{k+d}),
\end{aligned}
\tag{4}
$$

where β_i is a constant range in $[0, 1]$ and $\sum_{i=1}^{3} \beta_i = 1$, $S_{area}(\cdot)$, $S_{dis}(\cdot)$ and $S_{def}(\cdot)$, respectively, denote the similarity scores of area, distance and deformation of cells, which are defined as

$$S_{area}(p_u^k, p_m^{k+d}, p_n^{k+d}) = 1 - \frac{A(p_u^k) \cap A(p_m^{k+d}) - A(p_u^k) \cap A(p_n^{k+d})}{A(p_u^k) \cup A(p_m^{k+d}) + A(p_u^k) \cup A(p_n^{k+d})}, \tag{5}$$

$$S_{dis}(p_u^k, p_m^{k+d}, p_n^{k+d}) = 1 - \frac{d(p_u^k, p_m^{k+d}) - d(p_u^k, p_n^{k+d})}{d(p_u^k, p_m^{k+d}) + d(p_u^k, p_n^{k+d})}, \tag{6}$$

$$S_{def}(p_m^{k+d}, p_n^{k+d}) = 1 - \frac{1}{2}\left(\frac{|L_h(p_m^{k+d}) - L_h(p_n^{k+d})|}{L_h(p_m^{k+d}) + L_h(p_n^{k+d})} + \frac{|L_w(p_m^{k+d}) - L_w(p_n^{k+d})|}{L_w(p_m^{k+d}) + L_w(p_n^{k+d})}\right), \tag{7}$$

where $L_h(\cdot)$ and $L_w(\cdot)$, respectively, denote the length of major and minor axes of the estimated cell contour.

If the similarity score $S(p_u^k, p_m^{k+d}, p_n^{k+d})$ is above a prespecified threshold ε_1, two ants will select p_m^{k+d} and p_n^{k+d} respectively and the selected cells are disjoint with $p_m^{k+d} \cap p_n^{k+d} = \varnothing$. If no mitotic event is detected, that is, the similarity score $S(p_u^k, p_m^{k+d}, p_n^{k+d}) < \varepsilon_1$ or $|N_a^{k+d}| = 1$, each ant a at the current position p_u^k selects a candidate p_v^{k+d} according to

$$P_{p_u^k,p_v^{k+d}}^a = \frac{(\tau_{p_u^k,p_v^{k+d}})^\alpha (\eta_{p_u^k,p_v^{k+d}})^\beta}{\sum\limits_{p_w^{k+d} \in N_a^{k+d}} (\tau_{p_u^k,p_w^{k+d}})^\alpha (\eta_{p_u^k,p_w^{k+d}})^\beta},\tag{8}$$

where $\tau_{p_u^k,p_v^{k+d}}$ denotes the amount of trail pheromone on path (p_u^k, p_v^{k+d}) and $\eta_{p_u^k,p_v^{k+d}}$ denotes the heuristic information with $\eta_{p_u^k,p_v^{k+1}} = 1/E(p_u^k, p_v^{k+d})$. In our method, we first set $d = 1$. If $|N_a^{k+d}| = 0$, we expand the ant's step size as $d \leftarrow d + 1$, and then the ant repeats the above decision-making process.

Once ant a has made a decision, a local update process of trail pheromone is conducted on its visited path by

$$\tau_{p_u^k,p_v^{k+d}} \leftarrow (1 - \rho) \cdot \tau_{p_u^k,p_v^{k+d}} + \Delta\tau_c,\tag{9}$$

where $\Delta\tau_c$ denotes a fixed amount of pheromone.

When all ants in the colony complete their tours, an individual global trail pheromone update is defined as

$$\tau_{p_u^k,p_v^{k+d}} \leftarrow (1 - \rho) \cdot \tau_{p_u^k,p_v^{k+d}} + \Delta\tau_{p_u^k,p_v^{k+d}},\tag{10}$$

$$\Delta\tau_{p_u^k,p_v^{k+d}} = \begin{cases} \dfrac{Q_1}{E_{bt}}, & \text{if } (p_u^k, p_v^{k+d}) \in P_{bt} \\ 0, & \text{otherwise} \end{cases},\tag{11}$$

where Q_1 is a constant, E_{bt} denotes the cost of the best tour P_{bt}.

Once all ant colonies complete their foraging, a global update trail pheromone on all ant colonies is performed by

$$\tau_{p_u^k,p_v^{k+d}} \leftarrow (1 - \rho) \cdot \tau_{p_u^k,p_v^{k+d}} + \Delta\tau_{p_u^k,p_v^{k+d}},\tag{12}$$

$$\Delta\tau_{p_u^k,p_v^{k+d}} = \begin{cases} \dfrac{Q_2}{\sum\limits_{i=1}^{m} E_{bt}^i}, & \text{if } (p_u^k, p_v^{k+d}) \in P_{bt}^i \\ 0, & \text{otherwise} \end{cases},\tag{13}$$

where $\sum\limits_{i=1}^{m} E_{bt}^i$ denotes total cost of the set of best tours $\{P_{bt}^i\}_{i=1}^m$ of all ant colonies in current iteration, P_{bt}^i denotes the ith best tour of $\{P_{bt}^i\}_{i=1}^m$.

As iterations increase, the trail pheromone field is continuously strengthened. Once reaching the maximum value of iteration, the trails with high pheromone intensity above a prespecified threshold ε_2 are finally extracted by morphological operations. The main framework of our method is summarized in Algorithm 1.

Algorithm 1. Main steps for Ant-Inspired Track Recovery

Require: input the tracklets $T = \{T^{(i)}\}_{i=1}^{m}$, working ant colonies $\tilde{W} = \{\tilde{W}^{(i)}\}_{i=1}^{m}$
   initialization, the iteration parameter $t = 1$, and the maximum iteration parameter
   t_{max}, mitotic similarity threshold ε_1 and pheromone extracting threshold ε_2.
1: **while** $t \leq t_{max}$ **do**
2:    **while** $\tilde{W} \neq \varnothing$ **do**
3:       **for** each ant colony in $\tilde{W}$ **do**
4:          **for** a group of ant colony **do**
5:             **if** find candidates **then**
6:                **if** above two candidates **then**
7:                   Calculate mitotic similarity S via (4).
8:                   **if** $S > \varepsilon_1$ **then**
9:                      Mitotic decision made by two ants.
10:                   **else**
11:                      Migration decision made by an ant via (8).
12:                   **end if**
13:                **else**
14:                   Migration decision made by an ant via (8).
15:                **end if**
16:                Local pheromone update via (9).
17:             **else**
18:                The ant returns and completes current tour.
19:             **end if**
20:          **end for**
21:          Global pheromone update via (10).
22:       **end for**
23:    **end while**
24:    Global pheromone update via (12).
25:    $t = t + 1$
26: **end while**
27: Extract the trails lasting more than 3 frames with pheromone intensity above ε_2.

---

3   Experimental Results

To test the performance of our proposed track recovery method, we implemented it in MATLAB(R2014a) on a 2.6 GHz processor computer with 16G random access memory. In this section, we use two image sequences from publicly available website at http://www.celltrackingchallenge.net/. The two cell image sequences include real N2DL-Hela+ dataset and pancreatic stem cell dataset. With the reliable track fragments results, our track recovery method proved to be effective. The parameters used in our approach mainly focus on ant colony setting, we have $\alpha = 3$, $\beta = 2$, and $\rho = 0.3$. The initial value of the pheromone field is $c = 0.0005$. We set the mitotic similarity threshold $\varepsilon_1 = 0.85$, the pheromone extracting threshold $\varepsilon_2 = 0.05$ and the maximum iteration parameter $t_{max} = 20$. We find that three factors of similarity score in (4), i.e., area, distance and deformation of cells, are crucial to the recovery of mitotic events, which affects the track accuracy. To observe the effect of these factors on similarity score, we compare the performance of different combinations using several measure metrics.

The track recovery results on two cell image sequences are, respectively, shown in Fig. 2 and Fig. 3, which illustrate the track recovery results including lineages and cell contours based on the raw fragmented tracks.

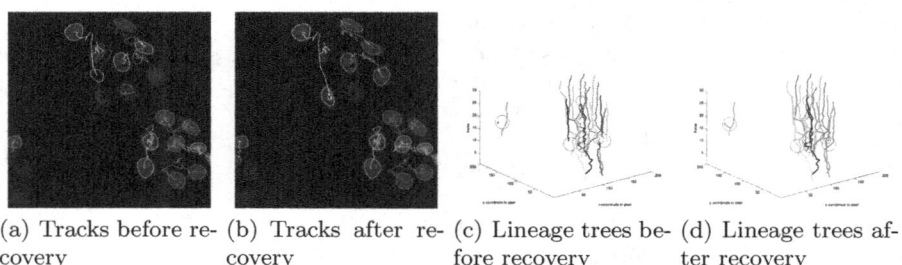

(a) Tracks before re-   (b) Tracks after re-   (c) Lineage trees be-   (d) Lineage trees af-
covery   covery   fore recovery   ter recovery

Fig. 2. Track recovery results of N2DL-Hela+ dataset

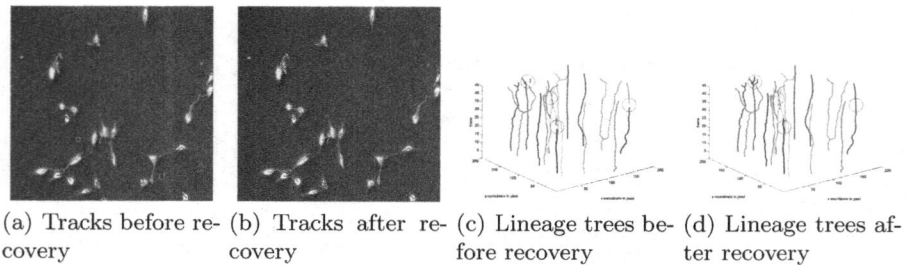

(a) Tracks before re-   (b) Tracks after re-   (c) Lineage trees be-   (d) Lineage trees af-
covery   covery   fore recovery   ter recovery

Fig. 3. Track recovery results of pancreatic stem cell dataset (Color figure online)

In N2DL-Hela+ dataset, there are 25 tracklets with different track colors before track recovery in Fig. 2(a), which is generated by cell erratic motion, cell division, and cell occlusion. After the proposed recovery method, the true reliable tracks have been stitched to be 19 entire trajectories as shown in Fig. 2(b). From the lineage trees as shown in Fig. 2(c), the track segments marked in red circles have been correctly linked into longer trajectories as illustrated in Fig. 2(d). In pancreatic stem cell dataset, the 35 tracks in Fig. 3(a) including false positives and false negatives have been recovered to be 25 entire tracks, and false positive tracks are removed as shown in Fig. 3(b). The comparison lineage trees are also shown in Fig. 3(c) and Fig. 3(d) with red circle marks.

Obviously, our track recovery method can fix broken tracks and restore mitotic events, and finally can obtain the whole reliable cell lineage trees. Figure 4 shows the resulting trail pheromone field. The color corresponds to pheromone intensity, and the trails with the amount of pheromone greater than a prespecified threshold are extracted.

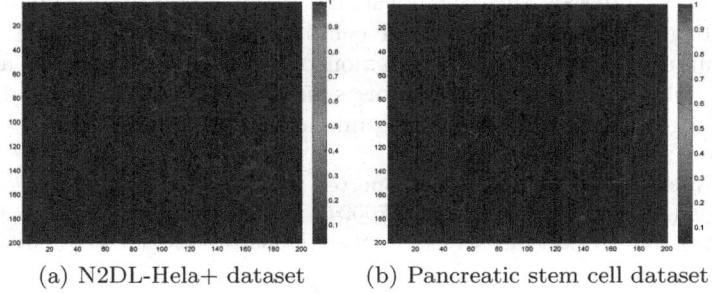

(a) N2DL-Hela+ dataset   (b) Pancreatic stem cell dataset

Fig. 4. 2-D trail pheromone field

For performance evaluation, we use the complete tracks (CT) [8], which shows how good an approach is at reconstructing complete reference tracks and is defined as $CT = \dfrac{2T_{rc}}{T_{gt} + T_c}$, where T_{rc} denotes the number of completely reconstructed reference tracks, T_{gt} denotes the number of all reference tracks and T_c denotes the number of all computed tracks. To jointly evaluate the errors of label and cardinality of tracks, the metric of optimal sub-pattern assignment metric for track (OSPA-T) [9] is introduced as well. We compare the performance of different combinations of three factors of similarity score in (4), i.e., area, distance and deformation of cells, as shown in Table 1. We observe that the performance is better when all three factors are taken into account simultaneously, in which the mitotic events are accurately detected.

Table 1. Performance measure of different combinations

	Dataset	Metric	
		CT	OSPA-T
Area and distance	N2DL-Hela+	0.76	2.56
	Pancreatic stem cell	0.84	2.95
Area and deformation	N2DL-Hela+	0.86	2.32
	Pancreatic stem cell	0.87	2.86
Distance and deformation	N2DL-Hela+	0.81	2.45
	Pancreatic stem cell	0.87	2.86
Area, distance and deformation	N2DL-Hela+	0.95	2.17
	Pancreatic stem cell	0.91	2.74

4   Conclusion

In this paper, we proposed an ant-inspired track recovery approach linking potential tracks through minimizing the cost function that mainly occurs on the fragmented intervals with the constraint of maximum interframe displacement. Through constant iterations, the completed repaired trails were obtained through minimizing total cost. It is demonstrated that our proposed approach successfully obtain reliable cell trajectories and lineage trees by stitching sets of true track segments and reconstructing missing mitosis branching.

Acknowledgement. This work was supported by National Natural Science Foundation of China (No. 61673075 and No. 61876024), 333 Project of Jiangsu Province (No. BRA2019284), and Project of talent peak of six industries (2017-DZXX-001).

References

1. Padfield, D., Rittscher, J., Roysam, B.: Coupled minimum-cost flow cell tracking for high-throughput quantitative analysis. Med. Image Anal. **15**(4), 650–668 (2011)
2. Benlian, X., Shi, J., Mingli, L., Cong, J., Wang, L., Nener, B.: An automated cell tracking approach with multi-bernoulli filtering and ant colony labor division. IEEE/ACM Trans. Comput. Biol. Bioinform. (2019). https://doi.org/10.1109/TCBB.2019.2954502
3. Reid, D.B.: An algorithm for tracking multiple targets. IEEE Trans. Autom. Control **24**(6), 1202–1211 (1979)
4. Fortmann, T.E., Bar-Shalom, Y., Scheffe, M.: Sonar tracking of multiple targets using joint probabilistic data association. IEEE J. Oceanic Eng. **8**(3), 173–184 (2003)
5. Magnusson, K.E.G., Jaldén, J., Gilbert, P.M., Blau, H.M.: Global linking of cell tracks using the Viterbi algorithm. IEEE Trans. Med. Imaging **34**(4), 911–929 (2014)
6. Huang, C., Wu, B., Nevatia, R.: Robust object tracking by hierarchical association of detection responses. In: Forsyth, D., Torr, P., Zisserman, A. (eds.) ECCV 2008. LNCS, vol. 5303, pp. 788–801. Springer, Heidelberg (2008). https://doi.org/10.1007/978-3-540-88688-4_58
7. Dorigo, M., Gambardella, L.M.: Ant colony system: a cooperative learning approach to the traveling salesman problem. IEEE Trans. Evol. Comput. **1**(1), 53–66 (1997)
8. Ulman, V., et al.: An objective comparison of cell-tracking algorithms. Nat. Methods **14**(12), 1141 (2017)
9. Ristic, B., Vo, B.-N., Clark, D., Vo, B.-T.: A metric for performance evaluation of multi-target tracking algorithms. IEEE Trans. Signal Process. **59**(7), 3452–3457 (2011)

An Ant Colony Optimization Algorithm Based Automated Generation of Software Test Cases

Saju Sankar S[1(✉)] and Vinod Chandra S S[2(✉)]

[1] Department of Computer Engineering, Government Polytechnic College, Punalur, India
tkmce@rediffmail.com
[2] Department of Computer Science, University of Kerala, Thiruvananthapuram 695581, India
vinod@keralauniversity.ac.in

Abstract. Software testing is an important process of detecting bugs in the software product thereby a quality software product is developed. Verification and Validation (V & V) activities are the effective methods employed to achieve quality. Static and dynamic testing activities are performed during V & V. During static testing, the program code is not executed while in dynamic testing (Black Box and White Box), the execution of the program code is performed. Effective test cases are designed by both these methods. Tables are employed to represent test case documentation. The most beneficial representation - State table based testing, for generating test inputs is explained with the help of state graphs and state tables. This technique is mainly employed in embedded system software testing, real time applications and web application based software product testing where time constraints are a major criteria. Automatic generation of test cases will help to reduce time overhead in testing activities. Our study is to develop optimum test cases by a modified Ant Colony Optimization (ACO) technique in an automated method and it ensures maximum coverage. The prediction model used in this paper ensures better accuracy of the design of test inputs. A comparison of the similar optimization techniques was also discussed that is used in automated test case generation. A case study of the various states during the execution of a task in an operating system has been presented to illustrate our approach.

Keywords: Ant Colony Optimization · Software · Automated · Test cases · Pheromone

1 Introduction

A software product should be reliable and measurable. These qualities are evaluated by way of effective testing activities. Hence testing is an important stage of Software Development Life Cycle (SDLC). Like SDLC, Software Testing Life Cycle (STLC) is also a process which detects bugs or faults so as to rectify them before delivery of the software product to the customer. The testing of the various phases of STLC by way of manual testing is difficult due to the overhead of time, cost and schedule slippage. Hence automated testing is complemented for majority of the testing activities [1]. This automated generation of test cases is necessary when a set of tests are to be

© Springer Nature Switzerland AG 2020
Y. Tan et al. (Eds.): ICSI 2020, LNCS 12145, pp. 231–239, 2020.
https://doi.org/10.1007/978-3-030-53956-6_21

done repeatedly, compatibility testing, regression testing etc. For this purpose, artificial intelligence techniques are adopted with a Meta heuristic approach. The problem of generating sets of test cases for functional testing, structural testing etc. are achieved by automated test case generation techniques [2].

In this paper, we propose an optimal algorithm for the automated generation of test cases based on Ant Colony Optimization (ACO). State table based testing - a black box testing technique is employed, which assures a higher level of functional testing of the individual modules. Here the process is categorized as – software environment modeling, test case selection, test case execution, test metrics and automated test suite reduction techniques [3].

A software product can be optimized by various algorithms such as genetic algorithms, ACO, Particle Swarm Optimization (PSO), Artificial Bee Colony (ABC) etc. The ACO algorithm is a metaheuristic intelligent optimization method. The algorithm is used for finding the optimal path in a graph. ACO is also employed for the optimization of test case generation techniques namely functional testing, Structural testing, Regression testing etc. [4]. Praveen et al. proposed an ACO based automated software testing technique which shows the generation of optimal test cases in an automated environment [5].

This paper proposes an automated method of generating test cases in functional testing technique mainly state table based testing, optimized by an ACO algorithm. The results are compared with other optimization models for effectiveness [6].

2 State Table Based Testing

State table based testing is defined as the black box testing technique in which changes in input conditions cause state changes in the application under test [7]. It is a convenient method for testing software systems where states and transitions are specified. Tables are used for representing information relating to the design of test cases. We have represented them using state transition diagrams and state tables. A state table representation has a) Finite State Machine (FSM), a model whose output is dependent on both previous and present inputs. An FSM model represents the software behavior and serves as a guide to design functional test cases. b) State transition diagram or state graph, is a software system which has different states depending on its input and time. The nodes in a state graph represent states. The nodes are connected by links denoted as transitions. With the help of nodes and transitions, a state graph is prepared. The pictorial representation of an FSM is depicted by a state graph and it represents the states that the system can assume. The state graph is converted to a tabular form known as state tables. They specify states, input events, transitions and outputs. The information contained in the state graph and the state table is converted into test cases.

The state table contains cells of valid and invalid inputs. Valid inputs causes a change of state and invalid inputs do not cause any change in transition in the state of a task. Due to the tremendous overhead of time and cost exhaustive testing is not possible. The solution is to formulate a strategy for test case reduction without affecting the functional coverage of the system under test. The genetic algorithms employed currently have to be modified for the above [8].

The method of state table based testing is depicted with a case study, showing the different states of a task in an operating system. A task or job assigned to an operating system has the states – New, Ready, Running, Waiting, Terminated. The state graph is drawn as the first step. The state graph can be represented as a directed graph G = (N, E), where N denotes the states (nodes) of the system under test and E denotes the edges or transition between the states.

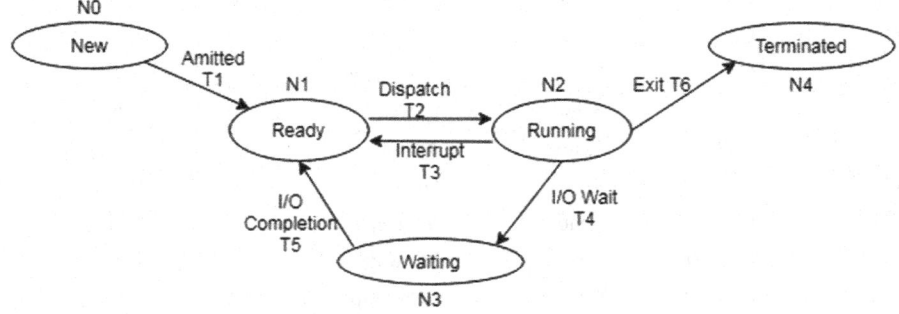

Fig. 1. State graph.

The transition events are Admitted T1, Dispatch T2, Interrupt T3, I/O Wait T4, I/O Completion T5 and Exit T6. From the state graph, a state table is prepared.

Table 1. State table

State/Input Event	Admit	Dispatch	Interrupt	I/O Wait	I/O Completion	Exit
New	Ready/T1	New/T0	New/T0	New/T0	New/T0	New/T0
Ready	Ready/T1	Running/T2	Ready/T1	Ready/T1	Ready/T1	Ready/T 1
Running	Running/T2	Running/T2	Ready/T3	Waiting/T4	Running/T2	Terminated/T6
Waiting	Waiting/T4	Waiting/T4	Waiting/T4	Waiting/T4	Ready/T5	Waiting/T4

Table 1 contains cells of valid and invalid inputs. From the state table, test cases are derived. The test cases generated are stored in a tabular form known as test case table and it contains six columns.

The test case table (Table 2) shows that 24 test cases are generated consisting of both valid and invalid test cases. We have to differentiate the valid and invalid test cases. Higher number of invalid test cases shows weak coverage. The solution can be obtained by reducing the test cases by prioritizing the test cases by following the rules.

a.   Develop test cases consisting of valid test cases that cause a change of state.
b.   Create test cases such that all test paths are executed at least once and the paths should be feasible.

Table 2. Test case table

Test case ID	Test source	Input		Expected Output	
		Current state	Event	Output	Next state
TC 1	Cell 1	New	Admit	T1	Ready
TC 2	Cell 2	New	Dispatch	T0	New
TC 3	Cell 3	New	Interrupt	T0	New
TC 4	Cell 4	New	I/O wait	T0	New
TC 5	Cell 5	New	I/O completion	T0	New
TC 6	Cell 6	New	Exit	T0	New
TC 7	Cell 7	Ready	Admit	T1	Ready
TC 8	Cell 8	Ready	Dispatch	T2	Running
TC 9	Cell 9	Ready	Interrupt	T1	Ready
TC 10	Cell 10	Ready	I/O wait	T1	Ready
TC 11	Cell 11	Ready	I/O completion	T1	Ready
TC 12	Cell 12	Ready	Exit	T1	Ready
TC 13	Cell 13	Running	Admit	T2	Running
TC 14	Cell 14	Running	Dispatch	T2	Running
TC 15	Cell 15	Running	Interrupt	T3	Ready
TC 16	Cell 16	Running	I/O wait	T4	Waiting
TC 17	Cell 17	Running	I/O completion	T2	Running
TC 18	Cell 18	Running	Exit	T6	Terminated
TC 19	Cell 19	Waiting	Admit	T4	Waiting
TC 20	Cell 20	Waiting	Dispatch	T4	Waiting
TC 21	Cell 21	Waiting	Interrupt	T4	Waiting
TC 22	Cell 22	Waiting	I/O wait	T4	Waiting
TC 23	Cell 23	Waiting	I/O completion	T5	Ready
TC 24	Cell 24	Waiting	Exit	T4	Waiting

c. The inputs which do not cause change in transition have to be identified from the state table.

As shown in Fig. 1, there are two paths which satisfy rule b.
1. N0 → N1 → N2 → N4
2. N0 → N1 → N2 → N3 → N1 → N2 → N4

3   ACO Algorithm for Test Case Generation

ACO is a probabilistic technique which searches for optimal path in a graph. Ant behavior is looking a shortest path between their colony and location of food source. The path is discovered by pheromone deposits when the ants move at random. More pheromone deposits on a path increases the probability of the path being followed. The path is selected based on the maximum pheromone deposit from start node and the path is analyzed for optimality [9].

The behavior of ants can be used for solving the problem. Selection of paths depends upon the theory of probability. Ants generate pheromone and deposits on the paths for further remembrance and it is a heuristic technique. The path visibility is accomplished by the level of pheromone intensity and heuristic information. The feasible path is selected based on highest pheromone level and heuristic information. The algorithm needs four parameters for selecting the valid transitions of the state graph – Probability, Heuristic information, Pheromone intensity and Visibility of the path [10].

Kamna et al. evaluated the performances of genetic algorithm (GA), Bee Colony optimization (BCO), ACO and modified ACO (m-ACO) for test case prioritization in terms of Average Percentage of Faults Detected (APFD) and Percentage of Test Cases Required (PTR) metric [6]. The metrics was evaluated by the case studies for triangle problem, quadratic equation problem etc. (Table 3).

Table 3. Comparison of GA, BCO, ACO and m-ACO for APFD and PTR.

	APFD				PTR			
	GA	BCO	ACO	m-ACO	GA	BCO	ACO	m-ACO
Triangle problem	0.88	0.95	0.93	0.97	18	12	16	12
Quadratic problem	0.86	0.91	0.89	0.93	20	18	18	16

The comparison shows that m-ACO algorithm shows better coverage than the other optimization algorithms.

In order to classify or to select the valid test cases, we used the modified algorithm 'Comprehensive Improved Ant Colony Optimization (ACIACO) for finding the effective optimization path and this path model is used to achieve highest coverage and reduce the number of iterations [11]. The establishment of transformation relationship makes effective use of ant colony algorithm for iterative optimization of test cases.

In this paper, generating the test cases from the state table is achieved by the modified ACO algorithm. The algorithm is for the effective traversing through the different states. Also the feasible test cases are generated so as to cover all transitions at least once. The procedure is given,

1. Initialize parameters.

    1.1   Set heuristic value (η).
    Initialize heuristic value of each transition in the state graph $\eta = 2$.

1.2 Set pheromone intensity (T).
Initialize pheromone value for each transition in the state graph (T=1).
1.3 Set visited status (V_s).
Initialize $V_s = 0$ (the condition in which ant not visited any state).
1.4 Set probability (P).
Initialize $P = 0$.
1.5 Initialize $\alpha = 1$, $\beta = 1$, the parameters which controls the desirability and visibility.
1.6 Set count = maximum number of possible transitions.

2. While (count > 0)

2.1 Update the paths or visited status of the paths $V_s [i] = 1$.
2.2 Evaluate feasible path F (P), if any from the first node to the next node in the state graph. Else go to step 6.
2.3 Evaluate probability of the path.

$$P_{ij} = \sum_{i}^{k}((Tik)^{\wedge}\alpha * (\eta ik)^{\wedge} - \beta).$$

The probability has values between 0 and 1.

3. Move to the next node.

3.1 Select the destination node. Ant will follow the rules.

3.1.1 If there is self-transition from $(i \rightarrow i)$, select it.
3.1.2 Else select the transition not visited. (V_s=0).
3.1.3 Else if two or more transition having the same visited status $V_s[j] = V_s[k]$, then random selection of the node.

4. Update values of Pheromone and heuristic.

4.1 Update pheromone intensity, $T_{ij} = (T_{ij})^{\alpha} * (\eta_{ij})^{-\beta}$
4.2 Update heuristic, $\eta_{ij} = 2 * (\eta_{ij})$.
4.3 Update count, Decrement count by one each step.

5. Go to step 2.
6. Stop.

4 Results and Discussion

We have discussed how the test cases are minimized while maximizing coverage of testing. If there are 'n' states in a state graph, then there will be a maximum of 'n*n' test cases both feasible and infeasible generated thereby increasing the testing time overhead. For the automated generation of test cases, we used an open source testing tool multidimensional modified condition/decision coverage which supports state graph based testing and generates test cases by traversing through the state transition graph [12].

The test cases given in Table 2, twenty four test cases both valid and invalid, which cause or do not cause change in transition from one state to another during the execution of a task has to be minimized.

4.1 Steps for Minimizing Test Cases

Wang's algorithm [13] was used for the effective reduction of test cases.

1. Calculate node coverage (NC) for each test case.
   Let NC (tc) = t_1, t_2 ... t_n, where t_1, t_2, ... t_n are transitions.
2. If a number of set tc = 0, then tc is included in the effective set of test cases.
3. Final set of test cases is generated.

   In our case study, the algorithm is implemented as
   N = {N0, N1, N2, N3, N4} representing the nodes.
   ID = {ID1, ID2, ... ID6} representing input data.
   OD = {OD1, OD2, ... OD6} representing output data.
   T = {T1, T2, ... T6} representing transitions.
   Ti is a transition from source node to the destination node.
   Ti = {Np, Nq}, where Np is the source node and Nq is the destination node.
   The next step is to extract each transition,
   T1 = {N0, N1} to T6 = {N2, N4}.

After completely extracting all the transitions, the next step is to generate the test cases from TC1 to TC24.

The last step is to reduce the set of generated test cases by calculating the node coverage for each test case and determining which test cases are covered by other test cases. i.e. from NC(TC1) to NC(TC24). The test cases are valid if the node coverage is empty. All other test cases are invalid and can be ignored.

Hence the six valid test cases which causes state transitions in the execution of a task in an operating system are Test Suite, TS = {TC1, TC8, TC15, TC16, TC18, TC23} as shown in Table 4.

Table 4. Cells containing valid test cases.

State/Input Event	Admit	Dispatch	Interrupt	I/O Wait	I/O Completion	Exit
New	Ready/T1					
Ready		Running/T2				
Running			Ready/T3	Waiting/T4		Terminated/T6
Waiting					Ready/T5	

This reduction in test suite helps saving of time in resource constrained software projects. The ACIACO algorithm effectively covered the criteria such as reduced test suite size, improved fault detection capability, reduced time, cost and highest coverage criteria. A comparison of the three kinds of coverage – statement coverage, branch coverage and modified condition/decision coverage shows that the modified ACIACO algorithm obtained better values as shown in Table 5. It is evident that the ACO optimization algorithm will effectively improve the quality of the test cases generated.

Table 5. The coverage of different ant numbers on ACIACO

ACIACO	Statement coverage	Branch coverage	Modified condition/Decision Coverage
8 ants	82.37%	64.30%	17.17%
32 ants	94.38%	80.23%	35.55%
56 ants	97.89%	87.77%	45.25%
88 ants	100.00%	100.00%	76.13%

5 Conclusion

We have proposed a modified ACO based approach for the automated and effective generation of valid test cases for the state transition based software testing. An FSM model is prepared. From the model, a state graph followed a state table and a test case table was generated. Also a test suite reduction algorithm is implemented thereby the optimization is achieved. ACO is a promising methodology for test case generation, selection and prioritization problem. ACO algorithm fully satisfies software coverage without having any redundancy. The power of nature inspired models in software engineering area is emerging because of its optimization outcome. The swarm based optimization is evolving in many of the software optimization fields. It is highly recommended, agent and swarm fused optimization algorithms can be used to generate efficient automated test environments.

References

1. Setiani, N., et al.: Literature review on test case generation approach. In: ICSIM 2019 Proceedings of the Second International Conference on Software Engineering and Information Management, pp. 91– 95, January 2019
2. Tahbildar, H., Kalita, B.: Automated software test data generation: direction of research. Int. J. Comput. Sci. Eng. IJCSES 2, 99–120 (2011)
3. Swain, T.R., et al.: Generation and optimization of test cases for object oriented software using state chart diagram, CS & IT – CSCP (2012)
4. Singh, G., et al.: Evaluation of test cases using ACO with a new heuristic function: a proposed approach. Int. J. Adv. Res. Comput. Sci. Softw. Eng. IJARCSSE (2014)

5. Srivastava, P.: Structured testing using ant colony optimization. In: Proceedings of the First International Conference on Intelligent Interactive Technologies and Multimedia, pp. 203–207. IITM, ACM India, December 2010
6. Kamna, S., et al.: A Comparative evaluation of 'm-ACO' technique for test suite prioritization. Indian J. Sci. Technol. **9**(30), 1–10 (2016)
7. Li, H., Lam, C.P.: An ant colony optimization approach to test sequence generation for state based software testing. In: Proceedings of the fifth international conference on quality software, QSIC. IEEE (2005)
8. Thakur, P., Varma, T.: A survey on test case selection using optimization techniques in software testing. Int. J. Innov. Sci. Eng. Technol. IJISET **2**, 593–596 (2015)
9. Vinod Chandra, S.S.: Smell detection agent based optimization algorithm. J. Insti. Eng. **97**(3), 431–436 (2016). https://doi.org/10.1007/s40031-014-0182-0
10. Srivastava, P.: Baby: automatic test sequence generation for state transition testing via ACO, IGI, Global (2010)
11. Shunkun et al.: Improved Ant algorithm for software testing cases generation. The Sci. World J. (2014)
12. Maheshwari, V., Prasanna, M.: Generation of test case using automation in software systems – a review. Indian J. Sci. Technol. **8**(35), 1 (2015)
13. Linzhang, W., et al.: Generating test cases from UML activity diagram based on gray-box method. In: Proceedings of the 11th Asia-Pacific Software Engineering Conference (APSEC04) (2004)

Brain Storm Optimization Algorithm

BSO-CLS: Brain Storm Optimization Algorithm with Cooperative Learning Strategy

Liang Qu[1], Qiqi Duan[1], Jian Yang[1], Shi Cheng[2], Ruiqi Zheng[1], and Yuhui Shi[1(✉)]

[1] Department of Computer Science and Engineering,
Southern University of Science and Technology, Guangdong 518055, China
qul@mail.sustech.edu.cn, shiyh@sustech.edu.cn
[2] School of Computer Science, Shaanxi Normal University, Xi'an 710062, China

Abstract. Brain storm optimization algorithms (BSO) have shown great potential in many global black-box optimization problems. However, the existing BSO variants can suffer from three problems: (1) large-scale optimization problem; (2) hyperparameter optimization problem; (3) high computational cost of the clustering operations. To address these problems, in this paper, we propose a simple yet effective BSO variant named Brain Storm Optimization Algorithm with Cooperative Learning Strategy (BSO-CLS). It is inspired by the new ideas generating process of brain storm in which the participators propose their own ideas by cooperatively learning other participators' ideas. Thus, BSO-CLS iteratively updates the candidate solutions by linearly combining other solutions with the weights deriving from the fitness values of other solutions. To validate the effectiveness of the proposed method, we test it on 6 benchmark functions with the 1000 dimensions. The experimental results show that BSO-CLS can outperform the vanilla BSO and the other BSO variant with the learning strategy.

Keywords: Cooperatively learning · Brain storm optimization · Large scale optimization

1 Introduction

Large scale black-box optimization problems play a very important role in many scientific and engineering applications. It can be formulated as follows [12]:

$$x^* = \arg min_{x \in R^D} f(x) \tag{1}$$

where x^* is the global minimizer to be searched and $f : R^D \to R$ is the evaluation function. In this paper, we focus on the large scale black-box optimization problem [11], i.e., the evaluation function f typically has three properties:

© Springer Nature Switzerland AG 2020
Y. Tan et al. (Eds.): ICSI 2020, LNCS 12145, pp. 243–250, 2020.
https://doi.org/10.1007/978-3-030-53956-6_22

- **Black-box:** When a candidate solution $x \in R^D$ is evaluated by f, we can only obtain the function evaluation value $f(x)$. Any other information of f, such as gradient information, is unavailable.
- **High-dimension:** The dimension D of the candidate solution x is typically larger than or equal to 1000 (i.e. $D \geq 1000$).
- **Multimodal:** The evaluation function f can have many local optima and global optima solutions.

Recently, swarm intelligence (SI) [6,7] has been a promising technique to solve the large scale black-box optimization problems [2,8]. Most existing SI algorithms such as particle swarm optimization (PSO) [14] and ant colony optimization (ACO) [5] are inspired by the swarm behaviours of the simple creatures in nature. However, BSO [3,4,15], a young and promising SI algorithm, is inspired by the brainstorming process of the high-level human being, which utilizes the clustering operation to simulate the brainstorming process and generates the new candidate solutions by learning other solutions from intercluster or intracluster randomly. In general, the existing BSO algorithms can suffer from three problems: (1) cannot obtain good performance on the high-dimension optimization problems; (2) several hyperparameters of algorithm itself need to be optimized; (3) the clustering operation (e.g. k-means [10]) is high computational cost.

To address the aforementioned problems, in this paper, we propose a novel BSO variant named BSO-CLS. It is inspired by the participators' ideas generating process of brain storm, i.e., each new idea is generated by cooperatively learning the ideas from other participators. Thus, for each candidate solution of BSO-CLS, it iteratively updates itself by linearly combining other solutions with the weights deriving from the function evaluation values of other solutions.

The contributions of this paper are summarized as follows:

- We introduce a novel cooperative learning strategy to simulate the new ideas generating process of brain storm. The analysis and experiment show that the novel learning strategy is effective and efficient.
- In order to validate the effectiveness of the proposed method, we test it on 6 benchmark functions with the 1000 dimensions. The empirical results show that BSO-CLS can outperform the vanilla BSO and the other BSO variant with the learning strategy.

The rest of this paper is organized as follows. Section 2 introduces the representative BSO variants. Section 3 introduces BSO-CLS in detail, and Sect. 4 presents and discusses the experimental setting and results. The conclusions are drawn in Sect. 5.

2   Related Work

In this section, we will introduce some representative BSO variants. In order to reduce the high computational cost of clustering operations, BSO-OS [13]

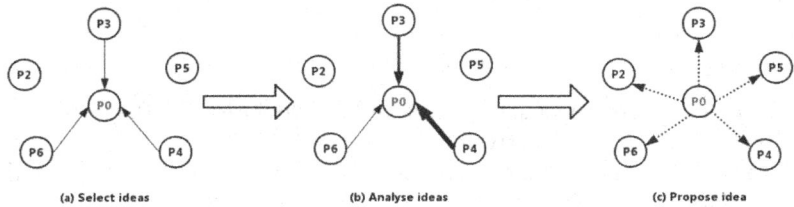

Fig. 1. The processes of the new ideas proposed in the brain storm.

proposed to cluster individuals in the objective space instead of in the solution space. MBSO [17] proposed a modified BSO which introduced the simple grouping method (SGM) with the idea difference strategy (IDS). RGBSO [1] proposed to utilize the random grouping strategy in clustering.

Recently, some learning based new solutions generating strategies have been proposed. BSOLS [16] proposed a novel learning strategy after updating operator to improve the diversity of population. OLBSO [9] introduced a orthogonal learning (OL) framework and incorporated it with BSO to improve the performance.

3   Proposed Method

In this section, we will introduce the proposed method in detail. The key idea of BSO-CLS is that it utilizes a novel method to simulate the new ideas generating process of the brain storm. Specifically, as shown in Fig. 1, during the brain storm process, the participators generally go through three processes to cooperatively learn other participators' ideas before proposing their own ideas. Taking participator $P0$ as an example, the first process is to listen to other participators' ideas and select the ideas that inspire him. The second process is to analyze the selected ideas. Some of them have a greater impact on him, and others have a smaller impact on him. The third process is to come up with his own ideas based on his analysis and share them with other participators. Thus, other participators can follow these three processes to come up with their own ideas until the brain storm is finished.

Based on the processes introduced above, the BSO-CLS can be implemented as follows:

Step 1: Randomly initialize N candidate solutions $X \in R^{P \times D}$ with D dimension.

Step 2: Evaluate the fitness $Y = f(X)$ using the evaluation function f.

Step 3.1: For each candidate solution, randomly select m other candidate solutions $x_1, x_2, \cdots, x_m$ as the learning objects.

Step 3.2: For each learning object x_i, calculate the learning weight w_i using the formula (2) by normalizing the fitness values $f(x_1), f(x_2), \cdots, f(x_m)$ of the learning objects.

$$w_i = \frac{f(x_i) - \mu}{\sigma} \tag{2}$$

where μ and σ are the mean and standard deviation of the fitness values $f(x_1), f(x_2), \cdots, f(x_m)$ respectively.

Step 3.3: Generate the new candidate solution x_{new} using the formula (3) and evaluate its fitness value.

$$x_{new} = \sum_{i=1}^{n} w_i x_i \tag{3}$$

Step 3.4: If N new solutions have not been generated, go to Step 3.1.
Step 4: If the stop condition is not met, return Step 3.1.
The procedures of BSO-CLS have been given in the Algorithm 1.

Algorithm 1. BSO-CLS

1: Randomly initialize N candidate solutions $X \in R^{P \times D}$ with D dimension
2: Evaluate the fitness $Y = f(X)$ using the evaluation function f
3: **while** not stopping condition **do**
4:     **for** i = 1 to P **do**
5:         Randomly select m candidate solutions $x_1, x_2, \cdots, x_m$ as learning objects and their fitness values $f(x_1), f(x_2), \cdots, f(x_m)$.
6:         Calculate the learning weights $w_1, w_2, \cdots, w_m$ using formula (2)
7:         Generate the new candidate solution according to the formula (3)
8:     **end for**
9: **end while**

---

4   Experiments

In this section, we will present and discuss the experimental settings and results.

4.1   Benchmark Functions

To validate the effectiveness of the BSO-CLS, we test it on the 6 benchmark functions including the unimodal function (Sphere) and the multimodal functions (Rosenbrock, Ackley, Rastrigin, Schwefel, and Ellipsoid). Furthermore, in order to test the proposed method's performance on the various dimensions, we vary the dimensions from 10 to 1000 for all benchmark functions. The information of the benchmark functions are summarized in Table 1.

Table 1. The information of benchmark functions

Benchmark function	Function	Search space
Sphere	$f(\mathbf{x}) = \sum_{i=1}^{n} x_i^2$	$[-5.12, 5.12]^D$
Rosenbrock	$f(\mathbf{x}) = \sum_{i=1}^{n} [10(x_{i+1} - x_i^2)^2 + (1 - x_i)^2]$	$[-5, 10]^D$
Ackley	$f(\mathbf{x}) = -20.exp(-0.2\sqrt{\frac{1}{n}\sum_{i=1}^{n} x_i^2}) -$ $exp(\frac{1}{n}\sum_{i=1}^{n} cos(2\pi x_i)) + 20 + exp(1)$	$[-32, 32]^D$
Rastrigin	$f(\mathbf{x}) = 10n + \sum_{i=1}^{n} (x_i^2 - 10cos(2\pi x_i))$	$[-5.12, 5.12]^D$
Schwefel	$f(\mathbf{x}), = 418.9829n - \sum_{i=1}^{n} x_i sin(\sqrt{|x_i|})$	$[-500, 500]^D$
Ellipsoid	$f(\mathbf{x}) = \sum_{i=1}^{n} 10^{6\frac{i-1}{n-1}} x_i^2$	$[-100, 100]^D$

4.2 Comparison Method

This paper aims to propose a novel learning mechanism to generate the new candidate solutions for BSO algorithms. Therefore, we choose the most representative SI algorithm PSO [14], the original BSO algorithm [15] and the other BSO variant BSOLS with learning strategy [16]. The hyperparameters setting for each algorithm is given in Table 2.

Table 2. The hyperparameters setting for each algorithm

Algorithm	Hyperparameters setting
BSO	k $= 20$, $\mu = 0$, $\sigma = 1$, p$_{replace} = 0.2$, $p_{one} = 0.2$, N $= 100$, M $= 5$, p$_{onecluster} = 0.4$, $p_{twocluster} = 0.5$
PSO	w $= 0.9{\sim}0.4$, c$_1 = c_2 = 2.0$, $V_{MAXd} = 0.2 \times$ Range, N $= 40$, global version
BSO-LS	N $= 100$, m $= 5$, P$_{replace} = 0.2$, $P_{one} = 0.8$, $P_{onecluster} = 0.4$, P$_{twocluster} = 0.5$, $P_{dynamic} = 0.5$
BSO-CL	m $= 10$

4.3 Experimental Setting

In order to fairly compare all algorithms, they are tested with the same population size 100 and the same maximum number of function evaluations $1E4 \times D$ in each run for each test function, where D is the dimension. In order to reduce the statistical error, each algorithm is tested 30 times independently, and the mean and standard deviation (std) are reported for comparison.

4.4 Results and Discussion

The experimental results are given in Table 3, and the best results are marked with **bold**.

Table 3. Solutions accuracy (mean and std) comparisons.

Funtions		BSO		PSO		BSO-LS		BSO-CLS	
		Mean	Std	Mean	Std	Mean	Std	Mean	Std
Sphere	10	3.66e−34	7.12e−34	5.90e−42	5.87e−42	**0.00e+00**	**0.00e+00**	1.74e−06	2.67e−06
	50	4.12e−12	9.06e−12	**2.18e−13**	**8.22e−13**	6.61e−12	5.12e−12	3.21e−05	4.89e−05
	100	1.45e+01	2.56e+01	5.23e+01	8.11e+01	2.11e+00	5.61e+00	**6.42e−05**	**8.82e−05**
	500	3.80e+03	4.77e+04	5.12e+03	9.01e+03	7.24e+03	6.24e+03	**1.60e−02**	**3.17e−02**
	1000	7.25e+04	3.21e+04	7.13e+04	8.23e+04	5.15e+04	8.14e+04	**1.83e−01**	**2.84e−01**
Rosenbrock	10	2.21+00	3.78+00	1.21e+00	2.42e+00	9.66e+00	2.22e+00	**1.10e−05**	**2.52e−05**
	50	4.56+01	5.21+e01	7.92e+01	9.21e+01	8.89e+01	6.12e+01	**1.95e−06**	**3.69e−06**
	100	6.13e+02	4.45e+01	2.98e+02	8.87e+01	9.55e+02	6.73e+02	**2.18e−07**	**2.94e−07**
	500	2.38e+04	5.02e+02	6.66+e04	7.78e+02	3.91e+04	6.67e+04	**1.17e−07**	**1.71e−07**
	1000	8.32e+05	4.18e+03	6.33e+05	9.12e+03	7.43e+05	1.10e+03	**3.81e−08**	**5.76e−08**
Ackley	10	5.71e−05	7.98e−05	8.75e−05	2.20e−05	**9.13e−06**	**4.32e−06**	7.31e−03	6.49e−03
	50	3.22e+00	2.18e+00	7.11e+00	9.10e+00	6.28e+00	8.13e+00	**1.71e−01**	**1.67e−01**
	100	5.13e+02	6.33e+02	9.12e+02	6.23e+02	1.22e+02	5.11e+01	**3.17e−01**	**2.48e−01**
	500	7.13e+03	6.12e+03	5.55e+03	8.12e+03	9.12e+03	7.18e+03	**1.15e+00**	**1.95e−01**
	1000	2.26e+04	5.21e+02	7.71e+04	7.91e+02	6.32e+04	8.12e+01	**1.17e+00**	**2.57e−01**
Rastrigin	10	4.22e−01	5.99e−01	4.21e+00	1.10e+00	8.32e−01	7.22e−01	**1.43e−03**	**2.86e−03**
	50	8.81e+01	7.21e+01	2.27e+01	4.32e+01	7.21e+01	3.33e+01	**1.45e−01**	**2.25e−01**
	100	6.44e+03	4.21e+02	5.07e+03	8.89e+02	9.22e+03	8.84e+02	**7.78e−01**	**1.33e+00**
	500	3.21e+04	7.21e+02	3.37e+04	1.09e+02	8.50e+04	7.79e+02	**4.24e+01**	**2.15e+01**
	1000	7.71e+06	5.22e+04	5.03e+06	9.91e+05	7.68e+06	3.28e+04	**8.68e+01**	**3.47e+01**
Schwefel	10	7.21e−02	8.84e−02	5.53e−02	4.77e−02	9.01e−03	4.32e−03	**8.98e−04**	**1.41e−03**
	50	6.11e+00	3.25e+00	5.88e+00	4.32e+00	7.76e+00	2.43e+00	**2.74e−03**	**3.86e−03**
	100	1.13e+02	6.61e+01	7.87e+01	4.11e+02	5.78e+01	6.54e+01	**4.37e−03**	**4.93e−03**
	500	4.28e+03	5.55e+02	7.14e+03	5.27e+02	9.01e+03	2.34e+02	**2.45e−02**	**3.70e−02**
	1000	1.98e+04	9.31e+04	3.16e+04	2.19e+03	8.13e+02	5.26e+02	**6.48e−02**	**7.57e−02**
Ellipsoid	10	1.45e+00	2.03e+00	5.54e+01	3.22e+00	5.17e+00	6.63e+00	**9.73e−01**	**1.45e+00**
	50	7.36e+02	2.54e+02	8.94e+02	6.58e+02	4.13e+02	3.69e+02	**8.02e+00**	**1.22e+00**
	100	6.62e+03	5.17e+02	7.96e+02	3.88e+03	5.25e+02	7.13e+02	**1.56e+01**	**2.90e+01**
	500	4.13e+04	8.83e+03	1.48e+04	9.22e+04	3.66e+03	7.87e+03	**2.51e+02**	**3.09e+02**
	1000	5.16e+05	2.86e+04	5.22e+05	1.18e+03	8.96e+05	7.41e+04	**1.11e+03**	**1.13e+03**

As shown in Table 3, we can clearly observe that: (1) The proposed method can obtain competitive performance on the low dimension problems against other methods. (2) The proposed method outperforms all the comparison methods on the high dimension problems. (3) With the dimension increasing, the proposed method obtains better results on the Rosenbrock test function.

5   Conclusion

In this paper, we proposed a novel BSO variant named BSO-CLS, which introduced a simple yet effective cooperative learning mechanism. The key concept is inspired by the new ideas generating process of brain storm which the participators propose their own ideas by cooperatively learning other participators' ideas. Thus, BSO-CLS iteratively updates the candidate solutions by linearly combining other solutions with the weights deriving from the fitness values of other solutions. The effectiveness of the proposed method was validated on 6 benchmark functions for both low-dimension and high-dimension settings. The empirical results showed that BSO-CLS can outperform the vanilla BSO and the other BSO variant with the learning strategy especially for the large-scale optimization problems.

In the future, we plan to validate the proposed method on more complex problems, such as the rotation and shifted benchmark functions. We intend to explore the reasons behind the better performance on Rosenbrock function with the dimension increasing. Furthermore, we will test the influence of different normalization functions.

Acknowledgement. This work is supported by the National Science Foundation of China under the Grant No. 61761136008, the Shenzhen Peacock Plan under the Grant No. KQTD2016112514355531, the Program for Guangdong Introducing Innovative and Entrepreneurial Teams under the Grant No. 2017ZT07X386, the Science and Technology Innovation Committee Foundation of Shenzhen under the Grant No. ZDSYS201703031748284, Guangdong Provincial Key Laboratory under Grant No. 2020B121201001.

References

1. Cao, Z., Shi, Y., Rong, X., Liu, B., Du, Z., Yang, B.: Random grouping brain storm optimization algorithm with a new dynamically changing step size. In: Tan, Y., Shi, Y., Buarque, F., Gelbukh, A., Das, S., Engelbrecht, A. (eds.) ICSI 2015. LNCS, vol. 9140, pp. 357–364. Springer, Cham (2015). https://doi.org/10.1007/978-3-319-20466-6_38
2. Cheng, R., Jin, Y.: A competitive swarm optimizer for large scale optimization. IEEE Trans. Cybern. **45**(2), 191–204 (2014)
3. Cheng, S., Qin, Q., Chen, J., Shi, Y.: Brain storm optimization algorithm: a review. Artif. Intell. Rev. **46**(4), 445–458 (2016). https://doi.org/10.1007/s10462-016-9471-0
4. Cheng, S., Shi, Y. (eds.): Brain Storm Optimization Algorithms. ALO, vol. 23. Springer, Cham (2019). https://doi.org/10.1007/978-3-030-15070-9
5. Dorigo, M., Birattari, M., Stutzle, T.: Ant colony optimization. IEEE Comput. Intell. Mag. **1**(4), 28–39 (2006)
6. Eberhart, R.C., Shi, Y., Kennedy, J.: Swarm Intelligence. Elsevier (2001)
7. Kennedy, J.: Swarm intelligence. In: Zomaya, A.Y. (ed.) Handbook of Nature-Inspired and Innovative Computing, pp. 187–219. Springer, Boston (2006). https://doi.org/10.1007/0-387-27705-6_6
8. Li, X., Yao, X.: Cooperatively coevolving particle swarms for large scale optimization. IEEE Trans. Evol. Comput. **16**(2), 210–224 (2011)
9. Ma, L., Cheng, S., Shi, Y.: Enhancing learning efficiency of brain storm optimization via orthogonal learning design. IEEE Trans. Syst. Man Cybern. Syst. (2020)
10. MacQueen, J., et al.: Some methods for classification and analysis of multivariate observations. In: Proceedings of the Fifth Berkeley Symposium on Mathematical Statistics and Probability, Oakland, CA, USA, vol. 1, pp. 281–297 (1967)

11. Omidvar, M.N., Li, X., Mei, Y., Yao, X.: Cooperative co-evolution with differential grouping for large scale optimization. IEEE Trans. Evol. Comput. **18**(3), 378–393 (2013)
12. Qian, H., Hu, Y.Q., Yu, Y.: Derivative-free optimization of high-dimensional nonconvex functions by sequential random embeddings. In: IJCAI, pp. 1946–1952 (2016)
13. Shi, Y.: Brain storm optimization algorithm in objective space. In: 2015 IEEE Congress on Evolutionary Computation (CEC), pp. 1227–1234, May 2015. https:// doi.org/10.1109/CEC.2015.7257029
14. Shi, Y., Eberhart, R.: A modified particle swarm optimizer. In: 1998 IEEE International Conference on Evolutionary Computation Proceedings. IEEE World Congress on Computational Intelligence (Cat. No.98TH8360), pp. 69–73, May 1998. https://doi.org/10.1109/ICEC.1998.699146 ·
15. Shi, Y.: Brain storm optimization algorithm. In: Tan, Y., Shi, Y., Chai, Y., Wang, G. (eds.) ICSI 2011. LNCS, vol. 6728, pp. 303–309. Springer, Heidelberg (2011). https://doi.org/10.1007/978-3-642-21515-5_36
16. Wang, H., Liu, J., Yi, W., Niu, B., Baek, J.: An improved brain storm optimization with learning strategy. In: Tan, Y., Takagi, H., Shi, Y. (eds.) ICSI 2017. LNCS, vol. 10385, pp. 511–518. Springer, Cham (2017). https://doi.org/10.1007/978-3-319-61824-1_56
17. Zhan, Z., Zhang, J., Shi, Y., Liu, H.: A modified brain storm optimization. In: 2012 IEEE Congress on Evolutionary Computation, pp. 1–8. IEEE (2012)

A Hybrid Brain Storm Optimization Algorithm for Dynamic Vehicle Routing Problem

Mingde Liu, Yang Shen, and Yuhui Shi[✉]

Department of Computer Science and Engineering,
Southern University of Science and Technology, Shenzhen 518055, China
{11849245,sheny3}@mail.sustech.edu.cn, shiyh@sustech.edu.cn

Abstract. The Dynamic Vehicle Routing Problem (DVRP) has many real-world applications and practical values. The objective of DVRP is to find the optimal routes for a fleet of vehicles to service the given customer requests, without violating the vehicle capacity constraint. In this paper, a hybrid algorithm is proposed for solving the DVRP with the objective to minimize the total distance of the vehicles. The Brain Storm Optimization in objective space (BSO-OS) is applied to guide the choice of different strategies for the periodic reoptimization of routes. In the BSO-OS procedure, Adaptive Large Neighborhood Search (ALNS) and Ant Colony System (ACS) are used to generate new solutions. The experiments on the DVRP benchmark and comparative studies are conducted, from which 12 out of 21 new best solutions are obtained by the proposed algorithm, and the other nine solutions are also very competitive. The experimental results show that the proposed algorithm is very effective and competitive.

Keywords: Brain storm optimization in objective space · Ant colony system · Adaptive Large Neighborhood Search · Dynamic vehicle routing problem

1 Introduction

In recent years, logistics has drawn considerable attention in both research and industry. The Vehicle Routing Problem (VRP) is a classic logistics problem that seeks to find the optimal set of routes for a fleet of vehicles to service a given set of customers. Generally, the objective function of the VRP is to minimize the total travel distance. The VRP is proved NP-hard [10], when the size of the problem increases, exact algorithms become very time consuming and maybe invalid [5]. Therefore, researchers tend to use heuristics to solve VRPs.

In real-world scenarios, logistics companies or ride-hailing companies are facing the Dynamic Vehicle Routing Problems (DVRPs) [9]. For DVRPs, new customer requests arrive dynamically when the vehicles have already started servicing existing customer requests. Therefore, the routes of the vehicles have to

© Springer Nature Switzerland AG 2020
Y. Tan et al. (Eds.): ICSI 2020, LNCS 12145, pp. 251–258, 2020.
https://doi.org/10.1007/978-3-030-53956-6_23

be replanned at run time to minimize the cost, i.e, the routes have to be reoptimized. The reoptimization of DVRPs can be classified into two categories: periodic reoptimization and continuous reoptimization [14]. Generally, periodic reoptimization methods start with a first optimization of the initially known customer requests, then an optimization procedure solves the static VRP periodically with a fixed time interval [8]. For continuous reoptimization, whenever the new customer requests arrive, the reoptimization procedure starts to solve the new incoming data to update the routes [20]. Continuous reoptimization requires extensive computational resources. Also, if the new customer requests arrive very frequently, continuous reoptimization methods may repeat running and fail to update the routes. The advantages of periodic reoptimization are: 1) it transforms DVRPs to static VRPs to solve, and there exists extensive research on static VRPs; 2) the reoptimization is run independently during each time interval; 3) computational resources would be enough for each time interval; 4) it is more similar to practical applications. In this paper, we address the periodic reoptimization of DVRPs.

Many researches have been carried out based on the benchmark for DVRPs proposed by Kilby et al. [8] and extended by Montemanni et al. [12]. An algorithm based on Ant Colony System (ACS) was first proposed by Montemanni et al. [12] for the DVRPs. The ACS makes use of the pheromone to track the good components of a good solution. When the next time interval comes, the good components can be used by the reoptimization procedure. In addition, Hanshar et al. applied Genetic Algorithm (GA) to solve the DVRP and compared it with Tabu Search (TS) [6]. The proposed DVRP-GA algorithm used inversion operator [11] for mutation and a problem-specific operator Best-Cost Route Crossover (BCRC) for crossover. Moreover, a comparative study was carried out between the Dynamic Adapted Particle Swarm Optimization (DAPSO) algorithm and the Variable Neighborhood Search (VNS) algorithm for the DVRPs [7]. In the comparative study, the proposed DAPSO algorithm uses adaptive memory to reuse the information from the previous solutions, and the VNS algorithm systematically changes neighborhoods to escape from local optima. Additionally, an enhanced GA-based system [1] for DVRP was proposed to improve the DVRP-GA. The main modifications include the initial population of the time slices, the selection process, swap mutation, and a Local Optimal Condition (LOC) detection and escape strategy.

Brain Storm Optimization (BSO) [16,18] was first proposed in 2011, which is inspired by the human brainstorming process. In DVRPs, choosing different strategies to optimize the current state is similar to the brainstorming process. In the BSO procedure, different strategies were applied for simulating the problem owners to choose good solutions that they believe in the brainstorming process. To reduce the computational cost, an enhanced BSO algorithm in objective space named BSO-OS [17] was proposed in 2015. In this paper, we applied the BSO-OS algorithm and proposed a hybrid BSO algorithm named BSO-DVRP for solving DVRPs. The overall frame of the algorithm is BSO, and in the BSO procedure, two popular VRP heuristics are applied to generate new solutions, which are Adaptive Large Neighborhood Search (ALNS) [15] and ACS [3].

The rest of this paper is organized as follows. Section 2 illustrates the definition and model of DVRP. Section 3 introduces the proposed BSO-DVRP algorithm. Section 4 first describes the benchmark and then evaluates the proposed algorithm. Section 5 concludes the paper.

2 Problem Definition

In this paper, we explore a DVRP model based on the benchmark proposed by Kilby et al. [8] and Montemanni et al. [12], i.e., the DVRP model is a periodic reoptimization model. A DVRP model has a sequence of static VRP instances which contain all the customer requests known at each particular time, the periodic reoptimization needs to process the unserved customer requests.

In the DVRP model, all vehicles depart from the same depot to service customer requests. A vehicle is allowed to return to the depot when all customer requests have been serviced or the capacity of the vehicle has exceeded.

The DVRP has three parameters which are different from static VRP [1], which are: 1) the *available time* indicating that when the customer request appeared; 2) the *duration* for each customer request; 3) the *working day*, which determines the available time to service the customer requests.

For periodic reoptimization, the working day is divided into time slices. When new customer requests arrive during a time slice, these requests are delayed to the end of the time slice. Similar to static VRP, the objective function of DVRP is to minimize the total distance of all the routes. To better understand the DVRPs, Fig. 1 shows an example of DVRP. At time $t0$, the routes of the vehicles were planned based on the initially known customer requests. At time $t1$, when vehicles were executing their routes, some new customer requests arrived, then the reoptimization procedure was executed to process the remaining unserved customers. At time $t2$, when all the customers were serviced, the vehicles returned to the depot.

3 Proposed BSO-DVRP Algorithm

For static VRPs, population based methods and local search or neighborhood search have been widely used. In the DVRPs, a difficult problem is when and how to choose good strategies to optimize the current state (time slice). A good strategy can not only avoid local optima, but also make use of the solutions obtained from previous time slice. In this paper, we choose BSO [17] as a framework to determine when and what strategy to choose, and choose ALNS [15] and ACS [3] from extensive heuristics for VRPs reported in literature as two good strategies to choose from.

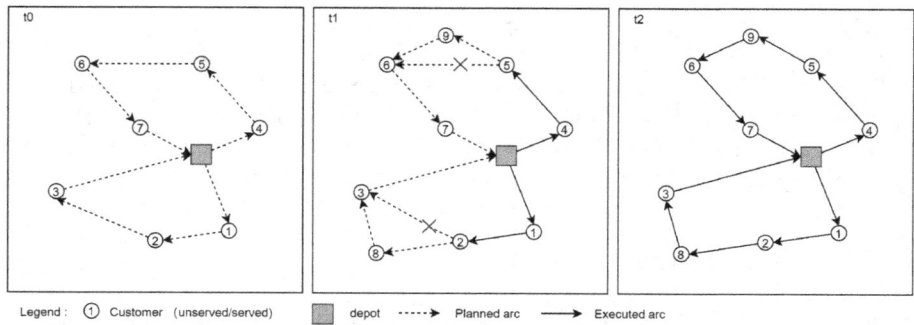

Fig. 1. An example of DVRP with

Algorithm 1. The BSO-DVRP Algorithm
___

1: initialize parameters and generate N solutions
2: **while** not terminated **do**
3:     evaluate and sort N solutions according to the fitness function (total distance)
4:     take the top $perc_e$ percentage as elitists, and set the remaining as normals
5:     **if** $rand(0,1) < p_{elitists}$ **then**   ▷ generate a new solution based on elitists
6:         **if** $rand(0,1) < p_{one}$ **then**
7:             randomly select a solution S_i in elitists
8:             $S' \leftarrow \text{ALNS}(S_i)$
9:         **else**
10:             randomly select two solutions S_i, S_j in elitists
11:             $S' \leftarrow \text{ACS}(S_i, S_j)$
12:         **end if**
13:     **else**   ▷ generate a new solution based on normals
14:         **if** $rand(0,1) < p_{one}$ **then**
15:             randomly select a solution S_i in normals
16:             $S' \leftarrow \text{ALNS}(S_i)$
17:         **else**
18:             randomly select two solutions S_i, S_j in normals
19:             $S' \leftarrow \text{ACS}(S_i, S_j)$
20:         **end if**
21:     **end if**
22:     **if** S' is better than S_i or S_i, S_j **then**
23:         replace S_i or the worse one between S_i and S_j
24:     **end if**
25: **end while**
26: **return** best solution in N solutions
___

ACS [3] is the most popular one among population based heuristics for VRP. The procedure of ACS is as the following: the ants depart from depot and select customers to service by pheromone one by one. When the ants can not service more customers, i.e., the vehicle capacity constraint can not be satisfied, the ants will return to the depot. Then, the ants will restart from the depot to service remained customers. The pheromone is updated after the ants completed their tours.

ALNS [15] is the most popular algorithm among neighborhood search for VRP. There are some heuristics to remove customer requests and some other heuristics to insert removed requests into routes in ALNS. The adaptive method is used to select the removal heuristics and inserting heuristics according to the history information.

BSO [16,18] is inspired by the human brainstorming process. In the BSO procedure, different strategies were applied for simulating the problem owners to choose good solutions that they believe in the brainstorming process. Since the clustering operation in the BSO algorithm is very time consuming, an enhanced version of BSO algorithm in objective space named BSO-OS [17] is proposed. In the BSO-OS algorithm, solutions are sorted according to their fitness values, and the top $perc_e$ percentage are set as elitists, while the remaining are set as normals. New solutions are generated in four ways: 1) generate a new solution based on one randomly selected elitist; 2) generate a new solution based on two randomly selected elitists; 3) generate a new solution based on one randomly selected normal; 4) generate a new solution based on two randomly selected normals.

To guide the choice of strategies, we applied the BSO-OS algorithm to choose different strategies, i.e., ALNS or ACS for the periodic reoptimization. In this paper, we propose a hybrid BSO algorithm named BSO-DVRP for solving the DVRPs. The pseudocode of the proposed algorithm is shown in Algorithm 1.

The overall frame of the algorithm is BSO-OS, in which ALNS and ACS are applied to generate new solutions. The new solutions are generated based on one solution or two solutions, either in elitists or in normals. If one solution S_i is selected, then ALNS is applied to perform a neighborhood search to generate a new solution. If two solutions S_i, S_j are selected, then these two solutions are sent to the ACS as the initial solution. By updating the pheromones, a new solution will be generated by ACS.

4   Experimental Results

4.1   Benchmark Description and Experiments Setup

In our experiments, we used the benchmarks proposed by Kilby et al. [8] and extended by Montemanni et al. [12], which were designed based on popular static VRP benchmarks proposed by Taillard [19], Christofides and Beasley [2], and Fisher [4]. There are three datasets in the benchmark: the first dataset has 12 instances with 75 to 150 customers; the second dataset consists of seven instances with 50 to 199 customers; and the third dataset contains two instances with 71 and 134 customers. In the DVRP instances, three types of data were introduced: 1) *available time* indicating that when the request first appeared; 2) *duration* for each request; 3) *working day*, which is the length of the day.

According to [13], when the number of time slices n_{ts} is set as 25, the trade-off between the total distance and the computational cost is well balanced. In addition, the working day is set as $16 \times 25 = 400$. The parameter settings of the BSO-OS algorithm are listed in Table 1.

Table 1. Parameter settings for BSO-OS

$perc_e$	$p_{elitists}$	p_{one}	max_iter
0.1	0.2	0.6	150

In Table 1, $perc_e$ is the percentage of elitists, $p_{elitists}$ is the probability of choosing elitists, p_{one} is the probability of choosing one solution, and max_iter is the maximum number of iterations.

The proposed algorithm was programmed in Python, and the DVRP experiments were conducted on an Intel Xeon E5-2650 CPU@2.30 GHz PC with 16 GB RAM.

4.2   Comparative Study

To evaluate the proposed algorithm, a comparative study has been conducted. The compared algorithms for DVRP are ACS [12], DVRP-GA and TS [6], DAPSO and VNS [7], and the GA-based DVRP [1]. The experimental results are given in Table 2, in which the best result for each instance is highlighted with bold fonts. The gap of the total distance (TD) is computed according to Eq. (1).

$$Gap = \frac{TD_{ours} - TD_{best}}{TD_{ours}} \tag{1}$$

where TD_{ours} is the total distance obtained by the proposed algorithm, and TD_{best} is the best total distance among all the compared algorithms for DVRP. A negative gap illustrates that the proposed algorithm outperforms all the other algorithms for DVRP, while a positive gap shows that the proposed algorithm is worse than the best result obtained by other algorithms.

As is observed from Table 2, 12 out of 21 new best solutions were found by the proposed algorithm, and the gap between our solutions and the previously best solutions ranges from -8.85% to -0.27%. From Table 2, the other nine solutions obtained by the proposed algorithm have a gap range from 0.11% to 6.91%, which are also competitive. All these results showed that the proposed algorithm is effective to generate high quality solutions for the DVRPs.

Table 2. Experimental results and comparison with literature for DVRP

Instance	ACS	DVRP-GA	TS	DAPSO	VNS	GA-based DVRP	BSO-DVRP	Gap (%)
c50	631.30	603.57	570.89	575.89	599.53	**566.01**	597.18	5.22
c75	1009.36	981.51	981.57	970.45	981.64	944.46	**938.79**	−0.60
c100	973.26	997.15	961.10	988.27	1022.92	943.89	**912.83**	−3.40
c100b	944.23	891.42	881.92	924.32	**866.71**	869.41	900.48	3.75
c120	1416.45	1331.80	1303.59	1276.88	1285.21	1288.66	**1173.10**	−8.85
c150	1345.73	1318.22	1348.88	1371.08	1334.73	1273.50	**1254.47**	−1.52
c199	1771.04	1750.09	1654.51	1640.40	1679.65	1646.36	**1631.23**	−0.56
tai75a	1843.08	1778.52	1782.91	1816.07	1806.81	1744.78	**1713.46**	−1.83
tai100a	2375.92	2208.85	2232.71	2249.84	2250.50	**2181.31**	2237.90	2.53
tai150a	3644.78	3488.02	3328.85	3400.33	3479.44	**3280.79**	3391.39	3.26
tai75b	1535.43	1461.37	1464.56	1447.39	1480.70	1441.35	**1426.93**	−1.01
tai100b	2283.97	2219.28	2147.70	2238.42	2169.10	2119.03	**2068.12**	−2.46
tai150b	3166.88	3109.23	2933.40	3013.99	2934.86	**2885.94**	2899.56	0.47
tai75c	1574.98	1406.27	1440.54	1481.35	1621.03	1433.73	**1392.96**	−0.96
tai100c	1562.30	1515.10	1541.28	1532.56	1490.58	1504.63	**1479.48**	−0.75
tai150c	2811.48	2666.28	2612.68	2714.34	2674.29	**2593.78**	2596.67	0.11
tai75d	1472.35	1430.83	**1399.83**	1414.28	1446.50	1408.48	1503.79	6.91
tai100d	2008.13	1881.91	1834.60	1955.06	1969.94	**1793.64**	1855.26	3.32
tai150d	3058.87	2950.83	2950.61	3025.43	2954.64	**2911.47**	3073.54	5.27
f71	311.18	280.23	301.79	279.52	304.32	288.30	**270.28**	−3.42
f134	15135.51	15717.90	15528.81	15875.00	15680.05	14871.40	**14831.29**	−0.27

5 Conclusions

In this paper, we proposed a BSO algorithm named BSO-DVRP for solving DVRPs. By cutting the working day into a certain number of time slices, the DVRP was transformed into static VRP to solve. To guide the choice of strategies for the periodic reoptimization, the BSO-OS algorithm was applied. In addition, two popular heuristics, ALNS and ACS were selected for generating new solutions in the proposed BSO procedure.

The experiments were conducted on the DVRP benchmark, and a comparative study with six algorithms for DVRP was carried out. A total of 12 out of 21 new best solutions were found by the proposed algorithm, and the other solutions obtained by the proposed algorithm were also competitive, which illustrated the effectiveness of the proposed algorithm.

Acknowledgment. This work is supported by the National Science Foundation of China under the Grant No. 61761136008, the Shenzhen Peacock Plan under the Grant No. KQTD2016112514355531, the Program for Guangdong Introducing Innovative and Entrepreneurial Teams under the Grant No. 2017ZT07X386, the Science and Technology Innovation Committee Foundation of Shenzhen under the Grant No. ZDSYS201703031748284.

258   M. Liu et al.

References

1. AbdAllah, A.M.F., Essam, D.L., Sarker, R.A.: On solving periodic re-optimization dynamic vehicle routing problems. Appl. Soft Comput. **55**, 1–12 (2017)
2. Christofides, N., Beasley, J.E.: The period routing problem. Networks **14**(2), 237–256 (1984)
3. Dorigo, M., Gambardella, L.M.: Ant colony system: a cooperative learning approach to the traveling salesman problem. IEEE Trans. Evol. Comput. **1**(1), 53–66 (1997)
4. Fisher, M.L., Jaikumar, R.: A generalized assignment heuristic for vehicle routing. Networks **11**(2), 109–124 (1981)
5. Golden, B.L., Raghavan, S., Wasil, E.A.: The Vehicle Routing Problem: Latest Advances and New Challenges, vol. 43. Springer, Heidelberg (2008)
6. Hanshar, F.T., Ombuki-Berman, B.M.: Dynamic vehicle routing using genetic algorithms. Appl. Intell. **27**(1), 89–99 (2007)
7. Khouadjia, M.R., Sarasola, B., Alba, E., Jourdan, L., Talbi, E.G.: A comparative study between dynamic adapted PSO and VNS for the vehicle routing problem with dynamic requests. Appl. Soft Comput. **12**(4), 1426–1439 (2012)
8. Kilby, P., Prosser, P., Shaw, P.: Dynamic VRPs: a study of scenarios. University of Strathclyde Technical Report, pp. 1–11 (1998)
9. Larsen, A.: The dynamic vehicle routing problem (2000)
10. Lenstra, J.K., Kan, A.R.: Complexity of vehicle routing and scheduling problems. Networks **11**(2), 221–227 (1981)
11. Mitchell, M.: An Introduction to Genetic Algorithms. MIT Press, Cambridge (1998)
12. Montemanni, R., Gambardella, L.M., Rizzoli, A.E., Donati, A.V.: A new algorithm for a dynamic vehicle routing problem based on ant colony system. In: Second International Workshop on Freight Transportation and Logistics, vol. 1, pp. 27–30 (2003)
13. Montemanni, R., Gambardella, L.M., Rizzoli, A.E., Donati, A.V.: Ant colony system for a dynamic vehicle routing problem. J. Comb. Optim. **10**(4), 327–343 (2005)
14. Pillac, V., Gendreau, M., Guéret, C., Medaglia, A.L.: A review of dynamic vehicle routing problems. Eur. J. Oper. Res. **225**(1), 1–11 (2013)
15. Ropke, S., Pisinger, D.: An adaptive large neighborhood search heuristic for the pickup and delivery problem with time windows. Transp. Sci. **40**(4), 455–472 (2006)
16. Shi, Y.: Brain storm optimization algorithm. In: Tan, Y., Shi, Y., Chai, Y., Wang, G. (eds.) ICSI 2011. LNCS, vol. 6728, pp. 303–309. Springer, Heidelberg (2011). https://doi.org/10.1007/978-3-642-21515-5_36
17. Shi, Y.: Brain storm optimization algorithm in objective space. In: 2015 IEEE Congress on Evolutionary Computation (CEC), pp. 1227–1234. IEEE (2015)
18. Shi, Y.: An optimization algorithm based on brainstorming process. In: Emerging Research on Swarm Intelligence and Algorithm Optimization, pp. 1–35. IGI Global (2015)
19. Taillard, É.: Parallel iterative search methods for vehicle routing problems. Networks **23**(8), 661–673 (1993)
20. Taillard, É.D., Gambardella, L.M., Gendreau, M., Potvin, J.Y.: Adaptive memory programming: a unified view of metaheuristics. Eur. J. Oper. Res. **135**(1), 1–16 (2001)

Determinative Brain Storm Optimization

Georgia Sovatzidi and Dimitris K. Iakovidis$^{(\boxtimes)}$

University of Thessaly, Papasiopoulou Street 2-4, 35131 Lamia, Greece
g.sovatzidi@gmail.com, diakovidis@uth.gr

Abstract. Brain Storm Optimization (BSO) is a swarm intelligence optimization algorithm, based on the human brainstorming process. The ideas of a brainstorming process comprise the solutions of the algorithm, which iteratively applies solution grouping, generation and selection operators. Several modifications of BSO have been proposed to enhance its performance. In this paper, we propose a novel modification enabling faster convergence of BSO to optimal solutions, without requiring setting an upper bound of algorithm iterations. It considers a brainstorming scenario where participating groups with similar ideas recognize that their ideas are similar, and together, collaborate for the determination of a better solution. The proposed modification, called Determinative BSO (DBSO), implements this scenario by applying a cluster merging strategy for merging groups of similar solutions, while following elitist selection. Experimental results using eleven benchmark functions show that the proposed modified BSO performs better than both the original and a state-of-the-art algorithm.

Keywords: Brain Storm Optimization · Swarm intelligence · Cluster merging

1 Introduction

Motivated by the way people cooperate to solve problems Shi [24] proposed a metaheuristic, swarm optimization algorithm, named Brain Storm Optimization (BSO) algorithm. BSO is a recent algorithm inspired by the human brainstorming process, which obeys the Osborn's four rules [20]. The members of a group that participate in the generation of an idea have to be open-minded and with an, as much as possible, diverse background. BSO possesses a great potential as an optimization tool and it has already been applied to solve successfully problems in various domains. Some of these applications include optimal design of efficient motors [8], optimization of satellite formation and reconfiguration [27], optimization of coverage and connectivity of wireless sensor networks [22], image fusion [19], prediction of protein folding kinetics [1], classification [15], and stock index forecasting [30].

Since the introduction of BSO, in 2011, many attempts have been made to improve its performance. Such an attempt is the Modified BSO (MBSO) [36], which uses a simple grouping method (SGM) for grouping ideas, instead of the k-means clustering algorithm used in the original BSO. Another attempt is the Quantum-behaved BSO (QBSO) [9], which has been proposed to cope with entrapment in local optima by an approach inspired by quantum theory. Zhou *et al.* [37] introduced an adaptive step-size coefficient,

© Springer Nature Switzerland AG 2020
Y. Tan et al. (Eds.): ICSI 2020, LNCS 12145, pp. 259–271, 2020.
https://doi.org/10.1007/978-3-030-53956-6_24

which can be utilized to balance the convergence speed of the algorithm. Various solution, generation and selection strategies have been proposed, mainly aiming to maintain the diversity for the whole population. In [35] two different mutation operators were considered to generate new individuals, independently, based on the Gaussian and the Cauchy distribution, respectively. The use of the latter distribution has a higher probability of making longer jumps than the former one, due to its long flat tails. Differential Evolution, Chaotic and hybrid mutation strategies have been considered to optimize the performance of BSO [7, 14, 32, 34] by avoiding premature convergence. In [8, 21], the predator-prey method has been proposed for better utilization of the global information of the swarm and diversification of the population. This method considers that the cluster centers play the role of predators, whereas the other solutions play the role of preys. Other approaches that have been proposed to maintain the population diversity include the Niche approach [38], the multiple partial re-initializations [6], and the Max-fitness Clustering Method (MCM) [13]. The latter is used to divide the solutions into sub-groups and obtain multiple global and local optima, in accordance with a self-adaptive parameter control. The control aims to adjust the exploration and exploitation, by reducing similar solutions in subpopulations. In [25] an objective space was used to reduce the computation time for convergence, instead of the solution space. A consequence of this approach is that the computation time becomes dependent on the size of the population, and not on the dimension of the problem. Multi-Objective Differential Brain Storm Optimization (MDBSO) algorithm [33] has been proposed as an extension of this approach using a differential mutation operation instead of the Gaussian. Global-best BSO (GBSO) uses the global-best idea for updating the population [11]. An elitist learning strategy of BSO has been proposed in [29]. According to this approach the first half individuals with better fitness values are maintained, while other individuals with worse fitness values can improve their performances by learning from the excellent ones. Cao *et al.* proposed a random grouping strategy as a replacement of the k-means clustering method [2], whereas Guo *et al.* proposed a self-adaptive Multiobjective BSO [12]. The combination of the information of one or more clusters has been considered in [5], using affinity propagation, which does not require to know in advance, the number of clusters. In [10] a stagnation-triggered re-initialization scheme has been proposed, where the search space information has been incorporated into the step size update. Agglomerative hierarchical clustering has been considered for BSO in [4], in order to avoid the use of a predefined number of clusters for the grouping of the generated solutions, and to enhance solution searching. In addition, an improved BSO (IBSO) algorithm [28] based on graph theory has been introduced, in order to enhance the diversity of the algorithm and help BSO escape from local optima. A GPU-based implementation of BSO using NVIDIA's CUDA technology has been investigated in [17]. In [18], an objective space-based cluster Multi-objective Brainstorm Optimization algorithm (MOBSO-OS), has been introduced for improving the computational efficiency, considering sparsity and measurement error as two competing cost function terms. The modification of BSO described in [31] is based on an orthogonal experimental design strategy, which aims to discover useful search experiences for improving the convergence and solution accuracy. The convergence of the BSO has also been analyzed by using the Markov model [39].

The termination of the original BSO algorithm and most of its current modifications usually depend on a predefined upper bound of algorithm iterations, whereas the role of clustering in the algorithm convergence has not been sufficiently investigated. To address these issues, in this paper we propose a novel modification of BSO, which considers a differentiated brainstorming scenario from the scenario considered in the original BSO. Specifically, it considers that during the brainstorming process, participating groups with similar ideas agree about the similarity of their ideas and collaborate for the determination of a better solution. This is implemented by following a cluster merging strategy per algorithm iteration, where the most similar clusters represent the groups with the similar ideas. This way, and by employing an elitist approach to the selection of the ideas, the algorithm is directed to convergence. In that sense, the proposed modification of BSO is called Determinative BSO (DBSO).

The rest of this paper is organized in four sections. Section 2 describes the principles of the original BSO, and Sect. 3 presents the proposed DBSO. The experiments performed and the results obtained are presented in Sect. 4. The conclusions of our study are summarized in Sect. 5.

2   Original BSO

Swarm intelligence algorithms have been inspired by the collective behavior of animals like ants, fish, birds, bees, etc. However, BSO is inspired by the most intelligent creature in the world, human being, and the way people brainstorm to find solutions to problems [24]. A facilitator, a brainstorming group of people and several problem owners are necessary to carry out the procedure. Moreover, in order to generate ideas and avoid inhibitions, Osborn's original four rules have to be obeyed. These rules are: 1) No judgment and evaluation should occur during the session; 2) Encourage the creativity of the members; 3) Combination of ideas and improvement are sought. Participants should suggest how ideas of other members can be improved; or how two or more ideas can be combined to create a new idea; 4) Go for quantity. Members should generate as many ideas as possible, because brainstorming mainly focuses on quantity of ideas, rather than their quality. The original BSO, in general, consists of the following four steps: initialization, grouping, generation and selection of solutions. All of them, except the first one, are repeated in each iteration, until a termination condition is met. More specifically, in the beginning, a population of N individuals is generated. Each of these individuals represents a different idea, randomly initialized within a search parameter space. Then, BSO evaluates these ideas according to a fitness function and uses the k-means clustering algorithm to group them into M clusters. The best idea in each cluster is recorded as the cluster center. A partial re-initialization is performed, as a randomly selected center is replaced by a new idea. In order to generate new individuals, BSO in a random way, in the beginning, chooses one or two clusters and then the cluster center that is selected is the one of them all that has higher priority or another idea in the cluster. The new individual generation is updated according to the formula:

$$X_{new}^d = X_{sel}^d + \xi \cdot n(\mu, \sigma)$$

(1)

where X_{new}^d is the dth dimension of individual newly generated, $n(\mu, \sigma)$ is the Gaussian random value with mean μ and standard deviation σ, X_{sel}^d is the dth dimension of individual selected to generate new individual and ξ is the step-size coefficient, which is a parameter controlling the convergence speed. Step-size is estimated as:

$$\xi = logsig\left(\frac{0.5 \cdot max_{it} - curr_{it}}{k}\right) \cdot p \qquad (2)$$

where $logsig$ is a logarithmic sigmoid transfer function, k adjusts the slope of the function, max_{it} and $curr_{it}$ denote the maximum number of iterations and current iteration number respectively. Variable p returns a random value within the range $(0, 1)$.

After the idea generation, the newly generated individual is compared with the existing individual, they are evaluated and the better one is kept and recorded as the new individual.

3 Determinative BSO

In the brainstorming process, a group of individuals gather and exchange their ideas, in order to find a solution for a given problem. During the brainstorming, there are many ideas produced by individuals of different background and as the process progresses, possible solutions are discussed and combined, in order to determine the best solution. However, it is common for a human brainstorming process not to be productive [26]. In this paper we consider a scenario where the brainstorming is performed by individuals that are willingly collaborate in order to converge faster to optimal solutions. To this end, individuals who have similar ideas, recognize and agree that their ideas are similar to each other, and they are grouped together to collaborate for the determination of an even better idea. This determinative BSO (DBSO) process is implemented by employing a cluster merging strategy in the grouping of the ideas and by selecting the best ideas per algorithm iteration. In addition, cluster merging is a method to identify general-shaped clusters [3].

Examining the process of the original BSO, described in the previous section, it can be observed that there is not any kind of directionality in the brainstorming process. Moreover, the BSO algorithm needs to be improved in the ability of preventing premature convergence and "jumping out" of local optima. In this paper, we propose a modification of BSO capable of automatically converging to optimal solutions. Particularly, clustering starts with a relatively large number of clusters, which represents possible ideas and whenever clusters are identified, the clusters are merged, after taking into consideration the criteria mentioned above. After the number of clusters has been reduced and there are not any other, different enough, possible solutions, the algorithm ends.

The detailed procedure of the DBSO is presented in Fig. 1, along with the basic steps of the original BSO [24]. The particular steps introduced in DBSO are highlighted with a red dashed line. In **step 1** the initialization of the parameters and the random generation of N individuals (potential solutions), are performed. In **step 2**, the clustering strategy separates the N individuals into $M < N$ clusters, using k-means. In **step 3**, the

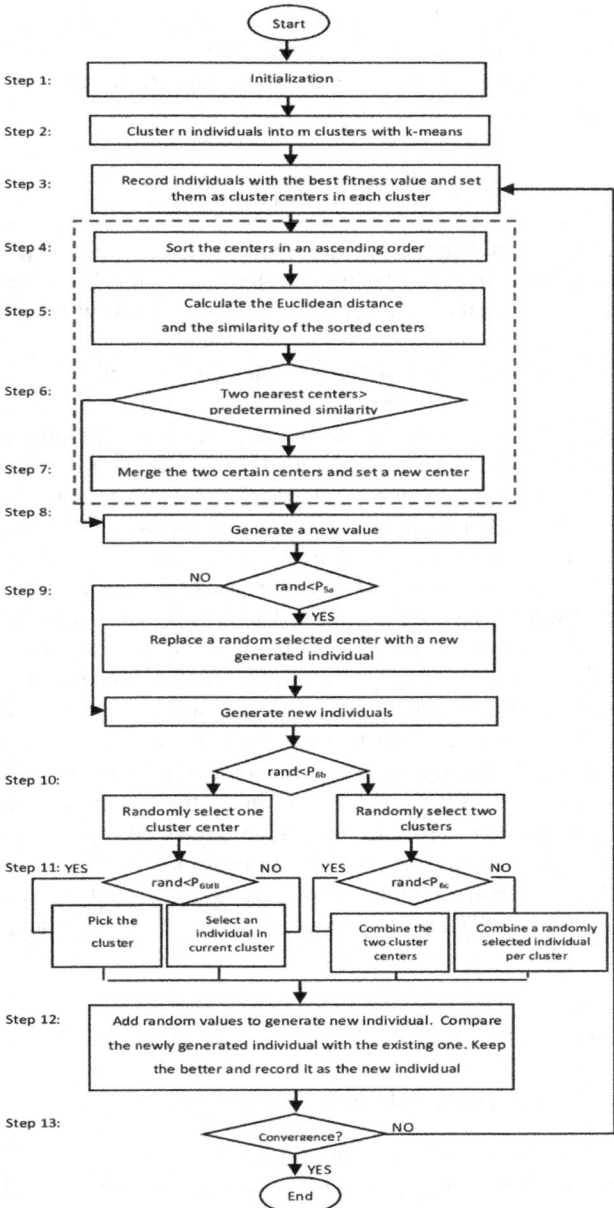

Fig. 1. Flowchart of DBSO algorithm

best individual is recorded as cluster center of each cluster, according to their fitness value. In **step 4**, the cluster centers are sorted in an ascending order. In **step 5**, the Euclidean distance of the centers and then the similarity, are calculated. The similarity S is calculated based on the follwing formula [23]:

$$S = \frac{1}{1 + dist(x, y)} \tag{3}$$

where *dist* is the Euclidean distance between two elements x, y. In **step 6**, the first two sorted centers are selected. In particular, the selected centers are the two centers with the smallest distance among all the sorted centers, which have also the biggest similarity, taking into consideration Eq. (3).

If they are similar enough, in **step 7**, merge the respective cluster centers and set as their new center, the center, which precedes in the ascending order between the two of them. Otherwise, go directly to step 8. In **step 8**, generate a new random value in the range [0, 1); In **step 9**, if the randomly generated value is smaller than a predetermined probability P_{5a}, randomly select a cluster center and then randomly generate an individual to replace the selected center. Then, generate new individuals, otherwise, generate directly new individuals. In **step 10**, randomly select one cluster, with probability P_{6b}, otherwise, select two clusters. In **step 11a**, for the case of the selection of one cluster, of step 10: if a random value generated is smaller than P_{6b3}, which is a probability to select the center of one selected cluster, pick the cluster center. Otherwise, randomly select an individual in the current cluster. Else, for the case of the selection of two clusters, of step 10, in **step 11b**, if a random value generated is smaller than P_{6c}, which is the probability to select the centers of two selected clusters, combine the two cluster centers. Otherwise, two individuals from each selected cluster are randomly selected to be combined. In **step 12**, add random values to the selected centers or individuals, in order to generate a new individual. Then, compare the newly generated individual with the existing ones. Keep the better one and record it as the new individual. In **step 13,** if there is no convergence to the best solution or a termination condition, repeat the algorithm from step 3, until there are not any other similar enough clusters that can be merged. Otherwise, end the algorithm.

4 Experiments and Results

4.1 Parameter Settings and Benchmark Functions

To evaluate DBSO a set of eleven benchmark functions were used, which are presented in Table 1, along with their bounds [16]. DBSO is compared not only with the original BSO, but also with a modified version, named IBSO [28]. For each benchmark function, both DBSO and BSO were executed 50 times, in order to obtain justifiable statistical results, as for different runs and values of parameters different results may be generated. Each of these functions has twenty independent variables, the population was set to be 50 individuals, the maximum number of generations were set to 1000 and the number of clusters 5. Moreover, the similarity degree for the clusters to be merged, which is referred in step 7 of the algorithm, was set to 65%, after preliminary experimentations,

Table 1. Benchmark Functions.

Function	Name	Bounds
f1	Alpine	[−10, 10]
f2	Dixon & Price	[−10, 10]
f3	Griewank	[−100, 100]
f4	Pathological function	[−100, 100]
f5	Schwefel 2.22	[−100,100]
f6	Schwefel 2.26	[−512, 512]
f7	Schwefel 2.21	[−100, 100]
f8	Zakharov	[−5,10]
f9	Ackley	[−35, 35]
f10	Matyas	[−10, 10]
f11	Sphere	[0, 10]

which indicated that it provides best results in most cases. In addition, DBSO was tested with a wider population in order to examine its performance.

The results of the experiments and the comparisons performed are summarized in Table 2, 3 and 4. The best results are indicated in boldface typesetting. The tables include the average values and the standard deviation (±) of the eleven benchmark functions that are presented below, obtained by DBSO in comparison with BSO and IBSO. The number of iterations of DBSO and BSO, in Table 2 and Table 3, shows the number of iterations that are needed in order the algorithm to converge.

4.2 Comparison of DBSO and BSO

In order to investigate the performance of DBSO and BSO on solving several types of problems, the two algorithms were tested on several benchmark functions, introduced in Table 1, with a wider number of population and clusters. Firstly, the experiments were done for a population of 50 and 5 clusters and then for a population of 500 and 10 clusters.

Table 1 includes functions that are multimodal and unimodal. Multimodal are the functions that have multiple local minima. As it can be noticed in Table 2, DBSO performs better than BSO, both in function minimization and the number of iterations required to converge, in multimodal functions (f1), (f6), (f9) and (f11). The presented results have been obtained by averaging, over 50 independent runs of the respective algorithms. For the multimodal functions (f3) and (f8) DBSO perform equivalently to the original BSO. For the unimodal benchmark functions (f2), (f5), (f7), (f10) DBSO exhibits also a better performance comparing to BSO. However, in (f4) BSO has provided better results than DBSO. As it can be noticed, DBSO converges earlier in most cases, taking into consideration the comparison with the original BSO. Furthermore, the convergence of

DBSO and BSO is illustrated indicatively on Fig. 2. The diagrams have been obtained by averaging the results of 50 independent runs of the respective algorithms.

Moreover, for the case of DBSO with a larger population and number of clusters, the similarity was set to be 60%. The results of the experiments are summarized in Table 3 and, indicatively, the convergence process is presented in Fig. 3. The presented results have been obtained by averaging, over 50 independent runs of the respective algorithms. DBSO, in this case, has a better performance in minimization on four out of four benchmark functions, in comparison with the original BSO. Moreover, considering the number of iterations required for convergence, DBSO converges in less iterations in (f4), (f7), (f11). However, in (f6), the required iterations of convergence for BSO seem to be less than those of DBSO. DBSO with a population of 500 individuals and 10 clusters appears to be more stable than DBSO with a population size equal to 50 and 5 clusters. In addition, the convergence is earlier in the latter case of Table 4 in comparison with the respective results presented in Table 2.

Table 2. Results of DBSO and BSO for a population of 50 individuals and 5 clusters.

Function	DBSO	BSO	Iterations of DBSO	Iterations of BSO
f1	**2.4E−01 ± 2.5E−01**	2.9E−01 ± 2.4E−01	**750**	754
f2	**7.4E−01 ± 1.2E−01**	7.9E−01 ± 2.1E−01	**465**	583
f3	**1.6E−01 ± 3.9E−01**	1.6E−01 ± 4.5E−01	**314**	395
f4	7E+00 ± 4.8E−01	**6.6E+00 ± 4.9E−01**	644	**543**
f5	**3.7E−03 ± 1.1E−02**	1.4E−02 ± 6.1E−02	**744**	890
f6	**3E+03 ± 6.5E+02**	3.3E+03 ± 834.8E+00	**256**	279
f7	**7.98E−03 ± 2E−02**	8.21E03 ± 7.4E−03	**740**	952
f8	**1.9E−01 ± 8.7E−01**	1.9E−01 ± 1.4E−01	**711**	831
f9	**6.9E−13 ± 4E−13**	8.3E−13 ± 4.1E−13	**879**	951
f10	**1E−26 ± 1E−26**	1.1E−26 ± 1.3E−26	**974**	990
f11	**2.8E−21 ± 9.7E−22**	2.9E−21 ± 9.7E−22	**94**	99

Table 3. Comparison of DBSO and BSO for a population of 500 individuals and 10 clusters.

Function	DBSO	BSO	Iterations of DBSO	Iterations of BSO
f4	**5.9E+00 ± 1.4E−01**	6.1E+00 ± 1.8E−01	**525**	620
f6	**2.8E+03 ± 5.7E+02**	2.9E+03 ± 6.7E+02	165	**116**
f7	**4E−15 ± 6.1E−16**	1.5E−11 ± 1.7E−12	**110**	126
f11	**5.8E−29 ± 1E−29**	8.6E−22 ± 1.7E−22	**110**	115

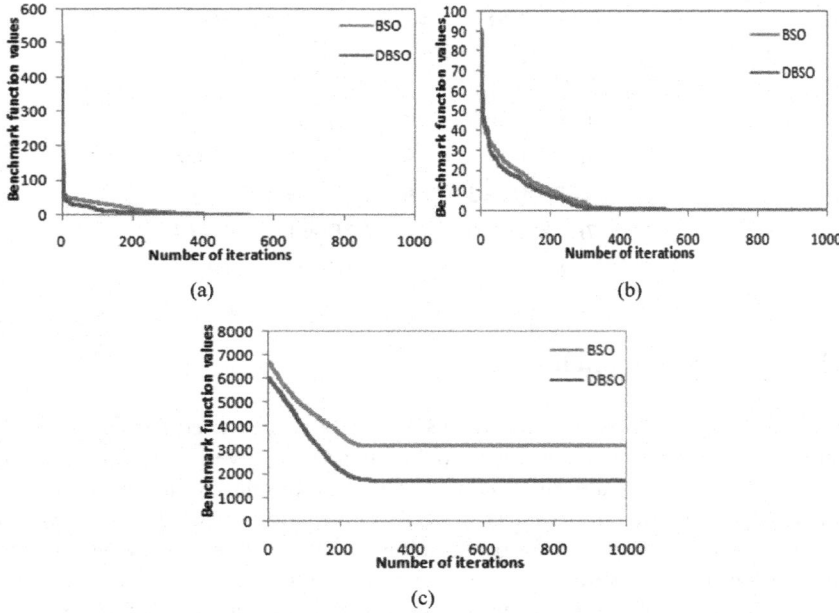

Fig. 2. Convergence of DBSO and BSO tested on benchmark functions for a population of 50 individuals and 5 clusters; (a) Dixon & Price, (b) Schwefel 2.21, (c) Schwefel 2.26.

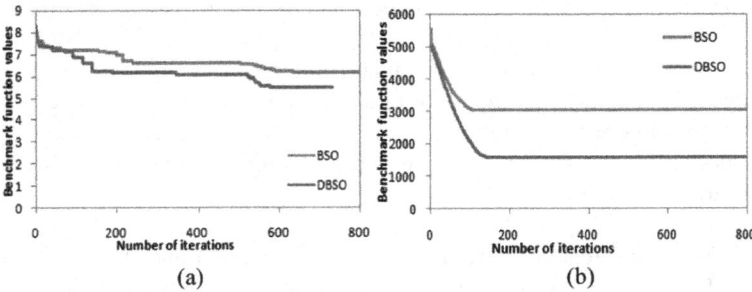

Fig. 3. Convergence of DBSO and BSO tested on benchmark functions for a population of 500 individuals and 10 clusters. (a) Pathological function, (b) Schwefel 2.26.

4.3   Comparison of DBSO and IBSO

The proposed DBSO algorithm was compared also with the state-of-the-art algorithm IBSO, which is a modified version of BSO based on graph theory [28]. The parameters of DBSO were set to the same values with those used in [28], for a fair comparison. The results of the comparison of DBSO and IBSO are presented in Table 4. As it can be observed from Table 4, DBSO has better results on six out of seven benchmark functions (*f1–f3*) and (*f5–f7*). IBSO, though, provides better results comparing to DBSO in (*f4*).

Table 4. DBSO and BSO tested on 5 benchmark functions

Function	DBSO	IBSO
f1	**2.4E−01 ± 2.5E−01**	3.5E−01 ± 3.1E−01
f2	**7.4E−01 ± 1.2E−01**	3.7E+00 ± 8.6E+00
f3	**1.6E−01 ± 3.9E−01**	1E+00 ± 2.4E−16
f4	7E+00 ± 4.8E−01	**6.7E+00 ± 4.7E−01**
f5	**3.7E−03 ± 1.1E−02**	6.4E−03 ± 1E−02

5   Discussion and Conclusions

In this paper, a new improved version of BSO is introduced, named DBSO. DBSO has been modified in order to converge more efficiently and effectively to optimal solutions. Specifically, the proposed algorithm considers that during the brainstorming process, participating groups with similar ideas agree about the similarity of their ideas and collaborate for the determination of a better solution. This is achieved by introducing a cluster merging strategy, per algorithm iteration, where the most similar clusters represent the groups with the similar ideas. Along with the elitist approach followed to the selection of the ideas, the proposed BSO modification provides a faster convergence compared to current BSO algorithms, while maintaining the diversity among the fittest solutions.

According to the results of the experiments and the comparisons performed:

• DBSO performs well both in multimodal and unimodal functions;
• The proposed method helps the algorithm find the best solution, while forces the algorithm converge in less iterations;
• DBSO succeeds a satisfactory stability in repeated experiments, after directing the solutions to the better one.

BSO possesses a great potential as an optimization tool and it has already been applied to solve successfully problems in various domains. It is a promising algorithm; however, it needs further investigation. With regard to future work, we plan to improve and investigate DBSO even more, addressing open questions related, but not limited to, the following:

• More benchmark functions with larger dimensions and wider population sizes;
• The development of hybrid models based on BSO for complicated real-time optimization problems;
• Comparisons of DBSO with other swarm intelligence algorithms, including other versions of BSO, e.g., chaotic, and state-of-the-art nature inspired approaches.

Acknowledgment. This research has been co-financed by the European Union and Greek national funds through the Operational Program Competitiveness, Entrepreneurship and Innovation, under the call RESEARCH—CREATE—INNOVATE (project code: T1EDK-02070).

References

1. Anbarasi, M., Saleem Durai, M.: Prediction of protein folding kinetics states using hybrid brainstorm optimization. Int. J. Comput. Appl. **2018**, 1–9 (2018)
2. Cao, Z., Shi, Y., Rong, X., Liu, B., Du, Z., Yang, B.: Random grouping brain storm optimization algorithm with a new dynamically changing step size. In: Tan, Y., Shi, Y., Buarque, F., Gelbukh, A., Das, S., Engelbrecht, A. (eds.) ICSI 2015. LNCS, vol. 9140, pp. 357–364. Springer, Cham (2015). https://doi.org/10.1007/978-3-319-20466-6_38
3. Celebi, M.E., et al.: A comparative study of efficient initialization methods for the k-means clustering algorithm. Expert Syst. Appl. **40**(1), 200–210 (2013)
4. Chen, J., Wang, J., Cheng, S., Shi, Y.: Brain storm optimization with agglomerative hierarchical clustering analysis. In: Tan, Y., Shi, Y., Li, L. (eds.) ICSI 2016. LNCS, vol. 9713, pp. 115–122. Springer, Cham (2016). https://doi.org/10.1007/978-3-319-41009-8_12
5. Chen, J., Cheng, S., Chen, Y., Xie, Y., Shi, Y.: Enhanced brain storm optimization algorithm for wireless sensor networks deployment. In: Tan, Y., Shi, Y., Buarque, F., Gelbukh, A., Das, S., Engelbrecht, A. (eds.) ICSI 2015. LNCS, vol. 9140, pp. 373–381. Springer, Cham (2015). https://doi.org/10.1007/978-3-319-20466-6_40
6. Cheng, S., et al.: Population diversity maintenance in brain storm optimization algorithm. J. Artif. Intell. Soft Comput. Res. **4**(2), 83–97 (2014)
7. Chu, X., Chen, J., Cai, F., Chen, C., Niu, B.: Augmented brain storm optimization with mutation strategies. In: Shi, Y., et al. (eds.) SEAL 2017. LNCS, vol. 10593, pp. 949–959. Springer, Cham (2017). https://doi.org/10.1007/978-3-319-68759-9_78
8. Duan, H., et al.: Predator–prey brain storm optimization for DC brushless motor. IEEE Trans. Magn. **49**(10), 5336–5340 (2013)
9. Duan, H., Li, C.: Quantum-behaved brain storm optimization approach to solving Loney's solenoid problem. IEEE Trans. Magn. **51**(1), 1–7 (2015)
10. El-Abd, M.: Brain storm optimization algorithm with re-initialized ideas and adaptive step size. In: 2016 IEEE Congress on Evolutionary Computation (CEC 2016), pp. 2682–2686 (2016)
11. El-Abd, M.: Global-best brain storm optimization algorithm. Swarm Evol. Comput. **37**(2017), 27–44 (2017)
12. Guo, X., Wu, Y., Xie, L., Cheng, S., Xin, J.: An adaptive brain storm optimization algorithm for multiobjective optimization problems. In: Tan, Y., Shi, Y., Buarque, F., Gelbukh, A., Das, S., Engelbrecht, A. (eds.) ICSI 2015. LNCS, vol. 9140, pp. 365–372. Springer, Cham (2015). https://doi.org/10.1007/978-3-319-20466-6_39
13. Guo, X., Wu, Y., Xie, L.: Modified brain storm optimization algorithm for multimodal optimization. In: Tan, Y., Shi, Y., Coello, C.A.C. (eds.) ICSI 2014. LNCS, vol. 8795, pp. 340–351. Springer, Cham (2014). https://doi.org/10.1007/978-3-319-11897-0_40
14. Guo, Y., et al.: Grid-based dynamic robust multi-objective brain storm optimization algorithm. Soft. Comput. **2019**, 1–21 (2019). https://doi.org/10.1007/s00500-019-04365-w
15. Ibrahim, R.A., et al.: Galaxy images classification using hybrid brain storm optimization with moth flame optimization. J. Astron. Telescopes Instrum. Syst. **4**(3), 038001 (2018)
16. Jamil, M., Yang, X.-S.: A literature survey of benchmark functions for global optimization problems. arXiv preprint arXiv:1308.4008 (2013)

17. Jin, C., Qin, A.K.: A GPU-based implementation of brain storm optimization. In: 2017 IEEE Congress on Evolutionary Computation (CEC 2017), pp. 2698–2705 (2017)
18. Liang, J., et al.: Multi-objective brainstorm optimization algorithm for sparse optimization. In: 2018 IEEE Congress on Evolutionary Computation (CEC 2018), pp. 1–8 (2018)
19. Madheswari, K., et al.: Visible and thermal image fusion using curvelet transform and brain storm optimization. In: Region 10 Conference (TENCON), 2016 IEEE (2016), pp. 2826–2829 (2016)
20. Osborn, A.F.: Applied Imagination, Scribner. Charles Scribner, New York (1953)
21. Qiu, H., et al.: Chaotic predator-prey brain storm optimization for continuous optimization problems. In: 2017 IEEE Symposium Series on Computational Intelligence (SSCI 2017), pp. 1–7 (2017)
22. Ramadan, R., Khedr, A.: Brain storming algorithm for coverage and connectivity problem in wireless sensor network. In: Communication, Management and Information Technology: International Conference on Communciation, Management and Information Technology, Cosenza, Italy, 26–29 April 2016 (ICCMIT 2016), p. 371 (2016)
23. Segaran, T.: Collective Intelligence-Building Smart Web 2.0 Applications. O'Reilly, Newton (2007)
24. Shi, Y.: Brain storm optimization algorithm. In: Tan, Y., Shi, Y., Chai, Y., Wang, G. (eds.) ICSI 2011. LNCS, vol. 6728, pp. 303–309. Springer, Heidelberg (2011). https://doi.org/10.1007/978-3-642-21515-5_36
25. Shi, Y.: Brain storm optimization algorithm in objective space. In: 2015 IEEE Congress on evolutionary computation (CEC 2015), 1227–1234 (2015)
26. Stroebe, W., et al.: Beyond productivity loss in brainstorming groups: the evolution of a question. Adv. Exp. Soc. Psychol. **43**, 157–203 (2010)
27. Sun, C., et al.: Optimal satellite formation reconfiguration based on closed-loop brain storm optimization. IEEE Comput. Intell. Mag. **8**(4), 39–51 (2013)
28. Wang, G.-G., et al.: An improved brain storm optimization algorithm based on graph theory. In: 2017 IEEE Congress on Evolutionary Computation (CEC 2017), pp. 509–515 (2017)
29. Wang, H., Liu, J., Yi, W., Niu, B., Baek, J.: An improved brain storm optimization with learning strategy. In: Tan, Y., Takagi, H., Shi, Y. (eds.) ICSI 2017. LNCS, vol. 10385, pp. 511–518. Springer, Cham (2017). https://doi.org/10.1007/978-3-319-61824-1_56
30. Wang, J., et al.: Improved v-support vector regression model based on variable selection and brain storm optimization for stock price forecasting. Appl. Soft Comput. **49**(2016), 164–178 (2016)
31. Wang, R., et al.: Brain storm optimization algorithm based on improved clustering approach using orthogonal experimental design. In: 2019 IEEE Congress on Evolutionary Computation (CEC 2019), pp. 262–270 (2019)
32. Wu, Y., Xie, L., Liu, Q.: Multi-objective brain storm optimization based on estimating in knee region and clustering in objective-space. In: Tan, Y., Shi, Y., Niu, B. (eds.) Advances in Swarm Intelligence. ICSI 2016. LNCS, vol. 9712, pp. 479–490. Springer, Cham (2016). https://doi.org/10.1007/978-3-319-41000-5_48
33. Wu, Y., Wang, X., Xu, Y., Fu, Y.: Multi-objective differential-based brain storm optimization for environmental economic dispatch problem. In: Cheng, S., Shi, Y. (eds.) Brain Storm Optimization Algorithms. ALO, vol. 23, pp. 79–104. Springer, Cham (2019). https://doi.org/10.1007/978-3-030-15070-9_4
34. Xie, L., Wu, Y.: A modified multi-objective optimization based on brain storm optimization algorithm. In: Tan, Y., Shi, Y., Coello, C.A.C. (eds.) ICSI 2014. LNCS, vol. 8795, pp. 328–339. Springer, Cham (2014). https://doi.org/10.1007/978-3-319-11897-0_39
35. Xue, J., Wu, Y., Shi, Y., Cheng, S.: Brain storm optimization algorithm for multi-objective optimization problems. In: Tan, Y., Shi, Y., Ji, Z. (eds.) ICSI 2012. LNCS, vol. 7331, pp. 513–519. Springer, Heidelberg (2012). https://doi.org/10.1007/978-3-642-30976-2_62

36. Zhan, Z., et al.: A modified brain storm optimization. In: 2012 IEEE Congress on Evolutionary Computation (CEC 2012), pp. 1–8 (2012)
37. Zhou, D., Shi, Y., Cheng, S.: Brain storm optimization algorithm with modified step-size and individual generation. In: Tan, Y., Shi, Y., Ji, Z. (eds.) ICSI 2012. LNCS, vol. 7331, pp. 243–252. Springer, Heidelberg (2012). https://doi.org/10.1007/978-3-642-30976-2_29
38. Zhou, H.J., et al.: Niche brain storm optimization algorithm for multi-peak function optimization. Adv. Mater. Res. **989**, 1626–1630 (2014)
39. Zhou, Z., et al.: Convergence analysis of brain storm optimization algorithm. In: 2016 IEEE Congress on Evolutionary Computation (CEC 2016), pp. 3747–3752 (2016)

Bacterial Foraging Optimization

An Adapting Chemotaxis Bacterial Foraging Optimization Algorithm for Feature Selection in Classification

Hong Wang$^{(\boxtimes)}$ and Yikun Ou

College of Management, Shenzhen University, Shenzhen 518060, China
ms.hongwang@gmail.com

Abstract. Efficient classification methods can improve the data quality or relevance to better optimize some Internet applications such as fast searching engine and accurate identification. However, in the big data era, difficulties and volumes of data processing increase drastically. To decrease the huge computational cost, heuristic algorithms have been used. In this paper, an Adapting Chemotaxis Bacterial Foraging Optimization (ACBFO) algorithm is proposed based on basic Bacterial Foraging Optimization (BFO) algorithm. The aim of this work is to design a modified algorithm which is more suitable for data classification. The proposed algorithm has two updating strategies and one structural changing. First, the adapting chemotaxis step updating strategy is responsible to increase the flexibility of searching. Second, the feature subsets updating strategy better combines the proposed heuristic algorithm with the KNN classifier. Third, the nesting structure of BFO has been simplified to reduce the computation complexity. The ACBFO has been compared with BFO, BFOLIW and BPSO by testing on 12 widely used benchmark datasets. The result shows that ACBFO has a good ability of solving classification problems and gets higher accuracy than the other comparison algorithm.

Keywords: Bacterial foraging optimization · Feature selection · Classification

1 Introduction

Data classification is an essential process in data works, the sorting scheme for large-scale data brings severe challenges. For example, a good searching engine needs to classify large-scale data in a webpage, such as Yahoo!'s webpage taxonomy, which has around 300 thousand categories [1]. Besides, many enterprises attach importance to the customer relationship management system to maintain a good relation with customers. Its core function of accurate identification needs a well classification method [2]. In summary, massive amount of data will to be processed, efficiency becomes an important factor in Internet environment.

Feature selection is a widely used tool for data classification with substantial efficiency and effectiveness [2]. It refers to many areas, including text classification, chest

© Springer Nature Switzerland AG 2020
Y. Tan et al. (Eds.): ICSI 2020, LNCS 12145, pp. 275–286, 2020.
https://doi.org/10.1007/978-3-030-53956-6_25

pathology identification, facial emotion recognition [3, 4], and so on. With the exponentially increasing time of data processing in classification problems, improving the computational speed while ensuring the accuracy is a hot issue. Feature selection methods select representative features from massive data and the generating optimized subsets can help improve the efficiency of computation in classification. Cutting down the irrelevant, redundant or the trivial features is the core of it [5–7]. Methods of feature selection can be classified into two main categories. One divides the methods into supervised, semi-supervised and unsupervised types by observing the number of features' label [8]. The other divides the methods into filter, wrapper and embedded by distinguishing the structure of the algorithms. [9, 10]. These methods have their own special characteristics, but are related to each other. Filter sorts and screens data before classification and delete the lower ranking features [13, 15]. Nevertheless, this method often loops over all data, which cost lots of time in solving high dimensional data. Different from this, wrapper randomly selecting features by combing classifiers with different heuristic algorithms such as PSO, ACO, GA [11, 12, 16] etc.

The classifiers often includes, naive Bayes classifier, SVM, random forest classifier and so on. Their combination reduces the amount of calculation. But the accuracy is decreased. To deal with this, embedded method has been created. It combines the advantage of filter and wrapper, aiming at improving calculating effectiveness of algorithms [17]. However, selecting an appropriate combination is very much depends on the researchers' practice experience [18].

As a popular heuristic algorithm, BFO is selected to be modified. It's proposed in 2002, inspired by the process of bacterial survival and reproduction [19]. This algorithm is good at randomly searching optimal solutions, because of its 'reproduction' and 'dispersal-elimination' strategies that can help the individual escapes from the local optima. Although, it can be applied into preprocessing the multidimensional data, the accuracy will not be increased if only use the original algorithm. Adding adaptive strategy can change the swimming method of each bacteria and makes their searching area more diversity [25]. Besides, a supervised classification method, KNN has been adapted as the classifier.

In sum up, this paper proposed a wrapper-supervised classification method, ACBFO (*Adapting Chemotaxis Bacterial Foraging Optimization*), which aims to realize the high efficiency of data classification. It is empirically faster and more accurate than the other methods in most of time, especially when dealing with large-scale data. In practice, this achievement is significant, which can save many computation costs in data works. The contribution in this research is a novel method that improves the classification efficiency of the heuristic algorithm (BFO). The main goals and organization of the paper are as follow.

1.1 Goals

Three classical heuristic algorithms will be compared: Bacterial Foraging Optimization (BFO) [19], Bacterial Foraging Optimization with linear chemotaxis (BFOLIW) [20], and Binary Particle Swarm Optimization (BPSO) [21]. The first two methods are bacterial foraging based algorithm, they adapt the same optimization framework but different in chemotaxis strategies, while BPSO employ the binary mechanism based on the PSO. The main aims of this research are listed below:

- A modified bacterial foraging based algorithm is proposed with adaptive chemotaxis to increase the accuracy of classification.
- An elite feature combination strategy are designed to adaptively reduce the dimension of feature subset to increase the classification efficiency.
- The reproduction and elimination mechanisms are redesigned to reduce the computation cost.

1.2 Organization

The other components of this paper are as follows: Sect. 2 introduces the basic information of Bacterial foraging optimization algorithm. Section 3 elaborates the concrete details of proposed algorithm. The experimental design and result are discussed in Sect. 4. Finally, the conclusion and future work are presented in Sect. 5.

2 Bacterial Foraging Optimization Algorithm

Combining heuristic algorithm with certain classifier is popular used in data classification nowadays. It will be implemented by means if feature selection methods. Feature selection can be realized by multitudinous approaches. Traditional approaches are based on statistics which sorts the features one by one through traversing entire dataset generating feature subsets and evaluating them by evaluation function [2]. This is appropriate for less quantity data.

Large amount of time will be cost when dealing with high dimension. Heuristic algorithms have exceptional performance in optimization which is good to be integrated with the evaluation function of feature selection. As one of common heuristic algorithm, bacterial foraging optimization is a heuristic distributed optimization algorithm. It emulates the social foraging habits of E. coli bacteria which contains chemotaxis, reproduction and elimination-dispersal nested processing [19].

Chemotaxis simulates the process of bacterial foraging. In this secession, bacteria swarming towards the place with high concentration of nutrients. One chemotaxis contains two steps [19], a tumble after tumble or a run after a tumble. They determine the nutrient concentration at the site by special pheromone. Once a unit find a good place, it will release attraction pheromone to inform other units [22]. On the contrary, if the nutrients is low concentration or is presenting noxious substances, it will release repulsive pheromone to notice other units to avoid approaching. In the BFO algorithm, this mechanism can help find the fitness of evaluation function more precisely. The step size of bacterial foraging optimization during chemotaxis stage is:

$$\theta^i(j+1, k, l) = \theta^i(j, k, l) + C(i)\frac{\Delta(i)}{\sqrt{\Delta^T(i)\,\Delta(i)}} \tag{1}$$

where the $\theta^i(j, k, l)$ indicates the concentration of nutrients in j_{th} chemotaxis, k_{th} reproduction and l_{th} elimination-dispersal. $C(i)$ is the chemotaxis step and $\Delta(i)$ is a random vector limited in $[-1,1]$. Formula of cell to cell effect of bacterial foraging optimization is:

$$J(i,j,k,l) = J(i,j,k,l) + J_{cc}\left(\theta^i(j,k,l), P(j,k,l)\right) \tag{2}$$

where $J(i,j,k,l)$ presents the pheromone of i_{th} bacteria. $J_{cc}\left(\theta^i(j,k,l), P(j,k,l)\right)$ controls the spreading rate of attractant or repelling agent [19].

Reproduction means the updating of bacterial group which contains two steps. Firstly, ranking the concentration of remaining nutrients in the environment [23]. Second, half of the bacterial are replaced by the reproduction of the top 50%. The change of bacterial foraging optimization nutrients:

$$J^i_{health} = \sum_{j=1}^{N_c+1} J(i,j,k,l) \tag{3}$$

where the J^i_{health} is the concentration of remaining nutrients, it presents the consumption of nutrients, the less J^i_{health}, the higher it ranks.

Elimination-dispersal happens randomly in a custom probability generation mechanism [24]. When the conditions are met, the position of bacterial will be reset to enhance the algorithm's ability of escaping from the local optimum. In the next section, the proposed methods for feature selection based on BFO will be introduced.

3 Adapting Chemotaxis Bacterial Foraging Optimization

The basic BFO can be used in training the classifier of feature selection. However, it often takes long time to do it due to the high dimension of data will increase the calculation cost with the nested structural BFO algorithm. Besides, the size of the training data also has impact on it which cannot be ignored. To improve these deficiencies, Adapting Chemotaxis Bacterial Foraging Optimization algorithm (ACBFO) which design an adapting learning strategy in chemotaxis section. Meanwhile, the K Nearest Neighbor algorithm holds the position of classifier for its fast speed and the characteristics of easy implement. The basic framework of ACBFO shows in Fig. 1.

3.1 Adapting Chemotaxis Mechanism

Basic chemotaxis step in BFO is fixed, but the movement of bacteria is not rigid in reality. Fixed step makes the bacteria easy to be caught in a same local place which is not benefit for the steady development of the population. A simple adaptive step changing method is adopted [26]. In the ACBFO, the initial step for each bacterium is:

$$\alpha = |(1 - (i \div S)) * (C_{start} - C_{end}) + C_{end}| \tag{4}$$

$$C_{step} = \frac{|J(i,j)|}{|J(i,j)| + \alpha} = \frac{1}{\left(1 + \frac{1}{|J(i,j)|}\right)} \tag{5}$$

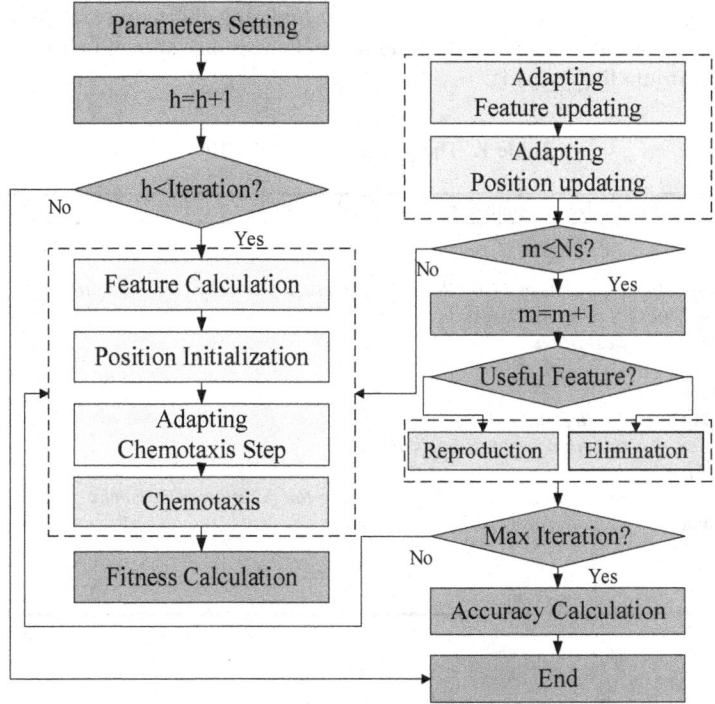

Fig. 1. The overall flow of Adapting Chemotaxis Bacterial Foraging Optimization.

It means that each bacterium i has different swimming step, which increasing the diversity of bacterial population.

During the foraging time, every unit needs to learning from others which can improving the probability to find a nutrient-rich place. The learning strategy is classical in particle swarm optimization algorithm.

$$C = C_{step} + c_1 R_1 (PBest_i - Pos_i) + c_2 R_2 (Best - Pos_i) \qquad (6)$$

where the $PBest_i$ is the personal optimal value for each bacterial colony and the $Best$ is the global best value for each iteration. The pseudo code of ACBFO is below.

3.2 Feature Combination Updating Mechanism

When dealing with high dimension data, reducing the features which are barely improving the classification is good to better training the classifier and reduce the calculation time. The basic position updating formula is:

$$Pos(i, j + 1) = Pos(i, j) + C(i) \frac{\Delta(i)}{\sqrt{\Delta^T(i)\Delta(i)}} \qquad (7)$$

after this step, a judge mechanism is design to updating the feature combination for next calculation of nutrient $J(i, j)$. The judge mechanism has shown in Table 1 and the calculating formula for $J(i, j)$ is:

Table 1. The pseudo code of ACBFO

Input dataset and initialize the parameters $(S=50, Nc=30, Ns=4, runs=3)$
For $j=1:Nc$
For $i=1:S$
Do the chemotaxis steps (4-6);Record bacteria position by (1);Get a fitness by (8)
If *new fitness < original fitness*
record the best fitness.
End
While *m<Ns*
If *fitness < threshold value*
Do reproduction same as basic BFO.
Else
Do elimination and dispersal by updating the position of Bacteria .
End
End
End
End

$$J(i, j) = Classifier_{KNN}(Pos(i, j+1)) \tag{8}$$

The pseudo code of feature combination updating is below (Table 2).

Table 2. The pseudo code of Feature combination updating

During the chemotaxis
Updating the position by (7);
Calculating the nutrient concentration by (8);
If $J(i, j) < J_{PBest}$
$J_{PBest} = J(i, j)$ *this is the fitness value of each bacteria*
End
Cell-cell attraction effect:
If *flag=0 (It means bacteria has information communication)*
Calculating J_{health}^i *by (2);*
End
Recording the classification effect of classifier in each run;
If *fitness > 0.6*
Delete the bad performance features and reset a new feature combination
If *times of bad performance combination >0*
Delete the combination and create a new combination
End
End

3.3 Bacterial Population Position Updating Mechanism

Bacterial population is updated after feature combination updating. During the bacterium swimming period, if the training performance of classifier is bad (e.g. training result leads the error rate lower than threshold value over certain times), elimination-dispersal will start. The population of bacterium needs reset. Otherwise, reproduce the bacterial population. The pseudo code of bacterial population updating is below (Table 3):

Table 3. The pseudo code of bacterial population updating

After the step of feature combination updating
While *m<Ns %m is the swimming times*
m=m+1;Updating the concentration of remaining nutrients by (3);
If *fitness>0.6*
New position = Randomly selected set of features(Elimination-dispersal)
Else
Reproduce the bacteria, half bad performance bacteria covered by good bacteria
End
End

4 Experimental Design and Result

In this section, the proposed algorithm is compared with three classical intelligent heuristic algorithms. This paper evaluate the ACBFO algorithm with binary PSO, standard BFO and its variants BFOLIW (with linear chemotaxis) empirically by comparing their classification accuracy and time. The parameter setting and datasets for testing are as follow.

4.1 Parameter Setting

The parameters setting of them are followed: The popular size S is 50, the dimension of datasets is averagely divided into 10 parts. For example, 11_Tumors datasets take the rule of '5:5:50', which means the number of selected features that be inputted into the algorithm is from 5 to 50, with the grow step of 5. The run times of algorithm in each dimension is 30. In this experiment, there is not much difference of accuracy between 5 iterations and 30 iterations. So, the iteration times of each runs is 5, because the amount of computation is enough under the appropriate population size and run times.

4.2 Datasets for Testing

The performance of the algorithms are evaluated by the classification accuracy based on 12 datasets which are widely used in testing the effect of feature selection algorithm. Table 4 shows the detail of the datasets, they are obtained from the http://www.gems-system.org/. which is used in testing the performance of a discrete bacterial algorithm for feature selection [27]. When training the classifier, randomly choosing 70% of the data as training set, the remain 30% are as testing set.

Table 4. Datasets for feature selection

Datasets	Feature	Instance	Class	Datasets	Feature	Instance	Class
11_Tumors	12533	174	11	Prostate_Tumor	10509	102	2
Brain_Tumor1	5920	90	5	Lung_Cancer I	12600	203	5
Brain_Tumor2	10367	50	4	DLBCL	5470	77	2
SRBCT	2309	83	4	Australian	15	690	2
Leukemia1	5328	72	3	German	25	1000	2
Leukemia2	11225	72	3	Lung Cancer large	12601	203	4

4.3 Experiment Result in Accuracy

The experiment was implemented in MATLAB, aims at analyzing the accuracy and run time of the proposed algorithm. The accuracy was measured by the rules 'Accuracy = 1- The error rate of classification'. The results are shown in Fig. 2. The abscissa represents the number of evaluated features in each evaluation and the ordinate represents the accuracy of classification. The proposed ACBFO algorithm performs well in most of time, especially in SRBCT, Lung Cancer Large and Leukemia 2 for their 'accuracy' is higher than 90%. These datasets has 50 ~ 200 instances, 3 ~ 11 classes and the average 'instances/feature attribution' rate is 1.2%. It reflects the ACBFO is good at dealing with multi-attribution data.

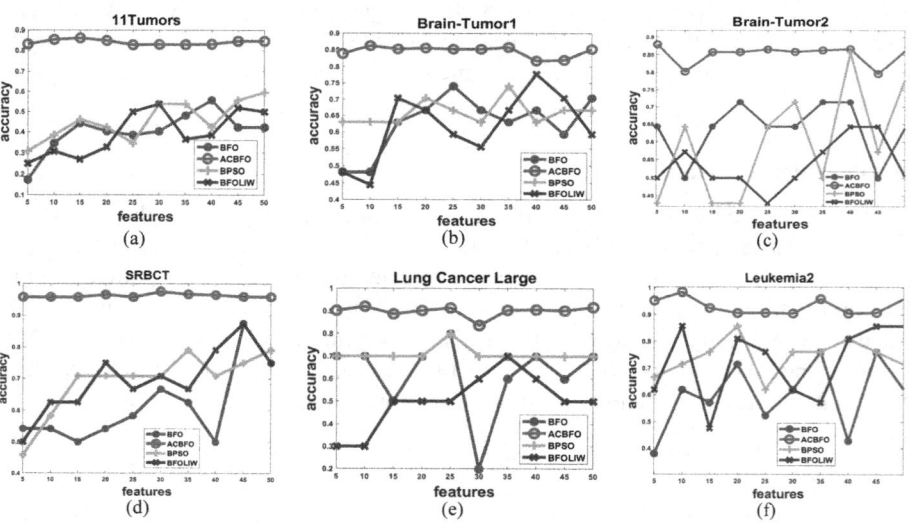

Fig. 2. Average classification accuracy of each algorithm on different datasets

As shown in Fig. 3, ACBFO does well in *(g), (h)* and *(l)* which has small ratio of 'instances/feature attribution'. However, it is unsteady when dealing with the data with little attributions. The accuracy lower than the compared algorithm serval times in 2 class datasets *(i)*, *(j)* and *(k)*. In conclusion, ACBFO can increase the accuracy and efficiency of data classification when dealing with high dimension datasets. But it's unstable if the classes of the dataset is less than 3.

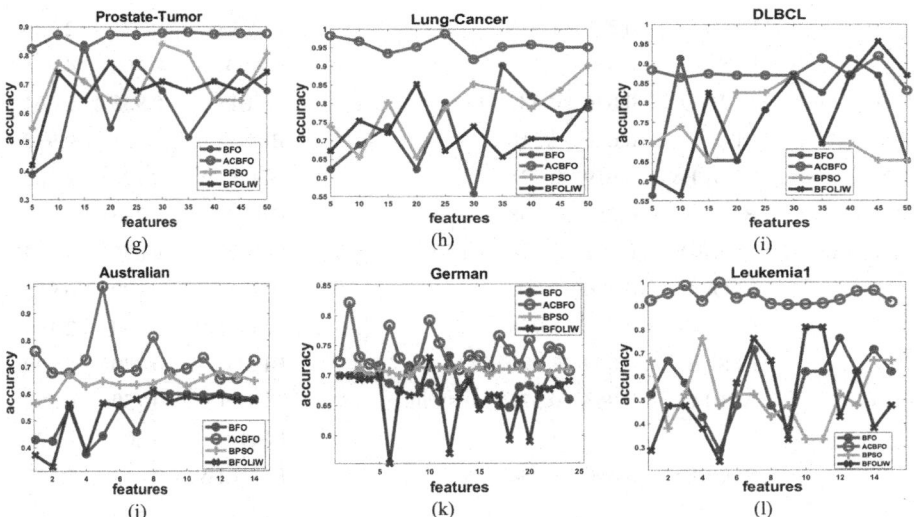

Fig. 3. Average classification accuracy of each algorithm on different datasets

4.4 Experiment Result in Efficiency

Table 5 shows the average accuracy and the average computation time of each compared algorithms. As shown in the results, the ACBFO still performance better than other compared algorithms in most time. Although, it seems to be surpassed several times in certain datasets, the overall performance in raising classification accuracy is good. On one hand, even BPSO is better than ACBFO in '*German*' datasets, the actual accuracy difference is only 0.002. On the other hand, the computational effective of ACBFO is well in nigh-twelfth of data.

What needs illustration is that the statistics below are acquired from a new experiment that the population size of each algorithm are set into 5. The data in Table 5 proof that, the proposed algorithm can get good result even the searching group is small.

Table 5. Accuracy and time of each algorithms

Datasets	Algorithm	Ac	Time	Datasets	Algorithm	Ac	Time
11_Tumors	ACBFO	**0.841**	1.799	Prostate_Tumor	ACBFO	**0.865**	**0.847**
	BFO	0.404	**1.399**		BFO	0.626	1.167
	BFOLIW	0.396	1.528		BFOLIW	0.677	2.380
	BPSO	0.458	4.421		BPSO	0.706	4.208
Brain_Tumor1	ACBFO	**0.846**	**0.487**	Lung_Cancer I	ACBFO	**0.955**	2.361
	BFO	0.626	2.216		BFO	0.731	**0.979**
	BFOLIW	0.619	2.225		BFOLIW	0.728	2.188
	BPSO	0.659	4.068		BPSO	0.785	4.477
Brain_Tumor2	ACBFO	**0.851**	**0.518**	DLBCL	ACBFO	**0.876**	**0.631**
	BFO	0.636	2.207		BFO	0.770	0.915
	BFOLIW	0.536	1.968		BFOLIW	0.770	2.194
	BPSO	0.600	3.870		BPSO	0.730	3.939
SRBCT	ACBFO	**0.963**	**0.376**	Australian	ACBFO	**0.739**	**0.590**
	BFO	0.613	2.297		BFO	0.504	1.125
	BFOLIW	0.696	0.934		BFOLIW	0.512	2.527
	BPSO	0.692	4.678		BPSO	0.629	0.961
Leukemia1	ACBFO	**0.939**	**0.519**	German	ACBFO	0.708	**0.576**
	BFO	0.514	2.127		BFO	0.694	1.175
	BFOLIW	0.500	1.220		BFOLIW	0.690	2.884
	BPSO	0.510	0.758		BPSO	0.710	21.621
Leukemia2	ACBFO	**0.931**	**0.912**	Lung Cancer large	ACBFO	**0.899**	2.266
	BFO	0.600	1.231		BFO	0.620	**0.895**
	BFOLIW	0.724	1.326		BFOLIW	0.500	2.200
	BPSO	0.743	6.123		BPSO	0.710	8.293

5   Conclusion and Future Work

Based on the basic BFO, a modified algorithm is proposed. ACBFO includes an adapting chemotaxis strategy and a feature updating strategy. It improves the performance of heuristic algorithm in feature selection and classification. After testing it in 12 popular basics datasets, the results shows that it can obtain better classification accuracy in the datasets of smaller 'instances/feature attribution' ratio. In theory, this research find a different way to make the BFO better connect with KNN classifier, acquiring a well computation accuracy and efficiency. In practice, this achievement can save many computation costs in data works. The contribution of this paper is a novel method that improves the classification efficiency of the heuristic algorithm (BFO). Comparing with

BFO, BFOLIW and BPSO, the performance of ACBFO should to be enhance by increasing the stability and further improving of computational accuracy. For example, designing a communicating mechanism in different bacterial groups to avoid bacterium units becoming too scattered, which is averse to result convergency.

Acknowledgments. This work is partially supported by the Natural Science Foundation of China (Grant no. 71901152), Natural Science Foundation of Guangdong Province (2018A030310575), Natural Science Foundation of Shenzhen University (85303/00000155).

References

1. Liu, T., Yang, Y., Wan, H., Zeng, H., Chen, Z., Ma, W.: Support vector machines classification with a very large-scale taxonomy. SIGKDD Explor. **7**, 36–43 (2005)
2. Saberi, M., Theobald, M., Hussain, O.K., Chang, E., Hussain, F.K.: Interactive feature selection for efficient customer recognition in contact centers: dealing with common names. Exp. Syst. Appl. **113**, 356–376 (2018)
3. Li, J., et al.: Feature selection: a data perspective. JACS **50**, 1–45 (2017)
4. Uysal, A.K.: An improved global feature selection scheme for text classification. Exp. Syst. Appl. **43**, 82–92 (2016)
5. Bar, Y., Diamant, I., Wolf, L., Lieberman, S., Komen, E., Greenspan, H.: Chest pathology identification using deep feature selection with non-medical training. Comput. Methods Biomech. Biomed. Eng.: Imaging Vis. **6**, 259–263 (2018
6. Nakariyakul, S., Casasent, D.P.: Improved forward floating selection algorithm for feature subset selection (2008)
7. Tan, P., Wang, X., Wang, Y.: Dimensionality reduction in evolutionary algorithms-based feature selection for motor imagery brain-computer interface. Swarm Evol. Comput. **52**, 100597 (2020)
8. Li, M., Wang, H., Yang, L., Liang, Y., Shang, Z., Wan, H.: Fast hybrid dimensionality reduction method for classification based on feature selection and grouped feature extraction. Exp. Syst. Appl. **150**, 113277 (2020)
9. Ashfaq, R.A.R., Wang, X.Z., Huang, J.Z., Abbas, H., He, Y.L.: Fuzziness based semi-supervised learning approach for intrusion detection system. Inf. Sci. **378**, 484–497 (2017)
10. Zhang, R., Nie, F., Li, X., Wei, X.: Feature selection with multi-view data: a survey. **50**, 158–167 (2019)
11. Tang, B., Zhang, L.: Local preserving logistic I-relief for semi-supervised feature selection. Neurocomputing (2020)
12. Banisakher, M., Mohammed, D., Nguyen, V.: A new optimization approach to resource distribution using semi-supervised learning graphs. Int. J. Simul.—Syst. Sci. Technol. **19** (2018)
13. Shahzad, W., Rehman, Q., Ahmed, E.: Missing data imputation using genetic algorithm for supervised learning. Int. J. Adv. Comput. Sci. Appl. **8**(3), 438–445 (2017)
14. Dong, W., Zhou, M.: A supervised learning and control method to improve particle swarm optimization algorithms. IEEE Trans. Syst. Man Cybern.: Syst. **47**, 1135–1148 (2016)
15. Tian, M., Bo, Y., Chen, Z., Wu, P., Yue, C.: A new improved firefly clustering algorithm for SMC-PHD filter. Appl. Soft Comput. **85**, 105840 (2019)
16. Moghaddasi, S.S., Faraji, N.: A hybrid algorithm based on particle filter and genetic algorithm for target tracking. Exp. Syst. Appl. **147**, 113188 (2020)

17. Labani, M., Moradi, P., Ahmadizar, F., Jalili, M.: A novel multivariate filter method for feature selection in text classification problems. Eng. Appl. Artif. Intell. **70**, 25–37 (2018)
18. Maldonado, S., López, J.: Dealing with high-dimensional class-imbalanced datasets: embedded feature selection for SVM classification. Appl. Soft Comput. **67**, 94–105 (2018)
19. Zhu, Q.H., Yang, Y.B.: Discriminative embedded unsupervised feature selection. Pattern Recogn. Lett. **112**, 219–225 (2018)
20. Passino, K.M.: Biomimicry of bacterial foraging for distributed optimization and control. IEEE Control Syst. Mag. **22**(3), 52–67 (2002)
21. Kora, P., Kalva, S.R.: Hybrid bacterial foraging and particle swarm optimization for detecting bundle branch block. SpringerPlus **4**(1), 1–19 (2015). https://doi.org/10.1186/s40064-015-1240-z
22. Too, J., Abdullah, A.R., Mohd Saad, N.: A new co-evolution binary particle swarm optimization with multiple inertia weight strategy for feature selection. In: Informatics: Multidisciplinary Digital Publishing Institute, vol. 21 (2019)
23. Zeema, J.L., Christopher, D.F.X.: Evolving optimized neutrosophic C means clustering using behavioral inspiration of artificial bacterial foraging (ONCMC-ABF) in the prediction of Dyslexia. J. King Saud Univ.-Comput. Inf. Sci. (2019)
24. Pourpanah, F., Lim, C.P., Wang, X., Tan, C.J., Seera, M., Shi, Y.: A hybrid model of fuzzy min–max and brain storm optimization for feature selection and data classification. Neurocomputing **333**, 440–451 (2019)
25. Pan, Y., Xia, Y., Zhou, T., Fulham, M.: Cell image segmentation using bacterial foraging optimization. Appl. Soft Comput. **58**, 770–782 (2017)
26. Majhi, R., Panda, G., Majhi, B., Sahoo, G.: Efficient prediction of stock market indices using adaptive bacterial foraging optimization (ABFO) and BFO based techniques. Exp. Syst. Appl. **36**(6), 10097–10104 (2009)
27. Wang, H., Jing, X., Niu, B.: A discrete bacterial algorithm for feature selection in classification of microarray gene expression cancer data. Knowl.-Based Syst. **126**, 8–19 (2017)

Bacterial Foraging Optimization Based on Levy Flight for Fuzzy Portfolio Optimization

Xinzheng Wu[1], Tianwei Zhou[2], and Zishan Qiu[1(✉)]

[1] College of Economics, Shenzhen University, Shenzhen, China
qiuzishan@163.com
[2] College of Management, Shenzhen University, Shenzhen, China

Abstract. In this paper, a new kind of bacterial foraging optimization that combines with levy flight (LBFO) is employed to solve a novel portfolio optimization (PO) problem with fuzzy variables and modified mean-semivariance model which includes the transaction fee (including the purchase fee and sell fee), no short sales and the original proportion of the different assets. First of all, a chemotaxis step size using levy distribution takes the place of fixed chemotaxis step size, which makes a good balance between local search and global search through frequent short-distance search and occasional long-distance search. Moreover, fuzzy variables are used to signify the uncertainty of future risks and returns on assets and some constrained conditions are taken into consideration. The results of the simulation show that the model can be solved more reasonably and effectively by LBFO algorithm than the original bacterial foraging optimization (BFO).

Keywords: Bacterial foraging optimization · Levy flight · Fuzzy portfolio optimization

1 Introduction

Portfolio optimization (PO) is a process to decide how to allocate wealth and which assets to invest can gain the maximum returns under the acceptable risk [1]. Markowitz proposed the mean-variance (M-V) model [2] that uses the variance of stock prices to measure the portfolio risk. With the defects of the mean-variance (M-V) model [2], alternative risk measures have been proposed, such as value-at-risk (VaR) [3], sparse and robust mean-variance [4], and vine copula liquidity-adjusted VaR (LVaR) optimization model [5]. To overcome NP-hard problem, swarm intelligence (SI) methodologies are applied to deal with PO, such as particle swarm optimization (PSO) [6], bacterial foraging optimization (BFO) [7], moth search algorithm (MSA) [8], etc.

BFO [9] is a good technique to solve optimization problems. It has been succeeded in solving many real-world problems including flexible job-shop scheduling problem [10], feature selection [11], and supply chain optimization problem [12]. According to its continuous nature and several successful applications in the continuous optimization domain, BFO is considered as a prospective algorithm in solving the PO problem.

© Springer Nature Switzerland AG 2020
Y. Tan et al. (Eds.): ICSI 2020, LNCS 12145, pp. 287–298, 2020.
https://doi.org/10.1007/978-3-030-53956-6_26

Levy flight which simulates the food searching path of numerous animals like deer, bumblebees, and albatross are added to SI algorithms to promote the performance of the algorithms such as PSO [13], cuckoo search algorithm (CSA) [14] and firefly algorithm (FA) [15].

Fuzzy set theory [16] can deal with decision-making problems since it allows us to describe and treat imprecise and uncertain elements. A growing number of researches show that it is hard to predict the future performance of assets exclusively based on historical data. So fuzzy logic [16] is applied to express uncertain knowledge that is suitable for representing the intrinsic uncertainty of the portfolio optimization problem. In a typical project, the return distributions of assets are usually skewed, which means a low possibility of high profits and a high possibility of low profits [24]. Substituting variance with semivariance can avoid sacrificing too much anticipated return in eliminating both high and low return extremes. In our approach, the uncertainty on returns and semivariance is set to trapezoidal fuzzy numbers.

Based on the analysis of the recent literature, the problem about how to improve the ability of original BFO to achieve high-quality solutions to more complicated PO problem attracts our attention. In this paper, we propose a new bacterial foraging optimization based on levy flight (LBFO) to solve a more complicated PO problem. The main contributions of this paper are listed below. First of all, levy distribution replaces the fixed chemotaxis step size to promote the optimization ability and efficiency of BFO through frequent short-distance exploration and occasional long-distance exploration. Next, transaction fee, no short sales and the original proportion of the different assets are used to modify mean-semivariance model. Finally, fuzzy variables are used to simulate the uncertain economic environment.

The rest of the paper is organized as follows. Section 2 is the introduction of some definitions. Section 3 gives a review of BFO and a description of LBFO. Section 4 describes the improved portfolio selection model and the detailed design of encoding and constrained boundary control. In Sect. 5, experimental settings and results are given. In the end, Sect. 6 concludes the paper and presents some future directions.

2 Preliminaries

In this section, we introduce some definitions that are needed in the following section. The assistance of a membership function $\mu_A(X) \rightarrow [0, 1]$ performs the degree of membership of the various elements, which means all elements in the interval between 0 and 1 are mapped.

Definition 1 [17]. A fuzzy number A is called trapezoidal with core interval $[a, b]$, left-width $\alpha > 0$ and right-width $\beta > 0$ if its membership function has the following form:

$$\mu_A(X) = \begin{cases} 1 - \frac{a-X}{\alpha}, & \text{if } a - \alpha \leq X \leq a \\ 1, & \text{if } a \leq X \leq b \\ 1 - \frac{X-b}{\beta}, & \text{if } b \leq X \leq b + \beta \\ 0, & \text{if otherwise} \end{cases} \quad (1)$$

and it is usually denoted by the notation $A = (a, b, \alpha, \beta)$. The family of fuzzy numbers is denoted by F. A fuzzy number A with γ-level set is expressed as $[A]^\gamma = [\alpha_1(\gamma), \alpha_2(\gamma)]$ for all $\gamma > 0$.

Definition 2 [18]. The above trapezoidal fuzzy number A is denoted by the notation $A = (a, b, \alpha, \beta)$ with core interval $[a, b]$, left-width α and right-width β and the γ-level set of A can be computed as:

$$[A]^\gamma = [a - (1 - \gamma)\alpha, b + (1 - \gamma)\beta](\gamma \in [0, 1]) \tag{2}$$

The possibilistic mean value of A is given by the following:

$$E(A) = \int_0^1 \gamma[\alpha_1(\gamma) + \alpha_2(\gamma)]d\gamma = \frac{a + b}{2} + \frac{\beta - \alpha}{6} \tag{3}$$

The upper and lower possibilistic semivariance of A is given respectively by the following:

$$Var^+(A) = \int_0^1 \gamma[E(A) - \alpha_2(\gamma)]^2 d\gamma = \left(\frac{b - a}{2} + \frac{\beta + \alpha}{6}\right)^2 + \frac{\beta^2}{18} \tag{4}$$

$$Var^-(A) = \int_0^1 \gamma[E(A) - \alpha_2(\gamma)]^2 d\gamma = \left(\frac{b - a}{2} + \frac{\beta + \alpha}{6}\right)^2 + \frac{\alpha^2}{18} \tag{5}$$

Assuming two fuzzy numbers A and B, with $[A]^\gamma = [\alpha_1(\gamma), \alpha_2(\gamma)]$ and $[B]^\gamma = [b_1(\gamma), b_2(\gamma)]$.

For all $\gamma \in [0,1]$, the upper and lower possibilistic covariance of A and B are given respectively:

$$Cov^+(A, B) = 2\int_0^1 \gamma[E(A) - \alpha_2(\gamma)] \cdot [E(B) - b_2(\gamma)]d\gamma \tag{6}$$

$$Cov^-(A, B) = 2\int_0^1 \gamma[E(A) - \alpha_1(\gamma)] \cdot [E(B) - b_1(\gamma)]d\gamma \tag{7}$$

Lemma 1 [18]. Assuming that A and B are two fuzzy numbers and let μ and λ be positive numbers. Then, the following conclusions can be drawn by using the extension principle:

$$E(\lambda A \pm uB) = \lambda E(A) \pm uE(B) \tag{8}$$

Theorem 1 [19]. Assuming that $A_1, A_2...A_n$ are fuzzy numbers, and $\lambda_1, \lambda_2,...\lambda_n$ are real numbers. Then, the following conclusions can be drawn by using the extension principle:

$$Var^+\left(\sum_{i=1}^n \lambda_i A_i\right) = \sum_{i=1}^n \lambda_i^2 Var^+(A_i) + 2\sum_{i<j=1}^n \lambda_i \lambda_j Cov^+(A_i, A_j) \tag{9}$$

$$Var^-\left(\sum_{i=1}^n \lambda_i A_i\right) = \sum_{i=1}^n \lambda_i^2 Var^-(A_i) + 2\sum_{i<j=1}^n \lambda_i \lambda_j Cov^-(A_i, A_j) \tag{10}$$

3 BFO and LBFO

3.1 Bacterial Foraging Optimization

BFO, a swarm intelligence algorithm, is based on the biology and physics underlying the foraging behavior of Escherichia coli. Four motile behaviors (chemotaxis, swarming, reproduction, and elimination and dispersal) are included in the bacterial foraging process. For more detailed information, please refer to [9].

3.2 Bacterial Foraging Optimization Based on Levy Flight

This part mainly explains the application of the random walk model of the levy flight strategy in algorithm improvement.

3.2.1 Levy Flight in Chemotaxis Step

The levy flight is a statistical description of motion. It is a kind of non-Gaussian random processes whose step length is drawn from levy stable distribution. This special walk strategy of levy flight is subject to the power-law distribution. There is an exponential relationship between the variance of levy flight and time.

$$Levy(s) \sim |s|^{-\lambda},\ 1 < \lambda \leq 3 \tag{11}$$

where s is the random step size of levy flight and λ is a real number.

In an algorithm proposed by Mantegna [20], the method of generating levy random step size is represented by:

$$S = \frac{u}{|v|^{1/\beta}} \tag{12}$$

where β is a real number. u and v are drawn from normal distributions. That is

$$u \sim N\left(0, \sigma_u^2\right),\ v \sim N\left(0, \sigma_v^2\right) \tag{13}$$

$$\sigma_u = \left\{ \frac{r(1 + \beta)\sin(\pi\beta/2)}{r[(1 + \beta)/2]\beta 2^{(\beta-1)/2}} \right\}^{1/\beta},\ \sigma_v^2 = 1,\ \beta \in [0.3, 1.99]$$

The improved chemotaxis step size formula is given as follows:

$$C(i) = scale * Levy(s) \tag{14}$$

$$scale = \frac{1}{10p} \sum_{d=1}^{\eta} \left| \theta_d^i(j, k, l) - \theta_d^*(j, k, l) \right| \tag{15}$$

In the formula, the $scale$ is the scale factor, $Levy\ (s)$ is the levy step size as the parameter, the D-dimensional paratactic value of the position of the ith bacteria is set to $\theta_d^i(j, k, l)$, and the D-dimensional paratactic value of the current optimal bacterial position is set to $\theta_d^*(j, k, l)$. p is the dimension of optimization. In order to make the levy chemotaxis step reach the opportune order of magnitude, the $scale$ utilizes the positional relationship between the optimal bacteria and the current bacteria.

4 Bacterial Foraging Optimization for Portfolio Selection Problems

4.1 Portfolio Selection Model

In this section, a model that considers the transaction fee and no short sales in portfolio optimization presented in [21] is introduced. The model can be described as following and the parameters and definitions of PO model are shown in Table 1.

Table 1. Parameters and definitions of PO model

Variables	Definitions
$f(X)$	The function that represents profit and pursuits the maximum value
$g(X)$	The function that represents risk and pursuits the minimum value
d	The number of assets
r_i	The expected yields of asset i
X_i	The proportion of investment of asset i
X_i^0	The initial holding proportion of investment of asset i
μ	$\mu = 1$: buy assets from market $\\$ $\mu = 0$: sell assets to market
k_i^b	The transaction cost of buying asset i from market
k_i^s	The transaction cost of selling asset i to market
σ_{ij}	The covariance of r_i and r_j

$$\mathrm{Min}F(X) = \min[\varphi g(X) - (1 - \varphi)f(X)]$$
$$\text{s.t.} \begin{cases} \sum_{i=1}^{n} X_i = 1 \\ X_i > 0 \end{cases} \tag{16}$$

$$f(X) = \sum_{i=1}^{d} r_i x_i - \sum_{i=1}^{n} \left[\mu \cdot k_i^b \cdot \left(x_i - x_i^0\right) + (1 - \mu) \cdot k_i^s \cdot \left(x_i^0 - x_i\right) \right]$$
$$and \ \mu = \begin{cases} 1 \ X_i \geq X_i^0 \\ 0 \ X_i < X_i^0 \end{cases} \tag{17}$$

$$g(X) = \sum_{i=1}^{d} \sum_{j=1}^{d} X_i X_j \sigma_{ij} \tag{18}$$

where $\varphi \in [0,1]$, representing risk aversion factors. When φ becomes smaller, inventors are willing to take more risks. The bigger the value of φ, the less risks will take.

4.2 Encoding

When LBFO is used to find the solutions of PO model, each particle is regarded as a potentially feasible solution. Three types of information, including the proportion of investment, the value of corresponding profit and the value of corresponding risk, are carried by each bacterium [22].

$$\theta = \left[X_1, X_2, X_3..X_d, f(X), g(X)\right] \tag{19}$$

$$s = \sum_{i=1}^{d} X_i$$

$$\theta' = \left[\frac{1}{s}(X_1, X_2, X_3 \ldots X_d), f(X)', g(X)'\right] \tag{20}$$

Equation (19) illustrates the coding of the bacteria. As is shown in Eq. (20), the proportions of all assets are summed up first and then every proportion of asset is divided by the s so that the sum of all asset proportions is equal to 1.

4.3 Constrained Boundary Control

$$\theta^i(j+1, k, l) = \begin{cases} D_{\min} + \text{rand}(D_{\max} - D_{\min}), & if \ P < 0 \\ \theta^i(j, k, l) + C(i)\frac{\Delta(i)}{\sqrt{\Delta^T(i)\Delta(i)}}, & if \ P \geq 0 \end{cases} \tag{21}$$

Boundary control guarantees that each proportion is a positive number. Bacteria change direction randomly in the process of chemotaxis, which may lead them to exceed the given area. If bacteria are permitted to leave the prescribed area, the border solutions may be infeasible. Otherwise, the border solutions may not be obtained. The boundary control rules are illustrated in Eq. (12, $D_{\min}$ and $D_{\max}$ are the lower and upper boundaries, separately. And the function *rand* (·) is used to generate a random number between 0 and 1.

5 Experiments and Discussions

In order to verify the performance of LBFO algorithm, the original BFO and PSO are selected for comparison. Both the algorithms shown in this paper were coded in MATLAB language.

5.1 Definition of Experiments

In the experiments, we assume that there are five assets to invest and the original proportion in every asset X_i^0 equals 0.2. Besides, the sum of the initialized ratio of each asset equals 1. Since we suppose that the future returns of the assets are trapezoidal fuzzy numbers, the left and right width and the core interval of the fuzzy numbers are needed to estimate. The estimation method proposed by Vercher et al. [23] is used to calculate the trapezoidal fuzzy return rates of the proposed model. According to Vercher et al., the historical returns are regarded as samples and the core and spreads of the trapezoidal fuzzy returns on the assets are approximated by sample percentiles. So the core of the fuzzy return r is set as the interval [40th, 60th], left-width (40th, 5th] and right-width

Table 2. The probability distribution of returns

The asset i	1	2	3	4	5
α	−0.32266	−0.18761	−0.29708	−0.0477	−0.14339
a	0.266462	0.303832	0.137969	0.176914	0.122531
b	0.687169	0.519906	0.37341	0.380465	0.375195
β	1.432592	1.107447	1.816847	0.926154	0.918654

(60th, 95th]. We consider the yearly returns over the examined period between January 2010 and December 2019. The probability distribution of returns is shown in Table 2.

In this paper, we assume that investors are risk-averse. Thus, the lower possibility semivariance is used to describe the risk. According to Theorem 1 and Definition 2, the risk of investment is shown as follows:

$$Var^-\left(\sum_{i=1}^{d} x_i r_i\right) = \sum_{i=1}^{d} x_i^2 Var^-(r_i) + 2\sum_{i<j=1}^{d} x_i x_j Cov^-(r_i, r_j)$$

$$= \left[\sum_{i=1}^{d} x_i \left(\frac{a_i - b_i}{2} + \frac{\alpha_i + \beta_i}{6}\right)\right]^2 + \frac{1}{18}\left(\sum_{i=1}^{d} x_i \alpha_i\right)^2 + 2\sum_{i<j=1}^{d} x_i x_j Cov^-(r_i, r_j)$$

$$\tag{22}$$

$$Cov^-(r_i, r_j) = \left(\frac{b_i - a_i}{2} + \frac{\beta_i - a_i}{6}\right)\left(\frac{b_j - a_j}{2} + \frac{\beta_j - a_j}{6}\right) + \frac{\alpha_j}{3}\left(\frac{b_i - a_i}{2} + \frac{\beta_i - \alpha_i}{6}\right)$$

$$+ \frac{\alpha_i}{3}\left(\frac{b_j - a_j}{2} + \frac{\beta_j - \alpha_j}{6}\right) + \frac{\alpha_i \alpha_j}{6}$$

$$\tag{23}$$

According to Eq. (3) and Eq. (14), the asset's probability means of return that is regarded as the expected yields of assets and the covariance of each asset's return is as follows:

$$r = [0.769357567, 0.627711275, 0.608011358, 0.440998792, 0.425870775]$$

$$\sigma = [0.162079, \quad 0.106683, \quad 0.152003, \quad 0.098973, \quad 0.103597;$$
$$0.106683, \quad 0.070256, \quad 0.100059, \quad 0.065359, \quad 0.068279;$$
$$0.152003, \quad 0.100059, \quad 0.142555, \quad 0.092867, \quad 0.097176;$$
$$0.098973, \quad 0.065359, \quad 0.092867, \quad 0.061722, \quad 0.063802;$$
$$0.103597, \quad 0.068279, \quad 0.097176, \quad 0.063802, \quad 0.066444]$$

Other parameter settings are the same as reference [1]. Three risk aversion factors that equal to 0.15, 0.5 and 0.85 respectively are used to identify three different kinds of investors. The transaction cost of buying asset $k_i^b = 0.00065$ and the transaction cost of selling asset $k_i^s = 0.00075$. In BFO, the number of chemotactic $N_c = 1000$. The number of elimination-dispersal $N_{ed} = 2$. The number of reproduction $N_{re} = 5$. The number of swimming $N_s = 4$. The elimination-dispersal frequency $P_{ed} = 0.25$. The swimming length $C = 0.2$. In PSO, inertia weight $w = 1$ and $c_1 = c_2 = 2$.

5.2 Experimental Results

Experimental results obtained by three algorithms of different λ and the final portfolio selection results are showed in Tables 3, 4 and 5. Figure 1 shows the convergence curves with various λ generated by BFO, LBFO and PSO.

Table 3. Experimental results of $\varphi = 0.15$

	BFO	LBFO	PSO
Min	−4.5740	**−4.8613**	−3. 2783E−01
Max	0	0	**−2.7206E−01**
Mean	−4.5740E−01	**−4.8613E−01**	−2.9714E−01
Std.	1.4464	1.5373	**2.8308E−02**
X_1	3.4661E−01	1.5205E−01	9.2883E−01
X_2	2.7350E−01	2.1958E−01	3.1142E−13
X_3	2.0433E−01	1.7316E−01	7.1166E−02
X_4	9.4721E−02	1.9758E−01	6.7232E−17
X_5	8.0839E−02	2.5764E−01	1.8993E−18
Return	6.3847E−01	5.5684E−01	7.5686E−01
Risk	1.1110E−01	8.9945E−02	1.0211E−01

Table 4. Experimental results of $\varphi = 0.5$

	BFO	LBFO	PSO
Min	−5.2977E−01	**−5.7620E−01**	−5.0209E−02
Max	0	0	**−3.1582E−02**
Mean	−5.2977E−02	**−5.7620E−02**	−3.9313E−02
Std.	**1.6753E−01**	1.8221E−01	9.7086E−03
X_1	1.5109E−01	1.1588E−01	9.6977E−01
X_2	2.4915E−01	2.2208E−01	4.5337E−21
X_3	2.0202E−01	3.2296E−01	3.0691E−01
X_4	3.1492E−01	2.5108E−01	1.9870E−05
X_5	8.2821E−02	8.7998E−02	5.3115E−14
Return	5.6938E−01	5.7285E−01	7.1899E−01
Risk	9.1322E−02	9.7371E−02	1.1718E−01

Table 5. Experimental results of $\varphi = 0.85$

	BFO	LBFO	PSO
Min	−2.7749E−02	−2.8004E−02	**−3.7393E−02**
Max	**0**	**0**	7.1282E−02
Mean	−2.7749E−03	− **2.8004E−03**	−1.1155E−03
Std.	**8.7750E−03**	8.8557E−03	6.2698E−02
X_1	7.7191E−02	2.1459E−01	4.8588E−11
X_2	3.8539E−01	2.0830E−01	9.8150E−10
X_3	1.3545E−01	1.8445E−01	4.9773E−01
X_4	2.9850E−01	1.9818E−01	5.9825E−17
X_5	1.0347E−01	1.9448E−01	5.0227E−01
Return	5.5896E−01	5.7819E−01	7.2298E−02
Risk	8.1073E−02	9.6231E−02	6.9586E−02

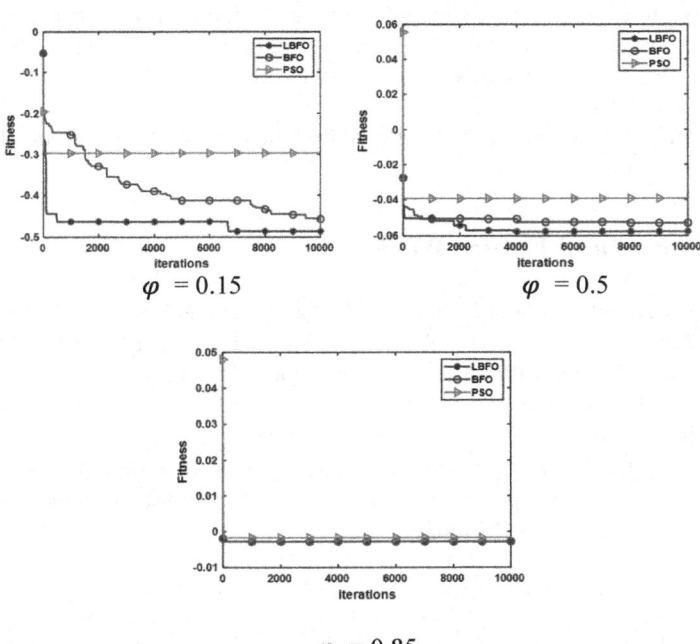

$\varphi = 0.15$ $\varphi = 0.5$

$\varphi = 0.85$

Fig. 1. The convergence curve of three algorithms

According to the tables and the figures, we can find that:

(1) The fitness values grow up with the increase of the risk aversion factor φ. The results illustrate that high returns involve increased risk.
(2) With the different φ, the proportion of the five assets is different. Different investors have different degrees of risk aversion, so they will make different investment decisions when facing the same assets and market conditions.
(3) By analyzing the tables and the convergence graphs, it is obvious that LBFO usually produces the best performance among these three algorithms and BFO is better than PSO. Detailed differences are listed as follows:

    a) On account of random search directions and fixed chemotaxis step size, the original BFO algorithm has a restrained global search capability and a weak convergence performance. Comparing to BFO, LBFO algorithm utilizes levy flight to balance global search and local search. The results illustrate that LBFO has higher convergence rate and solution accuracy.

    b) Due to the defects of algorithm performance, PSO algorithm shows worse results than BFO in this model. PSO algorithm is caught in local optimum through successive iterations and slow convergence rate appearing, which limits the accuracy of the algorithm. On the contrary, BFO algorithm has a more effective search capability, so it is easy to jump out of local optimum and find better results.

    c) It can be seen that LBFO can always find the best solution from the data of the mean value.

6   Conclusions and Future Work

In this paper, we employ original BFO and LBFO algorithms to solve PO problem with different risk aversion factors. The obtained results indicate that LBFO algorithm is a better choice to solve the difficult PO problem due to the levy flight strategy, whose characteristic is the frequent short-distance exploration and occasional long-distance exploration is utilized to adjust the chemotaxis step size.

Further work may consider more useful conditions such as inflation, fundamental analysis and focus on multi-period or dynamic objectives to satisfy demands from the real market to propose a new PO model.

Acknowledgments. This work was supported in part by Guangdong Basic and Applied Basic Research Foundation under Grant 2019A1515110401, in part by Natural Science Foundation of Shenzhen under Grant JCYJ20190808145011259, in part by Natural Science Foundation of Shenzhen University under Grant 860-000002110367, in part by Shenzhen Philosophy and Social Sciences Plan Project under Grant SZ2019D018, and in part by Guangdong Provincial Soft Science Project under Grant 2019A101002075.

References

1. Niu, B., Liu, J., Liu, J., Yang, C.: Brain storm optimization for portfolio optimization. In: Tan, Y., Shi, Y., Li, L. (eds.) ICSI 2016. LNCS, vol. 9713, pp. 416–423. Springer, Cham (2016). https://doi.org/10.1007/978-3-319-41009-8_45
2. Markowitz, H.M.: Portfolio selection. J. Finance 7(1), 77–91 (1952)
3. Jorion, P.: Value at Risk: the New Benchmark for Controlling Market Risk. Irwin Professional Pub (1997)
4. Dai, Z.F., Wang, F.: Sparse and robust mean-variance portfolio optimization problems. Phys. A 523, 1371–1378 (2019)
5. Al Janabi, M.A.M., Ferrer, R., Shahzad, S.J.H.: Liquidity-adjusted value-at-risk optimization of a multi-asset portfolio using a vine copula approach. Phys. A. 536, 122579 (2019)
6. Zhang, H.P.: Optimization of risk control in financial markets based on particle swarm optimization algorithm. J. Comput. Appl. Math. 368, 112530 (2020)
7. Niu, B., Fan, Y., Xiao, H., Xue, B.: Bacterial foraging based approaches to portfolio optimization with liquidity risk. Neurocomputing. 98, 90–100 (2012)
8. Strumberger, I., Tuba, E., Bacanin, N., Tuba, M.: Modified moth search algorithm for portfolio optimization. In: Zhang, Y.D., Mandal, J., So-In, C., Thakur, N. (eds.) Smart Trends in Computing and Communications 2020. SIST, vol. 165, pp. 445–453. Springer, Singapore (2020). https://doi.org/10.1007/978-981-15-0077-0_45
9. Liu, Y., Passino, K.M.: Biomimicry of social foraging bacteria for distributed optimization: models, principles, and emergent behaviors. J. Optim. Theory Appl. 115, 603–628 (2002)
10. Vital-Soto, A., Azab, A., Baki, M.F.: Mathematical modeling and a hybridized bacterial foraging optimization algorithm for the flexible job-shop scheduling problem with sequencing flexibility. J Manuf. Syst. 54, 74–93 (2020)
11. Chen, Y.P., et al.: A novel bacterial foraging optimization algorithm for feature selection. Exp. Syst. Appl. 83, 1–17 (2017)
12. Niu, B., Tan, L.J., Liu, J., Liu, J., Yi, W.J., Wang, H.: Cooperative bacterial foraging optimization method for multi-objective multi-echelon supply chain optimization problem. Swarm Evol. Comput. 49, 87–101 (2019)
13. Ning, Y., Liu, Z., Chen, Z., Zhao, C.: A novel competitive particle swarm optimization algorithm based on Levy flight. In: Jia, Y., Du, J., Zhang, W. (eds.) CISC 2019. LNEE, vol. 592, pp. 553–565. Springer, Singapore (2020). https://doi.org/10.1007/978-981-32-9682-4_58
14. Soto, R., Crawford, B., Olivares, R., Castro, C., Escárate, P., Calderón, S.: Cuckoo search via Lévy flight applied to optimal water supply system design. In: Mouhoub, M., Sadaoui, S., Ait, M.O., Ali, M. (eds.) IEA/AIE 2018. LNCS, vol. 10868, pp. 383–395. Springer, Cham (2018). https://doi.org/10.1007/978-3-319-92058-0_37
15. Pare, S., Bhandari, A., Kumar, A., Singh, G.K.: A new technique for multilevel color image thresholding based on modified fuzzy entropy and Lévy flight firefly algorithm. Comput. Electr. Eng. 70, 476–495 (2018)
16. Zadeh, L.A.: Fuzzy sets as a basis for a theory of possibility. Fuzzy Sets Syst. 1, 3–28 (1978)
17. Zadeh, L.A.: Fuzzy Sets. Int. J. Innov. Comput. Inf. Control. 8(3), 338–353 (1965)
18. Carlsson, C., Fuller, R.: On possibilistic mean value and variance of fuzzy numbers. Fuzzy Sets Syst. 122(2), 315–326 (2012)
19. Zhang, W.G., Wang, Y.L., Chen, Z.P., Nie, Z.K.: Possibilistic mean-variance models and efficient frontiers for portfolio selection problem. Inf. Sci. 177(13), 2787–2801 (2007)
20. Mantegna, R.N.: fast, accurate algorithm for numerical simulation of Lévy stable stochastic processes. Phys. Rev. E 49(5), 4677–4683 (1994)

21. Li, L., Xue, B., Tan, L., Niu, B.: Improved particle swarm optimizers with application on constrained portfolio selection. In: Huang, D.-S., Zhao, Z., Bevilacqua, V., Figueroa, J.C. (eds.) ICIC 2010. LNCS, vol. 6215, pp. 579–586. Springer, Heidelberg (2010). https://doi.org/10.1007/978-3-642-14922-1_72
22. Niu, B., Bi, Y., Xie, T.: Structure-redesign-based bacterial foraging optimization for portfolio selection. In: Han, K., Gromiha, M., Huang, D.-S. (eds.) ICIC 2014. LNCS, vol. 8590, pp. 424–430. Springer, Heidelberg (2014). https://doi.org/10.1007/978-3-319-09330-7_49
23. Vercher, E., Bermudez, J., Segura, J.: Fuzzy portfolio optimization under downside risk measures. Fuzzy Sets Syst. **158**, 769–782 (2007)
24. Walls, M.R.: Combining decision analysis and portfolio management to improve project selection in the exploration and production firm. J. Pet. Sci. Eng. **44**(1–2), 55–65 (2004)

Adaptive Bacterial Foraging Optimization Based on Roulette Strategy

Weifu Cao, Yingsi Tan[✉], Miaojia Huang, and Yuxi Luo

College of Management, Shenzhen University, Shenzhen 518061, China
Caowave@qq.com, 394461726@qq.com

Abstract. Bacterial foraging optimization has drawn great attention and has been applied widely in various fields. However, BFO performs poorly in convergence when coping with more complex optimization problems, especially multimodal and high dimensional tasks. Aiming to address these issues, we therefore seek to propose a hybrid strategy to improve the BFO algorithm in each stage of the bacteria's' foraging behavior. Firstly, a non-linear descending strategy of step size is adopted in the process of flipping, where a larger step size is given to the particle at the very beginning of the iteration, promoting the rapid convergence of the algorithm while later on a smaller step size is given, helping enhance the particles' global search ability. Secondly, an adaptive adjustment strategy of particle aggregation is introduced when calculating step size of the bacteria's swimming behavior. In this way, the particles will adjust the step size according to the degree of crowding to achieve efficient swimming. Thirdly, a roulette strategy is applied to enable the excellent particles to enjoy higher replication probability in the replication step. A linear descent elimination strategy is adopted finally in the elimination process. The experimental results demonstrate that the improved algorithm performs well in both single-peak function and multi-peak function, having strong convergence ability and search ability.

Keywords: Non-linear decreasing methods · Roulette gambling mechanism · Hybrid algorithm

1 Introduction

The past decades have witnessed numerous researchers sought different methods to tackle optimization problems. Mathematics methodology used to be a relatively good technique to solve these problems but its limitations turn out to be obvious as more and more practical optimization problems involve complexity, multi-minimum, strong constraint, non-linearity and a lot of variables and modeling difficulty. The traditional mathematics methodology is incapable of reaching the optimum in a reasonable computation time. Hence, developing new approaches has become one of the most important research directions. In recent years, a number of metaheuristics inspired from nature and

---

The original version of this chapter was revised: the author name was updated. The correction to this chapter is available at https://doi.org/10.1007/978-3-030-53956-6_64

© Springer Nature Switzerland AG 2020, corrected publication 2020
Y. Tan et al. (Eds.): ICSI 2020, LNCS 12145, pp. 299–311, 2020.
https://doi.org/10.1007/978-3-030-53956-6_27

biology has appealed numerous researches and have developed and come to widely used in different practice problems [1]. For example, genetic algorithm (GA) [2], is a probabilistic search algorithm, mimick-ing nature selection and biology evolution mechanism; particle swarm optimization (PSO) [3], is developed based on the swarming strategies of bird flocking and fish schooling.

Bacterial foraging optimization (BFO) [4], proposed by Passino is also belongs to this bio-mimetic algorithms group. It mimics the foraging strategy of Escherichia coli bacteria, involving four key processes, namely, chemotaxis, swarming, reproduction and elimination-dispersal steps, encouraging BFO to search the global optimum more efficiently than the traditional mathematical methods. BFO algorithm has been effectively applied to solve practical optimization problems in different fields, such as PID controller design [5], dynamic environment optimization [6],image processing [7, 8], vehicle routing [9], and machine learning [10]. Once emerged, BFO has been widely applied to various single-objective optimization problems [11–14] and multi-objective optimization problems [15].

The increasing interest for BFO has revealed that it is a promising, swarm-based optimization algorithm. However, there still exist several limitations in original BFO due to the fixed chemotaxis step-size, the less-efficient search direction for tumbling and the swarming strategy with a delay in approximating the global solution and a poor convergence rate, especially in tackling nonlinear, high-dimensional and multi-modal functions [1, 16–19]. Many scholars proposed corresponding im-provement strategies based on these problems, mainly aiming at the two key steps of chemotaxis and replication. Some of the current researches of improving BFO could be described as follows:

With regards to the chemotaxis process, Panda and Naik (2015) [16] proposed a modified BFO algorithm called adaptive crossover BFO algorithm, which incorporated adaptive chemotaxis an d inherited the crossover mechanism of genetic algorithm. W. G. Zhao, L.Y. Wang (2016) [1] reported an effective bacterial foraging optimization (EBFO) where a gravitational search strategy is incorporated into the chemotaxis step to adjust its unit length according to the swarm information. L.L. Wanga et al. [17] (2018) developed a bare bones bacterial foraging optimization (BBBFO) algorithm in which a chemotactic strategy based on Gaussian distribution is incorporated into this method through making use of both the historical information of individual and the share information of group. C.C. Yang et al. (2016) designed a new bacterial foraging optimizer using new chemotaxis and conjugation strategies (BFO-CC). Via the new chemotaxis mechanism, each bacterium randomly selects a standard-basis-vector direction for swimming or tumbling. At the same time, the step size of each bacterium is adaptively adjusted based on the evolutionary generations and the information of the globally best individual, which readily makes the algorithm keep a better balance between a local search and global search and significantly improve convergence. B. Pang et al. (2019) [18] improved BFO algorithm (LPBFO) based on the Lévy flight step-size and particle swarm optimization (PSO) operator. During the chemotactic process in LPBFO, each bacterium selects one dimension for tumbling randomly. The step-size of each bacterium is determined by the stochastic flight lengths of the improved Lévy flight which can generate small step-size with high frequency and big step-size occasionally and the stochastic step-size is reduced adaptively based on the evolutionary generations, which makes the bacteria transform from global search to local search.

In the reproduction step, W. G. Zhao, L.Y. Wang (2016) [1] designed a swarm diversity strategy to enhance the reproduction mode depending on the swarm diversity. The simulation results show that the proposed algorithm is more effective than its competitors and can be extended to other global optimization problems. Liang and H.S. Tian (2016) [19] presents a hybrid algorithm based on the combination of BFO algorithm and PSO algorithm. Due to the random change of the direction of search, and the migration of bacteria by selective replication at a certain probability, results show that the improved hybrid algorithm is better than the basic PSO algorithm and the basic BFO algorithm. Besides, the convergence rate is fast and has good robustness. L.L. Wanga et al. [17] (2018) introduced the swarm diversity in the reproduction strategy to promote the exploration ability of the algorithm. The comparative results reveal that the proposed approach is more superior to its counterparts.

Overall, the current optimization algorithm of bacterial foraging focuses on proposing novel chemotaxis step strategies, but pays less attention to the reproduction process, especially to enhancing the influence of particles that perform well, so as to accelerate the convergence rate and improve the searching capacity of the particles.

To improve the original BFO for tackling complex optimization problems. We incorporate three strategies into the traditional BFO in each stage of the bacteria's foraging behavior, seeking to achieve a valid balance between the exploration and the exploitation during the life cycle of search for global optima. Firstly, to ensure the convergence performance and local mining abilities of the algorithm, a non-linear descending strategy of step size is adopted in the process of chemotaxis, where a larger step size is given to the particle at the very beginning of the iteration, promoting the rapid convergence of the algorithm and a smaller step size is given later on to help enhance the particles' local search ability. Secondly, an adaptive adjustment strategy of particle aggregation is introduced when calculating step size of the bacteria's swimming behavior. In this way, the particles will adjust the step size according to the degree of crowding to achieve efficient swimming. Thirdly, a roulette strategy is applied to enable the excellent particles to enjoy higher replication probability in the replication step. A linear descent elimination strategy is adopted finally in the elimination process, thus avoiding premature and a trap into local extremum. Various benchmark functions are considered to verify the performance of the proposed improved strategies, the comparative results demonstrate that the improved algorithm has a significant enhancement over the original BFO, especially in single-peak function and multi-peak function, having strong convergence ability and search ability.

2   Standard BFO

Bacterial Foraging Optimization (BFO), a new swarm intelligence optimization algorithm proposed by Passino Kevin in 2002. The BFO algorithm simulates the foraging behavior of Escherichia coli in the human intestinal tract for mathematical modeling, so as to solve the optimization problem. Because of its simple structure and parallel processing, it has been widely used in many fields. According to the Theory of Bacterial Foraging, bacterial population has a strong tendency to nutrients. And every step of their movement is towards the position where they can get the maximum energy per unit time under the constraints of their own physiology and surrounding environment. Escherichia coli foraging behavior mainly includes four basic steps: Chemotaxis, Swarming, Reproduction, Elimination and dispersal.

2.1 Chemotaxis

Chemotaxis is a process that simulates Escherichia coli swimming and flipping. Escherichia coli migration can be divided into two processes: turnover and swimming, both of which are realized by flagella. If the flagella are counterclockwise rotation, Escherichia coli will be swimming; If the flagella were rotating clockwise, the bacteria would flip around in place looking for direction. After the bacteria find a new swimming direction by flipping, they will swim in that direction for the same length many times.

To define the direction of Chemotaxis, a unit length random direction is generated named $\varphi(j)$. Then in computational Chemotaxis, the movement of the bacterium could be represented by formula (1)

$$\theta^i(j+1, k, l) = \theta^i(j, k, l) + C(i)\varphi(j) \tag{1}$$

where $C(i)$ represents the size of the step taken in the random direction, $\theta^i(j, k, l)$ is the i th bacterium at j th chemotactic, k th reproductive, and l th elimination and dispersal step.

2.2 Swarming

In the process of bacteria approaching the optimal living environment, individuals of the colony release information, attractant and repellent, namely pheromone, to all other bacteria according to their current fitness value. This bacterium accepts the attractor and repulsor released by all other bacteria and modifies its adaptive value under the action of all its pheromones. Make sure to move to a better location for the local environment.

In a colony, the calculation method of pheromone concentration between the above individuals can be expressed as formula (2)

$$J_{cc}(\theta, P(j, k, l)) = \sum_{i=1}^{n} J_{cc}^i(\theta, \theta^i(j, k, l))$$

$$+ \sum_{i=1}^{n} [h_{repelent} \exp(-w_{repelent} \sum_{m=1}^{p} (\theta_m - \theta_m^i)^2]$$

$$+ \sum_{i=1}^{n} [-d_{attract} \exp(-w_{attract} \sum_{m=1}^{p} (\theta_m - \theta_m^i)^2] \tag{2}$$

where $J_{cc}(\theta, P(j, k, l))$ is a target function that changes with the population distribution state. When it is superimposed to the actual target function of the problem, it shows the trend of the relative distance between bacteria and the best individual. S is the size of the population; P indicates the dimensions of the optimization problem.

2.3 Reproduction

According to the principle of survival of the fittest, individuals with better performance (fitness) will reproduce, while those with poor performance will die.

First step of Reproduction's algorithm implementation is to calculate the health value, which is used to measure an individual's ability to explore. The health value of bacterium i determined as follows:

$$J^i_{health} = \sum_{j=1}^{N_c+1} J(i, j, k, l) \tag{3}$$

Then sorting the health values of the bacteria in descending order. The least half healthy bacteria die and the other half healthiest bacteria each split into two bacteria, which are placed in the same location. During the process of reproduction, the population of bacteria is constant.

2.4 Elimination and Dispersal

The number of bacterial populations changes gradually over time or with changes in the environment, such as nutrient depletion. When an emergency occurs, bacteria in an area may be eliminated or dispersed to new areas. The last step of Standard BFO algorithm is the simulation of this process. Bacterial migration occurs according to a certain probability P_{ed}, when a certain bacteria meets the migration conditions, the individual will be reallocated to another space.

3 Adaptive BFO Based on Roulette Strategy

In order to solve the problem of lack of learning direction and slow convergence speed in traditional bacterial foraging algorithm, this paper improve an adaptive bacterial foraging optimization algorithm based on roulette strategy (ARBFO) which improves BFO from chemotaxis, replication and elimination-diffusion. The ARBFO algorithm adopts roulette strategy and adaptive adjustment formula, which makes the algorithm have the ability of learning and adaptive adjustment to the environment. As a result, it accelerates the convergence speed and improves the search accuracy.

3.1 Chemotaxis: Two Non-linear Decreasing Methods

Chemotaxis step size controls the search range of the population. If the step size is not set properly, it will be trapped in local optimum or unable to converge to the optimal solution.

In the process of microbial foraging, the distance between each colony and the optimal solution in the initial population is larger, and the step size should be larger to help the rapid convergence of the microbial community. With the search, the distance between each colony and the optimal solution decreases, and the step size should be reduced at this time, so as to improve the accuracy of the microbial community search.

In this paper, two non-linear decreasing methods are used to adjust the step sizes of inversion and swimming in chemotaxis. In the process of inversion, with the increase of replication behavior, the newborn bacteria will search for a better range. At this time, the step size should be smaller to improve the search accuracy. The non-linear decline formula of step size should be adjusted:

$$C_i^k = C_{\min} + (C_{\max} - C_{\min})e^{(-4*(\frac{k}{Nre}))^3}$$ (4)

Among them, K is the current number of replication, and Nre is the largest number of bacterial replication. With the increase of k, the step size will decrease.

In the course of swimming, a strategy of non-linear adaptive adjustment of step size is adopted. Considering the current iteration and the maximum iteration number, the number of chemotactic steps in a given range is changed. With the increase of iteration number, the step size shows a downward trend. This strategy advances according to the number of iterations and the current nutritional status of particles. Adaptive adjustment [21], as follows:

$$C(j) = [(c_{\max} - c_{\min} - k_1 - k_2) * \cos(\frac{iter}{iter_{\max}} * \frac{\pi}{2}) + c_{\min} + k_2] + k_1 * \frac{\pi}{2} * \arctan\frac{J}{J_{avg}} - k2 * \frac{\min(J, J_t)}{\max(J, J_t)}$$ (5)

In this formula, besides the classical adaptive adjustment strategy, the parameters J, J_{avg}, J_t, adjusted according to the microbial nutrition environment are introduced. The swimming step is adjusted by the overall weight, the average microbial nutrition value, and the individual optimal fitness value, which enhances the learning ability of the operator. With the increase of iteration times, the step size is as a whole. The step size decreases with the increase of nutrient value of the bacterial community search, so as to improve the accuracy of the later stage of the search.

Among them, J and J_{avg} represent the current bacterial fitness and the average value of all bacteria respectively. J_t is the optimal fitness value of the previous individual. K1 and K2 are normal numbers. They are adjusted adaptively according to the average value of bacterial nutrition and the optimal fitness value of the individual. After experiments, they are set to 2,0.4 respectively.

3.2 Duplication: Roulette Gambling Mechanism

The replication strategy in the standard BFO algorithm, which retains half of the bacterial individuals with good fitness and eliminates the other half of the bacterial individuals with poor fitness, has not improved the optimal position of the current bacterial community; at the same time, this replication method reduces the diversity of the population in a half way by sacrificing the diversity of the population. The fast convergence of the algorithm can easily lead to the local optimum of the algorithm in the solution of high-dimensional and multi-peak functions.

In this paper, the roulette mechanism is used to improve the replication link in the flora foraging algorithm, improve the learning ability of the operator and improve the convergence speed. Roulette selection strategy, also known as proportional selection operator, has the basic idea that the probability of each individual being selected is proportional to the value of its fitness function.

If the population size is N and the fitness of individual Xi is f (xi), then the selection probability P (xi) of individual Xi is:

$$P(x_i) = \frac{f(x_i)}{\sum_{j=1}^{N} f(x_j)} \tag{6}$$

The roulette selection method can be realized by following process simulation:

(1) A uniformly distributed random number R is generated in [0,1].
(2) If r < q1, chromosome X1 is selected.
(3) If qk_1 < R < QK (2 < K < N), the chromosome XK is selected.
(4) Qi is called individual Xi (i = 1,2,... The cumulative probability of N) is calculated as follows:

$$q_i = \sum_{j=1}^{i} P(x_j) \tag{7}$$

In this process, the higher the fitness, the greater the chance that the particle will be selected, and vice versa, the smaller the chance that the particle will be selected. However, regardless of the fitness, the probability of being selected exists, allowing some particles with low nutritional value to survive. It is possible to improve the diversity of particles (Fig. 1).

3.3   Reproduction and Elimination: Linear Decreasing Adaptive Regulation Mechanism

Migration is the behavior that interferes with bacterial colonies and initializes the population randomly according to a certain probability. Migration probability describes the living environment of bacteria. Generally speaking, the change of nutrient value of bacterial colonies is not susceptible to the influence of bacteria, but decreases with the reproduction of bacteria. At the same time, the survival competition among bacteria has become more intense, and the more likely it is to disperse.

In this paper, a linear decreasing adaptive regulation mechanism is adopted. According to the linear decreasing of iteration number, the improved migration step simulates the change of environment during a bacterial foraging process according to probability formula (8). With the increase of iteration number, the migration probability decreases gradually, the chance of executing probability greater than the migration probability increases, and the bacteria are dispersed. The probability increases gradually to improve the diversity of particles and search accuracy.

$$Ped_j = Ped_{\min} + \frac{iter_{\max} - iter}{iter_{\max}} * (Ped_{\max} - Ped_{\min}) \tag{8}$$

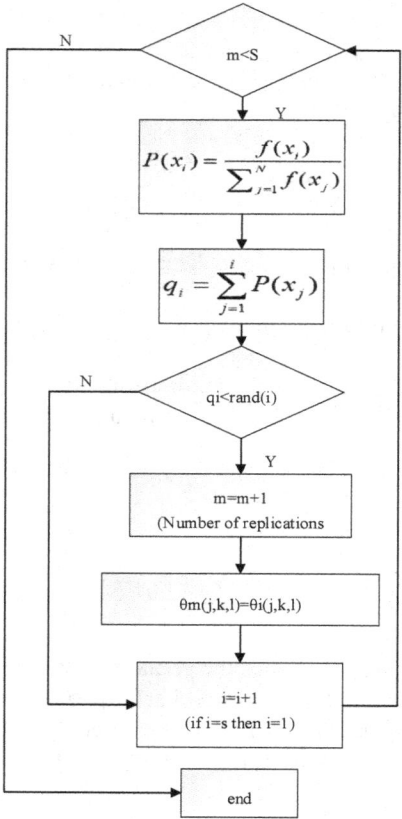

Fig. 1. Duplication flow chart after quoting roulette mechanism

Among them, Ped represents the probability of eliminating migration, ITER is the current number of iterations. Through this formula, the probability of eliminating migration can be adjusted adaptively according to the number of iterations to maximize the diversity of particles and search accuracy.

3.4 Benchmark Function

To verify the performance of the improved algorithm (ARBFO), this article introduce Sphere, Schwefel, Rosenbrock, Rotated-Hyper-Ellipse, Beale, General rastrigrin, Ackley, Griewank, Alpine, Three-hump Camel [17, 20] ten typical benchmark functions to conduct simulated contrast experiment. The minimum of ten benchmark functions is 0. Among them, Sphere, Schwefel, Rosenbrock, Rotated-Hyper-Ellipse, Beale are unimodal functions, General rastrigrin, Ackley, Griewank, Alpine, Three-hump Camel are multimodal functions. And the Rotated-Hyper-Ellipse is the only rotated function.

Table 1. Experiment Result

	Function		ASRBFO	BFOLDC	BFONDC	ARBFO
f_1	Sphere	Min	1.0448E+05	2.2529E+04	**1.7247E−02**	3.1663E−02
		Max	1.0448E+05	1.2522E+05	**2.4423E−02**	5.0875E−02
		Mean	1.0924E+05	5.8324E+04	**2.0858E−02**	3.9629E−02
		Std	2.4426E+03	2.8390E+04	**2.6759E−03**	5.6516E−03
f_2	Schwefel	Min	5.7970E+64	4.6761E+58	4.9436E+46	**4.4882**
		Max	5.7970E+64	3.5092E+72	4.7399E+52	**7.7279**
		Mean	3.9266E+67	4.0783E+69	8.5016E+51	**6.1735**
		Std	3.9535E+67	9.1487E+70	1.5520E+52	**9.6905E−01**
f_3	Rosenbrock	Min	3.8772E+10	1.5537E+09	5.1282E+01	**0**
		Max	3.8772E+10	5.5556E+10	1.0079E+03	**0**
		Mean	4.2359E+10	1.3921E+10	1.8286E+02	**0**
		Std	2.4723E+09	1.3059E+10	2.9506E+02	**0**
f_4	Rotated-Hyper-Ellipse	Min	2.5707E+06	4.4197E+05	**1.8046**	2.2840
		Max	2.5707E+06	3.0662E+06	1.9574E+02	**3.8138**
		Mean	2.6580E+06	1.3151E+06	9.2511E+01	**2.6105**
		Std	8.1457E+04	7.1888E+05	7.6209E+01	**4.5021E−01**
f_5	Beall	Min	3.1277E−02	3.5338E−01	3.8131E−10	**4.3665E−11**
		Max	3.1277E−02	1.9030E+05	1.9680E−03	**2.1881E−08**
		Mean	4.0331E−01	2.2927E+02	1.9682E−04	**4.8885E−09**
		Std	1.5528E−01	4.4009E+03	6.2233E−04	**6.1904E−09**
f_6	Generalized Rastrigin	Min	1.0278E+05	3.3723E+04	8.9868E+02	**5.00E+01**
		Max	1.0278E+05	1.2570E+05	1.2176E+03	**5.00E+01**
		Mean	1.0826E+05	6.5668E+04	1.0957E+03	**5.00E+01**
		Std	3.4972E+03	2.5350E+04	1.0088E+02	**0**
f_7	Ackley	Min	2.1225E+01	2.0015E+01	2.0017E+01	**1.9973**
		Max	2.1225E+01	2.1457E+01	2.0023E+01	**2.6504**
		Mean	2.1255E+01	2.0305E+01	2.0019E+01	**2.3840**
		Std	2.1945E−02	3.7634E−01	2.1066E−03	**2.1936E−01**
f_8	Griewank	Min	2.7011E+01	6.6180	**1.7503E−03**	3.5593E−03
		Max	2.7011E+01	3.2305E+01	**3.6206E−03**	7.8410E−03
		Mean	2.7887E+01	1.5600E+01	**2.7847E−03**	5.6189E−03
		Std	7.0130E−01	7.1150	**4.7405E−04**	1.3919E−03
f_9	Alpine	Min	8.5683E+02	9.4282E+01	1.1371E+02	**9.6447E−02**
		Max	8.5683E+02	1.1429E+03	1.5907E+02	**1.6201E−01**
		Mean	9.0606E+02	2.2713E+02	1.3368E+02	**1.2218E−01**
		Std	4.2282E+01	1.7135E+02	1.4184E+01	**2.1431E−02**
f_{10}	Three-Hump Camel	Min	9.1108E−03	5.9735E−02	2.0558E−10	**8.4751E−11**
		Max	9.1108E−03	4.4493E+01	6.3831E−09	**2.7885E−09**
		Mean	3.7530E−01	3.8030E−01	2.6565E−09	**1.1598E−09**
		Std	4.9494E−01	2.6250	1.7704E−09	**9.0145E−10**

3.5 Parameter Settings

The experimental environment is Inter(R) Core (TM) i5-7Y54 CPU @1.20 GHz, Windows 10,the running memory is 8BG, and it is completed under Matlab2018b.

To exam the performance of ARBFO, this article choose ASRBFO [21], BFOLDC [22] and BFONDC [23] to conduct the simulated contrast experiment, and record the minimum value, maximum value, average value and standard deviation. Each algorithm independently runs 10 times. Different BFO algorithms are set the same parameters.For BFOLDC, $Cmax = 0.2$, $Cmin = 0.01$. For BFONDC, $Cmax = 0.6$, $Cmin = 0.01$. For ASRBFO, maximum evaluation number $MaxFEs = 10000$; $Fre = 2000$, i.e. reproduce every 2000 iterations; $Fed = 3300$, i.e. dispel every 3300 iterations; initial step unit $Csz = 0.15$; swimming times $Ns = 10$, $Cmax = 0.3$, $Cmin = 0.15$, $k1 = 0.2$, $k2 = 0.15$. For ARBFO, $Cmax = 0.6$, $Cmin = 0.01$; $k1 = 0.2$, $k2 = 0.15$.

3.6 Analysis of Algorithm Convergence

Table 1 shows the minimum value (Min), maximum value (Max), average value (Mean) and standard deviation (Std) of four algorithms in 10 benchmark functions. The dimension of the particles is 50, and the optimal results will be marked in bold.

It can be seen from the data in Table 1 that, in terms of benchmark functions, ARBFO algorithm yields a compelling result in the convergence accuracy and stability of both unimodal functions and multimodal functions. Function 1–5 are unimodal functions and function 6-10 are multimodal functions.

Figure 2 shows the fitness curve of four algorithms. Combined Fig. 2 with Table 1, ARBFO outperforms other algorithms in functions 2, 4, 5, 6, 7, 9, and the optimization accuracy and stability of ARBFO algorithm are improved obviously. It is worth noticing that, the fitness curve of Rosenbrock has a breakpoint, because the ARBFO has converged to the minimum value of 0.

Compared with BFONDC algorithm, ARBFO fails to achieve the desired effect in convergence accuracy and stability. Therefore, future research will continue to improve ARBFO to better solve the existing problems on the part of the benchmark functions. The above analysis can prove that the proposed ARBFO algorithm in this paper demonstrates a far better convergence precision and optimal value than the BFO and it is an effective algorithm.

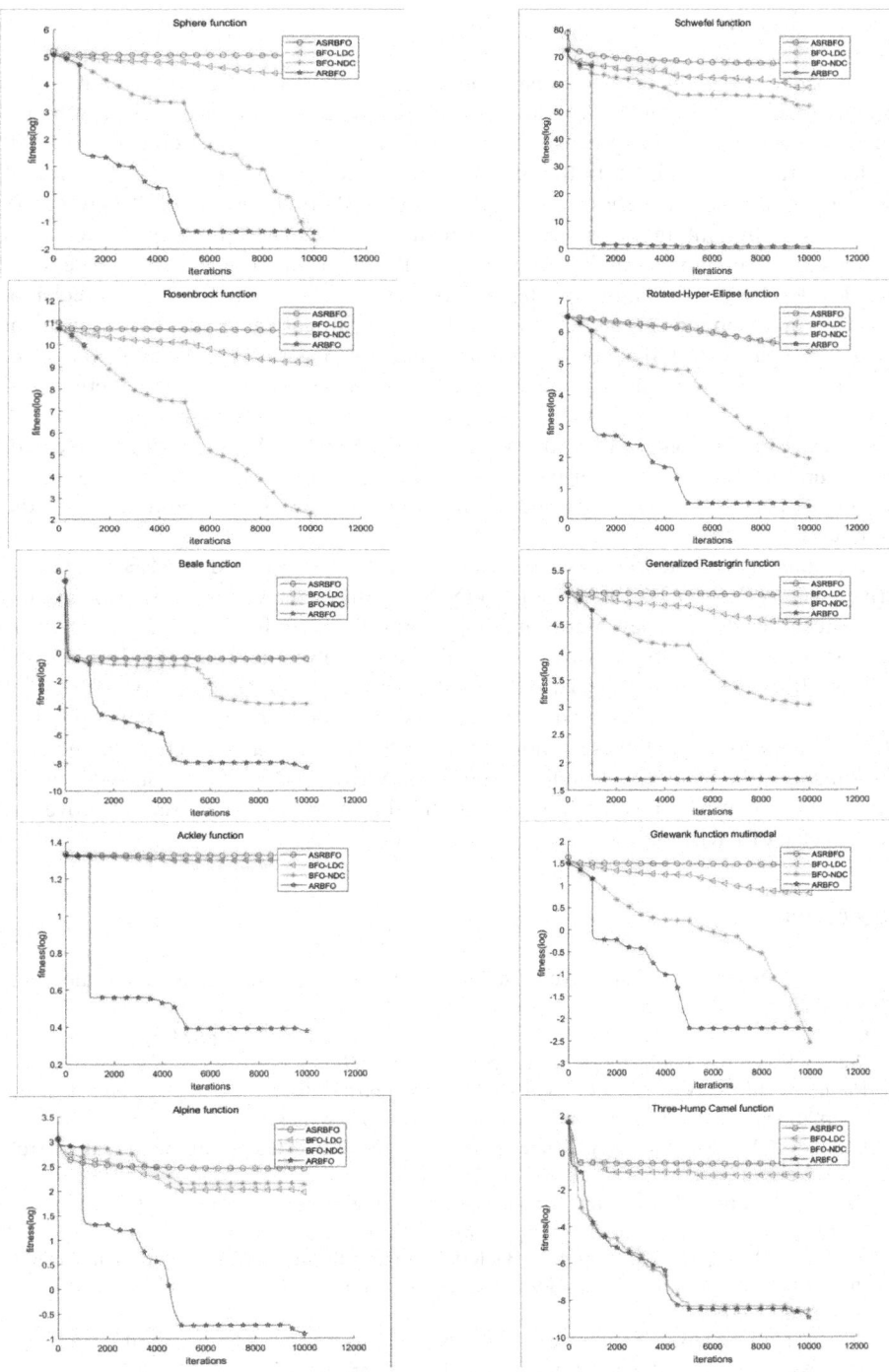

Fig. 2. Convergence curve on 50-Dim

4   Conclusion

In this paper, an adaptive mechanism and roulette strategy designed to improve the capacity of BFO is presented. The adaptive strategy is used to improve the search efficiency and accuracy in the process of tumbling, swimming, elimination and dispersal. Roulette strategy is adopted in the reproduction process to maximize the diversity of the group and avoid the algorithm falling into the local optimal value due to premature development. In tumbling, nonlinear descent strategy is adopted. In the early iterations particles are given larger step length, to prompt the algorithm to fast convergence, later particles will be given smaller step length, to strengthen the particles search precision. In swimming, step length calculation introduces nutritional value adaptive adjustment strategy, the particles will adaptively adjust step length according to the nutrition value, to realize efficient swimming. Roulette strategy is introduced in the reproduction process, therefore, the particles with better fitness value will have higher probability to reproduce, while the ones with worse fitness value have less chances to being selected, which enhances the diversity of particles and increases the search ability. In elimination and dispersal, the linear descending migration strategy is adopted to heighten the diversity of particles.

Ten benchmark functions has been used to test the performance of ARBFO in comparison with ASRBFO, BFOLDC and BFONDC. From the analysis and experiments, the result illustrates that this new algorithm outperforms the other four algorithms in convergence speed and accuracy in many cases, and it reach minimum value with Rosenbrock function. It can be concluded that ARBFO expressively improves the performance of BFO and lets out the better results on most optimization problems comparing with other BFO algorithms. However, more benchmark functions and practical application problems must be investigated in the future with ARBFO. The future work will underline more bio-heuristic mechanisms and application problems to entirely improve the performance of ARBFO.

References

1. Zhao, W., Wang, L.: An effective bacterial foraging optimizer for global optimization. Inf. Sci. **329**, 719–735 (2016)
2. Goldberg, D.E.: Genetic Algorithms in Search, Optimization and Machine Learning. Addison Wesley Longman, Publishing Co. Inc., New York (1989)
3. Kennedy, J.F., Eberhart, R.C.: Particle swarm optimization. In: Proceedings of IEEE International Conference of Neural Network, Perth, Australia (1995)
4. Passino, K.M.: Biomimicry of bacterial foraging for distributed optimization and control. IEEE Control Syst. Mag. **22**, 52–67 (2002)
5. Kim, D.H., Cho, J.H.: Biomimicry of bacterial foraging for distributed optimization and control. J. Adv. Comput. Intell. Intell. Inform. **9**(6), 669–676 (2005)
6. Tang, W.J., Wu, Q.H., Saunders, J.R.: Bacterial foraging algorithm for dynamic environments. In: IEEE Congress on Computational Intelligence 2006 (CEC 2006), Vancouver, Canada, 16–21 July 2006
7. Sanyal, N., Chatterjee, A., Munshi, S.: An adaptive bacterial foraging algorithm for fuzzy entropy based image segmentation. Exp. Syst. Appl. **38**(12), 15489–15498 (2011)

8. Verma, O.P., Hanmandlu, M., Kumar, P., Chhabra, S., Jindal, A.: A novel bacterial foraging technique for edge detection. Pattern Recogn. Lett. **32**(8), 1187–1196 (2011)

9. Tan, L., Lin, F., Wang, H.: Adaptive comprehensive learning bacterial foraging optimization and its application on vehicle routing problem with time windows. Neurocomputing **151**, 1208–1215 (2015)

10. Chana, R.I.: Bacterial foraging based hyper-heuristic for resource scheduling in grid computing. Future Gener. Comput. Syst. - Int. J. Grid Comput. Esci. **29**(3), 751–762 (2013)

11. Yi, J., Huang, D., Fu, S., et al.: Optimized relative transformation matrix using bacterial foraging algorithm for process fault detection. IEEE Trans. Ind. Electron. **63**(4), 2595–2605 (2016)

12. Verma, O.P., Parihar, A.S.: An optimal fuzzy system for edge detection in color images using bacterial foraging algorithm. IEEE Trans. Fuzzy Syst. **25**(1), 114–127 (2017)

13. Mam, M., Leena, G., Saxena, N.S.: Distribution network reconfiguration for power loss minimization using bacterial foraging optimization algorithm. IJEM-Int. J. Eng. Manuf. (IJEM) **6**(2), 18–32 (2016)

14. Panda, A., Tripathy, M.: Security constrained optimal power flow solution of wind-thermal generation system using modified bacteria foraging algorithm. Energy **93**(8), 816–827 (2015)

15. Lu, Y., Ni, Q.: An improved bacteria foraging optimization algorithm for high dimensional multi-objective optimization problems. In: Tan, Y., Shi, Y., Tang, Q. (eds.) ICSI 2018. LNCS, vol. 10941, pp. 540–549. Springer, Cham (2018). https://doi.org/10.1007/978-3-319-93815-8_51

16. Panda, R., Naik, M.K.: A novel adaptive crossover bacterial foraging optimization algorithm for linear discriminant analysis based face recognition. Appl. Soft Comput. **30**(C) 722–736 (2015)

17. Wanga, L.L., Zhaoa, W.G., Tianb, Y.L., Panc, G.Z.: A bare bones bacterial foraging optimization algorithm. Cogn. Syst. Res. **52**, 301–311 (2018)

18. Pang, B., Song, Y., Zhang, C., Wang, H., Yang, R.: Bacterial foraging optimization based on improved chemotaxis process and novel swarming strategy. Appl. Intell. **49**(4), 1283–1305 (2018). https://doi.org/10.1007/s10489-018-1317-9

19. Liang, Y., Tian, H.: An improved hybrid algorithm based on bacterial foraging and particle swarm optimization. Electron. Sci. Technol. (2017)

20. Tang, K., et al.: Benchmark Functions for the CEC 2008 Special Session and Competition on Large Scale Global Optimization. Technical Report (2007)

21. Jamil, M., Yang, X.S.: A literature survey of benchmark functions for global optimisation problems. Int. J. Math. Model. Numer. Optim. **4**(2), 150–194 (2013)

22. Tan, L.J., Yi, W.J., Yang, C., Feng, Y.Y.: Adaptive structure-redesigned-based bacterial foraging optimization. In: Huang, D.-S., Jo, K.-H. (eds.) ICIC 2016. LNCS, vol. 9772, pp. 897–907. Springer, Cham (2016). https://doi.org/10.1007/978-3-319-42294-7_80

23. Niu, B., Fan, Y., Wang, H., et al.: Novel bacterial foraging optimization with time-varying chemotaxis step. Int. J. Artif. Intell. **7**(11), 257–273 (2011)

An Improved Bacterial Foraging Optimization with Differential and Poisson Distribution Strategy and its Application to Nurse Scheduling Problem

Jingzhou Jiang[1], Xiaojun Xiong[2], Yikun Ou[2], and Hong Wang[2(✉)]

[1] College of Mathematics and Statistics, Shenzhen University, Shenzhen, China
[2] College of Management, Shenzhen University, Shenzhen, China
ms.hongwang@gmail.com

Abstract. Bacterial Foraging Optimization (BFO) has been predominately applied to some real-world problems, but this method has poor convergence speed over complex optimization problems. In this paper, an improved Bacterial Foraging Optimization with Differential and Poisson Distribution strategies (PDBFO) is proposed to promote the insufficiency of BFO. In PDBFO, the step size of bacteria is segmented and adjusted in accordance with fitness value to accelerate convergence and enhance the search capability. Moreover, the differential operator and the Poisson Distribution strategy are incorporated to enrich individual diversity, which prevents algorithm from being trapped in the local optimum. Experimental simulations on eleven benchmark functions demonstrate that the proposed PDBFO has better convergence behavior in comparison to other six algorithms. Additionally, to verify the effectiveness of the method in solving the real-world complex problems, the PDBFO is also applied to the Nurse Scheduling Problem (NSP). Results indicate that the proposed PDBFO is more effective in obtaining the optimal solutions by comparing with other algorithms.

Keywords: Bacterial Foraging Optimization · Differential strategy · Poisson Distribution · Nurse Scheduling

1 Introduction

In a seminal paper published in 2002, Passino showed how bacterial individuals and groups find nutrients and how to model it as a distributed optimization process, which he named the Bacterial Foraging Optimization (BFO) [1]. The algorithm is designed to simulate foraging behavior of animals in nature, which has excellent capability to search optimal value of functions with steep function images [2]. Moreover, in the standard BFO, bacteria can avoid falling into the local optimum to some extent and also cooperating [3]. However, this approach often leads to the problem of slow convergence speed [1]. In recent decades, many

© Springer Nature Switzerland AG 2020
Y. Tan et al. (Eds.): ICSI 2020, LNCS 12145, pp. 312–324, 2020.
https://doi.org/10.1007/978-3-030-53956-6_28

researchers have optimized BFO to enhance the performance. In the improvement of BFO scholars focus on two aspects: BFO's operational strategy and algorithm combination.

In terms of algorithm strategy improvement, Mishra et al. combined the fuzzy rule system of Takagi-Sugeno (TS) in the BFO and then put forward a Fuzzy Bacterial Foraging (FBF) algorithm [4]. Besides, compared with classical algorithms, adaptive chemotactic operators have better performance. Ben Niu proposed an improved BFO with adaptive chemotaixs step and a non-linearly decreasing exponential modulation model [5]. The BFO of automatic chemoattractant step size is brought up by Majhi [6].

In regards to algorithm combination, Tang suggested a multi-level threshold method using the modified Bacterial Foraging Optimization (MBFO) [7] so as to enhance the practicability of the optimal threshold technology. Researchers found that bacteria could learn from the best position in the population by integrating Particle Swarm Optimization (PSO) into each chemotactic step, which enhanced the global search capability of the algorithm [8]. D.H. Kim et al. combined the crossover and mutation operators of the Genetic Algorithm (GA) with the BFO [9]. Luh considered biological evolution and came up with Bacterial Evolutionary Algorithm (BEA) [10]. Combining the Bacterial Foraging and Particle Swarm Optimization, Biswas proposed the hybrid optimization algorithm and applied it to solve the optimization of multi-modal functions [11].

Despite the great efforts of the researchers, the problems of premature convergence and slow convergence speed remain tricky. In order to promote the development of BFO algorithm, this paper proposes an improved BFO with Differential and Poisson Distribution strategies (PDBFO) to shed some light on the problems. To begin with, differential operators are incorporated into standard BFO to increase the convergence accuracy. Meanwhile, the segmentation step size change strategy is adopted. Finally, the Poisson Distribution strategy is used to disperse the bacteria.

Optimization algorithms are widely used to solve practical problems with high complexity. Alireza Goli applied the Accelerated Cuckoo Algorithm to the vehicle routing problem [12]. Precup, R.E. suggests the use of Grey Wolf Optimizer algorithms to optimize the parameters of Takagi-Sugeno proportional-integral-fuzzy controllers [13]. To further demonstrate the effectiveness of PDBFO in solving the real-world problem, a real Nurse Scheduling Problem (NSP) which improves the working efficiency and quality of nurses is employed [14].

This paper is organized as follows. Section 2 introduces the standard BFO algorithm. Then, the proposed algorithm is illustrated in details in Sect. 3. Section 4 presents the model of NSP. Section 5 shows the performance comparisons. Finally, conclusions and further work are presented in Sect. 6.

2   Bacterial Foraging Optimization

2.1   Chemotaxis

Chemotaxis is the most important process of BFO, in which bacteria gradually approach the optimal value through rotation and swimming. This process simulates the behaviour of swimming and tumbling through flagella of E. coll. Suppose $\theta_i(j, k, l)$ represents the ith bacterium at jth chemotactic, kth reproductive, and lth elimination-dispersal process. The movement of ith bacterium is expressed as follows:

$$\theta_i(j + 1, k, l) = \theta_i(j, k, l) + C(i)\varphi(i) \tag{1}$$

where $C(i) > 0$ represents the step size of each step forward, and $\varphi(j)$ represents a random forward direction vector selected after tumbling.

2.2   Reproduction

For reproduction, bacteria are ranked according to their health degree $Jhealth$. The smaller $Jhealth$ is, the healthier the bacterium is. The larger half population will be replaced by the better half. In this way, the population of bacteria remains the same. The algorithm runs N_{re} times reproduction operations. The health degree of bacteria $Jhealth$ is calculated as follows:

$$Jhealth(i) = \sum_{j=1}^{N_c} J(i, j, k, l) \tag{2}$$

where J represents fitness value computed by objective function, i represents each individual, j represents the number of chemotactic, k represents the number of reproduction and l represents the number of migration.

2.3   Elimination-Dispersal

In the evolutionary process, elimination and dispersal events may occur, which bacteria in one area are killed or a group of them are dispersed to a new environment. Dispersal may disrupt chemotaxis, whereas may also assist chemotaxis since it may direct the bacteria approaching better places with fruitful nutrition. This operation simulates the migration of bacteria to new environments by water currents or other organisms and the bacteria will be dispersed to random locations within the search area. The algorithm runs the dispel operation N_{ed} times. The specific operation is to give a fixed value of P_{ed} which is chosen within [0,1]. When the random number of bacterial individual is less than P_{ed}, the bacteria will die. Otherwise, a new individual will be generated randomly so as to achieve the purpose of migration.

3 Improved Bacterial Foraging Optimization Algorithm

In order to improve the search capability and convergence speed of the BFO, step size segmentation strategies are introduced by adjusting the step size according to the fitness values. Additionally, the differential operators and greedy selection strategies are employed at the end of swimming operations. During the migration process, Poisson Distribution strategy is used to choose the individuals to be dispelled. The Pseudocode of PDBFO has been provided in Algorithm 1.

3.1 Segmentation Step Size Changes on Chemotaxis Operation

In [15], experiment results have indicated that with the change of the current fitness value, changing of Chemotaxis step size can lead to better convergence performance in comparison to the case when the step size is fixed. In this paper, Chemotaxis step size is exploited by adopting a segmentation strategy. The fitness values of the bacteria are sorted in ascending order. Individuals with the smaller fitness values indicate good localization and could be assigned with small step size, whereas individuals with larger fitness values indicate poor bacterial localization and are assigned with a large step size.

Thus, the Chemotaxis step size can be adjusted as follows:

$$C_i = \begin{cases} C_{max} + (N_c - j)\frac{C_{max}-C_{min}}{N_c}, & i \leq 0.2S \\ C_{min} - (N_c - j)(C_{max} - C_{min}), & i \geq 0.8S \\ 0.1, & i \in (0.2S, 0.8S) \end{cases} \tag{3}$$

where S represents the population number, N_c is the total number of swimming, j is the current swimming times, and C represents the step size.

3.2 Bacterial Foraging Algorithm Combined with Differential Strategy

From BFO, we can find that the chemotactic operator searches the field through random movement to ensure the local search capability of bacteria. However, the bacteria do not make full use of the information of other bacteria in the environment. Consequently, the convergence speed of the algorithm is slow, resulting in premature convergence of the algorithm and difficulty in obtaining the global optimal [16]. Therefore, differential operator and greedy selection mechanism are embedded in the proposed algorithm.

After the swimming operation, the bacteria enter the stage of differential operation. The differential vector is established first, and then the vector is synthesized with the individual to generate the new individual. Then the fitness values of each new individual and the corresponding original individual are compared, and the greedy strategy is used to retain the better performing individuals [17]. In addition, an adaptive scaling operator F is introduced in the process of generating intermediate individuals. The adaptive scaling factor changes according to the following equation:

$$F = 2F_0 \cdot e^{\frac{1-N_c}{N_c+1-j}} \tag{4}$$

where, F_0 is the initial mutation operator, $F_0 = 0.4$. N_c and j represent the total number of chemotaxis and the current number of chemotaxis.

The generation equation of intermediate individuals is

$$G_i = P_i + F \cdot (R_1 - R_2) \tag{5}$$

where, G is the intermediate individual, and P is the corresponding original individual. R_1 and R_2 are two random individuals which are different from P.

The selection process is expressed as follows:

$$P_{i+1} = \begin{cases} G_i, & \text{if } f(G_i) < f(P_i) \\ P_i, & otherwise \end{cases} \tag{6}$$

where, P_{i+1} is the location of the selected new individual, G_i is the location of the intermediate individual, and P_i is the location of the original individual.

PSEUDOCODE FOR PDBFO ALGORITHM

1   Initialize:
    (a) Set parameters: N_{ed}, N_{re}, N_c, N_s, S, C_{max}, C_{min}, F_0, Dim
    (b) Initialize bacterial population
2   **Eliminating and dispersal loop: for** $l = 1, 2, \cdots, N_{ed}$
3   **Reproduction loop: for** $k = 1, 2, \cdots, N_{re}$
4   **Chemotaxis Loop: for** $j = 1, 2, \cdots, N_c$
5   for $i = 1, 2, \cdots, S$
6   Compute Fitness Value $J(i, j, k, l)$, and set $Jlast = J(i, j, k, l)$
7   Tumble by Eq.(1), then compute and sort Fitness Value $J(i, j, k, l)$
8   **while** $m < N_s$
9   update P_i by Eq.(1) and Eq.(3)
10   **end while**
11   Compute F by Eq.(4) and G_i by Eq.(5)
12   Select G_i and P_i by Eq.(6)
13   **end for**
14   **end for**
15   Reproduction, compute the all bacteria' $Jhealth$ by Eq.(2) and sort bacteria
16   for $j = 1, 2, \cdots, S/2$
17   Rerandomize the location of bacteria P_j
18   **end for**
19   **end for**
20   Generate poisson distribution Numbers by Eq.(7) and compute $J(i, j, k, l)$
21   for $m = 1, 2, \cdots, S$
22   Eliminate each bacterium as described in subsection 3.3
23   **end for**
24 **end for**

3.3   Poisson Distribution in Elimination-Dispersal Operations

Elimination-dispersal is an integral part of BFO. By means of elimination-dispersal, the bacteria trapped in local optimum can reposition themselves to avoid premature convergence. Elimination-dispersal makes the algorithm have a better random searching capability, and increases the diversity of the population. However, for high-dimensional optimization problems, elimination-dispersal will greatly slow down the convergence speed due to the increasing of dimensionality and complexity. Worse still, it is possible to drive away the best-performing bacteria, resulting in redundant computation [18].

This paper proposes a bacterial selection mechanism based on Poisson Distribution (PD) strategy to solve this problem. When the algorithm enters the dissipation process, the bacteria are firstly sorted according to the fitness value from small to large. Generate S random numbers that conform to the PD, and then compare the serial number of the bacteria with the corresponding random number to determine whether the bacterium should be dispersed. Through this mechanism, it is possible to ensure that most of the excellent bacteria will not be dispersed, and the bad bacteria will have the opportunity to be retained for further search. The probability function for the PD is

$$P(X = k) = \frac{\lambda^k}{k!}e^{-\lambda}, k = 0, 1, 2 \cdots \tag{7}$$

where k is a random number, λ is the mean and variance of the PD. After experiments, when λ takes 25, the algorithm performs better.

4   Application of Improved Algorithm in Nurse Scheduling Problem

4.1   Problem Description

NSP refers to scheduling a specific group of nurses within a given scheduling period. The scheduling of nurses should meet some constraints (such as hard and soft constraints) and minimize the total salary of nurses [19].

The worksheet of nurse can be probably divided into three kinds: the early shift (0a.m.–8a.m.), the day shift (8a.m.–4p.m.) and the night shift (4p.m.–0p.m.). The wages are allocated by the level of nurses (Junior, Middle, Senior). The objective function of the Nurse Scheduling Problem is provided as follows [20]:

$$min f(x) = \sum_{i=1}^{nn}\sum_{j=1}^{sk}\sum_{k=1}^{ss}\sum_{d=1}^{sd} x_{ijkd} \cdot w_{jk} + c \cdot \sum_{i=1}^{nn}\sum_{j=1}^{sk}\sum_{k=1}^{ss}\sum_{d=1}^{sd} m_{jkd} \tag{8}$$

where, nn is the total number of nurses, sk is the grade, ss is the type of shifts and sd is the period of scheduling. x_{ijkd} represents the i nurse belonging to j level has k shift in the d day, w_jk is the wage of nurse on the k shift at the

j level and m_{jkd} means the amount of unsatisfied shifts. And c is the penalty coefficient, whose value is 1000.

Equations (9–11) are hard constraints of NSP and Eq. 12 is the soft constraint:

$$\sum_{k=1} X_{ijkd} \leq 1 \tag{9}$$

$$if \quad X_{i,j,3,d} = 1, \quad then \quad X_{i,j,3,d+1} = 0 \tag{10}$$

$$lp \leq \sum_{d=1}^{sd} \sum_{k=1}^{ss} X_{ijkd} \leq up \tag{11}$$

$$m_{ijkd} > 0 \tag{12}$$

Equation (9) means that each nurse can have no more than one shift per day. Equation (10) represents each nurse cannot be on consecutive shifts within two days. Equation (11) presents that the working hour of nurses cannot exceed the lower or upper limit in a scheduling period. Equation (12) shows that the number of nurses on one shift is no less than the actual demand.

5 Experment Results and Discussions

This section illustrates the PDBFO's performance and comparisons among the proposed PDBFO and the other BFOs, the GA [20], the HCO [21] and the PSO [22]. In this experiment, for above algorithms, the running times is 30, the swarm size is 50, 10000 is the maximum iterations and the dimension of the search space is 30. Specifically, as for GA, the crossover probability is 0.8 and the mutation probability is 0.1. While for BFO methods, the number of

Table 1. Function characteristics

Function	Name	Dimensions	Domain of definition
f_1	Ackley	30	$[-32.768, 32.768]$
f_2	Levy	30	$[-10, 10]$
f_3	Powell	30	$[-4, 5]$
f_4	Sphere	30	$[-5.12, 5.12]$
f_5	Sum of powers	30	$[-1, 1]$
f_6	Zakharov	30	$[-5, 10]$
f_7	Dixon-price	30	$[-500, 500]$
f_8	Griewank	30	$[-600, 600]$
f_9	Rotated hyper	30	$[-65.536, 65.536]$
f_{10}	Rastrigin	30	$[-5.12, 5.12]$
f_{11}	Sum squares	30	$[-10, 10]$

swimming, chemotaxis, reproduction and elimination-dispersal are respectively $N_s = 4$, $N_c = 1000$, $N_{re} = 5$ and $N_{ed} = 2$. In addition, in PDBFO, the λ in Eq. (7) is 25 and the F_0 in Eq. (4) is 0.4. While for PSO, the parameter setting is $c_1 = c_2 = 1.5$, $w = 0.8$. More parameters settings of HCO is: the maximum flow times is 3, the evaporation and rainfall probability is 0.2. We have selected eleven well-known benchmark functions [23]. Table 1 summarizes the search scope of all functions.

5.1   Experiment Results on Benchmark Functions

Table 2 provides the average results and the variances on benchmark functions over 30 runs. For the sake of observation, the results are treated with logarithms. Noted that the mean of minimum values and the variance of each group have been bolded to highlight the best performing algorithm.

From Table 2 and convergence Fig. 1, it can be observed that the PDBFO outperforms other algorithms. For one thing, PDBFO obtains high quality mean of results in comparison to those of other algorithms in most cases. Although PDBFO performs worse than GA in f_2, it still has the edge over its counterparts. When others BFOs, GA, PSO and HCO find a solution that is close to the optimal value, they get stuck in poor local optimal and have trouble getting rid of it, while PDBFO can improved its solutions steadily (such as in f_3, f_4 and f_6). Because differential operators and Poisson distribution strategies keep PDBFO from falling into poor local optima. Consequently, the proposed PDBFO

Table 2. The numerical results on benchmark functions f_1 through f_{11}

Function	Result	PDBFO	BFO	BFONIW	BFOLIW	PSO	GA	HCO
f_1	Variance	**1.01E−04**	1.82E−03	1.84E+00	4.18E−04	1.83E−01	1.52E−04	2.57E+00
	Mean	**1.00E−02**	1.96E+01	1.70E+01	1.90E+01	1.13E+01	9.82E−02	1.60E+00
f_2	Variance	2.08E−02	2.57E+00	9.70E−01	2.19E+00	6.59E+01	**9.78E−07**	2.13E−01
	Mean	1.44E−01	4.82E+01	2.69E+01	3.96E+01	8.01E+01	**4.94E−03**	4.61E−01
f_3	Variance	**1.09E−05**	2.12E+00	1.42E−02	1.44E−02	4.86E+04	1.05E−03	4.10E+01
	Mean	**3.30E−03**	6.87E+00	1.72E+00	4.03E−01	4.12E+02	1.22E−01	6.41E+00
f_4	Variance	**3.16E−08**	1.45E−03	7.90E−08	6.78E−13	1.83E+00	3.37E−05	7.76E−04
	Mean	**1.78E−04**	3.56E−01	6.71E−03	4.13E−03	6.72E+00	1.85E−02	2.79E−02
f_5	Variance	**1.11E−16**	6.56E−08	4.82E−02	1.27E−12	8.34E−11	5.60E−14	4.20E−16
	Mean	**2.41E−09**	5.21E−04	2.20E−01	6.68E−06	4.78E−05	2.65E−07	4.71E−09
f_6	Variance	**4.41E−06**	9.81E+00	1.85E+04	6.75E+02	7.55E+02	1.01E+05	2.50E+03
	Mean	**2.10E−03**	2.07E+02	5.27E+02	3.25E+02	7.19E+01	4.42E+02	5.00E+01
f_7	Variance	2.28E−01	7.99E−03	**1.09E−05**	2.42E−05	6.91E+08	1.02E+00	1.01E+06
	Mean	**4.78E−01**	9.13E+00	8.41E−01	7.58E−01	3.95E+04	2.27E+00	1.00E+03
f_8	Variance	**8.77E−11**	1.36E−05	4.22E−09	1.71E−10	4.06E−03	1.41E−10	2.29E−03
	Mean	**2.96E−05**	2.77E−02	4.97E−04	3.70E−04	9.33E−01	4.18E−04	4.79E−02
f_9	Variance	**1.83E−05**	3.08E−01	8.25E−04	2.80E−05	1.33E+04	1.94E−04	3.97E+00
	Mean	**1.35E−02**	6.42E+00	1.25E−01	9.22E−02	8.27E+02	1.83E−01	1.99E+00
f_{10}	Variance	**2.19E−03**	3.08E+00	1.53E+01	6.14E+00	2.28E+02	6.69E−02	3.92E+02
	Mean	**4.68E−02**	1.86E+02	1.83E+02	1.31E+02	1.81E+02	2.31E+00	1.98E+01
f_{11}	Variance	**1.46E−05**	5.33E−02	3.94E−04	3.53E−05	3.72E+04	2.96E−03	2.71E−01
	Mean	**3.83E−03**	7.11E+00	1.38E−01	1.15E−01	6.88E+02	1.45E−01	5.21E−01

has desirable global search capability and strong robustness. For another thing, although the convergence speed of PDBFO is slower than GA (such as in f_2 and f_7) or PSO (such as in f_9) in the early stage of some cases, PDBFO has a satisfactory convergence speed in comparison to other BFOs.

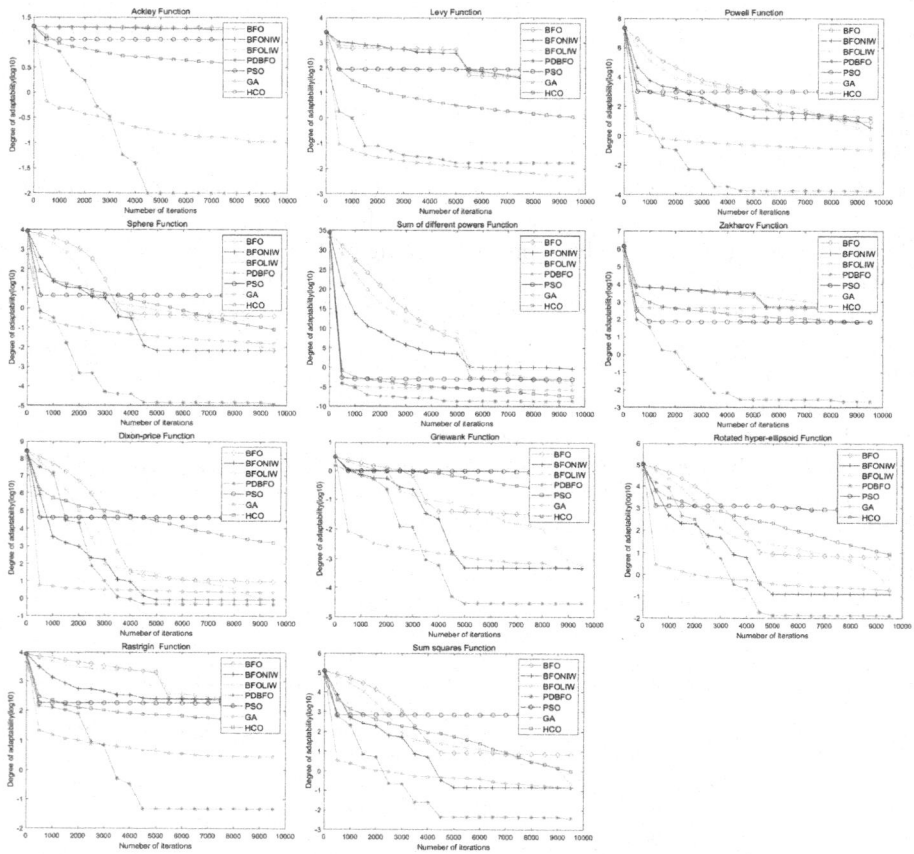

Fig. 1. The convergence results on benchmark function

Furthermore, PDBFO also has excellent performance in terms of stability. As can be seen from Table 2, in most cases, the variance given by PDBFO is much smaller than the corresponding variance given by other algorithms, which reflects that the PDBFO comes with very small volatility. Except that the variance of PDBFO is greater than GA in f_2, PDBFO shows sufficiently competitive stability in the other ten benchmark function experiments.

Overall, the PDBFO maintains splendid global searching capability and satisfactory convergence speed in most benchmark function experiments and hence it is more competitive than other algorithms. In addition, the low variance of

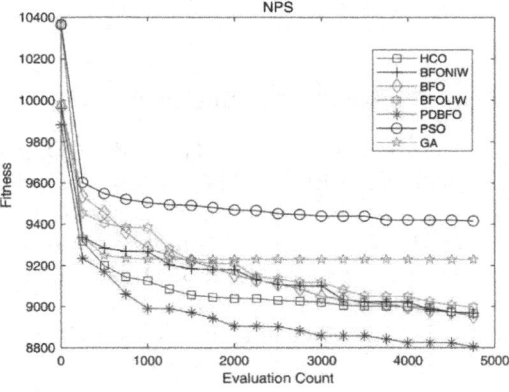

Fig. 2. The convergence results on the nurse scheduling problem

Table 3. The preferred schedule selected by PDBFO

Nurse number	Sun.	Mon.	Tue.	Wed.	Thu.	Fri.	Sat.
1	A	N	R	P	N	P	R
2	P	P	A	N	R	P	R
3	A	N	N	R	P	R	R
4	N	N	R	P	R	N	P
5	N	R	A	P	P	P	R
6	A	A	A	N	R	N	R
7	R	P	R	P	A	A	N
8	R	A	N	N	R	P	R
9	A	P	P	A	A	R	A
10	P	A	P	A	N	R	R
11	P	R	P	R	P	A	N
12	P	P	R	P	N	N	R
13	A	N	N	R	A	P	N
14	N	P	P	R	A	N	R
15	N	P	P	R	A	R	N
16	R	P	N	N	R	R	P
17	N	N	R	P	P	P	A
18	A	P	P	R	A	N	R
19	A	A	A	N	P	A	A
20	N	P	N	P	P	A	A

A, P, N and R represent morning work, noon work, evening work and rest respectively.

experimental results computed by PDBFO indicates that it is capable of delivering stable results.

5.2   Experiments on Nurses Scheduling Problem

PDBFO is compared with other BFOs, PSO, GA and HCO on solving the Nurse Scheduling Problem in this experiment. The schedule of 20 nurses for a week will be presented after calculation. Equation (8) is the objective function. The Function dimension is 30 dimension and the number of iterations is 5000.

As it is shown in Fig. 2, the proposed PDBFO has an edge over other algorithms on the Nurse Scheduling Problem. PDBFO has a better searching capability and convergence speed. An efficient shifts roster is shown in Table 3 to meet the needs of health care as well as improve the job satisfaction of nurses. The combination of scientific and reasonable nurse scheduling model and PDBFO can replace the low efficiency and low quality of manual scheduling scheme, contributing to enhancing the availability and optimization of the scheduling shifts. Due to the excellent search capability of PDBFO, an optimal scheduling scheme is more likely to be realized.

6   Conclusion and Future Work

PDBFO algorithm is proposed to improve the performance of BFO. The convergence speed is accelerated by introducing the change of segmentation step size. The Differential and Poisson Distribution strategies are used to reduce the problem of being trapped into local optimal. The benchmark function experiment results prove that the PDBFO significantly can deliver solutions with good quality and stability. Such an excellent performance demonstrates that PDBFO can balance different nursing requirements efficiently, making it an outstanding choice to solve the Nurse Scheduling Problem.

Due to the fact that PDBFO has shortcomings in the benchmark functions experiments, PDBFO can be further improved. More efficient bacterial swimming methods will be sought to improve the rate of convergence. Meanwhile, the improvement direction of the replication process will also be taken into consideration to improve the global optimization capability of the algorithm.

Acknowledgment. This work is partially supported by the Natural Science Foundation of China under Grant 71901152, Natural Science Foundation of Guangdong Province (2018A030310575), Natural Science Foundation of Shenzhen University (85303/00000155), Research Cultivation Project from Shenzhen Institute of Information Technology (ZY201717).

References

1. Passino, K.M.: Biomimicry of bacterial foraging for distributed optimization and control. IEEE Control Syst. Mag. **22**(3), 52–67 (2002)

2. Amjady, N., Fatemi, H., Zareipour, H.: Solution of optimal power flow subject to security constraints by a new improved bacterial foraging method. IEEE Trans. Power Syst. **27**(3), 1311–1323 (2012)
3. Liu, Q., Xu, J.: Traffic signal timing optimization for isolated intersections based on differential evolution bacteria foraging algorithm. Procedia-Soc. Behav. Sci. **43**(4), 210–215 (2012)
4. Mishra, S.: A hybrid least square-fuzzy bacterial foraging strategy for harmonic estimation. IEEE Trans. Evol. Comput. **9**(1), 61–73 (2005)
5. Niu, B., Wang, H., Tan, L., Li, L.: Improved BFO with adaptive chemotaxis step for global optimization. In: 2011 Seventh International Conference on Computational Intelligence and Security, pp. 76–80. IEEE (2011)
6. Majhi, R., Panda, G., Majhi, B., Sahoo, G.: Efficient prediction of stock market indices using adaptive bacterial foraging optimization (ABFO) and BFO based techniques. Expert Syst. Appl. **36**(6), 10097–10104 (2009)
7. Tang, K., Xiao, X., Wu, J., Yang, J., Luo, L.: An improved multilevel thresholding approach based modified bacterial foraging optimization. Appl. Intell. **46**(1), 214–226 (2016). https://doi.org/10.1007/s10489-016-0832-9
8. Raju, M., Gupta, M.K., Bhanot, N., Sharma, V.S.: A hybrid PSO-BFO evolutionary algorithm for optimization of fused deposition modelling process parameters. J. Intell. Manuf. **30**(7), 2743–2758 (2019)
9. Kim, D.H., Cho, J.H.: A biologically inspired intelligent PID controller tuning for AVR systems. Int. J. Control Autom. Syst. **4**(5), 624–636 (2006)
10. Zobolas, G., Tarantilis, C.D., Ioannou, G.: A hybrid evolutionary algorithm for the job shop scheduling problem. J. Oper. Res. Soc. **60**(2), 221–235 (2009)
11. Biswas, A., Dasgupta, S., Das, S., Abraham, A.: Synergy of PSO and bacterial foraging optimization—a comparative study on numerical benchmarks. In: Corchado, E., Corchado, J.M., Abraham, A. (eds.) Innovations in Hybrid Intelligent Systems. AINSC, vol. 44, pp. 255–263. Springer, Heidelberg (2007). https://doi.org/10.1007/978-3-540-74972-1_34
12. Goli, A., Aazami, A., Jabbarzadeh, A.: Accelerated cuckoo optimization algorithm for capacitated vehicle routing problem in competitive conditions. Int. J. Artif. Intell. **16**(1), 88–112 (2018)
13. Precup, R.E., David, R.C., Petriu, E.M., Szedlak-Stinean, A.I., Bojan-Dragos, C.A.: Grey wolf optimizer-based approach to the tuning of pi-fuzzy controllers with a reduced process parametric sensitivity. IFAC-PapersOnline **49**(5), 55–60 (2016)
14. Aickelin, U., Dowsland, K.A.: An indirect genetic algorithm for a nurse-scheduling problem. Comput. Oper. Res. **31**(5), 761–778 (2004)
15. Tong, Y.L.: Bacteria foraging optimization algorithm based on self-adaptive method. Value Eng. (2015)
16. Chatzis, S.P., Koukas, S.: Numerical optimization using synergetic swarms of foraging bacterial populations. Expert Syst. Appl. **38**(12), 15332–15343 (2011)
17. Dasgupta, S.: Analysis of a greedy active learning strategy. In: Advances in Neural Information Processing Systems, pp. 337–344 (2005)
18. Sahib, M.A., Abdulnabi, A.R., Mohammed, M.A.: Improving bacterial foraging algorithm using non-uniform elimination-dispersal probability distribution. Alexandria Eng. J. **57**(4), 3341–3349 (2018)
19. Chao, W., Dong, X.: Variable neighborhood search algorithm for nurse rostering problem. J. Comput. Appl. **33**(2), 338–341 (2013)
20. Booker, L.B., Goldberg, D.E., Holland, J.H.: Classifier systems and genetic algorithms. Artif. Intell. **40**(1–3), 235–282 (1989)

21. Yan, X., Niu, B.: Hydrologic cycle optimization part i: background and theory. In: Tan, Y., Shi, Y., Tang, Q. (eds.) ICSI 2018. LNCS, vol. 10941, pp. 341–349. Springer, Cham (2018). https://doi.org/10.1007/978-3-319-93815-8_33

22. Kennedy, J., Eberhart, R.: Particle swarm optimization. In: Proceedings of ICNN 1995-International Conference on Neural Networks, vol. 4, pp. 1942–1948. IEEE (1995)

23. Surjanovic, S., Bingham, D.: Virtual library of simulation experiments: test functions and datasets. http://www.sfu.ca/~ssurjano. Accessed 20 Feb 2020

Improved Bacterial Foraging Optimization Algorithm with Comprehensive Swarm Learning Strategies

Xiaobing Gan and Baoyu Xiao[✉]

College of Management, Shenzhen University, Shenzhen 518060, China
winsonxiao2019@163.com

Abstract. Bacterial foraging optimization (BFO), a novel bio-inspired heuristic optimization algorithm, has been attracted widespread attention and widely applied to various practical optimization problems. However, the standard BFO algorithm exists some potential deficiencies, such as the weakness of convergence accuracy and a lack of swarm communication. Owing to the improvement of these issues, an improved BFO algorithm with comprehensive swarm learning strategies (LPCBFO) is proposed. As for the LPCBFO algorithm, each bacterium keeps on moving with stochastic run lengths based on linear-decreasing Lévy flight strategy. Moreover, illuminated by the social learning mechanism of PSO and CSO algorithm, the paper incorporates cooperative communication with the current global best individual and competitive learning into the original BFO algorithm. To examine the optimization capability of the proposed algorithm, six benchmark functions with 30 dimensions are chosen. Finally, experimental results demonstrate that the performance of the LPCBFO algorithm is superior to the other five algorithms.

Keywords: Bacterial foraging optimization · Lévy flight · Comprehensive swarm learning strategies · Function optimization

1 Introduction

Bacterial foraging optimization (BFO) [1], a novel nature-oriented algorithm proposed by Passino, mainly simulates the behaviors of Escherichia coli in the process of searching for nutrients. During the foraging context, bacteria generally take four significant actions involved in chemotaxis, reproduction, elimination, and dispersal. Besides that, as for function optimization, the position of one bacterium can be regarded as a feasible solution in the search region. Bacteria adjust their own positions by tumbling based on random directions and swimming with certain step sizes to constantly find out the optimal location. Because of many advantages like the strong robustness and good performance in local search, the BFO algorithm has gradually become popular and until now, it has been applied to sorts of practical fields such as facility layout [2], feature selection [3], training kernel extreme learning machine [4] and so on.

© Springer Nature Switzerland AG 2020
Y. Tan et al. (Eds.): ICSI 2020, LNCS 12145, pp. 325–334, 2020.
https://doi.org/10.1007/978-3-030-53956-6_29

At present, relevant theoretical researches about the BFO algorithm are still in the initial stage. In other words, compared with the other traditional swarm intelligent algorithms such as particle swarm optimization (PSO) [5] and genetic algorithm (GA) [6], the development of the BFO algorithm is not enough mature. Moreover, researches have consistently shown that the BFO algorithm has poor capability both in convergence rate and optimization accuracy, especially for high-dimensional function problems. To elevate the performance of the original algorithm, plenty of improved methods and distinguished hybrid mechanisms [7–11] have been brought up. On the one hand, as the significance of the process of chemotaxis, numerous strategies were proposed to enhance it. Niu et al. [7, 8] improved the chemotactic step size through linear and non-linear decreasing strategies. Experimental results verified the improved algorithm had better performance than the standard BFO. In [9], Wang et al. proposed the other BFO variant (BFO-DX) that incorporates a novel mechanism of progressive exploitation into the chemotaxis operator for improving the ability of local exploration. Another part of the improvement is for the hybridization of the BFO algorithm with other algorithms. Biswas et al. [10] demonstrated an efficient optimization technique including BFO with PSO operator to enhance swarm learning and the global search ability of the original BFO algorithm. With the purpose to tackle with optimization problems more effectively, Zhao et al. [11] combined the gravitational search method with the BFO algorithm and then applied the proposed algorithm (EBFO) into optimizing the Lorenz system.

Although the above-proposed strategies have made great progress, there might have some potential demerits like poor performance of the convergence rate. As for the BFO algorithm, the chemotactic step size is set as a constant number regardless of what the condition of each bacterium is in. Aiming at coping with these disadvantages effectively, the paper introduces a linear-decreasing Lévy flight strategy to randomly generate the length of the motion route for each bacterium, which helps to balance the local and global search. More importantly, comprehensive swarm learning consisting of the cooperative communication with the current global best bacterium and the competitive learning mechanisms are adopted in the paper so as to improve the convergence accuracy of the BFO algorithm and furtherly increase the diversity of the general community to effectively alleviate the premature matter.

The rest of this paper is structured as follows: Sect. 2 briefly introduces relevant principles of the standard BFO algorithm. Section 3 details the proposed LPCBFO algorithm. Experimental results are described in Sect. 4. The final section draws the conclusion and future work.

2   The Standard Bacterial Foraging Optimization Algorithm

As a new heuristic optimization technique, the BFO algorithm [1] properly imitates the crucial actions of E. coli generating in the process of obtaining food, mainly including chemotaxis, reproduction, elimination, and dispersal.

2.1   Chemotaxis

Owing to far away from harmful materials efficiently and obtain nutrients in a faster way, each bacterium gradually moves towards the objectives through tumbling and swimming.

On the one hand, during choosing one direction randomly in the search space, bacteria continuously move on with fixed run lengths. After tumbling, bacteria could not insist on swimming along the same search direction until the updated position gets worse or the number of practicable movements is up to the limitation N_s. The new position of the bacterium i in $j + 1$th chemotaxis, kth reproduction and lth elimination and dispersal $\theta^i(j + 1, k, l)$ is shown as the Eq. (1) where $\theta^i(j, k, l)$ represents the last position of the bacterium i; $C(i)$ is the step size and $\Delta(i)$ means a random direction vector whose all elements range from -1 to 1.

$$\theta^i(j + 1, k, l) = \theta^i(j, k, l) + C(i) \times \frac{\Delta(i)}{\sqrt{\Delta^T(i)\Delta(i)}}. \tag{1}$$

2.2 Reproduction

Abiding by the main idea about "Survival of the Fittest" of Darwin's Evolutionary Theory, the process of reproduction in the BFO algorithm mirrors that the healthier bacteria are more likely to have the remarkable capability of reproduction to maintain the whole of swarm population while poor-nourished individual will be eliminated in the end. In the BFO algorithm, the health degree of the bacterium i is noted as $f_{i,health}$ that can be measured by the sum of fitness value among its lifecycle. Relatively, the corresponding mathematical expression can be presented as (2).

$$f_{i,health} = \sum_{j=1}^{N_c} J(i, j, k, l). \tag{2}$$

where N_c represents the total number of chemotaxis as the lifecycle of the bacterium i; $J(i, j, k, l)$ is the fitness value of the bacterium i in jth chemotaxis, kth reproduction, lth elimination and dispersal. Then through ascending order for the health value of all bacterium, half of healthier bacteria ($S_r = SS/2$) are able to split into two bacteria whose both of them have the same position while the rest of bacteria are given up.

2.3 Elimination and Dispersal

In reality, due to the dramatic change of its living environment all the time, bacteria might be confronted with lots of unpredicted risks including dynamic temperature change in the local region or invasion of kinds of detrimental substances. Therefore, when suffering from these adverse and unexpected conditions, a part of bacteria needs to disperse to another favorable location as soon as possible. Based on it, after the process of reproduction, the bacterium i randomly migrates to another new position θ' with a certain probability P_{ed}, otherwise it remains in the current location.

3 LPCBFO Algorithm

3.1 Linear-Decreasing Lévy Flight Strategy

Lévy flight strategy [12] sheds light on a stochastic motion process of certain objects in the search environment where the run length C strictly complies with Lévy distribution probability. The related mathematical equation [13] can be defined as (3) where μ ranges from 1 to 3.

$$f(C) = C^{-\mu}. \tag{3}$$

Up to now, the Lévy flight algorithm has been broadly used for imitating the trajectory of foraging behaviors about many creatures like bumblebees [14], and fruit flies [15] and so far, some favorable research developments have been achieved. Moreover, during the process of searching based on the Lévy flight method, objects can move on with smaller step sizes frequently and larger lengths occasionally, which is to a certain extent beneficial to balance the local exploration and global exploitation for optimization problems. According to these advantages of the Lévy flight strategy, the paper tries to add it to promote $C(i)$ as the Eq. (4) [12]. Furthermore, inspired by [7], we adopt the linear-decreasing Lévy flight strategy followed as the Eq. (5), seeking to improve the convergence accuracy of the standard BFO algorithm.

$$C(i) = \frac{u}{|v|^{1/\beta}}, \ \beta \epsilon [0.3, 1.99], \ u \sim N(0, \sigma_u^2), \ v \sim N(0, 1). \tag{4}$$

$$\sigma_u = \left\{ \frac{\Gamma(1+\beta)\sin\left(\frac{\pi\beta}{2}\right)}{\Gamma\left(\frac{1+\beta}{2}\right) \times 2^{\frac{\beta-1}{2}} \times \beta} \right\}^{1/\beta}.$$

$$C'(i) = \left(C_{min} + \frac{iter_{max} - iter_{current}}{iter_{max}} \right) \times C(i). \tag{5}$$

$$\theta^i(j+1, k, l) = \theta^i(j, k, l) + C'(i) \times \frac{\Delta(i)}{\sqrt{\Delta^T(i)\Delta(i)}}. \tag{6}$$

3.2 Cooperative Learning Strategy

As for the original BFO algorithm, there is a lack of swarm communication in the whole of the bacterial population, which may have a great negative impact on the convergence capability and accuracy. By contrast, when having great opportunities to communicate with other individuals during the process of searching for nutrients, bacteria could obtain so enough useful information that they could make appropriate adjustments for their current position in time. Consequently, with illumination by the group learning in PSO [5] and the hybridization algorithm based on PSO operator [10], the paper also incorporates corresponding cooperative learning mechanisms into the BFO algorithm. After tumbling and swimming of each bacterium, they have a chance to learn from the global best particle θ_{best} to adjust their current positions. Additionally, the linear-decreasing inertia weight [16] is conducted to modulate the velocity $v'(i)$ of each individual. The updating position of bacterium i $\theta^i(j+1, k, l)$ is as follows:

$$v'(i) = \left[\omega_{max} - \frac{iter_{current} \times (\omega_{max} - \omega_{min})}{iter_{max}} \right] \times v_i^{last} + c \times rand \times \left(\theta_{best} - \theta^i(j+1, k, l) \right). \tag{7}$$

$$\theta^i(j+1, k, l) = v'(i) + \theta^i(j+1, k, l). \tag{8}$$

where c means the study rate; θ_{best} represents the current global best position; *iter* means iterations.

3.3 Competitive Learning Strategy

Although the cooperative swarm learning mechanism can enhance the capability for global exploitation and the rate of convergence, bacteria are easy to trap into the local best solution. With regarding in the enhancement of premature problem effectively and improve the diversity of the whole bacterial population, we are inspired by the main principle of competitive swarm optimization (CSO) [17] which is proposed by Cheng and then adopt the pairwise bacterial competitive mechanism into the basic BFO algorithm. Firstly, when all of the bacteria *SS* accomplished the process of chemotaxis, they are randomly divided into $SS/2$ couples. After pairwise competition in each couple, the better individual called winner directly go to the next chemotaxis process while the loser with worse fitness value updates its current position by learning from the winner and then performs the next chemotaxis step. The competitive learning mechanism can be represented as:

$$v^{loser}(j+1, k, l) = \varepsilon\{rand1 \times v^{loser}(j, k, l) + rand2 \times \left[\theta_w(j, k, l) - \theta_{loser}(j, k, l)\right] \\ + \varphi \times rand3 \times \left[\theta_{w_{center}}(j, k, l) - \theta_{loser}(j, k, l)\right]\}. \tag{9}$$

$$\theta^{loser}(j+1, k, l) = v^{loser}(j+1, k, l) + \theta^{loser}(j+1, k, l). \tag{10}$$

where $\varepsilon = \frac{2}{2-c-\sqrt{c^2-4c}}$ [18], $\varphi = \varphi_{min} + (\varphi_{max} - \varphi_{min}) \times rand$, ε, φ are constraint factors; $\theta_w(j, k, l)$ is the position of the more competitive bacterium; $\theta_{w_{center}}(j, k, l)$ is the average position vector of total winners (Table 1).

4 Experimental Results and Discussion

To testify the optimization efficiency of the proposed LPCBFO algorithm, the convergency results of the LPCBFO algorithm are assessed by comparing with the original bacterial foraging optimization(BFO) [1] and other BFO variants involved the basic BFO algorithm with linear-decreasing strategy(BFO-LDC) [7], the algorithm improved by nonlinear-decreasing chemotactic step size(BFO-NDC) [8], the algorithm based on linear-decreasing Lévy flight strategy(LBFO) as well as the hybrid algorithm with PSO operator(BSO) [10]. In this paper, the population of bacteria *SS* for all involved algorithms is set in 50 and the total number of the process of chemotaxis N_C, reproduction N_{re}, elimination and dispersal N_{ed} respectively are 1000, 5 and 2. Thus, the total iteration in the experiment is $N_C \times N_{re} \times N_{ed} = 10000$. Besides, we also set $N_s = 4$, $P_{ed} = 0.25$. As for specified parameters settings in the LPCBFO algorithm, we set $C_{min} = 0.01$, $\beta = 1.99$, $\omega_{max} = 0.9$, $\omega_{min} = 0.4$, $\varphi_{min} = 0.01$, $\varphi_{max} = 0.2$, $c = 1.5$. In addition, other relevant parameters in the above improved BFO algorithms are as

Table 1. The pseudo code of the proposed LPCBFO algorithm

Initialize parameters and swarm of bacteria $\theta^i(j,k,l), i \in (1,2,3,\dots,SS)$
Evaluate the fitness value $J_i(j,k,l), i \in (1,2,3,\dots,SS)$, the global best position θ_{best} and the global best fitness value J_{best}
For $l = 1 : N_{ed}$
  For $k = 1 : N_{re}$
    For $j = 1 : N_c$
      For $i = 1 : SS$
        Update $J_i(j,k,l)$
        The bacterium i updates its position with the equation (6)
        Calculate the fitness value $J_i(j+1,k,l)$
        Let $m = 0$ (initialize counter for swim length)
        While $m < N_s$
          $m = m + 1$
          IF the updated fitness value $J_i(j+1,k,l)$ gets better
            The bacterium i preforms swimming using the equation (6)
          End
        End
        Perform the cooperative swarm learning using equations (7), (8)
        Update $J_i(j+1,k,l), \theta_{best}$ and J_{best}
      End
      Divide all bacterium into $SS/2$ couples (SS is an even number)
      Compare bacteria' fitness value of each couple respectively
      Perform pairwise competitive learning mechanism using equations (9), (10)
    End
    Calculate the health value for each bacterium $f_{i,health}$ using the equation (2)
    Sort out the bacteria $f_{i,health}$ in ascending order and perform reproduction
  End
The bacterium i is randomly located on a new position θ' with probability P_{ed}
End

---

follows. BFO-LDC settings: $C_{min} = 0.01$, $C_{max} = 1.5$; BFO-NDC: $C_{min} = 0.01$, $C_{max} = 1.5$, $\lambda = 4$; LBFO: $C_{min} = 0.01$, $\beta = 1.99$; BSO: the step length of each bacterium $iC(i) = 0.1$, $\omega = 0.8$, $c = 1.5$. According to the above parameter settings in each algorithm, six common benchmark functions in 30 dimensions are chosen to adequately identify the performance of the above six algorithms, involving four unimodal functions (Sphere, Rosenbrock, Schwefel's Problem and Sum of different powers) as well as two multimodal functions (Rastrigin, Ackley function). With regarding to the improvement of the results' reliability and availability, each algorithm is fully operated in 10 times for six benchmark functions.

After 10 runtimes in 30 dimensions, relevant experimental data results are illustrated in Table 2. In Table 2, there mainly contain four necessary measurement metrics including the minimum solution ('Best'), the worst fitness value ('Worst'), the average value ('Mean'), and standard deviation ('Std'). Additionally, the convergence results about six test functions with 30 dimensions are respectively shown in Fig. 1. Generally, in the initial iteration of some benchmark functions like Rosenbrock and Sum of different powers, the LPCBFO algorithm has slower convergence speed than others. This phenomenon might be contributed by the reason that bacteria with longer movement length in the early iteration stage are more committed to the global exploitation while they are poor in local search. However, we can observe that during the latter search period, the LPCBFO algorithm has greater capability to escape from the local best solution and its convergence accuracy is obviously more excellent than other algorithms'. It is likely to be accounted for comprehensive learning mechanisms and the enhancement of the diversity of the bacterial population.

Table 2. Comparison between LPCBFO and other algorithms with 30 dimensions

	BFO	BFO-LDC	BFO-NDC	LBFO	BSO	LPCBFO
Sphere	3.68e−01	6.26e−02	3.21e−03	5.88e−03	5.10e−06	**1.39e−92**
	5.62e−01	1.03e−01	4.72e−03	2.95e−02	2.47e−04	**3.83e−78**
	4.91e−01	8.57e−02	3.96e−03	1.74e−02	7.06e−05	**3.83e−79**
	7.07e−02	1.38e−02	5.01e−04	7.77e−03	7.84e−05	**1.21e−78**
Rosenbrock	6.09e+01	4.18e+01	1.43e+01	2.55e+01	2.29e+01	**5.99e−02**
	7.79e+01	7.22e+01	2.47e+01	2.81e+01	1.28e+02	**4.08e+00**
	7.10e+01	5.22e+01	2.12e+01	2.68e+01	3.69e+01	**1.71e+00**
	5.27e+00	8.10e+00	3.34e+00	**1.10e+00**	3.19e+01	1.99e+00
Schwefel	3.32e+00	2.42e+02	1.01e+02	1.25e+02	9.18e−02	**6.30e−35**
	5.14e+00	3.49e+04	2.65e+05	8.36e+02	2.52e−01	**8.28e−28**
	3.95e+00	1.04e+04	4.31e+04	3.00e+02	1.37e−01	**1.01e−28**
	5.03e−01	1.09e+04	8.73e+04	2.51e+02	5.36e−02	**2.61e−28**
Sum	1.58e−04	1.76e+03	1.21e+04	1.24e−07	1.49e−09	**1.73e−96**
	6.63e−04	5.48e+04	6.33e+06	3.20e−07	1.45e−07	**8.38e−61**
	3.91e−04	1.82e+04	9.32e+05	2.29e−07	2.22e−08	**8.38e−62**
	1.72e−04	1.82e+04	1.95e+06	5.96e−08	4.38e−08	**2.65e−61**
Rastrigin	1.07e+02	2.65e+02	1.48e+02	1.56e+02	2.99e+01	**1.49e+01**
	1.51e+02	3.50e+02	2.35e+02	1.86e+02	4.59e+01	**2.49e+01**
	1.36e+02	3.11e+02	1.84e+02	1.74e+02	3.73e+01	**1.92e+01**
	1.39e+01	2.74e+01	2.73e+01	9.71e+00	5.00e+00	**3.22e+00**
Ackley	1.68e+01	1.06e+01	1.83e+01	1.80e+01	6.18e+00	**1.16e+00**
	1.77e+01	1.96e+01	1.91e+01	1.806e+01	1.16e+01	**4.30e+00**
	1.74e+01	1.84e+01	1.89e+01	1.803e+01	9.49e+00	**2.407e+00**
	2.96e−01	2.77e+00	2.79e−01	**1.48e−02**	1.77e+00	8.26e−01

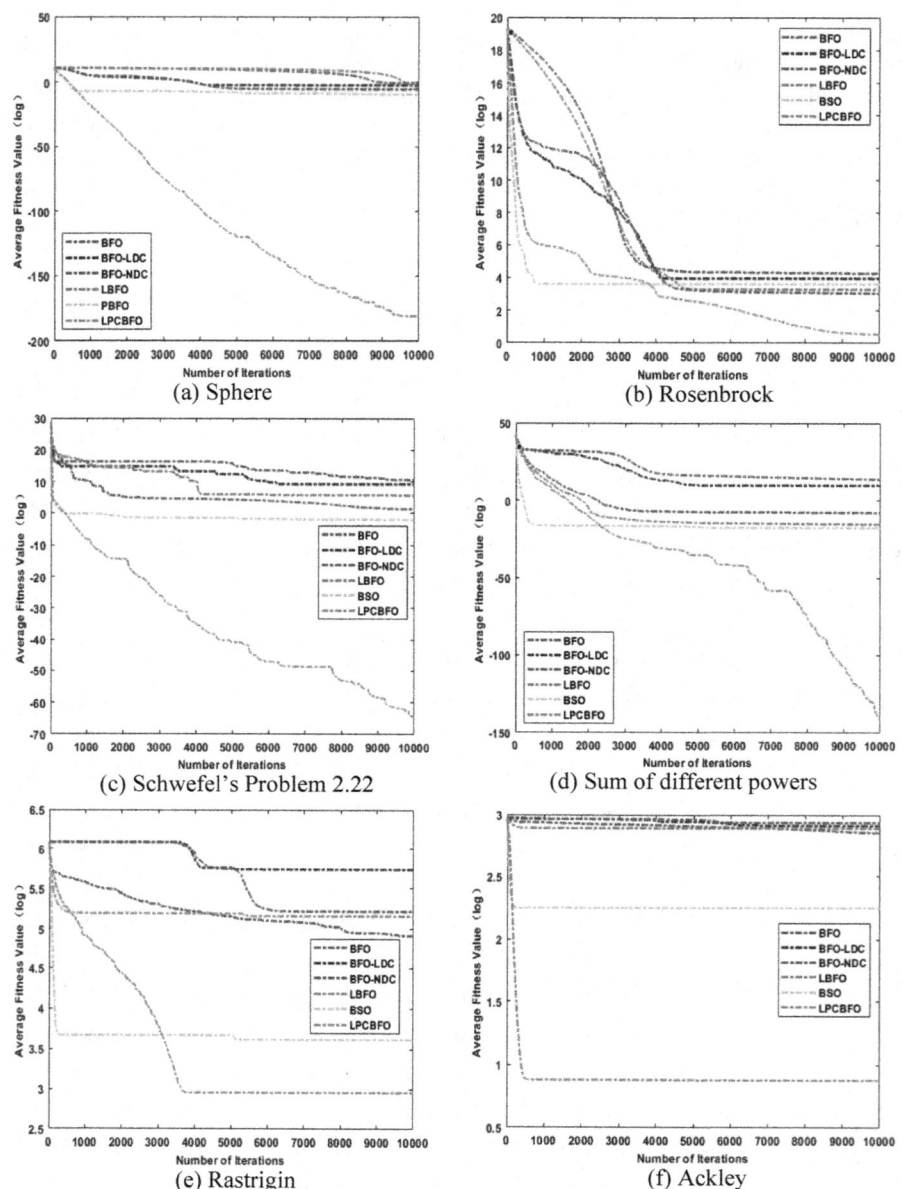

(a) Sphere

(b) Rosenbrock

(c) Schwefel's Problem 2.22

(d) Sum of different powers

(e) Rastrigin

(f) Ackley

Fig. 1. Convergence results of six different algorithms with 30 dimensions

5   Conclusion and Future Work

In the paper, the improved bacterial foraging optimization with comprehensive swarm learning mechanisms (LPCBFO) is proposed. Compared with the standard BFO algorithm, the paper incorporates the linear-decreasing Lévy flight method to randomly generate the run length of each bacterium, which is in favor of balancing the local exploration and global exploitation. Depending on improving the convergence speed and solution accuracy of the algorithm, the cooperative swarm strategy during learning with the current optimal individual is fully considered. To avoid the premature issue effectively and promote the diversity of the overall population, each bacterium can be pairwise allocated randomly to conduct competitive learning. Finally, six benchmark functions with 30 dimensions are chosen to measure the performance of the proposed LPCBFO algorithm compared with the BFO algorithm and the other four variants. Experimental results show that the optimization effectiveness of the LPCBFO algorithm outperforms others.

In the future, we will contribute to the improvement of the BFO algorithm and attempt to deal with practical problems likes airline scheduling, logistic delivery, and vehicle routing planning by improved algorithms.

References

1. Passino, K.M.: Biomimicry of bacterial foraging for distributed optimization and control. IEEE Control Syst. Mag. **22**, 52–67 (2002)
2. Turanoglu, B., Akkaya, G.: A new hybrid heuristic algorithm based on bacterial foraging optimization for the dynamic facility layout problem. Expert Syst. Appl. **98**, 93–104 (2018)
3. Chen, Y., Li, Y., Wang, G., et al.: A novel bacterial foraging optimization algorithm for feature selection. Expert Syst. Appl. **83**, 1–17 (2017)
4. Chen, H., Zhang, Q., Luo, J., et al.: An enhanced bacterial foraging optimization and its application for training kernel extreme learning machine. Appl. Soft Comput. **86**, 1–24 (2020)
5. Eberhart, R., Kennedy, J.: Particle swarm optimization. In: Proceedings of the IEEE International Conference on Neural Networks, pp. 1942–1948. IEEE Press, New York (1995)
6. Holland, J.H.: Adaptation in Natural and Artificial Systems: an Introductory Analysis with Applications to Biology, Control, and Artificial Intelligence. MIT Press (1992)
7. Niu, B., Fan, Y., Wang, H., et al.: Novel bacterial foraging optimization with time-varying chemotaxis step. Int. J. Artif. Intell. **7**, 257–273 (2011)
8. Niu, B., Wang, H., Tan, L., et al.: Improved BFO with adaptive chemotaxis step for global optimization. In: 2011 Seventh International Conference on Computational Intelligence and Security, pp. 76–80. IEEE Press, New York (2011)
9. Wang, D., Qian, X., Ban, X., et al.: Enhanced bacterial foraging optimization based on progressive exploitation toward local optimum and adaptive raid. IEEE Access **7**, 95725–95738 (2019)
10. Biswas, A., Dasgupta, S., Das, S., Abraham, A.: Synergy of PSO and bacterial foraging optimization—a comparative study on numerical benchmarks. In: Corchado, E., Corchado, J.M., Abraham, A. (eds.) Innovations in Hybrid Intelligent Systems. ASC, vol. 44, pp. 255–263. Springer, Heidelberg (2007). https://doi.org/10.1007/978-3-540-74972-1_34
11. Zhao, W., Wang, L.: An effective bacterial foraging optimizer for global optimization. Inf. Sci. **329**, 719–735 (2016)

12. Mantegna, R.N.: Fast, accurate algorithm for numerical simulation of Lévy stable stochastic processes. Phys. Rev. E **49**, 4677 (1994)

13. Viswanathan, G.M., Raposo, E.P., Da Luz, M.G.E.: Lévy flights and super-diffusion in the context of biological encounters and random searches. Phys. Life Rev. **5**, 133–150 (2008)

14. Edwards, A.M., Phillips, R.A., Watkins, N.W., et al.: Revisiting Lévy flight search patterns of wandering albatrosses, bumblebees deer. Nature **449**, 1044–1048 (2007)

15. Reynolds, A.M., Frye, M.A.: Free-flight odor tracking in drosophila is consistent with an optimal intermittent scale-free search. PLoS One **2**, e354 (2007)

16. Shi, Y., Eberhart, R.: A modified particle swarm optimizer. In: 1998 IEEE International Conference on Evolutionary Computation Proceedings, pp. 69–73. IEEE Press, New York (1998)

17. Cheng, R., Jin, Y.: A competitive swarm optimizer for large scale optimization. IEEE Trans. Cybern. **45**, 191–204 (2014)

18. Zhang, L., Yu, H., Hu, S.: A new approach to improve particle swarm optimization. In: Cantú-Paz, E., et al. (eds.) GECCO 2003. LNCS, vol. 2723, pp. 134–139. Springer, Heidelberg (2003). https://doi.org/10.1007/3-540-45105-6_12

Modified Bacterial Foraging Optimization for Fuzzy Mean-Semivariance-Skewness Portfolio Selection

Xinzheng Wu[1], Aiqing Gao[2(✉)], and Xin Huang[2]

[1] College of Economics, Shenzhen University, Shenzhen, China
[2] College of Management, Shenzhen University, Shenzhen, China
gaoaiqing_alina@163.com

Abstract. In this paper, a novel bacterial foraging optimization with decreasing chemotaxis step combined with sine function is employed to solve a fuzzy portfolio optimization with a modified mean-semivariance-skewness model which includes the transaction fee and no short sales. First of all, a decreasing chemotaxis step combined with sine function (BFO-SDC) takes the place of constant chemotaxis step size. It is a nonlinear decreasing strategy at every iteration of the algorithm. And then, the variance is replaced by semivariance and skewness is taken into account in order to generate asymmetry of return distributions to overcome the inadequacy of the standard mean-variance model. Finally, fuzzy variables are used to express the uncertain and imprecise elements in the decision-making process. The results of the simulation show that the model can be solved more reasonably and effectively by BFO-SDC than the original bacterial foraging optimization.

Keywords: Bacterial foraging optimization · Sine function · Fuzzy portfolio optimization · Mean-semivariance-skewness

1 Introduction

The mean-variance model (MVM) originally formulated by Markowitz [1] plays a critical and vital role in modern finance theory. Inspired by the Markowitz's idea, numerous extensions have been proposed, e.g., multi-period mean-variance formulation [2], behavioral mean-variance portfolio selection [3]. Nevertheless, one of the assumptions of MVM is that the returns of assets are symmetrically distributed. Actually, in reality, there are shreds of empirical evidence [4, 5] suggesting that many security returns follow the asymmetrical distribution. People start to considerate asymmetry of return distributions to overcome the inadequacy of the MVM. The one is that Ibbotson [6] and Prakash *et al.* [7] show that it can generate a higher return when skewness is considered in the decision-making process. As a result, some scholars such as Prakash *et al.* [7] extend MVM to mean–variance–skewness model (MVSM). The other directly use downside risk measure to avoid sacrificing a large amount of expected return in removing both high and low return extremes. Semivariance [8] which is clear, comparatively simple

© Springer Nature Switzerland AG 2020
Y. Tan et al. (Eds.): ICSI 2020, LNCS 12145, pp. 335–346, 2020.
https://doi.org/10.1007/978-3-030-53956-6_30

and direct in mirroring investors' intuition about risk is one of the well-known downside risk measures.

Moreover, another basic assumption of MVM is that the asset markets in the future can accurately reflect the asset data in the past. However, it is impossible to produce correct expectations for future risks and returns based on historical data exclusively in the uncertain economic environment. Thus, the fuzzy set theory [9] is well suited to deal with vagueness and uncertainty of any stock market attributes in portfolio optimization (PO).

As a fresh comer of swarm intelligence (SI), bacterial foraging optimization (BFO) [10] has gotten much attention from different areas, and widely used in many real-world problems including supply chain optimization problem [11], flexible job-shop scheduling problem [12], and vehicle routing problem [13]. And a modified BFO with linear decreasing chemotaxis step (BFO-LDC) has been already successfully applied to solve the PO [14].

Sine function, one of the trigonometric functions, has been applied in the generation of n-scroll attractors [15], the design of ship course-keeping autopilot [16], sound encryption scheme [17], etc.

Based on the analysis of the recent literature, the problems about how to modify MVM to become more suitable for the real stock market and promote the ability of BFO to achieve better solutions in the PO attracts our attention. In this paper, we propose a novel BFO with decreasing chemotaxis step combined with sine function (BFO-SDC) and build a more complex PO model. The main contributions of this paper are listed as follows. First of all, a decreasing strategy based on sine function replaces the constant chemotaxis step size to investigate the optimization ability of BFO through combing decreasing strategy with sine function to create a nonlinear decreasing strategy. Next, use semivariance to replace variance and take skewness into account to generate asymmetry of asset distributions. And then, transaction fees, no short sales are also included. Finally, fuzzy logic [18] is used to express uncertainty to make it suitable for representing the intrinsic vagueness nature of the PO problem.

The remainder of the paper is organized as follows. Section 2 provides some introductory definitions and concepts. Section 3 reviews BFO and describes BFO-SDC. Section 4 gives a description of the modified fuzzy mean-semivariance-skewness model and related computational steps. The experimental results and analyses are shown and discussed in Sect. 5. In the end, concluding remarks are given in Sect. 6.

2   Preliminaries

The theories related to the definitions needed in the rest of the paper are briefly introduced in this section. The assistance of a membership function $\mu_A(x) \rightarrow [0,1]$, which is a single value between zero and one represents the degree of membership of the various elements.

Definition 1 [19]. A trapezoidal fuzzy number A with tolerance interval $[a, b]$, left-width $\alpha > 0$ and right-width $\beta > 0$ is fully determined by the quadruplet (a, b, α, β).

And its membership function is given by

$$
\mu_A(X) = \begin{cases} 1 - \frac{a-X}{\alpha}, & \text{if } a - \alpha \leq X \leq a \\ 1, & \text{if } a \leq X \leq b \\ 1 - \frac{X-b}{\beta}, & \text{if } b \leq X \leq b + \beta \\ 0, & \text{if otherwise} \end{cases} \tag{1}
$$

Definition 2 [20]. A fuzzy number A with the γ-level set is expressed as $[A]^\gamma = [\alpha_1(\gamma), \alpha_2(\gamma)]$ for all $\gamma > 0$ and the γ-level set of A can be computed as

$$
[A]^\gamma = [a - (1 - \gamma)\alpha, \ b + (1 - \gamma)\beta](\gamma \in [0, 1]) \tag{2}
$$

The possibilistic mean value of A is given by the following.

$$
E(A) = \int\limits_0^1 \gamma[\alpha_1(\gamma) + \alpha_2(\gamma)]d\gamma = \frac{a+b}{2} + \frac{\beta - \alpha}{6} \tag{3}
$$

Definition 3 [21]. The upper and lower semivariances of A are defined as

$$
Var^+(A) = \int\limits_0^1 \gamma[E(A) - \alpha_2(\gamma)]^2 d\gamma = (\frac{b-a}{2} + \frac{\beta + \alpha}{6})^2 + \frac{\beta^2}{18} \tag{4}
$$

$$
Var^-(A) = \int\limits_0^1 \gamma[E(A) - \alpha_2(\gamma)]^2 d\gamma = (\frac{b-a}{2} + \frac{\beta + \alpha}{6})^2 + \frac{\alpha^2}{18} \tag{5}
$$

Definition 4 [22]. For any two given fuzzy numbers A with $[A]^\gamma = [\alpha_1(\gamma), \alpha_2(\gamma)]$ and B with $[B]^\gamma = [b_1(\gamma), b_2(\gamma)]$ for all $\gamma \in [0,1]$, the upper and lower possibilistic semicovariance between A and B are given as follows.

$$
Cov^+(A, B) = 2\int\limits_0^1 \gamma\Big[E(A) - \alpha_2(\gamma)\Big] \cdot [E(B) - b_2(\gamma)]d\gamma \tag{6}
$$

$$
Cov^-(A, B) = 2\int\limits_0^1 \gamma\Big[E(A) - \alpha_1(\gamma)\Big] \cdot [E(B) - b_1(\gamma)]d\gamma \tag{7}
$$

Especially, when A and B are symmetric fuzzy numbers, $Var^+(A) = Var^-(A)$, $Var^+(B) = Var^-(B)$ and $Cov^+(A,B) = Cov^-(A,B)$.

Lemma 1 [20]. Let A and B be two fuzzy numbers. For any real numbers μ and λ, the following conclusion can be drawn.

$$
E(\lambda A \pm uB) = \lambda E(A) \pm uE(B) \tag{8}
$$

Theorem 1 [23]. Let $A_1, A_2 \dots A_n$ be n fuzzy numbers, and let $\lambda_1, \lambda_2, \dots \lambda_n$ be n real numbers. Then

$$
Var^+\left(\sum\nolimits_{i=1}^n \lambda_i A_i\right) = \sum\nolimits_{i=1}^n \lambda_i^2 Var^+(A_i) + 2\sum\nolimits_{i<j=1}^n \lambda_i\lambda_j Cov^+(A_i, A_j) \tag{9}
$$

$$
Var^-\left(\sum\nolimits_{i=1}^n \lambda_i A_i\right) = \sum\nolimits_{i=1}^n \lambda_i^2 Var^-(A_i) + 2\sum\nolimits_{i<j=1}^n \lambda_i\lambda_j Cov^-(A_i, A_j) \tag{10}
$$

Definition 4 [24]. Let A be a fuzzy variable with finite expected value e. Then its skewness is defined as

$$
Sk(A) = E\Big[(A - e)^3\Big] \tag{11}
$$

3 BFO and BFO-SDC

3.1 Bacterial Foraging Optimization

Inspired by the social foraging behavior of the E. coli bacteria, BFO is an evolutionary optimization technique that has been applied to multitudinous optimization problems. Based on Liu and Passino's [10] discussion of how the control system of E. coli instructs and forages, bacteria migrate to nutrient-rich areas through the flagella. The cycle of optimization is divided into four steps: chemotaxis, swarming, reproduction, and elimination and dispersal. A brief introduction is as follows.

3.1.1 Chemotaxis

Bacteria "swim" or "tumble" via flagella. By switching between the two modes of motion, bacteria move randomly. Supposed $\theta^i(j, k, l)$ indicates the information of the ith bacterium including jth chemotaxis, kth reproduction, and lth elimination and dispersal step. C is the step size taken by swimming in a random direction. Δ represents the vector whose element is in the random direction of $[-1,1]$. When calculating chemotaxis, the mathematical expression of bacterial movement is

$$\theta^i(j+1,k,l) = \theta^i(j,k,l) + C(i)\frac{\Delta(i)}{\sqrt{\Delta^T(i)\Delta(i)}} \tag{12}$$

3.1.2 Swarming

Researchers have found that E. coli cells use complex communication mechanisms such as quorum-sensing, chemotactic signaling, and plasmid exchange to form highly structured colonies to improve environmental fitness. Swarming of bacteria can be represented by

$$J_{cc}(\theta, P(j, k, l)) = \sum_{i=1}^{n} J_{cc}^i\left(\theta, \theta^i(j, k, l)\right) + \sum_{i=1}^{n}[h_{repelent}exp(-w_{repelent}\sum_{m=1}^{p}(\theta_m - \theta_m^i)^2)]$$

$$+ \sum_{i=1}^{n}[-d_{attract}exp(w_{attract}\sum_{m=1}^{p}(\theta_m - \theta_m^i)^2)] \tag{13}$$

where $J_{cc}(\theta, P(j, k, l))$ is an objective function that changes with the population distribution state, reflecting the trend of the relative distance between bacteria and the optimal individual. S represents the population size, and P indicates the dimension of the optimization problem. $d_{attract}$, $w_{attract}$, $h_{replent}$ and $w_{replent}$ are different coefficients chosen properly.

3.1.3 Reproduction

The bacteria are ranked by their health, with half of the less healthy bacteria dying and each of the healthier half splitting into two, leaving the total number of bacteria unchanged.

3.1.4 Elimination and Dispersal

It is well known that the life of a bacterial population can change gradually. All bacteria in an area may be killed, or a colony may disperse and emerge in a new environment. Although this change can disrupt the chemotaxis process, it is beneficial for bacteria to jump out of the local optimal domain and improve the global search ability. In this process, some bacteria die by a given probability P_{ed} and then reappear randomly throughout the search space.

3.2 BFO with Decreasing Chemotaxis Step Based on Sine Function

This part mainly introduces the application of the decreasing chemotaxis step based on sine function in algorithm improvement.

3.2.1 Sine Function in Chemotaxis Step

Sine function is a trigonometric function that is a kind basic theory of trigonometry. And the function value changes nonlinearly.

In our proposed method, a decreasing chemotaxis step length combined with sine function is used over iterations. It starts with a large value and decreases to a small value at the maximal number of iterations. The mathematical representation of the BFO method is given as

$$C(i) = C_{\max} - (C_{\max} - C_{\min}) \cdot \sin(\frac{\pi}{2} \cdot \frac{j}{N_{ed} \cdot N_{re} \cdot N_c}) \tag{14}$$

In the formula, N_c denotes the number of chemotactic. N_{ed} is the number of elimination-dispersal. N_{re} represents the number of reproduction. C_{min} and C_{max} are real numbers and j is the current number of iterations.

4 Bacterial Foraging Optimization for Portfolio Selection Problems

4.1 Portfolio Selection Model

In this section, a mean–semivariance–skewness model that considers no short sales and the transaction fee in portfolio optimization is explained. The model can be described as follows.

$$\text{Min } F(X) = \min\{\lambda g(X) - (1 - \lambda)[f(X) + h(X)]\}$$

$$s.t. \quad \begin{cases} \sum_{i=1}^{d} X_i = 1 \\ X_i > 0 \end{cases} \tag{15}$$

$$f(X) = \sum_{i=1}^{d} r_i x_i - \sum_{i=1}^{n} [\mu \cdot k_i^b \cdot \left(x_i - x_i^0\right) + (1 - \mu) \cdot k_i^s \cdot (x_i^0 - x_i)]$$
$$and \ \mu = \begin{cases} 1 \ X_i \geq X_i^0 \\ 0 \ X_i < X_i^0 \end{cases} \tag{16}$$

$$g(X) = \sum_{i=1}^{d} \sum_{j=1}^{d} X_i X_j \sigma_{ij} \tag{17}$$

$$h(X) = \sum_{i=1}^{d} \sum_{j=1}^{d} \sum_{k=1}^{d} x_i x_j x_k s_{ijk} \tag{18}$$

Assuming that an investor will invest in d assets. λ represents the risk aversion factor. $f(X)$ represents investors' return function, $g(X)$ denotes risk function and $h(X)$ is skewness function. Let X_i be the proportion of investment of asset i, X_i^0 be the initial holding proportion of investment, r_i be the expected yields of ith asset, σ_{ij} be the covariance of r_i and r_j, s_{ijk} be the possibilistic co-skewness among r_i, r_j and r_k. k_i^s and k_i^b denote the transaction fee for selling and buying the asset i respectively.

4.2 Encoding

Encode the potentially feasible solution as ideas that individual generated in BFO-SDC. Four types of information including the value of corresponding profit, risk, and skewness, the proportion of investment are carried by each bacterium [25].

$$\theta = [X_1, X_2, X_3 \ldots X_d, f(X), g(X), h(X)] \tag{19}$$

$$s = \sum_{i=1}^{d} X_i$$
$$\theta' = [\frac{1}{s}(X_1, X_2, X_3 \ldots X_d), f(X)', g(X)', h(X)'] \tag{20}$$

Equation (19) introduces the coding of the bacteria. As is illustrated in Eq. (20), all the assets' proportions are summed up at the beginning and then each proportion of asset is divided by the s for the purpose of assuring all asset proportions' sum is equal to 1.

4.3 Constrained Boundary Control

$$\theta^i(j+1, k, l) = \begin{cases} D_{\min} + rand \cdot (D_{\max} - D_{\min}), & if \ P < 0 \\ \theta^i(j, k, l) + C(i) \frac{\Delta(i)}{\sqrt{\Delta^T(i)\Delta(i)}}, & if \ P \geq 0 \end{cases} \tag{21}$$

Boundary control assurances that every proportion is positive. Bacteria may exceed the given area since in the process of chemotaxis they change directions randomly. The rules of boundary control are shown in Eq. (21), $D_{\max}$ and $D_{\min}$ are the upper and lower boundaries. And $rand$ is a function that is used to generate a real number between 0 and 1.

5 Experiments and Discussions

For the purpose of testing the performance of the BFO-SDC algorithm, the original BFO and BFO-LDC are selected to compare. All the algorithms mentioned in this paper were coded in MATLAB R2018b.

5.1 Definition of Experiments

In the experiments, we assume that there are five assets can be selected to invest. Due to we suppose that the assets' future returns are trapezoidal fuzzy numbers, it's necessary to estimate the core interval, the right and left width of the fuzzy numbers. According to Vercher *et al.* [26], regard the historical returns as samples and use the sample percentile to approximate the spreads and core of the trapezoidal fuzzy returns. Thus, the interval of the 40th to 60th percentile is set as the core of the fuzzy return, the interval of the 5th to 40th percentile is set as the left-width and the interval of 40th to 95th percentile is set as the right-width. We consider the monthly returns over the tested period between January 2015 and December 2019. The trapezoidal fuzzy numbers are shown in Table 1.

Table 1. The trapezoidal fuzzy numbers

The asset i	1	2	3	4	5
α	−0.10516	−0.13309	−0.30344	−0.14459	−0.08656
a	−0.00244	−0.01443	0.013429	0.004195	0.020846
b	0.042983	0.026308	0.06576	0.045895	0.05327
β	0.220344	0.160453	0.543263	0.254134	0.169063

In this paper, we assume that investors are rational. Thus, the lower possibility variance is used to describe the risk. According to Theorem 1 and Definition 2, the risk of investment is shown as follows.

$$Var^- \left(\sum_{i=1}^{d} x_i r_i \right) = \sum_{i=1}^{d} x_i^2 Var^-(r_i) + 2 \sum_{i<j=1}^{d} x_i x_j Cov^-(r_i, r_j)$$

$$= [\sum_{i=1}^{d} x_i \left(\frac{a_i - b_i}{2} + \frac{\alpha_i + \beta_i}{6} \right)]^2 + \frac{1}{18} (\sum_{i=1}^{d} x_i \alpha_i)^2 + 2 \sum_{i<j=1}^{d} x_i x_j Cov^-(r_i, r_j)$$

$$(22)$$

$$Cov^-(r_i, r_j) = \left(\frac{b_i - a_i}{2} + \frac{\beta_i - a_i}{6} \right) \left(\frac{b_j - a_j}{2} + \frac{\beta_j - a_j}{6} \right) + \frac{\alpha_j}{3} \left(\frac{b_i - a_i}{2} + \frac{\beta_i - \alpha_i}{6} \right)$$

$$+ \frac{\alpha_i}{3} \left(\frac{b_j - a_j}{2} + \frac{\beta_j - \alpha_j}{6} \right) + \frac{\alpha_i \alpha_j}{6}$$

$$(23)$$

According to Liu *et al.* [27], the possibilistic skewness of the portfolio is

$$S\left(\sum_{i=1}^{d} x_i r_i\right) = \frac{19}{1089}\left[\left(\sum_{i=1}^{d} x_i \beta_i\right)^3 - \left(\sum_{i=1}^{d} x_i \alpha_i\right)^3\right]$$
$$+ \frac{1}{72}\left[\left(\sum_{i=1}^{d} x_i \alpha_i\right)\left(\sum_{i=1}^{d} x_i \beta_i\right)^2 - \left(\sum_{i=1}^{d} x_i \beta_i\right)\left(\sum_{i=1}^{d} x_i \alpha_i\right)^2\right]$$
$$+ \frac{1}{24}\sum_{i=1}^{d} x_i(b_i - a_i)\left[\left(\sum_{i=1}^{d} x_i \beta_i\right)^2 - \left(\sum_{i=1}^{d} x_i \alpha_i\right)^2\right] \tag{24}$$

In the decreasing chemotaxis step length based on sine function, $C_{min} = 0.01$, $C_{max} = 0.5$. The following parameter settings are the same as in corresponding reference [28]. To show various investors based on different preference to evaluate the final fortune, λ is set as 0.15, 0.5 and 0.85 respectively. $k_i^s = 0.00075$ and $k_i^b = 0.00065$. In BFO, $N_c = 1000$, $N_{ed} = 2$, $N_{re} = 5$, N_s (the number of swimming) = 4, P_{ed} (the elimination-dispersal frequency) = 0.25. C (the swimming length) = 0.2.

5.2 Experimental Results

Numerical results with different λ and the terminal portfolio selection results obtained by the original BFO, BFO-LDC, and BFO-SDC are showed in Tables 2, 3 and 4. Figure 1 shows the convergence curves with various λ generated by the three algorithms.

Table 2. Experimental results of $\lambda = 0.15$

	BFO	BFO-LDC	BFO-SDC
Min	−2.9076E+00	−1.7248E+01	**−2.1866E+01**
Max	0	1	0
Mean	−2.9076E−01	−1.7248E+00	**−2.1866E+00**
Std.	**9.1946E−01**	5.4544E+00	6.9147E+00
X_1	2.3619E−01	1.6276E−01	1.8054E−01
X_2	1.6315E−01	2.5461E−01	2.0436E−01
X_3	2.7044E−01	2.7919E−01	1.4639E−01
X_4	1.3663E−01	1.4928E−01	2.6812E−01
X_5	1.9360E−01	1.5416E−01	2.0059E−01
Return	1.0320E−01	1.0230E−01	9.1529E−02
Risk	3.3634E−03	3.3894E−03	2.7046E−03
Skewness	3.1849E−04	3.0871E−04	2.1187E−04

Table 3. Experimental results of $\lambda = 0.5$

	BFO	BFO-LDC	BFO-SDC
Min	−1.2345E+00	−3.0142E+00	**−6.2287E+00**
Max	0	0	0
Mean	−1.2345E−01	−3.0143E−01	**−6.2287E−01**
Std.	**3.9039E−01**	9.5319E−01	1.9697E+00
X_1	3.2366E−01	2.4145E−01	2.7598E−01
X_2	9.0457E−02	6.1790E−02	2.3570E−01
X_3	1.8598E−01	2.9873E−01	9.1497E−02
X_4	2.0407E−01	8.8298E−02	1.0163E−01
X_5	1.9583E−01	3.0973E−01	2.9520E−01
Return	9.6784E−02	1.0777E−01	8.2556E−02
Risk	2.9941E−03	3.4405E−03	2.2346E−03
Skewness	2.6747E−04	3.4922E−04	1.5155E−04

Table 4. Experimental results of $\lambda = 0.85$

	BFO	BFO-LDC	BFO-SDC
Min	−2.5908E−02	−2.6722E−02	**−2.7785E−02**
Max	0	0	0
Mean	−2.5908E−03	−2.6722E−03	**−2.7785E−03**
Std.	**8.1928E−03**	8.4501E−03	8.7863E−03
X_1	8.4933E−02	1.4236E−01	1.5807E−01
X_2	2.0848E−01	2.4435E−01	2.1004E−01
X_3	3.0795E−01	2.1466E−01	3.2087E−01
X_4	2.0448E−01	2.5917E−01	9.4012E−02
X_5	1.9415E−01	1.3945E−01	2.1701E−01
Return	1.0742E−01	9.7463E−02	1.0697E−01
Risk	3.5742E−03	3.1070E−03	3.5597E−03
Skewness	3.4445E−04	2.6401E−04	3.4545E−04

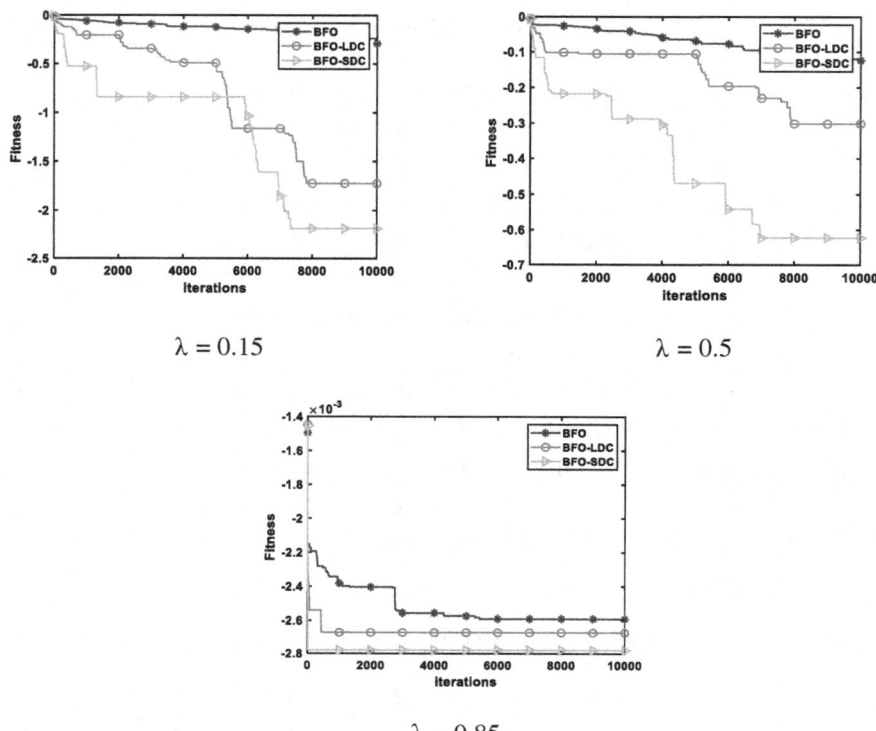

$\lambda = 0.15$ $\lambda = 0.5$

$\lambda = 0.85$

Fig. 1. The convergence curve of three algorithms

According to the tables and the figures, we can find that:

(1) The fitness value grows up with the increase of the risk-averse factor λ, and this trend keeps the same with the structure of the fitness function.
(2) With the different λ and different algorithm, the percentage of five assets is not the same. The results show that lower risk can be with the less profit.
(3) Comparing the numerical results shown in Tables 2 and 3, it verifies that BFO-SDC outperforms BFO and BFO-LDC in terms of mean value, minimum value and result qualify, which clarifies the effectiveness of the BFO-SDC.
(4) Comparing the convergence graphs shown in Fig. 1, BFO-SDC is superior to BFO-LDC and BFO for the three cases.

6   Conclusions and Future Work

In this paper, we pay attention to solving the PO problem by using BFO based methods. Based upon the standard mean-variance model, we take skewness and fuzzy set theory into consideration and use semivariance to take the place of variance. A decreasing chemotaxis step strategy based on sine function is included in the original BFO to solve this model. The obtained results indicate that BFO-SDC outperforms than BFO and BFO-LDC.

Further works may consider some biological mechanisms to promote the performance of BFO and propose novel models containing other conditions such as dynamic objectives or multi-period to meet the demands from the real-world.

Acknowledgements. This work is partially supported by Shenzhen Philosophy and Social Sciences Plan Project (SZ2019D018), Guangdong Provincial Soft Science Project (2019A101002075).

References

1. Markowitz, H.M.: Portfolio selection. J. Financ. **7**, 77–91 (1952)
2. Zhou, Z., Ren, T., Xiao, H., Liu, W.: Time-consistent investment and reinsurance strategies for insurers under multi-period mean-variance formulation with generalized correlated returns. J. Manag. Sci. Eng. **4**, 142–157 (2019)
3. Bi, J., Jin, H., Meng, Q.: Behavioral mean-variance portfolio selection. Eur. J. Oper. Res. **271**, 644–663 (2018)
4. Chunhachinda, P., Dandapani, K., Hamid, S., Prakash, A.J.: Portfolio selection and skewness: evidence from international stock markets. J. Bank. Financ. **21**, 143–167 (1997)
5. Simkowitz, M.A., Beedles, W.L.: Diversification in a three-moment world. J. Financ. Quant. Anal. **13**, 927–941 (1978)
6. Ibbotson, R.G.: Price performance of common stock new issues. J. Financ. Econ. **2**, 235–272 (1975)
7. Prakash, A.J., Chang, C.H., Pactwa, T.E.: Selecting a portfolio with skewness: recent evidence from US, European, and Latin American equity markets. J. Bank. Financ. **27**, 1375–1390 (2003)
8. Markowitz, H.: Portfolio Selection: Efficient Diversification of Investments. Wiley, New York (1959)
9. Ammar, E., Khalifa, H.A.: Fuzzy portfolio optimization a quadratic programming approach. Chaos, Solitons Fractals **18**, 1045–1054 (2003)
10. Liu, Y., Passino, K.M.: Biomimicry of social foraging bacteria for distributed optimization: models, principles, and emergent behaviors. J. Optim. Theory Appl. **115**, 603–628 (2002)
11. Niu, B., Tan, L.J., Liu, J., Liu, J., Yi, W.J., Wang, H.: Cooperative bacterial foraging optimization method for multi-objective multi-echelon supply chain optimization problem. Swarm Evol. Comput. **49**, 87–101 (2019)
12. Vital-Soto, A., Azab, A., Baki, M.F.: Mathematical modeling and a hybridized bacterial foraging optimization algorithm for the flexible job-shop scheduling problem with sequencing flexibility. J. Manuf. Syst. **54**, 74–93 (2020)
13. Tan, L., Lin, F., Wang, H.: Adaptive comprehensive learning bacterial foraging optimization and its application on vehicle routing problem with time windows. Neurocomputing **151**, 1208–1215 (2015)
14. Niu, B., Fan, Y., Xiao, H., Xue, B.: Bacterial foraging based approaches to portfolio optimization with liquidity risk. Neurocomputing **98**, 90–100 (2012)
15. Tang, W.K., Zhong, G., Chen, G., Man, K.F.: Generation of N-scroll attractors via sine function. IEEE Trans. Circuits Syst. I: Regular Pap. **48**, 1369–1372 (2001)
16. Zhang, X., Zhang, G.: Design of ship course-keeping autopilot using a sine function-based nonlinear feedback technique. J. Navig. **69**, 246–256 (2016)

17. Volos, C., Akgul, A., Pham, V., Stouboulos, I., Kyprianidis, I.: A simple chaotic circuit with a hyperbolic sine function and its use in a sound encryption scheme. Nonlinear Dyn. **89**, 1047–1061 (2017)
18. Zadeh, L.A.: Fuzzy sets as a basis for a theory of possibility. Fuzzy Sets Syst. **1**, 3–28 (1978)
19. Zadeh, L.A.: Fuzzy sets. Inf. Control **8**, 338–353 (1965)
20. Carlsson, C., Fuller, R.: On possibilistic mean value and variance of fuzzy numbers. Fuzzy Sets Syst. **122**(2), 315–326 (2001)
21. Saeidifar, A., Pasha, E.: The possibilistic moments of fuzzy numbers and their applications. J. Comput. Appl. Math. **2**, 1028–1042 (2009)
22. Zhang, W.G., Liu, Y.J., Xu, W.J.: A possibilistic mean-semivariance-entropy model for multi-period portfolio selection with transaction costs. Eur. J. Oper. Res. **222**, 341–349 (2012)
23. Zhang, W.G., Wang, Y.L., Chen, Z.P., Nie, Z.K.: Possibilistic mean-variance models and efficient frontiers for portfolio selection problem. J. Inf. Sci. **177**, 2787–2801 (2007)
24. Li, X., Qin, Z., Kar, S.: Mean-variance-skewness model for portfolio selection with fuzzy returns. Eur. J. Oper. Res. **202**, 239–247 (2010)
25. Niu, B., Bi, Y., Xie, T.: Structure-redesign-based bacterial foraging optimization for portfolio selection. In: Huang, D.-S., Han, K., Gromiha, M. (eds.) ICIC 2014. LNCS, vol. 8590, pp. 424–430. Springer, Cham (2014). https://doi.org/10.1007/978-3-319-09330-7_49
26. Vercher, E., Bermudez, J., Segura, J.: Fuzzy portfolio optimization under downside risk measures. J. Fuzzy Sets Syst. **158**, 769–782 (2007)
27. Liu, Y.J., Zhang, W.G., Zhao, X.J.: Fuzzy multi-period portfolio selection model with discounted transaction costs. Soft. Comput. **22**, 177–193 (2018)
28. Niu, B., Liu, J., Liu, J., Yang, C.: Brain storm optimization for portfolio optimization. In: Tan, Y., Shi, Y., Li, L. (eds.) ICSI 2016. LNCS, vol. 9713, pp. 416–423. Springer, Cham (2016). https://doi.org/10.1007/978-3-319-41009-8_45

Genetic Algorithm and Evolutionary Computation

A New Local Search Adaptive Genetic Algorithm for the Pseudo-Coloring Problem

Rodrigo Colnago Contreras[1], Orides Morandin Junior[2],
and Monique Simplicio Viana[2(✉)]

[1] University of São Paulo, São Carlos, Brazil
contreras@alumni.usp.br
[2] Federal University of São Carlos, São Carlos, Brazil
{orides,monique.viana}@ufscar.br

Abstract. Several applications result in a gray level image partitioned into different regions of interest. However, the human brain has difficulty in recognizing many levels of gray. In some cases, this problem is alleviated with the attribution of artificial colors to these regions, thus configuring an application in the area of visualization and graphic processing responsible for categorizing samples using colors. However, the task of making a set of distinct colors for these regions stand out is a problem of the NP-hard class, known as the pseudo-coloring problem (PsCP). In this work, it is proposed to use the well-known meta-heuristic Genetic Algorithm together with operators specialized in the local search for solutions as well as self-adjusting operators responsible for guiding the parameterization of the technique during the resolution of PsCPs. The proposed methodology was evaluated in two different scenarios of color assignment, having obtained the best results in comparison to the techniques that configure the state of the art.

Keywords: Genetic Algorithm · Local search · Adaptive operator · Visualization · Pseudo-coloring problem

1 Introduction

Many problems today consist of extracting visual patterns from images that are only available in gray levels. Thus, in this type of situation, a professional should view an image that presents details in the same tones and infer complex classification hypotheses. However, studies show that human vision has difficulty in differentiating monochrome tones [15]. This fact is related to the low capacity of the brain to categorize signals of similar frequencies. Therefore, many researchers have dedicated themselves to the development of specialized methodologies for assigning artificial colors to images originally arranged in gray levels to facilitate the extraction of visual patterns. For example, we can see advances in detecting edges in sonar images [2], detecting tumors in the chest [11], detecting weapons in baggage [10], visual enhancement of medical images [18], etc.

© Springer Nature Switzerland AG 2020
Y. Tan et al. (Eds.): ICSI 2020, LNCS 12145, pp. 349–361, 2020.
https://doi.org/10.1007/978-3-030-53956-6_31

In the aforementioned works, the central strategy used in the visual enhancement of information consists of the generation of a set of colors, which must be as distinct as possible, with a different coloring attributed to each region of the evaluated image. This situation is known as the Pseudo-Colorization Problem (PsCP), or construction of high contrast sets [7]. The main complication presented in PsCP is the similarity between colors used. That is, neighboring regions in an image may have similar colors and, consequently, their visualization may be compromised. To solve this need it is necessary to use some optimization technique in order to distance the colors used as far as possible. However, this optimization becomes unfeasible as the number of regions in the image increases, since this problem is contained in the class of problems NP-hard. In this way, many authors mitigate the problem with the use of meta-heuristics. Radlak and Smolka [17] propose a methodology using a measure of color contrast optimized with a Genetic Algorithm (GA). The method performs searches in the RGB color domain, making neighboring regions colored with the most distinct colors possible. However, simplified versions of GA can present several problems such as inefficient search and premature convergence [22].

To get around these problems, Asadzadeh [3] proposes aLSGA, which consists of a GA that uses specialized operators in local search to solve the combinatory problem Job Shop Scheduling. In detail, the author presents a GA with a local search operator who works in conjunction with the mutation operator and a local search operator who performs massive exploitation in search space. The methodology proved to be superior to traditional GA and similar evolutionary methods in solving this problem, which also belongs to the NP-hard class. In this work, we propose to improve aLSGA so that it is specialized in the PsCP solution. Also, we propose the addition of adaptive rules [23], [13], [19] so that the method developed makes automatic adjustments during its execution to perform the search process without premature convergence or inefficient search.

The paper is organized into 6 sections. Specifically, in Sect. 2 we describe the mathematical formulation of PsCP. In Sect. 3, the details of the proposed algorithm and each of the operators that compose it are presented. In Sect. 4, experiments, results, and comparison with other methods in the literature are presented in two different test scenarios. Finally, in Sect. 5, conclusions and possible directions for future work are presented.

2   Formulation of Pseudo-Coloring Problem

In this work, we will adopt a model similar to that of Radlak and Smolka [17] to approach PsCP. To this end, the objective is to allocate to a I image, already segmented into K disjoint regions, a set of K colors so that these colors are as distinct as possible in neighboring image regions. Mathematically, let I_1, I_2, ..., I_K be the pre-segmented sub-regions of I, and the neighborhood matrix Δ whose coordinates $\delta_{i,j}$ are equal to 1 if the region I_i is neighbor to I_j or $\delta_{i,j}$ are equal to 0 if the region I_i is not neighbor to I_j or in the case of $i = j$. Thus, the situation consists in determining a set of K colors $\mathcal{C} = \{c_1, c_2, ..., c_K\}$ to coloring the regions of I such that the value of the function F of Eq. (1) is the **largest** possible value, configuring this problem in a maximization problem.

$$F(\mathcal{C}) := \min \left\{ \delta_{i,j} \cdot d(c_i, c_j) \quad | \quad \delta_{i,j} \neq 0, \quad i, j \in \{1, 2, ..., K\} \right\}, \tag{1}$$

in which $d(\cdot, \cdot)$ is a distance function in some color space.

Specifically, each color $c_i \in \mathcal{C}$ is represented by a triple of integer values that define the RGB coloration to be associated to the region I_i. Thus, each color c_i belongs to the sRGB set , which in this work is represented by the set $\{0, 1, ..., 255\}^3$, and, consequently, $\mathcal{C} \subset \{0, 1, ..., 255\}^{3 \cdot K}$. Furthermore, it is common to define the distance function $d(\cdot, \cdot)$ to be the Euclidean distance between colors in the perceptually uniform color space CIELAB [8] with illuminant D50, since this space is favorable for performing visual distinction of colors [14].

3   Local Search Adaptive Genetic Algorithm for PsCP

In this section, we describe in detail the proposed algorithm, which was developed specifically to present good solutions for PsCP. In such a way that each operator of the method has in its description the explanation of the idea that composes the technique so that the reproducibility is done without difficulty. For the best of our knowledge, there is no record in the specialized literature of any GA-based technique that has a dedicated operator in carrying out a massive local search around the same individual and that its functioning is adjusted with an applied adaptative operator for the PsCP. Thus, this work has the main purpose of introducing a technique with these characteristics, which is entitled Local Search Adaptive Genetic Algorithm (LSAGA). Therefore, we present, in summary, the contributions of this work:

1. An adaptation of the Asadzadeh method [3] to PsCP. In particular, a new operator of massive local search for the best individual in the population is proposed;
2. Addition of an adaptation operator, inspired by [13], which coordinates the use of the basic operators of the algorithm in order to avoid premature convergence and optimize the method's exploitation and exploration capacity,
3. The advancement of experimental results in benchmarks that define the state-of-the-art.

3.1   Chromosome Decoding

In [17], three chromosome populations evolve in parallel in a GA, one dedicated to the R component, another to the G component and another to the B component of each of the K segmented regions in I. In our work, we propose that a single population of chromosomes is evolved during the execution of the method. In detail, each chromosome in the proposed modeling is associated with a set of colors for the regions in I. That is, each gene on a chromosome is formed by a color in sRGB which must be associated with a specific region of I. Mathematically, the genetic representation of a $\mathcal{C}$ chromosome adopted in this work follows the definition of Eq. (2).

$$\mathcal{C} = [(R_1, G_1, B_1), (R_2, G_2, B_2), ..., (R_K, G_K, B_K)], \qquad (2)$$

in which $(R_i, G_i, B_i) \in$ sRGB is the color to be associated with the region I_i.

It is important to note that, in practice, the proposed encoding models the chromosome as a vector of $3 \cdot K$ coordinates with values between 0 and 255 and not a subset of K colors in sRGB. As a consequence of this, the coordinates of each chromosome carry an order that refers to the sub-regions of I. That is, the first three coordinates of a chromosome represent the RGB color of the first region of I, the subsequent three coordinates represent the RGB color of the second region of I, and so on.

3.2   Fitness Function

The genetic representation proposed in the Sect. 3.1 makes it natural to define the fitness function as a simple isomorphism with the F function of the Eq. (1). Mathematically, we define the fitness of a chromosome $\mathcal{C} = [(R_1, G_1, B_1), (R_2, G_2, B_2), ..., (R_K, G_K, B_K)] \in$ sRGB^K the function $\bar{F}$, presented in Eq. (3).

$$\begin{aligned} \bar{F}: \quad \text{sRGB}^K \quad &\longrightarrow \quad \mathbb{R}_+ \\ (c_1, c_2, ..., c_K) &\longmapsto \bar{F}(c_1, c_2, ..., c_K) := F(\{c_1, c_2, ..., c_K\}) \end{aligned} \qquad (3)$$

3.3   Selection Process

The process of selecting individuals in evolutionary methods is important to ensure that individuals who are better adapted, or with better fitness value, have a greater chance of exchanging genetic information, or reproducing, during the crossover operator. Besides, the selection method is responsible for preserving individuals with good fitness values during the generation of new populations of the algorithm. In this paper, we make use of the roulette wheel method ensuring that the best individual in the current population will reproduce [21] and will also be transferred to the new population.

3.4   Crossover Operator

To ensure that the exchange of genetic information between two individuals is defined by valid colors, it is important that the individuals generated in the crossover process respect the limits of sRGB. For this, we propose an extension of the well-known convex crossover [9], in which each of the colors represented by the generated individuals is the result of the random convex combination of the colors represented by their parents. Specifically, two intermediate offsprings are generated, $\hat{\text{K}}\text{id}_1$ and $\hat{\text{K}}\text{id}_2$, which are the result of the convex combination between each of the parents' colors, Parent_1 and Parent_2, and therefore belong to $\mathbb{R}^{3K}$. Then, these individuals are projected in the feasible space sRGB^K using the function $\text{proj}_{\text{sRGB}^K}(\cdot)$, which projects a given vector from $\mathbb{R}^{3K}$ to the closest vector belonging to sRGB^K. This projection determines the Kid_1 and Kid_2 offsprings generated in this operator.

3.5   Mutation Operator

The mutation operator proposed in this work is based on the local search procedures presented for the first time in [3] and [16] to solve production scheduling problems. Our technique is an improvement that consists of the combination of these two methodologies. Therefore, the proposed mutation process consists of the eventual application of one of the following mutation subroutines:

– Mut_1: In this case, successive N_{Mut_1} applications of a mutation function, randomly determined in a set of mutation functions, are carried out on a chromosome so that the beneficial perturbation are maintained and the method proceeds from them;
– Mut_2: Unique and definitive application of a mutation function.

Thus, as soon as an individual is generated in the crossover operator, it has a probability p_{mut} of going through the mutation process. If selected, the individual also has a probability p_{LS} of going through a local search procedure, represented by the subroutine Mut_1, and a probability $1 - p_{\text{LS}}$ of receiving an only perturbation according to the subroutine Mut_2.

In Mut_1, a group of mutation functions in the form of $f_{\text{mut}}(\cdot, \cdot) : \text{sRGB} \times \{1, 2, ..., K\}^2 \longrightarrow \text{sRGB}$ must be defined. For this, we propose the use of the three most used mutation functions in solving combinatorial problems [3]: $f_{\text{swap}}(\cdot, \cdot)$, $f_{\text{invert}}(\cdot, \cdot)$ and $f_{\text{insert}}(\cdot, \cdot)$. In Fig. 1, an example of the perturbation caused by these functions on the same individual is presented. As these functions only perform permutations between the coordinates of a chromosome, it do not compromise the feasibility of the solutions generated.

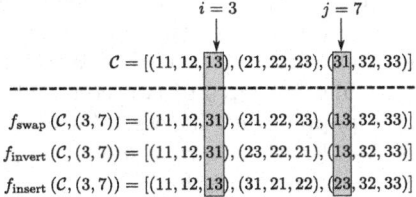

Fig. 1. Schematic diagram of the functioning of three mutation functions on the same chromosome $\mathcal{C}$.

In Mut_2, we propose to use only one mutation function. In this case, a simple Gaussian perturbation [4], $f_{\text{Gauss}}(\cdot)$, in which all genes on the chromosome receives a slightly random increase or decrease.

3.6   Massive Search Operator

This type of operator intends to carry out a more elaborate and systematic search around an individual from the population that presents a good adaptation, looking for neighbors of the same who are similar, but that has better fitness value. In other words, massive local search operators assume that around a good individual there may be better individuals more probability than in random regions of space. In [3], this operator performs successive swaps between the coordinates of the best individual in the population, maintaining beneficial perturbations. In our work, we propose a new massive local search operator specialized in looking for colors similar to the colors represented by the best individual in a population, through successive Gaussian perturbations. Specifically, considering $\mathcal{C}_{\text{Best}} = (c_1, c_2, ..., c_K)$ as the best individual in the population, the procedure consists of performing the following three steps for all colors c_i:

- **Step 1:** The color c_i receives a random addition, making it lighter;
- **Step 2:** The perturbation is maintained only if it is beneficial, increasing the fitness value from $\mathcal{C}_{\text{Best}}$,
- **Step 3:** If c_i was not modified in the previous step, then a random decrease in c_i is made, making it darker, which should only be maintained if it is beneficial.

3.7   Adaptive Rules

Adaptation strategies to control the occurrence of crossover and mutation are well-known methodologies in the specialized literature used to increase the genetic variability of the population and, consequently, prevent the occurrence of premature convergence. These techniques consist of changing the probability of mutation and crossover to control the ability of the meta-heuristic to properly perform exploitation and exploration, respectively. To this end, we propose to adjust the probabilities of mutation and crossover according to the improvement in the fitness value that individuals in a population have in relation to the fitness of the previous population. To model this improvement, we propose to use a measure based on how much the population of one generation of the method has improved compared to the population of the previous generation. Specifically, we propose that the improvement be measured by a weighted average between the differences of the following measures of two consecutive generations of the method: the average of the population's fitness values (μ), the best fitness (Λ), and the worst fitness (λ). Besides, this average should be multiplied by the standard deviation value of the current generation's fitness values, since this measure is a direct representation of the variability of the current population. Thus, the mathematical representation of the measure that represents the fitness improvement between two consecutive generations of the method is the value Improve$_{\text{it}}$, defined in Eq. (4).

$$\text{Improve}_{\text{it}} := \sigma_{\text{it}} \cdot \frac{\omega_1 \left| \mu_{\text{it}} - \mu_{\text{it}-1} \right| + \omega_2 \left| \Lambda_{\text{it}} - \Lambda_{\text{it}-1} \right| + \omega_3 \left| \lambda_{\text{it}} - \lambda_{\text{it}-1} \right|}{\omega_1 + \omega_2 + \omega_3}, \tag{4}$$

in which, "it" is the current generation of the method.

In this work, we consider that the most important measure to be considered is the difference between the best fitness values from one generation to the next. For this reason, we have adopted: $(\omega_1, \omega_2, \omega_3) := (1, 3, 1)$.

If the improvement is not contained between $\text{Improve}_{\min}$ and $\text{Improve}_{\max}$, then adaptive rules that control the probability of mutation and the probability of crossover must be applied with the intention of controlling the exploitation and exploration of the method, respectively. In detail, the adopted adaptive rules are applied in two cases:

- $\text{Improve}_{it} < \text{Improve}_{\min}$: In this case, 10% is added to the mutation probability value and 10% is reduced to the crossover probability value.
- $\text{Improve}_{it} > \text{Improve}_{\max}$: In this case, 10% is reduced to the mutation probability value and 10% is added to the crossover probability value.

3.8 Proposed Algorithm

The proposed method consists of using all the operators described in this text so that its structure consists of the standard scheme of a GA with additional operators. That is, the method generates an initial population of colors, selects individuals for reproduction, performs the crossover of these individuals, applies the mutation operator to a percentage of the population, performs a massive search in the region of the best individual, generates a new population with the best individuals and assesses the need to change the initial parameters using adaptive rules. Each of these steps is performed a fixed number of times.

4 Experiments and Results

To evaluate the proposed methodology, we defined two distinct test scenarios, as done in [17]. In the first scenario, the proposed method is evaluated on a set of images from the real world. In the second scenario, the proposed method is evaluated at 24 abstract images in which its sub-regions are fully-connected. Thus, the experiments must confirm that the proposed method obtains the best performance applied to real and synthetic problems.

4.1 Setup and Implementation

To perform the tests, the authors of [17] provided us their GA code. Thus, in all tests of this work, the technique compared is the technique of [17] and, for this reason, our technique has the most similar configuration possible with the configuration of the GA method. In detail, we use 30 individuals per population, which are taken randomly at sRGB^K; we started the technique with mutation probability $p_{\text{mut}} = 0.1$ and crossover probability $p_{\times} = 0.85$; 50% of individuals selected for mutation must go through the local search process ($p_{\text{LS}} = 0.5$), with $N_{\text{Mut}_1} = K$; improvement limits are $\text{Improve}_{\min} = 0.01$ and $\text{Improve}_{\max} = 122.5$; and the method runs for 10^4 generations. The computational implementation was done in the MATLAB environment on an i5-4460 PC with 8 GB of ram.

4.2   First Scenario

In this first case study, the proposed technique was evaluated on three images, originally arranged in gray levels, which are shown in the left column of Fig. 2. In detail, the images presented that make up the evaluation benchmark are: "brain" (Fig. 2a), with $K = 6$; "two brains" (Fig. 2e), with $K = 31$; and "mosaic" (Fig. 2i), with $K = 100$. The technique used for comparison is the basic GA [17] as it is the most recent technique and more similar to the proposed method.[1] Besides, two versions of the material developed in this work are evaluated, one disregarding the adaptive rules, the Local Search Genetic Algorithm (LSGA), and another technique considering these rules, the LSAGA. The best coloring obtained by each of these techniques after 50 executions of each one, is shown in Fig. 2.

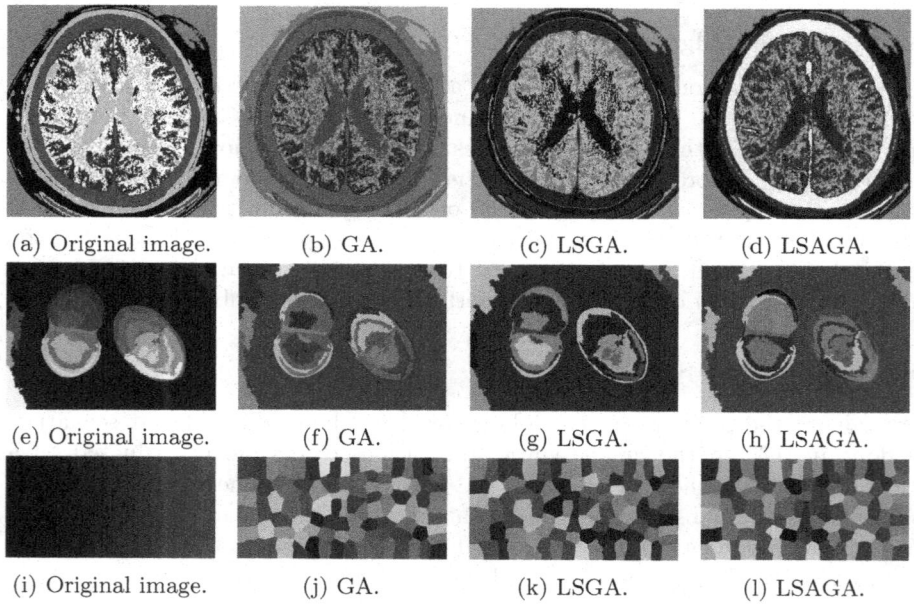

(a) Original image.   (b) GA.   (c) LSGA.   (d) LSAGA.

(e) Original image.   (f) GA.   (g) LSGA.   (h) LSAGA.

(i) Original image.   (j) GA.   (k) LSGA.   (l) LSAGA.

Fig. 2. Pseudo-Colored Images.

In all the raws of the images in Fig. 2 it is possible to see an evolution in the ease of detecting a greater number of regions if we observe the image in greyscale for the colored version by LSAGA. For example, concerning the images of the two brains (Figs. 2e–2h), we can see that basic GA presents some confusion in the colored regions in shades of pink and red in the midwest region of the image. Something similar occurs with the coloring obtained by LSGA in the central-east

---

[1] The technique presented in [6] is not used for comparison, since it performs optimization on pre-defined palettes and not on the sRGB space.

region of Fig. 2g, in which we can see that very dark shade of blue is close to a colored region in black. These complications are completely circumvented in the color obtained by the proposed LSAGA method.

Numerical evaluations confirm the superior performance of the proposed methodology. In detail, in Table 1, a set of statistical measures about the fitness value of each technique is presented after 50 executions of each. In all evaluated images, our LSAGA achieve the greatest best result in all cases, and also achieving the greatest worst fitness in two cases. Besides, on all occasions, our LSAGA achieved the best fitness average. This confirms that the adaptation operator tends to guide the LSGA to better solutions. In contrast, in the image "mosaic", which have a larger number of regions, we can see that the standard deviation (STD) of the fitness values of GA is the smallest. This is precisely because the solutions obtained by GA are restricted to a domain of lower fitness values since the average values presented by this technique are around 25 units less than the average values of the proposed techniques considering the image "mosaic".

Table 1. Statistics about the fitness in the first test scenario. **Bold** numbers are the best values in each situation.

Image	Method	Max	Min	Mean	STD	Average of time (seconds)
Brain	LSAGA	**111.5897**	**103.424**	**109.5214**	**2.356342**	44.4965625
	LSGA	**111.5897**	93.81592	107.9427	3.930504	**33.9584375**
	GA	110.4434	88.66374	100.2385	5.252312	66.953125
Two Brains	LSAGA	**105.3691**	74.19344	**87.03895**	**6.229127**	158.64375
	LSGA	103.2438	**74.92773**	85.71574	6.917277	144.0959375
	GA	92.47527	62.60709	78.36654	6.915184	**97.70625**
Mosaic	LSAGA	**83.7881**	**61.2706**	**73.5591**	6.286933	989.3925
	LSGA	81.51334	56.41686	72.11558	5.776788	936.844375
	GA	53.89128	43.38659	48.73923	**2.475167**	**331.4825**

With respect to time, in the case of the image "brain", the low number of regions ($K = 6$) causes the proposed methodology to present low complexity and, therefore, achieve better results in a shorter computational time, since the technique does not build a population for each RGB color component, as basic GA does. However, in more complex images, our methodology still achieves better results, but the computational time taken by these is longer than the time taken by the basic GA. This fact is due to the exaggerated number of generations for our techniques, as can be seen in the convergence analysis presented in Fig. 3, in which the evolution of the best fitness of the techniques in each of the evaluated images is represented. Note that our technique needs less than 20% of the total number of generations to achieve a result that is higher or at least close to the result obtained by GA with the 10^4 generations. Therefore, it is clear that the proposed methodology takes less time than GA to obtain a satisfactory solution in all images.

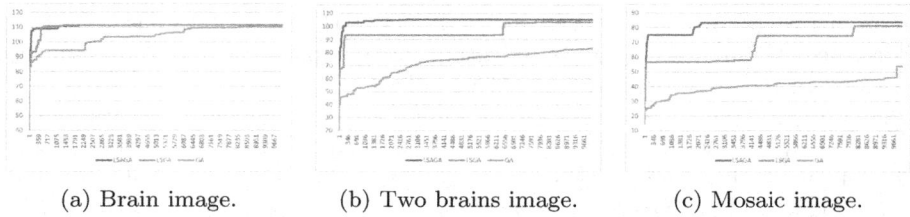

(a) Brain image.   (b) Two brains image.   (c) Mosaic image.

Fig. 3. Convergence analysis.

4.3   Second Scenario

The second scenario consists of evaluating the proposed techniques in 24 synthetic and abstract images, which are divided into fully-connected regions. In this evaluation, we compared the proposed techniques (LSGA and LSAGA), with basic GA [17] and a Greedy Algorithm [5]. Table 2 shows the maximum dissimilarity between K colors (fitness value) presented by each technique after 50 executions.

Table 2. Max distance of colors in a fully-connected images. Green numbers are the best values in raw and **red** numbers are the worst values in raw.

Regions (K)	LSAGA	LSGA	GA [17]	Greedy Algorithm [17]
2	249.2	249.2	249.2	**233.85**
3	166.11	166.11	166.11	**164.64**
4	130.64	**129.64**	130.21	**129.64**
5	111.59	111.59	111.43	**108.81**
6	102.58	102.58	102.48	**93.78**
7	94.7	93.75	93.04	**86.95**
8	86.15	86.13	84.78	**80.03**
9	81.49	80.43	78.68	**74.45**
10	77.8	74.9	74.65	**71.92**
11	69.43	68.1	66.71	**65.77**
12	65.61	64.65	64.84	**61.86**
13	64.26	62.5	63.13	**57.79**
14	60.89	59.1	58.8	**57.32**
15	57.16	56.7	**53.52**	55.27
16	55.82	51.53	**51.01**	53.4
17	53.56	52.55	**49.67**	51.32
18	50.56	50.47	**48.17**	49.42
19	50.5	48.24	**45.08**	47.9
20	49.26	45.83	**44.67**	47.57
21	45.68	44.78	**42.66**	46.54
22	46.36	44.87	**41.63**	44.23
23	43.62	43.28	**41.3**	44.74
24	43.86	42.22	**39.77**	43.61
25	43.09	41.82	**38.55**	41.98

In this scenario, LSAGA presented the best performance in 22 of the 24 images considered, having tied only in the first two ($K = 2$ and $K = 3$). In addition, LSGA had the worst performance on only one occasion ($K = 4$), and on other occasions, the Greedy Algorithm had the worst performance on images with the least number of regions ($2 \leq K \leq 14$) and GA had the worst performance in the most complex images ($15 \leq K \leq 24$). This demonstrates that the proposed methodology is robust both in images with a smaller number of regions and in images with a larger number of regions, surpassing the performance of GA and Greedy Algorithm in this case study.

5 Conclusion

In this work, we propose an adaptation of a GA with operators dedicated to local search and the adaptation of parameters to solve the well-known PsCP. All the necessary steps for the operation of the proposed method were presented with the amount of detail sufficient to make the technique reproducible.

As in [17], we evaluated the proposed material in two test scenarios: one consisting of images from the real world and the other with synthetic images with fully-connected regions. In both cases, the proposed methods, LSGA and LSAGA, exceeded the best techniques available in the specialized literature. In particular, the LSAGA method presents the best results in all the case studies of this work. This is due to the use of the adaptation rules in addition to the local search procedures, which helps the method to avoid premature convergence and to keep the genetic variability of the population high.

In future work, we intend to evaluate the addition of more elaborated diversity control operators at LSGA, such as operators with predator-prey models [12] or operators based on fuzzy rules [1]. Also, we intend to expand this work using the methodology proposed in real problems present in the literature that make direct use of artificial coloring such as weapon detection [20].

Acknowledgements. This study was financed in part by the Coordenação de Aperfeiçoamento de Pessoal de Nível Superior - Brasil (CAPES) - Finance Code 001.

References

1. Amali, S.M.J., Baskar, S.: Fuzzy logic-based diversity-controlled self-adaptive differential evolution. Eng. Optim. **45**(8), 899–915 (2013)
2. Anitha, U., Malarkkan, S., Premalatha, J., Manonmani, V.: Comparison of standard edge detection techniques along with morphological processing and pseudo coloring in sonar image. In: 2016 International Conference on Emerging Trends in Engineering, Technology and Science (ICETETS), pp. 1–4. IEEE (2016)
3. Asadzadeh, L.: A local search genetic algorithm for the job shop scheduling problem with intelligent agents. Comput. Ind. Eng. **85**, 376–383 (2015)
4. Bäck, T., Schwefel, H.P.: An overview of evolutionary algorithms for parameter optimization. Evol. Comput. **1**(1), 1–23 (1993)

5. Bianco, S., Citrolo, A.G.: High contrast color sets under multiple illuminants. In: Tominaga, S., Schettini, R., Trémeau, A. (eds.) CCIW 2013. LNCS, vol. 7786, pp. 133–142. Springer, Heidelberg (2013). https://doi.org/10.1007/978-3-642-36700-7_11

6. Bianco, S., Schettini, R.: Unsupervised color coding for visualizing image classification results. Inf. Vis. **17**(2), 161–177 (2018). https://doi.org/10.1177/1473871617700682

7. Carter, R.C., Carter, E.C.: High-contrast sets of colors. Appl. Opt. **21**(16), 2936–2939 (1982)

8. Connolly, C., Fleiss, T.: A study of efficiency and accuracy in the transformation from RGB to CIELAB color space. IEEE Trans. Image Process. **6**(7), 1046–1048 (1997)

9. Dioşan, L., Oltean, M.: Evolving crossover operators for function optimization. In: Collet, P., Tomassini, M., Ebner, M., Gustafson, S., Ekárt, A. (eds.) EuroGP 2006. LNCS, vol. 3905, pp. 97–108. Springer, Heidelberg (2006). https://doi.org/10.1007/11729976_9

10. Dmitruk, K., Denkowski, M., Mazur, M., Mikołajczak, P.: Sharpening filter for false color imaging of dual-energy x-ray scans. SIViP **11**(4), 613–620 (2017). https://doi.org/10.1007/s11760-016-1001-7

11. Etehadtavakol, M., Ng, E.Y.K.: Color segmentation of breast thermograms: a comparative study. In: Ng, E.Y.K., Etehadtavakol, M. (eds.) Application of Infrared to Biomedical Sciences. SB, pp. 69–77. Springer, Singapore (2017). https://doi.org/10.1007/978-981-10-3147-2_6

12. Li, X.: A real-coded predator-prey genetic algorithm for multiobjective optimization. In: Fonseca, C.M., Fleming, P.J., Zitzler, E., Thiele, L., Deb, K. (eds.) EMO 2003. LNCS, vol. 2632, pp. 207–221. Springer, Heidelberg (2003). https://doi.org/10.1007/3-540-36970-8_15

13. Lin, C.: An adaptive genetic algorithm based on population diversity strategy. In: 2009 Third International Conference on Genetic and Evolutionary Computing, pp. 93–96. IEEE (2009)

14. Mahyar, F., Cheung, V., Westland, S., Henry, P.: Investigation of complementary colour harmony in CIELAB colour space. In: Proceedings of the AIC Midterm Meeting, China (2007)

15. Moodley, K., Murrell, H.: A colour-map plugin for the open source, Java based, image processing package, imageJ. Comput. Geosci. **30**(6), 609–618 (2004)

16. Ombuki, B.M., Ventresca, M.: Local search genetic algorithms for the job shop scheduling problem. Appl. Intell. **21**(1), 99–109 (2004). https://doi.org/10.1023/B:APIN.0000027769.48098.91

17. Radlak, K., Smolka, B.: Visualization enhancement of segmented images using genetic algorithm. In: 2014 International Conference on Multimedia Computing and Systems (ICMCS), pp. 391–396. IEEE (2014)

18. Semary, N.A.: A proposed HSV-based pseudo-coloring scheme for enhancing medical images. In: Computer Science & Information Technology (2018)

19. Shojaedini, E., Majd, M., Safabakhsh, R.: Novel adaptive genetic algorithm sample consensus. Appl. Soft Comput. **77**, 635–642 (2019)

20. Xue, Z., Blum, R.S.: Concealed weapon detection using color image fusion. In: Proceedings of the 6th International Conference on Information Fusion, vol. 1, pp. 622–627. IEEE (2003)

21. Zames, G., et al.: Genetic algorithms in search, optimization and machine learning. Inf. Technol. J. **3**(1), 301–302 (1981)

22. Zang, W., Ren, L., Zhang, W., Liu, X.: A cloud model based DNA genetic algorithm for numerical optimization problems. Future Gener. Comput. Syst. **81**, 465–477 (2018)
23. Zhu, K.Q.: A diversity-controlling adaptive genetic algorithm for the vehicle routing problem with time windows. In: Proceedings of the 15th IEEE International Conference on Tools with Artificial Intelligence, pp. 176–183. IEEE (2003)

A Genetic Algorithm-Based Solver
for Small-Scale Jigsaw Puzzles

Wenjing Guo, Wenhong Wei$^{(\boxtimes)}$, Yuhui Zhang, and Anbing Fu

School of Computer, Dongguan University of Technology, Dongguan 523808, China
weiwh@dgut.edu.cn

Abstract. In this paper, we present a genetic algorithm-based puzzle solver, which is mainly used to solve small-scale puzzle problems. We introduce a new measurement function that improves its accuracy by normalizing the Mahalanobis distance and the Euclidean distance between two puzzle pieces. By calculating the difference between edges of two puzzle pieces and using the genetic algorithm to assemble pieces correctly, two "parent" solutions are merged into one improved "child" solution. Using the idea of local search, it avoids the problem of local optimum solutions brought by the genetic algorithm, which greatly improves the accuracy of the puzzle.

Keywords: Computational jigsaw puzzle · Genetic algorithm · Local search

1 Introduction

The Puzzle is a game everyone can play since they are little. A picture is divided into N pieces of different non-overlapping parts and shuffled the order. Players must use the shape and color information of each piece to reconstruct the original image. The Puzzle problem has been proved to be a Non-deterministic Polynomial (NP) complete problem [1]. Although it is often regarded as a game, the idea of solving puzzles usually plays an essential role in many fields like archeology and medicine, the repair of ancient artifact fragments, the restoration of fractures and displaced bones. With the latest development of computer science and engineering, researchers are able to create computer puzzle solvers. The algorithms of the puzzle solver are used to resolve the basic problems in various fields such as machine learning, computer vision, and bioinformatics.

Jigsaw puzzle was first produced in 1760 by a London engraving and mapmaker artist, John Spilsbury. Freeman [2] and Garder were the first people in the scientific community who tried solving the problem theoretically. In 1964, they introduced a square solver which can solve nine pieces of the puzzle. Shortly, the research focus has shifted from shape-based to color-based. Since then, more and more scholars have begun to study the puzzle problem. In 1988 [3], Wolfson H., et al. studied real-world puzzles, which were based on pieces with specific shapes and directions. Soon, Chung MG et al. [4] proposed a method of puzzle based on shape and color. Later, people began to study square puzzles, which pieces cannot distinguish directions. In 2010, Cho et al. proposed a probability-based puzzle solver that can handle up to 432 puzzle pieces and

© Springer Nature Switzerland AG 2020
Y. Tan et al. (Eds.): ICSI 2020, LNCS 12145, pp. 362–373, 2020.
https://doi.org/10.1007/978-3-030-53956-6_32

lead prior knowledge about puzzle problems. One year later, Yang et al. introduced a particle filtering-based puzzle solver, which improved their results. In the same year, Pomerantz [5] et al. first announced a fully automatic square puzzle solver, which can handle up to 3000 pieces of a puzzle. In 2012, Andalo, F. A., et al. [6] suggested a method to solve image problems based on a simple quadratic programming formula. In 2013, Sholomon et al. presented a large-scale puzzle problem based on genetic algorithms. Anne D [7] further explored this problem and considered a more general variant, that is, neither the direction of the pieces nor the size of the puzzle is known. [8] proposed a new method for solving small pieces of the puzzle. In 2019, [9] introduced a new puzzle solver, which performs well in the case of unknown direction and piece size.

In its most basic form, each puzzle solver needs a fitness evaluation function to determine the compatibility between adjacent puzzle pieces and find a puzzle strategy as accurate as possible. Those researchers mainly used (the Sum of Squared Distances (SSD) in LAB color space from Cho et al. [10]) the method of calculating the color distance in establishing the similarity measurement function. Color space distance refers to the difference between the two pieces. In general, the larger the distance, the greater differences between these two pieces, vice versa. When calculating the color distance, similar to calculating the Euclidean distance between two points, the value between the pieces calculated in this way is often not very effective. Therefore Gallagher [11] also proposed a powerful pairwise compatibility measure, Mahalanobis Gradient compatibility (MGC), which penalizes gradient changes when gradient changes exceed expectations. Gallagher mainly adopts the method of calculating Mahalanobis distance to construct compatibility function. Mahalanobis distance is created by P.C. Mahalanobis, an Indian statistician, which represents the distance between a point and a distribution. It is an effective method to calculate the similarity of two unknown sample sets since it takes into account the connections between various features. Based on this, we take the normalization treatment of color distance and Mahalanobis distance to build a new measurement function. Gallagher conducted a comparative study ([11], Table 4) with 432-piece-scale puzzles, and the results showed that the accuracy was only slightly improved compared to Pomeranz et al. (95.1% vs. 95.0%). Supplementary materials provided by Pomeranz et al. [12] showed there was much room for improvement in many puzzle problems. In this paper, we use the powerful technique of genetic algorithm [13] as a puzzle strategy. Toyama et al. tried the design of a ga-based solver, but it could only complete puzzles with a size of 64 pieces. We advanced a new puzzle solver based on the genetic algorithm, using the crossover puzzle strategy proposed in [14]. In addition to this, we improve it by adding a local search method, so that the final puzzle results can avoid falling into the local optimum. The research exhibits that our solver can complete the picture in small-scale puzzle problems.

2 Genetic Algorithm

A GA is a simulation of natural selection and the calculation of the mechanism of biological evolution, a method of searching through simulation of natural evolution. Because examining all possible solutions to a particular problem is generally considered infeasible, genetic algorithms provide a process of searching within solutions to a problem.

First, the initial population of a candidate solution, also known as a chromosome, is randomly generated. Each chromosome is a complete candidate solution to the puzzle problem, and arrange them into puzzle pieces, where each piece is viewed as a gene on the chromosome. By imitating the crossover, mutation, and evolution of biological heredity, the solution in the population is improved continuously. Thus, the optimal solution (i.e. correct image) is obtained.

In the process of simulating natural selection, the reproduction rate of chromosomes, where the number of times each chromosome is selected and reproduced, is proportional to its fitness value. The fitness value is a score obtained through the fitness measurement function, which measures and evaluates the quality of a given solution. Therefore, a "good" solution will produce more offspring than other solutions. Also, good chromosomes are more likely to reproduce with other good chromosomes, a process known as "crossover". Operators should allow both parents to pass on their better traits to offspring.

The success of the genetic algorithm mainly depends on the selection of appropriate chromosome representation, crossover operator and fitness function. The chromosome representation and the crossover operator must allow two excellent "parent solutions" to merge into a better "child" solution. The fitness function must correctly detect parts of the chromosome are more promising for transmission to the next generation.

3   The Puzzle Problem Based on Genetic Algorithm

By using the pseudo code of Algorithm 1, the underlying genetic algorithm framework for solving the puzzle problem is determined. As mentioned before, the genetic algorithm first defines and initializes a population, and each chromosome represents a possible solution. Specifically, our genetic algorithm starts from 1000 random placements. In each generation, the fitness function is used to evaluate the whole population (as described below), and a new offspring is generated through the selection and crossover of chromosome pairs. We use the common roulette wheel selection method to choose chromosomes. The probability of a chromosome is selected based on the value we calculated from the fitness function. The larger the value, the greater chances a chromosome will be chosen. Having provided a framework overview, we now describe the critical components of genetic algorithms, such as chromosome representations, fitness functions, and crossover mutation algorithms in detail.

Pseudo code

```
 1: population ← generate 1000 random chromosomes
 2: for generation number = 1 → 100
 3:    evaluate all chromosomes using the fitness function
 4:    new population ← NULL
 5:    copy 2 best chromosomes to new population
 6:    while size(new population) ≤ 1000 do
 7:       parent1 ← select chromosome
 8:       parent2 ← select chromosome
 9:       child ← crossover(parent1, parent2)
10:        add child to new population
11:    end while
```

```
12:    population ← new population
13:end for
```

3.1 Fitness Function

In the GA algorithm, fitness describes the relative probability an individual survives, and fitness functions are used to calculate it. Here, each chromosome represents a disorderly picture. In the puzzle, we are not aware of all the initial conditions, so calculating fitness is not a simple task. We accumulate the compatibility of every two adjacent pieces and divide the fitness factor by the result. (to make the chromosome with smaller difference obtain greater fitness).

We define the possibility of two pieces being adjacent pieces as compatibility. The greater the compatibility, the greater the probability of two pieces are adjacent pieces. For every given two pieces, we define a set of spatial direction {L, R, T, D} to represent the left, right, top, and down respectively. Then for each direction, we calculate the difference between the two pieces. $C(x_i, x_j, L)$ is used to represent the difference of x_i in the left direction of x_j. We will explain our difference measurement function later.

Based on the compatibility measurement function, many people have suggested suitable methods. Cho et al. [10] proposed to calculate the compatibility value of the two pieces by calculating the sum of the square of each pixel's spatial distance. Pomeranz et al. [12] also proposed some optimizations. It should be noted that using this method, for maximum compatibility, we need to calculate their minimum differences.

We propose a new compatibility measurement method. By calculating the sum of the color space distance and the Mahalanobis distance, we get a new set of differences. In order to make the color space distance and Mahalanobis distance comparable, we reduce the weight of the two methods by normalization so that they can get the best results. Suppose there are x_i and x_j represents two pieces of size $K * K * 3$, and K means the height and width of a piece (unit is pixel). So the difference measurement function is:

$$C(x_i, x_j, r) = D(x_i, x_j, r) + DG(x_i, x_j, r) \tag{1}$$

Here D represents x_i, x_j, the color space distance in the R direction:

$$D(x_i, x_j, r) = \sqrt{\sum_{k=1}^{K}\sum_{b=1}^{3} x_i(k, K, b) - x_j(k, 1, b)} \tag{2}$$

DG stands for Mahalanobis distance, a compatibility measurement algorithm proposed by [11], which calculates compatibility by calculating the gradient value of the color change of two pieces. The formula is as follows:

$$DG(x_i, x_j, r) = \sum_{s=1}^{K} (\Lambda_{LR}^{ij}(s) - E_{LR}^{ij}(s)) V_{LR} - (\Lambda_{LR}^{ij}(s) - E_{LR}^{ij}(s))^T \tag{3}$$

$$L_{LR}^{ij}(s) = \delta_j(s, 1) - \delta_i(s, K) \tag{4}$$

$$E_{LR}^{ij}(s) = 1/2 \, (\delta_i \, (s, \, K-1) - \delta_i \, (s, \, K-1) + \delta_j \, (s, \, 2) - \delta_j \, (s, \, 1)) \qquad (5)$$

It is worth mentioning that $C \, (x_i, \, x_j, \, r) \neq D \, (x_j, \, x_i, \, r)$. Obviously, for greater compatibility, the differences between the two pieces should be as small as possible.

The fitness function also needs to consider the calculation speed. When the program is running, it needs to calculate the fitness of each chromosome in each generation. This consumed time cannot be ignored. Since it's impossible to calculate the degree of difference between pieces for each fitness calculation, so we use a table to cache the degree of difference in the senior of $(n * m)^{\wedge 2} * 2$ and includes the difference degree between all pieces. In this way, we don't need to calculate the difference degree every time, but add the values in the cache.

This is our calculation formula of fitness

$$\sum_{i=1}^{N} \sum_{j=1}^{M-1} C \, (x_{i,j}, \, x_{i,j+1}, \, r) + \sum_{i=1}^{N-1} \sum_{j=1}^{M} C \, (x_{i,j}, \, x_{i+1,j}, \, r) \qquad (6)$$

Which r and d represent the right and down directions

3.2 Crossover and Mutation

Problem Definition

As mentioned above, we use an $(N * M)$ size chromosome to represent a disordered picture. During initialization, we will give each piece a number based on the original picture (mainly used for the result evaluation after the completion of the puzzle). This method is easy to use and suitable for the assessment. The main problem now is how to define a suitable crossover algorithm, as this method generates a child chromosome from a given two parent chromosomes. It should be able to retain the "good traits" of the parent generation to the child generation (such as complete pieces already been placed), to obtain a better puzzle result. If only a random algorithm is used, it may lead to a completely random selection from the parent's chromosome, causing some pieces to repeat or miss, and the puzzle to fail. Thus, as long as the problem of crossover is solved, the GA algorithm can be improved.

Even if the validity problem is solved, we still need to think carefully about the crossover operator. Crossover is based on the fitness of two chromosomes, which is determined by the compatibility between adjacent pieces. Therefore, crossover cannot precisely locate the correct position but select a piece with the highest similarity according to the fitness. The population is completely random from the beginning, and then gradually improves. We can reasonably assume that after several generations of evolution, more pieces will be placed in the correct position. Considering the limitations of the fitness function, it cannot fully determine whether a piece is in the right position. Hence, we predict some fragments may be the wrong position. So how to find a piece that belongs to the correct location is vital. A properly positioned piece should be considered a good feature and passed to the offspring. The crossover operation must consider how to transfer a correctly spelled fragment so it can move as a whole.

Once we solve the problem of moving a fragment, we need to solve the problem of fragment misplaced. What traits will pass to an offspring? Heuristics methods may be applied and used to distinguish whether prices are correct.

Proposed Methods

Given two parent chromosomes, for example, two completely different chromosomes (with the different distribution of internal pieces), the crossover operation will gradually build a word chromosome from the inside, and take the two parent chromosomes as the prototype to generate a complete offspring (Fig. 1).

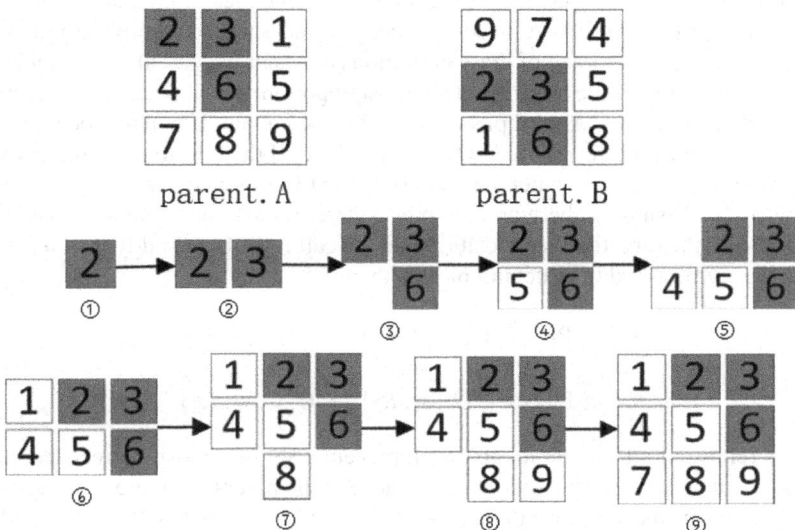

Fig. 1. Shows the process of crossover. Randomly select two parents, the parents have the same fragment, 2, 3, 6. We start with piece 2, and the algorithm will first select the same fragments around 2 piece in the parent generation (the number of adjacent fragments is the same in a certain direction). Based on this principle, we get ① ② ③ pictures. Next, we choose the best-buddy piece. When there is no best-buddy piece, we traverse all the boundaries to find the piece with the highest matching compatibility.

This crossover operation starts with a randomly selected piece. Then gradually acquire the available pieces (the highest possible unused adjacent pieces). Merging with neighboring pieces, a picture obtained by this method must be continuous and complete. This operation continuously seeks the most compatible piece from the candidate pool, until there are no more candidates, which the puzzle is completed. Because each piece can only appear once, which will not cause duplicate piece, and considering the size of the image is known, this operation will not exceed the original boundary. It also ensures this operation can generate an effective picture (no repeating or missing pieces). Depending on the kernel growth vector, the position of each piece may be moved before completing the picture. For example, if a lower-left corner is randomly selected as the first piece, then the kernel will tend to grow to the upper-right. The first piece may be in any four corners or any other location. With this feature, the position of a piece is independent, and the whole fragment can be shifted.

Based on previous thoughts, we still need to solve the following issues: (1) How to select a suitable piece from the candidate pieces, (2) and where to place it in the child generation. Given a starting point, an image with only one piece, we can mark all reachable boundaries. The boundary of this piece is composed of itself and directions, which is represented by a pair (x_i, R). The crossover process consists of three stages. The method proposed in [14] is used here. The first stage: For a known boundary, if the program detects a candidate pieces, this piece and the fragment composed this candidate pieces both exist in the parents (The parent has the same piece in the same direction). Then we believe that these two pieces are correct and should directly be retained in the offspring. If more than one of these conditions exists in the parent at the same time, choose one randomly (so the order is not the most important, because children generation will keep all such pieces). A used piece cannot be used again. If a match occurs with a used piece, then the piece is ignored. The second stage: If there is no piece matching the parents at the same time, then enter the second stage.[14] is quoted here as the best-buddy matching piece. Assuming there are two pieces here, if each piece is the best match to the other piece (the direction is opposite), then we call it the best-buddy match piece. If pieces x_i, x_j are best-buddy matching pieces, then:

$$\forall x_k \in \text{Pieces}, \ C(x_i, x_j, R_1) \geq C(x_i, x_k, R_1)$$
$$\text{and}$$
$$\forall x_p \in \text{Pieces}, \ C(x_j, x_i, R_2) \geq C(x_j, x_p, R_2)$$

Pieces represent all pieces, R_1 and R_2 represent a set of opposite directions. In the second stage, the program checks whether a piece in the parents so there is a best-buddy matching piece in the optional boundary. If it exists, the piece will be selected and retained in the offspring. At the same time, if the program detects multiple best-buddy matching pieces, it will choose one randomly to perform the puzzle problem first. If this candidate piece already used in the child generation, the process will skip this match and look for new matches or enter the third stage. The third stage: if no best-buddy matching piece is selected, the process will randomly select a piece and select the piece with the highest degree of matching in the current direction as its child generation.

We propose two new mutation methods. After the crossover stage is the mutation stage. For every child generation, we will select the best offspring for mutation operation according to the fitness. For each piece in the child chromosome, there is a chance to mutate. The mutation will select a piece and a direction. We will find the best matching piece, and exchange the best matching piece with the adjacent pieces in the same direction. If the fitness of the offspring increases after this exchange, it means the mutation succeeds, and the result will be retained. If the fitness after the exchange decreases, it means the mutation failed, and we will restore this mutation.

Ranking adjacent piece achieves another mutation method, and we call it the best boundary ranking. In the mutation stage, for each generation, we will select the best offspring for mutation operation according to the fitness. For each piece in the child chromosome, there is a chance of mutation. We will randomly select a piece, and calculate

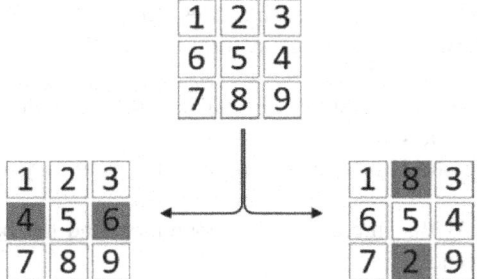

Fig. 2. Shows the process of mutation. There are two cases of mutation, successful mutation and mutation failure. When the mutation is successful, as shown in the left picture, the correct mutation will increase the compatibility of the picture, so that the mutation is retained. If the compatibility of the picture is reduced, as shown in the right figure, the mutation will be restored.

the sum of the similarity ranking of the two adjacent pieces (If these two pieces are the best-buddy matching pieces for all directions, the result is $4 + 4 = 8$). Then calculate the sum of the similarity ranking after this exchange. If the sum of the similarity rankings after this exchange is less than the sum of the previous similarity rankings, it means this mutation was successful, and the result is retained. Otherwise, it means that the mutation failed, and we will restore this mutation (Fig. 2).

(a) init   (b) 1 generation   (c) 2 generation   (d) 3 generation

(e) 4 generation   (f) 10 generation   (g) 50 generation   (h) 100 generation

Fig. 3. Shows the process of solving a 646 pieces puzzle. The pictures almost completed in the fourth generation.

In summary, the program repeats these three stages until there are no candidate pieces available, and the program ends. Crossover always take turns in the first, second, and third stage. We only consider starting the puzzle from the boundary to maintain the continuity of kernel growth, and after each successful match, we will return to the first stage. The code description for this stage as follows:

Code description:

The first stage: Within the assembled boundary, find whether two pieces are in the parent's chromosome at the same time.

If yes, add it to the child chromosome, update the boundary. Otherwise, enter the second stage.

The second stage: Within the assembled boundary, find the best-buddy matching piece in the parent chromosome

If yes, add it to the child chromosome, update the boundary. Otherwise, enter the second stage.

The third stage: Within the assembled boundary, randomly searching for the best matching piece to add to the child chromosome (Fig. 3).

Principle

In the GA framework, good traits should pass to the child generation. In this case, the good fragment of the parent generation can preserve well because this algorithm does not rely on the position. Each right fragment corresponds to the correct position of each puzzle piece. It should be noted that the relative spatial position of x_i and x_j is the key to solving the puzzle problem. However, every chromosome has all the pieces of the puzzle. Due to the randomness of the first generation, the program must actively seek the best features between pieces. We did some research. Assuming parents share a good characteristic, which is the reason for their survival and choice. In other words, if both parents have the same characteristic, we treat it as highly accurate and keep it to the offspring. Not all frequent features will pass to the next generation. Because of the kernel growth algorithm, some of the same pieces may match other pieces prematurely and occupied, so the correct pieces cannot match them. As for the second stage, without the same characteristics, people tend to randomly select a parent and start with it. Another option is to choose a piece with the highest compatibility or the best-buddy matching piece. Since the position of a piece in the parents is random, even the best-buddy matching piece may not be the correct match. Two pieces are the best-buddy matching pieces and have the same characteristics in the parents, which is a sign for a valid match. Another point of view is that each chromosome contains some correct fragments. Passing the right gene from parent to offspring is the core of the genetic algorithm. In addition, if each parent contains a correct fragment, and those fragments partially overlapped. The overlapping portion will pass to the child generation in the first stage, the parents complete the inheritance of the correct fragment in the second stage, and to form larger and more correct fragments. As for the third stage, we can conclude this: the genetic algorithm tries multiple puzzles at different locations simultaneously. Only fragments seem to be right can be passed on to the next generation, which embodies the principle of the fine traits of natural selection theory.

4   Experimental Result

Cho et al. [10] introduced three measures to evaluate the complete puzzle, two of which repeatedly used in the work. One is the direct comparison method, which measures the proportion of debris in the correct position. The other is the comparison of adjacent pieces, which measures the right proportion of adjacent pieces in the puzzle. In this experiment, we adopted the direct comparison method, since it's a more intuitive way to judge the completion of a puzzle.

In our experiments, we used the same genetic algorithm parameters as pseudocode 1. The population has 1000 chromosomes. In each generation, we kept the best 2 chromosomes (an elitist measure). The remaining population will be generated by the crossover operator with a mutation rate of 5%. Parent chromosomes are produced by roulette wheel selection, each time generating an offspring. GA runs 100 generations at a time.

We selected a set of image data, which contains 25 pictures, and divided each picture into different size pieces. We run the genetic algorithm 10 times on each image, each time using a different random seed, and record the best, worst, and average (and standard deviation). Table 1 lists the results of our genetic algorithm on each set. Interestingly, despite the random nature of GA, the results of different runs are close, which proves the robustness of genetic algorithms.

Table 1. Best, worst, and average results of variety pieces number

Number of pieces	Best	Worst	Average
256	100	99.21875	99.53125
646	99.69040	97.52311	98.45201
1196	87.95986	79.93311	84.94983

We compared the effectiveness of three compatibility measurement functions on different picture puzzles. The data collected from the 646 pieces puzzle showed in Table 2. We can conclude that the efficacy of using the color-space distance measurement function alone is not as good as using the Mahalanobis distance measurement function. The best result is achieved by combining the two functions with normalization. We can see that through the normalized function, the degree of restoration reached 98%, while using the Mahalanobis distance and color-space distance methods is 96% and 97%, respectively. Compared with the previous method, our method has greatly improved.

We also compared whether to use the local search for the puzzle. Using the local search as the mutation function, the data are shown in Table 3. When testing the data in this section, we use the 646 pieces puzzle, and the normalized measurement function of two distances as the benchmark.

Table 2. Best, worst, and average results of different measure function

	Best	Worst	Average
Color space distance based measure function	97.5232	95.04643	96.037142
Mahalanobis distance based measure function	98.7616	95.97523	97.647052
Proposed	99.69040	97.52311	98.45201

Each group of test pictures divided into pieces of different sizes, and Table 1 shows the results. Here are the best, worst, and average results.

Table 3. Best, worst, and average results of different mutation function

	Best	Worst	Average
No mutation	91.02167	83.90092	88.885448
Fitness based mutation function	99.69040	97.52311	98.45201
best boundary ran-king based mutation function	99.38080	97.21362	97.86377

Records the results of the puzzle using three different measurement functions. Using the 646 pieces puzzle, there are the best, worst, and average results under those three measurement functions.

Records the results obtained without mutation and utilizing different mutation algorithms. Using the 646 pieces puzzle, there are the best, worst, and average results under different mutation algorithms.

5   Discussion and Future Work

This article introduces a puzzle solver based on the genetic algorithm, which can accurately solve small-scale puzzle problems while significantly reduced the time. It improved the fitness function and the accuracy of the puzzle pieces. Based on our work, we can further study on solving the puzzle problem in more complex situations like unknown direction pieces, various missing pieces, and the accuracy of large-scale puzzles. To improve the efficiency of existing solver, solve the problem of unknown size and 3D Puzzle. It can also provide a reference for solving problems in other fields.

Acknowledgement. This work was supported by the Key Project of Science and Technology Innovation 2030 supported by the Ministry of Science and Technology of China (Grant No. 2018AAA0101301), the Key Projects of Artificial Intelligence of High School in Guangdong Province (No. 2019KZDZX1011) and Guangdong Provincial Science and Technology Plan Projects (No. 2016A010101034).

References

1. Demaine, E.D., Hearn, R.A.: Playing games with algorithms: algorithmic combinatorial game theory (2001)
2. Freeman, H., Garder, L.: Apictorial jigsaw puzzles: the computer solution of a problem in pattern recognition. IEEE Trans. Electron. Comput. **13**(2), 118–127 (1964)
3. Wolfson, H., Schonberg, E., Kalvin, A., Lamdan, Y.: Solving jigsaw puzzles by computer. Ann. Oper. Res. **12**(1), 51–64 (1988). https://doi.org/10.1007/BF02186360

4. Chung, M.G., Fleck, M.M., Forsyth, D.A.: Jigsaw puzzle solver using shape and color. In: Proceedings of the 1998 Fourth International Conference on Signal Processing. ICSP 1998. IEEE (1998)
5. Yang, X., Adluru, N., Latecki, L.J.: Particle filter with state permutations for solving image jigsaw puzzles (2011)
6. Andalo, F.A., Taubin, G., Goldenstein, S.: Solving image puzzles with a simple quadratic programming formulation. In: Graphics, Patterns & Images. IEEE Computer Society (2012)
7. Williams, A.D.: The Jigsaw Puzzle: Piecing Together a History. Berkley Publishing Group, New York (2004)
8. Son, K., Moreno, D., Hays, J., Cooper, D.B.: Solving small-piece jigsaw puzzles by growing consensus. In: 2016 IEEE Conference on Computer Vision and Pattern Recognition (CVPR), pp. 1193–1201. IEEE (2016)
9. Son, K., Hays, J., Cooper, D.B.: Solving square jigsaw puzzle by hierarchical loop constraints. IEEE Trans. Pattern Anal. Mach. Intell., 2222–2235 (2019)
10. Cho, T.S., Avidan, S., Freeman, W.T.: A probabilistic image jigsaw puzzle solver. In: The Twenty-Third IEEE Conference on Computer Vision and Pattern Recognition. CVPR 2010, San Francisco, CA, USA, 13–18 June 2010. IEEE (2010)
11. Gallagher, A.C.: Jigsaw puzzles with pieces of unknown orientation. In: 2012 IEEE Conference on Computer Vision and Pattern Recognition (CVPR). IEEE (2012)
12. Pomeranz, D., Shemesh, M., Ben-Shahar, O.: A fully automated greedy square jigsaw puzzle solver (2011)
13. Holland, J.H.: Adaptation in Natural and Artificial System. MIT Press, Cambridge (1992)
14. Sholomon, D., David, O., Netanyahu, N.S.: A genetic algorithm-based solver for very large jigsaw puzzles. In: IEEE Conference on Computer Vision and Pattern Recognition. CVPR 2013. IEEE (2013)

A New EDA with Dimension Reduction Technique for Large Scale Many-Objective Optimization

Mingli Shi, Lianbo Ma$^{(\boxtimes)}$, and Guangming Yang$^{(\boxtimes)}$

Northeastern University, Shenyang, China
305337697@qq.com, {malb,yanggm}@swc.neu.edu.cn

Abstract. The performance of many-objective evolutionary algorithms deteriorates appreciably in solving large-scale many-objective optimization problems (MaOPs) which encompass more than hundreds variables. One of the known rationales is the curse of dimensionality. Estimation of distribution algorithms sample new solutions with a probabilistic model built from the statistics extracting over the existing solutions so as to mitigate the adverse impact of genetic operators. In this paper, an Gaussian Bayesian network-based estimation of distribution algorithm (GBNEDA-DR) is proposed to effectively tackle continued large-scale MaOPs. In the proposed algorithm, dimension reduction technique (i.e. LPP) is employed in the decision space to speed up the estimation search of the proposed algorithm. The experimental results show that the proposed algorithm performs significantly better on many of the problems and for different decision space dimensions, and achieves comparable results on some compared with many existing algorithms.

Keywords: Estimation of distribution algorithm · Gaussian Bayesian network · Dimension reduction

1 Introduction

Many-objective optimization problems (MaOPs) refer to the problems that involve a large number of conflicting objectives to be optimized simultaneously. Due to the complexity and difficulty of MaOPs, it is meaningful to investigate the ways of dealing with a given difficult MaOP. The main difficulty associated with MaOPs is often referred to as the curse of dimensionality. Currently, scalability with respect to the number of objectives has attracted considerable research interests. This is due to the fact that in many-objective optimization, most candidate solutions become nondominated with each other, thus causing

L. Ma and G. Yang—This work is supported by the National Natural Science Foundation of China under Grant No. 61773103, Fundamental Research Funds for the Central Universities No. N180408019 and Huawei HIRP project under Grant No. HO2019085002.

© Springer Nature Switzerland AG 2020
Y. Tan et al. (Eds.): ICSI 2020, LNCS 12145, pp. 374–385, 2020.
https://doi.org/10.1007/978-3-030-53956-6_33

failure of dominance-based selection strategies in traditional MOEAs. To tackle the MaOPs, a number of new multiobjective evolutionary algorithms (MOEAs) have been proposed, such as NSGA-III [6], MOEA/D [22], Tk-MaOEA [12], IBEA [26], and KnEA [24]. However, in spite of the various approaches that are focused on the scalability of MOEAs to the number of objectives, scalability in terms of the number of decision variables remains inadequately explored.

Recently, large-scale optimization has already attracted certain interests in the single-objective optimization problem (SOP). Akin to the large-scale single-objective optimization [14,19], some authors have attempted to adapt existing techniques for large-scale single-objective optimization to the MaOPs context, such as MOEA/DVA [13], LMEA [23], WOF [25], MOEA/D-RDG [18] and CCGDE3 [2]. The main idea of these methods is divide-and-conquer strategy. Since the target of many-objective optimization is different from that of single-objective optimization [11]. Thus, it is not trivial to generalize such divide-and-conquer strategy proposed in single objective optimization problem (SOP) to solve MaOPs because the objective functions of an MaOP are conflicting with one another.

Deb et al. [4] concluded that the performances of MOEAs are significantly influenced by the genetic operators (i.e. crossover and mutation) which cannot ensure to generate promising offspring. Estimation of distribution algorithms (EDAs) are a relatively new computational paradigm proposed to generate new offspring. EDA generates new solutions by applying probabilistic models, which inferred from a set of selected solutions. These models capture statistics about the values of problem variables and the dependencies among these variables [9].

It has been observed that under mild smoothness conditions, the Pareto set of a continuous MOP is a piecewise continuous (m-1)-dimensional manifold, where m is the number of the objectives. In paper [21], it has shown that reproduction of new trial solutions based on this regularity property can effectively cope with the variable linkages in continuous MOPs. Hence, this characteristics of MOPs can be integrated into EDA to effectively solve large-scale MOPs. This paper proposes a new EDA applied to large-scale MOPs, called GBNEDA-DR. The idea is to combine EDA with dimension reduction methods (i.e. LPP [8]), which are responsible for embedding the solutions used on the probabilistic models in low dimension space.

The rest of this paper is organized as follows. In Sect. 2, we briefly recall some related work on MOEAs for solving large-scale MOPs. Section 3 describes the proposed algorithm GBNEDA/DR. Section 4 illustrates and analyzes the experimental results. Section 5 concludes this paper.

2   Related Works

2.1   Gaussian Bayesian Network

Bayesian networks [15] are multivariate probabilistic graphical models, consisting of two components.

1) The structure, represented by a directed acyclic graph (DAG), where the nodes are the problem variables and the arcs are conditional (in)dependencies between twins of variables;
2) The parameters, expressing for each variable X_i the conditional probability of each of its values, given different value-settings of its parent variables ($Pa(X_i)$) according to the structure, i.e.

$$p(x_i|pa(X_i)) \qquad (1)$$

where $Pa(X_i)$ is a value-setting for the parent variables in $Pa(X_i)$.

In domains with continuous-valued variables, it is usually assumed that the variables follow a Gaussian distribution. The Bayesian network learned for a set of variables, having a multivariate Gaussian distribution $p(x) = N(\mu, \Sigma)$ as their joint probability function, is called a Gaussian Bayesian network (GBN). Here, μ is the mean vector and Σ is the covariance matrix of the distribution.

The structure of a GBN is similar to any other Bayesian network. However, for each node the conditional probability represented by the parameters is a univariate Gaussian distribution, which is determined by the values of the parent variables [7]

$$p(x|pa(X_i)) = N(\mu_i + \sum_{X_j \in Pa(X_i)} \omega_{ij}(x_j - \mu_j), v_i^2) \qquad (2)$$

where μ_i is the mean of variable X_i, v_i is the conditional standard deviation of the distribution, and regression coefficients ω_{ij} specify the importance of each of the parents. x_j is the corresponding value of X_j in $Pa(X_i)$. These are the parameters stored in each node of a GBN.

2.2 Estimation of Distribution Algorithm

Traditional genetic operators used for generating new solutions in evolutionary algorithms act almost blindly and are very likely to disrupt the good subsolutions found so far which will affect the optimization convergence. This disruption is more likely to occur as the correlation between problem variables increases, rendering the algorithm inefficient for such problems. EDAs make use of probabilistic models to replace the genetic operators in order to overcome this shortcoming. A general framework of EDAs is illustrated in Algorithm 1.

Typically, the EDAs-based MOEAs are broadly classified into two categories based on their estimation models. The first category covers the Bayesian network-based EDAs. For example, multiobjective Bayesian optimization algorithm (BOA) [10]. The other category is often known as the mixture probability model-based EDAs. Such as, in [16], the multiobjective hierarchical BOA was designed by the mixture Bayesian network-based probabilistic model for discrete MOPs. It is believed that EDAs are capable of solving MaOPs without suffering the disadvantages of MOEAs with traditional genetic operators.

Algorithm 1. Framework of an EDA

1: $t = 0$
2: P_t=Randomly initialize the population
3: **while** termination is not satisfied **do**
4:    M = Built probabilistic models from P_t
5:    $t = t + 1$
6:    U_t = Generate offspring from M
7:    P_t = Select promising solutions from $U_t \cup P_{t-1}$
8: **end while**
9: **return** P_t

2.3 Locality Preserving Projections

Locality Preserving Projection (LPP) [8] is a general method for manifold learning. Though it is still a linear technique, it seems to recover important aspects of the intrinsic nonlinear manifold structure by preserving local structure. In many real-world applications, the local structure is more important. In this section, we give a brief description of LPP. The complete derivation and theoretical justifications of LPP can be traced back to [8]. LPP seeks to preserve the intrinsic geometry of the data and local structure. Given a set $x_1, x_2, ..., x_m$ in R^n, find a transformation matrix A that maps these m points to a set of points $y_1, y_2, ..., y_m$ in R^l. The objective function of LPP is as follows:

$$min \sum_{ij} (y_i - y_j)^2 S_{ij} \tag{3}$$

where the matrix S is a similarity matrix. The following restrictions are imposed on the equation (3):

$$y^T D y = 1 \tag{4}$$

D is a diagonal matrix, its entries are column sum of S, $D_{ii} = \Sigma_j S_{ij}$. A possible way of defining S is as follows:

$$S_{ij} = \begin{cases} exp(- \|x_i - x_j\|^2 / t), & \|x_i - x_j\|^2 < \varepsilon \\ 0 & \text{otherwise} \end{cases} \tag{5}$$

Here, ε defines the radius of the local neighborhood and t is a custom parameter.

3 Proposed Algorithm

In this section, the framework of the proposed algorithm, i.e., GBNEDA-DR, is given first. Then elaborate on the four important components in it, i.e., reducing the dimension of decision space, building the probability model, repairing and environmental selection.

3.1 Framework of the Proposed Algorithm

The framework of the proposed algorithm is listed in Algorithm 2. It consists of the following three main steps. First, a population of N candidate solutions is randomly initialized. Second, by constructing the Gauss Bayesian network model, N new individuals are sampled and generated. This step has many sub-steps. Algorithm 2 shows an overview of this step. Next, the main sub-steps are described in detail. Finally, an environmental selection strategy is used to select excellent individuals, thus, a set of solutions with a better quality in convergence and diversity are obtained. The three steps are performed one by one in a limit number of fitness evaluations. In addition, maximum fitness evaluation, population size and respective threshold for dimension reduction and model building need to be made available prior to the proposed algorithm running.

Algorithm 2. Main framework of GBNEDA-DR

Input: N(population size) $nSel$(the number of Sel_Pop)
Output: P(final population)
 1: P=Initialize(N)
 2: **while** termination criterion not fulfilled **do**
 3:    Sel_Pop = Selection($P, nSel$)
 4:    Sel_Pop' = LPP(Sel_Pop)
 5:    Φ = Establishing probability model in low dimensional space by Sel_Pop'
 6:    $offspring$ = sampling(Φ, N)
 7:    $offspring'$ = Inverse transformation of ($offspring$)
 8:    $offspring''$ = repairing($offspring'$)
 9:    P = Environmental Selection($P, offspring''$)
10: **end while**
11: **return** P

3.2 Reducing the Dimension of Decision Space

In this paper, LPP [8] is used to reduce the volume of exploration space to speed up the search of sampling new solutions. A set of Pareto solutions (PS) is selected to be the training data and then exploitation is performed in the subspace. In this paper, the LPP is employed because: 1) LPP is based on the inner geometric structure of manifolds, it shows the stability of embedding; 2) LPP algorithm is a linear dimension reduction method.

At the beginning of dimensionality reduction, the Pareto solutions, which are denoted by Sp, are selected from the population. For convenience of the development, a matrix X is used to represent Sp. Specifically, each row in X denotes one solution while the columns refer to the different dimension of decision variables.

In most PCA-based methods, none of solutions sampled from the reduced space needs to be operated in the original space. However, in the proposed design, the solutions must be transformed back to the original space for fitness evaluation. After the new offspring is projected back to its original space, it can participate in environmental selection.

The contribution should contain no more than four levels of headings. Table 1 gives a summary of all heading levels.

3.3   Building the Probability Model

The probabilistic model used in this paper for model learning is the Gaussian Bayesian network (GBN). A search+score strategy is used in GBNEDA-DR to learn the GBN from the data. In this strategy, a search algorithm is employed to explore the space of possible GBN structures to find a structure that closely matches the data. The quality of different GBN structures obtained in this search process is measured using a scoring metric, usually computed from data. A greedy local search algorithm is used to learn the structure of GBN. The algorithm finally returns the highest scoring network in all these subsearches. The Bayesian information criterion (BIC) [17] is used to score possible GBN structures.

The parameters of this type of GBN are computed from the mean vector and covariance matrix of the Gaussian distribution (GD) estimated for the joint vector of variables and objectives:$N(\hat{\mu}_{\langle 1,n+m \rangle}, \hat{\Sigma}_{\langle n+m,n+m \rangle})$. Usually the maximum likelihood (ML) estimation is used to estimate the parameters of GD (the mean vector and covariance matrix) from the data.

3.4   Repairing Cross-Border Values

After the new offspring is projected back to its original space, values in some dimensions are illegal. Repairing methods are commonly used to guarantee the feasibility of solutions. They modify (repair) a given individual to guarantee that the constraints are satisfied. In GBNEDA-DR the repairing procedure is invoked at every generation. In this paper, there are two methods to fix illegal values. The first method changes the values of each out of range variable to the minimum (respectively maximum) bounds if variables are under (respectively over) the variables ranges. The second method truncates the values of each out of range variable to a random value within the feasible range. Each method is triggered in a random way.

3.5   Environmental Selection

The purpose of environmental selection is for maintaining a size of population with the same number of initialized population. Figure 1 shows an example of the structure of an GBN. The set of arcs in the structure is partitioned into three subsets. The red arc represents the dependency of decision variables, the blue arc represents the dependency of objective variables, and the black arc represents the dependency between the decision variables and the objective variables. An analysis of the structures learnt by GBNEDA-DR along the evolution path show that the proposed algorithm is able to distinguish between relevant and irrelevant variables. It can also capture stronger dependencies between similar objectives. The dependencies learnt between objectives in the MOP structure can be used to analyze relationships like conflict or redundancy between sets of objectives.

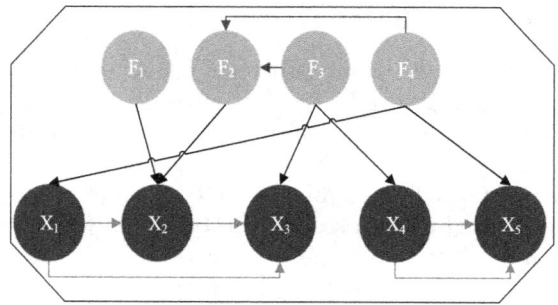

Fig. 1. An example of a Gaussian Bayesian network structure

With an increase of objective, almost the entire population acquires the same-rank of non-domination. This makes the Pareto-dominance based primary selection ineffective. Objective reduction approaches can solve this problem very well. In this paper, with the help of GBN, GBNEDA-DR can remove redundant objectives and make effective use of non-dominated sorting. In other words, if a class node in the GBN has no parent, it is not redundant, whereas if a class node (i.e. a objective) has a parent, it does not participate in the comparison in the non-dominant sort. For example, there are no arrows pointing at f1, f3 and f4 in Fig. 1. But there are arrows pointing at f2, therefore, f2 is redundant and can be ignored in non-dominant sort. The framework of the environmental selection in GBNEDA-DR is similar to that of VaEA [20]. This method performs a careful elitist preservation strategy and maintains diversity among solutions by putting more emphasis on solutions that have the maximum vector angle to individuals which have already survived (more details can be found in [20]).

4   Experiments

Since the proposed GBNEDA-DR is an EDA-based algorithm for solving large-scale MaOPs, we verify the performance of GBNEDA-DR by empirically comparing it with four state-of-the-art MOEAs covering two categories: 1) traditional MOEAs (MOEA/DVA [13] and NSGA-III [6]) and 2) EDA-based evolutionary algorithm (RM-MEDA [21] and MBN-EDA [9]). In the following sections, the selected benchmark test problems are introduced first. Then, the performance indicators and parameter settings are introduced and declared respectively. Finally, experiments on compared algorithms are performed and their results measured by the selected performance indicators are analyzed.

4.1   Test Problems and Performance Metrics

The experiments are conducted on 14 test problems taken from two widely used test suites, DTLZ and LSMOP. The DTLZ test suite is a class of widely used benchmark problems for testing the performance of MOEAs. The first four test problems are DTZL1-DTLZ4 taken from the DTLZ test suite. DTLZ test problems are considered less challengeable. LSMOP is a recently developed test suite for large-scale multiobjective and many-objective optimization. It can better reflect the challenges in large-scale MaOPs than existing test suits. Hence, the LSMOP1-LSMOP5 problems from the LSMOP test suit are included into the considered benchmark test problems.

One widely used performance metric, inverted generational distance (IGD) [3], which can simultaneously quantify the performance in convergence and diversity of the algorithms, is adopted in these experiments. The definition of the IGD from P^* (a set of uniformly distributed points in the objective space along the PF) to P (an approximation to the PF) is illustrated as follow,

$$IGD(P^*, P) = \frac{\sum_{v \in P^*} d(v, P)}{|P^*|} \tag{6}$$

where $d(v, P)$ represents the minimum Euclidean distance between v and the points in P.

4.2   Parameter Settings

In order to show the best effect of all algorithms, all compared algorithms adopt the recommended parameter values to achieve the best performance. To be specific, the parameter settings for all conducted experiments are as follows.

1) Crossover and Mutation: SBX [1] and polynomial mutations [5] are employed by traditional MaOEAs as the crossover operator and mutation operator, respectively. The crossover probability and mutation probability are set to P_c = 1.0 and $P_m = 1/D$, respectively, where D denotes the number of decision variables. In addition, the distribution index of NSGA-III is set to be 30 according to the suggestions in [6] while others are set to be 20.
2) Population Sizing: The population size of NSGA-III cannot be arbitrarily specified, which is equal to the number of reference vectors, other peer algorithms adopt the same population size for a fair comparison. Furthermore, the two-layer reference vector generation strategy is adopted here. The settings for reference vector and population size are listed in Table 1. $H1$ and $H2$ are the simplex-lattice design factors for generating uniformly distributed reference vectors on the outer boundaries and the inside layers, respectively.
3) Other Settings: The number of evaluations is used as the termination criterion for all considered algorithms. The maximum number of function evaluations is set to 100 000 in all experiments. On each test instance, 10 independent runs are performed for each algorithm to obtain statistical results. For MOEA/DVA, the number of interaction analysis and the number of control

property analysis are set to the recommended values, namely, $NIA = 6$ and $NCA = 50$. For RM-MEDA, the number of clusters in local PCA varies in [31 50 50].

Table 1. Settings for reference vectors and population size.

M	# of division		# of reference vectors	Population size
	H1	H2		
3	14	0	120	120
5	5	0	126	128
8	3	2	156	156
10	4	2	265	265

Table 2. Mean and standard deviation results of IGD obtained on DTLZ1-5 (Dimension of decision space is 100).

Problem	DTLZ1		DTLZ2		DTLZ3		DTLZ4	
Obj.	3	5	3	5	3	5	3	5
RM-MEDA	2.69e+1	2.21e+1	**2.43e-1**	4.62e+0	3.20e+3	3.12e+3	4.64e-1	3.38e+0
	(2.18e-1)	(5.97e-1)	**(1.80e-2)**	(5.76e-1)	(7.26e+1)	(2.48e+2)	(5.97e-2)	(2.45e-1)
MBN-EDA	5.10e+1	**1.58e+1**	2.47e-1	3.02e+0	**2.39e+2**	6.52e+3	**2.62e-1**	1.42e+0
	(1.88e-2)	**(4.20e-2)**	(2.05e-3)	(1.63e+0)	**(5.03e+1)**	(7.36e+2)	**(4.48e-4)**	(1.37e-1)
GBNEDA-DR	**2.17e+1**	3.82e+1	5.67e-1	**7.58e-1**	6.62e+3	**1.24e+3**	9.70e-1	**1.14e+0**
	(1.23+0)	(1.02e-2)	(1.17e-2)	**(9.80e-3)**	(9.13e+2)	**(1.18e+3)**	(7.14e-3)	**(3.54e-3)**

4.3 Results

Tables 2 present the results of the IGD metric values of the three compared algorithms on the five DTLZ test problems with 100 decision variables. As can be seen from the tables, the IGD values obtained by GBNEDA-DR on each test problem are consistently good as the number of objectives increases from 3 to 5, which confirms a promising scalability of GBNEDA-DR. The results on the eight LSMOP test problems with 1000 decision variables are given in Table 3, with both the mean and standard deviation of the IGD values averaged over 10 independent runs being listed for the five compared MOEAs, where the best mean among the five compared algorithms is highlighted. It is clearly shown in Table 3 that when the number of decision variables is increased, the proposed algorithm obtains all the best mean IGD results against its competitors over LSMOP1 and LSMOP4 with 5-, and 10-objective. In summary, the dimension reduction technique can significantly improve the performance of the proposed algorithm especially in solving large scale MaOPs.

Table 3. Mean and standard deviation results of IGD obtained on LSMOP1-8 (Dimension of decision space is 1000).

Problem	Obj.	NSGA-III	MOEA/DVA	RM-MEDA	MBN-EDA	GBNEDA-DR
LSMOP1	5	7.5893e+0 (2.64e-1)	9.9607e+0 (3.66e-1)	1.0004e+1 (3.07e-1)	9.9980e+0 (7.19e-1)	**4.1242e+0 (1.04e+0)**
	10	8.9901e+0 (2.33e-1)	9.6706e+0 (6.75e-1)	9.4195e+0 (1.74e-1)	9.0837e+0 (1.59e+0)	**7.3057e+0 (1.60e-1)**
LSMOP2	5	**8.9592e-2 (1.97e-5)**	1.2071e-1 (7.29e-3)	1.1071e-1 (1.98e-4)	1.0065e-1 (1.08e-3)	1.0832e-1 (1.35e-3)
	10	3.6174e-1 (1.37e-2)	3.8925e-1 (3.90e-4)	2.8695e-1 (2.29e-3)	2.5539e-1 (9.35e-3)	**2.0060e-1 (4.26e-4)**
LSMOP3	5	**1.4664e+1 (1.05e-1)**	7.2671e+1 (4.77e+1)	1.8609e+1 (1.35e-1)	2.0636e+1 (2.26e-1)	2.1846e+1 (6.18e-1)
	10	2.8425e+1 (1.95e+0)	1.3015e+3 (9.78e+2)	**2.4350e+1 (4.12e+0)**	2.4913e+1 (5.76e+0)	1.8471e+2 (1.04e+1)
LSMOP4	5	1.7878e-1 (1.31e-3)	1.9876e-1 (1.47e-4)	2.0692e-1 (2.99e-3)	1.9606e-1 (8.35e-5)	**1.6982e-1 (3.67e-4)**
	10	3.6897e-1 (7.09e-3)	3.8537e-1 (9.83e-3)	3.0729e-1 (2.11e-3)	2.9669e-1 (9.93e-3)	**2.3592e-1 (4.51e-4)**
LSMOP5	5	1.2234e+1 (1.75e-1)	8.7623e+1 (5.02e+0)	**6.4356e+0 (2.82e+0)**	9.5447e+0 (5.39e-2)	1.4250e+1 (3.61e-1)
	10	1.5426e+1 (9.83e-1)	4.8658e+1 (4.81e+1)	2.1896e+1 (2.10e-1)	1.8065e+1 (5.37e-1)	**7.3963e+0 (3.31e-1)**

From these results, we can see that GBNEDA-DR outperforms MOEA/DVA, RM-MEDA, MBN-EDA, and NSGA-III on DTLZ and LSMOP test problems in terms of IGD, especially for problems with more than 100 decision variables. Therefore, we can conclude that the proposed GBNEDA-DR is effective to handle large-scale MaOPs.

5   Conclusion

In this paper, we have proposed a Gaussian Bayesian network-based EDA, termed GBNEDA-DR, for solving large-scale MaOPs. GBNEDA-DR, the proposed algorithm, models a promising area in the search space by a probability model, which is used to generate new solutions. This model can capture the relationships between variables like other EDAs. It must be pointed out that the variables here are those in the low-dimensional space after dimensionality reduction. Because dimension reduction technique (i.e. LPP) is utilized to reduce the cost of exploitation and exploration. Through experimental evaluation we showed significant improvements of the performance on various benchmark problems compared to classical optimization methods as well as existing large scale approaches.

This paper demonstrates that the idea of using EDA to generates new solutions for large-scale MaOPs is very promising. In our future research, we would also like to further improve the computational efficiency of the dimension reduction procedure, which is the main computational cost of the proposed GBNEDA-DR.

References

1. Agrawal, R., Deb, K., Agrawal, R.: Simulated binary crossover for continuous search space. Complex Syst. **9**(2), 115–148 (2000)
2. Antonio, L.M., Coello, C.A.C.: Use of cooperative coevolution for solving large scale multiobjective optimization problems. In: 2013 IEEE Congress on Evolutionary Computation, pp. 2758–2765, June 2013
3. Bosman, P.A.N., Thierens, D.: The balance between proximity and diversity in multiobjective evolutionary algorithms. IEEE Trans. Evol. Comput. **7**(2), 174–188 (2003)
4. Deb, K., Sinha, A., Kukkonen, S.: Multi-objective test problems, linkages, and evolutionary methodologies. In: Proceeding of Genetic and Evolutionary Computation Conference, vol. 2, pp. 1141–1148, January 2006
5. Deb, K., Goyal, M.: A combined genetic adaptive search (GeneAS) for engineering design. Comput. Sci. Inf. **26** (1999)
6. Deb, K., Jain, H.: An evolutionary many-objective optimization algorithm using reference-point-based nondominated sorting approach, part I: solving problems with box constraints. IEEE Trans. Evol. Comput. **18**(4), 577–601 (2014)
7. Geiger, D., Heckerman, D.: Learning Gaussian networks. In: Proceedings of the Tenth International Conference on Uncertainty in Artificial Intelligence (UAI-1994), February 2013
8. He, X., Niyogi, P.: Locality preserving projections (LPP). IEEE Trans. Reliab. TR **16** (2002)
9. Karshenas, H., Santana, R., Bielza, C., Larrañaga, P.: Multiobjective estimation of distribution algorithm based on joint modeling of objectives and variables. IEEE Trans. Evol. Comput. **18**(4), 519–542 (2014). https://doi.org/10.1109/TEVC.2013.2281524
10. Khan, N., Goldberg, D., Pelikan, M.: Multiple-objective Bayesian optimization algorithm, p. 684, January 2002
11. Lianbo, M., Cheng, S., Shi, Y.: Enhancing learning efficiency of brain storm optimization via orthogonal learning design. IEEE Trans. Syst. Man Cybern. Syst., 1–20 (2020). https://doi.org/10.1109/TSMC.2020.2963943
12. Ma, L., et al.: A novel many-objective evolutionary algorithm based on transfer matrix with Kriging model. Inf. Sci. **509**, 437–456 (2020)
13. Ma, X., et al.: A multiobjective evolutionary algorithm based on decision variable analyses for multiobjective optimization problems with large-scale variables. IEEE Trans. Evol. Comput. **20**(2), 275–298 (2016)
14. Mahdavi, S., Shiri, M.E., Rahnamayan, S.: Metaheuristics in large-scale global continues optimization: a survey. Inf. Sci. **295**, 407–428 (2015)
15. Pearl, J.: Bayesian networks: a model of self-activated memory for evidential reasoning. In: Proceedings of the 7th Conference of the Cognitive Science Society (1985)
16. Pelikan, M., Sastry, K., Goldberg, D.: Multiobjective hBOA, clustering, and scalability. In: GECCO 2005 - Genetic and Evolutionary Computation Conference, March 2005

17. Schwarz, G.: Estimating the dimension of a model. Ann. Stat. **6**, 461–464 (1978)
18. Song, A., Yang, Q., Chen, W., Zhang, J.: A random-based dynamic grouping strategy for large scale multi-objective optimization. In: 2016 IEEE Congress on Evolutionary Computation (CEC), pp. 468–475, July 2016. https://doi.org/10.1109/CEC.2016.7743831
19. Tang, K., Li, X., Suganthan, P., Yang, Z., Weise, T.: Benchmark functions for the CEC 2008 special session and competition on large scale global optimization, December 2009
20. Xiang, Y., Zhou, Y., Li, M., Chen, Z.: A vector angle-based evolutionary algorithm for unconstrained many-objective optimization. IEEE Trans. Evol. Comput. **21**(1), 131–152 (2017)
21. Zhang, Q., Zhou, A., Jin, Y.: RM-MEDA: a regularity model-based multiobjective estimation of distribution algorithm. IEEE Trans. Evol. Comput. **12**(1), 41–63 (2008). https://doi.org/10.1109/TEVC.2007.894202
22. Zhang, Q., Hui, L.: MOEA/D: a multiobjective evolutionary algorithm based on decomposition. IEEE Trans. Evol. Comput. **11**(6), 712–731 (2008)
23. Zhang, X., Tian, Y., Cheng, R., Jin, Y.: A decision variable clustering-based evolutionary algorithm for large-scale many-objective optimization. IEEE Trans. Evol. Comput. **22**, 99 (2016)
24. Zhang, X., Tian, Y., Jin, Y.: A knee point driven evolutionary algorithm for many-objective optimization. IEEE Trans. Evol. Comput. **19**(6), 761–776 (2014)
25. Zille, H., Ishibuchi, H., Mostaghim, S., Nojima, Y.: A framework for large-scale multiobjective optimization based on problem transformation. IEEE Trans. Evol. Comput. (2017). https://doi.org/10.1109/TEVC.2017.2704782
26. Zitzler, E., Künzli, S.: Indicator-based selection in multiobjective search. In: Yao, X., et al. (eds.) PPSN 2004. LNCS, vol. 3242, pp. 832–842. Springer, Heidelberg (2004). https://doi.org/10.1007/978-3-540-30217-9_84

An Improved CMA-ES for Solving Large Scale Optimization Problem

Jin Jin$^{(\boxtimes)}$, Chuan Yang, and Yi Zhang

Chengdu Neusoft University, Chengdu 610844, China
jinjin@nsu.edu.cn

Abstract. In solving large scale optimization problems, CMA-ES has the disadvantages of high complexity and premature stagnation. To solve this problem, this paper proposes an improved CMA-ES, called GI-ES, for large-scale optimization problems. GI-ES uses all the historical information of the previous generation of individuals to evaluate the parameters of the distribution of the next generation. These estimates can be considered as approximate gradient information, which complete covariance information is not required. Thus GI-ES is friendly to large scale optimization problems. Comparative experiments have been done on state-of-the-art algorithms. The results proved the effectiveness and efficiency of GI-ES for large scale optimization problems.

Keywords: CMA-ES · Approximate gradients · Information utilization · Large scale optimization

1 Introduction

In the era of big data, large scale optimization has been applied more and more widely in many engineering and research fields. These optimization problems are difficult to obtain mathematical optimization models, such as simulation software, can be regarded as black box optimization problems. However, the stochastic global optimization method does not have high requirements on the characteristics of the optimization problem itself and does not depend on the specific problem. Therefore, it becomes a common method to solve optimization problems.

Among the stochastic global optimization methods, the most representative algorithm is evolutionary computation, which is a modern optimization algorithm [2]. Its main characteristics are parallelism and self-adaptability, self-learning habits and self-organization. Since 1960s when evolutionary computing was designed, it developed rapidly and formed many branches. These branches include genetic algorithm (GA)[8], evolutionary strategy (ES)[13], particle swarm optimization (PSO)[20], differential evolution algorithm (DE) [16], Covariance matrix adaptation evolutionary computation (CMA-ES) [6] and so on. These algorithms do not need the domain knowledge of the problem, only need to be able to calculate the fitness of the optimization target to be applied.

© Springer Nature Switzerland AG 2020
Y. Tan et al. (Eds.): ICSI 2020, LNCS 12145, pp. 386–396, 2020.
https://doi.org/10.1007/978-3-030-53956-6_34

But as the size of the problem increases, traditional evolutionary computation algorithms take hours or even days to find the optimal solution.

Covariance adaptive optimization algorithm is an optimization algorithm proposed in recent years [5]. The adaptive evolutionary strategy of covariance matrix can automatically adjust the standard deviation according to the distribution of the population. In addition, because CMA-ES can use the information of the optimal solution to adjust its parameters at the same time. CMA-ES as one of the most popular gradient-free optimization algorithms, has become the choice of many researchers and practitioners.

Although it has many advantages, CMA-ES has high space and time complexity when dealing with large scale optimization problems. Another obvious disadvantage is CMA-ES assessed some of the best individuals. Although it can speed up convergence to some extent, this strategy discards most of the information. We all know that great people in life have certain qualities that we can learn from, but some people who fail also keep a record of "not doing" something. It is important for better calculation and evaluation of the next generation. These two limitations may prevent large scale optimization using CMA-ES.

This paper proposes an evolutionary strategy based on gradient information utilization (GI-ES), which extends the application of CMA-ES in the field of large scale optimization.

To summarise, this work make the following contributions.

- The calculation of covariance matrix is replaced by the expected fitting degree scoring strategy.
- The gradient information is simulated through all individual information, and the approximate gradient information is used to guide the search direction.
- The extensive experiments are conducted on basic test problems. Experiments results prove the effectiveness and efficiency of the proposed algorithm.

Organization. Following the introduction section. We first discuss the related work of the utilization of the information of evolutionary computation in Sect. 2. Section 3 describes the detailed implementations of GI-ES. Thereafter, the simulation results on the benchmark test suites are conducted to evaluate the effectiveness of the proposed approach in Sect. 4. Finally, Sect. 5 summarizes this paper.

2   Related Work

Almost all evolutionary strategy (ES) frameworks are similar, with the main step being 1) to generate a number of candidates as needed, which can be either fixed or dynamic; 2) update the candidate scheme according to certain rules, and use the history information of the objective function in the update process. In the first step, information can be obtained according to the candidate scheme. In the second step, according to the information obtained, the algorithm can discard and retain the candidate schemes.

Many algorithms [4,12] that use objective function guidance information show that the use of this information plays an important role in the improvement of the algorithm. [11] proposed the information utilization ratio (IUR) to evaluate the performance of the heuristic algorithm. The IUR can be used as a metric to reflect how finely and advanced an algorithm is designed.

The research on gradient information originates from the Policy gradient proposed by Williams [18], which uses the reinforcement learning as a means of ES. Literature [15] adopts Policy Exploring Policy Gradients extends the using of gradient information. More extensions of ES that modify the search distribution use natural gradient or non-Gaussian (such as longtail distribution) search distributions [17]. [10] uses gradients information of a network with respect to the weights to increases the ability of traditional ES. Guided evolutionary strategies [12] uses the surrogate gradient information which combine the first-order methods and the random search.

In this study, information about the approximate gradient is used to optimize original CMA-ES. Our algorithm is different from these because our method estimates the gradient information but does not use first-order information. Because it is relatively difficult to solve the first order information of large scale optimization problems. The algorithm does not require absolute accuracy of the gradient, which is friendly for large scale problems.

3   Proposed Approach

The proposed algorithm GI-ES adopts the basic framework of CMA-ES, but makes some improvements to CMA-ES. In the proposed scheme, keep all the information about each scheme in each generation, good or bad. In this way, with these gradient signal assessments, we can move the whole scheme in a better direction for the next generation. Since we need to evaluate the gradient, we can use the standard stochastic gradient descent algorithm (SGD) applied to deep learning [3].

3.1   GI-ES

The fitness score was optimized for each sampling scheme in GI-ES. If the expected results are good enough, the best-performing scheme in the sampling generation may perform better. Maximization of the expected fitness score of a sampling scheme is actually equivalent to maximization of the whole fitness score.

3.2   Search Gradient Adaptation

GI-ES adopts approximate gradient as the direction of search, so that the algorithm can adapt to the fitness terrain dependent on variables. This process generates a fitting degree evaluation by the expected fitting degree score and obtains the gradient signal by the maximum likelihood estimation. It differs from traditional evolutionary computation in that it represents this "population" as a parameterized distribution, when it actually updates the parameters of this distribution using a search gradient, which is calculated using fitness values.

In the above derivation, the distribution is expressed as $\pi(z, \theta)$. In the actual scheme, the most typical distribution has multivariate normal distribution, but the algorithm can still extend to other distributions.

Multinormal Distribution. Multivariate normal distribution is the most widely used distribution in evolutionary computation. The fisher information matrix of multiple normal distribution can be easily solved. For normal distribution, the parameter θ is (μ, Σ), where $\boldsymbol{\mu} \in \mathbb{R}^d$ is the center of the alternative solution, and $\Sigma \in \mathbb{R}^{d \times d}$ is the covariance matrix. To sample more efficiently, you need a matrix $A \in \mathbb{R}^{d \times d}$, meet $\mathbf{A}^\top \mathbf{A} = \boldsymbol{\Sigma}$, then $\mathbf{z} = \boldsymbol{\mu} + \mathbf{A}^\top$ can transfer the standard normal distribution $\mathbf{s} \sim \mathcal{N}(0, \mathbb{I})$ to $\mathbf{z} \sim \mathcal{N}(\boldsymbol{\mu}, \boldsymbol{\Sigma})$. $\mathbb{I} = \mathrm{diag}(1, \ldots, 1) \in \mathbb{R}^{d \times d}$ denotes the identity matrix. $\pi(\mathbf{z}|\theta)$ represents the probability density function of the multinormal distribution.

$$
\begin{aligned}
\pi(\mathbf{z}|\theta) &= \frac{1}{(\sqrt{2\pi})^d |\det(\mathbf{A})|} \cdot \exp\left(-\frac{1}{2} \left\| \mathbf{A}^{-1} \cdot (\mathbf{z} - \boldsymbol{\mu}) \right\|^2 \right) \\
&= \frac{1}{\sqrt{(2\pi)^d \det(\boldsymbol{\Sigma})}} \cdot \exp\left(-\frac{1}{2}(\mathbf{z} - \boldsymbol{\mu})^\top \boldsymbol{\Sigma}^{-1}(\mathbf{z} - \boldsymbol{\mu})\right)
\end{aligned}
\tag{1}
$$

In order to calculate the gradient information of the multivariate gaussian variable, the logarithm of the probability density is obtained, so that the gradient can be estimated by summation:

$$
\log \pi(\mathbf{z}|\theta) = -\frac{d}{2} \log(2\pi) - \frac{1}{2} \log \det \boldsymbol{\Sigma} - \frac{1}{2}(\mathbf{z} - \boldsymbol{\mu})^\top \boldsymbol{\Sigma}^{-1}(\mathbf{z} - \boldsymbol{\mu})
\tag{2}
$$

So $\nabla_\mu \log \pi(\mathbf{z}|\theta)$ and $\nabla_\Sigma \log \pi(\mathbf{z}|\theta)$ can be obtained. Then update the parameters with the calculated gradient information.

$$
\theta \leftarrow \theta + \eta \nabla_\theta J
\tag{3}
$$

The algorithm can dynamically change the shape as needed to continue exploring or adjusting the solution space.

The Technique of GI-ES. Further, A can be decomposed into a scale parameter σ, and a normalized covariance factor B satisfying $det(B) = 1$. This decoupling form of two orthogonal components can be independently learned.

The advantage of overall information utilization is to prevent information loss, but outliers still need to be considered. In this method, according to the fitness value, the population individuals are ranked according to the fitness from small to large. Calculate the utility value according to the fitness value $u_1 \geq \cdots \geq u_{\lambda-2}$. Here, to reduce the impact of outliers on the performance of the algorithm. Get rid of the best and the worst.

$$u_i = \frac{u_i}{u_1 - u_{\lambda-2}} \tag{4}$$

The complexity of each covariance matrix update is $O(d^3)$. The complexity can be reduced to $O(d^2)$ by calculating the update of local non-exponential coordinates. In this case, the update of gradient information can be decomposed into the following components,

$$\nabla_\mathbf{M} J \leftarrow \sum_{k=1}^{\lambda-2} u_k \cdot \left(\mathbf{s}_k \mathbf{s}_k^\top - \mathbb{I}\right) \tag{5}$$

$$\nabla_\sigma J \leftarrow \mathrm{tr}\left(\nabla_\mathbf{M} J\right)/d \tag{6}$$

$$\nabla_\mathbf{B} J \leftarrow \nabla_\mathbf{M} J - \nabla_\sigma J \cdot \mathbb{I} \tag{7}$$

The Implementation of GI-ES. In this section, we summarize the pseudo-code of the proposed algorithm in Algorithm 1.

Algorithm 1: The pseudo-code of GI-ES

Require: $f(x)$: objective funtion; μ_{init}: initial μ; $\Sigma_{init} = \mathbf{A}^\top \mathbf{A}$;
Ensure: optimal x^*
Initial $\sigma \leftarrow \sqrt[d]{|\det(\mathbf{A})|}$ and $\mathbf{B} \leftarrow \mathbf{A}/\sigma$;
while *Iter* $\leq$ *MaxFE* **do**
  while $k = 1 \ldots \lambda$ **do**
    draw sample $\mathbf{s}_k \sim \mathcal{N}(0, \mathbb{I})$;
    $\mathbf{z}_k \leftarrow \mu + \sigma \mathbf{B}^\top \mathbf{s}_k$;
    evaluate the fitness value
  end
  sort the sampling particles according to the fitness value and compute utilities function u_k according to (4)
  compute gradients according to (5)-(7)
end

---

4   Experiments and Analysis

In this section, GI-ES is used to compare with the state-of-the-art algorithms to verify the effectiveness of the proposed algorithm.

4.1 Experiment and Settings

Parameter Setting. All parameters used in GI-ES are as follows,

$\lambda = 4 + \lfloor 3 \log(d) \rfloor$,

$\eta_\mu = \lfloor \frac{\lambda}{2} \rfloor$,

$\eta_\sigma = \eta_B = \frac{(9 + 3 \log(d))}{5 d \sqrt{d}}$,

$\eta_\delta = \frac{(3 + \log(d))}{5 \sqrt{d}}$.

Most of the parameters are recommended in [6].

In the algorithm, the number of population and the learning rate of gradient information are the parameters that need to be specified artificially.

Benchmark Function. Basic test problems. The test suite contains 11 classical problems that are widely used in evolutionary algorithms. As shown in Table 1 Sphere function is the simplest test function, which is used to test the basic performance of the algorithm. Ellipsoid Rosenbrock, and Cigar is a test of complex functions, used to test the function in the ill-conditioning, nonlinear scaling and flat region on the issue of test performance. Rotated function is through the rotating test function, matrix as references [14]. Persuasive in order to make the experiment. Each function is executed 21 times independently to record statistics. The end condition is the maximum number of iterations, MAXFE=10E08.

Table 1. Test problems

Set 1: Basic Test Problems	
Name	Functions
Sphere	$f_{\text{Sphere}}(\boldsymbol{x}) = \sum_{i=1}^{n} x_i^2$
Ellipsoid	$f_{\text{Elli}}(\boldsymbol{x}) = \sum_{i=1}^{n} 10^6 \frac{i-1}{n-1} x_i^2$
Rastrigin	$f_{\text{Ras}}(\boldsymbol{x}) = 10n + \sum_{i=1}^{n} (x_i^2 - 10 cos(2\pi x_i))$
Cigar	$f_{\text{Cigar}}(\boldsymbol{x}) = x_1^2 + 10^6 \sum_{i=2}^{n} x_i^2$
Rotated Ellipsoid	$f_{\text{RotElli}}(\boldsymbol{x}) = f_{\text{Elli}}(\boldsymbol{Rx})$
Rotated Cigar	$f_{\text{RotCigar}}(\boldsymbol{x}) = f_{\text{Cigar}}(\boldsymbol{Rx})$

* $\boldsymbol{R}$ is a rotation matrix by Gram-Schnidt orthogonalization

Algorithms for Comparison. CMA-ES and 2 algorithm variants for solving large scale optimization, including search direction adaptation evolution strategy(SDA-ES)[7]. Some other algorithms are not derived from CMA-ES, but are the state-of-the-art ones. For example, CC-based differential evolution (DECC-G) [19], the multiple offspring sampling(MOS)[9].

Effectiveness of the Gradient Information. The adaptation of the mutation strength is crucial for evolutionary calculation. It determines the direction of the next generation population and the convergence characteristics of the algorithm [1]. Before testing the overall performance of the GI-ES, we first investigate the effectiveness of gradient information. In the basic test section, the test algorithms we used were SDA-ES, MOS, DECC-G. The parameters of these algorithms are given in the original literature.

The 1000-dimensional sphere function f_{sphere} and Rastrigin function $f_{rastrigin}$ are used to test the effectiveness of gradient information. Sphere function is a spherical function, and many algorithms can be solved quickly, but the convergence performance of the algorithm is different. Rastrigin function is a relatively complex function with only one optimal solution, but there are many local optimizations in the fitness landscape of the function. In this part, we analyze the validity of gradient information by running GI-ES and ES-based algorithms.

To avoid the sensitivity of the algorithm to the origin, the test function is operated in the experimental design and shifted by 10. Units away from the origin. As can be seen from Fig. 1, DECC-G converge faster in the initial stage, because the DECC-G adopts the group-based problem decomposition strategy for searching. However the time required to reach the optimal solution is longer than GI-ES. As can be seen from Fig. 1(a), in the subsequent convergence curve, GI-ES showed better convergence characteristics. For large scale optimization problems, the solution complexity is high and the computation is large. The Sphere function test shows that the use of historical information by GI-ES is useful for solving large scale optimization problems.

The rastrigin function is a very complex function. There are many local optimal solutions with disturbing properties in the adaptive terrain. As can be seen from Fig. 1(b), DECC-G converges faster in the early convergence process, and other algorithms gradually fall into local optimal solution as the convergence process proceeds. And GI-ES has a very good ability to jump out of the local optimal solution.

In sphere and rastrigin function tests, GI-ES was superior to other algorithms. This shows that for the application of single locally optimal objective function and multiple locally optimal objective functions, it is effective for GI-ES to use gradient information to determine the direction of the next generation of individuals in the iterative process.

Effectiveness of the GI-ES. In this part, to further verify the effectiveness of the proposed algorithm, the performance of the algorithm is tested on the 1000d basic test problems. In order to verify the invariance of the algorithm, some basic test functions are rotated. In general, the test of the rotation function can well illustrate the invariance of the algorithm. And the use of rotation functions is common in many mainstream test functions.

A visual representation of the convergence comparison of several algorithms is given in Fig. 2. In general, GI-ES is good for rotating and non-rotating functions.

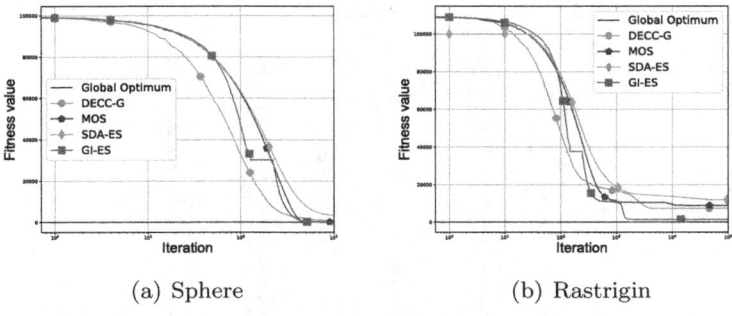

(a) Sphere   (b) Rastrigin

Fig. 1. Convergence plot on the 1000-d Sphere and Rastrigin function

Follows by DECC-G and MOS. On the Ellipsoid problem, GI-ES showed excellent performance in solving the rotation function. DECC-G shows sensitivity to the problem. DECC-G converges prematurely to the local optimal solution on the rotation function. However, GI-ES algorithm can jump out of local optimal solution in a short time after encountering local optimal solution, which benefits from the excellent ability of GI-ES algorithm to jump out of local optimal solution.

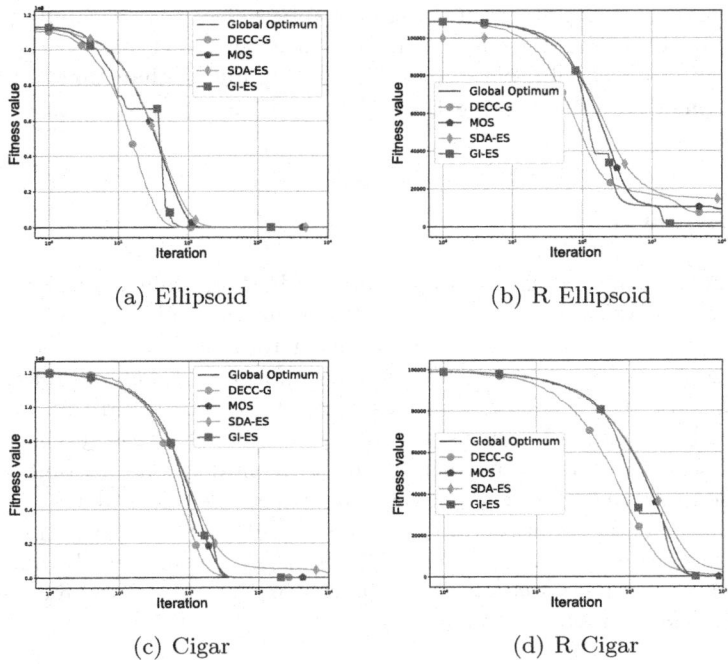

(a) Ellipsoid   (b) R Ellipsoid

(c) Cigar   (d) R Cigar

Fig. 2. Convergence plot on the 1000-d Ellipsoid and Cigar function

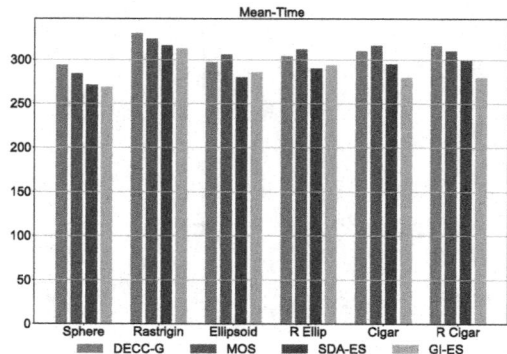

Fig. 3. Mean time consumed

Although the smooth of the cigar problem, it has a narrow ridge to be followed. And the overall shape deviates remarkably from being quadratic. DECC-G performs best for non-rotated cigar problem, but fails to GI-ES for rotated ones as shown in Fig. 2(c and d). In this case, the use of historical information can be a good guide for the algorithm to exploitation, so as to produce high-quality solutions.

The average running time of the algorithm is also a criterion that measures the performance of the algorithm. Figure 3 shows the average running time of the algorithm for each function. It can be seen from the figure that the average time of GI-ES on the Ellipsoid function is slightly higher than that of SDA-ES. For other functions, the average time of the GI-ES is less than that of other algorithms.

5   Conclusion

This research introduced the use of guiding gradient information to improve the performance of CMA-ES. The problem of low utilization of historical information by ES was solved by guiding the information to generate the distribution of the next generation solution. The guidance information was obtained by the approximation of the gradient. This strategy not only increased the diversity of knowledge, but also made full use of the optimal information in the heuristic algorithm. The theoretical analysis and experimental results showed that this method incorporating guidance information is accurate and stable.

The experimental results showed that the use of guiding information is effective. The algorithm was also compared with other typical meta-heuristic algorithms and demonstrated good average performance and pair-wise comparison performance across a wide range of test functions.

The experiments showed that this algorithm is an effective global optimization method for large scale problems, which makes it applicable to a large number of practical applications. The principle of using guidance information is simple, but effective, and has certain guiding significance for heuristic optimization algorithms.

References

1. Beyer, H.G., Hellwig, M.: The dynamics of cumulative step size adaptation on the ellipsoid model. Evol. Comput. **24**(1), 25–57 (2016)
2. Beyer, H.G., Schwefel, H.P.: Evolution strategies - a comprehensive introduction. Nat. Comput. **1**(1), 3–52 (2002). https://doi.org/10.1023/a:1015059928466
3. Bordes, A., Bottou, L., Gallinari, P.: SGD-QN: careful quasi-newton stochastic gradient descent. J. Mach. Learn. Res. **10**(Jul), 1737–1754 (2009)
4. Bringmann, K., Friedrich, T., Neumann, F., Wagner, M.: Approximation-guided evolutionary multi-objective optimization. In: Twenty-Second International Joint Conference on Artificial Intelligence (2011)
5. Hansen, N.: The CMA evolution strategy: a tutorial. arXiv preprint arXiv:1604.00772 (2016)
6. Hansen, N., Müller, S.D., Koumoutsakos, P.: Reducing the time complexity of the derandomized evolution strategy with covariance matrix adaptation (CMA-ES). Evol. Comput. **11**(1), 1–18 (2003)
7. He, X., Zhou, Y., Chen, Z., Zhang, J., Chen, W.N.: Large-scale evolution strategy based on search direction adaptation. IEEE Trans. Cybern., 1–15 (2019). https://doi.org/10.1109/tcyb.2019.2928563
8. Holland, J.H.: Genetic algorithms. Sci. Am. **267**(1), 66–73 (1992)
9. LaTorre, A., Muelas, S., Pena, J.M.: Multiple offspring sampling in large scale global optimization. In: 2012 IEEE Congress on Evolutionary Computation. IEEE, June 2012. https://doi.org/10.1109/cec.2012.6256611
10. Lehman, J., Chen, J., Clune, J., Stanley, K.O.: Safe mutations for deep and recurrent neural networks through output gradients. In: Proceedings of the Genetic and Evolutionary Computation Conference, pp. 117–124. ACM (2018)
11. Li, J., Tan, Y.: Information utilization ratio in heuristic optimization algorithms. arXiv preprint arXiv:1604.01643 (2016)
12. Maheswaranathan, N., Metz, L., Tucker, G., Sohl-Dickstein, J.: Guided evolutionary strategies: escaping the curse of dimensionality in random search. arXiv preprint arXiv:1806.10230 (2018)
13. Roubos, J., van Straten, G., van Boxtel, A.: An evolutionary strategy for fedbatch bioreactor optimization; concepts and performance. J. Biotechnol. **67**(2–3), 173–187 (1999). https://doi.org/10.1016/s0168-1656(98)00174-6
14. Salomon, R.: Evolutionary algorithms and gradient search: similarities and differences. IEEE Trans. Evol. Comput. **2**(2), 45–55 (1998). https://doi.org/10.1109/4235.728207
15. Sehnke, F., Osendorfer, C., Rückstieß, T., Graves, A., Peters, J., Schmidhuber, J.: Parameter-exploring policy gradients. Neural Netw. **23**(4), 551–559 (2010)
16. Storn, R., Price, K.: Differential evolution-a simple and efficient heuristic for global optimization over continuous spaces. J. Global Optim. **11**(4), 341–359 (1997). https://doi.org/10.1023/A:1008202821328

17. Wierstra, D., Schaul, T., Peters, J., Schmidhuber, J.: Natural evolution strategies. In: 2008 IEEE Congress on Evolutionary Computation (IEEE World Congress on Computational Intelligence). IEEE, June 2008. https://doi.org/10.1109/cec.2008. 4631255

18. Williams, R.J.: Simple statistical gradient-following algorithms for connectionist reinforcement learning. Mach. Learn. **8**(3–4), 229–256 (1992). https://doi.org/10. 1007/bf00992696

19. Yang, Z., Tang, K., Yao, X.: Large scale evolutionary optimization using cooperative coevolution. Inf. Sci. **178**(15), 2985–2999 (2008). https://doi.org/10.1016/j. ins.2008.02.017

20. Zeugmann, T., et al.: Particle swarm optimization. In: Sammut, C., Webb, G.I. (eds.) Encyclopedia of Machine Learning, pp. 760–766. Springer, Heidelberg (2011). https://doi.org/10.1007/978-0-387-30164-8_630

Archive Update Strategy Influences Differential Evolution Performance

Vladimir Stanovov[(⊠)], Shakhnaz Akhmedova, and Eugene Semenkin

Reshetnev Siberian State University of Science and Technology, "Krasnoyarskiy Rabochiy" av.
31, 660037 Krasnoyarsk, Russia
vladimirstanovov@yandex.ru, shahnaz@inbox.ru,
eugenesemenkin@yandex.ru

Abstract. In this paper the effects of archive set update strategies on differential evolution algorithm performance are studied. The archive set is generated from inferior solutions, removed from the main population, as the search process proceeds. Next, the archived solutions participate in the search during mutation step, allowing better exploration properties to be achieved. The LSHADE-RSP algorithm is taken as baseline, and 4 new update rules are proposed, including replacing the worst solution, the first found worse solution, the tournament-selected solution and individually stored solution for every solution in the population. The experiments are performed on CEC 2020 single objective optimization benchmark functions. The results are compared using statistical tests. The comparison shows that changing the update strategy significantly improves the performance of LSHADE-RSP on high-dimensional problems. The deeper analysis of the reasons of efficiency improvement reveals that new archive update strategies lead to more successful usage of the archive set. The proposed algorithms and obtained results open new possibilities of archive usage in differential evolution.

Keywords: Differential Evolution · Optimization · Archive set · Mutation · CEC benchmark

1 Introduction

The heuristic optimization techniques, which include evolutionary computation and swarm intelligence algorithms, are receiving significant attention from the scientific community in recent decades, mainly due to their high efficiency and ability to solve a wide range of optimization problems [1]. Among single-objective optimization techniques, the Differential Evolution (DE) algorithms represent an interesting class of approaches, due to their high efficiency and relatively simple implementation. The DE was first introduced in a pioneering work [2], which started further research in this direction. A variety of new mutation strategies, parameter adaptation techniques and other improvements have been proposed [3], making the DE often the prize-winning algorithm in many scenarios. Despite the fact that the No Free Lunch Theorem states [4] that no optimization algorithm could be considered as the best one, still there is a room for further improvement of DE algorithms, which could be important for practitioners.

© Springer Nature Switzerland AG 2020
Y. Tan et al. (Eds.): ICSI 2020, LNCS 12145, pp. 397–404, 2020.
https://doi.org/10.1007/978-3-030-53956-6_35

In this paper the effects of the archive set update strategies are studied in the LSHADE-RSP algorithm, originally proposed in [5]. The Success-History based Adaptive Differential Evolution (SHADE) [6] algorithm and those based on SHADE framework use an external archive of inferior solutions to improve the exploration properties of DE by using these stored solutions during the search. As shown in [7], the algorithms based on SHADE represent one of the most efficient DE variants. Still, these algorithms rely on random update of the archive set, where a randomly selected individual is replaced if the archive size is exceeded. This study proposes 4 new archive update strategies, which replace individuals in the archive based on fitness values, and shows that most of them are capable of improving the algorithm efficiency significantly. The experiments are performed in accordance with the CEC 2020 Competition on Single-Objective Numerical Optimization setup, which, unlike previous competitions, is focused on identifying the algorithms, capable of using large computational resource efficiently. The experimental results compare all proposed archive update strategies and show their effect on overall performance and archive successful usage rates.

The rest of the paper is organized as follows: Sect. 2 describes the basics of DE and LSHADE-RSP algorithm, Sect. 3 proposes the new archive update rules, Sect. 4 contains experimental setup and results, and Sect. 5 concludes the paper.

2   Differential Evolution and SHADE Framework

The DE is a population-based evolutionary algorithm, proposed for numerical optimization. The main idea of DE is to use the scaled difference vectors between the members of the population to produce new solutions. DE starts by randomly initializing a set of NP solutions $x_{i,j}$, $i = 1, ..., NP, j = 1, ..., D$, inside the given boundaries $[xmin_j, xmax_j]$, where D is the problem dimension. The original DE uses the *rand*/1 mutation strategy; however, nowadays the *current-to-pbest*/1 strategy is the most widely used. It was originally proposed in the JADE algorithm [8], and further applied in SHADE framework [6]. This strategy generates mutant vector v_i using scaling factor $F \subset [0,1]$ as follows:

$$v_{i,j} = F\left(x_{pbest,j} - x_{i,j}\right) + F\left(x_{r1,j} - x_{r2,j}\right), \tag{1}$$

where *pbest* is the randomly selected index from $pb*100\%$ best individuals, $r1$ is randomly selected from the population, and $r2$ is selected from either the population or the archive set. All indexes $i, pb, r1$ and $r2$ are mutually different from each other. After the mutation, the crossover is performed with probability $Cr \subset [0,1]$ as follows:

$$u_{i,j} = \begin{cases} v_{i,j} \ if \ rand(0, 1) < Cr \ or \ j = jrand \\ x_{i,j} \ otherwise \end{cases}, \tag{2}$$

where *jrand* is the randomly selected index from $[1, D]$, required to make sure that at least one coordinate is inherited from the mutant vector. After the crossover, the bound constraint handling method is applied, so that all vectors u_i would be inside the boundaries. For example, the parent's position could be used as follows:

$$u_{i,j} = \begin{cases} \frac{xmin_j + x_{i,j}}{2} \ if u_{i,j} < xmin_j \\ \frac{xmax_j + x_{i,j}}{2} \ if u_{i,j} > xmax_j \end{cases}. \tag{3}$$

After this the fitness values of trial vectors $f(u_i)$ are estimated, and the selection step is performed as follows:

$$x_{i,j}^{G+1} = \begin{cases} u_{i,j}^{G} \; if \, f\left(u_{i,j}^{G}\right) \le f\left(x_{i,j}^{G}\right) \\ x_{i,j}^{G} \; otherwise \end{cases}, \tag{4}$$

where G is the current generation number. The application of the DE mutation leads to the situation when the fitness of the population either improves or stays the same during the search.

The L-SHADE algorithm, proposed in [9], follows the ideas of JADE, and improves them by introducing the Success-History parameter adaptation with several memory cells containing pairs of successful parameter values, and the Linear Population Size Reduction (LPSR), aimed at improving the convergence properties of the algorithm closer to the end of the search. More details on SHA and LPSR could be found in [9].

In the LSHADE-RSP algorithm, proposed in [5], the usage of Rank-based Selective Pressure (RSP) is proposed. In this method, the indexes $r1$ and $r2$ in (1) have non-equal probabilities to be chosen from the population, but depend on the fitness values. Each individual receives rank value $rank_i = i$, and the probabilities p_i are calculated as follows:

$$p_i = \frac{rank_i}{\sum_{j=1}^{NP} rank_j}. \tag{5}$$

Other methods of probabilities assignment and their effect were studied in [10].

The algorithm used in this study also relies on the parameter adaptation techniques, proposed in the jSO algorithm [11], and the Distance-based Success-History Adaptation [12], described in the mentioned papers.

The SHADE class of algorithm, as well as JADE, L-SHADE and LSHADE-RSP use the external archive of inferior solutions. The archive A is initially empty, and is filled with parents – individuals $x_{i,j}$, which were replaced by their corresponding trial vectors. If the archive set size $|A|$ is equal to the maximum size, usually set to current population size, $NA = NP$, then a randomly chosen individual is replaced. The archive update rules, proposed in this study, aim at changing this update procedure.

3 Archive Update Strategies

The original archive update rule has relatively obvious drawbacks: the archive is updated with no respect to the fitness values of the individual in the archive or the added individual. This may lead to the situation, when better solutions are replaced by worse ones, or the some useless solutions are kept in the archive for too long. To resolve this issue, four new update rules are proposed.

In the first method, the random index of an individual in the archive r is generated until a worse solution is found:

```
Set attempts counter C = 0
The individual to be added is xᵢ
```

```
do
  r = randInt(|A|)
  C = C + 1
while(f(A_r) < f(x_i) or C < |A|)
Replace A_r with x_i
```

This algorithm replaces only worse individuals in the archive, and the search for these solutions is random. It is possible that the worst individual will not be replaced, as the search time is limited.

In the second method the worst individual in the archive is found and replaced. Although this may seem like a straightforward strategy, it may result in filling the archive with a set of very similar solutions.

In the third method, the binary tournament selection is used to find the individual to be replaced:

```
Set rand1 = randInt(|A|)
Set rand2 = randInt(|A|)
If(f(A_rand1) < f(A_rand2))
  rand1 = rand2
Replace A_rand1 with x_i
```

This approach represents a softer version of the first method, where the search for a worst solution in the archive only considers two randomly selected archived solutions, and it does not consider $f(x_i)$.

The fourth method holds a separate position for every individual with index i in the population, so that the A_i is always replaced by corresponding x_i. This strategy is somewhat similar to those used in PSO algorithms, where the best found solutions are stored separately, but here A_i holds worse solutions then x_i.

All the described archive update strategies have different ideas behind them, and should be tested against the baseline approach with random replacement. These Archive Update Strategies will be further referred to as AUS_0 (baseline) – AUS_4. The experimental setup and results are presented in the next section.

4 Experimental Setup and Results

The experiments were performed in accordance with the CEC 2020 competition rules, presented in [13]. The benchmark contains 10 functions, defined for D = 5, 10, 15 and 20, the computational resource NFE_{max} is set to $5 \cdot 10^5$ for $5D$, 10^6 for $10D$, $3 \cdot 10^6$ for $15D$ and 10^7 for $20D$. Functions 6 and 7 are excluded from the competition for $5D$. The main announced goal of CEC 2020 is to find the approaches capable of using the large computational resource efficiently.

For every test function 30 independent runs were performed, and the best achieved goal function values were recorded after every $D^{0.25k-3}NFE_{max}$ function evaluations, k = 0, … ,15. The population size NP was set to $30D^{1.5}$. The archive size NA was equal to NP, and decreased with the population size. The algorithm was implemented in C++

with GCC and run on PC with Ubuntu 19.04, Intel Core i7 8700 k processor and 48 GB RAM, results post-processing was performed using Python 3.6.

To compare the performance of different algorithms, the Mann-Whitney statistical test with significance level p = 0.01, tie correction, and normal distribution approximation was used. Table 1 shows the comparison of the baseline approach to newly developed AUS for all dimensions.

Table 1. Comparison of different archive update strategies, Mann-Whitney test, AUT_0 as baseline.

D	AUS_1	AUS_2	AUS_3	AUS_4
5	0+/8=/0−	0+/8=/0−	0+/8=/0−	0+/8=/0−
10	0+/10=/0−	1+/9=/0−	0+/10=/0−	0+/10=/0−
15	2+/8=/0−	1+/9=/0−	1+/9=/0−	1+/9=/0−
20	2+/8=/0−	2+/8=/0−	2+/8=/0−	1+/9=/0−

In Table 1 the "+" sign means that there was a statistically significant improvement against AUS_0, "=" means that there is no statistically significant difference, and "−" means that the performance was smaller. It could be seen that for 5D there is no difference in performance with proposed AUS, however, for larger dimensions there is a positive effect. The AUS_1 (search for worse for |A| steps), unlike other strategies, was able to deliver 2 improvements for 15D, while other methods gave only one improvement. On the other hand, the AUS_2 (replacing worst) delivered 1 improvement for *10D*. The improvements were mainly made on functions 5, 9 and 10. F5 is a composition function made of Shwefel's, Rastrigin's and High Conditioned Elliptic Function, and F9 combines Ackley's, High Conditioned Elliptic Function, Griewank's and Rastrigin's functions.

Additionally, the ranking procedure, applied in the Friedman statistical test was used to compare the algorithms. For this purpose, all the results of 5 different AUS methods were joined and sorted and ranked for every function, and the ranks were summed and normalized. This procedure was performed for all dimensions separately, and smaller ranks were assigned to better results. Table 2 contains the comparison of results.

From Table 2 it could be seen that for *5D* the AUS_1 strategy shows the best results, however, for *10D*, *15D* and *20D*, the AUS_2 (replacing worst) is better.

It is important to mention, that for *5D*, *15D* and *20D* all four proposed archive update strategies are better than the baseline approach with random replacing.

To demonstrate the efficiency of the proposed archive update strategies, the Archive Successful Usage Ratio (ASUR) was calculated. The ASUR metric was defined as the number of times when the trial vector, generated with particular individual from the archive, was better than the parent; the success values were set to zero when an individual in the archive was replaced, and the ASUR value was divided by the current archive size for normalization. The ASUR metrics were averaged over 30 algorithm runs.

From Fig. 1 one may see that replacing worst individual in the archive (AUS_2) leads to many successful usages, as the search proceeds. Moreover, the stages of the

Table 2. Comparison of different archive update strategies, Friedman ranking.

D	AUS_0	AUS_1	AUS_2	AUS_3	AUS_4
5	9.8627	**8.82352**	9.60784	9.62745	9.13725
10	11.8627	11.5098	**10.7941**	12.1470	12.5098
15	12.7254	11.5000	**11.0686**	11.1960	12.3333
20	13.0490	11.8627	**10.8725**	11.2451	11.7941

search process are very well seen. Application of AUS_1 (search for worse) gives more improvements at the beginning of the search, and in the middle of the search process, a significant increase in ASUR metrics is observed. It is difficult to say what the reasons for such behavior are; however, one idea is that at this stage some of the previously visited areas, captured in the archive, appeared to be helpful for improving the search. Such peaks of ASUR metrics were observed for AUS_1 for other functions and dimensions, including F5, where significant performance improvement was observed. Another example of ASUR metrics change is presented in Fig. 2.

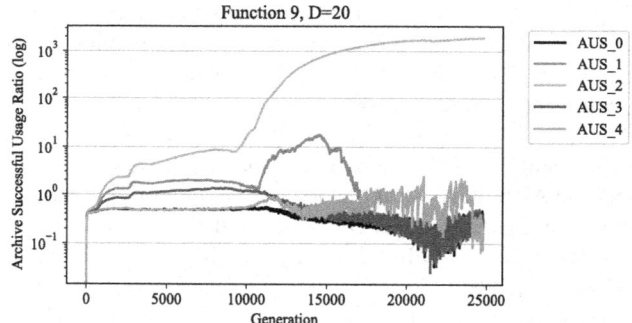

Fig. 1. Archive successful usage ratio for F9, 20D, all archive update strategies.

In Fig. 2 the change of archive successful usage ratio metrics change is shown for all five AUS methods. The difference from Fig. 1 is that here AUS_4 performs less similar to baseline method AUS_0 and relatively small modification AUS_3 (tournament-based replacement). Again, the AUS_1 method performs similarly to other methods at the beginning of the search, but further on there is a large increase in successful archive usage after 5000-th generation. Although the ASUR metrics provides important information about the archive usage dynamics, it does not consider the improvement value, so that the larger values for AUS_2 may simply mean that most of the archive set values is not replaced as often as in other archive update strategies.

The performed experiments and results post-processing show that archive update strategy significantly influences the DE performance, and should be further studied to improve the archive set usage efficiency.

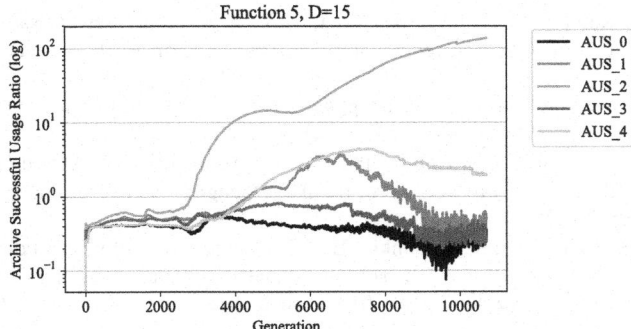

Fig. 2. Archive successful usage ratio for F5, 15D, all archive update strategies.

5 Conclusion

The archive set, used in many variants of Differential Evolution today, represent the memory of the algorithm about previous search. This memory could be successfully used during the search, so that the exploration properties of the algorithm could be improved. In this study several new archive handling techniques were proposed, in particular, the archive update strategies, and it was shown, that updating the archive by replacing the worst solution, or at least replacing the solution that is worse than current, gives significant performance improvement, and the archive set is used more efficiently. These modifications do not decrease the algorithm performance, but allow improvements on some functions. This proves that the archive handling techniques in DE should be further studied, as they represent an important part of the algorithm.

Acknowledgments. This work was supported by the Ministry of Science and Higher Education of the Russian Federation within limits of state contract № FEFE-2020-0013.

References

1. Del Ser, J., et al.: Bio-inspired computation: Where we stand and what's next. Swarm Evol. Comput. **48**, 220–250 (2019). https://doi.org/10.1016/j.swevo.2019.04.008
2. Storn, R., Price, K.: Differential evolution – a simple and efficient heuristic for global optimization over continuous spaces. J. Global Optim. **11**(4), 341–359 (1997). https://doi.org/10.1023/A:1008202821328
3. Das, S., Mullick, S.S., Suganthan, P.N.: Recent advances in differential evolution – an updated survey. Swarm Evol. Comput. **27**, 1–30 (2016)
4. Wolpert, D.H., Macready, W.G.: No free lunch theorems for optimization. IEEE Trans. Evol. Comput. **1**(1), 67–82 (1997)
5. Stanovov, V., Akhmedova, S., Semenkin, E.: LSHADE algorithm with rank-based selective pressure strategy for solving CEC 2017 benchmark problems. In: 2018 IEEE Congress on Evolutionary Computation (CEC), pp. 1–8 (2018). https://doi.org/10.1109/cec.2018.8477977
6. Tanabe, R., Fukunaga, A.: Success-history based parameter adaptation for differential evolution. In: Proceedings of the IEEE Congress on Evolutionary Computation, pp. 71–78 (2013)

7. Al-Dabbagh, R.D., Neri, F., Idris, N., Baba, M.S.: Algorithmic design issues in adaptive differential evolution schemes: review and taxonomy. Swarm Evol. Comput. **43**, 284–311 (2018)
8. Zhang, J., Sanderson, A.C.: JADE: adaptive differential evolution with optional external archive. IEEE Trans. Evol. Comput. **13**(5), 945–958 (2009)
9. Tanabe, R., Fukunaga, A.S.: Improving the search performance of SHADE using linear population size reduction. In: Proceedings of the IEEE Congress on Evolutionary Computation, pp. 1658–1665 (2014)
10. Stanovov, V., Akhmedova, S., Semenkin, E.: Selective pressure strategy in differential evolution: exploitation improvement in solving global optimization problems. Swarm Evol. Comput. **50** (2019). https://doi.org/10.1016/j.swevo.2018.10.014. ISSN 2210-6502
11. Brest, J., Maucec, M.S., Boskovic, B.: Single objective real-parameter optimization algorithm jSO. In: Proceedings of the IEEE Congress on Evolutionary Computation, pp. 1311–1318 (2017)
12. Viktorin, A., Senkerik, R., Pluhacek, M., Kadavy, T., Zamuda, A.: Distance based parameter adaptation for success-history based differential evolution. Swarm Evol. Comput. **50** (2019). https://doi.org/10.1016/j.swevo.2018.10.013
13. Yue, C.T., et al.: Problem definitions and evaluation criteria for the CEC 2020 special session and competition on single objective bound constrained numerical optimization. Technical report 201911, Computational Intelligence Laboratory, Zhengzhou University, Zhengzhou China and Technical Report, Nanyang Technological University, Singapore, November 2019

A Structural Testing Model Using SDA Algorithm

Saju Sankar S$^{1(\boxtimes)}$ and Vinod Chandra S S$^{2(\boxtimes)}$

^{1} Department of Computer Engineering, Government Polytechnic College, Punalur, India
tkmce@rediffmail.com
^{2} Department of Computer Science, University of Kerala, Thiruvananthapuram 695581, India
vinod@keralauniversity.ac.in

Abstract. Path testing is the most needed and useful coverage criterion in structural testing. Tracing and obtaining the resultant paths is the main problem in path coverage testing. Evolutionary techniques are adopted in many software product evaluation methods such as generating and selection of input test data. The priority of the feasible paths is also to be determined. In this paper, we proposes an optimization algorithm for identifying the effective test data execution paths in control flow graph for the program module under test and finding the most efficient test paths using modified smell detection agent based optimization algorithm. New innovations are being conducted for bio-motivated algorithmic techniques from the characteristics of animal behavior. Smell detection agent based algorithm helps to identify most feasible paths and it uses sequential search to obtain all paths in a graph. The tester achieves the paths to be tested through a number of smell spot values from the source node to the target node. We will use control flow graph to produce perfect test paths and cyclomatic complexity number for obtaining the number of feasible test paths. The best feasible paths are prioritized using smell detection agent algorithm such that all the paths are thoroughly tested which ensures structural testing. This algorithm generates paths equal to the cyclomatic complexity. It can be illustrated that the proposed approach guarantees full path coverage.

Keywords: Structural testing · Path testing · SDA algorithm · CFG

1 Introduction

Testing is considered as one of the most important process in the life cycle of software development [1]. There are different software testing techniques like structural, functional testing and its hybrid model. The most significant structural testing approach known as Basis Path Testing (BPT) focused into the many ways of evaluating software source code. The emphasis in this method is to develop test data inputs such that it produces all feasible efficient test paths connecting all the nodes and edges of the graph. Path testing has the advantages of thorough testing, more coverage, unit testing, integration testing, maintenance testing, regression testing etc. The main advantage is that the testing effort can be estimated in proportional to the logical complexity of the software.

© Springer Nature Switzerland AG 2020
Y. Tan et al. (Eds.): ICSI 2020, LNCS 12145, pp. 405–412, 2020.
https://doi.org/10.1007/978-3-030-53956-6_36

We used Control Flow Graph (CFG) in BPT and calculated cyclomatic complexity. From that value we will be able to determine all the possible paths from source node to the destination node [2].

McCabe developed the concept of path coverage based basis path testing in the period of 1980's which utilized cyclomatic complexity [3]. In path testing there are different paths from source to destination. Not all paths are feasible while understanding the functionality of the software. It varies depending upon the different types of control statements used in the module and its output boolean values. To prioritize the feasible and infeasible paths, we need a selection procedure. An algorithm can be designed to identify all the basis paths and its priority ranking will help effective testing. In most of the basis path testing techniques, the paths are identified without any prioritizing. An ant colony optimization algorithmic approach was used in identification of paths with its priority [4].

In this paper, we propose Smell Detection Agent (SDA) algorithm that selects all paths and prioritizes the feasible paths. The algorithm is a nature inspired optimization algorithm suitable for identification of optimal paths with its priority in a graph [5, 6].

2   Path Driven Testing

In this approach, the purpose is to test the different paths from the root node to the destination node by which all combinations of various decision or control statements are executed at least once. The technique is based on the logical structure of the program. A graph (CFG) is drawn with all the feasible paths and verified during testing.

Control Flow Graph (CFG): The logical complexity of the program module to be tested is drawn with a CFG. The CGF contains several nodes and edges. The nodes denote executable code lines whereas the edges denote the flow of control between the nodes. All efficient paths are generated with the aid of a CFG diagram.

Cyclomatic Complexity: The maximum number of possible paths in a graph with M predicate nodes is 2^M and if the CFG has any looping statements, then there will be countless number of test paths. The factor of cyclomatic complexity number is an important parameter to minimize the total count of feasible test paths. Cyclomatic complexity number is necessary for the validation of linearly independent test paths in a graph. There are two factors associated with a CFG, one is the cyclomatic number denoted by 'V' in graph theory and the other is the complexity value 'G' as a function of the graph.

The aim of testers is to evaluate all the feasible paths in the CFG. The major challenge in testing is to find the optimal and feasible paths. Hence to find the optimal path, a priority ranking is done for all the feasible paths. The path with highest priority will be initially selected for testing and it continues until the lowest priority path is tested.

Procedure of Basis Path Testing: A software module contains various independent paths to be tested. All these paths should be tested at least once in basis path testing.

Following are the various steps of testing process.

1. Develop the CFG of the program module to be evaluated.

2. Determine the cyclomatic complexity of the CFG, for finding the possible number of linearly independent test paths.
3. Create sets of basis test paths using the baseline method:

   a. Select the first feasible independent path to be tested.
   b. Back trace the independent paths by suddenly moving to each predicate node to create newer paths.

Evaluation of Normal Path Testing: Examine the software program "test" which uses switch case constructs. A CFG is drawn using join (J1, J2) and the graph is depicted using entry and exit criteria as shown in Fig. 1.

```
Program "test".
     1. read(x)
     2. if (x < 0) then
     3. print("negative");
        else
     4. print("positive")
        endif
     5. switch(x)
        case 1:
     6. print("SUN")
        break;
        case 2:
     7. print("MON')
        case 3:
     8. print("TUE")
             break;
       default:
     9. print("OTHER")
          end switch;
```

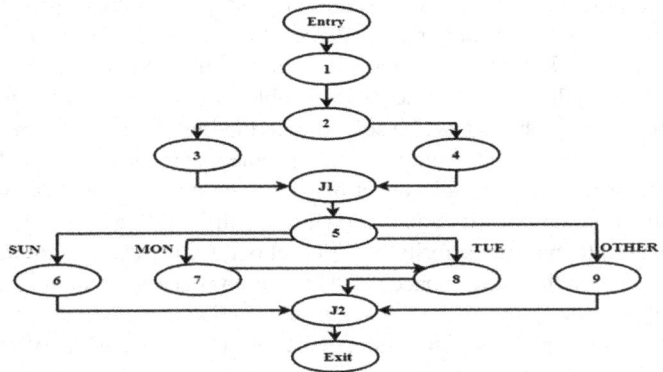

Fig. 1. CFG of program 'test'.

Cyclomatic complexity factor, V (G) = Edges−Nodes + 2, V (G) = 16 − 13 + 2 = 5.

The test paths generated are

Test Path TP1 Entry → 1 → 2 → 3 → J1 → 5 → 6 → J2 → Exit
Test Path TP2 Entry → 1 → 2 → 3 → J1 → 5 → 7 → 8 → J2 → Exit
Test Path TP3 Entry → 1 → 2 → 3 → J1 → 5 → 8 → J2 → Exit
Test Path TP4 Entry → 1 → 2 → 3 → J1 → 5 → 9 → J2 → Exit
Test Path TP5 Entry → 1 → 2 → 4 → J1 → 5 → 6 → J2 → Exit
Test Path TP6 Entry → 1 → 2 → 4 → J1 → 5 → 7 → 8 → J2 → Exit
Test Path TP7 Entry → 1 → 2 → 4 → J1 → 5 → 8 → J2 → Exit
Test Path TP8 Entry → 1 → 2 → 4 → J1 → 5 → 9 → J2 → Exit

In the above example, the number of paths identified is 8 (due to usage of switch case construct) and since the cyclomatic complexity obtained is only 5, we have to weed out infeasible paths. Saurabh et al. [7] proposed an approach using ant colony optimization algorithm, which selects only the feasible paths and prioritized the feasible paths. The algorithm used the factors such as path feasibility, past experience, path visibility and the visited status of path. The model is featured as a directed graph approach and the model also denotes the system to be tested and shows the various test paths of the model during its execution. The best sequence of the path is created automatically after the implementation of the optimization algorithm. The highest priority path is selected first and successively all the other linear paths in the control flow graph can be tested.

Jun yan et al. suggested another suitable and efficient method to create feasible paths for basis path testing [8]. There are two steps in creating feasible paths i) produce a limited set of feasible paths P which fulfills the coverage criteria, ii) obtain a minimum subset p of set P such that p fulfills the test coverage. Two conditions should be satisfied by a path when belonging to a basis path set: a) the test paths should be properly feasible and b) the test paths should be linearly independent of all other selected paths.

3   SDA Algorithm for Path Testing

Canines are considered as the earliest animal disciplined by human [5]. They helped men in hunting and its deep odour helped man in finding the exact position of the animal to be hunted. Now also, canines are used by police personnel for tracing the route of culprits from the area of crime. Many problems faced by men cannot be solved conventionally. These problems can be solved with the introduction of new algorithms. In such contexts, solution to the computational problems can be found by the usage of natural phenomena like animal habits or actions. It can be suitably used to solve problems having computational complexity and are asymptotically NP-hard.

Sniffing is used to evaluate priority of different paths which can be implemented by way of an algorithm in the search space [9]. This search space or domain of the problem to be remedied is treated as an area with smell trails and agents motivated from canines are taken to discover all paths, which points to the solution. The concept of canine's path tracing nature helps to develop necessary environments to solve problems regarding path identification. We can draw this nature-motivated technique in co-ordinate geometry. The search space is formed as a Cartesian rectangular plot with specific values mentioning the space and these values may be changed depending upon the specific constraints of the problem. Every coordinates in the area are not reachable, but some selected arbitrary points that can be visited by the SDAs. The coordinates are denoted as smell spots that help in solving the problem to a subset of points. The values of these smell spots are saved in two parameters. The first is a trailing value of smell from the destination node. The second is a signature value of the SDA that has been denoted as a smell spot.

We propose a SDA algorithm derived from the natural behavior of canines [5]. SDA is a multi-agent algorithm that can be used in any optimum path identification. The algorithm is modified to find the number of feasible paths in a CFG. There are two parameters associated with SDA algorithm i) the assigned signature value that can be used to specify smell spots and ii) the radius value that specifies their olfactory capability. The two parameters are stored in a data structure that is beneficial in the development of the algorithm – data structure (D_{sda}) of the SDA and data structure (D_{ss}) of the smell spot.

Algorithm

Let

N: Count of nodes in the CFG.
N1:   Count of SDAs.
N2:   Count of smell spots
N3:   Count of SDAs that are feasible and reaches the destination

R: radius of the smell spots in the increasing order to the destination
s: the smell value of each node minimum at the source.
P: priority of each path.

1. Assign initially the SDA's with integer values as signature indices and radius values in the increasing direction, thereby the SDA is treated in the progress of traversing in the nodes having highest radius.
2. Select N2 points (nodes) inside the region of the graph as Cartesian values (plots) as smell spots(s).

$$s = 1/(x + y * d)$$

Where 'd' is the Cartesian distance between the smell spots (nodes), the destination and x, y are proportionality constants.
3. Initialize each SDA to the source point.
4. For each SDA from 1 to N1

4.1 Select the unmarked point (within the radius) from the increasing order of smell value.
4.2 Move the SDA forward by earmarking the SDA signature (visiting status).
5.   Step 4 is repeated until all SDA's reach the destination in a way all independent paths are traversed at least once.

Path Sequence Generation and Prioritizing Using Modified SDA Algorithm
This algorithm adopted a sequential searching method to obtain test paths in the CFG. The SDA finds a test path from a collection of smell spot values from the root node

to the destination node. For 'n' agents, there will be 'n' paths returned by the algorithm. The feasible paths are prioritized from these 'n' paths. Also the final number of nodes is received. The initial smell value of each node is contained in the node location coordinates. The values get updated while traversing from source to the destination. Identification of the next source and destination nodes will provide the best path. For the calculation of smell value of each node from the destination node, the values of initial smell, decrement count which is inverse of total and effective distance are considered. The values of smell are updated; all the SDA's are initialized with ID value, current node and length. Based on the smell value of each node, each SDA finds a path.

Identification of the path is done by considering the node, which has the highest smell value from the current node. This identification results in assigning highest smell node as current node and this looping process will continue until the destination is reached. The SDA is assigned with a flag 'stop', when the SDA arrives at the destination. The unique paths are identified from the SDA's who have arrived the destination with highest smell value. The optimized path is found by comparing the total number of nodes visited by each SDA. For CFG, the number of nodes, weight assigned to each node, maximum smell value and maximum radius are considered. The weight of each edge is proportional to the maximum number of times; each node is visited by an SDA. The priority is top for the unique path having maximum smell value and depends on the weight assigned to each edge.

4 Results

In the CFG of the example program 'test', the SDA algorithm works as follows. Initially count of nodes N = 13, initial smell value, s = 1, count of SDAs, N1 = 1. The count of smell spots = N2 = N = 13, Radius or distance from source is initially zero. Figure 2 gives the working of our proposed algorithm for the example program 'test' discussed in Sect. 2.

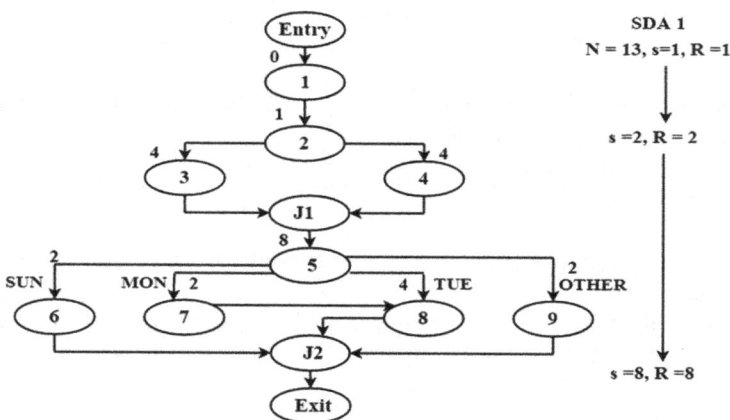

Fig. 2. CFG of program 'test' using modified SDA algorithm.

As per our modified SDA algorithm, the basic paths are traversed by the SDA and fix the priority. In basis path testing, all paths need to be tested, but one test engineer cannot be aware of all the important paths. The SDA algorithm proposed in our model gives all the identified feasible paths in the order of priority. Each edge of the CFG has a weight which depends on the smell spot value. Also, SDAs identify all the test paths in a CFG. In the above program 'test', our algorithm gives a priority wise list of path testing.

Test Path 1 Entry $\rightarrow$ 1 $\rightarrow$ 2 $\rightarrow$ 4 $\rightarrow$ J1 $\rightarrow$ 5 $\rightarrow$ 8 $\rightarrow$ J2 $\rightarrow$ Exit

Test Path 2 Entry $\rightarrow$ 1 $\rightarrow$ 2 $\rightarrow$ 4 $\rightarrow$ J1 $\rightarrow$ 5 $\rightarrow$ 7 $\rightarrow$ 8 $\rightarrow$ J2 $\rightarrow$ Exit

Test Path 3 Entry $\rightarrow$ 1 $\rightarrow$ 2 $\rightarrow$ 4 $\rightarrow$ J1 $\rightarrow$ 5 $\rightarrow$ 6 $\rightarrow$ J2 $\rightarrow$ Exit

Test Path 4 Entry $\rightarrow$ 1 $\rightarrow$ 2 $\rightarrow$ 4 $\rightarrow$ J1 $\rightarrow$ 5 $\rightarrow$ 9 $\rightarrow$ J2 $\rightarrow$ Exit

Test Path 5 Entry $\rightarrow$ 1 $\rightarrow$ 2 $\rightarrow$ 3 $\rightarrow$ J1 $\rightarrow$ 5 $\rightarrow$ 8 $\rightarrow$ J2 $\rightarrow$ Exit

Test Path 6 Entry $\rightarrow$ 1 $\rightarrow$ 2 $\rightarrow$ 3 $\rightarrow$ J1 $\rightarrow$ 5 $\rightarrow$ 7 $\rightarrow$ 8 $\rightarrow$ J2 $\rightarrow$ Exit

Test Path 7 Entry $\rightarrow$ 1 $\rightarrow$ 2 $\rightarrow$ 3 $\rightarrow$ J1 $\rightarrow$ 5 $\rightarrow$ 6 $\rightarrow$ J2 $\rightarrow$ Exit

Test Path 8 Entry $\rightarrow$ 1 $\rightarrow$ 2 $\rightarrow$ 3 $\rightarrow$ J1 $\rightarrow$ 5 $\rightarrow$ 9 $\rightarrow$ J2 $\rightarrow$ Exit

In Ant Colony Optimization (ACO) algorithm, the paths are selected randomly for the path generation from source to destination [10]. In our SDA algorithm, the selection of optimal paths is based on the maximum weight assigned to each most traversed edge of the CFG. In ACO algorithm, the routing is done based of decreasing pheromone value while in SDA algorithm, the olfactory capability is increasing from source to the destination node thereby time complexity is reduced [11, 12] (Table 1).

Table 1. Comparison of ACO and SDA algorithms employed in structural testing.

Algorithm	ACO	SDA
Count of independent paths	All independent paths are identified with some paths have equal priority	All the 8 independent paths are identified with priority from 1 to 8
Swarm communication	Ants communicate called stigmergy	Each Canine or agent has a territory
Algorithm applicability	ACO is suitable to problems where source and destination are predefined	Multiple agents are employed for a faster solution
Problem representation	A construction graph is used to mark ACO's solution space	Cartesian rectangular plot with specific values mentioning the area
Time complexity	$O(n^2)$	$O(|E| + |V|\log|V|)$

5 Conclusion

We have demonstrated the test paths creation methods for basis path testing in this paper and proposed a suitable optimization procedure for feasible test path generation in structural testing by using SDA optimization algorithm. After implementation of this method, the algorithmic process selects the best test path sequence based on its priority. The highest priority test path is selected first for test execution and in successive steps all the next priority independent paths in the control flow graph can be tested. The SDA Algorithm tends to be more beneficial for better path coverage in basis path testing. The model avoids duplicate paths based on SDA signature and the visited status of the nodes. The model can be modified by an automated method as a future work. The results shows that the SDA algorithm based structural testing can be extended for the generation of optimal and prioritized generation of test paths for multipath software modules.

References

1. Granno, G.: A new dimension of test quality - assessing and generating higher quality unit test cases. In: ISSTA 2019, China, pp. 15–19. Software Evolution and Architecture Lab, University of Zurich, Zurich, Switzerland (2019)
2. Wang, X., et al.: An efficient method for automatic generation of linearly independent paths in white box testing. School of Software and Engineering, University of Electronic Science and Technology of China (2015)
3. McCabe, T.J.: A complexity measure. IEEE Trans. Softw. Eng. **SE-2**(4) (1976)
4. Alshaheen, H.S.: Finding shortest path in routing problem by using ant colony optimization. J. Univ. Thi-Qar **8**(3) (2013)
5. Vinod Chandra, S.S.: Smell detection agent based optimization algorithm. J. Inst. Eng. (India) Ser. B **97**(4), 431–436 (2016). https://doi.org/10.1007/s40031-014-0182-0
6. Ananthalakshmi Ammal, R., Sajimon, P.C., Vinodchandra, S.S.: Application of smell detection agent based algorithm for optimal path identification by SDN controllers. In: Tan, Y., Takagi, H., Shi, Y., Niu, B. (eds.) ICSI 2017. LNCS, vol. 10386, pp. 502–510. Springer, Cham (2017). https://doi.org/10.1007/978-3-319-61833-3_53
7. Srivastava, S., Kumar, S., Verma, A.K.: Optimal path sequencing in basis path testing. Int. J. Adv. Comput. Eng. Netw. (2013)
8. Yan, J., Zhang, J.: An efficient method to generate feasible paths for basis path testing. State Key Laboratory of Computer Science, Institute of Software, Chinese Academy of Sciences, China 2008)
9. Salawudeen, A.T., et al.: From smell phenomenon to smell agent optimization (SAO): a feasibility study. In: Proceedings of ICGET (2018)
10. Kaur, S.: Shortest path finding algorithm using ant colony optimization. Int. J. Eng. Res. Technol. (IJERT) **2**(6), 317–326 (2013). ISSN 2278-0181
11. Cherkassky, B.V., Goldberg, A.V., Radzik, T.: Shortest paths algorithms: theory and experimental evaluation. Math. Program. **73**, 129–174 (1996). https://doi.org/10.1007/BF02592101
12. Donald, J.: A note on Dijikstra's shortest path algorithm. J. ACM **20**(3), 385–388 (1973)

Multi-objective Optimization

Multi-objective Particle Swarm Optimisation for Cargo Packaging in Large Containers

Vinod Chandra S S[1], S. Anand Hareendran[2(✉)], and Saju Sankar S[3]

[1] Computer Centre, University of Kerala, Trivandrum, India
vinod@keralauniversity.ac.in
[2] Department of Computer Science, MITS, Kochi, India
anandhareendrans@mgits.ac.in
[3] Department of Computer Engineering, Government Polytechnic College,
Punalur, India
tkmce@rediffmail.com

Abstract. Cargo management in all mode of transports like airlines, ships and trucks is a challenging task. The way in which an optimal allocation of packages in different containers are done using a software controlled method. An agent based software module is enabled as a service for the optimum allocation of cargo packages in the container terminals. There are multiple factors that will affect this allocation - size, shape, weight of the cargo packets and the container. When we design an optimal allocation module in a software these components need to be addressed along with capacity of the container. Hence, a multi-objective optimization algorithm will improve the performance of cargo management software. In this paper we suggest a Mixed Species Particle Swarm Optimisation (MSPSO) procedure for optimal allocation of cargo packages in containers of different size and capacity. The redesigned version of cargo management software performs well with search space on normal time complexity. The simulated results gives an improved optimised allocation than normalised allocation of cargo packets. The improved implementation performed better in terms of efficient cargo package allocation.

Keywords: PSO · Multi-objective PSO · Cargo management · Optimisation

1 Introduction

Optimised placement of cargo packets in containers is a challenging task. This is because size, shape and weight of the cargo packets are different. It is also noted that there may be difference in size, shape and capacity of the current selected container. When multiple containers are loaded in a terminal for shipment and different category cargo packers are trying to load, efficiency is a major concern

© Springer Nature Switzerland AG 2020
Y. Tan et al. (Eds.): ICSI 2020, LNCS 12145, pp. 415–422, 2020.
https://doi.org/10.1007/978-3-030-53956-6_37

[1]. This problem can be treated as a multi-objective task because more than one objective need to be considered while cargo packets are placed in a container. The size, shape and weight of the cargo packets as well as container are considered in the optimisation phase. Capacity of the container is also a major factor. Hence, space allocation in a container for each cargo packet is considered as a multi-objective optimal allocation problem.

To make cost-effective cargo carrier operations, a major challenge is to make profitable packing. There is a software controlled mechanism, which handle this work effectively. If this software is built as an optimised model, then the cost-effective performance can be increased. The agent based techniques are useful in optimum allocation of packets or in load balancing of the container. Genetic algorithm and Smell detection based optimum allocation techniques are making fruitful solution to this problem [2–4]. These agents generates single optimum solution by an objective function after operating a sequence of steps. But such intelligent agents cannot handle more than one objectives and cannot combine to form an optimised output. The cargo packets management in multiple containers is treated as multi-objective problem as we consider multiple sources (cargo packets in different size) and multiple destinations (containers in different shipment terminals).

There are optimised models which helps effective cargo management softwares [5,6]. The model works using integer linear programming based approach for effective load balancing. It is operated as a single objective optimisation technology. A multi-objective honey bee algorithm can be used to solve optimisation problems [7,8]. Multi-objective honey bee algorithm shows dynamic and distributed computing behaviour of honey bees at separate colonies in meeting various resources for meeting their demands at individual destinations by maximising the profit [8]. The multi-objective optimisation technique is effectively used in multi-dimensional transportation problems. In this paper, we have addressed the cargo management problem using a multi-objective particle swarm optimisation technique. Our technique is focused in multi-objective optimisation for both the cargo as well as its container.

2   Multi-objective PSO

The proposed model is referred as Mixed Species Particle Swarm Optimisation (MSPSO). Mixed species flocks preserve the principle of collision avoidance, velocity matching and flock cantering as followed by the single species flock. The individuals keep a distance from neighbours such that they don't plunge at others. They try to match the velocity of neighbours so that they do not fall out of the group and also try to move towards centre of the flock [9].

Figure 1 depicts the fleet of mixed species flocks of Rooks and Jackdaws with circles indicate paired a flight of Jackdaws. A mathematical model is derived from the mixed species flocking of birds. N species are assumed to flock together. Each species is expected to optimally arrive at the respective objectives. Same numbers of birds from each species participate in the flocking. Each bird is considered as a

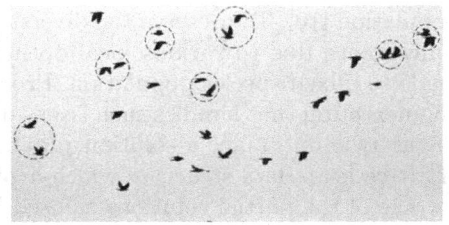

Fig. 1. Mixed species particle flocking of Rooks and Jackdaws

particle, $\mathbf{x}$ which occupy a random position in the search domain S^n as specified by $x \leftarrow random(s^n)$.

All particle species has an initial velocity, which is assigned randomly. Each species has a limiting factor in curbing the maximum limit that is $V_{max}(N)$ for each species N.

$$V_{max(N)} = random(V); V_{min}(N) \leq V \leq V_{max}(N) \qquad (1)$$

$V_{max}(N)$ and $V_{min}(N)$ are determined such as to permit fair movement of a particle in the search domain. Too small value of $V(N)$ leads to slow convergence and too high value causes the particle move fly out of the search domain. Each species N is assigned objective function $f(x(N))$.

Objective function is specified as Eq. 2

$$\text{Minimize}$$
$$(f_1(x), f_2(x), \ldots f_N(x))$$
$$x \in X, f : X \to R^k \qquad (2)$$
$$f(x) = f_1(x), f_2(x), \ldots f_d(x)$$
$$N \geq 2$$

In multi-objective optimisation, there is not an optimal solution which minimises all objective functions simultaneously. The objective is to determine Pareto optimal solutions which cannot improve any objective without degrading other objectives.

The Pareto optimal set is determined for a specific multi-objective optimisation problems should be closer to true Pareto front and also should preserve the diversity of solutions. These two conditions are contradictory - when tried to preserve diversity, converge speed is reduced. Mixed species population has to be controlled in such a way that the species span over the entire solution space. The presence of local optimum with in specific neighbourhood has a significant effect on the quality of Pareto front determined. Considering all these parameters a mathematical model based on mixed species flocking for multi-objective optimisation is proposed. This model has five significant stages. There is a basic optimisation algorithm which controls the fleet of particles in the search space and has an enumeration for detecting the global best particle of the mixed species population [10]. To preserve the diversity of solution set and to evade premature convergence due to various local optimum solutions, dynamic adaptations are made to mixed species population. Procedure for particle depletion and particle augmentation that handles such issues. In order to obtain Pareto efficiency closer to the true optimum, a solution ranking scheme is also used which makes use of a tree heap data structure which avoids an additional external repository for storage of the partial solutions as used by particle swarm based multi-objective optimisation algorithms.

2.1   Results

Loading of cargo packets in a container is not an issue but optimally inserting these packets are very hard. This problem is a two dimensional problem that have more than one objective of packing like

(1) maximum of I cargoes with width W and height H, (2) J items with $w_j \leq W, h_j \leq H$ and weight ξ_i.

The objectives are (1) minimise the number of cargoes used K and (2) minimise the average deviation between the overall centre of gravity and the desired one.

Usually the packets are placed randomly or placed one by one but not optimally placed. To solve the problem using multi-objective PSO, first we have to initialise the particles. In this work, we have to use solution from Bottom Left Fill (BLF) heuristic. To sort the rectangles for bottom left fill, according to some criteria like width, weight, area, perimeter etc. These criteria are aimed as objectives and the problem enters to a multi-objective problem. For an optimised output from these objectives create a multi-objective optimisation problem. Figure 2 gives the initialisation of bottom left fill. The items are moved to the top if intersection detected at the right. Figure 3(a) shows an item moved to the top if intersection detected at the right. In Fig. 3(b), the item moved if there is a lower available space for an insertion. Now the optimisation part is required to explore. In the PSO, velocity depends on either $pbest$(PB) or $gbest$(GB), never both at the same time. Figure 4 gives two different solution options.

We have to use the above multi-objective PSO procedure included into the cargo packing procedure. There are three stages in this procedure. In first stage of the procedure a partial swap between 2 cargoes followed by merge 2 cargoes then split 1 cargo. In the second stage randomly rotate the boxes in to the cargo and in the third stage a random shuffle is carried. Procedure for a particle the mutation modes are given below.

Cargo Packing Procedure

Start of mutation
If the probability < 0.33 then
    partial swap between 2 cargoes
If the probability between 0.33 and 0.66 then
    merge last filled two cargoes into 1 cargo
If the probability > 0.66 then
    split one cargo into 2 cargoes

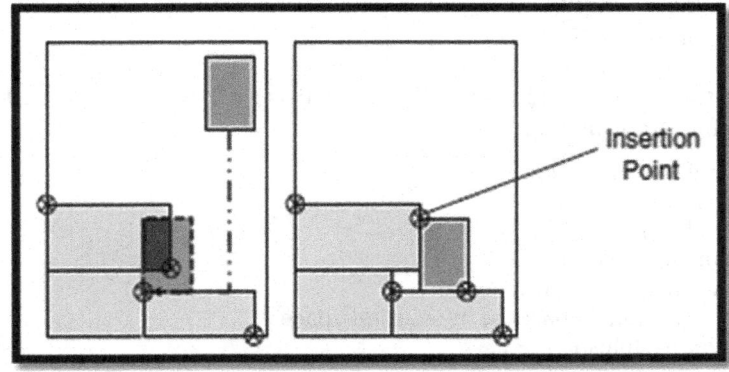

Fig. 2. If intersection detected at the top then item moved to the right

(a)   (b)

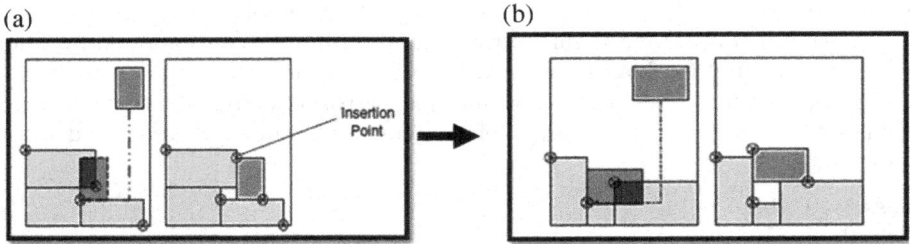

Fig. 3. (a) If intersection detected at the right then item moved to the top (b) Item moved if there is a lower available space for insertion

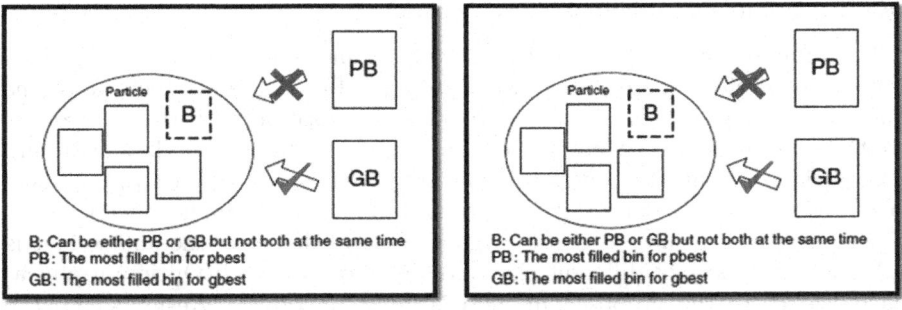

Fig. 4. Two choices of velocity selection

      Rotate boxes in the cargo
      Intra cargo shuffle
   End mutation

Procedure that included in a hybrid multi-objective PSO is proposed to solve cargo packing problem is given below

1. Build initial population
2. Cost function evaluation
3. Fitness sharing
4. Tournament selection
5. Generation of velocity vectors
6. Update position of particle in solution space
7. Mutation evaluation
8. Preservation of non-dominated particle in archive
9. If stopping criteria is not met go to step 2
10. End procedure

The multi-objective optimisation procedure for cargo packing is establishing the fitness of all particles and to stimulate the particle progress towards optimal locale, method to determine the globally best particle, method for particle depletion, procedure for particle augmentation and a routine for solution ranking. The process is repeated for Max number of iterations so that the particles move to their global optimal positions to optimise respective objective functions. In our simulated inputs, there are 8 classes with 50 instances randomly generated with a size range:

Class 1: [0, 100]
Class 2: [0, 250]
Class 3: [0, 500]
Class 4: [0, 750]
Class 4: [0, 1000]
Class 5: [250, 750]
Class 6: [250, 500]
Class 4: [500, 1000]
Class 2: small items → more difficult to pack

The proposed method is capable of evolving more optimal solution and its computational efficiency is good with a stopping function after 1000 iterations or no improvement in last 5 generations. This optimisation algorithm is a robust search optimisation algorithm that can create of variable length data structure with specialised mutation operator. The proposed algorithm performs consistently well with the best average performance on the performance metric.

The simulated results for 1000 cargo packets of different size and weight is loaded in containers of different size and capacity is tested. Optimum allocation efficiency of the proposed method is given in Table 1. Result shows the efficiency of cargo packet allocation in containers drastically improved when size and capacity of the container and cargo packets are different. This is because, the power of multi-objective optimisation PSO.

Table 1. Performance optimisation. Percentage of improvement in efficiency after implementing the multi-objective PSO in cargo management software

Cargo packets	Containers of same and different size and capacity			
	Before opt.	After opt.	Before opt.	After opt.
Same size and weight	74	85	84	92
Different size and weight	78	84	72	88

3   Conclusion

A problem with **N** objective functions and **P** particles in the search space, the computational complexity is linear and has $O(NP)$ complexity. It is further reduced as the non-dominated solutions are stored in heap tree where the worst case search complexity is only in terms of $O(n)$ where n is the size of solution set required. The space complexity is $O(n)$ which is the property of heap tree used for the storage of approximation set.

This method is a strong prospect to be used for general multi objective optimization problem. Population based approach follows the trajectory of global best particle to obtain the pareto dominant solution set. Software can be designed by integrating a module that uses a parallel optimization technique. Proposed model performs well with search space discontinuous optimal regions also. It also performs well on non-separable problems with multiple local optima. But there are a few limitations also. Application of the method to practical optimization problems requires the adaptation of parameters as per specific problem.

Acknowledgment. We thank to Girish Chandran, CEO of Kefi Tech Solutions, Technopark, Thiruvananthapuram for the help and test assistance that he had offered even between his busy schedule for data analysis and knowledge transfer phase.

References

1. Dahmani, N., Krichen, S.: Solving a load balancing problem with a multi-objective particle swarm optimisation approach: application to aircraft cargo transportation. Int. J. Oper. Res. **27**(1–2), 62–84 (2016)
2. Fong, S., Da Costa, M.G., Khoury, R.: Air cargo scheduling using genetic algorithms. In: International Symposium on Computational and Business Intelligence, New Delhi, pp. 170–173 (2013)
3. Vinod Chandra, S.S.: Smell detection agent based optimization algorithm. J. Inst. Eng. India Ser. B **97**, 431–436 (2016). https://doi.org/10.1007/s40031-014-0182-0
4. Ananthalakshmi Ammal, R., Sajimon, P.C., Vinodchandra, S.S.: Application of smell detection agent based algorithm for optimal path identification by SDN controllers. In: Tan, Y., Takagi, H., Shi, Y., Niu, B. (eds.) ICSI 2017. LNCS, vol. 10386, pp. 502–510. Springer, Cham (2017). https://doi.org/10.1007/978-3-319-61833-3_53
5. El Noshokaty, S.: Shipping optimisation systems (SOS): liner optimisation perspective. Int. J. Shipp. Transport Logist. **5**(3), 237–256 (2013)

6. Meijer, S.A., Mayer, I.S., van Luipen, J., Weitenberg, N.: Gaming rail cargo management: exploring and validating alternative modes of organization. Simul. Gaming **43**(1), 85–101 (2012)
7. Saritha, R., Vinod Chandra, S.S.: Multi dimensional honey bee foraging algorithm based on optimal energy consumption. J. Inst. Eng. Ser. B **98**(5), 517–525 (2017). https://doi.org/10.1007/s40031-017-0294-4
8. Saritha, R., Vinod Chandra, S.S.: Multi modal foraging by honey bees toward optimizing profits at multiple colonies. IEEE Intell. Syst. **34**(1), 14–22 (2018)
9. Raveendran, S., Vinodchandra, S.S.: An approach using particle swarm optimization and rational kernel for variable length data sequence optimization. In: Tan, Y., Shi, Y., Niu, B. (eds.) ICSI 2016. LNCS, vol. 9712, pp. 401–409. Springer, Cham (2016). https://doi.org/10.1007/978-3-319-41000-5_40
10. Kennedy, J.: The particle swarm: social adaptation of knowledge. In: Proceedings of IEEE International Conference on Evolutionary Computation, pp. 303–308 (1997)

Multi-objective Combinatorial Generative Adversarial Optimization and Its Application in Crowdsensing

Yi-nan Guo[1](✉), Jianjiao Ji[1], Ying Tan[2], and Shi Cheng[3]

[1] School of Information and Control Engineering, China University of Mining and Technology,
Xuzhou 221008, Jiangsu, China
guoyinan@cumt.edu.cn
[2] Peking University, Beijing 100091, China
[3] School of Computer Science, Shaanxi Normal University, Xi'an 710119, China

Abstract. With the increasing of the decision variables in multi-objective combinatorial optimization problems, the traditional evolutionary algorithms perform worse due to the low efficiency for generating the offspring by a stochastic mechanism. To address the issue, a multi-objective combinatorial generative adversarial optimization method is proposed to make the algorithm capable of learning the implicit information embodied in the evolution process. After classifying the optimal non-dominated solutions in the current generation as real data, the generative adversarial network (GAN) is trained by them, with the purpose of learning their distribution information. The Adam algorithm that employs the adaptively learning rate for each parameter is introduced to update the main parameters of GAN. Following that, an offspring reproduction strategy is designed to form a new feasible solution from the decimal output of the generator. To further verify the rationality of the proposed method, it is applied to solve the participant selection problem of the crowdsensing and the detailed offspring reproduction strategy is given. The experimental results for the crowdsensing systems with various tasks and participants show that the proposed algorithm outperforms the others in both convergence and distribution.

Keywords: Multi-objective · Combinatorial optimization · Generative adversarial network · Participant selection · Crowdsensing

1 Introduction

Multi-objective combinatorial optimization problems (MOCOPs), such as traveling salesman problem, vehicle routing planning, participant selection problem of crowdsensing and so on, is to find the optimal resource assignment that takes multiple objectives into consideration [1, 2]. To address the issues, the classical linear programming, metaheuristic search, evolutionary algorithm, and some other population-based intelligent optimization algorithms are introduced. However, with the increasing of the decision variables, the exploration ability of above-mentioned algorithms become limited due to

© Springer Nature Switzerland AG 2020
Y. Tan et al. (Eds.): ICSI 2020, LNCS 12145, pp. 423–434, 2020.
https://doi.org/10.1007/978-3-030-53956-6_38

the low efficiency for generating diverse offspring by a stochastic mechanism. Many researchers [3–7] employed the handcrafted strategies that were especially designed according to the characteristics of specific problems to improve the performance. However, such problem-specific methods depends a lot on the artificial experience. The recent advances [8–11] in machine learning algorithms have shown their strong ability of helping engineers to design optimization algorithms with learning ability to solve different problems with a relatively good performance. Based on this, various studies [12–14] have tried to utilize the neurol networks to learn the useful information about the fitness landscape or the distribution of the individuals to generate the more rational offspring. But a large number of the training data must be provided for building the learning models, which is always difficult or expensive to be achieved in practice.

The Generative Adversarial Networks (GAN) proposed by Goodfellow in 2014 is able to learn high-dimensional distributions efficiently with the limited training data by the following adversarial learning mechanism [15], which consists of a generator and a discriminator [16]. The former learns the distribution $P_{data}(x)$ of a real data x and generates a new sample $G(z)$ with the prior distribution $P_{prior}(x)$, while the latter works hard on identifying whether the sample is real or fake, and outputs a discriminant probability $D(x)$. More specifically, the generator tries to produce the samples as real as possible, with the purpose of decreasing the accuracy of a discriminator. By contrast, the discriminator makes an effort on enhancing its recognition ability. Both of them are trained in a minimax game manner as follows.

$$\min_{G} \max_{D} V(D, G) = E_{x \in P_{data}}[\log D(x)] + E_{z \in P_{prior}}[\log(1 - D(G(z)))] \qquad (1)$$

Various studies have been done on GAN-based optimization algorithms, in which the offspring is generated along the direction learned from the distribution of the better candidate solutions. Tan et al. [17] proposed a generative adversarial optimization framework for continuous optimization problems with a single objective. A new solution is produced from a candidate with the input noise by the generator, and then the discriminator predicts whether the fitness value of a generated solution is better than that of the original candidate. He et al. [15] first presented a GAN-based multi-objective evolutionary algorithm. The candidates are classified into two datasets that are labeled as real and fake, respectively. After training the generator with the above samples, the offspring is formed by it or the genetic operators with the same probability. Despite the application of GAN on continuous optimization problems, fewer works have been done on the combinatorial optimization problems. Probst [18] employed GAN to build the probability model that approximates the distribution of the candidates in the estimation of distribution algorithm. The offspring are gotten from the probability model, with the purpose of finding the optima for a scalar combinatorial optimization problem. Being different from it, a multi-objective combinatorial generative adversarial optimization algorithm (MOCGAO) is proposed for the MOCOPs in this paper. And the main contributions of this study are summarized as follows:

(1) MOCGAO takes advantage of the learning and generative abilities of GAN to generate superior solutions for the MOCOPs.

(2) A classification strategy is developed to identify the non-dominated solutions found in the evolution as the real samples for training GAN, as they provide the distribution information of the population.

(3) An offspring reproduction strategy is designed to form a new feasible solution from the decimal output of the generator for the MOCOPs.

(4) The proposed method is applied to solve the participant selection problem of the crowdsensing and the detailed offspring reproduction strategy is given.

The rest of the paper is organized as follows. In Sect. 2, the key issues of multi-objective combinatorial generative adversarial optimization are presented in detail. MOCGAO-based participant selection strategy for the crowdsensing is illustrated in Sect. 3. The experimental results are compared and further analyzed in Sect. 4. Finally, Sect. 5 concludes the whole paper and plans the topic to be researched in the future.

2 Multi-objective Combinatorial Generative Adversarial Optimization

According to the algorithm steps of MOCGAO shown in Algorithm 1, the initial population $P(0)$ is constructed by the randomly produced individuals and the optima of each objective obtained by the greedy algorithm. The latter ones provide the extremum for training GAN so as to speed up the convergence of the network. After training GAN by the classified individuals, the generator outputs the offspring $Q(t)$. N individuals selected from the combination of $P(t)$ and $Q(t)$ by the non-domination sort and elite selection strategy of NSGA-II, compose of the population in the next generation $P(t + 1)$. Finally, the Pareto-optimal solution is found until the termination condition is satisfied. Apparently, the key issues of the proposed method are to classify the population, train GAN and reproduce the offspring. The detailed selection strategy of NSGA-II refer to Ref. [19].

Algorithm 1: Multi-objective combinatorial generative adversarial optimization algorithm

Input: the population size N, the number of objectives M, the maximum termination iteration T

Output: PS

Net ← Randomly initialize the GAN;

$P(0)$ ← Randomly initialize $N-M$ individuals;

$P(0)$ ← Add the optimal individual of each objective by the greedy algorithm;

For t=1:T **do**

  X ← Classification($P(t)$);

  ($Q(t)$, Net) ← Training GAN (Net, X);

  $P(t+1)$ ← Selection($P(t) \cup Q(t)$, N);

End

Obtain the Pareto-optimal solutions PS.

2.1   The Classification of the Population

Both the real and fake samples provide effective information for training GAN. For image processing [20–22] and text generation [23], the real data distributions of the images and texts are normally obtained in advance. However, it is difficult to know the fitness landscape, even the true Pareto-optimal solutions before the evolution of actual multi-objective optimization problems. To address the issue, He et al. [15] partitioned the population in each generation into two datasets with the same size, and the one with the better convergence and diversity is treated as real samples. However, both the non-dominate individuals and the dominated ones with the even distribution are classified to form the training data. The latter is conducive to form the GAN that can produce the offspring with better diversity, but the distribution of the worse individuals also is learned by GAN, which slows down the convergence speed.

Different from it, only the non-dominated individuals are labeled as real and employed to form the real dataset x^r. The rest of the population are classified into the fake dataset x^f. Because GAN iteratively learns only the distribution of better solutions, the generated offspring may more approximate to the true Pareto solutions.

$$x_i \in \begin{cases} x^r & x_i \text{ is a non-dominated solution} \\ x^f & \text{otherwise} \end{cases} \tag{2}$$

2.2   Training GAN

The generator and discriminator of MOCGAO both consist of the feedforward neural network with a single hidden layer, as shown in Fig. 1. Each node in the hidden layer employs the ReLu activation function, while the nodes in the output layer adopt the sigmoid function.

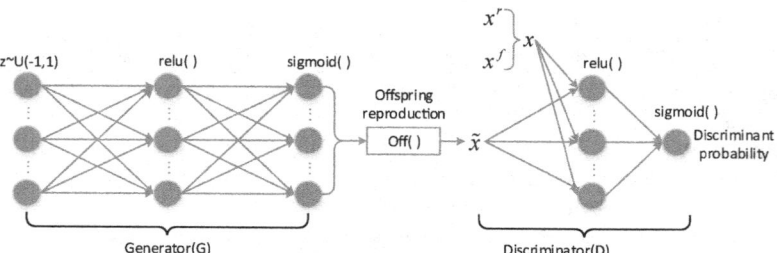

Fig. 1. The structure of GAN

The noise obeying the continuous uniform distribution $Z \sim U(-1, 1)$ is employed as the input signal to the generator. Following that, the output of $G(z)$ is transformed into an offspring $\tilde{x}$ by the offspring reproduction strategy $Off()$. The generated sample $\tilde{x}$ is utilized to calculate the loss function of the generator as follows.

$$\tilde{V}_G = \frac{1}{N} \sum_{i=1}^{N} \log(1 - D(Off(G(z_i)))) \tag{3}$$

Subsequently, the real samples x^r, the fake ones x^f and the generated ones $\tilde{x}$ are all employed to train the discriminator. The comprehensive loss function is defined.

$$\tilde{V}_D = \frac{1}{|x^r|} \sum_{i=1}^{|x^r|} \log D(x_i^r) + \frac{1}{|x^f|} \sum_{i=1}^{|x^f|} \log(1 - D(x_i^f)) + \frac{1}{N} \sum_{i=1}^{N} \log(1 - D(\tilde{x}_i)) \tag{4}$$

The parameters of GAN are learned by the Adam algorithm [24], in which each parameter remains the various learning rate, instead of the traditional gradient descent method.

2.3 The Offspring Reproduction Strategy

For most of the combinatorial optimization problems, a solution is normally encoded by the binary or the integer. However, the outputs of the generator in GAN is a decimal between 0 and 1, which cannot represent an individual of a combinatorial optimization problem directly. To this end, a novel offspring reproduction strategy is presented, with the purpose of forming an available individual based on the decimal output of GAN.

The number of neurons in the output layer of a generator is equal to the dimension of decision variables. For a binary-coded individual, the output of each neuron is treated as the probability of each gene being set to 1. In the offspring reproduction strategy, the output of all neurons in the generator are sorted in the descending order, and the variable corresponding to the first unselected one is labeled by 1. Different from it, the possible integer-values of the decision variables are assigned to the genes corresponding to the sorted neurons in the same descending order. That is, the maximum integer-value is first set to the gene corresponding to the neuron having the maximum output. As shown in Fig. 2, the same decimal output of a generator is mapped to the different offspring in terms of the encoding scheme of an individual.

The output of a generator	0.351	0.174	0.293
The binary individual	1	0	0
The integer-coded individual	1	3	2

Fig. 2. An example of an offspring reproduction strategy

3 MOCGAO-Based Participant Selection of a Crowdsensing System

To verify the effectiveness of the proposed MOCGAO algorithm, it is applied to the participant selection problem of Crowdsensing, which allocates all the sensing tasks to suitable participants that are selected from the sensing-user set. Assume that the sensing tasks denoted as $T = \{t_1, t_2, \ldots, t_m\}$ are published on the crowdsensing system, and the mobile users expressed by $U = \{u_1, u_2, \ldots, u_n\}$ want to participate the works as executors. Suppose that each task need to be fulfilled by ξ users, and each user is assigned to at most one task. Let e_{ij} and a_{ij} be the sensing ability and reward of the user u_j for the task t_i, respectively. Moreover, the sensing ability is determined by the distance between the task and the user, and the reward depends on the sharing mechanism of reward for the user and his cooperative friend. More details refer to Reference [25]. Based on this, a participant selection model that maximize both the sensing quality of tasks and the reward of participants can be constructed as follow:

$$\begin{cases} \max f_1 = \sum_i \sum_j e_{ij} x_{ij} \\ \max f_2 = \sum_i \sum_j a_{ij} x_{ij} \\ s.t. \ \xi = \sum_j x_{ij}, \forall i \in [1, m] \\ \quad \sum_i x_{ij} \leq 1, \forall i \in [1, n] \end{cases} \tag{5}$$

In the above formula, $[x_{ij}]_{m \times n}$ is the Task-User matrix, as shown in Fig. 3(a). $x_{ij} = 1$ means that the task is allocated to the jth user. The Task-User matrix is converted to the binary vector, as shown in Fig. 3(b), with the purpose of simplifying the training process of GAN.

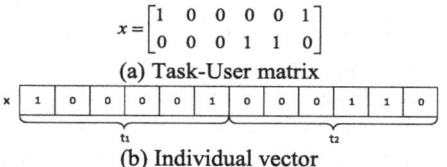

$$x = \begin{bmatrix} 1 & 0 & 0 & 0 & 0 & 1 \\ 0 & 0 & 0 & 1 & 1 & 0 \end{bmatrix}$$

(a) Task-User matrix

(b) Individual vector

Fig. 3. An example of an individual ($m = 2, n = 6, \xi = 2$)

According to the above-mentioned encoding scheme of the participant selection model, the output of each neuron in the output layer of a generator represents the probability of a user being assigned to a task. In order to obtain the feasible offspring by the proposed offspring reproduction strategy, the number of neurons is set to $m*n$. For each task, ξ unallocated users are selected to complete the task in the descending order of the corresponding probability, and the corresponding gene is set to 1.

As shown in Fig. 4, two tasks are allocated to six users in the crowdsensing system, and each task needs two participants. For the task t_1, the two users with the maximum probability, u_1 and u_6, are selected. The first and sixth genes are set to 1. u_4 and u_5 are chosen to carry out t_2. u_6 having a higher probability than u_5 is not employed by this task because of the constraint for the available users.

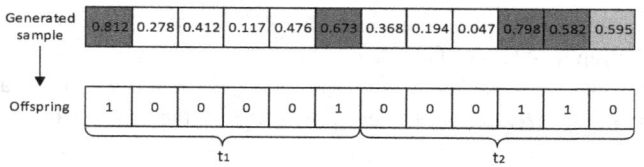

Fig. 4. An example of the offspring reproduction ($m = 2, n = 6, \xi = 2$)

4   Experimental Results and Discussion

Fully experiments are conducted to examine the performance of the proposed MOCGAO. The main experimental parameters are listed in Table 1, and the other parameters of the participant selection problem refer to paper [25]. Besides, the hypervolume (HV) and coverage(C) metrics [26] are employed to evaluate the performance of the proposed algorithm, and the best results are labeled by bold.

Table 1. The main parameters

Parameter	Value
m (the number of tasks)	{5, 10, 15, 20}
n (the number of users)	{100, 200, 300}
N (the population size)	100
T (the maximum termination iteration)	100
$iter$ (the training iteration)	3
β_1 (the preset constant for Adam)	0.9
β_2 (the preset constant for Adam)	0.999
ε (the preset constant for Adam)	10^{-8}
η (the initial learning rate)	0.001
$NodeG$ (the number of nodes for each layer of the Generator)	100, 128, m*n
$NodeD$ (the number of nodes for each layer of the Discriminator)	m*n, 128, 1

To verify the effectiveness of the Adam method, we compare the performances of MOCGAO with the Adam method (Adam) against one with the gradient descent method (Gradient). From the statistical results listed in Table 2, no matter how many users participate to complete the tasks, MOCGAO with the Adam method converges to the best Pareto solutions because the Adam adopts the adaptive learning rate for each parameter instead of the static on in the gradient descent method, which is more efficient for training GAN.

The rationality of the Greedy-based initialization method (Greedy) is analyzed by comparing the performance of MOCGAO with the random initialization strategy (Random), as listed in Table 3. Apparently, the extreme of each objective provides more information on the true distribution of the Pareto front, which is helpful for speeding up the training process of GAN and generating the more promising offspring. Thus, MOCGAO with the Greedy-based initialization method can found better Pareto-optimal solutions, showing the larger HV-values.

Two representative multi-objective evolutionary algorithms, including NSGA-II [19] and MOEA/D [27] are employed as the comparison algorithms. Figure 5 depicts the Pareto fronts obtained by the three compared algorithms. It can be observed that the Pareto-optimal solutions of all instances generated by NSGA-II have the worst convergence, while MOEA/D tends to generate the Pareto solutions distributed in a small

Table 2. Comparison of the performances for MOCGAOs with different learning methods

m*n	HV		C	
	Gradient	Adam	C(Gradient, Adam)	C(Adam, Gradient)
5*100	6.79	**222.76**	0.00	**1.00**
5*200	23.59	**202.64**	0.00	**1.00**
5*300	17.84	**253.20**	0.00	**1.00**
10*100	64.10	**642.33**	0.00	**1.00**
10*200	105.87	**462.18**	0.00	**1.00**
10*300	97.13	**617.41**	0.00	**1.00**
15*100	132.17	**1266.88**	0.00	**1.00**
15*200	110.66	**1882.61**	0.00	**1.00**
15*300	214.91	**2153.24**	0.00	**1.00**
20*100	181.11	**2664.65**	0.00	**1.00**
20*200	163.32	**1917.41**	0.00	**1.00**
20*300	219.70	**1873.09**	0.00	**1.00**

Table 3. Comparison of the performances for MOCGAOs with different initialization strategies

m*n	HV		C	
	Random	Greedy	C(Random, Greedy)	C(Greedy, Random)
5*100	222.76	**290.47**	0.00	**1.00**
5*200	202.64	**460.19**	0.00	**1.00**
5*300	253.20	**667.13**	0.00	**1.00**
10*100	642.33	**1326.42**	0.00	**1.00**
10*200	462.18	**1480.75**	0.00	**1.00**
10*300	617.41	**2074.57**	0.00	**1.00**
15*100	1266.88	**3304.06**	0.00	**1.00**
15*200	1882.61	**3906.53**	0.00	**1.00**
15*300	2153.24	**5068.72**	0.00	**1.00**
20*100	2664.65	**5187.26**	0.00	**1.00**
20*200	1917.41	**6313.68**	0.00	**1.00**
20*300	1873.09	**7486.02**	0.00	**1.00**

region, but with the better convergence. In contrast, the Pareto fronts found by the proposed MOCGAO achieve the best performance in both convergence and distribution for 11 out of 12 instances, except for the 10*100 instance. The statistical results of HV and

C summarized in Tables 4 and 5 confirm the above observations. Consequently, the proposed algorithm outperforms the other compared algorithms due to the better diversity of the offspring maintained by the improved GAN, especially for the problems with the large-scale participants.

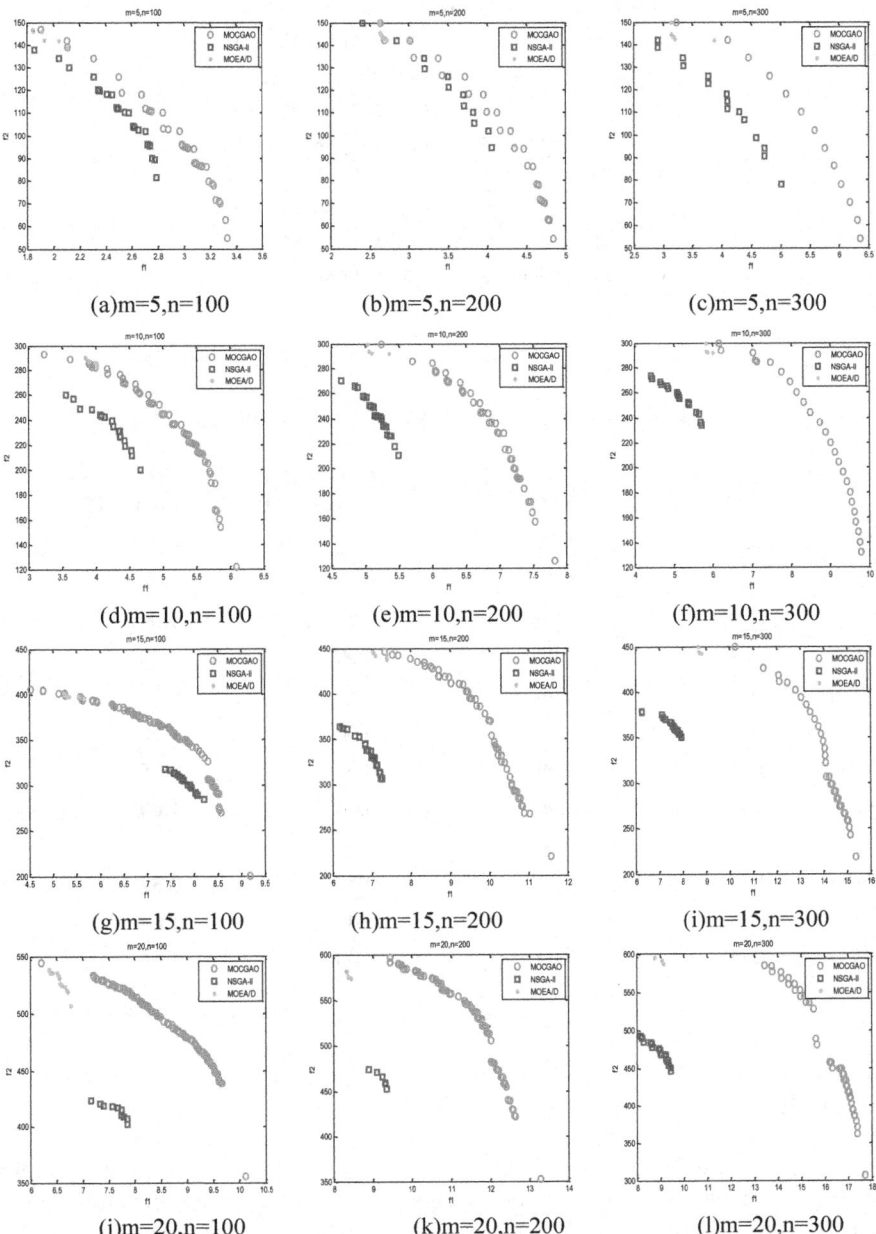

Fig. 5. The Pareto fronts found by different algorithms

Table 4. Comparison of HV for different algorithms

Algorithms	5*100	5*200	5*300	10*100
NSGA-II	255.91	401.69	555.19	995.15
MOEA/D	190.92	336.97	510.12	900.75
MOCGAO	**290.47**	**460.19**	**667.13**	**1326.42**
Algorithms	10*200	10*300	15*100	15*200
NSGA-II	1150.59	1436.14	2293.47	2282.35
MOEA/D	1361.30	1508.12	2021.01	2951.97
MOCGAO	**1480.75**	**2074.57**	**3304.06**	**3906.53**
Algorithms	15*300	20*100	20*200	20*300
NSGA-II	3050.39	3043.77	3981.00	4366.54
MOEA/D	3515.28	3144.68	4341.35	5000.99
MOCGAO	**5068.72**	**5187.26**	**6313.68**	**7486.02**

Table 5. Comparison of C for different algorithms

m*n	C(NSGA-II, MOCGAO)	C(MOCGAO, NSGA-II)	**C(MOEA/D, MOCGAO)**	C(MOCGAO, MOEA/D)
5*100	0.00	**1.00**	0.00	**0.57**
5*200	0.00	**1.00**	0.04	**0.38**
5*300	0.00	**1.00**	0.00	**1.00**
10*100	0.00	**1.00**	**0.09**	0.00
10*200	0.00	**1.00**	0.00	**0.75**
10*300	0.00	**1.00**	0.00	**1.00**
15*100	0.00	**1.00**	0.03	**0.85**
15*200	0.00	**1.00**	0.00	**1.00**
15*300	0.00	**1.00**	0.00	**1.00**
20*100	0.00	**1.00**	0.00	**0.39**
20*200	0.00	**1.00**	0.00	**1.00**
20*300	0.00	**1.00**	0.00	**1.00**

5 Conclusions

To overcome the weakness of the traditional evolutionary algorithms on solving multi-objective combinatorial optimization problems with the large-scale decision variables, a generative adversarial network that has the strong learning and generative abilities is introduced to construct a multi-objective combinatorial generative adversarial optimization algorithm. The extreme of each objective obtained by the greedy algorithm is combined with the randomly produced individuals to form the initial population, with the purpose of speeding up the training process of GAN. During the evolution, the optimal non-dominated solutions in the current generation are identified as the real samples, while the rest are fake. Classified solutions are employed to train GAN. More specifically, the Adam method with the adaptive learning rate is employed to update the parameters of GAN, and an offspring reproduction strategy is presented to obtain a feasible offspring from the decimal output of the generator. Following that, the proposed algorithm is utilized to solve the participant selection problem of the crowdsensing, and a detailed offspring reproduction strategy is given. The experiments are conducted on the crowdsensing system with the various tasks and participants, and the results show that the proposed algorithm superior to the others in both convergence and distribution. To combine the evolutionary operators with GAN will be our future work, with the purpose of generating the offspring with more uniform distribution.

Acknowledgements. This work is supported by National Natural Science Foundation of China under Grant 61973305, 61806119, National Key Research and Development Program under Grant 2016YFC0801406, and Six talent peaks project in Jiangsu Province under Grant No. 2017-DZXX-046.

References

1. Guo, Y., Cheng, J., Luo, S., et al.: Robust dynamic multi-objective vehicle routing optimization method. IEEE/ACM Trans. Comput. Biol. Bioinform. **15**(6), 1891–1903 (2018)
2. Blum, C., Puchinger, J., Günther, R.R.: Hybrid metaheuristics in combinatorial optimization: a survey. Appl. Soft Comput. **11**(6), 4135–4151 (2011)
3. Zhang, P., Tan, Y.: Immune cooperation mechanism based learning framework. Neurocomputing **148**, 158–166 (2015)
4. Precup, R.E., David, R.C., Petriu, E.M., et al.: Grey wolf optimizer-based approach to the tuning of pi-fuzzy controllers with a reduced process parametric sensitivity. IFAC PapersOnLine **49**(5), 55–60 (2016)
5. Goli, A., Aazami, A., Jabbarzadeh, A.: Accelerated cuckoo optimization algorithm for capacitated vehicle routing problem in competitive conditions. Int. J. Artif. Intell. **16**(1), 88–112 (2018)
6. Yang, M., Omidvar, M.N., Li, C., et al.: Efficient resource allocation in cooperative co-evolution for large-scale global optimization. IEEE Trans. Evol. Comput. **21**(4), 493–505 (2017)
7. Tian, Y., Zhang, X., Wang, C., et al.: An evolutionary algorithm for large-scale sparse multi-objective optimization problems. IEEE Trans. Evol. Comput. (2019). https://doi.org/10.1109/TEVC.2019.2918140
8. Cheng, R., He, C., Jin, Y., Yao, X.: Model-based evolutionary algorithms: a short survey. Complex Intell. Syst. **4**(4), 283–292 (2018). https://doi.org/10.1007/s40747-018-0080-1
9. Guo, Y., Huan, Y., Chen, M., et al.: Ensemble prediction-based dynamic robust multi-objective optimization methods. Swarm Evol. Comput. **48**, 156–171 (2019)
10. Zhang, J., Zhan, Z., Lin, Y., et al.: Evolutionary computation meets machine learning: a survey. IEEE Comput. Intell. Mag. **6**(4), 68–75 (2011)

11. Guo, Y., Zhang, X., Gong, D., et al.: Novel interactive preference-based multi-objective evolutionary optimization for bolt supporting networks. IEEE Trans. Evol. Comput. (2019). https://doi.org/10.1109/TEVC.2019.2951217

12. Li, K., Zhang, T., Wang, R.: Deep reinforcement learning for multi-objective optimization **14**(8), 1–10 (2019)

13. Nazari, M., Oroojlooy, A., Snyder, L., et al.: Reinforcement learning for solving the vehicle routing problem. In: Advances in Neural Information Processing Systems, pp. 9839–9849 (2018)

14. Ruiz-Rangel, J., Ardila, C., Gonzalez, L.M., et al.: ERNEAD: training of artificial neural networks based on a genetic algorithm and finite automata theory. Int. J. Artif. Intell. **16**(1), 214–253 (2018)

15. He, C., Huang, S., Cheng, R.: Evolutionary multi-objective optimization driven by generative adversarial networks. arXiv:1907.04482 [cs.NE] (2019)

16. Goodfellow, I., Pouget-Abadie, J., Mirza, M., et al.: Generative adversarial nets. In: Advances in Neural Information Processing System, pp. 2672–2680 (2014)

17. Tan, Y., Shi, B.: Generative adversarial optimization. In: Tan, Y., Shi, Y., Niu, B. (eds.) ICSI 2019. LNCS, vol. 11655, pp. 3–17. Springer, Cham (2019). https://doi.org/10.1007/978-3-030-26369-0_1

18. Probst, M.: Generative adversarial networks in estimation of distribution algorithms for combinatorial optimization. arXiv:1509.09235 [cs.NE] (2015)

19. Deb, K., Pratap, A., Agarwal, S.: A fast and elitist multiobjective genetic algorithm: NSGA-II. IEEE Trans. Evol. Comput. **6**(2), 180–197 (2002)

20. Ledig, C., Theis, L., Huszár, F.: Photo-realistic single image super resolution using a generative adversarial network. In: IEEE/CVF Conference on Computer Vision and Pattern Recognition (CVPR), pp. 4681–4690 (2016)

21. Zhang, D., Shao, J., Hu, G., Gao, L.: Sharp and real image super-resolution using generative adversarial network. In: Liu, D., Xie, S., Li, Y., Zhao, D., El-Alfy, E.S. (eds.) Neural Information Processing. ICONIP 2017. LNCS, vol. 10636, pp. 217–226. Springer, Cham (2017). https://doi.org/10.1007/978-3-319-70090-8_23

22. Li, R., Pan, J., Li, Z.: Single image dehazing via conditional generative adversarial network. In: 2018 IEEE/CVF Conference on Computer Vision and Pattern Recognition, pp. 8202–8211 (2018)

23. Press, O., Bar, A., Bogin, B.: Language generation with recurrent generative adversarial networks without pre-training. arXiv:1706.01399 [cs.CL] (2017)

24. Kingma, D., Ba, J.: Adam: a method for stochastic optimization. arXiv:1412.6980 [cs.LG] (2017)

25. Ji, J., Guo, Y., Gong, D., et al.: MOEA/D-based participant selection method for crowdsensing with Social awareness. Appl. Soft Comput. **87** (2019). https://doi.org/10.1016/j.asoc.2019.105981

26. Tian, Y., Cheng, R., Zhang, X., et al.: PlatEMO: a MATLAB platform for evolutionary multi-objective optimization. IEEE Comput. Intell. Mag. **12**(4), 73–87 (2019)

27. Zhang, Q., Li, H.: MOEA/D: a multiobjective evolutionary algorithm based on decomposition. IEEE Trans. Evol. Comput. **11**(6), 712–731 (2008)

Multi-objective Dynamic Scheduling Model of Flexible Job Shop Based on NSGAII Algorithm and Scroll Window Technology

Yingli Li and Jiahai Wang[✉]

School of Mechanical Engineering, Tongji University, Shanghai 201804, China
jhwang@tongji.edu.cn

Abstract. The production process is often accompanied by a lot of disturbances, which make it difficult for flexible job shop to execute production according to the original job plan. It is necessary to dynamically adjust the production plan according to real-time conditions. To this end, this paper proposes a multi-objective dynamic scheduling model. In this model, scroll window technology and NSGAII algorithm is adopted to adapt the dynamic production evironment. A specific chromosome retention strategy and a variable objective selection mechanism are designed to ensure that the proposed model can select different objectives according to different disturbance events to solve the optimal solution. Finally, a case test is used to verify the feasibility and effectiveness of the model.

Keywords: Flexible job-shop · Dynamic scheduling · Evolutionary algorithm

1 Introduction

The flexible job-shop scheduling problem (FJSP), as an extension of the job-shop scheduling problem (JSP), has been proved to be a NP-hard problem [1]. FJSP is usually divided into two categories [2]: static scheduling and dynamic scheduling. Static scheduling is an optimized job plan generated by the management system based on the determined resource information, while dynamic scheduling is a response to the emergency in production process based on real-time production information. Compared with static scheduling, due to the uncertainty of dynamic scheduling, solving the problem of dynamic scheduling is more complicated. It is of great significance to study the flexible job shop dynamic scheduling problem (FJDSP), as described below.

On the one hand, the production process is often accompanied by the occurrence of emergencies. The timing of these events and their impact on production are often uncertain. This makes it difficult for the job shop to carry out production according to original plan. Therefore, compared with static scheduling, dynamic scheduling is more in line with the actual situation of job shop production control [3]. On the other hand, scheduling is the core functional modules of manufacturing execution system (MES), and its performance is directly related to the effect of MES. Therefore, the study of FJDSP is conducive to improve MES management level.

© Springer Nature Switzerland AG 2020
Y. Tan et al. (Eds.): ICSI 2020, LNCS 12145, pp. 435–444, 2020.
https://doi.org/10.1007/978-3-030-53956-6_39

Due to its importance, many scholars paid much attention on FJDSP and established some dynamic scheduling models, including: genetic algorithm-based dynamic scheduling [4], particle swarm algorithm-based dynamic scheduling [5] and simulated annealing algorithm-based dynamic scheduling [6] and so on. However, the survey found that although many machining companies in China have deployed MES, they have not used the scheduling functions, and have only used resource management and monitoring modules. The reason is that the existing dynamic scheduling model has poor self-adaptability and cannot effectively respond to disturbances. The specific performance is that from static scheduling to dynamic scheduling, the optimization goal is single and fixed, which is the shortest maximum completion time, or the lowest penalty cost, or a combination of the two. This scheduling model with a single fixed objective will cause the algorithm ignoring other key issues when seeking the optimal solution, such as making a job unrestricted delay in order to achieve the shortest maximum completion time.

Aiming at the above existing problems of FJDSP, this paper uses NSGAII algorithm combined with scroll window technology to establish a multi-objective dynamic scheduling model DSNSGAII. This model can adaptively select optimization objectives for rescheduling according to different emergencies. This improves the reliability of production plan execution.

The rest of this paper is organized as follows: In Sect. 2, application scenarios is described. DSNSGAII is introduced in Sect. 3. In Sect. 4, case verification is presented. Section 5 are the conclusions.

2   Problem Description

The research object of this paper is flexible job shop, which characteristics are described as follows: There are $N_i(i \in (1, 2, \ldots n))$ jobs to be produced on M machines, where i is the index of job number. Each job has j operations, O_{ij} represents the *jth* operation of job i. There is a predefined sequence between any two-adjoining operations of each job. Each operation can be processed by multiple machines. $m_{ij}(m_{ij} \subset M)$ represents the candidate machine set of O_{ij}. Each machine can only process one operation at a time, and one operation can only be processed by one machine at a time. There are two subproblems, one is how to assign operations to suitable machine, and the other is to find optimal production sequence for all operations assigned to machines. The optimization objectives used in this paper mainly include the following.

(1)   Minimize makespan:

$$f_1(t) = min\{max(C_{ij})\}. \tag{1}$$

(2)   Minimize total tardiness:

$$f_2(t) = min \sum_{i=1}^{n} \left[max\left(0, C_i - T_i^J\right)L\left(N_i^{y1}\right) + max\left(0, C_i - T_i^{yJ}\right)L\left(N_i^{y2}\right)\right]. \tag{2}$$

$$\begin{cases} T_i^x \le T_i^J, L\left(N_i^{y1}\right) = 1, \ L\left(N_i^{y2}\right) = 0 \ if \ L(N_i) = 1 \\ T_i^x \le T_i^{yJ}, L\left(N_i^{y1}\right) = 0, \ L\left(N_i^{y2}\right) = 1 \ if \ L(N_i) = 0 \end{cases}. \tag{3}$$

(3) The shortest delay time for a single job:

$$f_3(t) = min\{max(0, C_k - D_k)\}. \tag{4}$$

C_{ij} represents the completion time of operation O_{ij}. $L(N_i)$ is the delay tag. T_i^x is the completion time of job i in the new plan. T_i^J is the actual completion time of job i before dynamic scheduling. T_i^{yJ} is the original planned completion time of job i. C_k is the completion time of job k. D_k is the due date of job k.

3   DSNSGAII Model

3.1   Job Processing

According to the scroll window technology [7], when dynamic scheduling is executed, the state of the operation set may have four, namely: finished processing, being processing, waiting processing and waiting scheduling, as shown in Fig. 1. For the operation sets that have been processed, it can be removed when performing rescheduling. For the operation sets that is waiting for processing and waiting for scheduling can be retained. The key problem lies in how to deal with the operation sets that are being processed. In this paper, whether the dynamic scheduling is triggered by machine failure, the operation set being processed is divided into two cases to deal with separately.

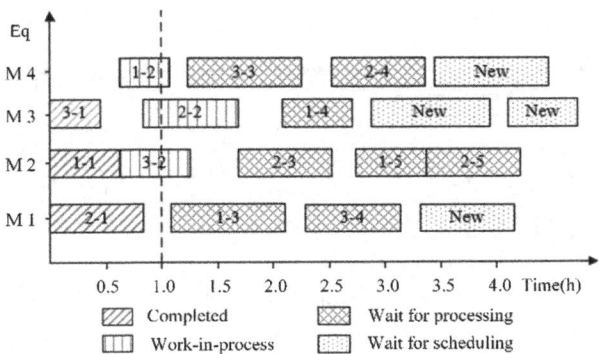

Fig. 1. Job status diagram based on scroll window technology.

(1) Dynamic scheduling is not trigged by machine failure
      In this case, the operation set of being processed is still completed by current machine. Its effect on dynamic scheduling is that the available time of this machine does not start from the dynamic scheduling trigger time, but the end time of the operation set of being processed. Its mathematical expression is shown in formula (5), where T_{MP} is the available start time of machine P after dynamic scheduling is triggered, t_c is the dynamic scheduling trigger time, t_{ijMP} is the required time

to complete the operation set of being processed when the dynamic scheduling is triggered.

$$T_{MP} = t_c + t_{ijMP}. \tag{5}$$

(2) Dynamic scheduling is trigged by machine failure

In this case, the operation set of being processed cannot continue processing on the original machine, so it needs to participate in dynamic scheduling. Its impact on dynamic scheduling is that part of the products in the operation set have been completed. Therefore, the processing time required by the operation set should be the original planned time minus the time consumed by the completed products. Its mathematical expression is shown in formula (6), where T_{ijx} is the time required to complete the new operation set after removing the finished product, T_{ij} is the required processing time of O_{ij} of a product. Q_i is the product quantity of the operation set, and q_i is the finished product quantity in the operation set.

$$T_{ijx} = T_{ij}(Q_i - q_i). \tag{6}$$

3.2 Encoding and Decoding

Encoding: The A-B string coding method that used by Zhang et al. is adopted [8]. The chromosome includes two parts: machine selection and operation sequence. The total length of chromosome is the twice sum of all operations. as shown in Fig. 2.

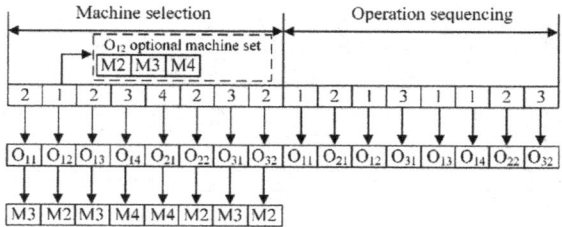

Fig. 2. Chromosome coding

In the machine selection section, machine numbers are arranged according to operation numbers. The number represents the location of the machine in the candidate machine set. For example, the second number 1 in the machine selection part represents the machine position number corresponding to the operation O_{12}. That is, the machine located in the first position is selected from the candidate machine set of operation O_{12}, and the machine selected at this time is M2. In the operation sequence, the number represents the job number, and the number of occurrences represents the corresponding operation number. For example, the first appearance of 1 represents operation O_{11}, and the second appearance of 1 represents operation O_{12}.

Decoding: It has been proved that the optimal solution is often within the set of active solutions [9]. In order to obtain the active solutions, the left shift interpolation method is adopted. The detail calculation method of left shift interpolation can reference to literature [8].

3.3   Genetic Manipulation

Population Initialization. In order to ensure the diversity of population, initial population is generated by the mixed method. Operation sequence is generated by mixing four methods: random generation method, shortest processing time priority rule, maximum remaining operation rule, and maximum remaining load rule. The respective proportions are: 50%, 20%, 20%, and 10%. The machine selection is generated by mixing three methods: random generation method, shortest processing time priority rule, and machine workload minimum priority rule. The respective proportions are: 50%, 30%, and 20%.

Chromosome Crossing. In order to make good individual genes inherited to offspring, a superior chromosome repetition crossover strategy is proposed. Step1: Build superior chromosome memory with capacity R. Step2: The chromosome with superior objective value are added to the chromosome memory. If the memory reaches the maximum capacity, the better chromosome replaces the poor one. Step3: An individual is selected in turn from the chromosome memory, and it is crossed with multiple non-memory chromosomes to obtain offspring. In addition, the operation of randomly selecting two chromosomes from all chromosomes for crossover remains. The two kinds of crossover methods account for 40% and 60%. The specific cross-operation adopts the IPOX and MPX methods proposed by Wang et al. [10].

Chromosome Mutation. Machine chromosome mutation uses a single point replacement method, which randomly selects one point from the chromosome as the mutation point and replaces the machine at the mutation point with the shortest processing time's machine in the candidate machine set. Operation chromosome mutation adopts two methods: double-point exchange and clockwork rotation, as shown in Fig. 3. Two-point exchange is to randomly select two different points from the operation chromosome as the exchange points and exchange the genes of these two points. The clockwork rotation mutation method is described as follows: randomly generate an integer n ($1 \leq n \leq L$), all genes in the operation sequence are moved n positions in a clockwise direction, and maintain the relative position invariant. The proportion of the two methods in chromosome mutations is 70% and 30% of the mutation size, respectively.

3.4   Chromosome Selection

There are generally three disturbances in job shop: normal order addition, urgent order insertion, and machine failure. Different disturbances have different requirements for rescheduling results. Therefore, these three cases are processed separately.

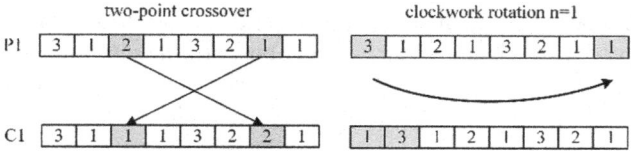

Fig. 3. The clockwork rotation mutation method

Normal Order Addition. In order to avoid the impact of new job addition on original job delivery time, a restriction rule is set. i.e. the original job was completed on time and still completed on time. The delay time of original delayed job in new plan cannot exceed the original delayed time. Thus, there are two objectives, one is that the original jobs have the shortest delay time in new plan, namely f_2, and the other is minimum the makespan, namely f_1. If there are individuals with f_2 of 0, add the individuals to next iteration and the chromosome memory. For other individuals, the chromosome is selected by fast non-dominant sorting and crowding distance calculation [11]. Finally, the solution with $f_1 = \min$ and $f_2 = 0$ is the optimal solution.

Insert Urgent Job. It is necessary to ensure that the urgent job is completed on time. In this case, the first objective is the shortest delay time for urgent job, namely f_3. The second objective is to minimize the total delay time of all jobs. In addition, to ensure that all jobs are completed quickly, this section sets the auxiliary objective, which is minimize makespan. If there are individuals with f_3 of 0, add the individuals to next generation population and the chromosome memory. For other individuals, the chromosome is selected by fast non-dominant sorting and crowding distance calculation. When outputting the optimal solution, the hierarchical selection method is used. First, f_3 must be the smallest and the screening result is the population q_1; then the individuals with the smallest total delay time is selected and its population is $q_2(q_1 \subset q_2)$; finally, the individuals $q_3(q_3 \subset q_2)$ with the smallest f_1 is selected.

Machine Failure. The dynamic scheduling triggered by machine failure has a great impact on the original job plan, mainly because the machine is production resource, the reduction of production resource may lead to the delay of multiple jobs. In order to mitigate the impact of machine failure on production plan, the shortest total delay time f_2 was taken as objective. In order to deal with the case that machine failure did not cause job delay, take minimum makespan as the second objective. The chromosome with the smallest objective function value ($min\ f_2(f_2 \neq 0)$ or $min\ f_1(f_2 = 0)$) is added to chromosome memory. The population that enters the next iteration is selected by fast non-dominated sorting and calculation of the crowded distance. Finally, the solution with $min\ f_2(f_2 \neq 0)$ or $min\ f_1(f_2 = 0)$ is the optimal solution.

4   Case Verification

To test the effectiveness of DSNSGAII, the benchmark case ka 4X5 [12] is adopted, the information of this case is shown in Table 1. J_5 is the job of normal additional

Table 1. The information of benchmark case.

Job no.	O_{ij}	Processing time per machine					Q_i	D_k
		M1	M2	M3	M4	M5		
J_1	O_{11}	2	5	4	1	2	20	190
	O_{12}	5	4	5	7	5		
	O_{13}	4	5	5	4	5		
J_2	O_{21}	2	5	4	7	8	20	240
	O_{22}	5	6	9	8	5		
	O_{23}	4	5	4	54	5		
J_3	O_{31}	9	8	6	7	9	10	120
	O_{32}	6	1	2	5	4		
	O_{33}	2	5	4	2	4		
	O_{34}	4	5	2	1	5		
J_4	O_{41}	1	5	2	4	12	30	100
	O_{42}	5	1	2	1	2		

and emergency insertion, its information shown in Table 2. The time of normal order addition, urgent order insertion and machine failure is generated randomly. The failure machine is also random selected.

Due to the optimization objectives in DSNSGAII is changed with the disturbances, it is hard to compare with other excellent algorithms directly, this paper only compares dynamic scheduling results with the classical genetic algorithm (MGA), which aims to minimize makespan and minimize total delay time. In the MGA, the weight of the two objectives is 0.6 and 0.4. In order to ensure the comparability of results, the DSNSGAII and the MGA adopt the same genetic methods, and the parameters adopts the same value: the population size is 200, crossover rate is 0.8, mutation rate is 0.8 and iterations is 100.

Table 2. The information of urgent insertion order.

Job no.	O_{ij}	Processing time per machine					Q_i	D_k
		M1	M2	M3	M4	M5		
J_5	O_{51}	2	4	3	5	2	20	230
	O_{52}	3	5	7	2	4		
	O_{53}	4	6	4	3	5		

On-time delivery is a guarantee to ensure customer satisfaction and improve enterprise credibility. Therefore, this paper takes the delay time as the evaluation index of the algorithm's advantages and disadvantages. The fewer the delay orders and the shorter the total delay time, the better the algorithm.

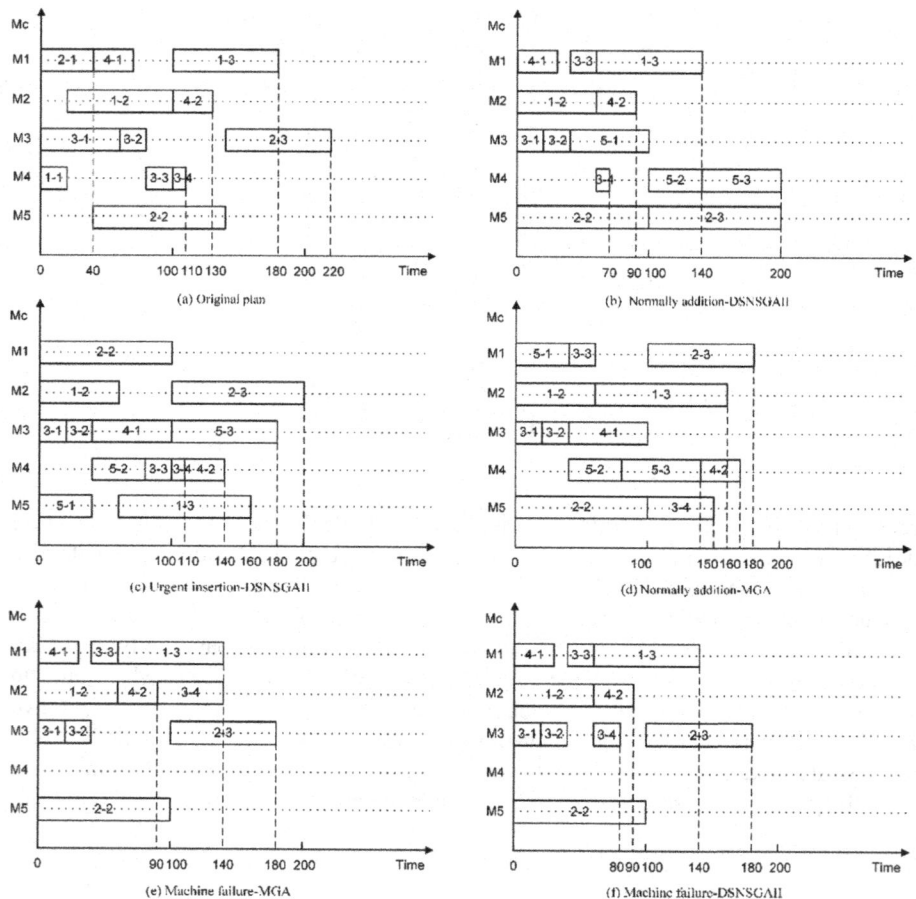

Fig. 4. The gantt chart of job-shop production plan

The experiment results are shown in Fig. 4. Figure 4(a) is the original production plan, as can be seen from this figure, dynamic scheduling is triggered at time 40, and only J_4 is delayed and its delay time is 30.

Normal order addition. After J_5 is added normally, the production plan obtained by DSNSGAII is shown in Fig. 4(b). Compared with Fig. 4(a), it can be seen that the original job was completed on time and still completed on time, such as J_1, J_2 and J_3. The original job is delayed, the new completion time of the job is no later than the original completion time, such as J_4. As can be seen from Fig. 4(b), only two job is delayed, and the total delay time is 40. The production plan obtained by MGA is shown in Fig. 4(d). It can be seen that due to the objective weights are difference, the optimal solution is more inclined to the objective with a large weight. Although the maximum completion time of the results obtained by MGA is 220 and it is smaller than DSNSGAII, the three jobs of J_1, J_3 and J_4 are delayed, and the total delay time is 190. This result not only leads to an increase of delay cost, but also affects customer satisfaction. Therefore, through comparison, we conclude that DSNSGAII is superior to MGA in normal order addition.

Urgent order insertion. After J_5 is added to production in the form of an urgent job, the production plan obtained by DSNSGAII is shown in Fig. 4(c). As can be seen from this figure, J_5 can complete on time, the three jobs of J_1, J_3 and J_4 are delayed, the total delayed time is 120. Compared with Fig. 4(d), the DSNSGAII has fewer delay orders and the total delay time while ensuring that urgent job is completed on time. So, it is concluded that DSNSGAII is superior to MGA algorithm in terms of emergency order insertion.

Machine failure. Figure 4(e) and Fig. 4(f) are Gantt chart of the production plan solved by MGA and DSNSGAII after machine M4 fault. From Fig. 4(e), it can be seen that MGA will give priority to minimize makespan when solving. At the same time, the optimization goal with the smallest total delay time is weakened, resulting in a delay of 60 for J_3 and 30 for J_4. The DSNSGAII can effectively balance the two goals. The maximum completion time is 220, which is the same as the result obtained by MGA. However, in the term of minimize total delay time, DSNSGAII only one job is delayed, and the total delay time is 30. Therefore, it is concluded that the DSNSGAII is more effective than MGA.

5 Conclusions

Dynamic scheduling is important for flexible job-shop production management. For solving dynamic scheduling effectively, this paper proposed a DSNSGAII model based on scroll windows technology and NSGAII algorithm. In the proposed model, a new crossover operator is designed to retain more good genes. A clockwork rotation mutation operator is adopted to generate good individuals. For different disturbances, different environment selection mechanism is designed to obtain the required optimal solution. Final, a case is given to verify the validity of the model.

Acknowledgement. This research is supported by the school-enterprise cooperation project of Tongji University under Grant No. kh0100020192160.

References

1. Mohan, J., Lanka, K., Rao, A.N.: A review of dynamic job shop scheduling techniques. Procedia Manuf. (2019). https://doi.org/10.1016/j.promfg.2019.02.006
2. Zambrano Rey, G., Bekrar, A., Prabhu, V., Trentesaux, D.: Coupling a genetic algorithm with the distributed arrival-time control for the JIT dynamic scheduling of flexible job-shops. Int. J. Prod. Res. (2014). https://doi.org/10.1080/00207543.2014.881575

3. Renna, P.: Job shop scheduling by pheromone approach in a dynamic environment. Int. J. Comput. Integr. Manuf. (2010). https://doi.org/10.1080/09511921003642170
4. Kundakci, N., Kulak, O.: Hybrid genetic algorithms for minimizing makespan in dynamic job shop scheduling problem. Comput. Ind. Eng. (2016). https://doi.org/10.1016/j.cie.2016.03.011
5. Al-Behadili, M., Ouelhadj, D., Jones, D.: Multi-objective particle swarm optimisation for robust dynamic scheduling in a permutation flow shop. In: Madureira, A.M., Abraham, A., Gamboa, D., Novais, P. (eds.) ISDA 2016. AISC, vol. 557, pp. 498–507. Springer, Cham (2017). https://doi.org/10.1007/978-3-319-53480-0_49
6. Naderi, B., Azab, A.: An improved model and novel simulated annealing for distributed job shop problems. Int. J. Adv. Manuf. Technol. (2015). https://doi.org/10.1007/s00170-015-7080-8
7. Nelson, R.T., Holloway, C.A., Mei-Lun Wong, R.: Centralized scheduling and priority implementation heuristics for a dynamic job shop model. AIIE Trans. (1977). https://doi.org/10.1080/05695557708975127
8. Zhang, G., Sun, J., Liu, X., Wang, G., Yang, Y.: Solving flexible job shop scheduling problems with transportation time based on improved genetic algorithm. Math. Biosci. Eng. **16**, 1334–1347 (2019). https://doi.org/10.3934/mbe.2019065
9. Gao, J., Sun, L., Gen, M.: A hybrid genetic and variable neighborhood descent algorithm for flexible job shop scheduling problems. Comput. Oper. Res. (2008). https://doi.org/10.1016/j.cor.2007.01.001
10. Wang, X., Gao, L., Zhang, C., Shao, X.: A multi-objective genetic algorithm based on immune and entropy principle for flexible job-shop scheduling problem. Int. J. Adv. Manuf. Technol. (2010). https://doi.org/10.1007/s00170-010-2642-2
11. Deb, K., Pratap, A., Agarwal, S., Meyarivan, T.: A fast and elitist multiobjective genetic algorithm: NSGA-II. IEEE Trans. Evol. Comput. (2002). https://doi.org/10.1109/4235.996017
12. Kacem, I., Hammadi, S., Borne, P.: Pareto-optimality approach for flexible job-shop scheduling problems: hybridization of evolutionary algorithms and fuzzy logic. Math. Comput. Simul. (2002). https://doi.org/10.1016/S0378-4754(02)00019-8

Optimal Reservoir Optimization Using Multiobjective Genetic Algorithm

Vinod Chandra S S[1], S. Anand Hareendran[2(✉)], and Saju Sankar S[3]

[1] Computer Centre, University of Kerala, Trivandrum, India
vinod@keralauniversity.ac.in
[2] Department of Computer Science, MITS, Kochi, India
anandhareendrans@mgits.ac.in
[3] Department of Computer Engineering,
Government Polytechnic College, Punalur, India
tkmce@rediffmail.com

Abstract. Scarcity of fresh water resources has thrown various challenges to hydrologist. Optimum usage of resource is the only way out to handle this situation. Among the various water resources the most controllable one is the dam reservoirs. This paper deals with optimal reservoir optimization using multi objective genetic algorithm (MOGA). Various parameters like reservoir storage capacity, spill loss, evaporation rate, water used for irrigation, water used for electricity production, rate of inflow, outflow all need to be managed in an optimal way so that water levels are managed and resource specifications are met. This is normally managed using a software, but sudden change in scenarios and change in requirements cannot be handled by such softwares. Hence we are incorporating an optimised software layer to handle such situation. Multi objective genetic algorithm was able to optimise the water usage within the usage constrains. The results were assessed based on reliability, vulnerability and resilience indices. In addition, based on a multi-criteria decision-making model, it was evaluated by comparing it with other evolutionary algorithms. The simulated result shows that MOGA derived rules are promising and competitive and can be effectively used for reservoir optimization operations.

Keywords: Reservoir optimization · Multi objective genetic algorithm · Resource optimisation · Nature inspired computing · Software optimisation

1 Introduction

There are times in the year where a specific place gets heavy rainfall during a quarter and goes dried up in another. Normally the rainwater is harvested in the dam and is used for power generation, agricultural usage and as a source

Supported by Machine Intelligent Research Group.

for drinking. When the rainfall is heavy and is too much concentrated, there are chances that the dams get filled and the engineers will be forced to open the shutters of the dam. This can cause serious threat for the physical assets or can lead to life threatening scenarios. Floods and resource disruption will be heavy. On the other hand - during summer season, the out flow should be regulated in such a way that enough water is available for drinking and irrigation purpose till the next rain. To control all such situation, an automated software for controlling the reservoir level, outflow of water are needed. But in many cases such a software alone doesnt fully meet the purpose. We need to have an intelligent optimization agent which runs on top of the software to have a perfect solution. In this work we propose an optimization technique which explores the possibilities of genetic algorithm for optimal reservoir level and flow.

Genetic algorithm is a directed search algorithms based on the mechanics of biological evolution developed by John Holland from University of Michigan in 1970's. It is a search technique used in computing to find true or approximate solutions to optimisation and search problems. This technique is categorised as global search heuristics used a particular class of evolutionary techniques inspired by evolutionary biology such as inheritance, mutation, selection, and crossover (also called recombination). Genetic algorithms are implemented as a computer simulation in which a population of abstract representations called chromosomes or the genotype or the genome of candidate solutions (called individuals, creatures, or phenotypes) to an optimisation problem evolves toward better solutions. Traditionally, solutions are represented in binary as strings of 0s and 1s, but other encodings are also possible. The evolution usually starts from a population of randomly generated individuals and happens in generations. In each generation, the fitness of every individual in the population is evaluated, multiple individuals are selected from the current population (based on their fitness), and modified (recombined and possibly mutated) to form a new population. The new population is then used in the next iteration of the algorithm. Commonly, the algorithm terminates when either a maximum number of generations has been produced, or a satisfactory fitness level has been reached for the population. If algorithm has terminated due to a maximum number of generations, a satisfactory solution may or may not have been reached.

2 Literature Survey

Until Oliveira and Loucks in 1997 explored much into the possibilities of using genetic algorithm (GA) for reservoir optimization, none of the water resource or dam engineers had given a though to it. There have been methods which made use of dynamic programming and linear programming but they all had constrains in the objective function. When the models turned to be stochastic, modelling need to be carried out strong to have a very specific target class. Scientists Karamouz and Houck has compared stochastic dynamic programming (SDP) and dynamic programming with regression for rule generations in reservoir optimization. The works actually concluded by the fact that for small reservoir stochastic model works well and for larger ones with high outflow dynamic process works well. Wardlaw and Sharif in 1999 has explored the various extremes of GA in formulating real time optimization in reservoir, but found that the objective function definition was a tough task while considering the various constrains.

Genetic algorithm has used in various type of water optimisation problems. In 1991 Wang has developed a model based on GA for calibrating the amount of water runoff during rainfall. Similarly GA has been used by McKinney and in to optimise the usage of ground water resource. During early 1997 Oliveira and Loucks has evaluated the rules generated by GA for multi reservoir system. The approach could be applied easily for non-linear and complex systems. Adeyemo and Otieno in 2009 has presented a multi objective differential evolutionary technique for farm land irrigation. The objective function basically pointed to minimising irrigation water use and maximising the total plant area coverage. In another study by Sharma and Jana in 2009, a fuzzy programming based genetic algorithm model was developed for decision making in farm land regarding the supply of nutrients through the water. The optimization results showed peak improvement in the proposed scheme. Various other studies also have shown applications of genetic algorithm in water resource management, the major works includes Tospornsampan et al. during 2005 and Simonovic et al. in 2004.

3   Methodology

Genetic algorithm is a directed search algorithms based on the mechanics of biological evolution developed by John Holland from University of Michigan in 1970's. It is a search technique used in computing to find true or approximate solutions to optimisation and search problems. This technique is categorised as global search heuristics used a particular class of evolutionary techniques inspired by evolutionary biology such as inheritance, mutation, selection, and crossover (also called recombination).

Genetic algorithms are implemented as a computer simulation in which a population of abstract representations called chromosomes or the genotype or the genome of candidate solutions (called individuals, creatures, or phenotypes) to an optimisation problem evolves toward better solutions. Traditionally, solutions are represented in binary as strings of 0s and 1s, but other encodings are also possible. The evolution usually starts from a population of randomly generated individuals and happens in generations. In each generation, the fitness of every individual in the population is evaluated, multiple individuals are selected from the current population (based on their fitness), and modified (recombined and possibly mutated) to form a new population. The new population is then used in the next iteration of the algorithm. Commonly, the algorithm terminates when either a maximum number of generations has been produced, or a satisfactory fitness level has been reached for the population. If algorithm has terminated due to a maximum number of generations, a satisfactory solution may or may not have been reached.

A typical genetic algorithm requires two things to be defined - a genetic representation of the solution domain, and a fitness function to evaluate the solution domain. The genetic algorithm is a probabilistic search algorithm that iteratively transforms a set or a population of mathematical objects (typically fixed-length binary character strings), each with an associated fitness value, into a new population of offspring objects using the Darwinian principle of natural selection and using operations that are patterned after naturally occurring genetic operations, such as crossover (sexual recombination) and mutation. In the scenario of water resource optimization, we may need to have a modified GA approach. The non-dominated classification of GA population need to be considered for optimization. This may also be termed as multi objective genetic algorithm. The non-dominant class is also taken for crossover. The offspring thus created gives a very unique class of classifier, which can be used in multi objective optimization.

Multi Objective Genetic Algorithm

> Generate initial population;
> Compute fitness of each individual;
> **Repeat** /* New generation /*
>> **for** population size/2 **do**
>>> Select two parents from old generation;
>>> /* biased to the fitter ones */
>>> Recombine parents for two offspring;
>>> Compute fitness of offspring;
>>> Insert offspring in new generation
>> **endfor**
>> **if** non dominated populatin exist **do**
>>> Select high ranked Parent with non-dominant for cross over;
>>> Recombine parents for offspring;
>>> Compute fitness of offspring;
>>> Insert offspring in new generation class
>> **Until** non dominant population has converged
> **Until** total population has converged

3.1   Modelling the Objective Function

In any optimization problem the primary challenge is to model the system. Here we need a mathematical model of the reservoir for generating the objective function. In this work genetic algorithm is explored to determine the optimal operating policies of the reservoir. Reservoir system can be modelled using the general equation

$$V_{t+1} = V_t + R_t + Sp_t - Loss_t \tag{1}$$

where V_{t+1} represents the volume of water stored at the end of the given time t, V_t shows the volume at the beginning of the period, Sp_t is the reservoir spill(overflow), R_t shows the amount of water released at time t and $Loss_t$ is the water lost in course of evaporation and transpiration from the reservoir surface.

Loss can be calculated by taking the product of net evaporation with the average surface area.

$$Loss_t = Eva_{net} * \bar{A} \tag{2}$$

Surface area and the reservoir storage also can be mathematically shown as

$$\bar{A} = aV_t^3 + bV_t^2 + cV_t^1 + d \tag{3}$$

where a, b, c and d are constants calculated by fitting the relationship between reservoirs surface and storage.

Electricity produced by the dam can be found out using the equation,

$$Pow_t = minimize[\frac{g * \theta * R_t}{PPF_t} * \frac{\bar{Level} - TWT}{1000}, PPC] \tag{4}$$

where Pow_t is the electricity produced, g is the acceleration due to gravity, θ is the efficiency of power plant, PPF_t is the power plant factor, Level represents the average water level in reservoir, TWT is sequence of water level and PPC is the power plant installation capacity.

Major constrains that need to be addressed are water released during the time t, R_t and V_t which represents the volume at the time t. The values of R_t and V_t should be bounded between the reservoir maximum and minimum limits. The total releases from reservoir cannot exceed the canal capacity and also reservoir storage volume in any time should be less than or equal to the maximum live storage capacity of the reservoir. Thus the deficiency minimisation objective function can be given as,

$$min_f = [1 - \frac{Pow_t}{PPC}]^2 \tag{5}$$

subjected to

$$R_{min,t} \leq R_t \leq R_{max,t}; t = 1, 2, 3...T \tag{6}$$

$$V_{min,t} \leq V_t \leq V_{max,t}; t = 1, 2, 3...T \tag{7}$$

If P_1, P_2 are the penalty functions and K_1, K_2 are corresponding penalty coefficients, then penalty functions can be derived as

$$P_1 = K_1(V_{t+1} - V_t)^2 \tag{8}$$

$$P_2 = K_2(V_{min} - V_{t+!})^2 \tag{9}$$

Thus the final optimization function is

$$min_f = [1 - \frac{Pow_t}{PPC}]^2 + P_1 + P_2 \tag{10}$$

Now we have an optimisation function and the needed constraints. So an optimisation algorithm will do the task of finding the most optimal water distribution plan. But genetic algorithm alone does not helps in doing so in a dynamic situation. Whenever we are having a unpredictable climatic situations prevailing the crossover and mutation parameters specifically identify the fitness function and does the needed optimal strategy to distribute apt quantity of water to each outlet. A very interactive graphical user interface can be developed at the operator end, which gives a hard copy of the results and operational directions for effective management. Figure 1 shows the sample block diagram of the proposed solution.

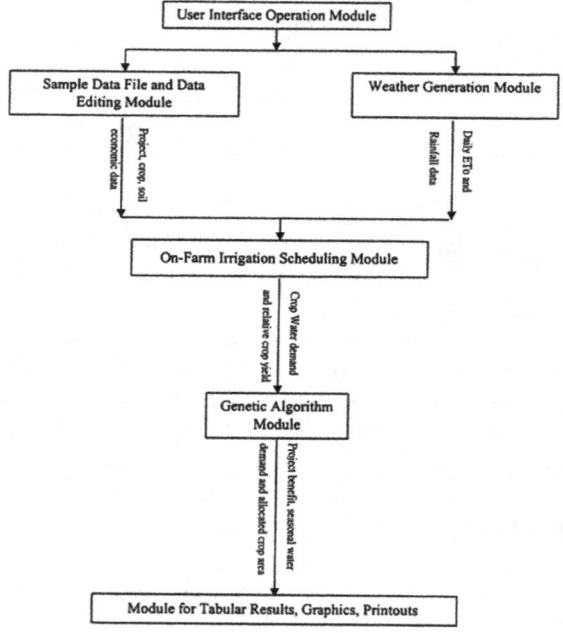

Fig. 1. Architecture details.

We have a user interface operation module which acts as the GUI to the system. Various indicators of soil condition and weather helps the on-farm irrigation module to schedule the water flow to the farm land. The GA module build on top helps in optimising the working. The final analytics and user results can be obtained from the result session.

4   Results and Discussion

Global Reservoir and Dam (GRanD) dataset has been used for simulation purpose. It contains 6,862 records of reservoirs and their associated dams with a cumulative storage capacity of 6,197 cubic km. The reservoirs were delineated from high spatial resolution satellite imagery and are available as polygon shape files. Dataset contains details regarding the various constraints like Pow_t - electricity produced, θ - efficiency of power plant, PPF_t - power plant factor, average water level in reservoir, TWT - sequence of water level and PPC - power plant installation capacity.

As the problem is solved using genetic algorithm approach we need to find the decision parameter that need to be measured. Here in reservoir optimisation the amount of water to be released through the release valve. Consider the Fig. 2, it clearly explains the routes through which water need to travel. When more power need to be generated G2 will be closed and when enough power is being generated more water flows through the bypass. G3 is the gate towards irrigation adn G4 towards the drinking purpose. Depending on the water levels, optimisation need to be carried out for maximum power generation along with water reaching the agricultural fields with minimum error. Drinking water reaching the urban/rural areas should also be monitored.

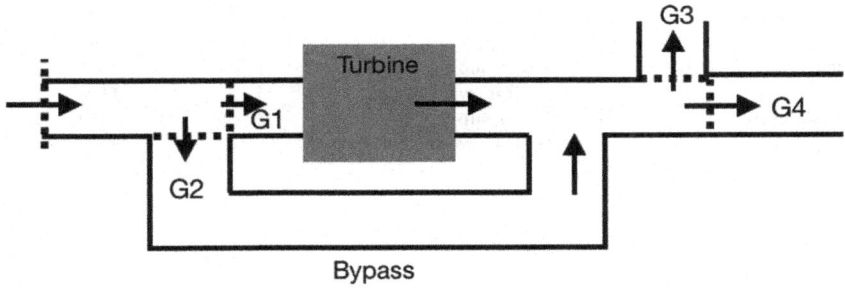

Fig. 2. Water distribution system.

Table 1, shows the optimised results obtained while simulating with GRanD dataset. Multiobjective genetic algorithm has given the maximum power generation with least shortage in irrigation and urban needs with least error rate.

Table 1. Accuracy of algorithms.

Algorithm	Total shortage (mcm/year)	Urban/rural shortage (mcm/year)	Electricity generated (10^8 kWh)	Irrigation shortage (mcm/year)	Error percentage in delivery (%)
Multiobjective genetic algorithm	2814	8	3.67	4	0.2
Particle swam optimisation	3127	14	3.42	11	4.4
Genetic algorithm	2989	11	3.59	6	1.7

Another statistics is also provided for comparison of various optimisation methods. Table 2 shows the best, worst and average solutions obtained while simulating the problem using multi objective genetic algorithm, particle swam optimisation and genetic algorithm. The results shows that multi objective genetic algorithm was capable of producing 10 feasible solutions for the simplest case of water-supply operation and 8 feasible solutions for the hydropower operation. In longer operation periods, the number of runs with a feasible solution decrease. Particle swam optimisation and Genetic algorithm was able to produce only one feasible solution for both water-supply and hydropower operation for the shortest operation period. For longer operation periods genetic algorithm couldn't even find feasible solutions.

Table 2. Solution rate of algorithms.

Algorithm used	Operation purpose	Best solution	Worst solution	Average of solutions
Multi objective genetic algorithm	Water supply	10.3	13.3	12
	Hydropower	7.91	8.06	8.00
Particle swam optimisation	Water supply	1.07	3.85	2.06
	Hydropower	9.26	14.3	11.3
Genetic algorithm	Water supply	0.775	0.936	0.870
	Hydropower	8.08	9.10	8.48

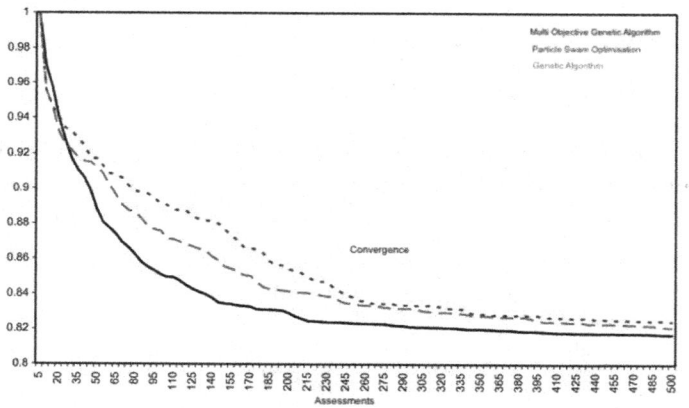

Fig. 3. Convergence trend.

Convergence trend of different methods at different assessments is also depicted in Fig. 3. Multi objective genetic algorithm converged after 215 assessments, while PSO and GA converged after 350 and 410 assessments, respectively, and after that the objective function value stays constant. Also, note that the displayed values show the average responses of different methods, in which the accuracy of MOGA results is higher than that of the other methods. Convergence trend analysis, Optimization accuracies are indicators which points to the fact that optimal reservoir optimization can be best done using multi objective genetic algorithm.

5 Conclusion

Reservoir water optimization using multi-objective genetic algorithm was attempted in this work. Water from the reservoir is being used for various purposes and the demand and supply varies according to situations. Optimising the software module with a better optimisation scheme was the primary objective of this work. Traditional evolutionary algorithms has also been used for comparative studies. Results were compared to confirm the superiority of this new method. Novelty of the present study is its introduction of the multi objective genetic algorithm for optimization of water resources management. This method increased the convergence of objective function as well as increased the accuracy rate of generating feasible solutions. Automatic constrain modelling can be seen as a future scope for this work.

Acknowledgment. Authors would like to thank all members in the Machine Intelligent Research Group, who has helped during the various phases of algorithm development and deployment. Also thank the Maniyar power plant engineers for the help they have extended during the various phases of knowledge transfer. Thanks extended to Columbia University for hosting the datasets for simulation and training.

References

1. Adeyemo, J.A.: Reservoir operation using multi-objective evolutionary algorithms-a review. Asian J. Sci. Res. **4**(1), 16–27 (2011)
2. Ahmed, J.A., Sarma, A.K.: Stochastic models for synthetic streamflow generation. In: Proceedings of the International Conference Recent Trends in Probability and Statistics: Theory and Applications, Guwahati, India (2002)
3. Ahmed, J.A., Sarma, A.K.: Genetic algorithm for optimal operating policy of a multipurpose reservoir. Water Resour. Manag. **19**(2), 145–161 (2005). https://doi.org/10.1007/s11269-005-2704-7
4. Bozorg-Haddad, O., Karimirad, I., Seifollahi-Aghmiuni, S., Loáiciga, H.A.: Development and application of the bat algorithm for optimising the operation of reservoir systems. J. Water Resour. Plan. Manag. **141**(8), 401–409 (2015)
5. Burn, D.H., Yulianti, J.S.: Waste-load allocation using genetic algorithms. J. Water Resource Plan. Manag. ASCE **127**(2), 121–129 (2001)
6. Haddad, O.B., Afshar, A., Mariño, M.A.: Multireservoir optimisation in discrete and continuous domains. Proc. Inst. Civ. Eng. - Water Manag. **164**(2), 57–72 (2011)
7. Khanmirzaei, Z., Teshnehlab, M., Sharifi, A.: Modified honey bee optimization for recurrent neuro-fuzzy system model. In: The 2nd International Conference on Computer and Automation Engineering, ICCAE 2010, pp. 780–785 (2010)

8. McKinney, D.C., Lin, M.D.: Genetic algorithm solution of groundwater management models. Water Resour. Res. **30**(6), 1897–1906 (1994)
9. Peng, Y.: An improved artificial fish swarm algorithm for optimal operation of cascade reservoirs. J. Comput. **6**(4), 740–746 (2011)
10. Tasgetiren, M.F., Pan, Q.K., Suganthan, P.N., Chen, A.H.L.: A discrete artificial bee colony algorithm for the total flow time minimisation in permutation flow shops. Inf. Sci. **181**(16), 3459–3475 (2011)

Success-History Based Parameter Adaptation in MOEA/D Algorithm

Shakhnaz Akhmedova[✉] and Vladimir Stanovov

Reshetnev Siberian State University of Science and Technology, "Krasnoyarskiy Rabochiy" av. 31, 660037 Krasnoyarsk, Russia
shahnaz@inbox.ru, vladimirstanovov@yandex.ru

Abstract. In this paper two parameter self-adaptation schemes are proposed for the MOEA/D-DE algorithm. These schemes use the fitness improvement ration to change four parameter values for every individual separately, as long as in the MOEA/D framework every individual solves its own scalar optimization problem. The first proposed scheme samples new values and replaces old values with new ones if there is an improvement, while the second one keeps a set of memory cells and updates the parameter values using the weighted sum. The proposed methods are testes on two sets of benchmark problems, namely MOEADDE functions and WFG functions, IGD and HV metrics are calculated. The results comparison is performed with statistical tests. The comparison shows that the proposed parameter adaptation schemes are capable of delivering significant improvements to the performance of the MOEA/D-DE algorithm. Also, it is shown that parameter tuning is better than random sampling of parameter values. The proposed parameter self-adaptation techniques could be used for other multi-objective algorithms, which use MOEA/D framework.

Keywords: Multi-objective optimization · Differential evolution · Parameter adaptation · Self-adaptation · MOEA/D

1 Introduction

The multi-objective and many-objective optimization techniques based on evolutionary algorithms (EA) and swarm intelligence algorithms (SI) have proved to be efficient for solving complex problems due to their population-based nature. The success of SPEA2 [1], NSGA-II [2], MOEA/D [3] and other methods developed later have shown that it is possible to find representative sets of points of the true Pareto set even for many objectives. However, very small attention has been paid to the underlying optimization techniques, used in the multi-objective optimization algorithms. In most cases, the multi-objective evolutionary algorithm relies on problem specific operators, for example, simulated binary crossover (SBX) and polynomial mutation [4, 5] form genetic algorithms (GA) or differential evolution (DE) mutation and crossover operators [6] in case of numerical optimization.

© Springer Nature Switzerland AG 2020
Y. Tan et al. (Eds.): ICSI 2020, LNCS 12145, pp. 455–462, 2020.
https://doi.org/10.1007/978-3-030-53956-6_41

The search operators taken from single-objective optimization algorithms have a set of parameter values, which influence the algorithm efficiency, and for single objective optimization various self-adaptation schemes have been proposed [7]. However, applying these techniques to multi-objective optimization is problematic due to difficulties in estimating the parameters influence on the algorithm performance. Moreover, MOEA aims to find a set of points, each in its own region of search space, while single-objective algorithms need to find only a single solution. To solve the mentioned problem some research have been made about adaptive operator selection (AOS) in MOEAs, for example JADE2 [8], MOSaDE [9], MODE/SN [10] and MOEA/D-FRRMAB [11].

In this study the scheme of operator efficiency estimation proposed in [11] is used to adaptively tune the search parameters of DE and GA operators, with a set of parameters kept separately for every point. The MOEA/D-DE algorithm is taken as baseline, and two approaches are proposed: the self-adaptation (SA) similar to the one used in [12], and the success-history adaptation, proposed in [13]. The experiments are performed on DTLZ and WFG sets of problems, the results are compared with statistical tests.

The rest of the paper is organized as follows: Sect. 2 describes the MOEA/D framework and search operators, Sect. 3 proposes the new parameter adaptation schemes, Sect. 4 contains experimental setup and results, and Sect. 5 concludes the paper.

2 MOEA/D Algorithm and Self-tuning

The multi-objective evolutionary algorithm based on decomposition (MOEA/D) was originally proposed in [3]. The main idea of this approach was to decompose the initial problem into a set of scalar problems. The multi-objective optimization problem (MOP) is formulated as follows:

$$minimize\ F(x)\ =\ (f_1(x),\ f_2(x),\ \ldots,\ f_m(x)) \atop subject\ to\ x\ \in\ \Omega, \tag{1}$$

where $\Omega \subset R^m$ is the variable space, x is a solution, and F: $\Omega \to R^m$ is a vector-function to be optimized.

The MOEA/D framework proposes several methods of problem decomposition, including weighted sum, Tchebycheff and penalized boundary intersection approaches [3]. The Tchebycheff approach is one of the commonly used methods, with scalar optimization problems defined as follows:

$$minimize\ g\left(x|\lambda,\ z^*\right)\ =\ \max_{1\le i\le m}\left\{\lambda_i\left|f_i(x)\ -\ z_i^*\right|\right\}, \tag{2}$$

where λ is a weight vector, z^* is a reference point. The MOEA/D algorithm defines a set of weight vectors λ^j, $j = 1 \ldots N$, N is the population size. In this manner, the algorithm optimizes N scalar problems in one run, allowing finding representative distribution of points in the Pareto front, if the corresponding weight vectors are evenly distributed.

The variation operators, used in MOEA/D, should it be the SBX crossover or DE mutation operators, use a neighborhood of size T, which is defined based on distances between the weight vectors λ. So, for every individual i = 1...N a set of vectors B(i) = $\{i_1, \ldots, i_T\}$, where $(\lambda^{i1} \ldots \lambda^{iT})$ are T closest vectors to λ^i. In case of SBX crossover one of B(i) is chosen, and in case of DE all 3 vectors are chosen from B(i) to perform mutation.

The implementation of self-tuning in multi-objective framework requires the definition of improvement rates, i.e. feedback values, which could be used to drive parameters towards optimal values at every stage of the search. In [14] the fitness improvement rates (FIR) were proposed to solve this problem, defined as follows:

$$FIR_{i,t} = \frac{pf_{i,t} - cf_{i,t}}{pf_{i,t}}, \tag{3}$$

where $pf_{i,t}$ is the fitness of parent, $cf_{i,t}$ is the fitness of child for individual i at step t. As long as MOEA/D solves a set of N scalar optimization problems, it is possible to calculate improvements rates in a similar manner to single-objective optimization algorithms.

Further in this study the DE will be used as the main optimization engine. The main idea of DE is to use the scaled difference vectors between the members of the population to produce new solutions. Classical DE uses rand/1 mutation strategy:

$$v_{i,j} = x_{r1} + F(x_{r2,j} - x_{r3,j}), \tag{4}$$

where r1, r2 and r3 are mutually different indexes chosen from B(i), and F is the scaling factor, v_i is the mutant vector. The crossover is performed with probability Cr:

$$u_{i,j} = \begin{cases} v_{i,j} & if\ rand\ (0,\ 1) < c_r\ or\ j = j\ rand \\ x_{i,j} & otherwise \end{cases}, \tag{5}$$

where *jrand* is the randomly selected index from [1, D], required to make sure that at least one coordinate is inherited from the mutant vector, u_i is the trial vector.

The polynomial mutation is performed with probability pm and scale parameter η. This operator is applied after the crossover step to produce an offspring. Totally, there are 4 numeric parameters to be tuned: scaling factor F, crossover rate Cr, mutation probability pm and mutation parameter η.

The next section contains the description of the proposed self-adaptation schemes for the MOEA/D-DE algorithm.

3 Proposed Parameter Self-adaptation Schemes

Among single-objective EAs, it is well known that adaptation of parameter values to the problem in hand is an important part of every algorithm. However, for multi-objective algorithms the typical scenario is to use fixed parameters, or probably use several operators, as described in [14] to adapt the algorithm to the problem being solved. One more important difference of MOPs is that each point in the population is a part of the final solution, and its optimal position is in an area of search space, different from other areas, so that the properties of fitness functions landscape could vary significantly for every individual, especially for decomposition-based approaches.

Taking into account these considerations, one may come up with an idea of parametric adaptation, where every individual has its own set of parameter values, which could be considered as suboptimal for the problem in hand. Similar are already known from literature, where in jDE algorithm [12] pairs of F and Cr parameters were stored for every individual separately. As the search proceeded, these F and Cr were updated in pursuit of finding best possible values. Another well-known approach for parameter adaptation was proposed in the SHADE algorithm [13]. In SHADE algorithm, as well as those developed based on it, a set of H memory cells (usually H = 5) is maintained to keep the most suitable parameter values. The memory cells are used to sample new parameter values, and are updated with respect to the fitness improvement rates.

Based on these ideas, the first parameter self-adaptation method is proposed. For every individual $i = 1, ..., N$ in the population the a set of parameter values $[F_i, Cr_i, pm_i, \eta_i]$ is maintained. Initially all these memory cells set to fixed values, for example [0.5, 1, 1/D, 20]. For every individual, new parameters are sampled using normal distribution:

$$
\begin{aligned}
F_i^{new} &= rnorm(F_i, \, 0.2) \\
Cr_i^{new} &= rnorm(Cr_i, \, 0.2) \\
pm_i^{new} &= rnorm(pm_i, \, 0.2) \\
\eta_i^{new} &= rnorm(\eta_i, \, 5)
\end{aligned}
\tag{6}
$$

If some of the parameters were sampled below 0, then they were sampled again. However, if F, Cr or pm were above 1, then the value of 1 was kept.

After the application of combination and variation operators, the fitness value of the child is compared to the parent's fitness, and if there is an improvement, then the new parameter values replace the old ones. This approach will be further referred to as MOEA/D-DE-SA.

The second self-adaptation approach uses the idea of success-history based adaptation, where the parameter values are averaged over several last steps. For every individual a set of H = 5 memory cells is maintained, with $MF_{i,h}$, $MCr_{i,h}$, $Mpm_{i,h}$ and $M\eta_{i,h}$ values, $i = 1, ..., N$, $h = 1, ..., H$. Memory cell initialization and sampling is performed in the same way as in MOEA/D-DE-SA, however, the update scheme is changed. The FIR values from Eq. 3 are calculated and used as weights $w_{i,h}$ for the update, performed as follows:

$$
\begin{aligned}
F_i^{new} &= \tfrac{1}{2}\Big(F_i^{old} + \frac{\sum_{k=1}^{H} w_{i,k}(MF_{i,k}^{new})^2}{\sum_{k=1}^{H} w_{i,k}MF_{i,k}^{new}}\Big) \\
\eta_i^{new} &= \tfrac{1}{2}\Big(\eta_i^{old} + \frac{\sum_{k=1}^{H} w_{i,k}M\eta_{i,k}^{new}}{\sum_{k=1}^{H} w_{i,k}}\Big)
\end{aligned}
\tag{7}
$$

where F_i^{new} and F_i^{old} are the new and old values of F parameter. The update scheme for Cr and pm parameters is the same as for F. Note that if there was no improvement, i.e. FIR < 0, the weight was set to zero, and if all weights were zero, there was no parameter update. The h index responsible for the memory cell index to write the temporary parameter values is incremented every generation, and if the h value exceeds H = 5, then it is reset back to 1. This algorithm will be further referred to as MOEA/D-DE-SHA.

In addition to the described algorithm, the approach with random sampling was used, i.e. the parameters were generated as shown in Eq. 6, but no memory cells update schemes were applied. This approach will be further referred to as MOEA/D-DE-RS. The experimental setup and results are presented in the next section.

4   Experimental Setup and Results

The experiments were performed on a set of benchmark problems proposed in [14] for the MOEA/D-DE algorithm, as well as on a set of WFG problems [15]. The population size was set to 100, actual population size depended on the number of objectives. The maximum number of function evaluations was set to 10000 for all problems. The algorithms were implemented using the PlatEMO 2.5 system [16].

Table 1. Comparison of MOEA/D to the proposed approaches, MOEA/D-DE-SHA as baseline, IGD metric.

Problem	MOEA/D-DE	MOEA/D-DE-RS	MOEA/D-DE-SA	MOEA/D-DE-SHA
MOEADDE1	**1.061e-2 (3.59e-3)** +	1.096e-2 (2.55e-3) =	1.162e-2 (2.88e-3) =	1.210e-2 (3.72e-3)
MOEADDE2	1.579e-1 (3.61e-2) -	1.013e-1 (2.23e-2) -	9.355e-2 (1.94e-2) =	**9.309e-2 (1.48e-2)**
MOEADDE3	1.097e-1 (4.32e-2) -	9.156e-2 (4.22e-2) -	**6.614e-2 (1.63e-2)** =	6.631e-2 (2.81e-2)
MOEADDE4	1.103e-1 (3.72e-2) -	9.483e-2 (3.18e-2) -	8.092e-2 (2.49e-2) -	**7.945e-2 (1.61e-2)**
MOEADDE5	7.272e-2 (2.41e-2) -	**5.975e-2 (1.51e-2)** =	6.054e-2 (1.33e-2) =	6.037e-2 (1.78e-2)
MOEADDE6	1.572e-1 (3.64e-2) -	1.583e-1 (4.37e-2) =	1.452e-1 (2.84e-2) =	**1.435e-1 (3.25e-2)**
MOEADDE7	3.489e-1 (1.14e-1) =	3.762e-1 (1.42e-1) =	**2.612e-1 (9.58e-2)** +	3.122e-1 (6.91e-2)
MOEADDE8	2.462e-1 (5.23e-2) +	2.831e-1 (6.11e-2) =	**2.457e-1 (5.74e-2)** +	3.127e-1 (5.96e-2)
MOEADDE9	1.503e-1 (2.74e-2) -	1.076e-1 (2.61e-2) -	9.414e-2 (2.06e-2) =	**9.359e-2 (2.66e-2)**
WFG1	1.546e+0 (3.10e-2) -	1.452e+0 (7.00e-2) -	1.368e+0 (8.58e-2) =	**1.338e+0 (8.86e-2)**
WFG2	3.593e-1 (2.96e-2) =	**3.372e-1 (1.61e-2)** +	3.563e-1 (2.20e-2) =	3.514e-1 (2.00e-2)
WFG3	2.759e-1 (3.74e-2) -	2.073e-1 (2.55e-2) -	1.919e-1 (2.13e-2) =	**1.837e-1 (1.87e-2)**
WFG4	3.962e-1 (1.59e-2) -	3.941e-1 (1.06e-2) +	**3.929e-1 (1.43e-2)** +	4.022e-1 (1.40e-2)
WFG5	**3.362e-1 (4.97e-3)** =	3.369e-1 (6.47e-3) =	3.363e-1 (5.43e-3) =	3.373e-1 (6.31e-3)
WFG6	4.385e-1 (2.14e-2) =	4.405e-1 (2.04e-2) =	**4.339e-1 (1.57e-2)** +	4.414e-1 (1.46e-2)
WFG7	3.839e-1 (1.25e-2) -	3.743e-1 (9.08e-3) =	**3.730e-1 (9.69e-3)** =	3.742e-1 (1.01e-2)
WFG8	4.878e-1 (4.08e-2) -	4.479e-1 (2.00e-2) =	4.334e-1 (1.30e-2) =	**4.302e-1 (1.05e-2)**
WFG9	**3.468e-1 (9.42e-3)** =	3.489e-1 (2.04e-2) =	3.613e-1 (3.18e-2) =	3.557e-1 (2.78e-2)
Total	2+/6=/10-	2+/10=/6-	4+/14=/0-	

For every test function 30 independent runs were performed, and the inverted generational distance (IGD) and hypervolume (HV) metrics were calculated. All WFG functions had m = 3 objectives, while all MOEA/D-DE functions had 2 objectives except for F6, which had 3 objectives.

To compare the performance of different algorithms, the Wilcoxon rank sum statistical test with significance level p = 0.05 was used. Table 1 shows the IGD values for all test problems, and Table 2 shows HV values.

The best average values in Tables 1 and 2 are marked. If the MOEA/D-DE-SHA was significantly better than the other algorithm, then the "+" sign was used, if worse, then "−" sign, otherwise "=". From Tables 1 and 2 it could be seen that MOEA/D-DE-SA and MOEA/D-DE-SHA outperform both standard MOEA/D-DE with fixed parameters and the MOEA-D/DE-RS with random sampling. However, even the random sampling is most of the times better than fixed parameter values.

Comparing MOEA/D-DE-SA and MOEA/D-DE-SHA, in terms of IGD metric the former has shown better results, i.e. significantly better on 4 problems out of 18, but for HV metric the two approaches have similar performance, i.e. 3 wins and 3 losses. But, it

Table 2. Comparison of MOEA/D to the proposed approaches, MOEA/D-DE-SHA as baseline, HV metric.

Problem	MOEA/D-DE	MOEA/D-DE-RS	MOEA/D-DE-SA	MOEA/D-DE-SHA
MOEADDE1	7.0899e-1 (5.55e-3) =	**7.0944e-1 (3.78e-3) +**	7.0872e-1 (3.68e-3) =	7.0805e-1 (5.07e-3)
MOEADDE2	5.0146e-1 (3.85e-2) -	5.6748e-1 (3.07e-2) =	5.7485e-1 (3.01e-2) =	**5.7629e-1 (2.39e-2)**
MOEADDE3	6.1718e-1 (2.60e-2) -	6.2621e-1 (2.48e-2) -	6.4138e-1 (1.22e-2) =	**6.4330e-1 (1.66e-2)**
MOEADDE4	6.1748e-1 (2.52e-2) -	6.2907e-1 (1.83e-2) =	6.3283e-1 (1.82e-2) =	**6.3679e-1 (1.13e-2)**
MOEADDE5	6.4418e-1 (1.38e-2) =	**6.5126e-1 (9.65e-3) =**	6.4800e-1 (1.12e-2) =	6.5056e-1 (1.22e-2)
MOEADDE6	3.8415e-1 (3.59e-2) =	3.8533e-1 (3.73e-2) =	3.9858e-1 (2.53e-2) =	**3.9884e-1 (3.00e-2)**
MOEADDE7	2.6923e-1 (8.38e-2) =	2.6947e-1 (7.96e-2) =	**3.7552e-1 (1.17e-1) +**	2.9384e-1 (7.79e-2)
MOEADDE8	3.6255e-1 (7.55e-2) +	3.1275e-1 (8.94e-2) +	**3.7399e-1 (8.55e-2) +**	2.6100e-1 (8.97e-2)
MOEADDE9	2.2668e-1 (3.47e-2) -	2.7780e-1 (4.21e-2) -	2.9973e-1 (3.10e-2) =	**3.0060e-1 (3.72e-2)**
WFG1	2.6741e-1 (1.49e-2) -	2.9960e-1 (2.32e-2) -	3.2444e-1 (2.71e-2) =	**3.3359e-1 (2.83e-2)**
WFG2	8.5717e-1 (1.60e-2) -	**8.6870e-1 (9.08e-3) =**	8.6731e-1 (8.38e-3) =	8.6816e-1 (8.78e-3)
WFG3	2.8778e-1 (2.32e-2) -	3.3166e-1 (1.32e-2) -	3.3926e-1 (9.56e-3) -	**3.4490e-1 (8.68e-3)**
WFG4	4.4927e-1 (7.59e-3) -	4.6641e-1 (7.35e-3) -	4.8247e-1 (5.48e-3) -	**4.8606e-1 (6.45e-3)**
WFG5	4.5894e-1 (4.32e-3) =	4.5837e-1 (3.81e-3) =	4.6025e-1 (4.28e-3) =	**4.6048e-1 (3.84e-3)**
WFG6	3.8575e-1 (2.20e-2) +	3.8426e-1 (2.68e-2) =	**4.0163e-1 (3.33e-2) +**	3.7719e-1 (2.12e-2)
WFG7	4.5816e-1 (9.43e-3) -	4.8504e-1 (6.75e-3) -	4.9494e-1 (6.22e-3) =	**4.9605e-1 (5.45e-3)**
WFG8	3.4231e-1 (2.05e-2) -	3.8402e-1 (1.11e-2) -	3.9655e-1 (7.70e-3) -	**4.0106e-1 (5.33e-3)**
WFG9	4.5905e-1 (1.13e-2) +	**4.6384e-1 (2.49e-2) =**	4.5031e-1 (4.10e-2) =	4.5777e-1 (3.48e-2)
Total	3+/5=/10-	2+/9=/7-	3+/12=/3-	

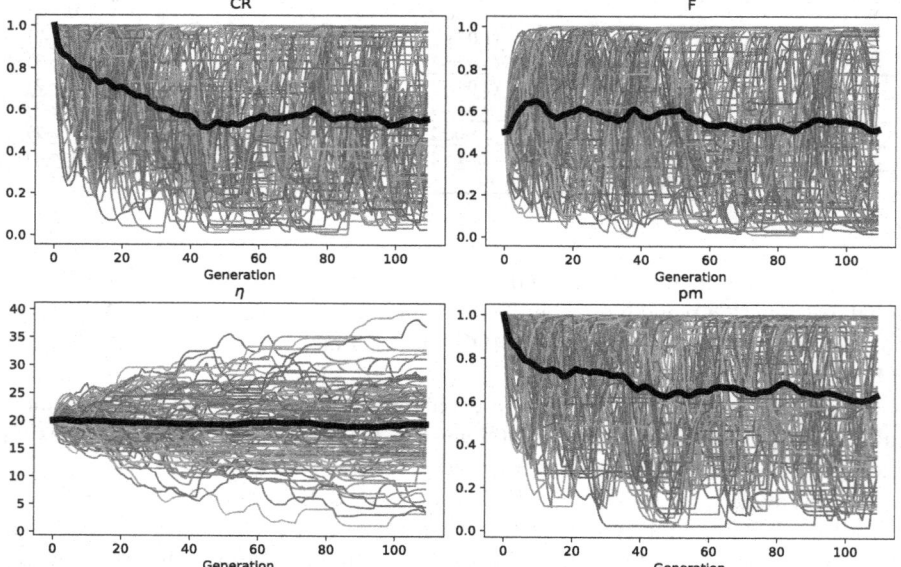

Fig. 1. Change of parameters of the MOEA/D-DE-SHA algorithm during one of the runs, WFG8 problem.

is important to mention that MOEA/D-DE-SHA has achieved better IGD and HV more often than other methods.

Figure 1 shows the change of parameters of the MOEA/D-DE-SHA algorithm during one of the runs. Cr and pm parameters start from 1 and gradually reduce to around 0.5–0.7, while for F value the average value, shown by black line, oscillates near 0.5. It is seen, especially on the η graph, that some of the parameter values gradually increase, while others decrease, allowing each point to adapt to its own part of the goal function landscape.

Similar graphs were obtained for other test problems, and the general trend is that the average values of parameters do not change much. For the MOEA/D-DE-SA algorithm, the parameter changes are sharper, as the previous parameter value does not influence the new one directly.

5   Conclusion

The parameter adaptation mechanism is an important part of every single-objective evolutionary and swarm intelligence search algorithm, which allows significant improvement of efficiency. Likewise, for multi-objective optimization, the parameter adaptation scheme allows receiving more representative Pareto sets, as demonstrated in this study. The proposed parameter adaptation schemes, MOEA/D-DE-SA and MOEA/D-DE-SHA use the improvement ratio, which is relatively easy to calculate for the MOEA/D framework, however, the ideas of these algorithms could be used for other multi-objective optimization approaches.

This study shows that there is a potential in improvement of MOEAs by developing new parameter adaptation schemes, as well as new improvement ration estimation approaches. Further studies in this direction may include testing the proposed SA and SHA algorithms on algorithms using SBX crossover, or other problem-specific operators, which have numerical parameters.

Acknowledgments. The is work was supported by the internal grant of Reshetnev Siberian State University of Science and Technology for the support of young researchers.

References

1. Zitzler, E., Laumanns, M., Thiele, L.: SPEA2: improving the strength Pareto evolutionary algorithm. Technical report TIK-Report103, Swiss Federal Institute of Technology, Zurich, Germany (2001)
2. Deb, K., Pratab, A., Agrawal, S., Meyarivan, T.: A fast and elitist multiobjective genetic algorithm: NSGA-II. IEEE Trans. Evol. Comput. **6**(2), 182–197 (2002)
3. Zhang, Q., Li, H.: MOEA/D: a multiobjective evolutionary algorithm based on decomposition. IEEE Trans. Evol. Comput. **11**(6), 712–731 (2007)
4. Deb, K., Agrawal, R.B.: Simulated binary crossover for continuous search space. Complex Syst. **9**(2), 115–148 (1995)
5. Deb, K., Deb, D.: Analysing mutation schemes for real-parameter genetic algorithms. Int. J. Artif. Intell. Soft Comput. **4**(1), 1–28 (2014)
6. Das, S., Mullick, S.S., Suganthan, P.N.: Recent advances in differential evolution – an updated survey. Swarm Evol. Comput. **27**, 1–30 (2016)

7. Eiben, A.E., Hinterding, R., Michalewicz, Z.: Parameter control in evolutionary algorithms. IEEE Trans. Evol. Comput. **3**(2), 124–141 (1999)
8. Zhang, J., Sanderson, A.C.: Self-adaptive multiobjective differential evolution with direction information provided by archived inferior solutions. In: Proceedings of the IEEE Congress on Evolutionary Computation, pp. 2806–2815, July 2008
9. Huang, V.L., Qin, A.K., Suganthan, P.N., Tasgetiren, M.F.: Multiobjective optimization based on self-adaptive differential evolution algorithm. In: Proceedings of the IEEE Congress on Evolutionary Computation, pp. 3601–3608, May 2007
10. Li, K., Kwong, S., Wang, R., Cao, J., Rudas, I.J.: Multiobjective differential evolution with self-navigation. In: Proceedings of the IEEE nternational Conference on Systems, Man, and Cybernetics, pp. 508–513, October 2012
11. Li, K., Fialho, A., Kwong, S., Zhang, Q.: Adaptive operator selection with bandits for a multiobjective evolutionary algorithm based on decomposition. IEEE Trans. Evol. Comput. **18**(1), 114–130 (2014)
12. Brest, J., Greiner, S., Bošković, B., Mernik, M., Žumer, V.: Self-adapting control parameters in differential evolution: a comparative study on numerical benchmark problems. IEEE Trans. Evol. Comput. **10**(6), 646–657 (2006)
13. Tanabe, R., Fukunaga, A.: Success-history based parameter adaptation for differential evolution. In: Proceedings of the IEEE Congress on Evolutionary Computation, pp. 71–78 (2013)
14. Li, H., Zhang, Q.: Multiobjective optimization problems with complicated Pareto sets MOEA/D and NSGA-II. IEEE Trans. Evol. Comput. **13**(2), 284–302 (2009)
15. Huband, S., Hingston, P., Barone, L., While, L.: A review of multiobjective test problems and a scalable test problem toolkit. IEEE Trans. Evol. Comput. **10**(5), 477–506 (2006)
16. Tian, Y., Cheng, R., Zhang, X., Jin, Y.: PlatEMO: a MATLAB platform for evolutionary multi-objective optimization. IEEE Comput. Intell. Mag. **12**(4), 73–87 (2017). https://doi.org/10.1109/mci.2017.2742868

Machine Learning

Image Clustering by Generative Adversarial Optimization and Advanced Clustering Criteria

Eva Tuba, Ivana Strumberger, Nebojsa Bacanin, Timea Bezdan,
and Milan Tuba[(✉)]

Singidunum University, Danijelova 32, 11000 Belgrade, Serbia
tuba@ieee.org

Abstract. Clustering is the task that has been used in numerous applications including digital image analysis and processing. Image clustering refers to the problem of segmenting image for different purposes which leads to various clustering criteria. Finding the optimal clusters represented by their centers is a hard optimization problem and it is one of the main research focuses on clustering methods. In this paper we proposed a novel generative adversarial optimization algorithm for finding the optimal cluster centers while using standard and advance clustering criteria. The proposed method was tested on seven benchmark images and results were compared with the artificial bee colony, particle swarm optimization and genetic algorithm. Based on the obtained results, the generative adversarial optimization algorithm founded better cluster centers for image clustering compared to named methods from the literature.

Keywords: Image clustering · Swarm intelligence · Generative adversarial optimization

1 Introduction

Digital images are a big part of the modern world since they have been part of almost every scientific field as well as an important part of everyday life. There are countless benefits that the usage of digital images has brought. Fast and relatively simple but precise analysis of digital images enabled their usage in some unexpected fields such as agriculture [15] while in some other fields where images have been used even before such as medicine, they brought huge improvements [21]. Besides digital images taken by mobile phones or cameras that capture the visible light which are the most common digital images in everyday life, in science various other modalities are used such as X-ray, ultrasound, magnetic resonance imaging (MRI), etc.

The final goal of digital image processing application can be the detection of plant diseases [9], tumor recognition [3], bleeding detection [20], fire detection [22], and many more. In order to achieve these goals which are rather different, some standard and common image processing methods adjusted for the specific

© Springer Nature Switzerland AG 2020
Y. Tan et al. (Eds.): ICSI 2020, LNCS 12145, pp. 465–475, 2020.
https://doi.org/10.1007/978-3-030-53956-6_42

problem are used. All digital image processing methods and algorithms can be categorized as low, middle or high-level algorithms and usually, methods from more than one category are used in one application. Usually, pre-processing represents the first step in all applications where the digital image is enhanced for further processing. Low-level methods such as contrast adjustment, changing the brightness, binarization of the digital image are frequently used in the pre-processing step and they have a common factor which is that all these methods manipulate with the pixel values without any further understanding of the objects in the image. Methods from the middle-level category represent a higher level of digital image processing where certain characteristics such as shapes, textures, edges and contours are recognized. Again, there is no further knowledge about what is on the image. An example can be detecting faces by finding rounded objects in skin color. High-level digital image processing methods use artificial intelligence for recognizing elements that were detected by methods of low and middle processing levels such as recognizing persons based on the detected faces. Each of the steps, pre-processing, detection and recognition are important for the success of the final application. One of the important tasks in middle-level processing is segmentation. Segmentation is the participation of the digital image into meaningful parts. Due to the similarity of the segmentation and clustering problems, clustering algorithms have been widely used for digital image segmentation. In both cases the goal is to divide data into clusters so the data from one cluster are more similar to each other than to data from other clusters. In the case of segmentation, data can be pixels or regions.

Currently, there are numerous clustering methods proposed and used in various applications such as hierarchical clustering, DBSCAN, many distributions based clustering algorithms, k-means, and others. In this paper we used the modified and optimized k-means algorithm for digital image segmentation. It is well-known that the quality of clustering by the k-means algorithm is determined by initial cluster centers. Finding the optimal cluster centers is a hard optimization problem and many optimization techniques have been proposed for solving it, including swarm intelligence algorithms [3, 6, 19]. When using swarm intelligence algorithms it is important to define fitness function according to the considered problem. In this paper, a novel swarm intelligence algorithm, generative adversarial optimization is used for finding optimal cluster centers and three different fitness functions have been used, two standards and one proposed especially for digital image segmentation proposed in [13].

The rest of this paper is organized as follows. Short literature review is given in Sect. 2. Section 3 defines the generative adversarial optimization algorithm used for image segmentation along with the used fitness functions. A comparison of the proposed method with other approaches from the literature is presented in Sect. 4. The conclusion of this paper is given in Sect. 5.

2   Literature Review

Image clustering represents common problem in various applications that deal with the standard, medical, satellite or other images. Since it is a very common task in image processing applications, numerous methods can be found in the literature.

One of the well-known clustering algorithms is k-means and it was widely used for the image segmentation. The method for 2-level segmentation was proposed in [4]. Before applying the clustering algorithm, images were preprocessed by the partial stretching enhancement method while the initial cluster centers were determined by the subtractive clustering method and the segmentation was enhanced by using median filter. Similar approach was presented in [23] for fish image segmentation.

Even though the k-means algorithm is one of most commonly used clustering algorithms it has one big drawback - it is highly sensitive to the choice of the initial cluster centers. Due to this issue, k-means algorithm is frequently combined by the optimization metaheuristics such as swarm intelligence algorithms.

Combination of the k-means algorithm and the particle swarm optimization and ant colony optimization algorithm was proposed and tested in [11]. In [7], the k-means algorithm was optimized by the firefly algorithm while in [10] instead of the original k-means algorithm, fuzzy k-means method was proposed.

Besides optimizing the k-means algorithm was data clustering, this method was also used for the image segmentation problem. In [2], hybridization of the particle swarm optimization and the k-means algorithm was proposed in [2] and it was used for the image segmentation. The obtained segmentation was further enhanced by the spatial gray-level information used for the correction of misclassified pixels.

The gravitation search algorithm was used to automatically determine the number of segments, i.e. clusters and to optimize the k-means algorithm for the image segmentation problem.

The k-means algorithm was also used for medical image applications in [5,14,17]. In [14] adaptive k-means algorithm was used for breast cancer detection while in [5] fuzzy k-means algorithm combined by the genetic algorithm and particle swarm optimization was applied to noisy MRI images. The method used in [5] was based on the results presented in [1] where different soft computing methods were combined by the fuzzy k-means algorithm and applied to MRI image segmentation. Another method for the medical image segmentation was proposed in [16] where genetic algorithm used for optimizing the k-means algorithm and the proposed method was applied to brain tumor detection in MRI images.

3   Generative Adversarial Optimization for Image Clustering

The generative adversarial optimization (GAO) algorithm represents one of the recent swarm intelligence optimization algorithm proposed by Tan and Shi in 2019 [18]. Currently, there are only two papers that apply the GAO algorithm for support vector machine optimization [21] and image compression [8]. In the paper where the GAO algorithm was presented it was tested on standard benchmark functions for bound constrained optimization problems. Based on the comparison with the other optimization methods from the literature, it was concluded that the GAO is a competitive metaheuristic for solving hard optimization problems. While the majority of the optimization metaheuristics use random sampling or guiding vectors for generating new solutions, the GAO algorithm has a drastically different approach by using the generative adversarial network as an inspiration. In the GAO algorithm, a generator is used for searching new solutions and the discriminator tries to predict if the new solution is better than the previous one. Feedback from the discriminator is used as the guiding vector that provides better solutions. The GAO algorithm is presented in Fig. 1.

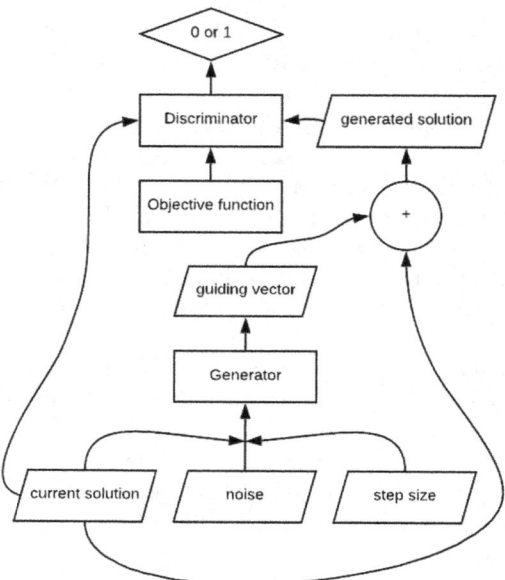

Fig. 1. The GAO algorithm

Inputs for the generator G are the current solution denoted as x_c, a noise vector z and the step size l. Output produced by the generator represents a guiding vector g, i.e. $g = G(x_c, z, l)$. The whole population is updated based on the output of the generator G presented in Fig. 2(a). As it can be seen from the Fig. 2(a), guided vector g is obtained after the concatenation of the current solution and the noise used as an input for fully-connected layer denoted by FC whose output is combined with the step size l:

$$g = G(x_c, z, l) = FC([x_c^T, z^T]^T) \cdot l. \tag{1}$$

In the GAO algorithm, new solutions are generated by adding the guiding vector g to the current solution x_c.

After generating new solutions, the discriminator D is used to make a prediction is the new solution better than the current solution. Labels used for the training are set by the following function:

$$y^i = \begin{cases} 1, & f(x_g) < f(x_c) \\ 0, & else, \end{cases} \tag{2}$$

where x_g is generated solution and f is objective function. The discriminator's scheme is shown in Fig. 2(b), The discriminator D contains two fully-connected layers denoted by $FC1$ and $FC2$. Inputs for the $FC1$ are the current x_c and generated solutions x_g. The output of the $FC1$ is subtracted from x_g and that is the input for the $FC2$. The output of D represents a prediction if the new solution improves the value of the objective function.

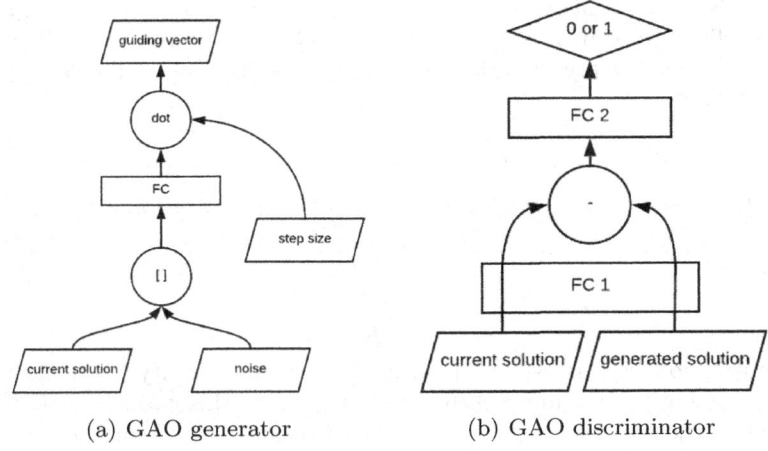

(a) GAO generator   (b) GAO discriminator

Fig. 2. The GAO generator and descriptor

In this paper, we used the GAO algorithm for finding the optimal cluster centers for image clustering task. The dimension of the problem is equal to the number of clusters. Pixels are assigned to the cluster which center is closest to it by theirs pixel intensity values. Solutions are ranked based on three different objective functions.

3.1   Objective Functions

In clustering algorithms there are three main criteria that are used for determining the quality of the clusters, comprising error measure, inter-cluster distance and intra-cluster separation. The first fitness function that will be used as objective function for the generative adversarial optimization algorithm combines these three criteria in weighted sum [12]:

$$f_1(x_i, Z) = w_1 d_{max}(Z, x_i) + w_2(z_{max} - d_{min}(Z, x_i)) + w_3 J_e, \qquad (3)$$

where Z denotes the image i.e. set of pixel values, x_i is the ith solution which is K cluster centers, z_{max} represents the maximal intensity value of the pixels in the image which is for the s-bit image equal to $2^s - 1$. Parameters w_1, w_2 and w_3 are redetermined weights that controls the influence of each criterion. Value of d_{max} represents the maximal average distance between pixels and their corresponding centers:

$$d_{max}(Z, x_i) = \max_k (\sum_{\forall z_p \in C_{i,k}} \frac{d(z_p, m_{i,k})}{n_{i,k}}), \qquad (4)$$

where $n_{i,k}$ is total number of elements in the cluster $C_{i,k}$ and $d(z_p, m_{i,k})$ represents Euclidean distance between pixel z_p and cluster center $m_{i,k}$. The value of d_{min} in the Eq. 3 represents the minimal average Euclidean distance between any two clusters:

$$d_{min}(Z, x_i) = \min d(m_{i,j}, m_{i,l}), \quad j \neq l, \ j, l = 1, 2, 3, \ldots, K. \qquad (5)$$

The third part of the first objective function is quantization error J_e defined as:

$$J_e = \frac{\sum_{k=1}^{K} \sum_{\forall z_p \in C_k} d(z_p, m_k)/n_k}{K}. \qquad (6)$$

This quantization error is used to determine the overall quality of the clustering.

The second objective function that is considered in this paper is more flexible compared to the first one since there are no parameters (except the number of clusters) that need to be set. It is defined as:

$$f_2(x_i, Z) = \frac{d_{max}(Z, x_i) + J_{e,i}}{d_{min}(Z, x_i)}. \qquad (7)$$

The third objective function was proposed in [13]. This objective function was proposed with intention to include benefits while eliminating drawbacks of the previous two fitness functions. The third objective function uses mean square error combined by the quantization error. It was designed to maximize d_{max} while minimizing d_{min}. Definition of the third objective function is as follows:

$$f_3(x_i, Z) = J_e \frac{d_{max}(Z, x_i)}{d_{min}(Z, x_i)}(d_{max}(Z, x_i) + z_{max} - d_{min}(Z, x_i) + MSE), \qquad (8)$$

where MSE is the mean square error of cluster centers and actual pixel values.

4   Experimental Results

The method proposed for digital image clustering by generative adversarial optimization algorithm was tested on Intel ® Core^{TM} i7-3770K CPU at 4GHz, 8GB RAM, Windows 10 Professional OS computer. The proposed GAO clustering method was implemented in Python 3.7.

The proposed GAO clustering method is compared to other state-of-the-art methods presented in [13]. In [13] the proposed objective function defined by Eq. 8 was used with the artificial bee colony (ABC) algorithm while it was compared by particle swarm optimization (PSO) and genetic algorithm (GA). Images used in [13] have been used in our test too. Test images are standard benchmark images: airplane, house, Lena, Morro Bay and MRI along with two images from the Berkeley segmentation dataset named 42049 and 48025. Test images are shown in Fig. 3. The number of clusters K for all images was set to 5. Parameters for the ABC, PSO and GA are listed in [13]. The weights for the first objective function were set as follow: $w_1 = 0.4$, $w_2 = 0.2$, $w_3 = 0.4$. Parameters of the GAO algorithm were set based on the recommendations in [18]: a total number of solutions kept for the next iteration was $n = 5$ while in each iteration $\beta = 30$ new solutions are generated and the selection process control parameter was $\alpha = 2$. Fine tuning of the parameters can be the part of future work since it is known that adequate choice for the parameters is the crucial for the optimal results of any optimization algorithm. For each image, the algorithm was started 30 times. Comparisons of the results obtained for different fitness functions are presented in Table 1, Table 2 and Table 3.

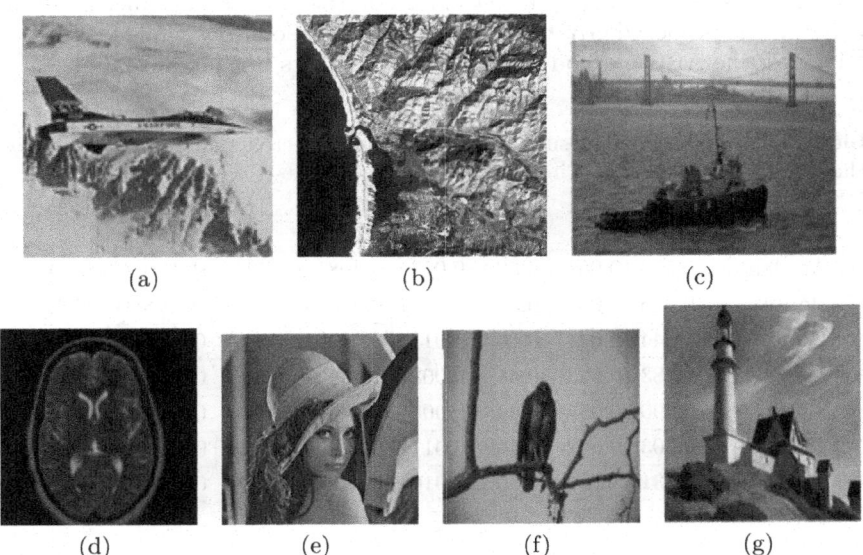

Fig. 3. Test images

Table 1. Comparison of the results with the first objective function of the proposed method and method proposed in [13]

	GA	PSO	ABC	GAO
Airplane	47.328 (1.741)	46.275 (0.273)	46.159 (0.079)	**46.124 (0.283)**
House	51.732 (0.993)	51.116 (0.841)	50.795 (0.155)	**50.623 (0.314)**
Lena	50.666 (0.616	50.087 (0.236)	50.065 (0.088)	**50.049 (0.113)**
Morro Bay	50.741 (0.522)	50.168 (0.186)	50.097 (0.104)	**50.083 (0.167)**
MRI	40.929 (0.466)	40.448 (0.096)	40.490 (0.073)	**40.442 (0.089)**
42049	52.089 (1.065	**50.768 (0.170)**	50.789 (0.058)	50.774 (0.111)
48025	51.675 (0.562)	51.074 (0.277)	**51.064 (0.104)**	51.072 (0.197)

Based on the results presented in Table 1, we can see that the proposed GAO method outperformed all three algorithms used for comparison for standard benchmark images, while for the images from the Berkeley dataset PSO and ABC methods obtained slightly better results. It should be noticed that for all test images (also for all objective functions) ABC algorithm has a smaller standard deviation compared to the proposed GAO algorithm. This should be further investigated and possibly outcast this drawback. One of the possible solution is fine tuning the GAO parameters and adjusting them to the considered problem rather than using the same parameters as in [18] were the GAO was applied to benchmark functions.

In the case when the second fitness function was sed (Eq. 7), our proposed GAO and ABC have comparable results. For the images airplane, house and Morro bay, the proposed GAO method found better solutions while for the other test images, the ABC method achieved better results but just for 0.001.

Table 2. Comparison of the results with the second objective function of the proposed method and method proposed in [13]

	GA	PSO	ABC	GAO
Airplane	0.570 (0.059	0.500 (0.013)	0.498 (0.005)	**0.496 (0.007)**
House	0.545 (0.053)	0.505 (0.047)	0.490 (0.008)	**0.483 (0.007)**
Lena	0.544 (0.044)	0.503 (0.011)	**0.503 (0.006)**	0.504 (0.003)
Morro Bay	0.483 (0.023)	0.458 (0.008)	0.454 (0.006)	**0.450 (0.004)**
MRI	0.490 (0.055)	0.448 (0.005)	**0.446 (0.003)**	0.447 (0.003)
42049	0.603 (0.092	0.488 (0.011)	**0.487 (0.005)**	0.488 (0.007)
48025	0.531(0.029)	0.506 (0.016)	**0.505 (0.007)**	0.505 (0.009)

At the end, we used the objective function proposed in [13] defined by Eq. 8. It can be noticed that the values of the fitness function are much higher compared to the cases when the first and the second objective function were used. When the third objective function is used, PSO outperformed ABC for airplane, Lena and 42049 images while ABC outperformed the proposed GAO algorithm only for Morro Bay image.

Table 3. Comparison of the results with the third objective function of the proposed method and method proposed in [13]

	GA	PSO	ABC	GAO
Airplane	924.596 (133.109)	777.767 (8.676)	790.618 (8.789)	**768.248 (9.103)**
House	1192.324 (212.851)	1085.34 (137.140)	1070.080 (11.840)	**1062.982 (33.345)**
Lena	1025.065 (100.002)	899.365 (11.464)	919.307 (13.987)	**881.634 (15.239)**
Morro Bay	998.267 (130.435)	898.866 (64.648)	**886.052 (9.825)**	887.213 (14.920)
MRI	595.781 (61.695)	523.751 (16.786)	523.145 (7.282)	**522.928 (12.837)**
42049	714.839 (45.818)	667.083 (9.110)	673.370 (7.785)	**664.396 (12.441)**
48025	1332.130 (202.390)	1202.15 (24.536)	1192.57 (16.602)	**1186.751 (20.498)**

5   Conclusion

Digital images found their purpose in various scientific fields which resulted by numerous research works and applications in this domain. One of the common tasks in digital image processing applications is segmentation which can be done by clustering algorithms. In this paper we proposed usage of novel generative adversarial optimization algorithm for finding optimal cluster centers. The proposed method was tested with three different fitness functions and compared to the genetic algorithm, particle swarm optimization and artificial bee colony algorithm. The best results were obtained while using standard clustering objective function and improved clustering fitness. Based on the results, it can be concluded that the proposed GAO algorithm is more suitable for image clustering tasks compared to other state-of-the-art methods.

References

1. Agrawal, S., Panda, R., Dora, L.: A study on fuzzy clustering for magnetic resonance brain image segmentation using soft computing approaches. Appl. Soft Comput. **24**, 522–533 (2014)
2. Benaichouche, A.N., Oulhadj, H., Siarry, P.: Improved spatial fuzzy c-means clustering for image segmentation using pso initialization, mahalanobis distance and post-segmentation correction. Digit. Sig. Process. **23**(5), 1390–1400 (2013)
3. Capor Hrosik, R., Tuba, E., Dolicanin, E., Jovanovic, R., Tuba, M.: Brain image segmentation based on firefly algorithm combined with k-means clustering. Stud. Inform. Control **28**, 167–176 (2019)
4. Dhanachandra, N., Manglem, K., Chanu, Y.J.: Image segmentation using k-means clustering algorithm and subtractive clustering algorithm. Procedia Comput. Sci. **54**, 764–771 (2015)

5. Forouzanfar, M., Forghani, N., Teshnehlab, M.: Parameter optimization of improved fuzzy c-means clustering algorithm for brain MR image segmentation. Eng. Appl. Artif. Intell. **23**(2), 160–168 (2010)
6. Hancer, E., Ozturk, C., Karaboga, D.: Artificial bee colony based image clustering method. In: Congress on Evolutionary Computation (CEC), pp. 1–5. IEEE (2012)
7. Hassanzadeh, T., Meybodi, M.R.: A new hybrid approach for data clustering using firefly algorithm and k-means. In: The 16th CSI International Symposium on Artificial Intelligence and Signal Processing (AISP 2012), pp. 007–011. IEEE (2012)
8. Huang, C., Liu, H., Chen, T., Shen, Q., Ma, Z.: Extreme image coding via multiscale autoencoders with generative adversarial optimization. In: 2019 IEEE Visual Communications and Image Processing (VCIP), pp. 1–4. IEEE (2019)
9. Lukic, M., Tuba, E., Tuba, M.: Leaf recognition algorithm using support vector machine with Hu moments and local binary patterns. In: 2017 IEEE 15th International Symposium on Applied Machine Intelligence and Informatics (SAMI), pp. 000485–000490. IEEE (2017)
10. Nayak, J., Nanda, M., Nayak, K., Naik, B., Behera, H.S.: An improved firefly fuzzy C-means (FAFCM) algorithm for clustering real world data sets. In: Kumar Kundu, M., Mohapatra, D.P., Konar, A., Chakraborty, A. (eds.) Advanced Computing, Networking and Informatics- Volume 1. SIST, vol. 27, pp. 339–348. Springer, Cham (2014). https://doi.org/10.1007/978-3-319-07353-8_40
11. Niknam, T., Amiri, B.: An efficient hybrid approach based on PSO, ACO and k-means for cluster analysis. Appl. Soft Comput. **10**(1), 183–197 (2010)
12. Omran, M.G., Engelbrecht, A.P., Salman, A.: Particle swarm optimization for pattern recognition and image processing. In: Abraham, A., Grosan, C., Ramos, V. (eds.) Swarm Intelligence in Data Mining, vol. 34, pp. 125–151. Springer, Heidelberg (2006). https://doi.org/10.1007/978-3-540-34956-3_6
13. Ozturk, C., Hancer, E., Karaboga, D.: Improved clustering criterion for image clustering with artificial bee colony algorithm. Pattern Anal. Appl. **18**(3), 587–599 (2014). https://doi.org/10.1007/s10044-014-0365-y
14. Patel, B.C., Sinha, G.: An adaptive k-means clustering algorithm for breast image segmentation. Int. J. Comput. Appl. **10**(4), 35–38 (2010)
15. Shen, Q., Kirschbaum, M.U., Hedley, M.J., Arbestain, M.C.: Testing an alternative method for estimating the length of fungal hyphae using photomicrography and image processing. PloS One **11**(6), e0157017 (2016)
16. Sinha, K., Sinha, G.: Efficient segmentation methods for tumor detection in MRI images. In: Conference on Electrical, Electronics and Computer Science, pp. 1–6. IEEE (2014)
17. Sulaiman, S.N., Isa, N.A.M.: Adaptive fuzzy-K-means clustering algorithm for image segmentation. IEEE Trans. Consumer Electron. **56**(4), 2661–2668 (2010)
18. Tan, Y., Shi, B.: Generative adversarial optimization. In: Tan, Y., Shi, Y., Niu, B. (eds.) ICSI 2019. LNCS, vol. 11655, pp. 3–17. Springer, Cham (2019). https://doi.org/10.1007/978-3-030-26369-0_1
19. Tuba, E., Dolicanin-Djekic, D., Jovanovic, R., Simian, D., Tuba, M.: Combined elephant herding optimization algorithm with K-means for data clustering. In: Satapathy, S.C., Joshi, A. (eds.) Information and Communication Technology for Intelligent Systems. SIST, vol. 107, pp. 665–673. Springer, Singapore (2019). https://doi.org/10.1007/978-981-13-1747-7_65
20. Tuba, E., Tuba, M., Jovanovic, R.: An algorithm for automated segmentation for bleeding detection in endoscopic images. In: International Joint Conference on Neural Networks (IJCNN), pp. 4579–4586. IEEE (2017)

21. Tuba, M., Tuba, E.: Generative adversarial optimization (GOA) for acute lymphocytic leukemia detection. Stud. Inform. Control **28**(3), 245–254 (2019)
22. Tuba, V., Capor-Hrosik, R., Tuba, E.: Forest fires detection in digital images based on color features. Int. J. Educ. Learn. Syst. **2** (2017)
23. Yao, H., Duan, Q., Li, D., Wang, J.: An improved k-means clustering algorithm for fish image segmentation. Math. Comput. Model. **58**(3–4), 790–798 (2013)

A Tool for Supporting the Evaluation of Active Learning Activities

Waraporn Jirapanthong[✉]

College of Creative Design and Entertainment Technology, Dhurakij Pundit University, Bangkok, Thailand
Waraporn.jir@dpu.ac.th

Abstract. Active learning becomes a strategical approach for an educational principle. The student engagement become a wider concern. Many researches have been proposed to support the approach. However, one of issues is how to effectively evaluate the performance and progress of students' learning. Although, having student engagement in a classroom is vital, the evaluation of students' performance is more important. However, keeping up the details or records of students' progress is a difficult task. We therefore propose a support for instructors to evaluate the performance of their students. In particular, a prototype tool is designed and developed in order to facilitate the evaluation of activities based on an active learning class. The tool also encompasses the web service for a function of face feature recognition. Two scenarios of active learning classrooms are created in order to evaluate the prototype tool. We also plan to create a larger number of scenarios which involve different class objectives. The results show that the tool can detect and determine students with high precision values. However, the prototype tool takes a long time to be processed depending on the size and number of photos.

Keywords: Active learning · Education method · Facial recognition · Facial features recognition · Student engagement

1 Introduction

The concept of student engagement is becoming a concern. Active-learning techniques have emerged as strategies for instructors to promote engagement during learning classes. The engagement of students at high level increases learning and retention of the students. The engagement with students may occur outside the classroom. For in the classroom, student engagement involves the participation of students such as interaction between instructors and students or between students themselves.

The advantages of active learning are numerous: i) classroom time can be utilized in discussing higher order thinking skills rather than wasting time on lower order activities; ii) collaboration, communication and leadership skills are enhanced amongst learners; iii) students are actively engaged in a realistic learning experience.

Even though the active learning is becoming as an important approach for educational learning, it has still some challenges which include resistance from students, unprepared

© Springer Nature Switzerland AG 2020
Y. Tan et al. (Eds.): ICSI 2020, LNCS 12145, pp. 476–484, 2020.
https://doi.org/10.1007/978-3-030-53956-6_43

students, lack of access to technology, and heavy workload prior to and during class. Moreover, the evaluation method for the active learning approach is also concerned. Our research relies on the method and supporting tool for enhancing the active learning approach to be successful. In this paper, we present a tool for supporting instructors to evaluate the learning progress. This is to facilitate the tasks of evaluation on learners. The instructors therefore can identify participating learners and analyse the learners' performances more effectively.

In this paper, the background of active learning and facial recognition analysis is provided in Sect. 2. Our approach is presenting in Sect. 3. The experimental results, discussion and future work are following.

2 Background

2.1 Active Learning

Active learning is generally defined as any instructional method that engages students in the learning process. In short, active learning requires students to do meaningful learning activities and think about what they are doing [1]. While this definition could include traditional activities such as homework, in practice active learning refers to activities that are introduced into the classroom. The core elements of active learning are student activity and engagement in the learning process. Active learning is often contrasted to the traditional lecture where students passively receive information from the instructor.

Active learning methods that can be incorporated in the classroom: i) having multiple pauses during lectures to allow students time to reflect on what is being learnt and to consolidate their notes; ii) having brief demonstrations, or ungraded exercises, followed by a class discussion to increase student engagement; iii) incorporating small group study periods during lectures to stimulate creativity and discuss the subject matter; and iv) using case studies to involve students in doing things and thinking about what they are doing [1]. The researchers introduced engaging activities throughout traditional lectures as they stimulate learning and retention, improve students' attitudes regarding education, and enhances academic achievement [1–5]. An active learning environment notably increases student participation and collaboration with peers, where knowledge is enthusiastically shared [6]. It has further been known to stimulate creativity by promoting individual and group ideas [6]. Therefore, in a time when individuals need to be critical thinkers and problem-solvers, Active Learning provides students with the necessary tools to develop those life skills that were not necessarily on the forefront with traditional education methods.

2.2 Facial Recognition Analysis

Facial recognition systems become more common. Industries and organizations are provides the services embedded with facial recognition systems.

However, some experts are still concerned regarding the algorithms, particularly when it comes to performance on faces with darker skin. Some research published by the MIT Media Lab found that some facial recognition systems performed worse when identifying an individual's gender if they were female or darker-skinned by MIT's Joy Buolamwini. Particularly, in the research, it focused on Amazon Rekognition [7] that the testing system made no mistakes when identifying the gender of lighter-skinned men. Otherwise, it mistook women for men 19% of the time and mistook darker-skinned women for men 31 percent of the time. Considering with the facial analysis software built by Microsoft, IBM, and Chinese firm Megvii, they are concerned to improve identifying similar racial and gender biases. Recently, a number of tech companies have voiced concern about the problems with facial recognition. As bias in algorithms is often the result of biased training data. However, many researches keep studying to improve the regulation and to ensure higher standards.

Although, there are little to engage with this performance, many applications and systems are still suggested to apply with the technology. A lot of researches are going on to find out the best outcome for benefits in use. For example, the gender identification test was facial analysis which spots expressions and characteristics like facial hair.

Basically, the following are the types of detection and recognition that common recognition analysis software are provided. Firstly, Labels: A label refers to any objects (e.g. flower, tree, or table), events (e.g. a wedding, graduation, or birthday party), concepts (e.g. a landscape, evening, and nature) or activities (e.g. getting out of a car). The software can detect labels in images and videos. However activities are not detected in images.

Secondly, Custom Labels: the software can identify the objects and scenes in images that are specific to some business needs by training a machine learning model. For example, a user can train a model to detect logos or detect engineering machine parts on an assembly line.

Thirdly, Faces: the software can detect faces in images and stored videos. The software shall learn where faces are detected in an image or video, facial landmarks such as the position of eyes, and detected emotions such as happy or sad. Moreover, some software have provided face searching function which is indexed into a collection of faces. The software can then be matched with faces detected in images, stored videos, and streaming video. Particularly, some software can identify the celebrities in images and stored videos.

Fourthly, People Paths: the software can track the paths of people detected in a stored video. Some software provides path tracking, face details, and in-frame location information for people detected in a video.

Fifthly, Text Detection: the software can detect text in images and convert it into machine-readable text. This allows the analysis is further applied in other systems.

Sixthly, Unsafe Content: the software can identify images or videos for adult and with violent content.

3 Approach

To support the evaluation of activities during active learning, we proposed a tool to facilitate instructors to evaluate the performance and competency of learners. The prototype tool is developed. It can analyze images that are supplied as image bytes or images stored in a source folder. As shown in the figure, a part of source code allows a user to choose an image and view the estimated ages of faces that are detected in the image. The chosen image is loaded by using the displaying the image. This example shows how to unencode the loaded image bytes. The program then estimated orientation of an image and to translate bounding box coordinates. An image is loaded and its height and width are determined. The bounding box coordinates of the face for the rotated image.

The program is implemented with JavaScript and JSON. Particularly, it encompasses the Amazon web service [7] which provides a function of image recognition.

The steps to execute the program are: i) provide photos capturing the activities in the classroom in the images folder. ii) provide photos of each student in the classroom in the ref folder. iii) execute the program, entitled node; which implements the algorithm as shown in Figs. 1 and 2. iv) the program calls the web services of face recognition to identify the picture of a face. Particularly, the photos including students in various gesture are computed. When single facial features are identified, the face features are determined comparing with the individual photos. The overall configuration can be described by a vector representing the position an size of the main facial features, such as eyes and eyebrows, nose, mouth, and the shape of face outline. And v) the feature matching based on measured distances between features will be then concluded. The sets of photos for each student are created.

```
function DetectFaces(imageData) {
  AWS.region = "RegionToUse";
  var rekognition = new AWS.Rekognition();
  var params = {
    Image: {
    Bytes: imageData
    },
    Attributes: [
      'ALL',
    ]    };
  rekognition.detectFaces(params, function (err, data) {
    if (err) console.log(err, err.stack); // an error occurred
    else {
      var table = "<table><tr><th>Low</th><th>High</th></tr>";
      // show each face and build out estimated age table
      for (var i = 0; i < data.FaceDetails.length; i++) {
        table += '<tr><td>' + data.FaceDetails[i].AgeRange.Low +
          '</td><td>' + data.FaceDetails[i].AgeRange.High + '</td></tr>';
      }
      table += "</table>";
      document.getElementById("opResult").innerHTML = table;
    }
}); }
```

Fig. 1. A part of web service to unencode the image files.

```
function ProcessImage() {

    AnonLog();

    var control = document.getElementById("fileToUpload");

    var file = control.files[0];

    // Load base64 encoded image

    var reader = new FileReader();

    reader.onload = (function (theFile) {

      return function (e) {

          var img = document.createElement('img');

          var image = null;

          img.src = e.target.result;

          var jpg = true;

          try {

            image = atob(e.target.result.split("data:image/jpeg;base64,")[1]);

          } catch (e) {

            jpg = false;

          }

          if (jpg == false) {

            try {

                image = atob(e.target.result.split("data:image/png;base64,")[1]);

            } catch (e) {

                alert("Not an image file Rekognition can process");

                return;

            }    }

          //unencode image bytes for Rekognition DetectFaces API

          var length = image.length;

          imageBytes = new ArrayBuffer(length);

          var ua = new Uint8Array(imageBytes);

          for (var i = 0; i < length; i++) {

                ua[i] = image.charCodeAt(i);

          }

          //Call Rekognition

          DetectFaces(imageBytes);

    };

    })(file);

    reader.readAsDataURL(file);

}
```

Fig. 2. A part of web service to estimated orientation of an image and to identify bounding box coordinates

4   Experimental Results

To work with the program, an instructor has to capture photos during activities of active learning in a classroom. The photos then become resources for the program. As shown in Fig. 3, the photos are taken during the activities in the classroom. To evaluate the prototype, we created two scenarios of classroom. Firstly, we have a classroom with 54 students. The class is run based on active learning. Totally, the students involved the class twelve hours. The 39 photos are captured during the activities. Also, the photos of each student are provided.

Fig. 3. Example of a set of photos capturing the activities in the classroom

Secondly, we have established a small classroom based on active learning. The class objectives are accomplished in three hours. The activities are performed according to the class. The photos are captured during the learning and provided as a resource. There are four learners participating in the classroom. Snapshots of each learner's face are provided as shown in Fig. 4. There are 9 photos taken from the class.

Boon   Boss   Bright   Mhee

Fig. 4. A snapshot of each learner presenting face features are provided.

As shown in Fig. 5, the program computes by analyzing each picture. In particular, it detects the face features of each student based on reference photos. The program then create a folder of photos for each student as shown in Fig. 6.

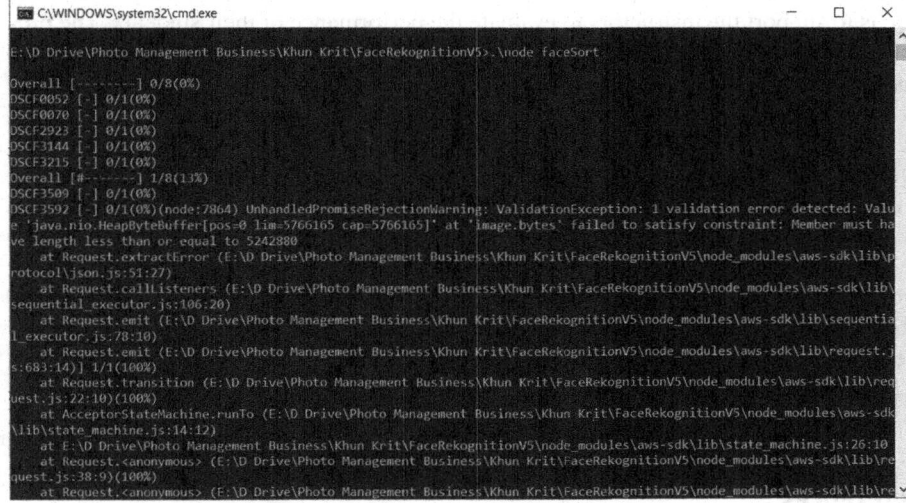

Fig. 5. All photos are computed by the program

Name	Date modified	Type	Size
Boon	1/8/2020 10:24 PM	File folder	
Boss	1/8/2020 10:24 PM	File folder	
Bright	1/8/2020 10:24 PM	File folder	
Mhee	1/8/2020 10:24 PM	File folder	

Fig. 6. Photos of each learner are analyzed and identified.

For the first scenario, there are 54 students with 39 taken photos. 54 folders are created by the prototype. The photos of each student are detected based on their face features. There are 51 folders identified the student correctly 100%. Otherwise, recognition of other 3 folders are partly incorrect. One folder included 1 mismatched photo. Other two folders includes 2 mismatched photos. For the second scenario, there 4 learners with 9 photos taken during the activities. There are four folders created by the prototype. The photos of each student are detected based on their face features completely. They are totally corrected identified.

On average, the performance of our approach in terms of precision measurements in two scenarios seems to be consistently high (ranging from 94% to 100%).

5   Discussion and Future Work

Our research focuses on how to support the active learning approach. One of remaining issues is how to evaluate the performance or participating of learners effectively. Basically, recording the details of students' progress is a clumsy and tedious task. Our work here is to support the instructors to evaluate the performance of their students. The prototype tool is implemented in JavaScript in order to facilitate the evaluation of activities based on an active learning class. The tool also encompasses the Amazon web service for a function of face feature recognition. The photos of students during participating the activities in the classrooms are captured and the prototype tool then generates the folders of each student collecting only the student's photos. This assists the instructors to determine the performance and participating of each student. They then can evaluate the students' progress more effectively.

We plan to create a larger number of scenarios which involve different class objectives. It is therefore believed that the approach could be extended and enhanced to support a better way. In addition, sophisticated techniques for visualization could support the use of the prototype tool more efficiently. However, the prototype tool takes a long time to be processed depending on the size and number of photos. More work needs to be done to optimize the processing time.

References

1. Bonwell, C.C. (n.d.): Active Learning: Creating Excitement in the Classroom. https://www.ydae.purdue.edu/lct/HBCU/documents/Active_Learning_Creating_Excitement_in_the_Classroom.pdf. Accessed 12 July 2014
2. Eison, J.: Using Active Learning Instructional Strategies to Create Excitement and Enhance Learning (2000). http://www.cte.cornell.edu/documents/presentations/Active%20Learning%20%20Creating%20Excitement%20in%20the%20Classroom%20-%20Handout.pdf. Accessed 12 July 2014
3. Michael, J.A., Modell, H.I.: Active Learning in Secondary and College Science Classrooms: A Working Model for Helping the Learner to Learn. Lawrence Erlbaum Associates, Mahwah (2003)
4. Sutherland, T.E., Bonwell, C.C. (eds.): Using Active Learning in College Classes: A Range of Options for Faculty. Jossey-Bass, San Francisco (1996)
5. Thomas, J.: The variation of memory with time for information appearing during a lecture. Stud. Adult Educ. **4**, 57–62 (1972)
6. Park, E.L., Choi, B.K.: Transformation of classroom spaces: traditional versus active learning classroom in colleges. High. Educ. **68**, 749–771 (2014). https://doi.org/10.1007/s10734-014-9742-0
7. https://docs.aws.amazon.com/sdk-for-javascript/v2/developer-guide/getting-started-browser.html

Inferring Candidate CircRNA-Disease Associations by Bi-random Walk Based on CircRNA Regulatory Similarity

Chunyan Fan[1], Xiujuan Lei[1(✉)], and Ying Tan[2]

[1] School of Computer Science, Shaanxi Normal University, Xi'an 710119, China
xjlei@snnu.edu.cn
[2] School of Electronics Engineering and Computer Science, Peking University, Beijing 100871, China

Abstract. Identification of associations between circular RNAs (circRNA) and diseases has become a hot topic, which is beneficial for researchers to understand the disease mechanism. However, traditional biological experiments are expensive and time-consuming. In this study, we proposed a novel method named BWHCDA, which applied bi-random walk algorithm on the heterogeneous network for predicting circRNA-disease associations. First, circRNA regulatory similarity is measured based on circRNA-miRNA interactions, and circRNA similarity is calculated by the average of circRNA regulatory similarity and Gaussian interaction profiles (GIP) kernel similarity for circRNAs. Similarly, disease similarity is the mean of disease semantic similarity and GIP kernel similarity for diseases. Then, the heterogeneous network is constructed by integrating circRNA network, disease network via circRNA-disease associations. Subsequently, the bi-random walk algorithm is implemented on the heterogeneous network to predict circRNA-disease associations. Finally, we utilize leave-one-out cross validation and 10-fold cross validation frameworks to evaluate the prediction performance of BWHCDA method and obtain AUC of 0.9334 and 0.8764 ± 0.0038, respectively. Moreover, the predicted hsa_circ_0000519-gastric cancer association is analyzed. Results show that BWHCDA could be an effective resource for clinical experimental guidance.

Keywords: CircRNA-disease associations · Bi-random walk · CircRNA regulatory similarity

1 Introduction

Circular RNAs (CircRNAs) are a type of non-coding RNAs with closed loop structures formed by back splicing [1]. Recently, large number of circRNAs are widely found in various livings [2], and they could regulate gene expression at transcriptional or post-transcriptional levels by titrating microRNAs (miRNAs) [3], regulating transcription and splicing [4, 5], even several circRNAs could translate to produce polypeptides [6]. Increasing researches have demonstrated that the mis-regulation of circRNAs may cause

© Springer Nature Switzerland AG 2020
Y. Tan et al. (Eds.): ICSI 2020, LNCS 12145, pp. 485–494, 2020.
https://doi.org/10.1007/978-3-030-53956-6_44

abnormal cellular functions and associated with various diseases [7]. Thus, disease-associated circRNAs are becoming a class of promising biomarkers for disease diagnosis and treatment.

However, it is costly and laborious to identify the disease-related circRNAs with biomedical experiments. Recently, several computational approaches have been developed. Lei *et al.* [8] firstly designed a path weighted approach named PWCDA to predict circRNA-disease associations. Likewise, KATZHCDA [9] is developed based on KATZ model to measure the probability for each pair of circRNA-disease associations, in which the circRNA expression similarity and disease phenotype similarity matrices are used as priori knowledge to establish the circRNA-disease heterogeneous network. DWNN-RLS [10] is designed based on Kronecker regularized least squares to predict the associations between circRNAs and diseases. iCircDA-MF [11] is developed based on non-negative matrix factorization by integrating the circRNA-gene, gene-disease and circRNA-disease relationships. Wang *et al.* [12] utilized a recommendation algorithm PersonalRank to measure the relevance between circRNAs and diseases based on circRNA expression profiles and functional similarity. Although several methods have developed for the circRNA-disease association prediction, it is still a challenge to obtain sufficiently accurate results.

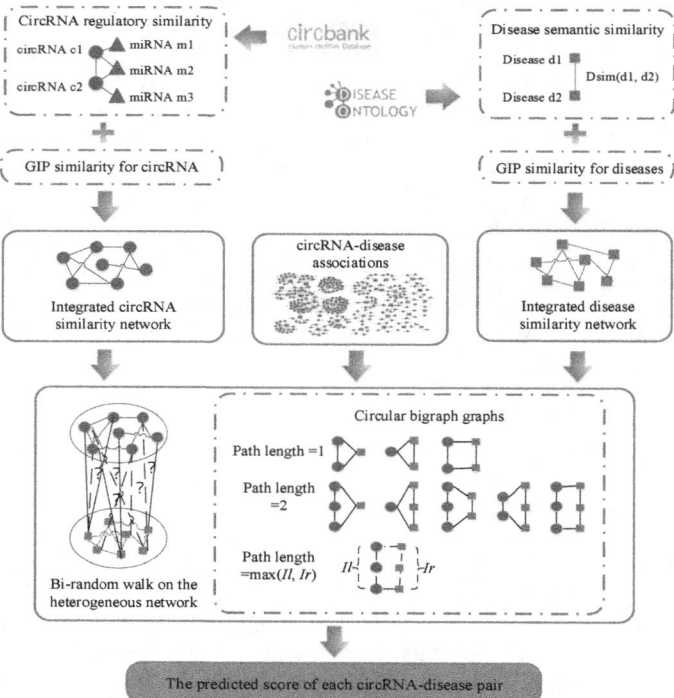

Fig. 1. The flowchart of BWHCDA method.

In this study, we developed a novel framework for forecasting circRNA-disease associations named BWHCDA, which integrated multiple similarity measures and implemented bi-random walk algorithm (Fig. 1). First, circRNA regulatory similarity is effective measured based on circRNAs may play essential roles in regulating miRNA function in disease occurrence and progression. Moreover, combined with Gaussian interaction profiles (GIP) kernel similarity for circRNAs, the integrated circRNA similarity is effectively measured. Similarly, disease similarity is denoted as the average of disease sematic similarity and GIP kernel similarity for diseases. Subsequently, the heterogeneous network is constructed by combing the circRNA network, disease network and circRNA-disease associations. Then, circular bigraph (CBG) patterns are introduced in bi-random walk algorithm to predict the missing associations based on the heterogeneous network. The results show that BWHCDA could be considered as a powerful tool for predicting circRNA-disease associations.

2 Methods

2.1 Human CircRNA-Disease Associations

The experimentally validated human circRNA-disease associations are extracted from the CircR2Disease database [13]. Then, we choose the associations that circRNAs have been recorded in circBase database [14] and disease name recorded in disease ontology database [15]. Finally, we retained 371 circRNA-disease associations between 325 circRNAs and 53 diseases as the gold standard dataset. The circRNA-disease adjacency matrix $A(i,j)$ is established, if there is an association between circRNA and disease, $A(i,j)$ is set as 1, otherwise 0.

2.2 CircRNA Regulatory Similarity

The miRNA-circRNA interactions are downloaded from the CircBank database [16], and the interactions overlapped with disease-related circRNAs are selected to measure the regulatory similarity of circRNAs. It is measured as follows:

$$SC\_RG(c_i, c_j) = \frac{card(M_i \cap M_j)}{\sqrt{card(M_i)} \cdot \sqrt{card(M_j)}} \tag{1}$$

where the set of M_i have relationship with circRNA c_i and the set of miRNA M_j have relationship with circRNA c_j.

2.3 Disease Semantic Similarity

The disease names are described as hierarchical directed acyclic graph (DAG) based on the Medical Subject Headings (MeSH) descriptions for diseases. And disease semantic similarity is calculated by the DOSE [17] tool with Wang *et al.* method.

2.4 GIP Kernel Similarity

Based on the assumption that similar circRNAs (diseases) are tend to have similar inter-action or non-interaction pattern with diseases (circRNAs) [18], the GIP kernel similarity for circRNAs and diseases are respectively calculated as follows:

$$SC\_cGIP(c(i), c(j)) = exp(-\gamma_c \|c(i) - c(j)\|^2)$$
$$\gamma_c = \frac{1}{(\frac{1}{n_c} \sum_{i=1}^{n_c} \|c(i)\|^2)} \quad (2)$$

$$SD\_dGIP(d(i), d(j)) = exp(-\gamma_d \|d(i) - d(j)\|^2)$$
$$\gamma_d = \frac{1}{(\frac{1}{n_d} \sum_{i=1}^{n_d} \|d(i)\|^2)} \quad (3)$$

where $c(i)$ (or $d(i)$) denotes the circRNA (disease) interaction profiles, which is the i-th row (column) of the adjacency matrix A. The parameters γ_c and γ_d are used to control the kernel bandwidth. n_c (or n_d) is the number of circRNAs (diseases).

2.5 Integrated Similarity for CircRNAs and Diseases

The new circRNA similarity scores (SC) are calculated with the average scores of the circRNA regulatory similarity and GIP kernel similarity for circRNAs. Similarly, the integrated disease similarity (SD) is denoted as the mean of the disease semantic sim-ilarity and GIP kernel similarity for diseases. Then, the integrated circRNA similarity and integrated disease similarity are adjusted with the logistic function [19].

$$S(x) = \frac{1}{1 + e^{cx+d}} \quad (4)$$

where x is the value of element of matrix SC or SD. Parameters c and d control the adjustment effects, and we set c as -15 and set d as $\log(9999)$, respectively.

2.6 The Construction of Heterogeneous Network

According to the circRNA similarity and disease similarity measures, the circRNA network and disease network can be constructed. Next, the weighted heterogeneous circRNA-disease network is constructed based on the circRNA network, disease net-work via gold standard circRNA-disease associations. The heterogeneous network could be considered as a bipartite graph, the nodes represent circRNAs or diseases, the edges represent three types of interactions of circRNA-circRNA, disease-disease and circRNA-disease.

2.7 BWHCDA Method

Based on the topology and structure characteristics of circRNA network and disease network, the concept of CBG was introduced. A CBG is described as a subgraph of a circRNA path $\{c_1, c_2, ..., c_n\}$ and a disease path $\{d_1, d_2, ..., d_m\}$, in which the two ends connected by circRNA-disease associations (c_1, d_1) and (c_n, d_m). The CBG indicates a vicinity relation between the two association (c_1, d_1) and (c_n, d_m), which is generalized by their distance to other associations in the circRNA network and disease network. The length of CBG patterns (l, r) is determined by the longer length of circRNA path and the disease path. In this study, we hypothesize that most potential associations tend to be covered by many shorter CBGs in the unknown circRNA-disease network. If there are more CBG patterns between circRNAs and diseases, the higher possibility of circRNA-disease associations are.

By iteratively adding the circRNA path and disease path, we calculates the CBGs weighted by decay factor α that ranges from 0 to 1. Because of different structures and topologies in the circRNA network and disease network, disparate optimal number of random walk steps are generated. Therefore, parameters l and r are introduced to restrict the number of random steps in circRNA similarity network and disease similarity network, respectively. The iterative process of bi-random walk is described as follows:

$$\text{On the circRNA network: } Cc = \alpha \cdot SC_L \cdot CD_{t-1} + (1 - \alpha)A \tag{5}$$

$$\text{On the disease network: } Dd = \alpha \cdot CD_{t-1} \cdot SD_L + (1 - \alpha)A \tag{6}$$

where α is the decay factor that controls the importance of CBG for different paths, SL_L and SD_L represent the normalized matrix by using Laplace regularization.

$$SC_L = Dc^{-1/2}(S_c)Dc^{-1/2} \tag{7}$$

$$SD_L = Dd^{-1/2}(S_d)Dd^{-1/2} \tag{8}$$

where $Dc(i,i)$ (or $Dd(i,i)$) is the diagonal matrix of circRNA similarity matrix S_c (S_d).

By combining the propagation scores of matrices Cc and Dd, the relevance scores of unknown circRNA-disease associations could be obtained. The BWHCDA algorithm is outlined as Table 1.

3   Results

3.1   Prediction Performance

To assess the performance of BWHCDA method, leave-one-out cross validation (LOOCV) and 5-fold cross validation (10-fold CV) framework are performed on the gold standard datasets. For LOOCV, each known circRNA-disease association is removed in turn as testing sample, and the other associations are regarded as training samples. Then, the unknown circRNA-disease associations are considered as candidate associations, and the prediction performance is assessed by the predicted rank of test sample. In the framework of 10-fold CV, circRNA-disease associations are randomly divided into ten subsets, and each subset is utilized in turn as test set and the remaining as the train set on each time. To decrease the sample division bias, we perform 100 times repetitions of 10-fold CV. The receiver operating characteristic (ROC) curves are plotted to show the prediction performance by calculating the true positive rate (TPR) and false positive rate (FPR). Furthermore, the area under the curves (AUCs) are calculated to evaluate the overall performance.

Table 1. The pseudocode of BWHCDA algorithm

Algorithm: BWHCDA
Input: circRNA-disease association interaction adjacency matrix A, circRNA-circRNA regulated similarity matrix SC_RG, disease semantic similarity matrix DS_Dss, parameter α, iteration step I_l and I_r
Output: predicted interaction matrix CD
BWHCDA $(A, SC\_RG, DS\_Dss, \alpha, I_l, I_r)$
1. Calculate GIP similarity matrix SC_cGIP and SD_dGIP with A;
2. The integrated circRNA similarity matrix SC is obtained based on SC_RG and SC_cGIP, while the disease similarity SD is calculated based on DS_Dss and SD_dGIP;
3. Obtain the matrix by logistic function S_c and S_d;
4. Obtain the normalized matrix SC_L and SD_L by Laplacian normalization operation.
5. $CD_0 = A/\text{sun}(A)$;   // CD_0 is the initial probability
6. //Iteration process;
7. $Max\_Iter = \max([I_l, I_r])$
8. **for** $t = 1$ to Max_Iter
9. $m = n = 0$;
10. //Random walk in circRNA similarity network
11. **if** $(t <= I_l)$
12. $m = 1$;
13. $Cc = \alpha*SC_L*CD_{t-1}+(1-\alpha)*A$;
14. **end if**
15. // Random walk in disease similarity network
16. **if** $(t <= I_r)$
17. $n = 1$;
18. $Dd = \alpha*CD_{t-1}*SD_L+(1-\alpha)*A$;
19. **end if**
20. //combination of results
21. $CD_t = (m* Cc+ n*Dd)/(m+n)$
22.**end for**
23.**return** CD;

3.2 Effects of Parameters

There are three parameters in the BWHCDA method, including α, I_l, I_r. To test the effects of the three parameters, we set α value as $\{0.2, 0.4, 0.6, 0.8\}$, and I_l, I_r are set from 1 to 5, respectively. Then, we could calculate AUC values based on LOOCV and the effects of these parameters are shown in Tables 2, 3, 4 and 5. The results indicate that α has little effects on prediction performance. When $\alpha = 0.4$, $I_l = 4$ and $I_r = 5$, the AUC value of LOOCV is the highest with step length less than five. When $\alpha = 0.4$, $I_l = 3$, $I_r = 4$, AUC value of LOOCV is the highest within step length less than four. The AUC value of LOOCV is the highest within step length than three steps when $\alpha = 0.4$, $I_l = 2$, $I_r = 3$. And when $\alpha = 0.6$, $I_l = 1$, $I_r = 2$, the AUC value of LOOCV is the highest within two steps. Finally, we set three parameters as $\alpha = 0.4$, $I_l = 2$, $I_r = 3$, respectively.

3.3 Comparison with Other Methods

To further evaluate the prediction performance of BWHCDA, we compare it with other five methods including KATZHCDA [9], PageRank [20], NCP [21], BDSILP [22] and

Table 2. When α is set as 0.2, the effect of parameters I_l and I_r for LOOCV AUC.

$\alpha = 0.2$	$I_r = 1$	$I_r = 2$	$I_r = 3$	$I_r = 4$	$I_r = 5$
$I_l = 1$	0.9084	0.9278	0.9126	0.9046	0.9009
$I_l = 2$	0.6851	0.9097	0.9295	0.9137	0.9050
$I_l = 3$	0.3462	0.7035	0.9099	0.9298	0.9138
$I_l = 4$	0.1645	0.3678	0.7057	0.9099	0.9298
$I_l = 5$	0.1429	0.1666	0.3706	0.7059	0.9099

Table 3. When α is set as 0.4, the effect of parameters I_l and I_r for LOOCV AUC.

$\alpha = 0.4$	$I_r = 1$	$I_r = 2$	$I_r = 3$	$I_r = 4$	$I_r = 5$
$I_l = 1$	0.9084	0.9314	0.9209	0.9116	0.9058
$I_l = 2$	0.7788	0.9109	**0.9334**	0.9243	0.9138
$I_l = 3$	0.5692	0.8018	0.9116	**0.9341**	0.9253
$I_l = 4$	0.3632	0.6156	0.8056	0.9116	**0.9343**
$I_l = 5$	0.2076	0.4049	0.6259	0.8062	0.9115

Table 4. When α is set as 0.6, the effect of parameters I_l and I_r for LOOCV AUC.

$\alpha = 0.6$	$I_r = 1$	$I_r = 2$	$I_r = 3$	$I_r = 4$	$I_r = 5$
$I_l = 1$	0.9084	**0.9322**	0.9254	0.9165	0.9095
$I_l = 2$	0.8194	0.9119	0.9331	0.9285	0.9209
$I_l = 3$	0.6887	0.8428	0.9118	0.9328	0.9296
$I_l = 4$	0.5445	0.7381	0.8476	0.9108	0.9324
$I_l = 5$	0.4094	0.6150	0.7506	0.8480	0.9100

Table 5. When α is set as 0.8, the effect of parameters I_l and I_r for LOOCV AUC.

$\alpha = 0.8$	$I_r = 1$	$I_r = 2$	$I_r = 3$	$I_r = 4$	$I_r = 5$
$I_l = 1$	0.9084	0.9318	0.9261	0.9180	0.9098
$I_l = 2$	0.8422	0.9123	0.9299	0.9273	0.9203
$I_l = 3$	0.7543	0.8653	0.9109	0.9261	0.9255
$I_l = 4$	0.6670	0.8022	0.8694	0.9078	0.9229
$I_l = 5$	0.5789	0.7359	0.8158	0.8688	0.9046

HeteSim [23]. Consequently, BWHCDA method achieve the best performance among these six approaches based on AUC values of LOOCV and 10-fold CV with the same datasets (Figs. 2 and 3). Therefore, BWHCDA method is better than other five methods.

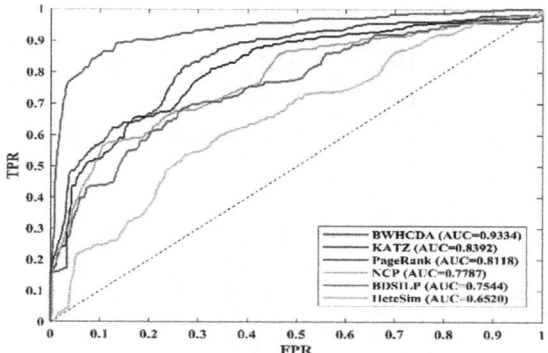

Fig. 2. Comparison of BWHCDA and other methods in terms of ROC curves in LOOCV.

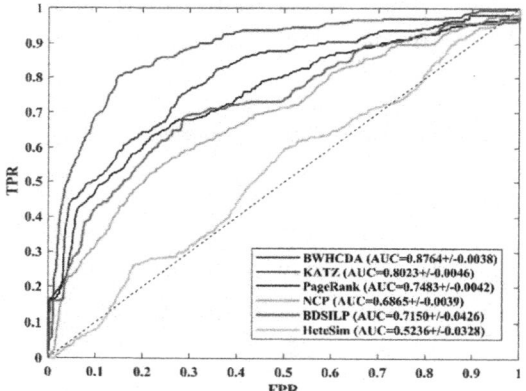

Fig. 3. Comparison of BWHCDA and other methods in terms of ROC curves in 10-fold CV.

3.4 Case Studies

To further assess the prediction performance of BWHCDA method, we analyze the predicted hsa_circ_0000519-gastric cancer association. As shown in Fig. 4, hsa_circ_0000519 may interact with miRNAs including hsa-miR-1233, hsa-miR-1258, hsa-miR-1296, hsa-miR-146b-3p, hsa-miR-521 to play their biological roles. The miRNA targets gene of these miRNAs have been validated related with gastric cancer, including hsa-miR-1258 target HPSE, hsa-miR-146b-3p target PER1 and IRAK1, hsa-miR-521 target ERCC8, hsa-miR-1296-5p target ERBB2. In addition, hsa-miR-1296 has been validated associated with gastric cancer. Therefore, hsa_circ_0000519 may be a potential biomarker for gastric diagnosis and prognosis.

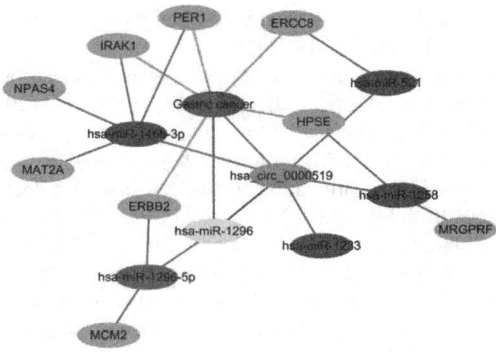

Fig. 4. The hsa_circ_0000519-miRNA-mRNA-gastric cancer interaction network.

4 Conclusion

Prioritizing the potential associations between circRNAs and diseases is benefit to the development of the understanding of the disease mechanism, diagnose and treatment for diseases. The reasons that why BWHCDA method has better performance is shown as following aspects. First, bi-random explored the CBG patterns with iteratively implement random walk on the circRNA similarity network and disease similarity network. In addition, BWHCDA is a multi-task learning method that could forecast potential circRNA-disease associations simultaneously rather than mine candidate circRNAs for specific diseases. Therefore, BWHCDA could be an effective method for biomedical research.

Acknowledgements. This work was supported by the National Natural Science Foundation of China (61972451, 61672334, 61902230) and the Fundamental Research Funds for the Central Universities, Shaanxi Normal University (GK201901010).

References

1. Barrett, S.P., Wang, P.L., Salzman, J.: Circular RNA biogenesis can proceed through an exon-containing lariat precursor. eLife **4**, e07540 (2015)
2. Memczak, S., et al.: Circular RNAs are a large class of animal RNAs with regulatory potency. Nature **495**, 333–338 (2013)
3. Salmena, L., Poliseno, L., Tay, Y., Kats, L., Pandolfi, P.P.: A ceRNA hypothesis: the Rosetta Stone of a hidden RNA language? Cell **146**, 353–358 (2011)
4. Zhang, Y., et al.: Circular intronic long noncoding RNAs. Mol. Cell **51**, 792–806 (2013)
5. Conn, V.M., et al.: A circRNA from SEPALLATA3 regulates splicing of its cognate mRNA through R-loop formation. Nat. Plants **3**, 17053 (2017)
6. Sun, P., Li, G.: CircCode: a powerful tool for identifying circRNA coding ability. Front. Genet. **10**, 981 (2019)
7. Meng, S., et al.: CircRNA: functions and properties of a novel potential biomarker for cancer. 16

8. Lei, X., Fang, Z., Chen, L., Wu, F.X.: PWCDA: path weighted method for predicting circRNA-disease associations. Int. J. Mol. Sci. 19 (2018)

9. Fan, C., Lei, X., Wu, F.X.: Prediction of CircRNA-disease associations using KATZ model based on heterogeneous networks. Int. J. Biol. Sci. **14**, 1950–1959 (2018)

10. Yan, C., Wang, J., Wu, F.X.: DWNN-RLS: regularized least squares method for predicting circRNA-disease associations. BMC Bioinform. **19**, 520 (2018)

11. Wei, H., Liu, B.: iCircDA-MF: identification of circRNA-disease associations based on matrix factorization. Briefings Bioinform. (2019)

12. Wang, Y., Nie, C., Zang, T., Wang, Y.: Predicting circRNA-disease associations based on circRNA expression similarity and functional similarity. **10** (2019)

13. Fan, C., Lei, X., Fang, Z., Jiang, Q., Wu, F.X.: CircR2Disease: a manually curated database for experimentally supported circular RNAs associated with various diseases. Database: J. Biol. Databases Curation **2018** (2018)

14. Glazar, P., Papavasileiou, P., Rajewsky, N.: circBase: a database for circular RNAs. RNA (New York, N.Y.) **20**, 1666–1670 (2014)

15. Schriml, L.M., et al.: Disease ontology: a backbone for disease semantic integration. Nucleic Acids Res. **40**, D940–D946 (2012)

16. Liu, M., Wang, Q., Shen, J., Yang, B.B., Ding, X.: Circbank: a comprehensive database for circRNA with standard nomenclature. RNA Biol. **16**, 899–905 (2019)

17. Yu, G., Wang, L.-G., Yan, G.-R., He, Q.-Y.J.B.: DOSE: an R/Bioconductor package for disease ontology semantic and enrichment analysis. Bioinformatics **31**, 608–609 (2015)

18. van Laarhoven, T., Nabuurs, S.B., Marchiori, E.: Gaussian interaction profile kernels for predicting drug-target interaction. Bioinform. (Oxford, England) **27**, 3036–3043 (2011)

19. Vanunu, O., Magger, O., Ruppin, E., Shlomi, T., Sharan, R.: Associating genes and protein complexes with disease via network propagation. PLoS Comput. Biol. **6**, e1000641 (2010)

20. Page, L., Brin, S., Motwani, R., Winograd, T.: The PageRank citation ranking: Bringing order to the web. Stanford InfoLab (1999)

21. Gu, C., Liao, B., Li, X., Li, K.: Network consistency projection for human miRNA-disease associations inference. Sci. Rep. **6**, 36054 (2016)

22. Zhang, W., Yang, W., Lu, X., Huang, F., Luo, F.: The bi-direction similarity integration method for predicting microbe-disease associations. IEEE Access **6**, 38052–38061 (2018)

23. Fan, C., Lei, X., Guo, L., Zhang, A.: Predicting the associations between microbes and diseases by integrating multiple data sources and path-based HeteSim scores. Neurocomputing **323**, 76–85 (2019)

Methods of Machine Learning in System Abnormal Behavior Detection

Pavel A. Savenkov$^{(\boxtimes)}$ ⓘ and Alexey N. Ivutin$^{(\boxtimes)}$ ⓘ

Department of Computer Technology, Tula State University, Tula, Russia
pavel@savenkov.net, alexey.ivutin@gmail.com

Abstract. The aim of the research is to develop mathematical and program support for detecting abnormal behavior of users. It will be based on analysis of their behavioral biometric characteristics. One of the major problems in UEBA/DSS intelligent systems is obtaining useful information from a large amount of unstructured, inconsistent data. Management decision-making should be based on real data collected from the analysed feature. However, based on the information received, it is rather difficult to make any management decision, as the data are heterogeneous and their volumes are extremely large. Application of machine learning methods in implementation of mobile UEBA/DSS system is proposed. This will make it possible to achieve a data analysis high quality and find complex dependencies in it. A list of the most significant factors submitted to the input of the analysing methods was formed during the research.

Keywords: DLP · UBA · Big data · Data science · Software · Information system · Machine learning · Unstructured data · Dynamic model · Neural network · K-nearest neighbors algorithm

1 Introduction

Over the past few years there has been a sustained increase in interest in data security challenges in enterprise information systems. Many experts in the field of information security (IS) show a trend of increased number of internal incursions compared to external ones. Concerns about the issue are reinforced by the fact that companies usually focus on protecting against external threats, while analysts point out that more than half of intrusion and computer security breaches are caused by their own employees or others with legitimate access to the information system. Theft and sale of confidential information, dissemination of information with limited asses are only a small part of IS-incidents directly related to internal threats [1].

Thus, information security internal threats are caused by harmful actions of users (insiders) who have legitimate access to the corporate network. This type of attack is usually distinguished from attacks that result from compromising the company employees' accounts, where the intruder (hacker) gets access to corporate IT resources using stolen accounts.

In the case of an internal attack, the insider usually acts maliciously and most likely knows that he is violating his company's security policy. However, when internal threats

© Springer Nature Switzerland AG 2020
Y. Tan et al. (Eds.): ICSI 2020, LNCS 12145, pp. 495–505, 2020.
https://doi.org/10.1007/978-3-030-53956-6_45

are classifying, a group of threats is sorted out. There are threats committed without malicious intent (random), by negligence or due to technical ignorance.

The sources of internal threats can be referred to different categories of users who have or have had access to the corporate network. The group of potentially malicious users of the corporate network is difficult to identify, and it can be much wider than it may seem at first glance [2].

In addition, the amount of data that can be the goal of internal attacks is constantly increasing at a high speed. Financial reports, customer or employee data, product technical documentation, and etc. can be examples of such vulnerable data. Similar data may be located in different locations on the corporate network at the same time time, as they are required for processing by different departments/employees, they are stored on corporate mail servers, backed up and etc.

Data breach is one of the most dangerous internal threats for modern companies. The number and complexity of internal attacks continues to grow. In 2015 it was registered an increase of about 64% more attacks than in 2014. According to research provided by the Ponemon Institute, which was supported by IBM, the company suffered an average loss of $4 million per incident in 2016, while the average value of a lost or stolen document was estimated at $158. The data were based on an analysis of 383 companies in 12 countries.

1.1 Typical Data Breach Stages

As show modern researches, from the moment the user decides to steal the data to directly the data forwarding, it takes from weeks to months to prepare the breach and this time is spent on breach preparation stage. Therefore, more experts now agree that data breaches need to be identified even before the stage of data transfer beyond the company's information technologies sphere [3].

We will describe the typical stages of data loss more detailed. (see Fig. 1). A legitimate employee becomes an insider beginning at some crucial point, for example at the moment after social media/email communication with one of company's competitors (the "Start of internal invasion" phase). After that, the employee-insider enters the research phase ("Research phase"), where he attempts to find and access information, in which he is interested, herewith using his current rights or trying to expand them in legitimate ways. At this stage, cases in which an insider under various excuses asks his colleagues to give assess to their rights to reach a certain category of information often appear there, and Edward Snowden's actions are usually used as an example of such behaviour. It will also be relevant to note here the importance of the users' authenticating task, i.e. determining that the user is the one on behalf of whom he or she has authorized. The insider's "Research phase" may continue for weeks and months, but as time goes on, he tends to find a way to gain access to the data which he is interested in.

After getting access to the desired information, the "Data hiding" phase begins. At this stage, the main goal of the insider is to test the existing information security systems of the company and find the optimal way to safely exfilter the received information. No attempt had been made to transfer data beyond the information perimeter of the organization before this stage, so traditional Data Loss Prevention (DLP) protection did not work. To achieve the goal of "Data hiding" stage it will be suitable for the insider to use

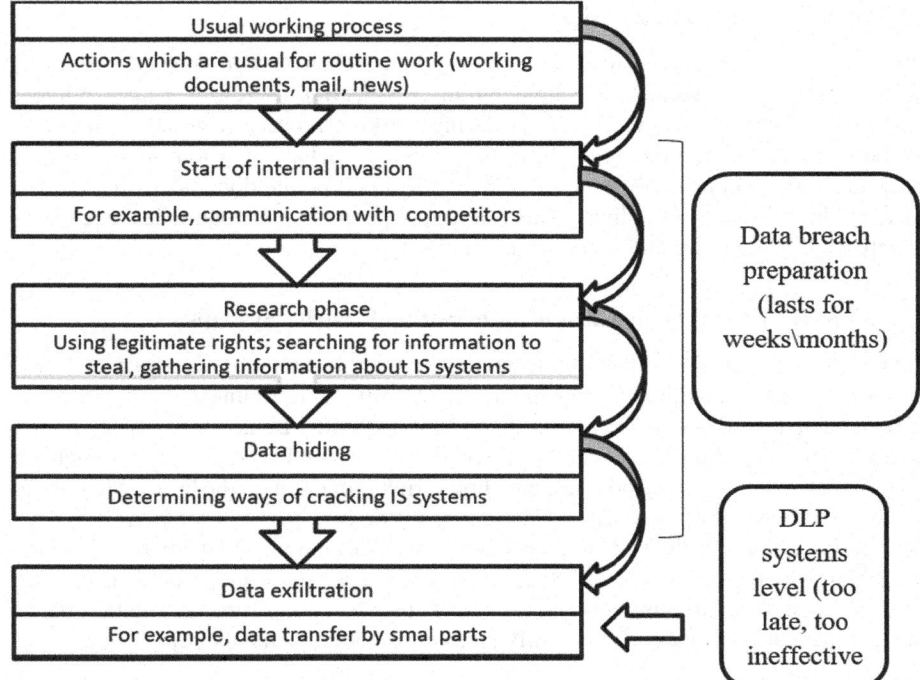

Fig. 1. Scheme of typical data breach

any actions which can be justified with carelessness (negligence) or ignorance (technical incompetence) in case of their disclosure, i.e. to reduce to unintentional violation. Insiders often use fairly simple techniques, such as creating "fictive" data which are similar in content structure to data planned for exfiltration, but that is not confidential at the same time. The insider will repeat such attempts to transfer data with a certain frequency until he can determine the method of transmission, at which the IS systems do not work properly. Then, having access to the relevant confidential information and choosing the method of its theft, the insider goes to the final stage of leakage - "Data exfiltration".

1.2 Abnormal User Behavior

It follows from the description of the data breach scenario that in most cases the actual theft of information is preceded by abnormal (though possibly permitted) behavior of the user, i.e. the user even before the theft of information begins to take actions that are not typical for his previous activity both according to the set of performed operations and to the content of the processed information. Also, the very stage of data breach preparation during which abnormal behavior of the user is observed usually takes quite a long time, up to several months. Therefore the direction of user behavior analysis for detecting anomalies has been actively developed over the past few years [4].

1.3   Purpose of Internal Invasions

The purpose of internal intrusions is usually to gain access to textual information (financial reports, contracts, technical documentation, e-mail, etc.). Therefore, the key moment is to detect abnormal behavior of users during working process with data. Abnormal behavior may indicate that the user is not the one on behalf of whom he authorized (user authentication task), or the user is interested in corporate documents that are not related to his current work activity. This is a sign of potential information leakage (early detection of information theft attempts task) [5].

1.4   UBA as a Stand-Alone Class of Information Security Systems

At present, an independent class of information security systems has been formed, based on machine learning methods which are used to identify signs of unusual user behavior. Gartner designates this system class as UBA (User and Entity Behavior Analytics). UBA systems, unlike DLP, monitor a wide range of user actions and make decisions which are not based on expert security policies, but choose right direction on the basis of historical data on legitimate user performance. These systems detect early signs of breach, so their main purpose is not to block user actions, but to provide analytical data to the IS service describing why the detected actions are abnormal to a particular user. As defined in the Gartner report, UBA systems construct and apply user behaviors (profiles) models based on machine learning methods to identify signs of abnormal behavior [6].

1.5   Early Signs Detection of Abnormal Behavior

It is relevant to develop the direction of users abnormal behavior early signs detection based on machine learning methods to solve the following problems of information security:

1. The task of early attempts to steal information detection is the procedure of detecting the facts of abnormal or suspicious behavior of insiders, who may precede or be directly part of the organization attempting to steal information.
2. The user authentication task is validity evaluation procedure. It examines if the user working with the protected computer system is really the person on whose behalf he authorized.

When analyzing a user's behavioral image, a large amount of real data is collected. However, it is quite difficult to make any decision on their basis, as the data are heterogeneous and the number of parameters for analysis is extremely large.

To solve the problem of anomaly search by means of users behavioral biometric characteristics analysis, it is proposed to use methods of machine learning and intelligent data processing [7].

1.6   Factors of Users Abnormal Behavior

To solve the problem of detecting anomalies in user behavior, we will determine the factors of users abnormal behavior. These factors are shown in Table 1.

Table 1. Factors for abnormal user behavior

Data source	User behavioural sign
Used applications	Changing of the activity time in different applications
Visited sites	Changing of the visited sites list; Visiting sites of another user group
Camera, images	Finding prohibited fragments in the image (photos of documents with signatures, stamps)
Calls, dictophone records	Finding prohibited key phrases, or phrases belonging to another user group
Typed and received text	Phrases which are prohibited to input
GPS coordinates	Change of location

The following scenario is common practice in the field of experimental studies in the internal threats detection sphere.

1. All actual behavioral data which was collected is considered to be legitimate.
2. Data modeling pre-specified internal threats are added to the collected behavioral data.
3. The users daily activity is analyzed and the task of binary classification is considered: it is necessary to determine days with abnormal users activity, which corresponds to specified threats.

2 Anomaly Search Methods Determination

For the implemented UBA system with DSS functionality, based on the analysis of behavioral biometric characteristics of the enterprise personnel due to the large volume of input analyzed data it is proposed to use machine learning methods and intelligent data processing. Such actions will reduce the number of resulting parameters.

Collecting input data is implemented through a mobile application installed on the mobile device with OC Android of a certain employee of the enterprise. For behavioral analysis, it is proposed to use the following methods for data analysis:

- The k method of the nearest neighbors:
  - (a) the used applications;
  - (b) GPS coordinates (employee's travel history);
  - (c) the visited sites;
  - (d) the typed text;
  - (e) the received text.
- neural networks:
  - (a) – calls, dictophone records;
  - (b) – camera, image.

The software indicates certain deviations of the user's behavioural characteristics, suggests to perform a number of actions to the administrator. In some cases the system administrator decides to block the user.

Neural networks are used to analyze data such as recorded calls, recorded sound from a dictaphone and photos. In order to find deviations the network preliminary training takes place.

To find deviations from the user's reference profile in such data as Employee Movement History (GPS), typed text, the resulting text the k method of the nearest neighbors is used. You can reduce the data analysis load as well as bring down the number of iterations in training applying this method. During training this method only stores training data. Classification is performed when new untagged data is obtained at the input of the method. In this case, the data received from the user is checked and it starts process of finding if it belongs to a specific users' group or user.

User characteristics are compared by searching Euclidean distance to all records from the obtained sample [6].

$$d(p, q) = \sqrt{(p_1 - q_1)^2 + (p_2 - q_2)^2 + (p_3 - q_3)^2} \tag{1}$$

Then k records are selected, for which the Euclidean distance from the current record to the new one will be minimal.

The sum of the class weights (distances) is calculated by the formula:

$$Z_{classN} = \sum w(x_{(i)}) \tag{2}$$

Z_{classN} – is sum of class weights from a new point to N class;
$w(x_{(i)})$ – is weight of i-th object of class N falling into the area of nearest k objects.

Then the sum of the inverse squares of the distances between the records of this class and the new one is counted for each user. The class is given to the new record for which the sum of the inverse squares is the largest. In Fig. 2. it is shown an example of assigning a new object to one of two existing classes with k = 6.

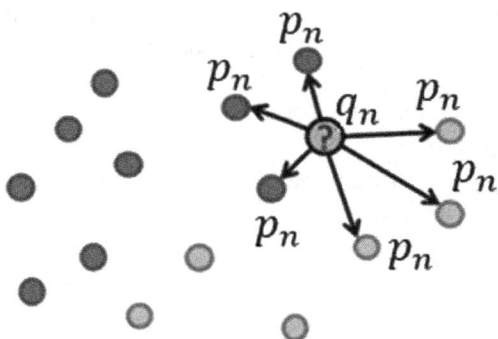

Fig. 2. Representing the k-nearest neighbors method in a two-dimensional factor space

In this case knn method uses such parameters as:

- d (p, q) is the distance between points;
- p_n is the coordinate of the p point along the axis n;
- q_n is the coordinate of the q point along the axis n.

If the user or group ID assigned by the method k of the analyzed record corresponds to the user or group ID obtained by the initial authorization in the system, it is considered that the obtained characteristics correspond to the reference performances and there were found no deviations from these ones.

In case the ID obtained by the initial authorization in the system does not correspond to the ID assigned by the method k of the newly generated record, it is considered that the obtained characteristics differ from the reference performances or belong to another user or group of users.

Based on the selected data, the software offers to implement a number of actions indicating certain deviations of the user from the reference profile. Thereby the administrator should be informed about this range of actions. In some cases the system administrator can make the decision to block the user.

3 Software Implementation of Experimental Client-Server Software Sample

3.1 Basic Structure of the Client-Server Software Exploratory Prototype

To collect behavioral biometric user characteristics collecting software agents are used, they are installed directly on mobile devices of users (data sources) and transmit the collected information to a single repository for its subsequent processing.

Behavioral information processing during the user's working process with data consists of three stages:

1. Collecting of user behavioral data. Software agents should implement the collecting and intermediate local memory storage of behavioral information in order to optimize the load on the data network or in case if there is no connection with the single storage.
2. Sending of the collected behavioral information to the server. Transfer of behavioral data from different mobile devices of users to a single repository.
3. Reception of behavioral information from monitoring agents and storing it in a single centralized repository.

In Fig. 3 the basic diagram of connections in the system is presented.

A mobile agent application is installed on each mobile device connected to the system. After the application is installed on the employee's mobile device, the system administrator gives the user the list of parameters collected from his device for its identification. The set of analysed parameters that will be collected on the device and analysed on the server differs, it depends on the user/group of users. The system administrator generates the list of analyzed parameters and user groups.

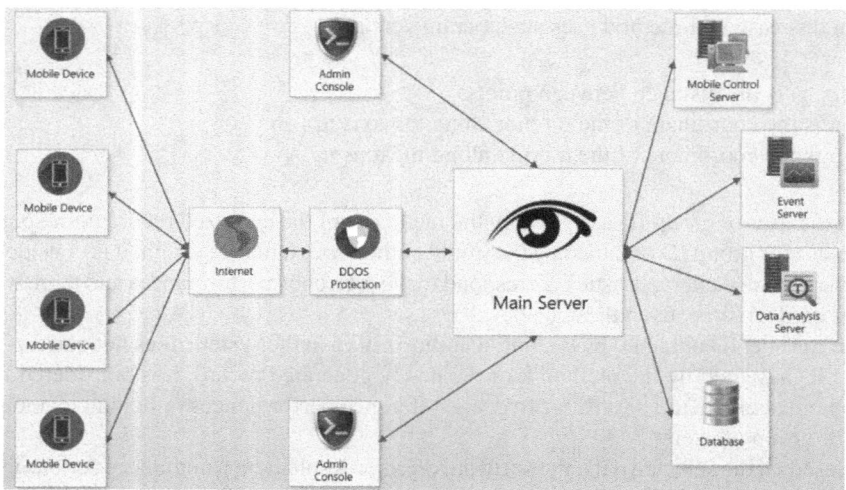

Fig. 3. Scheme of a system communications

The mobile application starts when the Mobile Device begins its work as a foreground service. The mobile device requests a list of commands from the server once in N minutes. The instruction fetch period dynamically varies, it depends on the level of user activity. After selecting the list of commands which are available for realization on the employee's device, they are further processed, information is received and data are sent to the Main Server. The commands (Event Server) have different order of operations priorities. Commands have different statuses such as running once and cycle operation with a timer. After sending the data, the central Main Server receives this information, processes it, then analyzes this one with the Data Analysis server and writes the source and result parameters to the Data Base. If an error occurs, this command is realized again on the mobile device.

The Admin Console panel is directly connected to the master server and has certain capabilities such as:

- Ability to manage a group or user-defined Mobile Control Server;
- Adding new Event Server commands to the run;
- Generation of reports.

Direct access to the server provides continuous access to management in case of DDOS attack bypassing DDOS attack filtering by the "DDOS Protection" module.

Based on the selected data the software offers to realize a number of actions to the administrator therewith indicating certain deviations of the user's behavior from the reference profile. In some cases the system administrator decides to block the user.

3.2 Monitoring Agent Architecture

The monitoring agent is implemented in the high-level programming language C# with the help of using the mobile application development framework "XAM-ARIN.ANDROID." A monitoring agent distribution to collect behavioral biometric information is an "apk" format file designed to be installed on an employee's mobile device. The distribution contains all components and libraries which are necessary for employee monitoring and includes such modules as:

- Data Collection Module;
- Local Database;
- TCP/IP Exchanger.

The Data Collection Module is a module that collects and pre-processes information from an employee's mobile device before making a record in a local database.

Local Database is a module that temporarily stores data to unload the network channel when information is transmitted to the main server. Also it stores data if there is no connection to the server.

TCP/IP Examiner is a module which is responsible for the client server exchange and power saving during the process of data sharing over the network. Figure 4 shows the basic structure of the mobile agent.

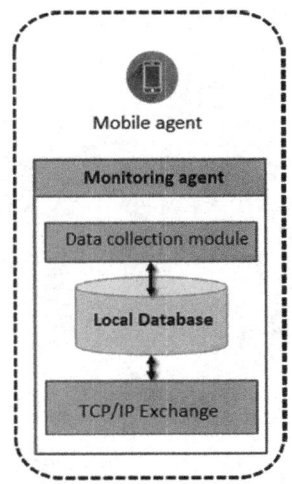

Fig. 4. Basic mobile agent structure

3.3 Main Server and Its Child Units Operation Scheme

The "Main Server" is a central server that receives data from client devices with installed mobile agent applications. "Main Server" can be installed on the Windows operating system. The "Main Server" is implemented on the basis of Web API ASP.NET technology in C # language. The "Main Server" is connected with all major system modules such as:

- Event Server;
- Mobile Control Server;
- Data Analysis Server;
- Database;
- Admin Console.

4 Conclusion

During the study, a list of the most significant factors submitted to the input of the analysing methods was formed. With the increase of the signs number, the number of objects that must be in the learning sample to cover all kinds of situations has exponentially increased. Number of input parameters reducing helped to lower the amount of learning sample for the knn method. The diagram of user identification correctness is shown on Fig. 5.

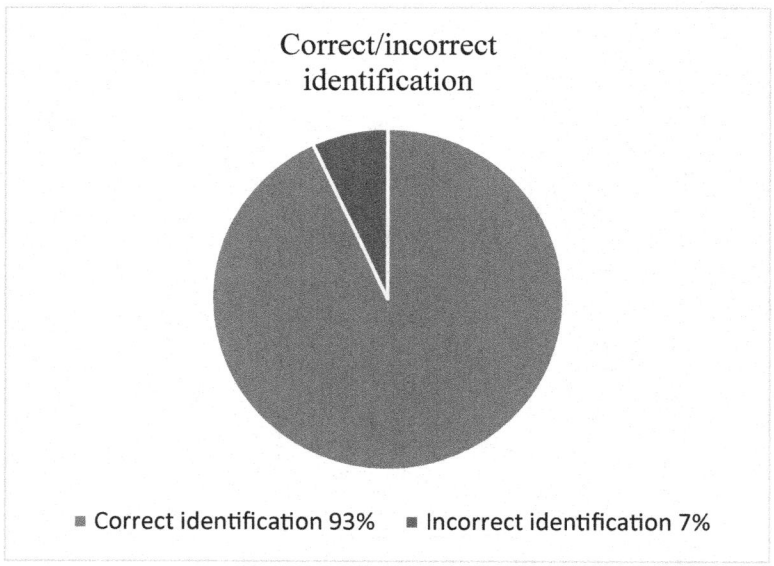

Fig. 5. Correctness of identification diagram

User data was correctly identified in 93% of cases and incorrect in 7% of cases on average. Due to the decrease in the number of output data and the increase in the correctness of user identification by their characteristics, the average time to obtain useful data in the management decision support system was reduced.

Moreover, the basic architecture of the server software complex client was built and it provides high stability in data processing.

Early anomaly detection will allow the system administrator to make balanced management decisions, reduce operational costs, and increase enterprise competitiveness.

Due to the application of various algorithms and methods of data analysis and machine learning in mobile UBA it has been possible to improve the informativity of the resulting data. Early anomaly detection will allow the system administrator to make balanced management decisions, reduce operational costs, and increase enterprise competitiveness [8].

Acknowledgments. The reported study was funded by RFBR, project number 19-37-90111.

References

1. Szaniawska, K., Lehmann, M.: The human factor in managing the security of information. In: Ahram, T., Karwowski, W. (eds.) AHFE 2019. Advances in Intelligent Systems and Computing, vol. 960, pp. 38–47. Springer, Cham (2019). https://doi.org/10.1007/978-3-030-20488-4_4
2. Magklaras, G.B., Furnell, S.M.: A preliminary model of end user sophistication for insider threat prediction in IT systems. Comput. Secur. **24**(5), pp. 371–380 (2005)
3. Hu, Q., Tang, B., Lin, D.: Anomalous user activity detection in enterprise multi-source logs. In: 2017 IEEE International Conference on Data Mining Workshops (ICDMW), pp. 797–803. IEEE (2017)
4. Ryan, J., Lin, M.J., Miikkulainen, R.: Intrusion detection with neural networks. In: Advances in Neural Information Processing Systems, pp. 943–949 (1998)
5. McGough, A.S., et al.: Insider threats: identifying anomalous human behaviour in heterogeneous systems using beneficial intelligent software (ben-ware). In: Proceedings of the 7th ACM CCS International Workshop on Managing Insider Security Threats, pp. 1–12 (2015)
6. Kambhampaty, K.K.: Detecting Insider and Masquerade Attacks by Identifying Malicious User Behavior and Evaluating Trust in Cloud Computing and IoT Devices: дис. – North Dakota State University (2019)
7. Savenkov, P.A., Ivutin, A.N.: Methods and algorithms of data and machine learning usage in management decision making support systems. In: 2019 8th Mediterranean Conference on Embedded Computing (MECO), pp. 1–4. IEEE (2019)
8. Ivutin, A.N., Savenkov, P.A., Veselova, A.V.: Neural network for analysis of additional authentication behavioral biometrie characteristics. In: 2018 7th Mediterranean Conference on Embedded Computing (MECO), pp. 1–3. IEEE (2018)

Use of the Industrial Property System in Colombia (2018): A Supervised Learning Application

Jenny-Paola Lis-Gutiérrez[1,2,5]([⊠]), Melissa Lis-Gutiérrez[2,3],
Adriana Patricia Gallego-Torres[4], Vladimir Alfonso Ballesteros Ballesteros[5],
and Manuel Francisco Romero Ospina[5]

[1] Universidad de la Costa, Barranquilla, Colombia
jlis@cuc.edu.co
[2] Universidad Nacional de Colombia, Bogota, Colombia
{jplisg,mlisg}@unal.edu.co
[3] Corporación Universitaria del Meta, Villavicencio, Colombia
melissa.lis@unimeta.edu.co
[4] Universidad Distrital Francisco José de Caldas, Bogota, Colombia
adpgallegot@udistrital.edu.co
[5] Fundación Universitaria Los Libertadores, Bogota, Colombia
{jplisg,vladimir.ballesteros,mfromeroo}@libertadores.edu.co

Abstract. The purpose of this paper is to establish ways to predict the spatial distribution of the use of the intellectual property system from information on industrial property applications and grants (distinctive signs and new creations) and copyright registrations in 2018. This will be done using supervised learning algorithms applied to information on industrial property applications and grants (trademarks and new creations) and copyright registrations in 2018. Within the findings, 4 algorithms were identified with a level of explanation higher than 80%: (i) Linear Regression, with an elastic network regularization; (ii) Stochastic Gradient Descent, with Hinge loss function, Ringe regularization (L2) and a constant learning rate; (iii) Neural Networks, with 1,000 layers, with Adam's solution algorithm and 2,000 iterations; (iv) Random Forest, with 10 trees.

Keywords: Spatial distribution · Distinctive signs · New creations · Supervised learning · Machine learning

1 Introduction

According to the World Intellectual Property Organization (WIPO, 2016), intellectual property (IP) refers to all creations of the intellect, which include (i) inventions, (ii) literary, artistic and scientific works, (iii) symbols, names and images used in commerce. Under the traditional protection scheme, IP is divided into three branches: industrial property, copyright and related rights, and plant varieties [1].

© Springer Nature Switzerland AG 2020
Y. Tan et al. (Eds.): ICSI 2020, LNCS 12145, pp. 506–514, 2020.
https://doi.org/10.1007/978-3-030-53956-6_46

Specifically, Colombia is characterized by low levels of use of copyright and industrial property protection systems [2]. According to the World Intellectual Property Organization [3, 4], in 2017 Colombia ranked 48th out of 129 countries in terms of applications for patent registrations, 36th in terms of trademark applications and 69th in terms of industrial registrations.

The use of the industrial property system by residents in Colombia is significantly lower than the use given by foreigners. Therefore, the purpose of this paper is to establish how to predict the spatial distribution of the use of the intellectual property system from information on industrial property applications and grants (distinctive signs and new creations) and copyright registrations in 2018.

The data used correspond to records from the Superintendence of Industry and Commerce [5], on new creations and distinctive signs requested and granted at the departmental level in 2018, and information from the different types of copyright records in 2018 from the National Copyright Directorate [6].

In order to achieve this purpose, several supervised learning algorithms are applied [7], such as (Random Forest, KNN, Support Vector Machines, linear regression, neural networks, among others [8]).

2   Literature Review

2.1   Intellectual Property

Some of the most recent studies on intellectual property include the following. [9] found that reforms in IP systems in some countries led to a significant reduction in the cost of debt in IP-intensive industries, through lower rates of borrowing. [10] employed a dynamic panel, for 70 countries with data between 1965 and 2009, establishing that patent rights have no effect on productivity growth.

There is also the study of [11]. These authors found that the enforcement of intellectual property rights is positively related to increased exports to advanced economies [12], but has negative effects in developing countries, associated with reduced speed of technology transfers and incentives to invest in R&D. [13] established that rich countries and small or poor countries apply intellectual property rights for different reasons. The former to protect innovations, the latter seeking access to foreign markets. According to these authors, emerging countries have greater flexibility in the application of IP systems. For their part, [14] showed that most large developers employ a combination of informal mechanisms and formal intellectual property rights (copyright, patents and trademarks).

With respect to the use of trademarks, the study by [15], who were able to establish that trademarks allow for the measurement of the degree of innovation and the capacity of response in foreign markets, stands out. [16], based on 712 observations from a cross-sector sample of European companies, applied a panel data model. The results revealed a positive relationship between the companies' international performance and the company's attitude towards enriching its portfolio with externally developed trademarks. [17], through a survey of 48 Portuguese companies located in S&T parks and incubators, analyzed the direct and indirect effects of intellectual property rights protection mechanisms. Contrary to most studies, they found that formal protection of intellectual property rights is detrimental to the competitiveness of firms, but other non-formal mechanisms such as trade secrets do encourage it.

The paper by [18], uses data from 14,065 Chinese companies between 2007 and 2013. The authors use a discrete time risk model and analyze the effects of differences in internal and external innovation mechanisms, specifically the efficiency of innovation and the spillover effect of trade, on the probability of survival of firms.

As can be seen, the analysis of intellectual property is ongoing and the means of analysis are diverse, but generally involve the use of quantitative tools. The methods proposed in this paper are related to machine learning. A brief state of the art on its applications is presented below.

2.2 Machine Learning

In recent literature there are several machine learning applications that include medicine, energy, education, intellectual property, among others. [19] used machine learning algorithms to predict and diagnose heart disease in India. They compared the accuracy of four machine learning algorithms using 14 attributes obtained from intensive care unit data. A similar study, but applied to fatty liver disease, considering 577 patients was developed by [20].

From other fields, in [21], they apply different algorithms to public transport data from EUBra-BIGSEA (Europe-Brazil Collaboration of Big Data Scientific Research Through Cloud-Centric Applications). [22] applied decode-based learning for machine translation. [23] predict the energy produced in a wind farm from line regression, decision tree, K-neighbor, and cross-validation to reduce variance.

As for the applications of machine learning to intellectual property, in [24], they reviewed 57 papers on artificial intelligence, automatic and in-depth learning associated with intellectual property. In [25], the employed algorithms were Support Vector Machines, Neural Networks and Decision Trees.

3   Method

This section describes the data used, the design of the study, the procedure and the indicators and models used for the analysis.

3.1 Data

This paper uses as its primary source the records of the Superintendence of Industry and Commerce [5], on new creations and distinctive signs requested and granted at the departmental level in 2018 and information from the different types of copyright registrations in 2018 from [6]. Table 1 presents the data, sources and units used for the following sections. The free software used was Orange (Demsar et al. 2013).

3.2 Study Design

This study is quantitative and its scope is descriptive and predictive. The design is non-experimental and cross-sectional. The units of analysis are the departments of Colombia.

Table 1. Data sources and units used

Variable	Unit	Source
Projected population 2018	Number of inhabitants	[27]
Application for patents of invention	Ratio for every 10,000 inhabitants	[5]
Application for utility model patents	Ratio for every 10,000 inhabitants	[5]
Granting of patents of invention	Ratio for every 10,000 inhabitants	[5]
Granting of utility model patents	Ratio for every 10,000 inhabitants	[5]
Chemical Invention Patents Filed	Ratio for every 10,000 inhabitants	[5]
Electricity/Electronics Patents Filed	Ratio for every 10,000 inhabitants	[5]
Industrial design application	Ratio for every 10,000 inhabitants	[5]
Industrial designs awarded	Ratio for every 10,000 inhabitants	[5]
Designations of origin submitted	Ratio for every 10,000 inhabitants	[5]
Commercial School presented	Ratio for every 10,000 inhabitants	[5]
Commercial slogans presented	Ratio for every 10,000 inhabitants	[5]
Collective brand presented	Ratio for every 10,000 inhabitants	[5]
Trademarks presented	Ratio for every 10,000 inhabitants	[5]
Certification brand submitted	Ratio for every 10,000 inhabitants	[5]
Trade names presented	Ratio for every 10,000 inhabitants	[5]
Trade names granted	Ratio for every 10,000 inhabitants	[5]
Certification brand awarded	Ratio for every 10,000 inhabitants	[5]
Trademark granted	Ratio for every 10,000 inhabitants	[5]
Collective brand granted	Ratio for every 10,000 inhabitants	[5]
Commercial slogan granted	Ratio for every 10,000 inhabitants	[5]
Commercial teaching granted	Ratio for every 10,000 inhabitants	[5]
Phonogram registration	Ratio for every 10,000 inhabitants	[6]
Registration of artistic work	Ratio for every 10,000 inhabitants	[6]
Registration of unpublished literary work	Ratio for every 10,000 inhabitants	[6]
Registration of musical work	Ratio for every 10,000 inhabitants	[6]
Registration of contract and other acts	Ratio for every 10,000 inhabitants	[6]
Registration of audiovisual works	Ratio for every 10,000 inhabitants	[6]
Registration of published literary work	Ratio for every 10,000 inhabitants	[6]
Software Registration	Ratio for every 10,000 inhabitants	[6]

Note: filing refers to the application, and granting to the distinctive signs that actually obtained registration before [5] and [6].
Source: Prepared by the Office on the basis of [5, 6, 27]

3.3 Procedure

Information on the statistics of new creations and distinctive signs was searched on the page of [5], and on copyright registrations on [6]. The most recent information was identified, i.e., data available from 2018. The information was organized considering the departments as units of analysis.

In order to control by the number of inhabitants of each department, the ratio of respective applications or concessions per 10,000 inhabitants was calculated. Different methods (algorithms) of supervised learning were applied for information processing: AdaBoost, Random Forest, SVM (Support Vector Machines), Neural Network, Stochastic Gradient Descent, Linear Regression, KNN and decision tree learning algorithm [28, 29].

4   Results

In this section, the different algorithms used to predict the number of trademarks are analyzed. The novelty of the analysis lies in the use of other information related to the use of industrial property and copyright protection systems, and the handling of artificial intelligence for projection.

In Fig. 1, the results for each of the algorithms used are presented. The results show the root mean square error (RMSE), the root mean absolute error (MAE) and R2, i.e. the proportion of the variance in the dependent variable that is predictable from the independent variables.

The different types of sampling used for prediction are shown: leave one out, test on the training data, boostraping of 100 repetitions with a training sample of 50% and 50% prediction, cross validation of 10 and 20 folds.

Based on the above, the evaluation is carried out considering R2 and the lowest MAE. The algorithms that presented the best behavior were:

– Linear Regression, with an elastic network regulation
– Stochastic Gradient Descent, with Hinge loss function, Ringe regularization (L2) and a constant learning rate
– Neural networks, with 1,000 layers, with Adam's solution algorithm and 2,000 iterations.
– Random forests, with 10 trees

The AdaBoost algorithm has an over-adjustment to the data, so it should not be considered. The algorithms with less predictive capacity were: SVM, KNN and decision trees. The prediction results are presented in Annex 2.

Test & Score

Settings

Sampling type: Leave one out

Scores

Model	MSE	RMSE	MAE	R2
Linear Regression	0.504	0.710	0.527	0.942
SGD	1.226	1.107	0.713	0.858
Neural Network	1.524	1.234	0.780	0.824
Random Forest	2.557	1.599	0.964	0.704
AdaBoost	2.613	1.617	0.916	0.698
Tree	5.174	2.275	1.382	0.401
SVM	6.404	2.531	1.283	0.259
kNN	7.357	2.712	1.858	0.148

Test & Score

Settings

Sampling type: No sampling, test on training data

Scores

Model	MSE	RMSE	MAE	R2
AdaBoost	0.057	0.239	0.133	0.993
Neural Network	0.064	0.252	0.186	0.993
SGD	0.070	0.264	0.195	0.992
Linear Regression	0.106	0.325	0.259	0.988
Tree	0.470	0.686	0.294	0.946
Random Forest	0.668	0.818	0.424	0.923
SVM	4.170	2.042	0.814	0.517
kNN	4.551	2.133	1.398	0.473

Test & Score

Settings

Sampling type: Stratified Shuffle split, 100 random samples with 50% data

Scores

Model	MSE	RMSE	MAE	R2
Linear Regression	1.180	1.086	0.690	0.867
Neural Network	2.602	1.613	1.021	0.707
AdaBoost	4.051	2.013	1.079	0.545
Random Forest	4.427	2.104	1.145	0.502
SGD	4.702	2.168	1.066	0.471
SVM	7.470	2.733	1.487	0.160
kNN	9.951	3.155	2.170	-0.119
Tree	9.557	3.091	1.784	-0.074

Fig. 1. Algorithm results. Source: own elaboration using Orange [26].

Test & Score

Settings

Sampling type: Stratified 10-fold Cross validation

Scores

Model	MSE	RMSE	MAE	R2
Linear Regression	0.587	0.766	0.567	0.932
SGD	1.094	1.046	0.687	0.873
Neural Network	1.644	1.282	0.885	0.810
AdaBoost	2.931	1.712	0.964	0.661
Random Forest	3.376	1.837	1.009	0.609
SVM	6.314	2.513	1.312	0.269
kNN	7.308	2.703	1.848	0.154
Tree	8.987	2.998	1.822	-0.040

Test & Score

Settings

Sampling type: Stratified 20-fold Cross validation

Scores

Model	MSE	RMSE	MAE	R2
Linear Regression	0.500	0.707	0.529	0.942
SGD	1.269	1.127	0.697	0.853
Neural Network	1.533	1.238	0.790	0.823
AdaBoost	2.829	1.682	0.933	0.673
Random Forest	3.574	1.890	1.019	0.586
SVM	6.407	2.531	1.286	0.258
kNN	7.366	2.714	1.866	0.147
Tree	8.239	2.870	1.663	0.046

Fig. 1. (*continued*)

5 Discussion and Conclusions

In the case of supervised learning it was possible to identify 4 algorithms with a level of explanation higher than 80%, these are: (i) Linear Regression, with an elastic network regularization; (ii) Stochastic Gradient Descent, with Hinge loss function, Ringe regularization (L2) and a constant learning rate; (iii) Neural Networks, with 1,000 layers, with Adam's solution algorithm and 2,000 iterations; (iv) Random Forest, with 10 trees. The results found in this study are consistent with those of [25], and some algorithms are added.

The originality of this study lies in: (i) the transformation in ratios of the variables, since the other studies on intellectual property make the analysis in absolute values; (ii) the compendium of the information of the systems of protection of the intellectual property in Colombia; (iii) application of the artificial intelligence (machine learning) for the description and projection.

It is suggested that for future research a multivariate spatial analysis be conducted, for example using a geographically weighted regression or a panel data analysis, to determine the behavior of the innovation of the record and granting of distinctive signs in the light of other variables. Similarly, it would be appropriate to extend the study to a greater number of years and to the possibility of predicting other variables.

References

1. Lis-Gutiérrez, J.P., Zerda-Sarmiento, A., Balaguera, M., Gaitán-Angulo, M., Lis-Gutiérrez, M.: Uso del sistema de propiedad industrial para signos distintivos en Colombia: un análisis departamental (2000–2016). En: Campos, G., Castaño, M., Gaitán-Angulo, M. & Sánchez, V. (Comps). Diálogos sobre investigación: avances científicos Konrad Lorenz, pp 193–215. Bogotá: Konrad Lorenz Editores (2019)
2. Lis-Gutiérrez, J.P., Lis-Gutiérrez, M., Gaitán-Angulo, M., Balaguera, M.I., Viloria, A., Santander-Abril, J.E.: Use of the industrial property system for new creations in colombia: a departmental analysis (2000–2016). In: Tan, Y., Shi, Y., Tang, Q. (eds.) DMBD 2018. LNCS, vol. 10943, pp. 786–796. Springer, Cham (2018). https://doi.org/10.1007/978-3-319-93803-5_74
3. WIPO. World intellectual property indicators. Ginebra: OMPI (2018)
4. WIPO. Datos y cifras de la OMPI sobre PI, edición de 2018. Ginebra: OMPI (2019)
5. Superintendencia de Industria y Comercio. Estadísticas PI [base de datos] (2019)
6. Dirección Nacional de Derechos de Autor (DNDA). Estadísticas en línea [Base de datos]. Bogotá: DNDA (2019)
7. Moros Ochoa, A., Lis-Gutiérrez, J.P., Castro Nieto, G.Y., Vargas, C.A., Rincón. J.C.: La percepción de calidad de servicio como determinante de la recomendación: una predicción mediante inteligencia artificial para los hoteles en Cartagena. En: G. Campos, M.A. Castaño, M. Gaitán-Angulo, V. Sánchez (comp). Diálogos sobre investigación. Bogotá: Editorial Konrad Lorenz (2020)
8. Lis-Gutiérrez, J.P., Aguilera-Hernández, D., Escobedo David, L.R.: Análisis de las demandas de los integrantes del Ejército colombiano en calidad de víctimas; una aplicación de machine learning. En: G. Barbosa Castillo, M. Correa, y A. Ciro Gómez (eds.), Análisis de las demandas de los integrantes del Ejército en calidad de víctimas: una aplicación de "machine learning", pp. 437–468. Universidad Externado de Colombia, Bogotá (2020)
9. Alimov, A.: Intellectual property rights reform and the cost of corporate debt. J. Int. Money Finance **91**, 195–211 (2019)
10. Sweet, C., Eterovic, D.: Do patent rights matter? 40 years of innovation, complexity and productivity. World Dev. **115**, 78–93 (2019)
11. Auriol, E., Biancini, S., Paillacar, R.: Universal intellectual property rights: too much of a good thing? Int. J. Ind. Organ. **65**, 51–81 (2019)
12. Campi, M., Dueñas, M.: Intellectual property rights, trade agreements, and international trade. Res. Policy **48**(3), 531–545 (2019)
13. Papageorgiadis, N., McDonald, F.: Defining and measuring the institutional context of national intellectual property systems in a post-trips world. J. Int. Manag. **25**(1), 3–18 (2019)
14. Miric, M., Boudreau, K.J., Jeppesen, L.B.: Protecting their digital assets: the use of formal & informal appropriability strategies by App developers. Res. Policy **48**(8), 103738 (2019)
15. Barroso, A., Giarratana, M.S., Pasquini, M.: Product portfolio performance in new foreign markets: the EU trademark dual system. Res. Policy **48**(1), 11–21 (2019)

16. Denicolai, S., Hagen, B., Zucchella, A., Dudinskaya, E.C.: When less family is more: trademark acquisition, family ownership, and internationalization. Int. Bus. Rev. **28**(2), 238–251 (2019)
17. Teixeira, A.A., Ferreira, C.: Intellectual property rights and the competitiveness of academic spin-offs. J. Innov. Knowl. **4**(3), 154–161 (2019)
18. Zhang, D., Zheng, W., Ning, L.: Does innovation facilitate firm survival? Evidence from chinese high-tech firms. Econ. Model. **75**, 458–468 (2018)
19. Kannan, R., Vasanthi, V.: Machine learning algorithms with roc curve for predicting and diagnosing the heart disease. Soft Computing and Medical Bioinformatics. SAST, pp. 63–72. Springer, Singapore (2019). https://doi.org/10.1007/978-981-13-0059-2_8
20. Wu, C.C., et al.: Prediction of fatty liver disease using machine learning algorithms. Comput. Methods Programs Biomed. **170**, 23–29 (2019)
21. Alic, A.S., et al.: BIGSEA: a big data analytics platform for public transportation information. Future Gen. Comput. Syst. **96**, 243–269 (2019)
22. Banik, D., Ekbal, A., Bhattacharyya, P.: Machine learning based optimized pruning approach for decoding in statistical machine translation. IEEE Access **7**, 1736–1751 (2019)
23. Aguilar, R., Torres, J., Martín, C.: Aprendizaje Automático en la Identificación de Sistemas. Un caso de estudio en la generación de un parque eólico. Revista iberoamericana de automática e informática industrial **16**(1), 114–127 (2018)
24. Aristodemou, L., Tietze, F.: The state-of-the-art on Intellectual Property Analytics (IPA): a literature review on artificial intelligence, machine learning and deep learning methods for analysing intellectual property (IP) data. World Patent Inf. **55**, 37–51 (2018)
25. Havermans, Q.A., Gabaly, S., Hidalgo, A.: Forecasting European trademark and design filings: An innovative approach including exogenous variables and IP offices' events. World Patent Inf. **48**, 96–108 (2017)
26. Demsar, J., et al.: Orange: data mining toolbox in Python. J. Mach. Learn. Res. **14**(Aug), 2349–2353 (2013)
27. Departamento Administrativo Nacional de Estadística (DANE). Proyecciones de Población Departamental [Base de datos]. Bogotá: Dane (2020)
28. Quitian, O.I.T., Lis-Gutiérrez, J.P., Viloria, A.: Supervised and unsupervised learning applied to crowdfunding. Adv. Intell. Syst. Comput. **1108**, 90–97 (2020)
29. Viloria, A., Lis-Gutiérrez, J.P., Gaitán-Angulo, M., Stanescu, C.L.V., Crissien, T.: Machine learning applied to the H index of colombian authors with publications in scopus. Smart Innov. Syst. Technol. **167**, 388–397 (2020)

Imbalanced Ensemble Learning for Enhanced Pulsar Identification

Jakub Holewik[1], Gerald Schaefer[1(✉)], and Iakov Korovin[2]

[1] Department of Computer Science, Loughborough University, Loughborough, UK
[2] Southern Federal University, Taganrog, Russia

Abstract. Pulsars can be detected based on their emitted radio waves. Machine learning methods can be employed to support automated screening of a large number of radio signals for pulsars. This is however a challenging task since training these methods is affected by an inherent imbalance in the acquired data with signals relating to actual pulsars being in the minority.

In this paper, we demonstrate that ensemble classification methods that are dedicated to imbalanced classification problems can be successfully employed for pulsar identification. Classifier ensembles combine several individual classifiers to yield more robust and improved classification, while class imbalance can be addressed through careful sampling or through cost-sensitive classification. Experimental results, based on HTRU2 data, show that the investigated ensembles outperform methods that do not consider class balance, and suggest their use for other applications in astrophysics.

Keywords: Pattern classification · Ensemble classifier · Class imbalance · Astrophysics · Pulsar identification

1 Introduction

Pulsars are rare neutron stars detectable through the radio waves they emit [23]. To allow for automated screening of a large number of radio signals, machine learning methods can be adopted. However, this is hampered by a considerable amount of noise as well as radio frequency interference. Interference is so common that the large majority of signals detected turn out to not stem from pulsars. This makes the use of common machine learning algorithms challenging since they are not designed to take into account such a class imbalance.

Class imbalance is a common issue in pattern classification tasks. When collecting data for training, in particular for binary classification (i.e., tasks where patterns are separated into exactly two classes as in "pulsar" and "not pulsar"), the ideal scenario is that the split of patterns across the classes will be approximately equal. Unfortunately, when collecting data for pulsar candidates, only a handful of observations will correspond to true pulsars. Standard classifiers struggle to learn successfully from such imbalanced datasets and in particular

© Springer Nature Switzerland AG 2020
Y. Tan et al. (Eds.): ICSI 2020, LNCS 12145, pp. 515–524, 2020.
https://doi.org/10.1007/978-3-030-53956-6_47

to learn well from the minority class, which for our problem here (real pulsars) is the one of interest.

In this paper, we show that ensemble classification methods, i.e. methods that combine several individual classifiers, that are dedicated to imbalanced classification problems can be successfully employed for pulsar identification. Our results demonstrate that such dedicated ensembles yield better results compared to methods that do not consider class balance, and suggest their use for other applications in the field of astrophysics.

2   Background

Searching for pulsars is conducted through collecting pulsar candidates, that is, sets of statistical information about certain radio emissions captured from space [18]. Search techniques used to isolate these look for periodic broadband signals that appear dispersed. The collected signals are analysed to determine which of them are actual pulsars. Signals that are determined to be likely coming from pulsars are then passed on for further observation. Traditionally, this analysis was conducted manually by human experts. Unfortunately, the majority of captured signals do not come from pulsars, leading to a lot of time dedicated to discarding noisy candidates. In addition, technological advancements have significantly increased the number of candidates being discovered [26], leading to the manual approach becoming infeasible.

Consequently, various automated approaches have been developed for pulsar classification. For example, [12] describes a computer program for candidate selection as early as 1992. However these methods were not intelligent enough, since after initial filtering of candidates, the selected samples still needed to be manually checked. The use of advanced machine learning approaches leads to more reliable detection. Examples include an artificial neural network for pulsar classification [8], PICS, a method which utilises image pattern classification approaches to recognise pulsars from diagnostic plots [30], and SPINN, a high-performance solution that is also based on neural networks [19].

While such machine learning approaches have shown potential to greatly reduce the work needed for identifying pulsars, none of these solutions address the fundamental problem of data imbalance present in the candidate selection task with true pulsars being greatly outnumbered by noisy samples. It is this aspect that we specifically address in this paper.

3   Imbalanced Classification

Many real-life datasets are imbalanced so that patterns of interest (commonly referred as the positive class) are outnumbered (making it the minority class) by "other" patterns (referred to as the negative class and majority class). In our pulsar detection task, there are many more noise samples compared to those that represent a true pulsar. This is challenging as classification algorithms typically try to maximise accuracy over all samples and thus tend to be biased towards the majority class, leading to poor recognition of minority class samples.

A common approach to address class imbalance is sampling which tries to "fix" the dataset. The goal here is to create a new training dataset with equal class distribution. In undersampling approaches, this is achieved by removing patterns of the majority class, at the cost of discarding potentially useful data [29]. On the other hand, in oversampling, the number of patterns of the minority class is increased to match more closely that of the majority class. The key obstacle here is how to obtain useful new minority class samples.

SMOTE (for Synthetic Minority Over-sampling TEchnique) [4] generates new, artificial patterns of the minority class that are designed to be similar to the actual patterns in the dataset. For this, it uses a nearest neighbour approach, creating new patterns by combining features from existing neighbouring patterns. SMOTE has been widely used and is known to help with generalisation in imbalanced classifiers [4, 29].

A different approach to address class imbalance is cost-sensitive classification which is based on the idea of assigning a cost to misclassifications [20]. Conventional classifiers try to reduce the number of misclassifications but do not pay attention to which class they belong. Introducing class costs is a common approach to reflect the varying degrees of importance among classes. In most imbalanced classification problems, the minority class is the class of interest and is thus assigned a higher cost so that the resulting classifier will focus more on reducing the error rate of that class.

4 Classifier Ensembles

Traditionally, a single classifier is used in pattern recognition problems. However, classifiers are rarely perfect and designing a classifier that generalises well is a difficult problem. On the other hand, different classifiers can complement each other when it comes to achieving high performance [10]. This observation leads to the development of multiple classifier systems, also known as ensemble classifiers. Using separate classification methods simultaneously, and then combining their outputs, these methods can deal particularly well with noisy inputs and yield more robust classification [11].

In general there are three reasons for why ensemble methods are worth using [7]:

- *Statistical argument:* This is relevant in problems that suffer from data sparsity. With a limited number of patterns, training could produce many different classifiers with similar performance. But some of them will be better than others at generalisation. Combining these classifiers into an ensemble is better than picking one and risking that it will not perform well on unseen data.
- *Computational argument:* This argument applies to methods that use some sort of hill-climbing or random search, for example neural networks with gradient descent or decision trees with greedy splitting rules. These techniques are inherently difficult to optimise and a common issue is the search getting

stuck in a local optimum. This is where an ensemble can be beneficial by utilising multiple classifiers which begin searching in different places, thus improving the likelihood of finding the global optimum.

– *Representational argument:* It may be impossible to obtain an optimal classifier. For example, for a dataset with a non-linear decision boundary, there is no linear classifier that can achieve perfect classification. In a situation like this, there are two solutions. One is to train a classifier of higher complexity, while the other is to combine some imperfect classifiers with the aim of increasing the overall performance.

The most common approaches of ensemble learning are bagging and boosting. In bagging [1], the idea is that each classifier is not trained on the full dataset. Instead, the dataset is randomly sampled multiple times (with replacement), and each classifier trained on a different subset. All classifiers' outputs are then combined. Boosting revolves around "weak learners", i.e. classifiers that are only slightly better than a random guess [24]. These can be effectively transformed, or "boosted", into strong learners by iteratively training ensemble members, with each of them focussing on specific data patterns that were difficult to learn for the previous classifiers.

5   Ensemble Classifiers for Imbalanced Data

In this paper, we investigate a number of ensemble classifiers that specifically address class imbalance. In the following, we briefly describe the algorithms that we use.

5.1   SMOTEBagging

SMOTEBagging combines a bagging ensemble with various sampling strategies [28]. The main idea is to employ a bagging scheme that trains individual classifiers on subsets of the training data so that each class is equally represented. SMOTE is applied to the minority class, and all original samples along with the generated patterns are used alongside a random subset of the majority class when training each classifier. Experimental results in [28] show that SMOTE effectively improves the diversity and performance of a bagging ensemble.

5.2   SMOTEBoost

[5] proposes a method that also utilises SMOTE, but in combination with an AdaBoost classifier. SMOTE is employed to improve the performance on the minority class, while boosting is used make up for the loss of general accuracy. SMOTEBoost is more sophisticated than just simply running SMOTE on a dataset and then training an ensemble on it. SMOTE is instead used separately for each classifier, and all synthetically generated patterns are discarded before training the next classifier. Unlike standard AdaBoost, which treats all

misclassifications equally, misclassified minority class patterns are focussed on. Particularly hard to learn minority patterns will have "similar" synthetic patterns with similar weights added to the training set, thus enabling classifiers to better learn them, while implicitly creating more diversity in the ensemble (since every classifier is trained on a number of exclusive patterns that will be discarded afterwards).

5.3   EasyEnsemble

[16] proposes an effective ensemble which focusses on undersampling rather than oversampling. EasyEnsemble can be seen as a fusion between bagging and boosting but is somewhat unique in that it technically generates an ensemble of ensembles. During each iteration, it uses random undersampling with replacement to generate a subset of the majority class training data. This subset is then used together with the full minority class data as a training set for an AdaBoost ensemble. This way, a set of diverse AdaBoost ensembles is generated, each trained on different majority class data. Finally, the outputs of all classifiers predicting the same class are summed, and the class with higher support is chosen.

5.4   Balanced Random Forest

In a similar fashion to EasyEnsemble, the Balanced Random Forest algorithm [6] adapts standard the Random Forest algorithm [2] for imbalanced data. The algorithm uses undersampling on the majority class, and so each tree receives a subset with an equal spread between the classes.

5.5   AdaC2

AdaC2 utilises AdaBoost with a cost-sensitive approach to address data imbalance [27]. The goal is to adjust the weights so that misclassified minority class patterns are the main focus. The algorithm uses a cost value for each pattern which represents the penalty to the classifier for misclassifying that pattern with minority class costs higher than majority class costs. These costs are then incorporated into the weights as

$$w_i^{k+1} = \frac{w_i^k e^{\beta_i} C_i}{Z}, \tag{1}$$

where w_i^{k+1} is the weight of pattern i in the next classifier, w_i^k is that pattern's weight in the current classifier, Z is a normalisation factor, β is a parameter such that $\beta_i = \alpha_k$ if pattern i was misclassified by classifier k, and $\beta_i = -\alpha_k$ otherwise, with α_k a parameter that is some predefined function of the classifier's error rate.

5.6 AdaCost

AdaC2 and related algorithms are actually simplified variants of another cost-sensitive method, namely AdaCost [9]. In this algorithm, the AdaBoost cost function is

$$w_i^{k+1} = \frac{w_i^k e^{\beta_i D_i}}{Z}. \tag{2}$$

Here, instead of introducing a constant cost for each pattern, a cost adjustment function D_i is used, which is designed to have higher values when the pattern was misclassified. An interesting aspect of this algorithm is that, unlike AdaC2, it does not reduce to AdaBoost when both the majority and minority class are given the same weight [27].

6 Pulsar Classification

In this paper, we perform pulsar classification based on the HTRU2 study which produced a large database of pulsar candidates collected in the dedicated High Time Resolution Universe Survey [13].

The features are extracted from the pulse profile which describes the longitude-resolved version of a the signal, averaged in frequency and time. The DM-SNR curve represents the correlation between the dispersion measure (DM; the integrated density of free electron columns between the pulsar and the point of observation) and the signal-to-noise ratio (SNR) from the given pattern.

Specifically, we use eight attributes that represent the various features of each pulsar candidate [19], namely:

- mean of the integrated pulse profile;
- standard deviation of the integrated pulse profile;
- excess kurtosis of the integrated pulse profile;
- skewness of the integrated pulse profile;
- mean of the DM-SNR curve;
- standard deviation of the DM-SNR curve;
- excess kurtosis of the DM-SNR curve;
- skewness of the DM-SNR curve.

The dataset[1] comprises 16,259 bogus patterns (caused by radio frequency interference and noise) and 1,639 real pulsar patterns which have been manually verified, thus exhibiting significant class imbalance.

7 Experimental Results

In a binary classification problem, there are four basic measures which are used to define various performance metrics [25]:

---

[1] https://archive.ics.uci.edu/ml/datasets/HTRU2/.

- *True Positives (TP):* Number of patterns from the positive class that are correctly classified;
- *True Negatives (TN):* Number of patterns from the negative class that are correctly classified;
- *False Positives (FP):* Number of patterns from the negative class that are incorrectly classified as the positive class;
- *False Negatives (FN):* Number of patterns from the positive class that are incorrectly classified as the negative class.

From these, we can calculate [25]:

- *Accuracy:* is the overall percentage of correctly classified patterns and is defined as
$$Acc = \frac{TP + TN}{TP + FN + FP + TN};$$ (3)
- *Precision:* is the percentage of patterns classified as positive that are correct and is defined as
$$Prec = \frac{TP}{TP + FP};$$ (4)
- *Recall* or *Sensitivity:* is the percentage of positive patterns classified correctly and is defined as
$$Rec = Sen = \frac{TP}{TP + FN};$$ (5)
- *Specificity:* is the percentage of negative patterns classified correctly and is defined as
$$Spec = \frac{TN}{TN + FP}.$$ (6)

For imbalanced classification problems, the following measures are more useful:

- *F-score* [22]: is defined as the harmonic mean of precision and recall,
$$F = \frac{2 * Prec * Rec}{Prec + Rec};$$ (7)
- *G-mean* [15]: is defined as the geometric mean of sensitivity and specificity,
$$G = \sqrt{Sen * Spec}.$$ (8)

As base classifiers, we employ decision trees and support vector machines (SVMs), except for the Balanced Random Forest which is inherently based on tree classifiers. For comparison, we also implement conventional AdaBoost as a standard ensemble classifier.

The obtained results are given in Table 1 for tree classifiers and in Table 2 for SVMs.

From Tables 1 and 2, we can see that AdaBoost gives fairly good performance. This confirms that the extracted features provide a good basis for successful pulsar identification. However, ensembles that are dedicated to imbalanced classification problems do, with the exception of the Balanced Random Forest, give

Table 1. Experimental results using decision trees as base classifiers.

	Accuracy	Precision	Recall	Specificity	G-mean	F-score
AdaBoost	97.96	94.80	81.21	99.57	89.92	87.48
SMOTEBagging	96.66	76.64	89.11	97.39	93.16	82.40
SMOTEBoost	96.63	76.48	88.93	97.37	93.06	82.24
Balanced Random Forest	96.15	73.84	86.96	97.04	91.86	79.86
EasyEnsemble	95.89	71.10	89.60	96.50	92.99	79.29
AdaC2	97.82	90.41	84.08	99.14	91.30	87.13
AdaCost	97.82	90.41	84.08	99.14	91.30	87.13

Table 2. Experimental results using SVMs as base classifiers.

	Accuracy	Precision	Recall	Specificity	G-mean	F-score
AdaBoost	96.82	94.64	67.52	99.63	82.02	78.81
SMOTEBagging	97.33	81.84	89.44	98.09	93.67	85.48
SMOTEBoost	96.97	81.29	84.95	98.12	91.30	83.08
EasyEnsemble	97.22	80.76	89.68	97.95	93.72	84.99
AdaC2	98.04	94.20	82.80	99.51	90.77	88.14
AdaCost	97.96	92.58	83.44	99.36	91.05	87.77

significantly better results, in particular in terms of yielding both high G-mean and F-score results combined with high sensitivity, thus confirming the usefulness of the presented approaches. Looking more closely at the different ensembles, we can see that EasyEnsemble correctly recognises the highest number of true pulsars, though at the trade-off of misclassifying more patterns from the majority class. Overall, SMOTEBagging gives the best balance and provides good classification for both classes, while the use of SVMs as base classifiers is generally superior to decision trees.

8   Conclusions

In this paper, we have shown that ensemble classifiers that address class imbalance represent a useful approach for finding true pulsars among the candidates in the HTRU2 study. Since the investigated methods are essentially agnostic with respect to the application, we expect that they can also be successfully employed for other astrophysical applications such classification of photometric variable stars [21], supernovas [17] or globular clusters [3]. We also currently investigate these ensemble classifiers for imbalanced classification problems in object classification and video analysis [14].

Acknowledgements. This paper is published due to the financial support of the Federal Target Programme of the Ministry of Science and Higher Education of Russian Federation, project unique identifier RFMEFI60819X0281.

References

1. Breiman, L.: Bagging predictors. Mach. Learn. **24**, 123–140 (1996)
2. Breiman, L.: Random forests. Mach. Learn. **45**, 5–32 (2001)
3. Cavuoti, S., et al.: Astrophysical data mining with GPU. A case study: genetic classification of globular clusters. New Astron. **26**, 12–22 (2014)
4. Chawla, N., Bowyer, K., Hall, L., Kegelmeyer, W.: SMOTE: synthetic minority over-sampling technique. J. Artif. Intell. Res. **16**, 321–357 (2002)
5. Chawla, N.V., Lazarevic, A., Hall, L.O., Bowyer, K.W.: SMOTEBoost: improving prediction of the minority class in boosting. In: Lavrač, N., Gamberger, D., Todorovski, L., Blockeel, H. (eds.) PKDD 2003. LNCS (LNAI), vol. 2838, pp. 107–119. Springer, Heidelberg (2003). https://doi.org/10.1007/978-3-540-39804-2_12
6. Chen, C., Liaw, A., Breiman, L.: Using random forest to learn imbalanced data. Technical report, UC Berkeley (2004)
7. Dietterich, T.G.: Ensemble methods in machine learning. In: Kittler, J., Roli, F. (eds.) MCS 2000. LNCS, vol. 1857, pp. 1–15. Springer, Heidelberg (2000). https://doi.org/10.1007/3-540-45014-9_1
8. Eatough, R., et al.: Selection of radio pulsar candidates using artificial neural networks. Mon. Not. R. Astron. Soc. **407**, 2443–2450 (2010)
9. Fan, W., Stolfo, S., Zhang, J., Chan, P.: AdaCost: misclassification cost-sensitive boosting. In: 16th International Conference on Machine Learning, vol. 99, pp. 97–105 (1999)
10. Ho, T., Hull, J., Srihari, S.: Combination of structural classifiers. In: IAPR Workshop on Syntactic and Structural Pattern Recognition, pp. 123–136 (1990)
11. Ho, T., Hull, J., Srihari, S.: Decision combination in multiple classifier systems. IEEE Trans. Pattern Anal. Mach. Intell. **16**, 66–75 (1994)
12. Johnston, S., et al.: A high-frequency survey of the southern galactic plane for pulsars. Mon. Not. R. Astron. Soc. **255**, 401–411 (1992)
13. Keith, M., et al.: The high time resolution universe pulsar survey I. System configuration and initial discoveries. Mon. Not. R. Astron. Soc. **409**, 619–627 (2010)
14. Korovin, I.S., Khisamutdinov, M.V., Ivanov, D.Y.: A basic algorithm of a target environment analyzer. In: 2nd International Conference on Advances in Artificial Intelligence, pp. 7–11 (2018)
15. Kubat, M., Matwin, S.: Addressing the curse of imbalanced training sets: one-sided selection. In: 14th International Conference on Machine Learning, pp. 179–186 (1997)
16. Liu, X., Wu, J., Zhou, Z.: Exploratory undersampling for class-imbalance learning. IEEE Trans. Syst. Man. Cybern. Part B **39**, 539–550 (2009)
17. Lochner, M., McEwen, J., Peiris, H., Lahav, O., Winter, M.: Photometric supernova classification with machine learning. Astrophys. J. Suppl. Ser. **225**, 31 (2016)
18. Lyon, R.J., Stappers, B., Cooper, S., Brooke, J., Knowles, J.: Fifty years of pulsar candidate selection: from simple filters to a new principled real-time classification approach. Mon. Not. R. Astron. Soc. **459**, 1104–1123 (2016)
19. Morello, V., Barr, E., Bailes, M., Flynn, C., Keane, E., van Straten, W.: SPINN: a straightforward machine learning solution to the pulsar candidate selection problem. Mon. Not. R. Astron. Soc. **443**, 1651–1662 (2014)

20. Nakashima, T., Yokota, Y., Ishibuchi, H., Schaefer, G., Drastich, A., Zavisek, M.: Constructing cost-sensitive fuzzy rule-based classification systems for pattern classification problems. J. Adv. Comput. Intell. Intell. Inf. **11**, 546–553 (2007)

21. Richards, J., et al.: Active learning to overcome sample selection bias: application to photometric variable star classification. Astrophys. J. **744**, 192 (2011)

22. Rijsbergen, C.J.V.: Information Retrieval, 2nd edn. Butterworth-Heinemann, Oxford (1979)

23. Roberts, N., et al.: Handbook of Pulsar Astronomy. Cambridge Observing Handbooks for Research Astronomers. Cambridge University Press, Cambridge (2005)

24. Schapire, R.E.: The strength of weak learnability. Mach. Learn. **5**, 197–227 (1990)

25. Sokolova, M., Lapalme, G.: A systematic analysis of performance measures for classification tasks. Inf. Process. Manag. **45**(4), 427–437 (2009)

26. Stovall, K., Lorimer, D., Lynch, R.: Searching for millisecond pulsars: surveys, techniques and prospects. Class. Quantum Gravity **30**, 224003 (2013)

27. Sun, Y., Kamel, M., Wong, A., Wang, Y.: Cost-sensitive boosting for classification of imbalanced data. Pattern Recogn. **40**, 3358–3378 (2007)

28. Wang, S., Yao, X.: Diversity analysis on imbalanced data sets by using ensemble models. In: IEEE Symposium on Computational Intelligence and Data Mining, pp. 324–331 (2009)

29. Weiss, G.: Mining with rarity: a unifying framework. SIGKDD Explor. **6**, 7–19 (2004)

30. Zhu, W., et al.: Searching for pulsars using image pattern recognition. Astrophys. J. **781**, 117 (2014)

Computational Analysis of Third-Grade Liquid Flow with Cross Diffusion Effects: Application to Entropy Modeling

K. Loganathan[1]([✉]) [iD], A. Charles Sagayaraj[2], Amelec Viloria[3,4], Noel Varela[3], Omar Bonerge Pineda Lezama[5], and Luis Ortiz-Ospino[6]

[1] Department of Mathematics, Faculty of Engineering,
Karpagam Academy of Higher Education, Coimbatore 641021, Tamilnadu, India
loganathankaruppusamy304@gmail.com
[2] Department of Mathematics, Sri Vidya Mandir Arts and Science College,
Katteri, Uthangarai, Tamilnadu, India
[3] Universidad de la Costa, Barranquilla, Colombia
[4] Universidad Peruana de Ciencias Aplicadas, Lima, Peru
[5] Universidad Tecnológica Centroamericana (UNITEC), San Pedro Sula, Honduras
[6] Universidad Simon Bolivar, Barranquilla, Colombia

Abstract. The key goal of this current study is to analyze the entropy generation with cross diffusion effects. The third-grade type non-Newtonian fluid model is used in this study. The current flow problem is modelled with stretching plate. Modified Fourier heat flux is replaced the classical heat flux. The appropriate transformation is availed to convert the basic boundary layers equations into ODEs and then verified by homotopy algorithm. The consequences of various physical quantities on temperature, velocity, entropy and concentration profile are illustrated graphically.

Keywords: Third grade fluid · Linear stretching sheet · Homotopy Analysis Method (HAM) · Soret and Dufour effects · Entropy generation

1 Introduction

Third grade fluid is one of the notable sub kinds of non-Newtonian fluids. The non-Newtonian fluid flow due to the stretching surface is the important area of research due to its broad applications in many industrial and production domains such as, rolling of polymer films, extrusion of metallic sheets, etc. The study on 2nd grade fluid which passed through the stretching sheet is numerically discussed including the variations in thermophysical properties like thermal conductivity, viscosity [1]. It is shown that Eckert number increases the heat transport rate. Hydromagnetic mixed convective heat transfer of 3rd-grade fluid with gyrotactic microorganism is examined [2]. Unsteady flow of power law fluid with uniform velocity is evaluated [3]. With the consideration of heat source and

© Springer Nature Switzerland AG 2020
Y. Tan et al. (Eds.): ICSI 2020, LNCS 12145, pp. 525–534, 2020.
https://doi.org/10.1007/978-3-030-53956-6_48

heat sink of MHD flow over a oscillatory stretching sheet is numerically studied
[4]. With the impact of chemical reaction, the fourth grade fluid through porous
plate of MHD radiative fluid is investigated [5]. In addition to MHD nanofluid,
the electrically conductive fluid that of second grade with suction parameter is
developed [6]. For the application of bio magnetic the third grade fluid is correlated numerically [7]. The modified Fourier heat flux model for the study of
carreau fluid is explored numerically [8]. The various features and applications
of non-Newtonian fluids are studied in ref's [9–15].

There are several techniques available to solve nonlinear problems. The homotopy analysis method (HAM) is initially constructed by Liao [16] in 1992. Moreover, he altered with a non-zero auxiliary parameter [17] . This parameter shows
the way to calculate the convergence rate. It also offers great independence to
choose the base functions of the solutions. A few more studies about this technique was seen in previous works [18, 19].

Inspired by the above literature surveys, we are constructing a steady 3rd-
grade liquid flow with considering radiation, and convective heating effects.
Dufour and Soret effects are examined. The system of entropy is discussed briefly
for various parameters.

2   Mathematical Formation

The steady third grade incompressible two dimensional chemically reactive fluid
flow due to stretchy surface is considered. The sheet to be stretchy by the pair
of same and inverse forces with velocity $(u_w = ax), a > 0$, a is known as stretchy
rate. The free stream velocity is u_∞. (C_∞) and (T_∞) are the free stream concentration and temperature and in order. The governing equations with boundary
conditions are listed below

$$\frac{\partial u}{\partial x} + \frac{\partial v}{\partial y} = 0 \tag{1}$$

$$u\frac{\partial u}{\partial x} + v\frac{\partial u}{\partial y} = \mu\frac{\partial^2 x}{\partial y^2} + \frac{\alpha_1^*}{\rho}\left(u\frac{\partial^3 u}{\partial y^2 \partial x} + v\frac{\partial^3 u}{\partial y^3} + \frac{\partial u}{\partial x}\frac{\partial^2 u}{\partial y^2} + 3\frac{\partial u}{\partial y}\frac{\partial^2 u}{\partial y^2}\right)$$
$$+2\frac{\partial_2^*}{\rho}\frac{\partial u}{\partial y}\frac{\partial^2 u}{\partial x \partial y} + 6\frac{\beta^*}{\rho}\left(\frac{\partial u}{\partial y}\right)^2\frac{\partial^2 u}{\partial y^2} + g\Big[\beta_T(T - T_\infty)$$
$$+\beta_C(C - C_\infty)\Big] \tag{2}$$

$$\frac{\partial T}{\partial x}u + \frac{\partial T}{\partial y}v = \frac{Q}{\rho c_p}(T - T_\infty) + \frac{k}{\rho c_p}\frac{\partial^2 T}{\partial y^2} - \frac{1}{\rho c_p}\frac{\partial q_r}{\partial y} + \frac{D_m k_m}{c_s c_p}\frac{\partial^2 C}{\partial y^2} \tag{3}$$

$$\frac{\partial u}{\partial x}u + \frac{\partial C}{\partial y}v = D_m\frac{\partial^2 C}{\partial y^2} + \frac{D_m k_m}{T_m}\frac{\partial^2 T}{\partial y^2} - k_m(C - C_\infty) \tag{4}$$

The boundary points stated as $u = (u_w(x) = ax), (v = 0), (-k\frac{\partial T}{\partial y} = h_f(T_f - T_w)), (C = C_w)$ at $(y = 0)$,

$$u(\to 0), T(\to T_\infty), (C \to C_\infty) \text{ as } y(\to \infty) \tag{5}$$

where u & v(=velocity components along the x & y-direction), μ (=kinematic viscosity), $(\alpha_1^*, \alpha_2^* \& \beta_1^*)$(=material parameters), ρ (=fluid density), (β_T, β_C) (=coefficient of thermal and concentration expansions), c_p (=specific heat), c_s (=concentration susceptibility), Q (=heat capacity of ordinary fluid), q_r (= radiative heat flux), C (=concentration), C_w (= fluid wall concentration), D_m (=mass diffusion coefficient), k_m (=first order chemical reaction parameter). Incorporating the Cattaneo-Christov heat flux into energy equation, we get

$$u\frac{\partial T}{\partial x} + v\frac{\partial T}{\partial y} + 2uv\frac{\partial^2 T}{\partial x \partial y} + \lambda\Big(u^2\frac{\partial^2 T}{\partial x^2} + v^2\frac{\partial^2 T}{\partial y^2} + \Big(u\frac{\partial u}{\partial x} + v\frac{\partial u}{\partial y}\Big)\frac{\partial T}{\partial x}$$

$$+ \Big(u\frac{\partial v}{\partial x} + v\frac{\partial v}{\partial y}\Big)\frac{\partial T}{\partial y}\Big) = \frac{k}{\rho c_p}\frac{\partial^2 T}{\partial y^2} - \frac{1}{\rho c_p}\frac{\partial q_r}{\partial y} + \frac{D_m k_T}{c_s c_p}\frac{\partial^2 C}{\partial y^2} + \frac{Q}{\rho c_p}(T - T_\infty). \tag{6}$$

Consider the transformations given below

$$\eta = \sqrt{\frac{a}{\mu}}y, v = -\sqrt{a\mu}F(\eta), u = axF'(\eta), \phi(\eta) = \frac{C - C_\infty}{C_w - C_\infty}, \theta(\eta) = \frac{T - T_\infty}{T_f - T_\infty} \tag{7}$$

Using the above mentioned transformations we retrive the ODE system as follows

$$-F'^2 + FF'' + (3\alpha_1 + 2\alpha_2)F''^2 + 6\beta ReF'''F''^2 + F''' \quad +\alpha_1(2F'F''' - FF^{iv})$$
$$+\lambda_1(\theta + N\phi) = 0 \tag{8}$$

$$\Big(1 + \frac{4}{3}Rd\Big)\theta'' + Prf\theta' + Q_H\theta - \gamma(FF'\theta' + F^2\theta'') + PrD_F\phi'' = 0 \tag{9}$$

$$\frac{1}{Sc}\phi'' + F\phi' - C_r\phi + Sr\theta'' = 0 \tag{10}$$

Boundary conditions are

$$F'(\eta) = 1, F(\eta) = 0, \theta'(\eta) = -Bi(1 - \theta(\eta)), \phi(\eta) = 1 \text{ at } \eta = 0$$
$$F'(\eta) \to 0, \theta(\eta) \to 0, \phi(\eta) \to 0 \text{ as } \eta \to \infty \tag{11}$$

where $\alpha_1 = \alpha_1^*a/\rho\mu, \alpha_2 = \alpha_2^*a/\rho\mu$ and $\beta = \beta^*a^2/\rho\mu$ (=fluid parameters), $Re = ax^2/\mu$ (=Reynolds number), $Pr = \rho\mu c_p/k$ (= Prandtl number), $Q_H = Q/a\rho c_p$ (=Heat generation), $\gamma = \lambda a$ (=thermal relaxation), $Sc = \mu/D_B$ (=Schmidt number), $C_r = k_m/a$(=Chemical reaction), $\lambda 1 = Gr/Re^2$ (=local buoyancy parameter), $Gr = g\beta_T(T_w - T_\infty)x^3/\mu^2$ (=Grashof number), $N = \beta_C(C_w - C_\infty)/\beta_T(T_w -$

T_∞)(=buoyancy ratio parameter), $Rd = 4\sigma_1 T_\infty^3/kk_*$ (=Radiation parameter), $D_F = D_m k_T/\mu c_s c_p \frac{C_w - C_\infty}{T_w - T_\infty}$ (= Dufour number), $Sr = \frac{D_m k_T}{\mu T_m} \frac{(T_w - T_\infty)}{(C_w - C_\infty)}$ (= Soret number).

Heat and mass transfer rate in dimensionless forms are

$$Re^{\frac{-1}{2}} Nu_x = -\left(1 + \frac{4}{3} Rd\right) \theta'(0), Re^{\frac{-1}{2}} Sh_x = -\phi'(0).$$

3   Analytical Procedure and Convergence Study

HAM has been used last twenty years to solve the non-linear system of ODE occurring in various fields. The nonlinear ODE are solved with the aid of HAM algorithm. This algorithm is computed through MATHEMATICA software in our personal computer with 8 GB RAM and 2.30 GHz Processor.

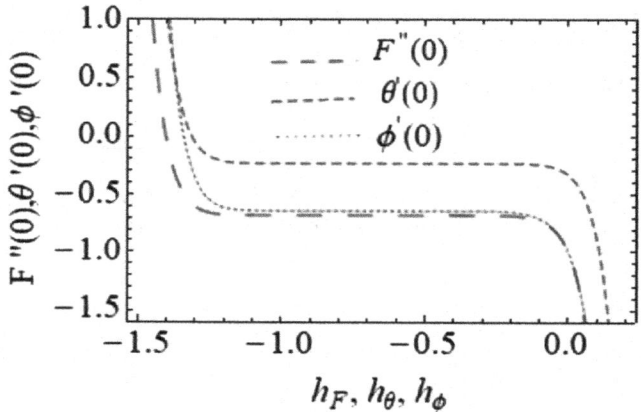

Fig. 1. h-curves for $h_{F,\theta,\phi}$.

Based on the Fig. 1, the auxiliary parameters have the range $-1.2 \leq h_F \leq 0.3, -1.3 \leq h_\theta \leq 0.1, -1.3 \leq h_\phi \leq 0.3$. Approximatley we fixed the h values as $h_F = h_\theta = h_\phi = -0.7$ (Table 1).

4   Entropy Optimization

The entropy minimization optimization for fluid friction, heat and mass transfer irreversibility's are given below:

$$S_{gen}''' = \frac{K_1}{T_\infty^2}\left[\left(\frac{\partial T}{\partial y}\right)^2 + \frac{16\sigma^* T_\infty^3}{3kk^*}\left(\frac{\partial T}{\partial y}\right)^2 + \frac{\mu}{T_\infty} + \left[\left(\frac{\partial u}{\partial y}\right)^2 + \frac{RD}{C_\infty}\left(\frac{\partial c}{\partial y}\right)^2 + \frac{RD}{T_\infty}\left(\frac{\partial T}{\partial y}\right)\left(\frac{\partial c}{\partial y}\right)\right.$$

Table 1. Displays the convergence solutions of HAM in order of approximation when $Pr = 0.9, \alpha_1 = 0.1, Sc = 0.9, D_F = 0.5, Re = 0.1, \beta = 0.1, \alpha_2 = 0.1, \gamma = 0.1, Bi = 0.5, Rd = 0.3, \lambda_1 = 0.2, N = 0.1, Sr = 0.3, Q_H = -0.3, h = -0.7, C_r = 0.1$.

Order	$-F''(0)$	$\theta'(0)$	$-\phi'(0)$
1	0.72116	0.23913	0.72777
5	0.67605	0.23555	0.63669
10	0.67817	0.23648	0.63945
15	0.67803	0.23643	0.63897
20	0.67801	0.23644	0.63901
25	0.67803	0.23644	0.63903
30	0.67803	0.23644	0.63903
40	0.67803	0.23644	0.63903
50	0.67803	0.23644	0.63903

Dimensionless system of entropy generation is defined as:

$$E_G = Re\left(1 + \frac{4}{3}Rd\right)\theta'^2 + Re\left(\frac{Br}{\Omega}\right)f''^2 + Re\left(\frac{\zeta}{\Omega}\right)^2\lambda\phi'^2 + Re\frac{\zeta}{\Omega}\lambda\phi'\theta'$$

5   Validation

In order to validate our numerical procedure, the results are validated with earlier report of Maria et al. [10]. The comparison results are given in Table 2.

Table 2. Comparison in absence of $D_F = 0, SR = 0, \omega = 0, Rd = 0, C_r = 0, \lambda_1 = 0, N = 0, Q_H = 0$.

Order	$-f''(0)$		$-\theta'(0)$		$-\phi'(0)$	
	Ref. [10]	Current	Ref. [10]	Current	Ref. [10]	Current
1	0.81450	0.81450	0.72778	0.72778	0.72778	0.72778
5	0.81221	0.81221	0.58070	0.58070	0.64933	0.64933
8	0.81235	0.81235	0.57779	0.57779	0.64835	0.64835
14	0.81235	0.81235	0.57871	0.57871	0.64873	0.64873
17	0.81235	0.81235	0.57878	0.57878	0.64873	0.64873
25	0.81235	0.81235	0.57878	0.57878	0.64873	0.64873
30	0.81235	0.81235	0.57878	0.57878	0.64873	0.64873
35	0.81235	0.81235	0.57878	0.57878	0.64873	0.64873

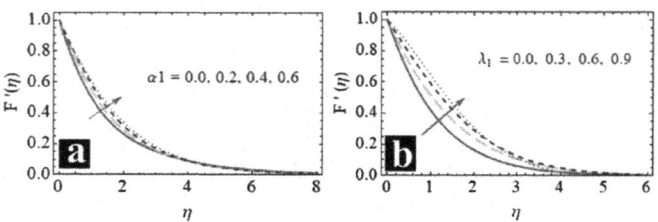

Fig. 2. Variation in $(F'(\eta))$ for α_1 & λ_1.

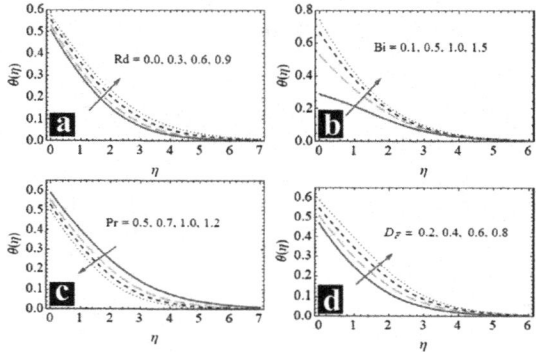

Fig. 3. Variation in $(\theta(\eta))$ for Rd, Bi, Pr and D_F.

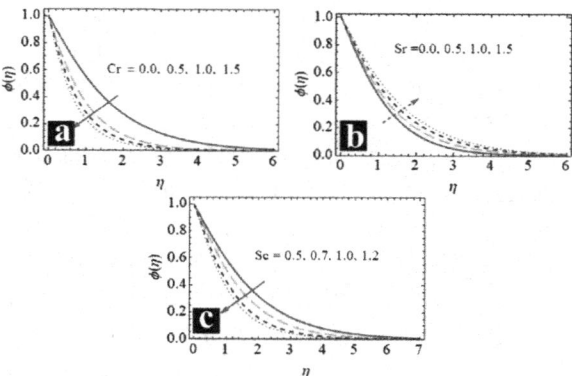

Fig. 4. Variation in $(\phi(\eta))$ for Cr, Sr and Sc.

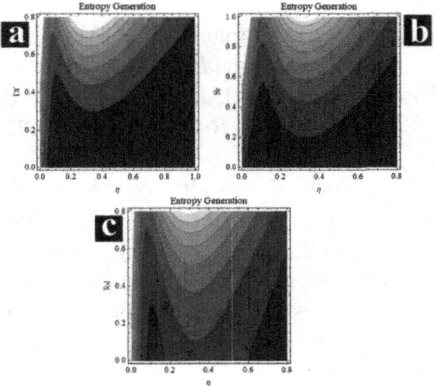

Fig. 5. Variation in (E_G) for D_F, Sr and Rd.

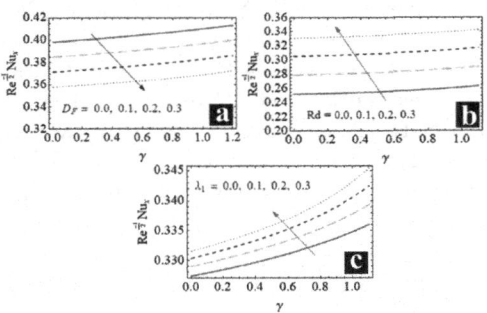

Fig. 6. Effect of Nu_x for values of D_F, Rd and λ_1.

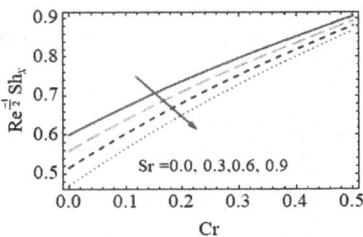

Fig. 7. Effect of Sh_x for values of Cr and Sr.

6 Results and Discussion

In this section, we examine the impacts of physical quantities on temperature($\theta(\eta)$), velocity ($F'(\eta)$), entropy(E_G) and concentration profiles($\Phi(\eta)$) with the fixed values $Pr = 0.9$, $Sc = 0.9$, $Re = 0.14$, $\alpha_1 = 0.1$, $\alpha_2 = 0.1$, $\beta = 0.1$, $\gamma = 0.1$, $D_F = 0.5$, $Sr = 0.3$, $Bi = 0.5$, $Rd = 0.3$, $\lambda_1 = 0.2$, $N = 0.1$, $Q_H = -0.3$, $h = -0.7$ and $Cr = 0.1$.

Figure 1 describes the effect of velocity profile ($F'(\eta)$) on material fluid parameter (α_1) and mixed convection parameter (λ_1). From Fig. 1(a & b), we have seen an increase in α_1 and λ_1 the velocity profile ($F'(\eta)$) rises. Figure 2 revels the temperature profile ($\theta(\eta)$) for different parameters. In Fig. 2(a, b, d), we note that, the ($\theta(\eta)$) enhances for the augmentation in Rd, Bi and D_F and it diminishes for the higher values of Prandtl number Pr as shown in Fig. 2c. Figure 3 depicts the different effects of Cr, Sr, and Sc on concentration profile. From Fig. 3(a) and Fig. 3(c) concentration profile ($\Phi(\eta)$) is inversely proportional to the higher Cr and Sc. Whereas in Fig. 3(b), it is found that ($\Phi(\eta)$) increases with augments in Sr. Figures 4(a–c) shows the effects of D_F, Sr and Rd on E_G (entropy generation profile). From these plots we obtain that the system of entropy enhances for the larger values of D_F, Sr and Rd.

From Fig. 5(a) we note that the Nusselt number (Nu_x) decreases with increases in D_F. Also, in Fig. 5(b) and Fig. 5(c), it is noted that Nu_x decrease with upsurge in Rd and γ. By increasing the D_F, fluid resits to move the hotter side of the sheet that subsequently Nu_x decreases. In addition, it is noted that as we increase the Rd and γ the Nu_x enhances. Figure 6 exposes the mass transfer rate for the combined parameters Sr and Cr. We noted that decreasing trend in mass transfer for larger Sr and mass transfer rate enhance for Cr.

7 Conclusion

The salient outcomes of 3rd-grade fluid flow with Soret and Dufour effects along with entropy calculation is stated as follows:

1 Higher range of mixed convection parameter(λ_1) and fluid parameter(α_1) intensifying the velocity profile.
2 Entropy of the system enhances with radiation, Sored and Dufour numbers.
3 Mass transfer rate rises with chemical reaction and reduces with Soret number.

References

1. Akinbobola, T.E., Okoya, S.S.: The flow of second grade fluid over a stretching sheet with variable thermal conductivity and viscosity in the presence of heat source/sink. J. Niger. Math. Soc. **34**(3), 331–342 (2015). https://doi.org/10.1016/j.jnnms.2015.10.002

2. Alzahrani, E.O., Shah, Z., Dawar, A., Malebary, S.J.: Hydromagnetic mixed convective third grade nanomaterial containing gyrotactic microorganisms toward a horizontal stretched surface. Alexandria Eng. J. **58**(4), 1421–1429 (2019). https://doi.org/10.1016/j.aej.2019.11.013

3. Ahmed, J., Mahmood, T., Iqbal, Z., Shahzad, A., Ali, R.: NU SC. J. Mol. Liq. (2016). https://doi.org/10.1016/j.molliq.2016.06.022

4. Ali, N., Ullah, S., Sajid, M., Abbas, Z.: MHD flow and heat transfer of couple stress fluid over an oscillatory stretching sheet with heat source/sink in porous medium. Alexandria Eng. J. (2016). https://doi.org/10.1016/j.aej.2016.02.018

5. Arifuzzaman, S.M., Khan, S., Al-mamun, A., Rezae-rabbi, S., Biswas, P., Karim, I.: Hydrodynamic stability and heat and mass transfer flow analysis of MHD radiative fourth-grade fluid through porous plate with chemical reaction. J. King Saud Univ. Sci. (2018). https://doi.org/10.1016/j.jksus.2018.12.009

6. Cortell, R.: Flow and heat transfer of an electrically conducting fluid of second grade over a stretching sheet subject to suction and to a transverse magnetic field. Int. J. Heat Mass Transf. **49**, 1851–1856 (2006). https://doi.org/10.1016/j.ijheatmasstransfer.2005.11.013

7. Ghosh, S.K.: Unsteady non-Newtonian fluid flow and heat transfer: a bio-magnetic application Sushil Kumar Ghosh. J. Magn. Magn. Mater. (2017). https://doi.org/10.1016/j.jmmm.2017.07.050

8. Nazir, U., Saleem, S., Nawaz, M., Sadiq, M.A., Alderremy, A.A.: Study of transport phenomenon in Carreau fluid using Cattaneo-Christov heat flux model with temperature dependent diffusion coefficients. Phys. A Stat. Mech. its Appl. 123921 (2020). https://doi.org/10.1016/j.physa.2019.123921

9. Waqas, M., Hayat, T., Farooq, M., Shehzad, S.A., Alsaedi, A.: Cattaneo-Christov heat flux model for flow of variable thermal conductivity generalized Burgers fluid. J. Mol. Liq. **220**, 642–648 (2016). https://doi.org/10.1016/j.molliq.2016.04.086

10. Imtiaz, M., Alsaedi, A., Shafiq, A., Hayat, T.: Impact of chemical reaction on third grade fluid flow with Cattaneo-Christov heat flux. J. Mol. Liq. **229**, 501–507 (2017). https://doi.org/10.1016/j.molliq.2016.12.103

11. Bhuvaneswari, M., Eswaramoorthi, S., Sivasankaran, S., Rajan, S., Saleh Alshomrani, A.: Effects of viscous dissipation and convective heating on convection flow of a second-grade liquid over a stretching surface: an analytical and numerical study. Sci. Iran. B **26**(3), 1350–1357 (2019)

12. Loganathan, K., Rajan, S.: An entropy approach of Williamson nanofluid flow with Joule heating and zero nanoparticle mass flux. J. Therm. Anal. Calorim. (2020). https://doi.org/10.1007/s10973-020-09414-3

13. Eswaramoorthi, S., Sivasankaran, S., Bhuvaneswari, M., Rajan, S.: Soret and Dufour effects on viscoelastic boundary layer flow over a stretchy surface with convective boundary condition with radiation and chemical reaction. Sci. Iran. B. **23**(6), 2575–2586 (2016)

14. Loganathan. K, Mohana. K, Mohanraj, M., Sakthivel, P., Rajan, S.: Impact of 3rd-grade nanofluid flow across a convective surface in the presence of inclined Lorentz force: an approach to entropy optimization. J. Therm. Anal. Calorim. (2020), https://doi.org/10.1007/s10973-020-09751-3

15. Elanchezhian, E., Nirmalkumar, R., Balamurugan, M., Mohana, K., Prabu, K.M., Viloria, A.: Heat and mass transmission of an Oldroyd-B nanofluid flow through a stratified medium with swimming of motile gyrotactic microorganisms and nanoparticles. J. Therm. Anal. Calorim. (2020). https://doi.org/10.1007/s10973-020-09847-w

16. Liao, S., Tan, Y.A.: General approach to obtain series solutions of nonlinear differential. Stud. Appl. Math. **119**(4), 297–354 (2007)
17. Liao, S.J.: An explicit, totally analytic approximation of Blasius viscous flow problems. Int. J. Non-Linear Mech. **34**, 759–778 (1999)
18. Loganathan, K., Sivasankaran, S., Bhuvaneswari, M., Rajan, S.: Second-order slip, cross-diffusion and chemical reaction effects on magneto-convection of Oldroyd-B liquid using Cattaneo-Christovheat flux with convective heating. J. Therm. Anal. Calorim. **136**(1), 401–409 (2019)
19. Loganathan, K., Prabu, K.M., Elanchezhian, E., Nirmalkumar, R., Manimekalai, K.: Computational analysis of thermally stratified mixed convective non-Newtonian fluid flow with radiation and chemical reaction impacts. J. Phys: Conf. Ser. **1432**, 012048 (2020)

Data Mining

Aula Touch Game: Digital Tablets and Their Incidence in the Development of Citizen Competences of Middle Education Students in the District of Barranquilla-Colombia

Paola Patricia Ariza Colpas[1]([⊠]), Belina Annery Herrera Tapias[1],
Andres Gabriel Sanchez Comas[1], Marlon Alberto Piñeres Melo[2],
and Judith Martinez Royert[3]

[1] Universidad de la Costa, CUC, Barranquilla, Colombia
{pariza1,bherrera,asanchez}@cuc.edu.co
[2] Universidad del Norte, Barranquilla, Colombia
pineresm@uninorte.edu.co
[3] Universidad Simon Bolivar, Barranquilla, Colombia
Judith.martinez@unisimonbolivar.edu.co

Abstract. Citizen competences are considered as a fundamental aspect in the social development of man with his environment, which allows him to carry out actions that are articulated with the different guidelines established by law, which leads the citizen to live in a coherent and peaceful way in a nation that tends for freedom of thought framed in a democratic society. That is why it is considered of high importance that in educational establishments there are spaces that tend for training in peaceful coexistence framed in the law of the educated. This article resulted from the research project: "Social Appropriation of citizen and mathematical competences making use of MIDTablets", in which the mediation of Information and Communication Technologies is proposed to support the training of citizens with competences citizens who ensure adequate behavior in society. This project was developed in 31 educational institutions in the district of Barranquilla-Colombia, with support from resources of both the Ministry of Information Technology and Communications (MinTic), and the Secretariat of District Education of Barranquilla, in compliance with national goals, departmental and district regarding the quality of education of the national population

Keywords: Digital tablets · Citizen competences · Social appropriation · Middle education · Learning software

1 Introduction

Postmodernity and globalization have brought with it the application of technological tools that have the property of making available to people an accumulation of information that facilitates the construction and transfer of knowledge [1]. The inclusion of these technologies in the teaching and learning processes allows education to reach more and

© Springer Nature Switzerland AG 2020
Y. Tan et al. (Eds.): ICSI 2020, LNCS 12145, pp. 537–546, 2020.
https://doi.org/10.1007/978-3-030-53956-6_49

more remote places [2]. The use of different technological and communication tools that have proliferated in recent years through the internet and the increasing incorporation of different resources and tools other than the computer, such as mobile devices: Tablets, Ipad, Cellular, Smartphone, among other devices, they make possible their incorporation into education and have given a new dimension to learning. In fact, this has to do with the desire of the human being to stay educated and updated throughout his life not only through face-to-face training scenarios but also through virtual media training scenarios, which allows them to access information and knowledge from anywhere and at any time with basic technical conditions of access [3, 4].

The National government is aware of the need to improve the quality of education at all levels, which is evidenced in the Sector Plan (2016–2019) of the Ministry of National Education, which highlights that the quality of education is related to multiple factors: the teaching and learning methodologies, the training of its educators, the evaluation systems implemented, the way in which the levels of training are articulated, the institutional capacity and infrastructure and the conceptual and legal framework that organizes and supports the educational system, through which it is made explicit that quality education is a right that all citizens must access. Consequently, teacher qualification in the educational incorporation of tablets in the classroom that responds to a pedagogical model, will contribute to improving the educational quality in the district of Barranquilla.

The District of Barranquilla has 152 educational institutions at levels ranging from early childhood to secondary education, institutions that according to studies by the District Mayor in its program "A Safer Barranquilla" has identified problems of violence and conflicts that threaten the human rights of children and adolescents, the fracture of the social fabric, the quality of life in our local environment. Against this background, it has been shown that education is the most important instrument for the recognition and management of conflict through peaceful mechanisms that generate school environments of reconciliation, democracy and peace, so that direct action is necessary that It can generate a social appropriation of mechanisms that contribute to the construction of satisfactory, reciprocal and participatory solutions of school actors who present antagonistic arguments, which in many cases leads to mutual psychological, physical and sexual aggression; and thus reflect a change in the behaviors of communities traditionally do not have developed citizen competencies.

In this project, 31 district educational institutions of strata 1 and 2 of the District of Barranquilla were intervened, in addition to generating conceptual, technological and methodological tools, within the framework of the development of citizen competencies through the conceptualization of friendly and peaceful solutions of the controversies that threaten human rights, for the integration of a network that generates direct actions on the community, in which the academic, research and innovation experience in the environment would be combined, as a form of positive intervention in the face of the social need of the District of Barranquilla and its metropolitan area.

2   The Conflict Resolution, National Bet for Coexistence

Conflict resolution is a fundamental aspect in which respect for the needs, tastes, points of view and values of different individuals converge, which is why it is quite probable that they can be generated [5, 6]. There are different stages to be addressed to support conflict resolution, which are focused on mitigating or reducing the consequences that may arise from their appearance [7, 8].

In the Barranquilla district, a phenomenon of conflicts has been identified with reference to school coexistence and human resources in district institutions. Regarding bullying among school students, the World Health Organization (WHO), in data from 35 countries, reports that 15% of 11-year-olds and 9% of 15-year-olds have been intimidated at some point. According to UNESCO statistics, in works carried out between 2009 and 2018, they show that in Latin America 51% of the 6th grade students surveyed say they have been the victim of insults, threats, bulling and different situations of conflict. In Colombia, 29% of fifth-graders and 15% of ninth-graders have been bullied in the past two months, according to a study of 50,000 students reported by the Colombian Parent-Parent Corporation RedPaPaz. The experts cited agree that bullying or bullying is not a problem of children, isolated, but of society, with a common denominator: violence. Consequently, it is possible to assume the problem from an integrated approach to the understanding and approach for the resolution and prevention of school conflict, identifying the factors that generate conflict and its components, valuing the role of communication as a means of conflict resolution, as well as the importance of the mediation process from a systemic perspective in the educational context, reflecting on the different roles and strategies of intervention in the face of school conflict and proposing institutional strategies and alternatives for the development of conflict intervention plans and school mediation [9, 10].

3   Mediation of ICT in the Development of Citizen Skills

Through the strategic alliance with government entities in order to implement a program which through the use of digital content in the middle school classrooms of the city, the learning of the student population and educational quality is strengthened of the public institutions of the city. The digital content was developed according to the requirements of the Barranquilla District Education Secretaries, implemented on smart mobile devices, and deployed with a training process for the teachers and staff of these Educational Institutions, see Fig. 1.

Operationally and technically, digital content is installed directly on smart mobile devices through an internet link, which will be downloaded through exclusive permits granted to educational institutions attached to the program. The download will be made from a repository maintained and supported by the Universidad de la Costa Corporation, which will provide a support service and technical assistance during the year of service. With the renewal of the program, digital content will be automatically updated via the internet after the feedback process and quality improvement of these contents. In the same way, new digital content can be installed either to strengthen new themes or other subjects of educational institutions.

Functionally, digital content allows the registration of each student who uses digital content in educational institutions, in order to monitor the student's learning process, in the context of what is being worked on in digital content, as well as the use and exploitation of the student, see Fig. 2. At the end of the year, reports on the use and exploitation of digital content by the institution will be issued.

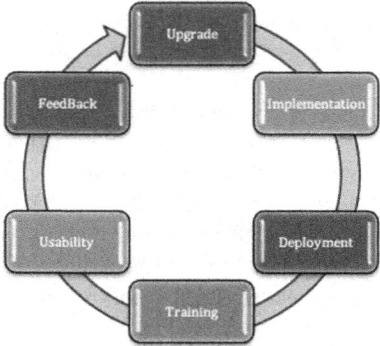

Fig. 1. Application work cycle

Fig. 2. Components of the solution architecture

4 Technical Specifications of the Application

The training strategy was carried out in three ways: use of support applications for the reinforcement and development of learning activities in the areas of mathematics and citizen skills, use of digital content developed by teachers and students in class sessions using the tablets and the use of Digital Content and learning activities developed by the ally that are accessed through a Digital Classroom Touch Classroom. The application has the following characteristics:

- A parameterized Technology Platform was developed that will be hosted in the Cloud (Administrator panel in the Cloud and the client will be developed in the Android Operating System)
- A pilot was carried out with the subjects in the areas of mathematics and Citizen Competencies, emphasizing violence and society, however, the platform will allow Parameterization in such a way that in a future term other subjects in the different areas of knowledge can be referenced that are taught in basic and secondary education.
- An accessed Android client application was installed on the tablets and each of these tablets will have a specific username and password, which will allow the student to access three (3) sessions separated by academic grade (9th, 10th, 11th). Once the user

enters the platform, the identification code of the mobile device will be linked to the FDI for the purpose of measuring results and statistics.

- A topic was selected: once the grade has been selected, the information regarding the subjects delimited in the previous investigation will be displayed (subject selection, select the Units and then select the specific topic to reinforce).
- Each subject contained content of the respective subject in the formats (Document (PDF), Podcast, MP3, Videos), it will contain a session of examples and evaluation exercises.
- The exercises were developed with 3 degrees of difficulty (basic, medium and advanced), so that the student can advance from one grade to another, they must previously carry out the exercises in the order of the grades, this will allow the motivation of the students as a challenge. that leads to learning. The platform will issue the student a report of their achievements and mistakes made, giving them the opportunity to retake the exercises.
- The exercises were developed taking into account the form of the Saber ICFES tests through questionnaires that will allow students to have a setting of the question and several multiple-choice answers, however the student must carry out the procedure of the exercise prior to selecting the answer. In case the student cannot solve the exercise, the application gives him the opportunity to show how it is solved and gives him the opportunity to do the exercises again. There will be a bank of random questions, this means that the questions are not repeated and that the student may know other options.
- For the administration of the WEB portal, an administrator was assigned to him who, by means of a user and a password, was enabled to create courses, modify, update, upload resources, delete, display and hide and finally enable and disable courses, exercises, topic, among others (upon request of the thematic experts) the following options were included: Creation of courses, units, topics, exercises and questionnaires.
- Taking into account that access is via the Internet, a 2 Mb connection is required, Android operating system.
- All resources (PDF, Videos, PODCAST) can be downloaded by students.
- The client application was created with high usability standards, allowing students greater navigability of the platform, since it will be delimited by specific sessions that will allow them to appropriate the information provided.
- For each student, statistics of student achievement are kept as long as it is arranged with the schools the delivery of the database of the students of 9th, 10th and 11th), this will allow the school to know the academic status of these students. for decision making (Fig. 3).

5   Methodology for the Development of the Application

Three phases were carried out for the development of this application, which are detailed below:

- **First phase:** access to different web pages in order to obtain information on the results of the "Saber 11ᵒ" tests, the competences that the ICFES evaluates in the areas of mathematics and citizen competences and the guidelines contemplated in the basic

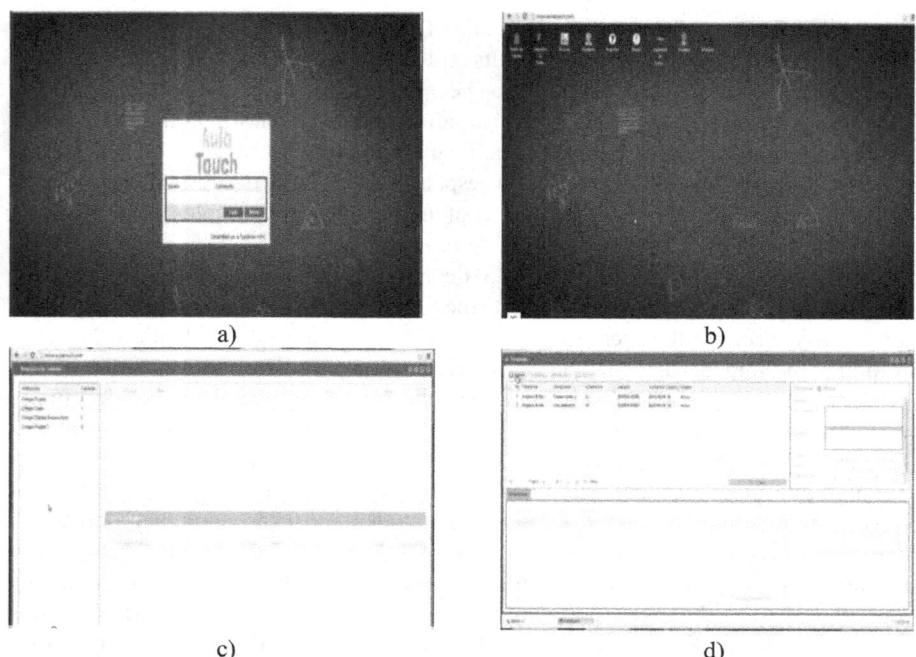

Fig. 3. Aula Touch images: a) Main page of Aulatouch, b) Main menu Aulatouch, c) Adding resources Aulatouch, d) Adding questions AulaTouch

competency standards of the Ministry of National Education where the competences that students must develop in these two areas of knowledge are established.

- **Second phase:** Review and analysis of the results of the Saber 11° tests obtained by the 31 Educational Establishments benefiting from the project during 2018, which are shown below in the Fig. 4. In Figs. 4, it is observed that the average obtained in the math tests by the 31 schools was 45.68, of which 16 institutions (51.61%) obtained results below this average. Similarly, the national average in the social area, in which the citizen competencies are located, was 43.80, of which 16 (51.61%) obtained results below the average. These low results demonstrate the need for FDI to reinforce these two areas, for which the strategy of incorporating tablets in the classroom with complementary content constitutes an extremely important opportunity.

- **Third phase:** Review of the Competences to evaluate in the tests Knowing 11° in the country: In the Mathematics Area, according to the ICFES, in middle education in the mathematics area, three competences are evaluated: Communication, reasoning and problem solving in the components (variational, geometric-metric and random number). In the area of Citizen Competences: According to ICFES, citizen competences are cognitive, emotional and communicative capacities that, integrated with each other and related to knowledge and attitudes, make it possible for citizens to act actively, in solidarity and democratically in society.

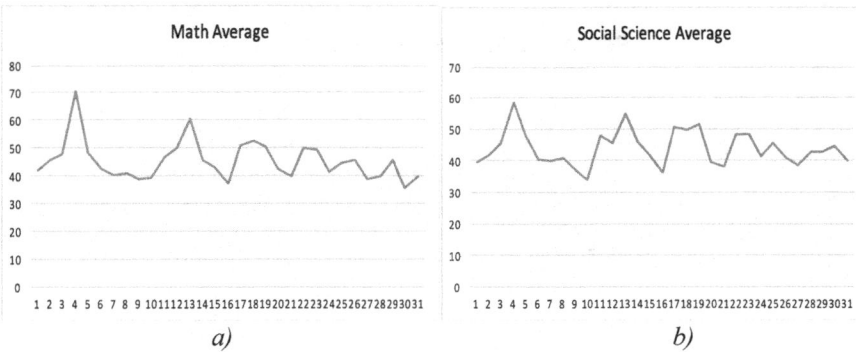

Fig. 4. a) Math Average, b) Social Science Average.

The identification of the problems associated with the areas of Citizen Competences and Mathematics, allowed us to have basic information to select the topics that in these two areas needed to be reinforced in the students. Mathematical problems are learning difficulties that a primary and secondary school student may encounter. It can be for some of the cognitive, physical or mental type, or any social problem in which the students are.

When there is a difficulty in learning mathematics, it is necessary to make a diagnosis, which allows us to know what is really the difficulty that the student presents, or if it refers to a disease, such as dyslexia, dysgraphia, dyspraxia, or other difficulties. It has been determined that in many cases the learning difficulties of the students are associated with many factors, including the methodology used by the teachers, the content, the motivation of the students and the resources made available by the same institution.

In the area of mathematics, it is necessary for students to develop a way of thinking that allows them to mathematically interpret and communicate situations that are presented to them in various sociocultural environments, using appropriate techniques to recognize, pose and solve problems. For the learning of the Citizen Competences, it is necessary that the teachers use innovative pedagogical strategies that allow the students, in addition to acquiring the cognitive competences, to appropriate these concepts and apply it to contextual problems.

6   Development of the Application Deployment and Launch of the Application

The students and teachers of the 31 district educational establishments of the project, recognized, developed and approved the citizen competences and after this diagnosis defined strategies that generated significant cultural changes in the students such as: identifying, evaluating and respecting the differences and similarities between the citizens according to the plurality of the Colombian Political Constitution, comply with the minimum standards of coexistence, reject situations of exclusion and discrimination in the classroom, strengthen the recognition and exercise of citizenship, identify mechanisms for citizen participation and express their opinions.

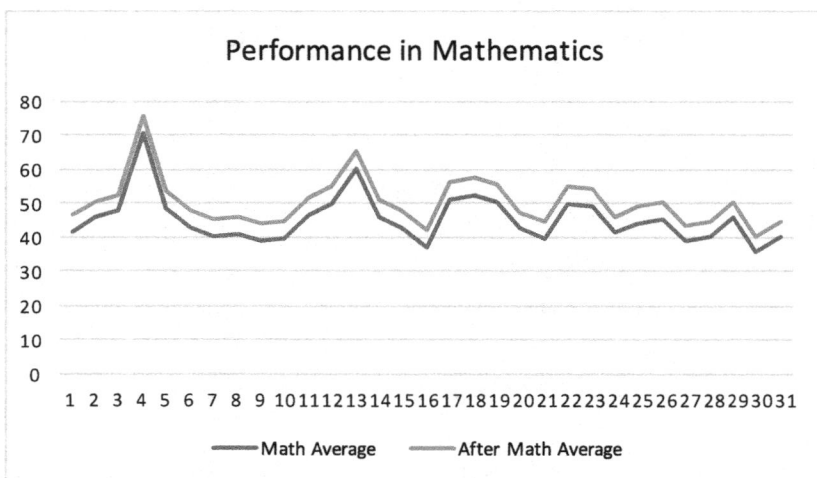

Fig. 5. Comparison of performance in mathematics before and after the use of the tool

Based on the results obtained, a proposal was prepared with the use of Tablets that leads to the development of citizen competencies and the improvement of student results in the Saber 11° tests. The project is expected to impact the academic community of the Educational Institutions of the Barranquilla district and society in general not only academically but also socially by training committed citizens, respectful of difference and defenders of the common good.

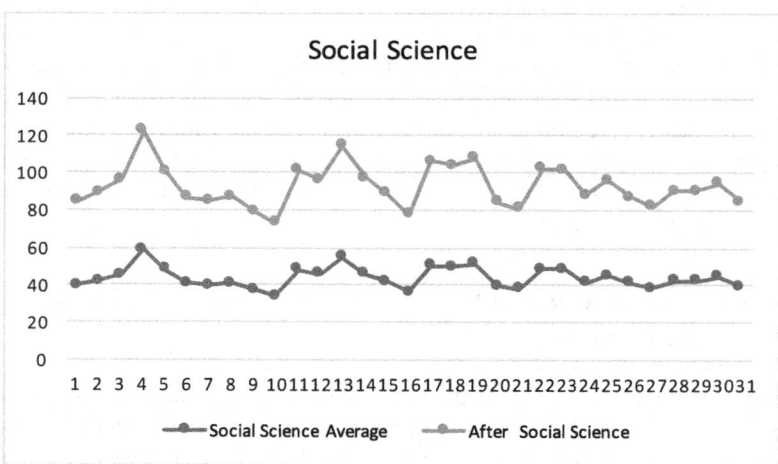

Fig. 6. Comparison of performance in Social Science before and after the use of the tool

As a result of the implementation of the project, better student performance was achieved in the math and social science tests, as can be seen in the following Figs. 5 and 6.

7 Conclusions

- The didactic strategies with the use of tablets incorporated into the educational practice constitutes a significant contribution for the Educational Establishments of the Barranquilla District, since they contribute to the development of the competences of the mathematical students and citizen competences of the students.
- To achieve success in a process of incorporating digital tablets, it is necessary to coherently link technology with pedagogy, since when developing a learning activity with the use of technology, clear pedagogical guidelines must be given and with a pedagogical intention.
- The use of tablets in the classroom during the development of a training process arouses the interest of the students, the debate and the argumentation that allow to improve the way in which the students achieve the learning.
- The use of didactic strategies supported by the use of Tablets, allows a greater interaction between students and teachers during the development of cooperative and collaborative projects.
- With the educational incorporation of ICT in the training processes, it constitutes a fundamental element for the development of collaborative projects aimed at improving the skills of students in the area in which they are used.

References

1. Zakaria, F., Zukiman, W.W., Shah, A.M.: SAT-482'UR-ine'Town board game: learning AKI the fun way!!! Kidney Int. Rep. **5**(3), S201 (2020)
2. Lee, D.: Comparison of reinforcement learning algorithms for a 2D racing game learning agent. J. Inst. Internet Broadcast. Commun. **20**(1), 171–176 (2020)
3. Sopy, H., Hasibuan, S.: Development of game learning media e-learning basketball based on students class X of SMA Negeri 3 Medan. In: 1st Unimed International Conference on Sport Science (UnICoSS 2019), pp. 11–13. Atlantis Press, March 2020
4. Pardede, E.Y.: Development of the snake game model for basic movement skills in SD medan struggle students. In: 1st Unimed International Conference on Sport Science (UnICoSS 2019), pp. 146–147. Atlantis Press, March 2020
5. Nuryasintia, I.: EFEK Moderasi Keaktifan Belajar Siswa Pada Pengaruh Media Monopoly Accounting Game Terhadap Pemahaman Konsep, Doctoral dissertation, Universitas Pendidikan Indonesia (2019)
6. Echeverri-Ocampo, I., Urina-Triana, M., Patricia Ariza, P., Mantilla, M.: El trabajo colaborativo entre ingenieros y personal de la salud para el desarrollo de proyectos en salud digital: una visión al futuro para lograr tener éxito (2018)
7. Morales Ortega, R., Ariza Colpas, P.P., Piñeres-Melo, M., Ayala-Mantilla, C., Peluffo-Martínez, G., Mendoza Palechor, F., Diaz Martinez, J.L.: CBT system (Computer Based Training) of the aircraft a-37b, used in the earth course of the combat air command No. 3 (CAMCOM-3) of the Colombian Air Force (FAC) (2020)

8. Wang, H., Chen, W.W., Sun, C.T.: Play teaches learning?: a pilot study on how gaming experience influences new game learning. In: Interactivity and the Future of the Human-Computer Interface, pp. 147–168. IGI Global (2020)

9. Lubay, L.H., Purnama, A.D.: An effort to improve the playing skill through the application of tool modification in small ball game (a classroom action research). In: 4th International Conference on Sport Science, Health, and Physical Education (ICSSHPE 2019), pp. 403–405. Atlantis Press, February 2020

10. Masyhuri, S.F., Suherman, W.S.: The traditional game learning model for the elementary school student character building. In: 4th International Conference on Sport Science, Health, and Physical Education (ICSSHPE 2019), pp. 9–13. Atlantis Press, February 2020

Case Classification Processing and Analysis Method for Respiratory Belt Data

Jinlong Chen[1] and Mengke Jiang[2(✉)]

[1] Guangxi Key Laboratory of Cryptography and Information Security,
Guilin University of Electronic Technology, Guilin, Guangxi, China
[2] Guangxi Key Laboratory of Trusted Software,
Guilin University of Electronic Technology, Guilin, Guangxi, China
446084066@qq.com

Abstract. Human respiratory signal is the important physiological indicator to reflect the physical condition. The respiratory belt, compared with the other human respiratory data measurement methods, has the advantages of being portable, cheap, non-invasive, etc. However, it is unclear which features of the breathing data can effectively classify the normal/abnormal state of breathing state. To solve the problem, we proposed a novel approach based on long-short-term-memory (LSTM) and breathing features of respiratory data. First, LSTM structure were used, then compared the result with the traditional method which extract the feature to experiment (in our paper which is RIE (ratio of inspiratory time to expiratory time)). In the end, a novel methodology proposed which combined the RIE feature with the LSTM structure. Experiment the three methods above using 342 normal and abnormal 24-h breathing data, the results show that the third method has higher classification accuracy.

Keywords: Respiratory belt · Respiratory data · Case classification

1 Introduction

The intensity, shape, rate and other aspects of human respiratory signals largely reflect other human functions such as cardiopulmonary function [1]. Through the analysis of human respiratory signals, it can effectively prevent or serve as the basis for other diseases found. Traditionally, there are several methods for measuring the breathing: (1) Wet temperature detection [2]. The method for detecting respiration based on nano-temperature and humidity sensing materials has poor adaptability, it is susceptible to external interference, and has low detection sensitivity. (2) Impedance detection. Impedance detection is currently the most commonly used respiratory detection method in the clinic. It can work stably and only needs to measure the respiratory signal through two electrodes, which is convenient and simple to use. However, this kind of method not only requires high on electrodes, but also causes problems in which the ratio is difficult to determine due to disturbance of cardiac blood flow [1]. (3) Extracting the respiratory signal from the ECG signal. This is an emerging detection method with non-invasive advantages, such as S.

© Springer Nature Switzerland AG 2020
Y. Tan et al. (Eds.): ICSI 2020, LNCS 12145, pp. 547–555, 2020.
https://doi.org/10.1007/978-3-030-53956-6_50

Leanderson [3] extracting respiratory signals from the ECG vector map and estimating the respiratory rate from the power spectrum of the respiratory signal. However, this measurement accuracy is not high, and the electrocardiographic electrode is prone to cause skin irritation of the patient. Therefore, the medical community currently lacks a method to measure the respiratory function in a natural state, long-term, non-invasively. The respiratory belt compensates for the above problems to some extent.

The respiratory belt is shown in Fig. 1. Usually, the weight is ≤30 g. The user binds it to the outside of the underwear that is close to the skin of the abdomen. Above the belt, the flexible breathing force sensor can be used to obtain the breathing waveform of the person by abdominal pressure. An example of a breathing belt and acquired breathing data is shown in Fig. 1.

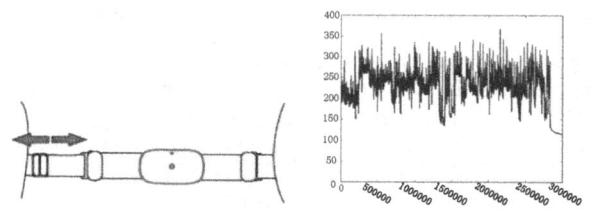

Fig. 1. Example of breathing belt (left) and breathing data (right)

The respiratory belt has the following characteristics compared to the above method: (1) non-invasive, direct and continuous. Detection is the direct, continuous collection of human bio signals performed without any trauma to the patient. (2) Portable and inexpensive. This device measures the respiratory motility by placing a tension sensor in the subject's belt. The current low price of sensors and data storage devices allows these instruments to be purchased and used by most subjects. (3) Robust, stable and sensitive under natural conditions. Because it is bound to the waist of the subject, the subject can perform most of the daily activities without being affected, and has good stability and sensitivity for the measurement of respiratory data.

Based on the above advantages of the respiratory belt, and the current analysis of the respiratory belt data is insufficient, this paper will explore the data obtained using the respiratory belt to analyze, trying to effectively distinguish the normal and abnormal breathing data.

2   Related Work

The normal inspiratory time is 0.8–1.2 s and the exhalation time is 0.5–1 s. That is, the normal breathing time is 1.3–2.2 s, plus the breathing interval is about 1–2 s, and the breathing time is 3.5 s a time. The ratio of inspiratory time to expiratory time is about 1:1.5–2. The expiratory time takes longer than inspiratory time because the exhaling generally does not require extra work, only the chest automatically retracted. However, the ratio of people with abnormal breathing state may reach 1:4 or higher, and the respiratory data obtained through the breathing belt can be further analyzed based on the similar parameter information.

Most researchers currently focus on the acquisition of respiratory data or on disease warning through real-time respiratory data. Sebastijan Sprager [4] proposed a method for detecting respiration from optical interference signals. A. Raji [5] used two temperature sensors to indirectly obtain respiratory data, and to determine the occurrence of asthma by abnormality in real-time respiration rate, Agnel John K. J and Pamela. D [6] proposed a sleep apnea monitoring system based on single-chip microcomputer to detect sleep apnea. These studies are mainly to detect the real-time respiratory data to determine the onset of respiratory disease, not the overall evaluation of the patient's respiratory system. In order to judge whether the overall respiratory state of the subject is normal or abnormal, this paper uses the respiratory belt to observe the daily behavioral respiratory data of the subject, analyzes and processes the data to find the appropriate distinguishing features to evaluate the respiratory condition of the subject.

3   Related Methods

For the problem of case classification based on the respiratory data acquired by the respiratory belt, this paper firstly filters the original respiratory signal, removes the corresponding abnormal value and baseline drift, and then uses the LSTM network, the absorption ratio combined with LSTM, the absorption ratio combined with SVM, respectively. The corresponding methods will be introduced separately below.

3.1   Filtering

Usually, the raw data has a phenomenon such as baseline drift. Baseline drift is generally caused by human breathing, electrode movement, etc., and needs to be removed from the original data before further research and analysis to obtain data that more reflects the original respiratory characteristics. Commonly used removal methods include median filtering, wavelet transform, and morphological filtering [7]. In this paper, wavelet transform is used to perform filtering processing.

Wavelet transform is widely used in signal processing, image processing, pattern recognition and other fields. Through the telescopic translation operation, the signal (function) is gradually multi-scale refined, and finally reaches the time division at high frequency, and the frequency division at low frequency, which can automatically adapt to the requirements of time-frequency signal analysis, so that it can focus on any detail of the signal. The wavelet transform is an inner product of a square integrable function and a wavelet function with good local properties in the time-frequency domain, as shown in Eq. (1).

$$W_f(a, b) = \langle f, \psi_{a,b} \rangle = \frac{1}{\sqrt{a}} \int_{-\infty}^{+\infty} f(t) \psi^* \left(\frac{t - b}{a} \right) dt \tag{1}$$

Where a > 0 is the scale factor, b is the displacement factor, * means the complex conjugate, and $\psi_{a,b}(t)$ is the wavelet basis function.

3.2   Ratio of Inspiratory Time to Expiratory Time (RIE)

RIE is a commonly used index for current respiratory data analysis, and the value is the ratio of the inspiratory time to the expiratory time in one breathing cycle. Therefore, we identify the crests and troughs of the data. The trough to the crest is an "inspiration" process, and the crest to the trough is an "expiration" process, as shown in the following figure.

3.3   Support Vector Machine (SVM)

The goal of the paper is to classify respiratory data as normal or abnormal by breathing characteristics. For this two-class problem, SVM is a suitable method. SVM is a two-class classification model. It is one of the more mainstream domain classifiers before the widespread use of deep neural networks. It has been widely used in visual model recognition and many other fields [8].

The SVM can map the linear indivisible problem of the original data into the higher-dimensional feature space through the kernel function, and transform it into a quadratic programming problem for solving linear constraints. Given a set of training samples $D = ((x_1, y_1), (x_2, y_2), \ldots\ldots, (x_m, y_m))$, $y_i \in \{-1, 1\}$, suppose we can use a hyperplane in a certain space: $w \cdot x = 0$ divides the training set into two categories. The most suitable hyperplane is the maximum margin hyperplane [9]. By solving the Eq. (2), the optimal values of w and b can be obtained.

$$f(x) = \text{sgn}\left(\sum_{i=1}^{n} a_i y_i K(x, x_i) + b\right) \tag{2}$$

Where $K(x, x_i)$ is a kernel function, which corresponds to constructing an optimal segmentation plane in the input space, and a_i and b are solved by the SVC learning algorithm [9].

3.4   Long Short-Term Memory (LSTM)

The respiratory data acquired by the respiratory belt is continuous data with time series characteristics. According to this feature, the LSTM network suitable for processing time series is also proposed for classification.

LSTM is a special RNN that solves the problem of gradient explosion and gradient disappearance of RNN. This is mainly because LSTM eliminates the "multiply" calculation method in simple RNN and changes it to "accumulate" mode [10]. LSTM introduces a memory unit so that the network can control when to forget unwanted information, when to update the memory unit with new input information, and to protect and control information through forgetting, input, and output gates. The LSTM update method at time t is as follows:

$$
\begin{aligned}
f_t &= \sigma\left(W_f \cdot \left[h_{t-1}, x_t\right] + b_f\right) \\
i_t &= \sigma\left(W_i \cdot \left[h_{t-1}, x_t\right] + b_i\right) \\
\tilde{C}_t &= \tanh\left(W_C \cdot \left[h_{t-1}, x_t\right] + b_C\right) \\
C_t &= f_t * C_{t-1} + i_t * \tilde{C}_t \\
o_t &= \sigma\left(W_o \cdot \left[h_{t-1}, x_t\right] + b_o\right) \\
h_t &= o_t * \tanh(C_t)
\end{aligned}
\tag{3}
$$

Where h_{t-1} is the output of the previous moment, x_t is the input of time t, and σ is the activation function. The forgotten gate f_t controls how much information each unit needs to forget, the input gate i_t controls new information, and the output gate o_t controls the output information (Fig. 2).

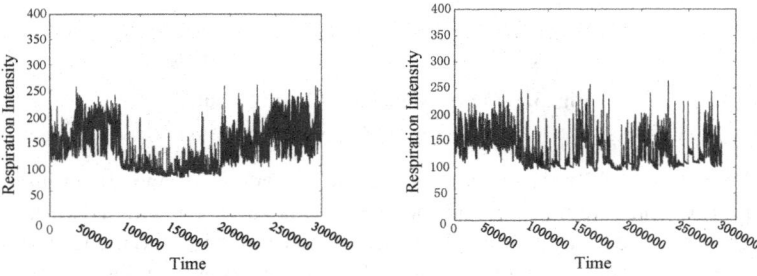

Fig. 2. Example of normal and abnormal data of breathing.

4   Experiment

4.1   Data Sources

The data used in the experiments in this paper were from 342 samples of normal and abnormal breathing data collected by the Academy of Chinese Medicine, including 55 abnormal samples and 287 normal samples, each with a decimal data of about 24 h. The visualization results of the data are shown in the following figure. Since the difference between the sample can not be clearly distinguished from the naked eye, it is necessary to perform appropriate processing on the data and then use a certain analysis method to perform the discrimination.

4.2   Data Preprocessing

Firstly, the original data is filtered. For our data, the wavelet transform method is selected to remove the baseline drift operation. The wavelet transform result is shown in Fig. 3.

4.3   LSTM

Our goal is to determine whether the breathing is abnormal based on the data, to treat it as a sequence classification task, and because the respiratory data is time-correlated, we decided to use LSTM network structure. Using an LSTM unit, the parameter is set to 32 (unit_num), the training data is in one-to-one correspondence with the label, the training

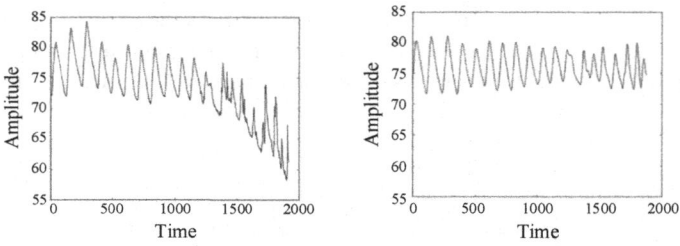

Fig. 3. Original signal and filtering result.

sample dimension is (7200, 10), the label is one-hot encoded, and (0, 1) indicates an exception, (1, 0) indicate normal, and the step size is set to 10. The network structure design is shown in the figure below. The processed data is input into the LSTM network of different hidden neurons, and the classified results are shown in Table 1 (Fig. 4).

Table 1. Experimental results

Method	Accuracy
LSTM (10+32+2)*	60.2
LSTM (10+64+2)	63.1
LSTM (10+128+2)	61.5
LSTM (10+32+64+2)	65.4
LSTM (10+64+64+2)	67.8
RIE+SVM	72.8
RIE+LSTM (10+32+2)	73.5
RIE+LSTM (10+64+2)	75.7
RIE+LSTM (10+128+2)	73.1
RIE+LSTM (10+32+64+2)	76.8
RIE+LSTM (10+64+64+2)	**79.2**
RIE+LSTM (10+64+128+2)	75.5

*Here is the number of hidden layer neural units, the first 10 is the dimension of the input data at each time point of the input layer, and the last 2 means that the input layer is the binary network, the middle number is the hidden layer and the number of neurons in each layer. For example, (10+32+2) means that the hidden layer is 1, and the number of hidden units is 32.

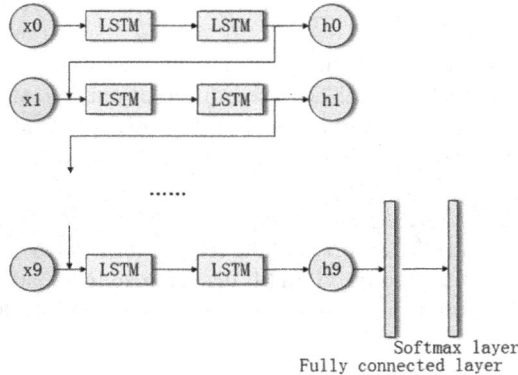

Fig. 4. LSTM network structure diagram.

4.4 RIE+SVM

The crests and troughs are identified according to the filtered result, then the respiratory time and the expiratory time of each breathing cycle can be obtained, and the RIE is calculated according to Eq. (2), as shown in Fig. 5. The result is input into the SVM, and the classification accuracy is 73%, which is 6% higher than that of the single LSTM structure.

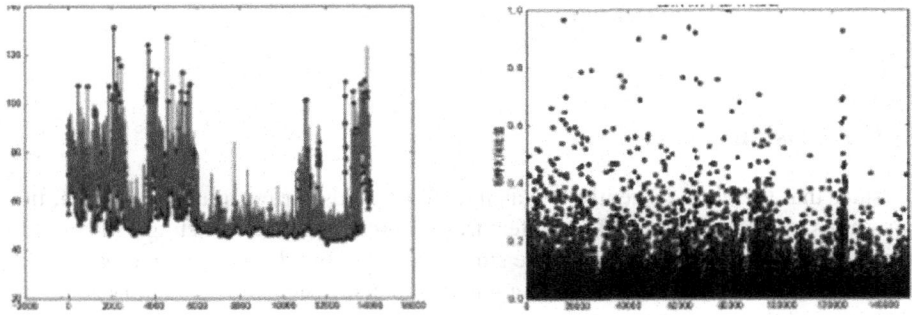

Fig. 5. Example of trough identification, and RIE characteristic.

4.5 RIE+LSTM

The result of RIE is input into the part 4.3 designed LSTM network structure. According to the experimental results, when the LSTM hidden layer is 2 layers and the number of hidden units is 64+64, the classification effect is the best, about 80%, which has improved the accuracy by about 15% compared with simply using LSTM structure, and about 5% higher than the RIE+SVM. The results are shown in Table 1.

4.6 Discussion

In this paper, the processed respiratory data were tested by LSTM, RIE+SVM, RIE+LSTM. The hidden layer of LSTM used different number of neural unit, some experimental results of the loss curve are shown in Fig. 6. It can be seen that the method with the highest accuracy has the fastest and lowest drop in the RIE+LSTM (10+64+64+2) loss. The accuracy results are shown in Table 1, from the results that the accuracy of using LSTM alone is not very high, about 62%, and the 64 hidden units has the best classification result. The accuracy of the combination of RIE and SVM increased to about 75%. After SVM changed to LSTM, the accuracy is greatly improved. When the nerve units set to 64+64 the accuracy is the best, reaching about 80%.

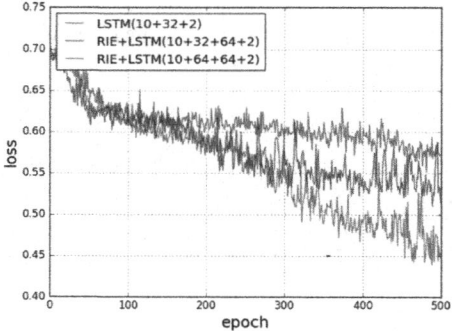

Fig. 6. Comparison of loss descent curve.

5 Conclusion

Consider that there are currently few analytical methods for respiratory belt data, this paper aims to find relatively effective features for breathing data to distinguish between normal and abnormal populations. The single LSTM network structure compared with the traditional method which extracting features to distinguish the respiratory state, the result proved the effectiveness of that kind of network structure. At last combined the LSTM structure with the manual features. Through the above experimental results, it can be concluded that the classification effect of the third method is better than the others, and the accuracy rate is about 79%. Compared with the single LSTM structure, the accuracy is improved by about 15%, which proves the effectiveness of the proposed algorithm. The effectiveness also provides good data support for the next breath clinical trials and pathological tests. In the future, we consider using other network structures such as recurrent neural trees, random forests, etc., and discussing with medical personnel to find other features other than RIE and expect better classification results.

Acknowledgements. This research work is supported by the grant of Guangxi science and technology development project (No: AB17195027), the grant of Guangxi scientific research and technology development plan project (No: AB18221011), the grant of

Guangxi Key Laboratory of Trusted Software of Guilin University of Electronic Technology (No: KX201620), the grant of Guilin science and technology projectResearch and application demonstration of key technologies of somatosensory interaction based on gesture (No: 20180107-4).

References

1. Zhenbao, L, Xiaohui Qi, Weina, L. et al.: Study on respiratory signal detection belt based on PVDF. Piezoelectr. Acoust. Opt. **36**(1), 72–75 (2014)
2. Lin, F., Xiangdong, C., Ning, L.: Wireless breath detection system based on rapid response humidity sensor. Sens. Microsyst. **34**(3), 84–86 (2015)
3. Leanders, S., Laguna, P., Sornmo, L.: Estimation of the respiration frequency using spatial inform sction in the VCG. Med. Eng. Phys. **25**(6), 501–507 (2003)
4. Sebastijan, Š., Damjan, Z.: Heartbeat and respiration detection from optical interferometric signals by using a multimethod approach. IEEE Trans. Biomed. Eng. **59**(10), 2922–2929 (2012)
5. Raji, A., Devi, P.K., Jeyaseeli, P.G., et al.: Respiratory monitoring system for asthma patients based on IoT. In: Proceeding of the Online International Conference on Green Engineering and Technologies. IEEE (2017)
6. Agnel John, K.J., Pamela, D.: Arduino uno Based Obstructive Sleep Apnea Detection Using Respiratory signal. Int. J. Res. Eng. Technol. **4**(3), 599–603 (2015)
7. Ping, C., Jilun, Y., et al.: Comparison of baseline drift removal methods and algorithm implementation in ECG signal. Chin. J. Med. Devices **42**(5), 326–329 (2018)
8. Schuldt, C., Laptev, I., Caputo, B.: Recognizing human actions a local SVM approach. In: Proceedings of the 17th International Conference on Pattern Recognition (2004)
9. Vapnik, V.N.: Statistical Learning Theory. A Wiley-Interscience Publication, New York (1998)
10. Dunlap, J.C.: Molecular bases for circadian clocks. Cell **96**(2), 271–290 (1999)

Target Tracking Algorithm Based on Density Clustering

Jinlong Chen, Qinghao Zeng$^{(\boxtimes)}$, and Xingguo Qin

Guangxi Key Laboratory of Trusted Software, Guilin University of Electronic Technology,
Guilin 541004, China
641577329@qq.com, 529045053@qq.com

Abstract. The traditional Siamese network-based target tracking algorithm needs to use the convolution feature of the target to scan around the target location when predicting the location of the target in the next frame image, and perform similarity calculation to obtain the similarity score matrix with the highest score. It is the next frame target position. The highest similarity score often does not represent the precise target position of the target, which is often affected by the sliding step size during scanning. Aiming at this problem, this paper proposes a target tracking method based on density clustering. By combining the Siamese network to predict the next frame target position, and adding the target's motion trajectory information, the direction of the target motion is given more weight, the other directions are given a smaller weight, and finally the target position is predicted by the density clustering method. The results show that the proposed algorithm effectively improves the accuracy of the target location prediction of the Siamese network when tracking targets.

Keywords: Target tracking · Siamese network · Clustering

1 Introduction

In recent years, with the development of science and technology and the increasingly diversified needs of people's living environment, the rapid development of artificial intelligence technology has been promoted. As an important branch of artificial intelligence, computer vision technology has attracted more and more scholars and experts to study. As an indispensable part of the field of computer vision, target tracking technology has a wide range of applications in video surveillance, autonomous driving, military reconnaissance, medical and life. The target tracking is to predict the position and width and height information of the target in the subsequent frames of the video according to the coordinate information of the target image of the first frame of the video without prior knowledge. The target tracking process can be roughly divided into three steps, namely feature extraction, model building, and adaptive update model. The main problem of target tracking is how to achieve accurate positioning targets in scenes with occlusion, illumination changes, motion blur, complex background and target deformation.

Y. Tan et al. (Eds.): ICSI 2020, LNCS 12145, pp. 556–563, 2020.
https://doi.org/10.1007/978-3-030-53956-6_51

Over the years, target tracking has become a hot issue in the field of computer vision, and more and more related methods, but how to track the position of the target more accurately under various conditions is still a problem. At the current location, the method of target tracking can be roughly divided into two categories. One is the traditional target tracking method based on machine learning. This kind of method usually consists of three parts: appearance model, running model and search strategy. The appearance model is used to estimate the possible state of a specific location. The motion model is used to describe the state information of the target's possible change with time. The search strategy is used to locate the target position of the next frame. Traditional target tracking methods are characterized by faster speeds, but the accuracy of tracking targets is not sufficient. In the KCF [1] algorithm, an appearance model is established by a discriminative correlation filter, and the target is located according to the correlation of the filter and the target directly. In the Kalman [2] filter algorithm, a sequential random approach is established for linear and Gaussian observation noise, and then statistical methods are used to locate the target, but the nonlinear motion template cannot be tracked. High-order particle filtering is introduced in the HOPF [3] method to track targets, but the classifier training costs are too high and result in data loss. The second type of method is a target tracking method based on deep learning. Deep neural network has made great progress in image classification, target detection and recognition, and target tracking in recent years because of its powerful feature extraction ability. This type of method extracts to the target's effective feature representation through a large amount of data training, thereby regressing or classifying the target position through these features and neural networks. One of the more representative ones is the SiamFC [4] method, which calculates the similarity matrix of the target and the next frame image through the fully convolved Siamese network [5] to locate the target. Later, the SiamRPN [6] method was added to the RPN structure in the Faster-RCNN [7] to return the target frame width to a more accurate tracking target. Although SiamFC proposed a very constructive idea to introduce the Siamese network to target tracking, it is still not accurate enough for the target positioning, and the target frame of the tracking has always been close to the initial frame, and it is unable to adapt to the change of the target. In order to solve this problem, this paper adds a clustering method, first extracts the target features through the Siamese network, assigns corresponding weights according to the target's motion trajectory, and then uses the similarity score matrix and density clustering algorithm to locate the target. Tracking the target by clustering instead of the initial frame achieves the goal of improving the accuracy of the target location in the target tracking, and can adapt to the change of the target.

2 Introduction

2.1 Siamese Network

The Siamese network is a depth-based similarity measure that learns similarity measures in data and then uses the learned knowledge to compare and match samples of new unknown categories. The Siamese network is composed of two identical networks. The two networks share weights. Just like a conjoined person, there are two people's thoughts, but they share a body. In 2016, the Siamese network was applied to the target tracking technology. In the tracking process, the convolution feature of the target image is used to scan the convolution feature of the next frame image by a certain step size, and then the similarity score of the current target image at each position of the next frame image is calculated. Finally, the position of the target is located according to the similarity score matrix.

As shown in Fig. 1, Network1 and Network2 are a group of neural networks with the same structure and shared weights. In this paper, a convolutional neural network (CNN) is used. The input of the network is two different images, and the corresponding convolution feature representation is obtained through the neural network output. The vector, by calculating the distance between the two vectors, obtains the similarity between the images. The more similar the two images are, the smaller the distance will be, and the bigger the difference. The distance is calculated as shown in Eq. (1):

$$D_w(x_1, x_2) = \|G_w(x_1) - G_w(x_2)\| \tag{1}$$

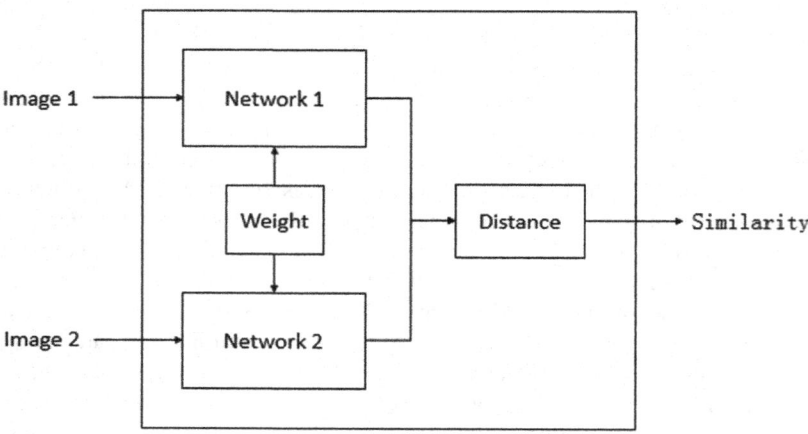

Fig. 1. Siamese network.

Where x_1 and x_2 are two pictures of the same size input by the network, w is the weight of the network training, G_w (x) is the vector obtained by the picture through the network, and D_w (x_1, x_2) is the vector of the two network outputs. The Euclidean distance between the two is used to judge the similarity between the two images. In the target tracking, you need to enter the current target and the next frame image. In the vector outputted by the network, the vector obtained by the network convolution of the target will be smaller than the vector obtained by convolving the next frame image. The vector requiring the target is scanned on the vector of the next frame according to a certain step size to obtain a similarity score matrix. And in order to cope with the change of the target's movement, it will be calculated on multiple scales when calculating the similarity score.

2.2 Density-Based Clustering Method

Clustering is the process of dividing a collection of data objects into one or more similar clusters, so that each object in the same cluster has a high similarity, and objects in different clusters have higher dissimilarity. According to the scale of clustering, clustering methods can be roughly divided into three categories, namely distance-based, interconnect-based, and density-based. The distance-based clustering method usually evaluates the similarity between the targets by the distance between the targets. The density-based clustering method mainly uses the density function to determine the similarity between targets. Interconnectivity-based clustering methods typically combine highly connected objects into one class based on a graph or hypergraph model. In 2014, the Alex Rodriguez [8] team published a text on Science about density-based clustering, which argues that cluster centers are surrounded by lower-density neighbors and farther away from other denser points. The method proposes two keywords, namely local density and distance. The local density is the number of other points within a certain distance from the point. The distance is the smallest cluster of points to any other denser point.

$$\rho_i = \sum_j F\left(d_{ij} - d_c\right) \tag{2}$$

$$F(x) = \begin{cases} 1, x < 0; \\ 0, x \geq 0; \end{cases} \tag{3}$$

Where ρ_i is the density of point i, d_ij is the distance from point i to point j, and d_c is a truncation distance. If the difference between d_ij and d_c is less than 0, F(x) is equal to 1, otherwise F(x) is equal to 0. However, in target tracking, only the target position of the next frame needs to be located, so only one cluster needs to be clustered (Fig. 2).

| Original image | Clustering | Target location |

Fig. 2. Density-based clustering.

In the method of this paper, the motion trajectory information before the target is added in the clustering process, so the clustering part of this paper will be clustered twice. The first clustering is to cluster the target's scoring matrix with the target's trajectory information to get the exact location of the target. The second clustering is a clustering of the target's width and height, and obtaining the target's accurate width and height information.

$$\rho_i = \sum_j F\left(\varphi_{ij}\left(s_{ij}, w_{ij}\right) - \varphi_c(s, w)\right) \tag{4}$$

Where s_ij is the difference between the similarities of the i point and the j point, and w_ij is the difference between the weights of the i point and the j point. In this paper, the motion trajectory information of the target is added to the prediction target process, and the density calculation changes the distance into the difference between the density and the weight product. For weight setting, since the target tracking is a continuous process, the weight of the direction before the target should be larger, and the weight of the opposite direction should be smaller. At the same time, we also cluster the width and height, combined with the width and height information of the prediction frame, combined with the weight of the prediction frame, to calculate the final target frame, so that the target tracking is more accurate.

The overall structure of the proposed method is shown in Fig. 3. The current target image and the target image of the next frame are input to the network, and the similarity score matrix of the target on the next frame image is calculated by the Siamese network. Then, according to the motion trajectory before the target, the scoring matrix is given corresponding weights. Finally, the density clustering algorithm is used to cluster the target position and width and height, and the exact position of the target is obtained, and the moving direction information of the target is updated.

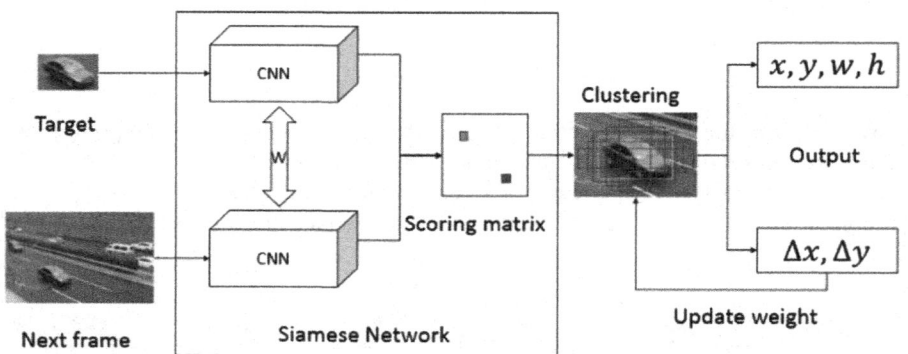

Fig. 3. Overall structure of the algorithm.

3   Experiment

The training and detection data of the method in this paper are from the public VOT dataset, and we randomly select part of the video data for training. The algorithm in this paper mainly improves on the traditional target tracking algorithm based on Siamese network, hoping to track the target more accurately (Fig. 4).

We randomly selected part of the video data from the VOT dataset to test on our method, SiamFC method, and particle filtering-based target tracking method. The image marked with a red box in the picture is the real position of the target during video tracking. The image with a yellow box is the tracking effect of our algorithm. The image with a blue box is the effect of the SiamFC method. The effect of particle filter on target tracking

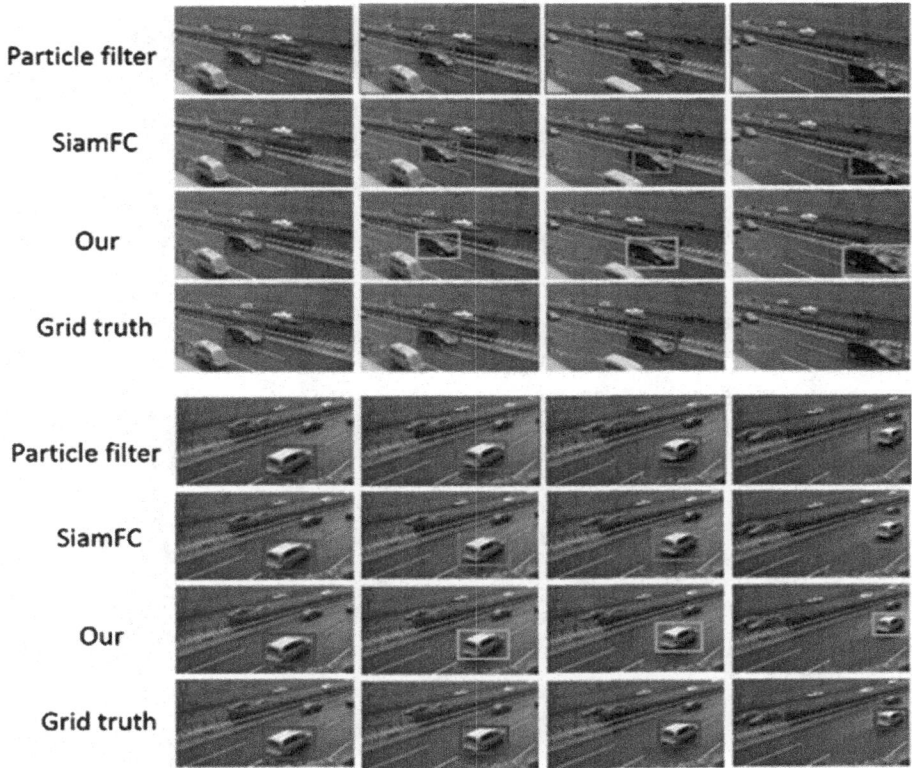

Fig. 4. Experimental comparison.

method. It can be seen from the figure that although the SiamFC method and particle filtering-based target tracking method can track the target during the tracking process, the tracking accuracy is low, and the tracking frame is always close to the frame marked by the initial frame Size, little change. In the method of this paper, both the center point and the width and height of the target are clustered. As can be seen from the figure, the box obtained by the clustering can well adapt to the change of the target (Figs. 5 and 6).

We compared Particle filter, SiamFC and our method. Statistics on accuracy and IOU. It can be seen that our method is 5%–10% higher in accuracy than Particle filter, slightly better than SiamFC. However, our method on IOU is about 10% higher than Particle filter and SiamFC. It can be seen that this paper proposes to add clustering and target motion trajectory information, which can make tracking more accurate in target tracking.

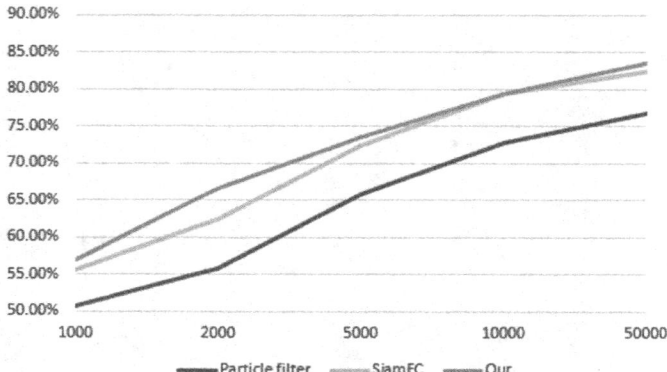

Fig. 5. Target tracking accuracy increases with training samples.

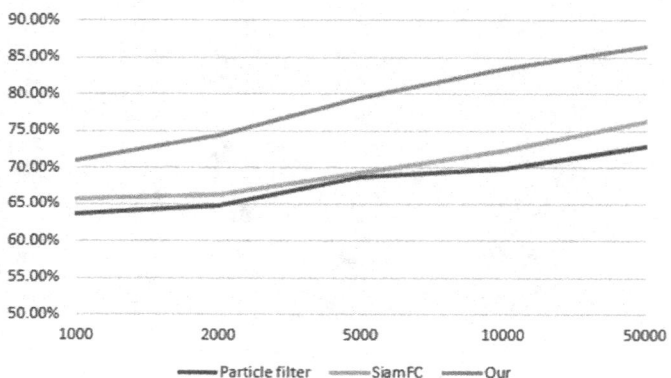

Fig. 6. Target tracking increases in IOU with training samples.

4 Conclusion

For the traditional Siamese network-based target tracking method, when tracking the target, the target position prediction is affected by the sliding step and the accuracy is low. This paper proposes the motion rule information before the predicted target position is added to the target, and better predicts the target position. And the density-based clustering method is added to locate the target frame, and the target center position and the target width and height are respectively clustered to better predict the position of the target in the next frame image. The experimental results show that the proposed method can effectively improve the accuracy of the prediction of the target position of the next frame without losing the success rate of tracking. In the next phase of the study, we can introduce the idea of online learning in the tracking process, while tracking the target, while updating the network weights, and constantly learning the new characteristics of the target in the movement process.

Acknowledgements. The National Natural Science Foundation of China (61866007), the Natural Science Foundation of Guangxi District (2018GXNSFDA138006). Research and application demonstration of intelligent recommendation system for tourist routes based on user preferences Guangxi Scientific Research and Technology Development Plan Project (Guike AB17195027). Research and application demonstration of key technologies for indoor positioning and location service of intelligent guides in karst cave scenic areas Guangxi Scientific Research and Technology Development Plan Project (Guike AB18221011). Funded by the research project of Guangxi Trusted Software Key Laboratory (No. kx201620). (Guilin Key Laboratory of Trustworthy Software, Guilin University of Electronic Technology, Guilin, Guangxi 541004). Guilin Scientific Research and Technology Development Plan Project 20180107-4.

References

1. Henriques, J.F., Caseiro, R., Martins, P.: High-speed tracking with kernelized correlation filters. IEEE Trans. Pattern Anal. Mach. Intell. **37**, 583–596 (2015)
2. Bi, H.Y., Ma, J.W., Wang, F.J.: An improved particle filter algorithm based on ensemble Kalman filter and Markov chain Monte Carlo method. J. Sel. Top. Appl. Earth Obs. Remote Sens. **8**(2), 447–459 (2017)
3. Xiao, Q.L., Fang, Y.L., Liu, Q.: Online machine health prognostics based on modified duration-dependent hidden semi-Markov model and high-order particle filtering. Int. J. Adv. Manuf. Technol. **94**, 1–15 (2017)
4. Bertinetto, L., Valmadre, J., Henriques, J.F., Vedaldi, A., Torr, P.H.S.: Fully-convolutional siamese networks for object tracking. In: Hua, G., Jégou, H. (eds.) ECCV 2016. LNCS, vol. 9914, pp. 850–865. Springer, Cham (2016). https://doi.org/10.1007/978-3-319-48881-3_56
5. Chopra, S. Hadsell, R. LeCun, Y.: Learning a similarity metric discriminatively, with application to face verification. In: IEEE Computer Society Conference on Computer Vision and Pattern Recognition, pp. 539–546 (2005)
6. Li, B., Yan, J.J., Wu, W.: High performance visual tracking with siamese region proposal network. In: IEEE Computer Society Conference on Computer Vision and Pattern Recognition, pp. 8971–8980 (2018)
7. Ren, S.Q., He, K., Girshick, R.: Faster R-CNN: Towards real-time object detection with region proposal networks. IEEE Trans. Pattern Anal. Mach. Intell. 1137–1149 (2017)
8. Alex, R., Alessandro, L.: Clustering by fast search and find of density peaks. Science **344**, 1492–1496 (2014)
9. Bo, L. Wei, W. Qiang, W.: SiamRPN ++: evolution of siamese visual tracking with very deep networks. In: Proceeding of 2019 IEEE Conference on Computer Vision and Pattern Recognition (2019)
10. Wang, N., Yeung, D.Y.: Learning a deep compact image representation for visual tracking. In: International Conference on Neural Information Processing Systems, pp. 809–817 (2013)

A Method for Localization and Classification of Breast Ultrasound Tumors

Wanying Mo[1]([✉]), Yuntao Zhu[2], and Chaoyun Wang[2]

[1] Computer Science and Technology College, Jilin University, Changchun 130012, China
mowanying@163.com
[2] School of Automation, Harbin Engineering University, Harbin 150000, China

Abstract. Ultrasound instruments are suitable for large-scale examination of breast tumors, especially for women from Asian whose glands are dense. However, ultrasound images have the low contrast and resolution, blurred boundary and artifacts, which bring great difficulties to the interpretation of the junior doctor. However, traditional methods of breast ultrasound tumor recognition often use manually extracted features to gradually realize ROI region location and tumor classification with low accuracy, poor robustness and weak universality. Deep learning is limited to the location of tumor ROI region or the classification of a given tumor ROI region. In this paper, YOLOV3 algorithm is used for breast ultrasound tumor recognition, which could realize ROI localization and tumor classification at the same time. In addition, K-Means is optimized by K-Means++ and K-Mediods algorithm to generate anchor boxes of YOLOV3, and based on the Darknet-53 network structure of YOLOV3, ResNet and DenseNet are combined to design ResNet-DenseNet_Darknet-53. The proposed method is tested on the breast ultrasound tumor data set. Experiments show that the improved YOLOV3 algorithm shows better detection results on multiple evaluation indicators.

Keywords: Breast tumor recognition · YOLOV3 · Anchor boxes · ResNet-DenseNet_Darknet-53

1 Introduction

According to the American Cancer Statistics of 2016 published by the American Cancer Society, breast cancer is the most common malignant tumor in women and is expected to monopolize 29% of all new women's cases [1]. Therefore, screening and early diagnosis of breast cancer are very necessary. At this stage, the main methods to diagnose breast cancer are MRI, PET, ultrasound imaging and X-ray, Compared with MRI, PET and X-ray, ultrasound imaging technology is not only inexpensive and non-radioactive, but also can show most of the lesion areas in each section, especially for more compact breast tissues of young Asian women [2, 3].

Although ultrasound imaging has become the main tool for early diagnosis, it still faces great challenges:

(1) Ultrasound images have a lot of noise;

© Springer Nature Switzerland AG 2020
Y. Tan et al. (Eds.): ICSI 2020, LNCS 12145, pp. 564–574, 2020.
https://doi.org/10.1007/978-3-030-53956-6_52

(2) the boundaries in the ultrasound image is blurred;

(3) Because the acoustic impedance of different human tissues and organs has large differences, it is easy to cause artifacts in the ultrasound image [4].

In order to solve this problem, researchers have proposed different methods.

2 Related Work

In recent years, with the rise of deep learning, some researchers have proposed a method based on deep learning for tumor recognition. But the methods of breast cancer recognition based on deep learning are basically limited to use image segmentation to locate ROI region or classify a given ROI region as benign or malignant, but they can not simultaneously locate ROI region and classify tumors, which brings great inconvenience to the diagnosis of medical staff. Recently, Yap et al. and Chiao et al. proposed to use improved FCN-AlexNet and improved Mask R-CNN semantics segmentation model to realize end-to-end ultrasound tumor recognition [5, 6], which locate and classify tumors at the same time, not only accurately locate the boundary of ultrasound tumors, but also realize the recognition of benign and malignant tumors. However, this method of image semantics segmentation requires manual labeling of a large number of tumor segmentation data sets, and the process of making the segmentation data sets is very cumbersome, which greatly increases the burden of professional doctor labeling.

In this paper, we propose a target detection algorithm based on deep learning for breast cancer recognition based on YOLOV3[7], which is the best target detection algorithm among all the other methods and could realize ROI localization and tumor classification at the same time. In addition, K-Means [8] is optimized by K-Means++ [9] and K-Mediods [10] algorithm to generate anchor boxes of YOLOV3 to solve the problem of instability of the initial center point and the problem of outlier sensitivity, respectively, and then based on the Darknet-53 network structure of YOLOV3, ResNet and DenseNet [11] are combined to design ResNet-DenseNet_Darknet-53 to solve the problem that features of ultrasound image of breast tumor are more difficult to extract than other images.

3 Method

3.1 Traditional YOLOV3 Algorithm

The YOLOV3 algorithm combines the tasks of classification and location into a step to directly predict the position and category of objects. It includes a new feature extraction network Darknet-53 and three scales of YOLO layer, which are used for feature extraction and multi-scale prediction, respectively. Its network structure is shown in Fig. 1 [11].

The Darknet-53 layer consists of one convolution block DBL and five residual blocks resn (n = 1, 2, 4, 8). DBL is a collection of convolution (conv), batch normalization (BN), and activation function (Leaky relu), which is the smallest component in YOLOV3. After feature extraction from Darknet-53 network, output the feature map with size of 13 * 13 * 1024. After upper sampling and shallow feature map splicing (see concat

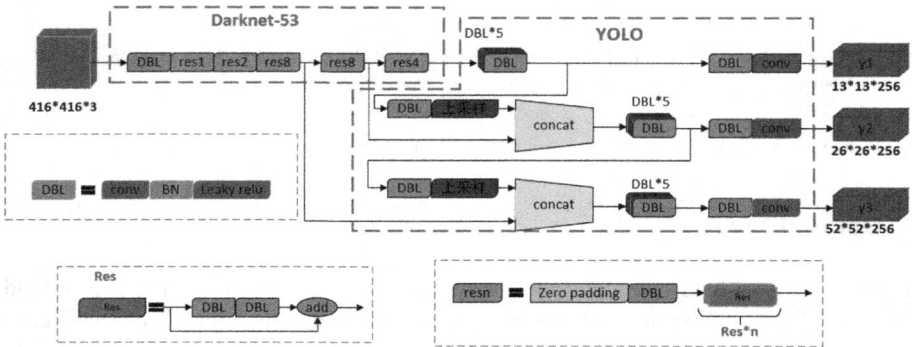

Fig. 1. YOLOV3 network architecture

in Fig. 1) [12], the feature map with three scales is output for predicting the results of YOLO layer detection. That is to say, each box is responsible for the regression of three anchor boxes.

3.2 Optimization of Anchor Box

The anchor box is used as a priori box to predict the target boundary and is designed according to different data sets. The existing YOLOV3 uses K-Means algorithm to cluster the annotated data of COCO dataset. First, it reads the data set file of PASCLA VOC format to get the category and border of the target. Then, it normalizes the border data to get the width w and height h of the target, which is used as the data to be clustered. The normalization process is shown in the formulas (1-1) and (1-2)where x_{min}, y_{min} and x_{max}, y_{max} represent the upper left corner coordinates and the lower right corner coordinates of the border, respectively. *width* and *height* represent the image size, respectively.

$$w = \frac{x_{max} - x_{min}}{width} \tag{1-1}$$

$$h = \frac{y_{max} - y_{min}}{height} \tag{1-2}$$

After that, nine clustering centers are initialized, each of which describes the length and width of the rectangular box. Computing *IOU* (the intersection and parallelism ratio) of rectangular boxes described by clustering center and data to be classified, using distance D as clustering basis, updating clustering center by means of in-cluster mean, and getting the final anchor box by optimizing the minimum clustering loss function J. The *IOU* expression is (1-3), the distance calculation formula D is (1-4), and the loss function J is (1-5).

$$IOU = \frac{area\ (box \cap centroid)}{area\ (box \cup centroid)} \tag{1-3}$$

$$D = 1 - IOU_{(box,centriod)} \tag{1-4}$$

$$J = \sum_{k=1}^{k} \sum_{i=1}^{n_k} D_i \tag{1-5}$$

where, 'box' represents the real target box, 'centroid' the candidate box, J the clustering loss function, K the number of categories, and n_k the number of sample points in a cluster.

In order to make the network better to learn the location and feature size of the target, this paper uses K-Means++ algorithm and K-Mediods algorithm to optimize the original K-Means algorithm to obtain a merger anchor box with higher intersection. The specific steps of the improved algorithm based on K-Means are as follows (where K = 9):

Step 1: Obtain m samples $(Q_m = \{(x_1, y_1), (x_2, y_2), \ldots \ldots, (x_m, y_m)\})$ which are clustered with normalized pretreatment of breast ultrasound tumor data sets;
Step 2: Select a sample $c_i = (x_i, y_i)(i \in [1, m])$ randomly from the data set as the clustering center;
Step 3: Calculate the distance d_j between each sample point c_j and c_i and the probability p_j according to the formulas in Formulas (1-6) and (1-7), respectively, where $j \in [1, m]$ and $j \neq i$;

$$d_j = 1 - IOU_{(c_j, c_i)} \tag{1-6}$$

$$p_j = d_j^2 \tag{1-7}$$

Step 4: Select the sample points with the largest probability p_j as the new clustering center.
Step 5: Repeat step 2 and step 3 until K cluster centers are selected. The corresponding K clusters are generated at the same time. The K-Means++ algorithm process is over.
Step 6: Calculate the distance $\hat{d}_j$ from center c_j of each sample in Q_m to cluster centers $n_1, n_2, \ldots .. n_k$, according to formula (1-6), corresponding samples to minimum distance are assigned to M_i in the cluster to form K clusters;
Step 7: Calculate the distance from each sample point $\hat{x}_i$ ($i \in (1, n_i)$, n_i denotes the number of all sample points) to all other sample points in each M_i according to formula (1-8), and use the sample point with the smallest distance to all other sample points as a new clustering center to update K clustering centers $(n_1, n_2, \ldots n_k)$

$$n_i = \arg\min_{\hat{x}_i \in M_i} \sum_{\hat{y} \in M_i} (1 - IOU(\hat{x}_i, \hat{y})) \tag{1-8}$$

Step 8: If the objective function E in formula (1-9) does not change, it will be optimal, otherwise, the algorithm will repeat step 7 and step 8.

$$E = \sum_{i=1}^{K} \sum_{j=1}^{m} (1 - IOU(n_i, c_j)) \tag{1-9}$$

where n_i denotes the number of sample points in cluster i.

3.3   Design of ResNet-DenseNet_Darknet-53

In this section, based on the existing Darknet-53 network structure, we use ResNet and the DensetNet to design a method named ResNet_ DenseNet-Darknet-53 for recognizing ultrasound images.

(1)   ResNet-DenseNet_Darknet-53

In traditional Darknet-53, when the feature map of the previous layer is input to resn ($n = 1, 2, 4, 8$), a conv3 down-sampling operation is first performed, and then transmitted to a network containing n ($n = 1, 2, 4, 8$) residuals Res to obtain the final output, The output of each residual network Res is constructed by feature fusion of a conv1 and a conv3 with short connections. But unlike Inception and other networks, this fusion does not use tensor splicing. It directly adds the pixels of each channel, so the number of channels will not be changed, as shown in Fig. 2.

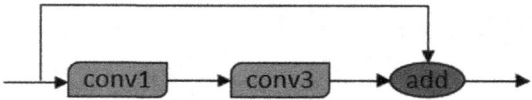

Fig. 2.   Structural diagram of Res network

In order to describe the ResNet-DenseNet_Darknet-53 conveniently, this paper takes res4 as an example to explain this process in detail. res4 consists of a conv3 and four Res. And the size of the input feature graph of res 4 is 26 * 26 * 512. First, a conv3 is used to downsample the feature graph to make its size 13 * 13 * 1024. Then, the output result is obtained after four consecutive Res processing of the feature graph. Because the corresponding channel pixels are directly added in Res, the input and output sizes remain to be unchanged after each Res, as shown in Fig. 3.

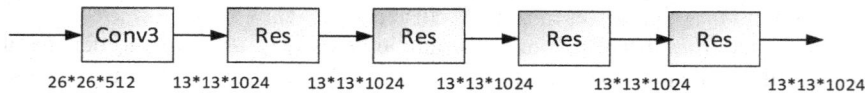

Fig. 3.   Structural diagram of res4 network

After introducing ResNet and DensetNet, the improved res4 network is shown in Fig. 4. The size of input feature graph is 26 * 26 * 512. After conv3 down-sampling, it becomes 13 * 13 * 1024. It should be pointed out that the number of conv1 and conv3 in each Res in the improved res4 is 256, so the output dimension of each Res is 256. Now all Res outputs are connected in pairs, so that each layer of the network output accepts the characteristics of all the layers in front of it as input. After the output of each residual network Res is spliced by features, the output feature maps are 13 * 13 * 1280, 13 * 13 * 1536, 13 * 13 * 1792 and 13 * 13 * 2048, respectively. Considering the output of the last residual network Res, the dimension of the feature map after feature splicing is twice as large as that of the feature map after conv3 downsampling. Drawing on the idea of pixel addition of the corresponding channel of ResNet, the feature map of the output after the first conv3 downsampling and the feature map after the conv1 feature reduced dimension are added to the corresponding channel pixels (as shown by the green line in the figure). Finally, a feature graph of 13 * 13 * 1024 size is output.

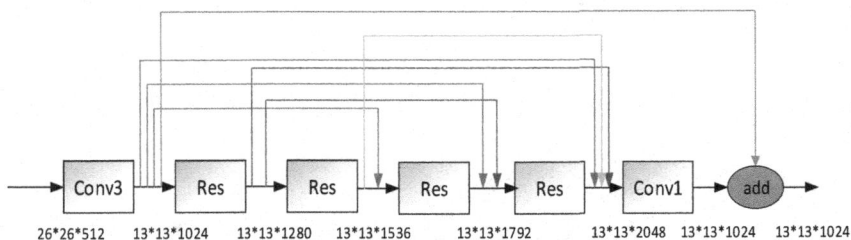

Fig. 4. Structural diagram of improved res4 network

Since res1 contains only one Res, no improvement is needed. Similarly, other resns (n = 2, 8) are improved according to the idea of res4. The difference is that the number of conv1 and conv3 in each Res is different. The number of the first res2, the first res8, the second res8 and the first res4 are 64, 32, 64 and 256, respectively. Thus, we construct a new Darknet network based on the ResNet and the DenseNet.

4   Experiments and Results Analysis

4.1   Data Set

The breast ultrasound data used in the experiment have been screened and eliminated from the 2011 original cases of different ages, regions and ethnicities by professional doctors of Harbin Medical University from 2015 to 2019. There are 13,586 original images with a size of 768*576. The effective images are 3259 pictures containing tumors, including 1199 benign patients and 2060 malignant patients. The data set is directly divided into training set and test set according to 4: 1. As shown in Table 1, there are 2608 training sets, including 960 benign training sets and 1648 malignant training sets. There are a total of 651 test sets, including 239 benign tests and 412 malignant tests.

4.2   Anchor Box Calculation

The average cross-and-merge ratio (Avg-IOU) is used as the evaluation index (the average of the cross-and-merge ratio between the calculated anchor box and all data). In order to improve the coincidence between the priori box and the data set, and to verify the effectiveness of the algorithm, eight experiments are repeated. As shown in Fig. 5, the maximum Avg-IOU of the original method is 0.8322, and the maximum Avg-IOU of this method is 0.8421, which improves the coincidence between anchor box and data set, and makes tasks easier to learn.

Table 1. Breast ultrasound data set partition

	Benign	Malignant	Total
The training set	960	1648	2608
The testing set	239	412	651
Total	1199	2060	3259

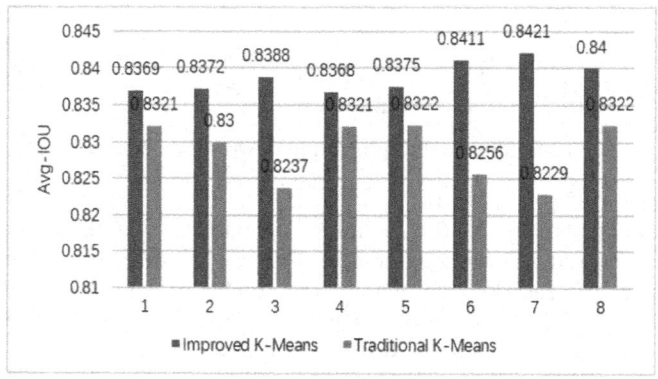

Fig. 5. Avg-IOU of traditional K-Means and improved K-Means

Anchor box obtained from the largest cluster experiment of Avg-IOU is used as a priori box in this paper. The results of clustering experiments are shown in Fig. 6. Different clusters are marked with different colors and clustering centers are drawn with black forks. After inverse transformation, nine anchor boxes are obtained as follows:(52,51), (79,72), (93,102), (122,94), (125,135), (159,117), (160,164), (190,225), (204,166).

4.3 Results Analysis Based on Index

In this paper, Faster R-CNN [13] algorithm and YOLOV3 algorithm with different configurations are selected for 1000 training sessions. The different network configurations are shown in Table 2. YOLOV3 (1) is the original YOLOV3 algorithm without optimizing anchor box and using ResNet-DenseNet_Darknet-53; YOLOV3 (2) is the YOLOV3 algorithm with introducing anchor box optimization; YOLOV3 (3) is the YOLOV3 algorithm with optimizing anchor box and using ResNet-DenseNet_Darknet-53 at the same time. In order to accelerate the training speed of the network and prevent over-fitting, this paper uses Adma algorithm to do gradient optimization. The initial learning rate is set to 0.001. After every 100 iterations, the learning rate decreases to 1/10 of the original, the impulse is 0.9, the attenuation coefficient is 0.0002, and the batch_size is 100. Then, the performance of the model is evaluated on the test set according to multiple evaluation indicators.

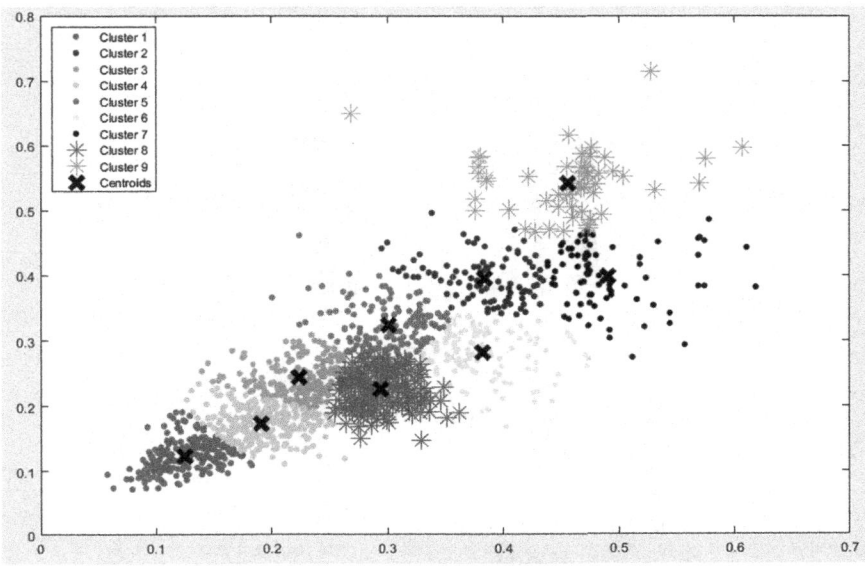

Fig. 6. Clustering experiment

Table 2. Performance configuration of different networks

	Faster R-CNN	YOLOV(1)	YOLOV (2)
Optimizing anchor box	×	×	√
Using ResNet-DenseNet_Darknet-53	×	×	×

By setting different confidence thresholds, AP of benign samples and malignant samples on training set and test set can be calculated, respectively. Compared with Fig. 10 and Fig. 11, the AP value of malignant samples is higher than that of benign samples, whether in training set or test set. This is Because the number of malignant samples in the training set is larger than that of benign samples.

From Fig. 7 and Fig. 8, it can be seen that the positive and malignant AP of YOLOV3 (1) algorithm are 87.85% and 90.25% respectively in the training set and 83.01% and 88.25% respectively in the test set, which are superior to Faster R-CNN algorithm, showing that the performance of YOLOV3 algorithm is better. The benign and malignant AP of YOLOV3 (2) algorithm is 2.03% and 2.76% higher than that of YOLOV3 (1) in training set, and 2.67% and 2% higher than that of YOLOV3 (1) in test set. This is because in YOLOV3 (2) algorithm, better anchor box can be obtained after clustering optimization. Compared with YOLOV3 (2) algorithm, the benign and malignant AP of YOLOV3 (3) algorithm is improved by 0.71% and 2.2% in training set and 1.37% and 3.22% in test set, respectively.

After calculating the AP of benign and malignant samples, the mAP of the model can be obtained. As shown in Fig. 9, in the four algorithms, the mAP on the training

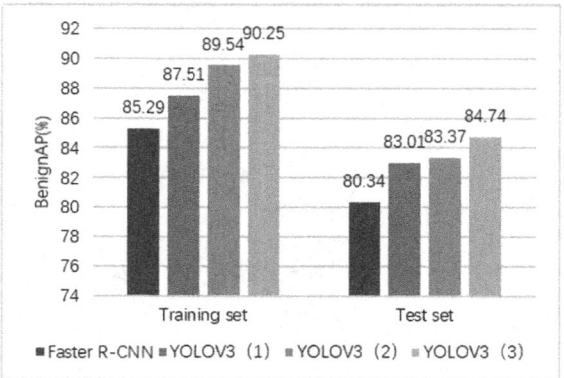

Fig. 7. Benign AP on training set and test set

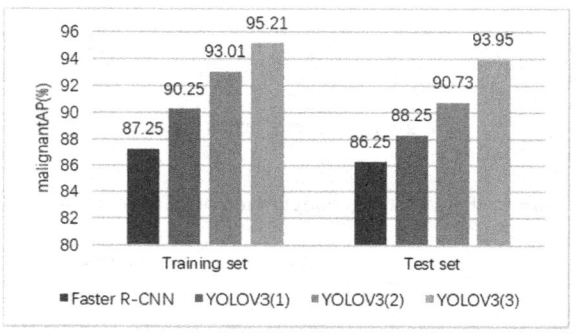

Fig. 8. malignant AP on training set and test set

set is higher than that on the test set, which is consistent with the reality. The mAP of YOLOV3 (1) algorithm is higher than that of Faster R-CNN in training set and test set. Compared with YOLOV3 (1) algorithm, the mAP of YOLOV3 (2) algorithm increased by 2.4% and 1.42% in training set and test set, indicating the effectiveness of optimizing anchor box. Compared with YOLOV3 (2), the mAP of YOLOV3 (3) algorithm increases by 1.45% and 2.25% in training set and test set respectively.

4.4 Results and Analysis Based on Prediction

One malignant samples are randomly selected from database and the above four algorithms are run, respectively. As shown in Fig. 10, the first image is the original image, and the second image is a label image labeled sample by a professional doctor. The blue area in the image is the location of the tumor. The third, fourth, fifth and sixth pictures are the results of running Faster R-CNN, YOLOV3 (1), YOLOV3 (2) and YOLOV3 (3), respectively. The four algorithms in Fig. 10 identify it as malignant with confidence levels of 87.25%, 95.91%, 96.72%, and 97.85%, respectively.

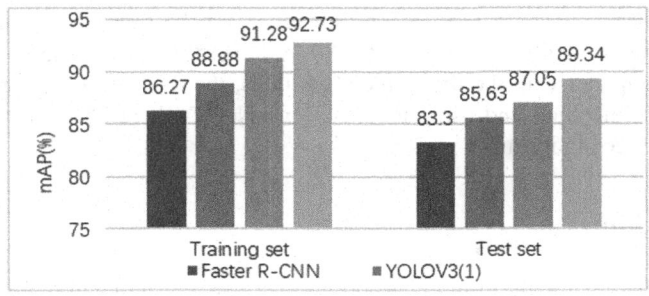

Fig. 9. Benign and malignant mAP on training and test set

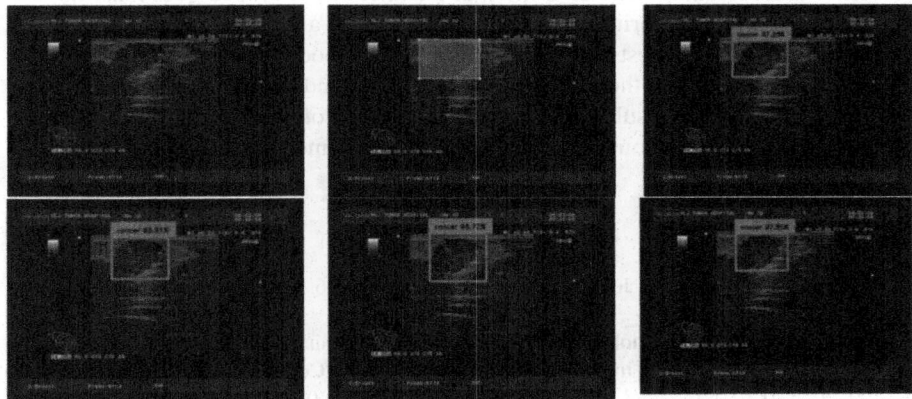

Fig. 10. Recognition effect under four different algorithms

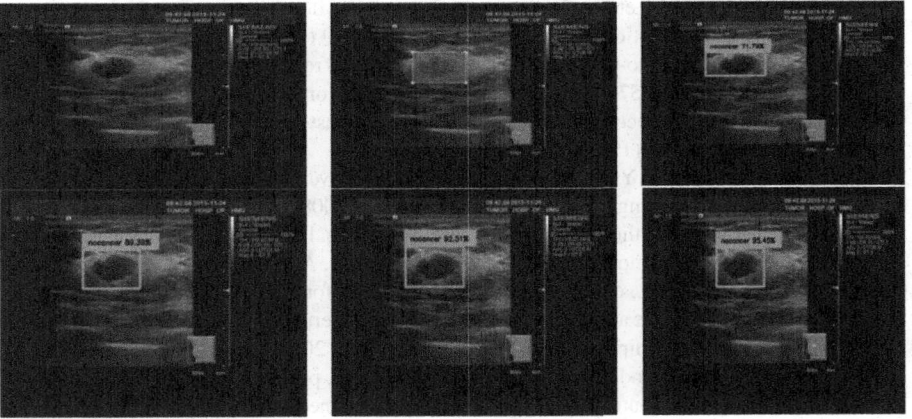

Fig. 11. Recognition results under different algorithms

Then, one benign samples are randomly selected from database, and the above four algorithms are run, respectively. As shown in Figs. 11, the order of the six images is the same as that in Fig. 10. Figures 11 shows that all the four algorithms recognize it as benign, with confidence of 71.79%, 89.39%, 92.51% and 95.45% respectively. Obviously, compared with the first three algorithms, the YOLOV3 (3) algorithm after anchor box optimization and using ResNet-DenseNet_Darknet-53 is obviously better than the first three algorithms.

5   Conclusions

In this paper, YOLOV3 algorithm is proposed to classify benign and malignant tumors and locate ROI regions simultaneously. It improves YOLOV3 algorithm by optimizing anchor and designing ResNet_DenseNet-Darknet-53 for related questions. Experiments show YOLOV3 algorithm after optimizing anchor and using ResNet_DenseNet-Darknet-53 achieves the best results. The proposed method not only realizes the localization of ROI region and the classification of benign and malignant tumors, but also achieves good detection results. It makes the application of artificial intelligence closer to the breast cancer detection in actual operating environment.

References

1. Siegel, R.L., Miller, K.D., Jemal, A.: Cancer statistics, 2016. CA Cancer J. Clin. **66**(1), 7–30 (2016)
2. Ikedo, Y., Morita, T., Fukuoka, D., et al.: Automated analysis of breast parenchymal patterns in whole breast ultrasound images: preliminary experience. Comput. Assist. Radiol. Sur. **4**(3), 299–306 (2009). https://doi.org/10.1007/s11548-009-0295-0
3. Huang, Y.L., Jiang, Y.R., Chen, D.R., et al.: Computer-aided diagnosis with morphological features for breast lesion on sonograms. Ultrasound Obstet. Gynecol. **32**(4), 565–572 (2008)
4. Ting, X., Lei, L., Kai, L., et al.: Comparison of transferred deep neural networks in ultrasonic breast masses discrimination. Biomed. Res. Int. **2018**, 1–9 (2018)
5. Yap, M.H., et al.: End-to-end breast ultrasound lesions recognition with a deep learning approach. Proc. SPIE **10578**, 1057819 (2018). https://doi.org/10.1117/12.2293498
6. Chiao, J.-Y., et al.: Detection and classification the breast tumors using mask R-CNN on sonograms. Medicine **98**(19), pe15200 (2019)
7. Redmon, J., Farhadi, A.: YOLOv3: an incremental improvement (2018)
8. Jain, A.K.: Data Clustering: 50 years beyond k-means (2008)
9. Arthur, D.: K-Means++: the advantages of careful seeding. In: Proceedings of the Eighteenth Annual ACM-SIAM Symposium on Discrete Algorithms. ACM (2007)
10. Zhou, Z., Si, G., Chen, J., et al.: A novel method of transformer fault diagnosis based on K-Mediods and decision tree algorithm. In: IEEE 2017 1st International Conference on Electrical Materials and Power Equipment (ICEMPE), Xian, China 2017 1st International Conference on Electrical Materials and Power Equipment (ICEMPE), pp. 369–373 (2017)
11. Gao, H., Zhuang, L., Maaten, L.V.D., et al.: Densely connected convolutional networks. In: IEEE Conference on Computer Vision & Pattern Recognition (2017)
12. Zhao, Y., Zhu, H., Shen, Q., et al.: Practical adversarial attack against object detector. **24** (2018)
13. Ren, S., He, K., Girshick, R., Sun, J.: Faster R-CNN: towards real-time object detection with region proposal networks. In: NIPS (2015)

Deep Learning Strategies for Survival Prediction in Prophylactic Resection Patients

S. Anand Hareendran[1(✉)], Vinod Chandra S S[2], Sreedevi R. Prasad[3], and S. Dhanya[1]

[1] Muthoot Institute of Technology and Science, Kochi, India
{anandhareendrans,dhanyas}@mgits.ac.in
[2] University of Kerala, Trivandrum, India
vinodchandrass@gmail.com
[3] Rajadhani Institute of Engineering and Technology, Attingal, India
sreedevirp@rietedu.in

Abstract. Human race is looking forward to an era where science and technology can wipeout the threats laid by lethal diseases. Major statistics shows that about 10 million people die from various forms of cancer annually. Every sixth death in the world is caused by cancer. Treatment to cancer always depend on its type and spread. Treatment includes single or combination of surgery, chemotherapy and radiation therapy. In this paper, survival prediction in prophylactic resection patients are carried out using various deep learning methods. Prophylactic resection has been found to be very effective in colon cancer, breast cancer and ovarian cancer. In this paper, we try to validate the results in a test environment using multi layered deep neural network. Classical Navie Bayer's algorithm has been used to classify the dataset and convolution neural network (CNN) has been used to create the survival prediction model. Results affirm better survival results in prophylactic resection patients.

Keywords: Survival prediction · Naive Bayer's algorithm · Classification · Heath informatics · Prophylactic resection · Deep learning

1 Introduction

Over the years, cancer research has seen tremendous improvement. From challenging treatment scenarios to early detection of symptoms have surly given a positive sign in the treatment process. With the advancement in technology and availability of immense data, medical research community has grown to a bigger level of early screening and prediction of disease.

Supported by MITS, Kochi.

Y. Tan et al. (Eds.): ICSI 2020, LNCS 12145, pp. 575–583, 2020.
https://doi.org/10.1007/978-3-030-53956-6_53

Treatment of cancer always depends on the staging system. Inaccurate staging diagnosis can lead to life threatening situations. Most of the time surgery and removal of the affected part is a vital part in the treatment process. But there are various cases where such removal doesnt meet the purpose. Early detection of cancer can provide doctors insights on removing a particular part/organ which can prevent the occurrence of disease. Such surgeries are termed as prophylactic resections. For various type of cancer like colon, breast and ovary this process has been seen very effective. Accurate and robust predictions of overall survival, using automated algorithms can provide valuable guidance for diagnosis, treatment planning, and outcome prediction. It is however difficult to have the reliable and accurate attributes for the prediction process. Medical imaging, clinical data, family history, drug and other disease history always contribute to it. Hence having a perfect decision making model for prediction can help the physician. Not only prophylactic resections, survival prediction of patients after this process can also lead to have a positive impact on the treatment process.

Deep learning strategies has been used for initial detection from the medical imaging. CNN is a variation of deep neural network which is highly dependent on the correlation of neighbouring pixels. At start, it make use of randomly defined patches as input and later modifies the same during the training process. When the training is finished, the model uses the new modified patches for predicting and validating the result. From the clinical dataset, Naive Bayers algorithm helps in predicting to which class the cells need to be classified. Thus a combined model provides accurate prediction module.

2   Literature Survey

Many approaches and techniques have been proposed in the field of cancer detection and prediction. The following methods have been able to detect cancer detection at early stage with higher accuracy. In [1] A prototype of lung cancer prediction system is developed using data mining classification techniques. The system extracts hidden knowledge from a historical lung cancer disease database. The most effective model to predict patients with Lung cancer disease appears to be Naïve Bayes followed by IF-THEN rule, Decision Trees and Neural Network.

The [2] is a skin cancer diagnosis using machine learning by imputing skin cancer images are given to the sheartlet transformation module, which decomposes the given input images to obtain the sub-band coefficients. After that feature extraction stage selects the features according to their rank by t-test. Then the selected features are classified by naïve Bayes classifier as normal or abnormal.

In [3] Brest cancer is predicted using Naive Bayes classifier an inductive learning algorithms for machine learning and data mining. Navies Bayes classifier uses large quantities of data related to breast cancer characteristics, in order to obtain an optimal prediction of recurrent events.

Neural networks and related techniques have a vast contribution when it comes into health informatics. Over the past few decades, Convolution Neural

Networks have been employed increasingly by more and more researchers, and become an active research area. ANNs have afforded numerous successes with great progress in Cancer classification and diagnosis in the very early stages. A typical ANN model is made up of a hierarchy of layers: input, hidden and output layers. Extensive research had been done with backpropagation artificial neural network (BP-ANN) method and its variations in breast cancer diagnosis. The technique, however, has some limitations such as no guarantee to global optima, a lot of tuning para-meters, and long training time. Single Hidden Layer Neural Networks (SFLN) was proposed by Huang and Babri to tackle the mentioned problems with tree steps learning process that called extreme learning machine (ELM). Standard and best parameterised ELM model were proposed for breast cancer early prediction. Results showed that it generally gave better accuracy, specificity, and sensitivity compared to BP ANN. However, most existing works focus on prediction performance with limited attention with medical professional as end user and applicability aspect in real medical setting.

3   Methodology

Symptoms leads to treatment. When ever a patient approaches the doctor, the initial step is to get the vital and other relevant clinical information. From such data and results of primary investigation, physician can generally conclude his initial diagnosis. He thus classifies the patient who can possibly affected by the disease. Those who are more prone to be affected will be reviewed frequently and treatments as and when needed will be suggested. This can be medicine intake or even surgery/removal of organs/parts etc.

Initial phase is to find the apt classifier which classifies the cells into malignant or benign. In this study we are selecting support vector machine (SVM), C4.5, Naive Bayers and K-Nearest Neighbourhood algorithm. Sien Luei dataset for classification is used for the study. It has 700 instances, with two classes benign and malignant. 10 fold cross validation is done, which means in evaluating predictive models the original set is split into a training sample to train the model, and a test set to evaluate it. The following table provides the results obtained while performing the test process in the 700 instance. Time taken to build the model and accurate classification are the attributes considered for the performance. Table 1 shows the detailed data obtained during the classification.

Table 1. Perfomance measures.

Perfomance indicators	Algorithms used			
	SVM	C4.5	Naive Bayers	Nearest neighbourhood
Time to build the model	0.091	0.085	0.035	0.027
Correctly classified instances	677	669	688	671
Accuracy	96.71	95.57	98.28	95.85

For more accurate learning; Kappa statistics, Mean absolute error, Root mean squared error has also been calculated. These values provide how accurate the instances were classified and also forecasts and predicts the eventual outcome. Table 2 shows the error measures and deviations.

Table 2. Perfomance measures.

Perfomance measures	Algorithms used			
	SVM	C4.5	Naive Bayers	Nearest neighbourhood
Kappa statistic	0.95	0.85	0.93	0.84
Mean absolute error	0.026	0.073	0.035	0.042
Root mean square error	0.14	0.25	0.17	0.24

The result statistics have been well analysed and for classification to benign and malignant cells, Naive Bayers classifier has been selected.

Once the classifier is build, a CNN model need to be build for predicting the survival of patients who are under going prophylactic resection. Our CNN model contains 3 convolutional layers which is followed by 2 fully connected layers and an output layer and is implemented over the AlexNet platform. Figure 1 shows the basic architecture of the model designed.

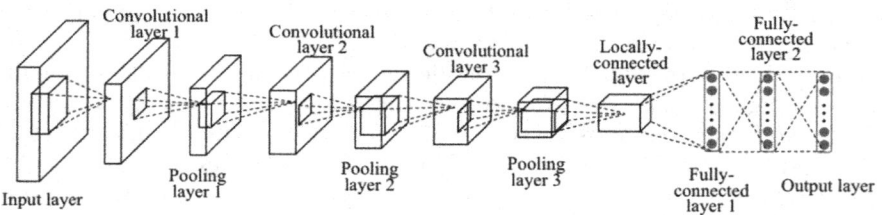

Fig. 1. Architecture details.

Standard survival regression models like Cox proportional hazards model is compared to the Deep neural network. Negative log of Cox partial likelihood was used as a loss function to train the network, and Rectified linear unit (ReLu) was used as the nonlinear activation function in the convolutional and fully connected layers. The deep learning model was trained with out Sien Luei dataset. The survival regression models were validated using 10-fold cross validation, and concordance index was used to evaluate the survival regression results. The C-Index obtained by the deep CNN model was 0.673 while the CPH model had a C- index of 0.592.

3.1   Dataset

Sien Luei survival dataset has been used for the prediction. Data consist of 4327 instances of 8 attributes. Age of the patient, operation date, number of positive auxiliary nodes detected, family history, drug used, survival in years were the top attributes used. Dataset has been specific for each analysis. For the prediction of breast cancer - the attributes used are mean radius, mean perimeter, mean compactness, smoothness, concave points, symmetry etc. Figure 2 shows the basic classification on the entire dataset with respect to each attributes. This dataset is used for the entire prediction model building.

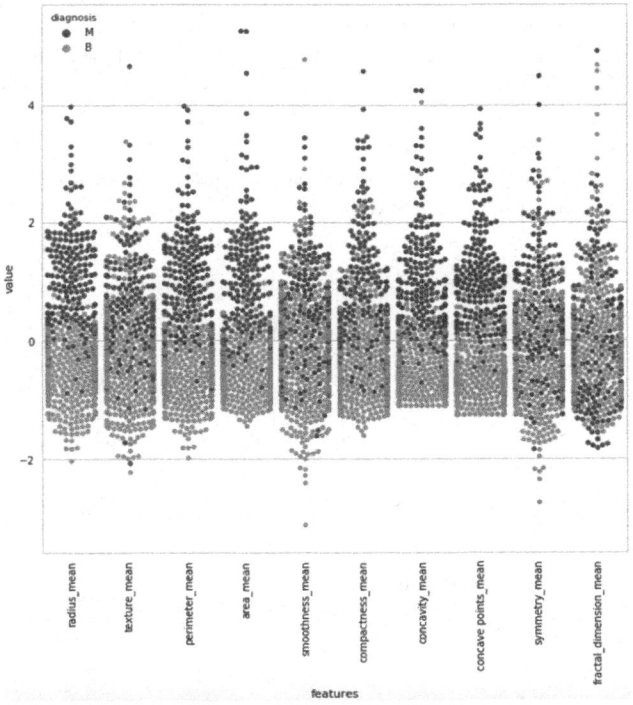

Fig. 2. Seaborn plot of attributes.

4   Results and Discussion

Setting and evaluating the various performance measure is a serious task which evaluates the entire model. Four different algorithms have been used for the classification. Table 3 shows the accuracy, precision, specificity and recall.

From Table 1 we can see that Naive Bayers takes 0.035 second to build the model. Even though time taken is higher than k-NN which about 0.027 second

Table 3. Perfomance measures.

Algorithm	Perfomance measure			
	Accuracy	Precision	Specificity	Recall
SVM	96.71	0.961	0.692	0.966
C4.5	95.57	0.949	0.827	0.985
Naive Bayers	98.28	0.983	0.916	0.990
K-nearest neighbour	95.85	0.952	0.875	0.882

we prefer NB by the fact that K-NN is a lazy learner algorithm which doesnt gets much learning during the training phase. Other than the time to build the model, accuracy obtained for Naive Bayes tops the list by 98.28% and have the highest number of correctly classified instance. Error rates can be studied from Table 2, which clearly indicates the variation from the correct classification. Naive Bayer and SVM shows the least deviation which makes them more preferred for the classification. But Naive Bayers has the best compatibility between the reliability of the data collected and their validity.

Table 4. Confusion matrix values.

Algorithm	Benign	Malignant	Class
SVM	438	20	Benign
	15	227	Malignant
C4.5	436	22	Benign
	12	230	Malignant
Naive Bayers	446	7	Benign
	5	242	Malignant
K-nearest neighbour	439	20	Benign
	22	219	Malignant

Once the model is created the efficiency of the algorithm need to be measured. Table 4 shows confusion matrix, which states the true positive and true negative split while using the four algorithms. The results affirm the use of Bayers algorithm to be more efficient when compared to others. Out of the 700 instances, 446 benign and 242 malignant has been correctly classified.

That is why the accuracy of Bayers was high when compared to other classification techniques. It outperforms with clear distinction other classifiers in accuracy, sensitivity, specificity and precision and in this work Naive Bayers was the best one which had the distinct split ratio. Figure 3 shows the box plot analysis of performance measure.

As the classification part was successful, next focus need to be given for building the CNN for survival prediction. Patients under scanner are underdone

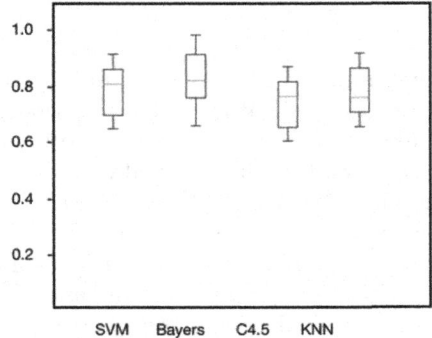

Fig. 3. Boxplot representation of performance

routine checkups and their vitals are used to create the survival models. Prophylactic resection will be suggested by doctors if they see any major changes during the checkup. System will have a close monitor on such details and creates a background knowledge from such information. This knowledge acts as the inductive logic base for prediction activities. Figure 4 shows the survival prediction curves with respect to the vital attributes.

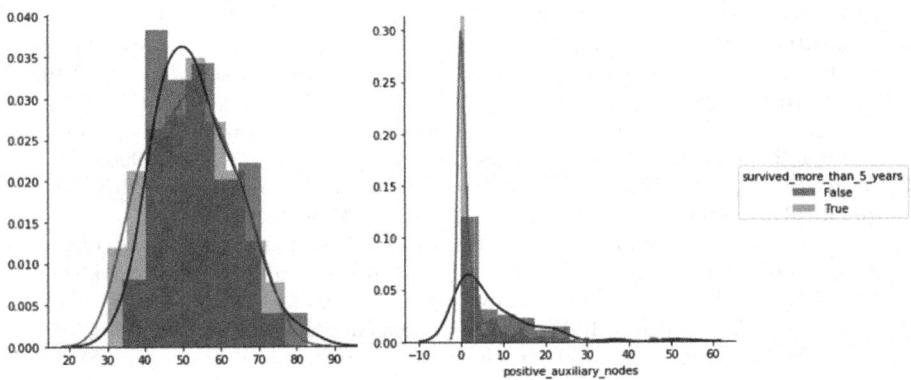

Fig. 4. Survival prediction

Experimental results on patients with ovarian, breast and colon cancer have demonstrated that the deep CNN survival analysis method could correctly predict the recurrence/risk better than state-of-the-art methods. Thus the resurrection procedure predicted by the model was found to be accurate. Experimental results demonstrate an accuracy of 98.6% and the classification model delivered an accuracy of 97.6%. A combined model of classification and survival prediction using Naive Bayers and Convolution neural network thus can be used effectively in Prophylactic Resection Patients.

5   Conclusion

Emergence of machine learning and usage of data mining techniques have helped to analyse and develop various medical related applications. An important challenge in data mining and machine learning areas is to build accurate and computationally efficient classifiers. Classifiers are always dependent to application and datasets, here even with very strong dataset Bayers classifier provided efficient classification when compared with SVM and KNN. The survival prediction model also when built showed perfectly aligned prediction results. Deep neural networks with a feedback loops are always efficient in the prediction strategies. Survival rates have been increased tremendously with the addiction of every single data record.

References

1. Krishnaiah, V., Narsimha, G., Subhash Chandra, N.: Diagnosis of lung cancer prediction system using data mining classification techniques? Int. J. Comput. Sci. Inf. Technol. (IJCSIT) **4**(1), 39–45 (2013)
2. Mohan Kumar, S., Ram Kumar, J., Gopalakrishnan, K.: Skin cancer diagnostic using machine learning techniques - shearlet transform and Naïve Bayes classifier? Int. J. Eng. Adv. Technol. (IJEAT), **9**(2) (2019). ISSN 2249-8958
3. Dumtru, D.: Prediction of recurrent events in breast Cancer using Naïve Bayesisan classification (2009)
4. Khalvati, F., et al.: Prognostic value of CT radiomic features in resectable pancreatic ductal adenocarcinoma. Nat. Sci. Rep. (2019). https://doi.org/10.1038/s41598-019-41728-7
5. George, B., Seals, S., Aban, I.: Survival analysis and regression models. J. Nucl. Cardiol. **21**(4), 686–694 (2014). https://doi.org/10.1007/s12350-014-9908-2
6. Aerts, H.J., et al.: Decoding tumour phenotype by noninvasive imaging using a quantitative radiomics approach. Nat. Commun. **5**, 4006 (2014)
7. Katzman, J.L., et al.: DeepSurv: personalized treatment recommender system using a Cox proportional hazards deep neural network. BMC Med. Res. Methodol. **18**, 24 (2018). https://doi.org/10.1186/s12874-018-0482-1
8. Krizhevsky, A., Sutskever, I., Hinton, G.E. Imagenet classification with deep convolutional neural networks. In: Advances in Neural Information Processing Systems, pp. 1097–1105 (2012)
9. Schröder, M.S., Culhane, A.C., Quackenbush, J., Haibe-Kains, B.: survcomp: bioconductor package for performance assessment and comparison of survival models. Bioinformatics **27**(22), 3206–3208 (2011)
10. Sinha, T., Verma, B., Haidar, A.: Optimization of convolutional neural network parameters for image classification. In: Proceedings of IEEE Symposium Series on Computational Intelligence, SSCI 2017, vol. 2018, pp. 1–7 (2018)
11. Amer, M., Maul, T.: A review of modularization techniques in artificial neural networks. Artif. Intell. Rev. **52**(1), 527–561 (2019). https://doi.org/10.1007/s10462-019-09706-7
12. Huang, G., Liu, Z., Van Der Maaten, L., Weinberger, K.Q.: Densely connected convolutional networks. In: Proceedings of 30th IEEE Conference on Computer Vision Pattern Recognition, CVPR 2017, vol. 2017, pp. 2261–2269 (2017)

13. Srivastava, R.K., Greff, K., Schmidhuber, J.: Highway Networks (2015)
14. Pang, J., Chen, K., Shi, J., Feng, H., Ouyang, W., Lin, D.: Libra R-CNN: towards balanced learning for object detection (2020)
15. Mikolov, T., Karafiát, M., Burget, L., Cernocky, J., Khudanpur, S.: Recurrent neural network based language model. In: Eleventh Annual Conference of the International Speech Communication Association (2010)

Method Based on Data Mining Techniques for Breast Cancer Recurrence Analysis

Morales-Ortega Roberto Cesar[1], Lozano-Bernal German[2],
Ariza-Colpas Paola Patricia[1（✉）], Arrieta-Rodriguez Eugenia[3],
Ospino-Mendoza Elisa Clementina[1], Caicedo-Ortiz Jose[1],
Piñeres-Melo Marlon Alberto[4], Mendoza-Palechor Fabio Enrique[1],
and Roca-Vides Margarita[1]

[1] Universidad de la Costa, CUC, Barranquilla, Colombia
{rmorales1,pariza1,eospino14,jcaicedo,fmendoza,mroca}@cuc.edu.co
[2] Universidad Simón Bolívar, Barranquilla, Colombia
glozano3@unisimonbolivar.edu.co
[3] Universidad del Sinú, Cartagena, Colombia
Investigacionsistemas@unisinucartagena.edu.co
[4] Universidad del Norte, Barranquilla, Colombia
pineresm@uninorte.edu.co

Abstract. Cancer is a constantly evolving disease, which affects a large number of people worldwide. Great efforts have been made at the research level for the development of tools based on data mining techniques that allow to detect or prevent breast cancer. The large volumes of data play a fundamental role according to the literature consulted, a great variety of dataset oriented to the analysis of the disease has been generated, in this research the Breast Cancer dataset was used, the purpose of the proposed research is to submit comparison of the J48 and randomforest, NaiveBayes and NaiveBayes Simple, SMO Poli-kernel and SMO RBF-Kernel classification algorithms, integrated with the Simple K-Means cluster algorithm for the generation of a model that allows the successful classification of patients who are or Non-recurring breast cancer after having previously undergone surgery for the treatment of said disease, finally the methods that obtained the best levels were SMO Poly-Kernel + Simple K-Means 98.5% of Precision, 98.5% recall, 98.5% TPRATE and 0.2% FPRATE. The results obtained suggest the possibility of using intelligent computational tools based on data mining methods for the detection of breast cancer recurrence in patients who had previously undergone surgery.

Keywords: Breast cancer · Data mining · Classification · Cluster · Dataset

1 Introduction

Cancer is a disease in constant evolution, which affects a large number of people worldwide. According to the world health organization 8.2 million people died from this disease where you can see the usual occurrence of cancer such as lung, liver, colon and

© Springer Nature Switzerland AG 2020
Y. Tan et al. (Eds.): ICSI 2020, LNCS 12145, pp. 584–596, 2020.
https://doi.org/10.1007/978-3-030-53956-6_54

breast stomach, approximately 30% of cancer deaths are due to five behavioral and food risk factors (high body mass index, insufficient consumption of fruits and vegetables, lack of physical activity and consumption of tobacco and alcohol) [1]. In Colombia, according to the report issued by the National Cancer Observatory, the mortality rate for breast cancer in Colombia on average is 11.49 * 100,000 for the year 2014 in women, in addition there is a tendency to increase for the last 10 years [2].

The diagnosis and prognosis of breast cancer is a great challenge for researchers. The implementation of machine learning and data mining methods have generated great changes revolutionized the entire process of breast cancer detection and prediction [3]. Different authors have made great efforts at the research level for the implementation of innovative methods based on artificial intelligence, machine learning, data mining, big data among others, where it is necessary to highlight the innovations made in biomedical technologies, Software and Hardware which allows the collection of information for the construction of large volumes of data as mentioned in [4], which allows the design of methods based on computational intelligence for the prediction or efficient detection of the disease as can be seen in the contributions made by [3, 5–10]. The large volumes of data play a fundamental role for the design of tools that allow the detection of breast cancer, according to the literature consulted, a wide variety of dataset oriented to the analysis of the disease has been generated, among which we can highlight the sets of data used in different experiments such as: SEER [4], Breast Cancer Wisconsin [8], Breast Cancer [11]. Data mining, understood as the discipline responsible for analyzing large volumes of data, is used as an alternative to support decision-making processes for the early and successful detection of breast cancer. In the proposed research, the implementation of classification methods, which are integrated with segmentation methods to detect the recurrence of breast cancer in patients whose information is collected in the Breast cancer Wisconsin dataset, is taken as a fundamental axis. The structure of the proposed work is presented below: Sect. 2 Previous Works, where you can find the relevant literary sources associated with breast cancer screening, Sect. 3. Materials and methods, in this section you will be able to appreciate the description of the data set used as well as the conceptual framework of the data mining methods used, Sect. 4 methodology, the process followed for the design and implementation of the proposed model is presented, Sect. 5 Results, contains the findings result of the exploratory process of the data, Sect. 7 conclusion, highlights the results achieved by the proposed model for the detection of breast cancer recurrence.

2   Brief Review of Literature

Different authors seeking to propose solutions for the early and efficient detection of breast cancer have made great contributions through the use of data mining, machine learning, artificial intelligence and bigdata methods. According to the literary analysis different studies are associated with the analysis of breast cancer using different Dataset, SEER is used in [4] where a study is presented for the prediction of breast cancer survival, a study where mining methods are compared of data DT decision trees, artificial neural networks and the statistical method of logistic regression, the best results achieved are associated with the DT method reaching a level of 93.6% accuracy, then the second best result is obtained by RNA with 91.2% and finally Logistic Regression with 89.2%. In [5] the authors present an analysis of the prediction of the survival rate in patients using data mining methods, the methods used for the experimentation process were Naive Bayes NB, Back-Propagated RNA and DT the best results were achieved by the DT method reaching an accuracy level of 86.7%, while Back-Propagated RNA achieved an 86.5% accuracy level and finally the NB method obtained an 84.5%. In [6] an analysis of breast cancer using statistical and data mining methods is presented, according to the authors there are three methods for the diagnosis of said disease which correspond to mammography, FNA (fine needle aspirate) and biopsy, which sometimes are usually expensive and unpleasant, the method that presents the best results is the biopsy with an accuracy level of approximately 100%, however it is possible to obtain better results easily through the implementation of integrated FNA with Data mining methods such as attribute selection, DT, AR association rules and statistical methods such as Principal component PCA analysis, PLS linear regression analysis. In [7] it is presented to the implementation of data mining for the discovery of breast cancer patterns based on the use of RNA and multivariable adaptive regression splines, according to the authors the RNAs have been very popular for prediction tasks and classification, the basis of the analysis is, first, to use MARS to model the classification problem, then the significant variables obtained are used as input variables of the designed neural network model. To demonstrate that the inclusion of important variables obtained from MARS would improve the accuracy of the classification of networks, diagnostic tasks are performed in a breast cancer data set with fine needle aspiration cytology.

In [8] a system for the automatic diagnosis of breast cancer based on the AR Association Rules method as attribute reduction technique and Neural Network NN as classification technique is presented, the data set used corresponds to Wisconsin Breast Cancer During the training and validation process, the 3-fold cross-validation method was used, the findings resulting from the experimentation carried out indicate that the AR + NN method achieves a correct classification rate of 95.6%. In [12] the same data set is used, where the authors propose a model for the prediction of benign and malignant ash cancer through the implementation of the Naive Bayes NB, RBF Network and J48 algorithms, the results obtained indicate that NB is the best predictor with 97.3 accuracy while RBF Network obtained 96.77% and finally the j48 algorithm achieves an accuracy level of 93.41%, during the experimentation process cross validation with 10 folds was used. In [13] an application of ML machine learning algorithms using the breast cancer Wisconsin data set for breast cancer detection is presented, for which 6 ML algorithms were submitted for comparison which correspond to GRU-SVM, Linear Regression, Multilayer Perceptron MLP, NN, Softmax Regression and Support Vector Machine SVM, in the proposed experimentation the data set is divided into 70% for the training phase and 30% for the test phase, the algorithms that obtained the best results It corresponds to MLP who achieved an accuracy level of 99.04%.

In [14] a novel approach to the detection of breast cancer using data mining techniques is presented, the objective of the proposed study is to compare three classification techniques using the Weka tool where the algorithms of SMO, IBK and BF Tree are used, the data set used corresponds to Breast Cancer Wisconsin, the results obtained show that

SMO achieves the best 96.2% accuracy results. A comparative study between the methods of K-means and fuzzy C-Means FCM for the detection of breast cancer is presented in [15], said study is focused first on comparing the performance of K-clustering algorithms means and FCM and, secondly, the integration of different computational measures is considered that allow to improve the grouping accuracy of the aforementioned techniques, FCM obtains better results compared to K-means considering that it achieves a 97% level of accuracy compared to the other technique that achieves 92%. A study for the prediction of breast cancer recurrence using data mining techniques is presented in [16], the study proposed proposes the use of different classification algorithms such as C5.0, KNN, Naive Bayes, SVM and as K-Means, EM, PAM, Fuzzy C-means clusterirng method, the experimentation performed evidence that the best results are achieved by C5.0 with an accuracy level of 81.03%.

3   Materials and Methods

3.1   Dataset Description

The set of breast cancer is provided in [17], according to the literature consulted, it is important to highlight the use of various data sets which have been made with the aim of generating significant contributions in the successful and early detection of the disease of breast cancer based on the application of artificial intelligence methods, machine learning, data mining, for the realization of classification, prediction, segmentation and association processes taking into account the heterogeneity of the variables related to the pathology in question, as You can see in [4, 18–20] where the authors present the studies of different data set alternatives for the analysis of the disease under study. For the investigation carried out, the data set called Breast Cancer taken from [17] is used, which contains 286 records of people who after having undergone surgeries present or not recurrences in the occurrence of breast cancer disease, the set of data has 201 records of people who do not show recurrence in the disease and 85 records in which there is evidence of recurrence as can be seen in Fig. 1.

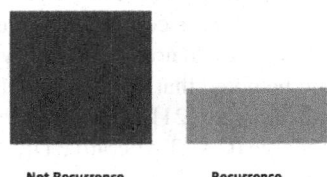

Not Recurrence   **Recurrence**

Fig. 1. Distribution of patients classified as recurring and non-recurring.

The data set has 9 attributes plus 1 class variable which limbs are described in Table 1 below.

Table 1. Description of data set attributes

Attribute	Value
Age	Ranges between: 10–19, 20–29, 30–39, 40–49, 50–59, 60–69, 70–79, 80–89, 90–99
Menopause (Time when menopause occurs)	Lt40, Ge40, Premeno
Size Tumor (tumor size expressed in mm)	Ranges between: 0–4, 5–9, 10–14, 15–19, 20–24, 25–29, 30–34, 34–39, 40–44, 45–49, 50–54, 55–59
PCCNL (Presence of cancer cells in lymph nodes)	Ranges between: 0–2, 3–5, 6–8, 9–11, 12–14, 15–17, 18–20, 21–23, 24–26, 27–29, 30–32, 33–35, 36–39
CCACNL (Cancer cells passed through lymph node capsule)	Yes, no
GHT (Histological Grade of the tumor)	1, 2, 3
Breast (Affected Breast)	Left, Right
Breast (Quadrant of the affected breast)	Left – Top, Left – Bottom, Right – Superior, Right – Bottom, Center
RT (Radio therapy)	Yes, No
Recurrencia (Variable de Clase)	Recurrence, Not recurrence

In the investigation carried out, the use of different classification and segmentation methods is proposed through the implementation of the DT, SVM, Naive Bayes, Simple K-Means algorithms, which is why in Sect. 4 the procedure and the changes made are described about the data set for its optimal behavior with the techniques mentioned.

3.2 Decision Trees

Decision tree is responsible for the recursive partition of a data set for which subdivisions are generated, generally the tree structure is composed of a main node called root and a node set that grow from the root called child nodes, Finally, within the tree structure there are the terminal nodes, it should be noted that each node of the tree has only one parent node and two or more descendant nodes [21]. According to [22] some DT algorithms are: classification and regression tree (CART), iterative Dichotomiser 3 (ID3), C4.5 and C5.0, Automatic detection of Chi-square interaction (CHAID), Decision stump, M5, Conditional decision trees. The following is a diagram of the structure of a decision tree.

According to [23] a decision tree supports the decision-making process. In [24] they mention that decision trees represent a supervised approach to classification that has a simple structure composed of terminal nodes or nodes, the nodes represent tests on one or more attributes and the terminal nodes present the results of the decisions.

3.3 Vector Support Machines

It is a method of classification that was proposed by Vapnik [25], It is based on the use of a hyperplane separator or a decision. The plane is responsible for defining the limits of decision between a set of data points classified with different labels according to what is mentioned in [22], they express the simple geometric explanation of this approach is to determine an optimal separation plane or hyperplane that separates the two classes or groups of data points fairly and is equidistant from both of them. SVM was first defined for the linear distribution of data points, additionally through the use of the kernel function it is possible to implement it to address problems with non-linear data. SVM has been applied by different agents in tasks such as recognition of Vapnik manuscript digits [25], used in object recognition problems [26], text classification [27]. According to [28], one of the advantages of SVM is considered to be the availability of powerful tools and algorithms to find the solution quickly and efficiently. SVM vector support machines have a strong theoretical foundation and excellent empirically results [24].

3.4 Naive Bayes

It is a supervised classification method developed using the Conditional Probability Theorem, they perform well in different situations, such as text classification and spam detection. Only a small amount of training data is necessary to estimate certain parameters [22]. Bayesian networks are considered an alternative to classic expert systems oriented to decision making and prediction under uncertainty in probabilistic terms [29]. The NB algorithm is a probabilistic classifier that calculates a set of probabilities based on the frequency and combination of the values given on the dataset [30], the algorithm uses the Bayes theorem and assumes that all data are independent of the values of class variable [31], rarely the assumption of conditional independence is met in real world applications, this is a naïve characterization, but the algorithm tends to work properly and learn fast in several supervised classification problems [32]. The most common algorithms that implement this method are: Naive Bayes, Gaussian Naive Bayes, Multinomial Naive Bayes, Averaged One-Dependence Estimators (AODE), Bayesian Belief Network (BBN), Bayesian Network (BN) [22].

3.5 Cluster

The cluster method is considered the most popular unsupervised learning task, which is based on the construction of a set of physical or abstract objects that have matching characteristics or attributes [33]. According to [34] the product of a good grouping, high quality groups with high intra-class similarities and low class similarities should be generated. The implementation of clustering algorithms for unsupervised data analysis has become a useful tool to explore and solve different problems in data mining. According to [22] Some of the algorithms implemented for cluster methods are: K-Means, K-Medians, Affinity Propagation, Spectral Clustering, Ward hierarchical clustering, Agglomerative clustering. DBSCAN, Gaussian Mixtures, Birch, Mean Shift, Expectation Maximization (EM).

4   Methodology

For the development of the proposed research, we initially start with obtaining the data set called Breast Cancer Wisconsin taken from [17], within which it was necessary to perform the data preprocessing stage called phase number 1 where we highlight the realization of a analysis of the balancing of the data, later in phase number 2 the training process and test of the classification methods used where the DT, NB and SVM algorithms were compared through the metrics of precision, coverage evaluation, true positive rate, false positive rate, finally in phase 3 the best classification method is taken with the simple cluster method k-means and the result obtained is compared in relation to the results obtained only by the classification. The experimentation process was performed using the WEKA data mining tool. The aspects mentioned above are detailed below:

4.1   Phase No 1. Preprocessing

Within the problems found in the data set we can see that the data is not balanced with respect to the class variable called recurrence which contains two possible recurring and non-recurring values, the foregoing considering that the non-recurring variable contains 201 records representing 70.27% of the total data, on the other hand, the recurring variable only has 85 data which corresponds to 29.7% of the records, the above can be evidenced in Fig. 1. the Previous figures mentioned are a problem for the method since it would learn to correctly identify the non-recurrence variable, which is why balancing the data is proposed. Next, in Fig. 2 the configuration used in the SMOTE filter for the data balancing process is presented.

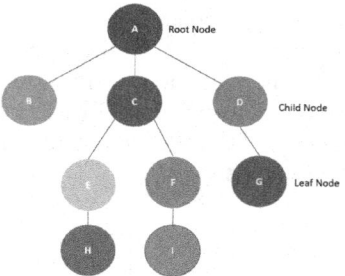

Fig. 2. DT structure representation.

Once the SMOTE filter has been implemented for the balancing process of the data, the recurrence class variable has a homogeneous distribution in terms of the number of records, so in the non-recurrence value there are 201 records (50.7%) and in recurrence 195 records (49.3%), in Fig. 3 the number of records per class is presented after the data balancing process. The data were subjected to verification where it was evidenced that it was not necessary to replace atypical data and missing data (Fig. 4).

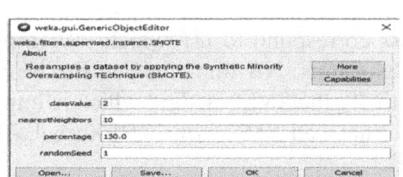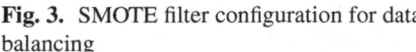

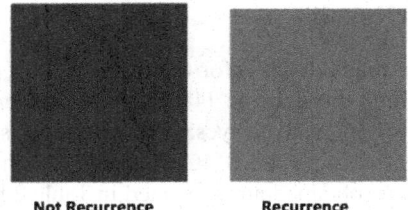

Not Recurrence   **Recurrence**

Fig. 3. SMOTE filter configuration for data balancing

Fig. 4. Balanced data distribution with SMOTE filter

4.2 Phase No 2. Training and Testing of Classification Algorithms

During the training and testing process of the selected methods, the cross-validation method was used as a test option where a part of the data set is randomly taken for the training process and the other part for the test this procedure is repeated according to the number of stipulated folds which in this case correspond to 10, then in Fig. 5. A scheme of the cross-validation process is presented.

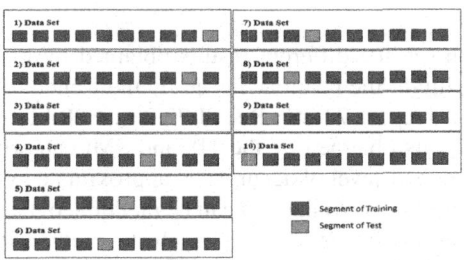

Fig. 5. Cross validation process scheme

Additionally, during this phase different evaluation metrics were taken into account such as level of accuracy, coverage, true positive rate, false positive rate.

4.3 Phase No 3. Integration of Classification and Segmentation Techniques

During this phase, the Simple K-means cluster method was integrated with the different classification algorithms, with the purpose of validating whether, by integrating both methods, better results are obtained in the evaluation metrics used during the experimentation process. In session V results, a description of the centroids corresponding to the clusters will be made.

5   Results

The methods used for the classification process correspond to DT which was implemented through the J48 and RandomForest algorithms, NB implemented the Naive-Bayes and NaiveBayesSimple algorithms and finally the SVM method which is implemented using the SMO algorithms with Polikernel and SMO with RBFKernel. The results obtained are presented in Table 2 below.

Table 2. Results classification methods

Method	Algorithm	TPRATE	FPRATE	PRECISION	RECALL
DT	J48	70,7%	29,2%	72,0%	69,2%
	RandomForest	73,7%	26,2%	73,8%	73,7%
NB	NaiveBayes	69,7%	30,4%	69,7%	69,7%
	NaiveBayesSimple	69,7%	30,4%	69,7%	69,7%
SVM	SMO - PoliKernel	70,7%	29,3%	70,7%	70,7%
	SMO - RBF Kernel	69,9%	30,3%	70,3%	69,9%

In Table 2, you can see the different results obtained by the classification methods where we must highlight the result achieved by the RandomForest algorithm who obtained a level of Accuracy of 73.8%, Recall 73.7%, TPRATE 73.7% and FPRATE 26.2%, however, the results obtained by the J48 and SMO algorithms with polikernel are promising given that their level of accuracy is approximate to the level achieved by RandomForest. After the results obtained, it can be mentioned that these are acceptable, additionally the classifiers are integrated with the cluster method in search of improving the levels in the evaluation metrics used. Next, in Fig. 6 the distribution of the data with respect to the generated clusters which are described in Table 3 can be seen.

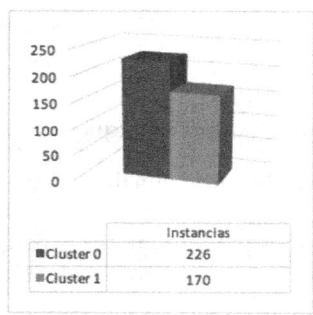
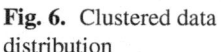
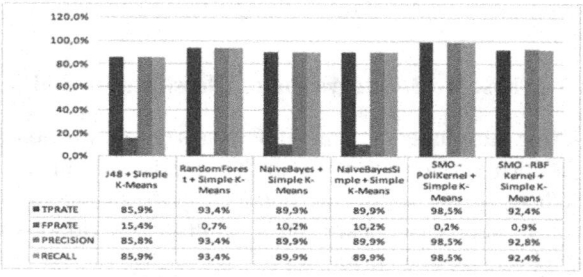

Fig. 6. Clustered data distribution

Fig. 7. Classification methods results.

The result of the classification methods used during the experimentation with the cluster algorithm which corresponds to Simple K-means is presented in Fig. 7.

Table 3. Cluster description

Cluster	Description
Cluster 0	Represents those whose age range is approximately between 40 and 49 years, the time at which menopause occurs is generally at 40, the size of the tumor expressed in mm corresponds to 30 and 34, whose presence of cancer cells in lymph nodes is 0 and 2.3, do not have cancer cells that cross the lymph node capsule, with a histological grade of the tumor 3 (high level), which has the affected left breast in the lower left quadrant, was not subjected to radius therapy and is recurrent
Clúster 1	It represents those whose age range corresponds to 30 to 39 years, who are in premenopausal condition, whose tumor size expressed in mm corresponds to 25 to 29, with presence between 0 and 2.3 cancer cells in lymph nodes, they do not have cancer cells that have passed through lymph node capsules, the affected breast corresponds to the right in the lower left quadrant, they have not undergone radiotherapy and are non-recurring patients

6 Discussion

Breast cancer is a problem that affects many women worldwide, which has generated great interest in the scientific field in order to take advantage of technological advances and thus generate intelligent tools or methods that allow diagnosis or prevention of Successful form of said disease. Data mining is a discipline in constant development, through this a large number of solutions have been generated for the analysis of different diseases that society suffers worldwide. In the proposed work, a model based on data mining techniques is proposed for the detection of recurrent or non-recurring persons after having undergone surgery in a period prior to 5 years.

According to the results, an analysis was initially carried out through classification methods such as DT, NB and SVM where different algorithms were used for the implementation of the aforementioned techniques. Taking into account the results, the levels of precision achieved are not the best since randomforest only reached a 73.8% level of accuracy, followed by J48 and SMO with 72% and 70.7% respectively, consequently, it was determined the alternative of integrating the classification methods with the simple cluster method k-means with the purpose of obtaining improvements with respect to the previously obtained results.

After the integration of the classification methods with the cluster algorithm, a significant improvement is observed in the levels of precision achieved, taking into account that, for example, the randomforest method went from having an accuracy of 73.8% to 93.4%, on the other hand, all the algorithms increased their values in the precision assessment metric, which indicates that an alternative for the successful identification of breast cancer is the joint use of classification methods with cluster methods. In previous works such as [8, 12–14] the study of breast cancer is proposed using classification methods which show good results, however it is possible to explore the possibility of integrating the proposed methods with cluster methods. This cluster method approach with classification method is also explored prior research for the determination of other pathologies that affect different societies [35, 36].

7 Conclusions

Cancer is a disease in constant evolution, which affects a large number of people worldwide. According to the world health organization 8.2 million people died from this disease where you can see the usual occurrence of cancer such as lung, liver, colon and breast stomach [2], large volumes of data play a role Fundamental for the design of tools that allow the detection of breast cancer, according to the literature consulted, a wide variety of dataset oriented to the analysis of the disease has been generated. In this investigation, the Breast Cancer data set taken from [17] was used, which was preprocessed for the validation of the data quality where it was necessary to perform data balancing, the algorithms implemented for the classification process correspond to J48 and randomforest (DT), NaiveBayes and NaiveBayes Simple (NB), SMO Poly-kernel and SMO RBF-Kernel (SVM), the Simple K-Means algorithm was used as a cluster method which was integrated with the classification methods In order to obtain the best results, finally the methods that obtained the best levels were SMO Poly-Kernel + Simple K-Means 98.5% Precision, 98.5% recall, 98.5% TPRATE and 0.2% deFPRATE. The results obtained suggest the possibility of using intelligent computational tools based on data mining methods for the detection of breast cancer recurrence in patients who had previously undergone surgery.

References

1. Facts and figures of cancer. https://www.who.int/cancer/about/facts/es/
2. Kourou, K., Exarchos, T.P., Exarchos, K.P., Karamouzis, M.V., Fotiadis, D.I.: Machine learning applications in cancer prognosis and prediction. Comput. Struct. Biotechnol. J. **13**, 8–17 (2015)
3. Gupta, S., Kumar, D., Sharma, A.: Data mining classification techniques applied for breast cancer diagnosis and prognosis. Ind. J. Comput. Sci. Eng. (IJCSE) **2**(2), 188–195 (2011)
4. Delen, D., Walker, G., Kadam, A.: Predicting breast cancer survivability: a comparison of three data mining methods. Artif. Intell. Med. **34**(2), 113–127 (2005)
5. Bellaachia, A., Guven, E.: Predicting breast cancer survivability using data mining techniques. Age **58**(13), 10–110 (2006)
6. Xiong, X., Kim, Y., Baek, Y., Rhee, D.W., Kim, S.H.: Analysis of breast cancer using data mining & statistical techniques. In: Sixth International Conference on Software Engineering, Artificial Intelligence, Networking and Parallel/Distributed Computing and First ACIS International Workshop on Self-Assembling Wireless Network, pp. 82–87. IEEE (2005)
7. Chou, S.M., Lee, T.S., Shao, Y.E., Chen, I.F.: Mining the breast cancer pattern using artificial neural networks and multivariate adaptive regression splines. Expert Syst. Appl. **27**(1), 133–142 (2004)
8. Karabatak, M., Ince, M.C.: An expert system for detection of breast cancer based on association rules and neural network. Expert Syst. Appl. **36**(2), 3465–3469 (2009)
9. Hung, P.D., Hanh, T.D., Diep, V.T.: Breast cancer prediction using spark MLlib and ML packages. In: Proceedings of the 2018 5th International Conference on Bioinformatics Research and Applications, pp. 52–59. ACM (2018)
10. Shadman, T.M., Akash, F.S., Ahmed, M.: Machine learning as an indicator for breast cancer prediction, Doctoral dissertation, BRAC University (2018)
11. Alwidian, J., Hammo, B.H., Obeid, N.: WCBA: weighted classification based on association rules algorithm for breast cancer disease. Appl. Soft Comput. **62**, 536–549 (2018)

12. Chaurasia, V., Pal, S., Tiwari, B.B.: Prediction of benign and malignant breast cancer using data mining techniques. J. Algorithms Comput. Technol. **12**(2), 119–126 (2018)
13. Agarap, A.F.M.: On breast cancer detection: an application of machine learning algorithms on the wisconsin diagnostic dataset. In: Proceedings of the 2nd International Conference on Machine Learning and Soft Computing, pp. 5–9. ACM (2018)
14. Chaurasia, V., Pal, S.: A novel approach for breast cancer detection using data mining techniques (2017)
15. Dubey, A.K., Gupta, U., Jain, S.: Comparative study of K-means and fuzzy C-means algorithms on the breast cancer data. Int. J. Adv. Sci. Eng. Inf. Technol. **8**(1), 18–29 (2018)
16. Ojha, U., Goel, S.: A study on prediction of breast cancer recurrence using data mining techniques. In: 2017 7th International Conference on Cloud Computing, Data Science & Engineering-Confluence, pp. 527–530. IEEE (2017)
17. Lichman, M.: UCI machine learning repository, University of California, School of Information and Computer Science, Irvine, CA (2019). http://archive.ics.uci.edu/ml/datasets/breast+cancer
18. Abbass, H.A.: An evolutionary artificial neural networks approach for breast cancer diagnosis. Artif. Intell. Med. **25**(3), 265–281 (2002)
19. Akay, M.F.: Support vector machines combined with feature selection for breast cancer diagnosis. Expert Syst. Appl. **36**(2), 3240–3247 (2009)
20. Polat, K., Güneş, S.: Breast cancer diagnosis using least square support vector machine. Digit. Sig. Proc. **17**(4), 694–701 (2007)
21. Friedl, M.A., Brodley, C.E.: Decision tree classification of land cover from remotely sensed data. Remote Sens. Environ. **61**(3), 399–409 (1997)
22. Das, K., Behera, R.N.: A survey on machine learning: concept, algorithms and applications. Int. J. Innov. Res. Comput. Commun. Eng. **5**(2), 1301–1309 (2017)
23. Magerman, D.M.: Statistical decision-tree models for parsing. In: Proceedings of the 33rd Annual Meeting on Association for Computational Linguistics, pp. 276–283. Association for Computational Linguistics (1995)
24. Tong, S., Koller, D.: Support vector machine active learning with applications to text classification. J. Mach. Learn. Res. **2**(Nov), 45–66 (2001)
25. Vapnik, V.: Statistical Learning Theory. Wiley, Hoboken (1998)
26. Papageorgiou, C., Oren, M., Poggio, T.: A general framework for object detection. In: Proceedings of the International Conference on Computer Vision (1998)
27. Joachims, T.: Text categorization with support vector machines: learning with many relevant features. In: Nédellec, C., Rouveirol, C. (eds.) ECML 1998. LNCS, vol. 1398, pp. 137–142. Springer, Heidelberg (1998). https://doi.org/10.1007/BFb0026683
28. Bekele, E., et al.: Multimodal adaptive social interaction in virtual environment (MASI-VR) for children with Autism spectrum disorders (ASD). In: 2016 IEEE virtual reality (VR), pp 121–130 (2016). https://doi.org/10.1109/vr.2016.7504695
29. Picard, R.W., et al.: Affective learning—a manifesto. BT Technol. J. **22**(4), 253–269 (2004). https://doi.org/10.1023/B:BTTJ.0000047603.37042.33
30. Patil, T.R., Sherekar, S.S.: Performance analysis of Naive Bayes and J48 classification algorithm for data classification. Int. J. Comput. Sci. Appl. **6**(2), 256–261 (2013)
31. O'Reilly, K.M.A., Mclaughlin, A.M., Beckett, W.S., Sime, P.J.: Asbestos-related lung disease. Am. Fam. Phys. **75**(5), 683–688 (2007)
32. Peddabachigari, S., Abraham, A., Grosan, G., Thomas, J.: Modeling intrusion detection system using hybrid intelligent systems. J. Netw. Comput. Appl. **30**(1), 114–132 (2007)
33. Han, J., Kamber, M.: Data mining: concepts and techniques, 2nd edn. Morgan Kaufmann Publishers, San Francisco (2001)

34. Hastie, T., Tibshirani, R., Friedman, J.H.: The Elements of Statistical Learning: Data Mining, Inference and Prediction. Springer, New York (2001). https://doi.org/10.1007/978-0-387-848 58-7

35. Palechor, F.M., De la Hoz Manotas, A., Colpas, P.A., Ojeda, J.S., Ortega, R.M., Melo, M.P.: Cardiovascular disease analysis using supervised and unsupervised data mining techniques. JSW **12**(2), 81–90 (2017)

36. Mendoza-Palechor, F.E., Ariza-Colpas, P.P., Sepulveda-Ojeda, J.A., De-la-Hoz-Manotas, A., Piñeres Melo, M.: Fertility analysis method based on supervised and unsupervised data mining techniques (2016)

Parasite-Guest Infection Modeling: Social Science Applications

Cesar Vargas-García[1], Jenny Paola Lis-Gutiérrez[2,3(✉)], Mercedes Gaitán-Angulo[3,4],
and Melissa Lis-Gutiérrez[5]

[1] Agrosavia, Mosquera, Colombia
Cavargas@agrosavia.co
[2] Universidad de La Costa, Barranquilla, Colombia
jlis@cuc.edu.co, e.jennypaolalis@go.ugr.es
[3] Universidad de Granada, Melilla, Spain
e.mercedesgaitan@go.ugr.es, m_gaitan689@cues.edu.co
[4] Corporación Universitaria de Salamanca, Barranquilla, Colombia
[5] Corporación Universitaria del Meta, Villavicencio, Colombia
melissa.lis@unimeta.edu.co

Abstract. In this study we argue that parasite-host infections are a major research topic because of their implications for human health, agriculture and wildlife. The evolution of infection mechanisms is a research topic in areas such as virology and ecology. Mathematical modelling has been an essential tool to obtain a better systematic and quantitative understanding of the processes of parasitic infection that are difficult to discern through strictly experimental approaches. In this article we review recent attempts using mathematical models to discriminate and quantify these infection mechanisms. We also emphasize the challenges that these models could bring to new fields of study such as social sciences and economics.

Keywords: Infection modeling · Parasite-host infections · Mathematical model

1 Introduction

Considering that the evolution of parasites and pathogens is important for human health, agricultural systems and wildlife [1, 2], there is a theory that focuses on how the mechanisms of infection can evolve. Because viruses are the most abundant and simple entities on the planet, they are often used as models to study the evolution of parasitic infections. In particular, parameters such as replication, mortality rate of the infected host, infection rate (absorption rate), among others, have been suggested as possible control parameters used by parasites to optimally infect hosts [3–6]. This paper reviewed the different mathematical models that describe the traditional and recently proposed infection mechanisms. In addition, we reviewed how these are used in the optimal dispersion of infections through susceptible host populations.

In the first section, the classic theory of the evolution of the parasite is reviewed. This theory states that natural selection maximizes the number of secondary infections

© Springer Nature Switzerland AG 2020
Y. Tan et al. (Eds.): ICSI 2020, LNCS 12145, pp. 597–603, 2020.
https://doi.org/10.1007/978-3-030-53956-6_55

resulting from infection of a susceptible host through free channels that do not involve direct contact between infected and susceptible hosts [7]. One way of doing this is by the evolution of the infection rate, which is the probability of a parasite infecting a host after direct contact. In restricted environments, the classical theory predicts that a parasite will evolve to an infinite maximum infection rate. However, experiments using bacteria as a host and viruses as parasites show the unexpected appearance of viruses with a moderate or intermediate infection rate [8, 9]. How and under what conditions this intermediate rate evolves is still an open question. The proposed section reviews the classical and recent models that try to explain this phenomenon

It has been suggested that infection channels between infected and susceptible hosts may provide an advantage, either by allowing parasites to evade the host's immune response [10], reducing antiviral drug activity [11], or simply having a more efficient mode of infection.

In the second section, a novel model of parasite-host interactions is proposed that accounts for transmission, both through free channels (not involving contact between infected and susceptible hosts), and through infections produced by contact between hosts. The last section examines the possible social and economic science applications that could result from this modeling.

2 Dynamics of Traditional Infection: The Host Free Mode of Transmission

First consider a basic model for parasite dynamics introduced by [12]. Let H, I and P be the number of healthy and infected hosts and parasites, respectively.

$$\dot{H} = \underbrace{\lambda}_{\substack{\text{Host} \\ \text{production}}} - \underbrace{d_H H}_{\text{Host death}} - \underbrace{rHP}_{\substack{\text{Host - free} \\ \text{infection}}} \tag{1}$$

$$\dot{I} = \underbrace{rHP}_{\text{Host - free}} - \underbrace{d_I I}_{\text{infection}} \tag{2}$$

$$\dot{P} = \underbrace{Bd_I I}_{\substack{\text{Parasite} \\ \text{Production}}} - \underbrace{d_P P}_{\substack{\text{Parasite} \\ \text{death}}} \tag{3}$$

A healthy host reproduces at a rate λ and dies at a d_H rate. The parasite attacks hosts at a rate of rPH, where r is the rate of infection. Once the infected host dies (with latency period $1/d_I$), a set of B-size parasites is released. Alternatively, the term $Bd_I I$ in (3) can be replaced by BI in situations where infected hosts release parasites throughout their life cycle rather than dying before releasing them. Parasites that are free in the environment (outside the infected host) can die at a d_P rate. The level of parasites in the steady state system is:

$$\lim_{t \to \infty} P = \frac{\lambda r(B - 1) - d_H d_P}{d_P r}. \tag{4}$$

Equation (4) can be seen as a way of measuring the parasite's ability to infect. Note, that for the parasite to develop its maximum infective capacity, the infection rate should be infinite (the maximum population of the parasite in a stable state is $\lambda(B - 1)/d_P$).

Alternatively, the number of secondary infections can be used to represent the performance of the parasite. Remember that the infection-free steady state, given by $H = \lambda/d_H$, $I = 0$, y $P = 0$, is an unstable point (meaning that infection will take place) if

$$R_0 = \frac{B\lambda r}{d_H d_P} > 1, \tag{5}$$

Where R_0 is the number of secondary infections and can be interpreted as the number of newly infected hosts produced by an infection. R_0 can be used to infer the evolutionary outcome of the system (3). For example, from (5) it is derived that the parasite should evolve towards infinite infection rates to obtain the maximum fit.

3   Ad Modeling of Effects Produced by Spatial Host Structures

The experiments shown in the literature challenge the theory that parasites can evolve to an infinite infection rate, suggested by the previous model. These experiments show the unexpected appearance of parasites with moderate or low infection rates [8, 9]. Intermediate infection rates can be explained by the presence of the spatial structure of the host [13]. Presumably, parasites with high infection rates tend to create a shielding effect in which the local availability of healthy hosts is reduced, resulting in more interactions with the parasite-infected host, leading to a rate of new parasites equal to zero [7]. Figure 1 shows the shielding effect. This shielding effect can be incorporated into the previous model, assuming the number of parasites released by the death of an infected host as a function of the infection rate [14].

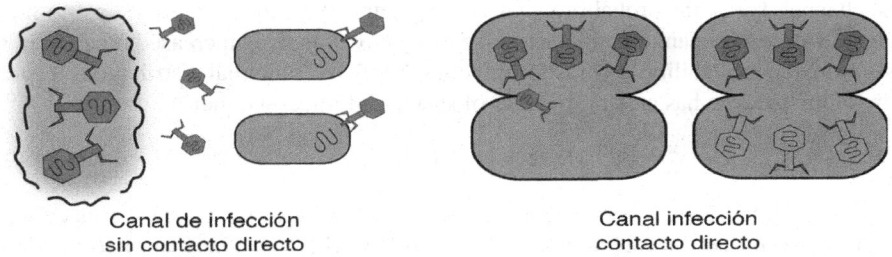

Canal de infección
sin contacto directo

Canal infección
contacto directo

Fig. 1. Screening effect. Channel of infection without direct contact Channel of infection with direct contact. Source: Own elaboration

$$B(r) = b\frac{d_f}{d_f + r\bar{\bar{X}}}. \tag{6}$$

Where b is the maximum number of parasites released that can be obtained from the death of infected cells. d_f represents the ability of the newly released parasite to escape from the harmful residues produced by the death of the infected host. A larger d_f means that the parasite has a high probability of finding a healthy host to infect and reproduce. $\bar{X}$ represents the average amount of waste generated by the death of a single infected host.

This modification produces a new level of parasites in a stable state with an optimal finite infection rate given by (7)

$$r^* = \frac{df \sqrt{d_H d_P}}{\sqrt{b\lambda d_f \bar{X}} - \bar{X}\sqrt{d_H d_P}}. \tag{7}$$

In addition, there is an optimal number of secondary infections given this finite rate of reproduction [14].

4   Mode of Transmission Between Guests

The Our system (1–3) was modified to include the ability of the parasite to carry out transmission by direct contact between infected and susceptible hosts. Let s the number of parasites sent through the channel formed between an infected and a susceptible host. In addition to the infections produced by the traditional mechanism of infection (without direct contact) $r\,P\,H$, we add an additional production of infections represented by $p(s)\beta P H$. Here β is the rate of interaction between infected and uninfected hosts. The $p(s)$ function is the probability that an uninfected host will become infected by receiving s parasites through the channel formed between an infected and a susceptible host. The probability $p(s)$ is defined as:

$$p(s) = f(s)\sigma(s), \tag{8}$$

Where $\sigma(s)$ is the probability that the infected and uninfected host will form a host-to-host channel. $f(s)$ is the probability that sending pathogens through a given host-to-host channel will result in an infection, and can be any monotonously increased function in s. Assuming the probability of parasites infecting a cell as a binomial distribution. If each copy of the parasite has an r probability of successful infection, then

$$f(s) = \left(1 - (1 - r)^s\right), \tag{9}$$

That is, f(s) is the probability that at least one of the parasites will have a successful infection given that there is an enabled host-to-host channel. There are two possible scenarios for host-to-host channel formation: channels between infected and uninfected hosts; and channels between infected hosts. The first scenario leads to an infection with probability p(s). Therefore, there is a reduction in the number of s $\sigma(s)$ H I parasites that cannot be used in other infections. The other scenario arises because there is no discrimination mechanism that causes the infected host to form channels with the uninfected host. Channels between infected hosts produce a waste of parasites s $\sigma(s)$ s $\sigma(s)$ rI^2 that does not produce additional infections, because both cells are already infected. Figure 2 shows the three possible routes of infection from host to host: transmission of parasites without involving direct contact between hosts; transmission of parasites

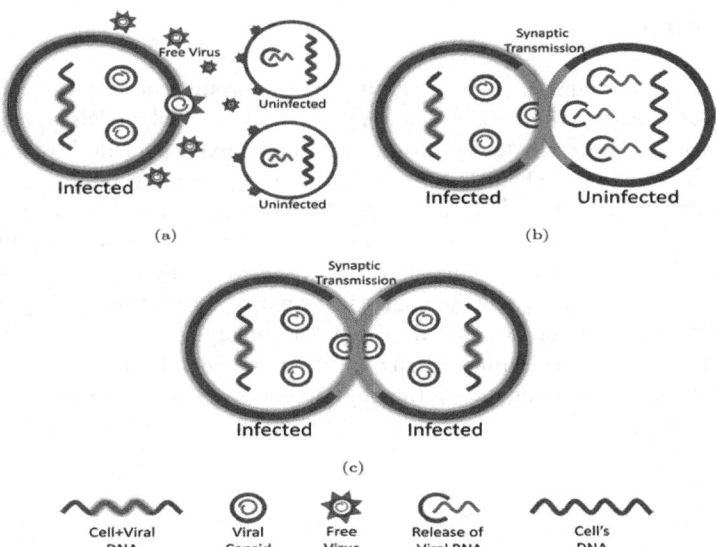

Fig. 2. Mechanisms of infection. Source: Own elaboration (Color figure online)

through channels between infected and uninfected hosts; and transmission of parasites through channels between infected hosts.

Including the mechanism described above in the system (1–3) results in the increased. An application to the AIDS virus of this augmented system is available at work [15].

$$\dot{H} = \lambda - d_H H - rHP - \underbrace{p(s)\beta HI}_{} \qquad (10)$$

$$\text{Host - to - host}$$
$$\text{Infection}$$

$$\dot{I} = rHP - d_I I + \underbrace{p(s)\beta HI}_{} \qquad (11)$$

$$\text{Host - to - host}$$
$$\text{Infection}$$

$$\dot{P} = kI - \underbrace{s\sigma(s)\beta(H+I)I}_{\text{Parasite wasted}} - d_P P. \qquad (12)$$

According to Fig. 2, a parasite has the ability to infect cells through (a) a free channel without direct interaction; (b) through contact. In the former, infected cells produce chains of RNA (red lines) that use information from the parasite stored in their genome (blue and red line), encapsulate them (blue and red concentric circles) and send these out of the cell. Uninfected cells absorb them and release strands of RNA parasites (blue open circle) that integrate with the cell's DNA (blue line). Interactions can occur between infected and uninfected cells (b) or between infected cells (c). Copies of the parasite in (b) sent through contact are not used in the infection of other cells.

5 Discussion

This paper reviewed current approaches in ecology through the use of mathematical tools such as Ordinary Differential Equations (ODEs). Extended models were presented that address issues under debate in ecology, such as optimizing parasite-host interactions and why host infection mechanisms can be beneficial to parasites.

Whether these models and their projections of infection spread can be applied to fields such as economics, business administration and public policy is relevant for future research. For example, recent studies have suggested studying crime in a region in a manner similar to an epidemic. One could, for example, predict how many additional crimes occur in a given season and design public policy using these models. In the medical field, one could determine which transmission model (host-to-host or non-host) is most effective in spreading and mitigating infections, or in agronomic science [16, 17].

References

1. Wodarz, D.: Computational Modeling Approaches to the Dynamics of Oncolytic Viruses. Wiley Interdisciplinary Reviews: Systems Biology and Medicine, pp. 242–252 (2016)
2. Bogitsh, B.J., Carter, C.C., Oeltmann, T.N.: Chapter 2 - parasite–host interactions. In: Human Parasitology, 5th ed, pp. 15–34 (2019)
3. Chao, L.: Fitness of RNA virus decreased by Muller's ratchet. Nature **348**, 454–455 (1990)
4. García-Villada, L., Drake, J.W.: Experimental selection reveals a trade-off between fecundity and lifespan in the coliphage Qß. Open Biol. **3**(6), 130043 (2013)
5. Vargas Garcia, C., Zurakowski, R., Singh, A.: Conditions for invasion of synapse-forming HIV variants. In: IEEE 52nd Conference on Decision and Control (CDC), pp. 7193–7198 (2013)
6. Roychoudhury, P., Shrestha, N., Wiss, V.R., Krone, S.M.: Fitness benefits of low infectivity in a spatially structured population of bacteriophages. Proc. R. Soc. B: Biol. Sci. **281**, 20132563 (2014)
7. Lion, S., Boots, M.: Are parasites "prudent" in space? Ecol. Lett. **13**, 1245–1255 (2010)
8. Boots, M., Mealor, M.: Local interactions select for lower pathogen infectivity. Science **315**, 1284–1286 (2007)
9. Du Toit, A.: Viral infection: changing sides to get in. Nat. Rev. Microbiol. **14**, 476–477 (2016)
10. Martin, N., Sattentau, Q.: Cell-to-cell HIV-1 spread and its implications for immune evasion. Curr. Opin. HIV AIDS **4**(2), 143–149 (2009)
11. Sigal, A., et al.: Cell-to-cell spread of HIV permits ongoing replication despite antiretroviral therapy. Nature **477**(7362), 95–98 (2011)
12. Nowak, M.A., Bangham, C.R.: Population dynamics of immune responses to persistent viruses. Science **272**(5258), 74–79 (1996)
13. Taylor, B.P., Penington, C.J., Weitz, J.S.: Emergence of increased frequency and severity of multiple infections by viruses due to spatial clustering of hosts. bioRxiv (2016)
14. Vargas-García, C.A., Agbemabiese, C., Singh, A.: Optimal adsorption rate: implications of the shielding effect. In: American Control Conference (ACC), pp. 2140–2145 (2017)
15. Vargas-Garcia, C., Zurakowski, R., Singh, A.: Synaptic transmission may provide an evolutionary benefit to HIV through modulation of latency. J. Theor. Biol. **455**, 261–268 (2018)

16. Kokla, A., Melnyk, C.W.: Developing a thief: Haustoria formation in parasitic plants. Dev. Biol. **442**, 53–59 (2018)

17. Viloria, A., Angulo, M.G., Kamatkar, S.J., de la Hoz – Hernandez, J., Guiliany, J.G., Bilbao, O.R., Hernandez-P, H.: Prediction rules in e-learning systems using genetic programming. In: Vijayakumar, V., Neelanarayanan, V., Rao, P., Light, J. (eds.) Proceedings of 6th International Conference on Big Data and Cloud Computing Challenges. SIST, vol. 164, pp. 55–63. Springer, Singapore (2020). https://doi.org/10.1007/978-981-32-9889-7_5

Multi-agent System and Robotic Swarm

Research on Sliding Mode Control of Underwater Vehicle-Manipulator System Based on an Exponential Approach Law

Qirong Tang[(✉)], Yang Hong, Zhenqiang Deng, Daopeng Jin, and Yinghao Li

Laboratory of Robotics and Multibody System, School of Mechanical Engineering, Tongji University, Shanghai 201804, People's Republic of China
qirong.tang@outlook.com

Abstract. To improve the performance of underwater vehicle-manipulator system (UVMS), which is subject to system uncertainties and time-varying external disturbances in trajectory tracking control, a sliding mode controller is proposed in this paper. Firstly, in order to reduce a influence of system uncertainties and external disturbances, a sliding mode controller is designed based on an exponential approach law. Then the error asymptotic convergence of the trajectory tracking control is proven by the Lyapunov-like function. Finally, the effectiveness of the sliding mode controller is verified by rich simulation. Results show that the designed controller can not only realize the coordination control of UVMS accurately, but also can eliminate the chattering of control signal.

Keywords: UVMS · Trajectory tracking · Sliding mode controller · Exponential approach law

1 Introduction

With the development of marine exploration in the world, autonomous underwater vehicle (AUV) has been widely used in the ocean. However, its application has certain limitations. It usually can only perform tasks such as underwater search and monitoring, rather than operation. The underwater vehicle-manipulator system (UVMS) is then attracting more attentions than AUVs because it carries one or even several manipulators to work more flexible. Therefore, more and more countries have carried out systematic studies on UVMS in recent years.

In order to complete various complex tasks, high-precision trajectory tracking controller is then demanded. However, UVMS is strongly coupled and with high nonlinearity [1]. When the manipulator is working, it will disturb the vehicle and even cause interference to the entire system [2]. Therefore, it is urgent to design a reasonable control system for underwater vehicle's trajectory tracking.

© Springer Nature Switzerland AG 2020
Y. Tan et al. (Eds.): ICSI 2020, LNCS 12145, pp. 607–615, 2020.
https://doi.org/10.1007/978-3-030-53956-6_56

In recent years, various controllers have been proposed for UVMS control, including PID control [3,4], fuzzy control [5,6], adaptive control [7,8], robust control [9,10], sliding mode control [11,12] and neural network based control [13]. The response PID control system is slow, and the control precision is limited. Fuzzy control belongs to a kind of experience control. Its control accuracy depends on the perfection of the summarized experience. Although it can have strong interference ability, it is rarely applied to the actual control system alone, and most of them are combined with other control methods. In addition, adaptive control is not very stable. The robust controller synthesis process is time-consuming and cannot be completed online, usually. The initial weight of the neural network based methods have high randomness and a long learning process, so they are difficult to be applied in practice. In comparison, sliding mode control has the advantages of simple implementation, fast response, small perturbation of model parameters and strong robustness, so it is very suitable for the trajectory tracking control of underwater robots. However, its discontinuous switching characteristics will cause chattering in the system. Therefore, it is necessary to tackle of the chattering problem of sliding mode control through certain methods.

In this study, a new control scheme based on an exponential approach law is proposed. The approach law can reduce arrival time and eliminate chattering. Based on this, a sliding mode control scheme for UVMS trajectory tracking control is designed.

The remainder of this paper is organized as follows. Section 2 presents the dynamic model of the concerned UVMS. In Sect. 3, presents the design of sliding mode controller based on the exponential approach law (SMC-EAL). In Sect. 4, the effectiveness of the proposed the SMC-EAL is evaluated through adequate simulations. While Sect. 5 concludes the paper.

2   Dynamic Modelling of UVMS

2.1   Lagrangian Dynamics Modelling of UVMS

The coordinate system of our study object which is equipped with a 2-DOFs manipulator is shown in Fig. 1. And the 3D model of UVMS is shown in Fig. 2. Here $\sum E$, $\sum V$ represent the earth-fixed frame and the vehicle frame, respectively. The position and orientation of UVMS are considered in the inertial frame, i.e.,the earth-fixed frame. The linear velocities and angular velocities of UVMS, as well as the external forces applied to UVMS are considered in the vehicle frame.

The UVMS system consists of two parts: the underwater vehicle and the manipulator, and its generalized coordinates and generalized control force are defined as follows,

$$\boldsymbol{\xi} = [x \; y \; z \; \varphi \; \theta \; \psi \; q_1 \; \cdots \; q_n]^T , \tag{1}$$

$$\boldsymbol{\tau} = [F_x \; F_y \; F_z \; W_x \; W_y \; W_z \; \tau_1 \; \cdots \; \tau_n]^T , \tag{2}$$

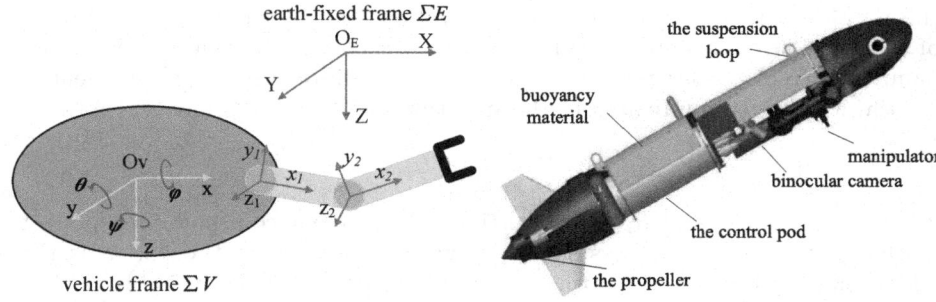

Fig. 1. Coordinate system of UVMS

Fig. 2. Three dimensional model of UVMS

where $\boldsymbol{\xi} = [\eta_T \; q_T]^T \in \mathbb{R}^{6+n}$ is the generalized position vector of UVMS, including the position, attitude and joint variables of the underwater vehicle. Define vector $\boldsymbol{\eta} = [x \; y \; z \; \varphi \; \theta \; \psi]^T$, x, y and z represent the three dimension position of the vehicle, φ, θ and ψ represent the roll angle, longitudinal inclination angle and heading angle of underwater vehicle, respectively. And vector $\mathbf{q} = [q_1 \; \cdots \; q_n]^T \in \mathbb{R}^n$ is the joint angle variable of manipulator. Meanwhile, $\boldsymbol{\tau} \in \mathbb{R}^n$ is the generalized control force term of the system, including the generalized thrust forces of the underwater vehicle and the joint driving forces of the manipulator.

The dynamic equation of UVMS is established according to the second type of Lagrange equation as follow,

$$\frac{d}{dt}(\frac{\partial L}{\partial \dot{\xi}}) - \frac{\partial L}{\partial \xi} = Q, \tag{3}$$

where L is the Lagrange function, $L = T - V$, T is system kinetic energy and V is system potential energy, Q is the generalized force corresponding to the conservative active force, which mainly includes the generalized control force, the restoring torque and the water resistance of the system. Through derivation, the whole dynamic equation of the system is defined as follow,

$$\mathbf{M}(\boldsymbol{\xi})\ddot{\boldsymbol{\xi}} + \mathbf{C}(\boldsymbol{\xi},\dot{\boldsymbol{\xi}})\dot{\boldsymbol{\xi}} + \mathbf{D}(\dot{\boldsymbol{\xi}})\dot{\boldsymbol{\xi}} + \mathbf{G}(\boldsymbol{\xi}) = \boldsymbol{\tau}, \tag{4}$$

where $\mathbf{M}(\boldsymbol{\xi}) \in \mathbb{R}^{(6+n)\times(6+n)}$ is the inertia matrix of UVMS, $\mathbf{C}(\boldsymbol{\xi},\dot{\boldsymbol{\xi}})\dot{\boldsymbol{\xi}} \in \mathbb{R}^{6+n}$ is the centripetal force and corioli term, and $\mathbf{D}(\dot{\boldsymbol{\xi}})\dot{\boldsymbol{\xi}} \in \mathbb{R}^{6+n}$ is the resistance term. Since the center of gravity of UVMS does not coincide with buoyancy, the restoring torque will be generated, and $\mathbf{G}(\boldsymbol{\xi}) \in \mathbb{R}^{6+n}$ is the restoring force term generated by the combined torque of gravity and buoyancy of UVMS.

2.2 Determination of Hydrodynamic Coefficient

It is difficult to calculate the hydrodynamic coefficient fully in underwater hydrodynamics, so it is necessary to determine which coefficients are important. Inertial hydrodynamics are only related to the acceleration of each moving part of the UVMS. It is linearly related to acceleration, and in the opposite direction of acceleration. Similar to the conventional mass concept, the inertial hydrodynamic force and acceleration are defined as the additional mass and moment of inertia, which are only related to the structure of UVMS, and have the form of

$$R_i = -\lambda_i \cdot U_i, \tag{5}$$

where $i = 1, 2, ..., 6$, and R_i is the inertial hydrodynamic coordinate component in the moving coordinate system, U_i is the acceleration of UVMS, λ_i is the additional inertia mass or inertia moment of UVMS, as shown in Table 1.

Table 1. The UVMS additional mass and additional inertial moment

λ_i	λ_1(kg)	λ_2(kg)	λ_3(kg)	λ_4(kg·m^2)	λ_5(kg·m^2)	λ_6(kg·m^2)
Calculation results	29.13	247.04	462.66	2.01	48.6	23.455

Viscous hydrodynamic force is mainly the water resistance applied to UVMS. It is mainly affected by the velocity and the square term of the moving system, so the higher order term of the velocity is usually ignored. In the system dynamics model, the viscous flow resistance is defined as follow,

$$\begin{aligned} \mathbf{D}(\dot{\xi}) &= -\mathbf{diag}\{X_u, Y_v, Z_w, K_p, M_q, N_r\} \\ &= -\mathbf{diag}\left[X_{u|u|}|u|, Y_{v|v|}|v|, Z_{w|w|}|w|, K_{p|p|}|p|, M_{q|q|}|q|, N_{r|r|}|r|\right\}, \end{aligned} \tag{6}$$

where $X_u, Y_v, Z_w, K_P, M_q, N_r$ represent the hydrodynamic coefficient terms in different directions, respectively. By introducing the force and torque of UVMS measured in the ship model test into the fitting formula of hydrodynamic coefficient, the hydrodynamic coefficients are obtained as shown in the Table 2.

Table 2. The hydrodynamic coefficients obtained by the ship model test

Hydrodynamic item	$X_{u|u|}$	$Y_{v|v|}$	$Z_{w|w|}$	$M_{q|q|}$	$N_{r|r|}$
Fitting results	0.00735	−0.1765	−0.1940	−0.0655	−0.0148

3   Design of Sliding Mode Controller

3.1   Sliding Mode Variable Structure Control

The basic principle of sliding mode variable structure control is that the controller limits the current state or state error of the system to the sliding mode surface and makes it stable on the sliding mode surface. Since the sliding mode motion characteristics are designed in advance according to the requirements, and the trajectory given at the same time has nothing to do with the control object parameters and external disturbance changes. Therefore, sliding mode control is insensitive to parameter changes and disturbances, and the system is extremely robust. However, in the actual control system, due to the mass inertia and time delay and other factors, the sliding mode variable structure control will have chattering in the sliding mode.

The process of implementing sliding mode variable structure control mainly includes determining the sliding mode arrival condition of the system, selecting the sliding mode surface and obtaining the system controller law, then establishing the controller.

3.2 Design of UVMS Sliding Mode Controller

The designed exponential approach law is applied to the sliding mode controller of UVMS, and compensation is carried out in the controller to improve the control accuracy, reduce the gain of sliding mode control, and thus reduce the chattering of the system. The proposed sliding mode control system is shown in Fig. 3.

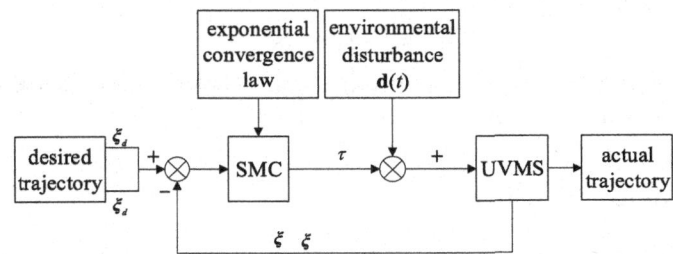

Fig. 3. The implementation structure of the sliding mode controller

Firstly, the expected trajectory of UVMS is set as follow $\boldsymbol{\xi}_d(t)$, $t \in \begin{bmatrix} 0 \ T \end{bmatrix}$. The corresponding velocity is $\dot{\boldsymbol{\xi}}(t)$, exists and continues throughout the time period. The trajectory tracking error and trajectory tracking error change rate are set as follow,

$$\begin{cases} \mathbf{e} = \boldsymbol{\xi}_d - \boldsymbol{\xi} \\ \dot{\mathbf{e}} = de/dt = \dot{\boldsymbol{\xi}}_d - \dot{\boldsymbol{\xi}}, \end{cases} \tag{7}$$

meanwhile, the linear sliding mode surface is selected, as shown in Eq. (8),

$$\mathbf{s} = \mathbf{c}\mathbf{e} + \dot{\mathbf{e}}, \tag{8}$$

and

$$\begin{cases} \mathbf{s} = \begin{bmatrix} s_1 \ s_2 \ \cdots \ s_N \end{bmatrix}^T \\ \mathbf{c} = \mathbf{diag} \left\{ c_1 \ c_2 \ \cdots \ c_N \right\}, \end{cases} \tag{9}$$

where **s** is the sliding mode surface vector of the control system, and **c** is the parameter matrix of the sliding mode surface of the system. In order to improve the dynamic quality of the sliding mode surface and reduce the chattering, the controller is designed based on the exponential approach law, which is shown in Eq. (10),

$$\dot{\mathbf{s}} = d\mathbf{s}/dt = -\varepsilon sgn(\mathbf{s}) - k\mathbf{s}, (\varepsilon > 0, k > 0), \tag{10}$$

where

$$sgn(\mathbf{s}) = \begin{cases} 1, & s > 0 \\ 0, & s = 0 \\ -1, & s < 0 \end{cases}, \tag{11}$$

combining Eqs. (6)–(8) and (10), the sliding mode controller law is designed as follows,

$$\begin{aligned} \mathbf{u} = \boldsymbol{\tau} = \mathbf{M}(\boldsymbol{\xi})(\mathbf{c}\dot{\mathbf{e}} + \varepsilon sgn(\mathbf{s}) + k\mathbf{s} + \ddot{\boldsymbol{\xi}}_d) \\ + \mathbf{C}(\boldsymbol{\xi}, \dot{\boldsymbol{\xi}})(\mathbf{c}\mathbf{e} - \mathbf{s} + \dot{\boldsymbol{\xi}}_d) \\ + \mathbf{D}(\dot{\boldsymbol{\xi}})(\mathbf{c}\mathbf{e} - \mathbf{s} + \dot{\boldsymbol{\xi}}_d) + \mathbf{G}(\boldsymbol{\xi}). \end{aligned} \tag{12}$$

In order to satisfy the sliding mode arrival condition and have certain stability, Lyapunov stability condition needs to be satisfied. Lyapunov function of the system is selected as

$$\dot{V} = -\varepsilon |\mathbf{s}| - k\mathbf{s}^2, \tag{13}$$

since $\varepsilon > 0, k > 0, \dot{V} < 0$, if and only if s = 0. The system satisfies Lyapunov stability condition, so the system is gradually stable.

4   Simulation Studies

In order to verify the effectiveness of the designed sliding mode control strategy, the expected trajectory is set under the simulation condition, and the actual trajectory is compared with the expected trajectory.

4.1   Simulation Object

To illustrate the effectiveness of the proposed SMC, comparative simulations in presence of environmental disturbances have been performed on a UVMS, which consists of a 6-DOFs vehicle and a 2-DOFs rotary joint manipulator. The specific parameters of the system are listed in Table 3 and Table 4.

In the simulation, expected trajectory of UVMS is set as $\boldsymbol{\xi}_d = [x_d \; y_d \; z_d \; \varphi_d \theta_d \; \psi_d \; q_{1d} \; q_{2d}]^T$, where $x_d=4cos(0.04\pi t)$, $y_d=4sin(0.04\pi t)$, $z_d=0.5t$, $\varphi_d=0$, $\theta_d=0$, $\psi_d=0$, $q_{1d}=10°$, $q_{2d}=20°$.

The design trajectory is a three-dimensional spiral with a turning period of 50 s. The UVMS adjusts its attitude during the dive, and the manipulator is deployed during the dive. The initial pose vector of UVMS is $\boldsymbol{\xi}_0 = [2 \; 2 \; 0 \; 10° \; 20° \; 0 \; 0 \; 0]^T$.

Table 3. Main parameters of UVMS

Items	Vehicle	Link 1	Link 2
m/kg	85.2	2.603	3.159
$I_{xx}/\text{kg}\cdot m^2$	35.040	0.0062	0.177
$I_{yy}/\text{kg}\cdot m^2$	2.140	0.0061	0.177
$I_{zz}/\text{kg}\cdot m^2$	35.667	0.0071	0.0047
$I_{xy}/\text{kg}\cdot m^2$	−0.0063	0	0
$I_{xz}/\text{kg}\cdot m^2$	0	0	0
$I_{yz}/\text{kg}\cdot m^2$	−0.0233	0	0.00559

Table 4. D-H parameters of manipulator in UVMS

joint	θ_i (rad)	α_i (rad)	α_{i-1} (rad)	d_i (mm)
1	0	$\pi/2$	0	0
2	π	$\pi/2$	0	0.312

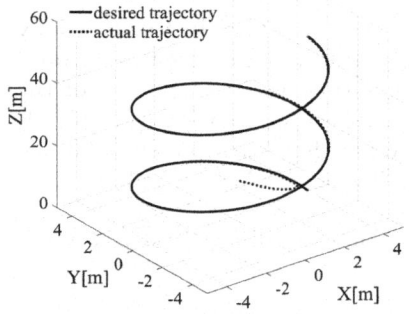

Fig. 4. 3D trajectory tracking result of UVMS

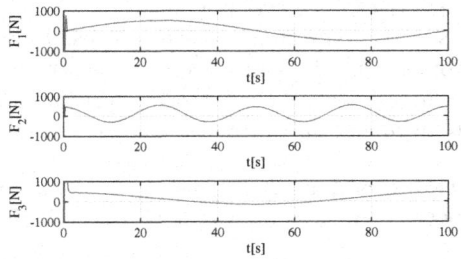

Fig. 5. Position control inputs of UVMS in separate dimension

4.2 Analysis of Simulation Results

In the simulation, SMC's gain is set as $k = 20$, and trajectory tracking result shown in Fig. 4. The desired trajectory is well stacked under SMC-ELA. And Figs. 5, 6 and 7 represent the position and attitude of UVMS, and the control inputs of each joint of the manipulator in each single degree of freedom, respectively. It can be seen from Figs. 4, 5, 6 and 7 that the sliding mode controller with exponential approach law is feasible for the control of UVMS with a relatively acceptable accuracy. The control switching gain in the sliding mode control simulation process is small, and the chattering of the control signal can be significantly suppressed.

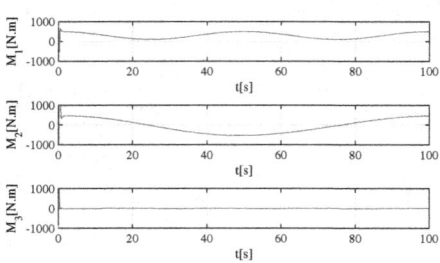
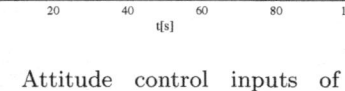

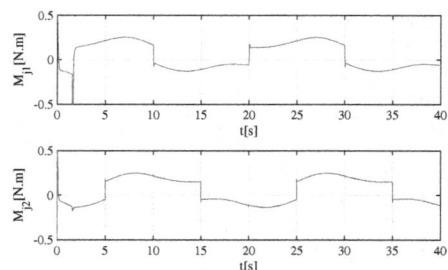

Fig. 6. Attitude control inputs of UVMS in separate dimension

Fig. 7. Joint motion control inputs of UVMS

5   Conclusion

This study presents a sliding mode controller. It is validated in this study by the trajectory tracking control of UVMS, which is subject to system uncertainties and environment disturbances. In the simulation, the effectiveness of the proposed method has been demonstrated. Moreover, the proposed controller is featured with higher tracking accuracy of UVMS with regard to environmental disturbances and provides a reference for the following UVMS control.

Acknowledgements. This work is supported by the projects of National Natural Science Foundation of China (No. 61603277, No. 61873192, No. 51579053).

References

1. Dai, Y., Yu, S.: Design of an indirect adaptive controller for the trajectory tracking of UVMS. Ocean Eng. **151**, 234–245 (2018)
2. Liu, H., Li, M., Liu, X.: Control of underwater robot attitude in wave based on fuzzy sliding mode method. J. Donghua Univ. **27**(2), 143–147 (2010)
3. Lashin, M., Fanni, M., Magdy, M., Mohamed, A.: PD type of fuzzy controller for a new 3DOF fully decoupled translational manipulator. In: Proceedings of the 2016 International Conference on Control, Automation and Robotics (ICCAR), Hong Kong, China, 28–30 April, pp. 263–267 (2016)
4. Han, J., Chung, W.: Active use of restoring moments for motion control of an underwater vehicle-manipulator system. IEEE J. Oceanic Eng. **39**(1), 100–109 (2014)
5. Xu, B., Pandian, S., Sakagami, N., Petry, F.: Neuro-fuzzy control of underwater vehicle-manipulator systems. J. Franklin Inst. **27**(3), 1125–1138 (2012)
6. Kazuo, T., Hua, W.: Fuzzy control systems design and analysis: a linear matrix inequality approach. Automatica **39**(11), 2011–2013 (2001)
7. Yong, C., Junku, Y.: A unified adaptive force control of underwater vehicle-manipulator systems (UVMS). In: Proceedings of the IEEE/RSJ International Conference on Intelligent Robots and Systems (IROS), 27–31 October Las Vegas, USA, pp. 553–558 (2003)

8. Mai, T.-L., Wang, Y.: Adaptive-backstepping force/motion control for mobile-manipulator robot based on fuzzy CMAC neural networks. Control Theory Technol. **12**(4), 368–382 (2014). https://doi.org/10.1007/s11768-014-3181-4

9. Xu, B., Abe, S., Sakagami, N., Pandian. S.: Robust nonlinear controller for underwater vehicle-manipulator systems. In: Proceedings of the 2005 International Conference on Advanced Intelligent Mechatronics, 24–28 July, Monterey, USA, pp. 711–716 (2005)

10. Taira, Y., Sagara, S., Oya, M.: A robust controller with integral action for underwater vehicle-manipulator systems including thruster dynamics. In: Proceedings of the 2014 International Conference on Advanced Mechatronic Systems (ICAMechS), 10–12 August Kumamoto, Japan, pp. 415–420 (2014)

11. Yang, Q., Su, H., Tang, G., Gao, D.: Robust optimal sliding mode control for AUV system with uncertainties. Inf. Control **47**(2), 176–183 (2018)

12. Kim, D., Choi, H.-S., Kim, J.-Y., Park, J.-H., Tran, N.-H.: Trajectory generation and sliding-mode controller design of an underwater vehicle-manipulator system with redundancy. Int. J. Precis. Eng. Manuf. **16**(7), 1561–1570 (2015). https://doi.org/10.1007/s12541-015-0206-y

13. Ge, S., Hong, F., Lee, T.: Adaptive neural network control of nonlinear systems with unknown time delays. In: Proceedings of the 2003 American Control Conference, 4–6 June, Denver, USA, pp. 4524–4529 (2003)

A Parallel Evolutionary Algorithm with Value Decomposition for Multi-agent Problems

Gao Li[✉], Qiqi Duan, and Yuhui Shi

Department of Computer Science and Engineering,
Southern University of Science and Technology, Shenzhen, China
lg16@qq.com, shiyh@sustech.edu.cn

Abstract. Many real-world problems involve cooperation and/or competition among multiple agents. These problems often can be formulated as multi-agent problems. Recently, Reinforcement Learning (RL) has made significant progress on single-agent problems. However, multi-agent problems still cannot be easily solved by traditional RL algorithms. First, the multi-agent environment is considered as a non-stationary system. Second, most multi-agent environments only provide a shared team reward as feedback. As a result, agents may not be able to learn proper cooperative or competitive behaviors by traditional RL. Our algorithm adopts Evolution Strategies (ES) for optimizing policy which is used to control agents and a value decomposition method for estimating proper fitness for each policy. Evolutionary Algorithm is considered as a promising alternative for signal-agent problems. Owing to its simplicity, scalability, and efficiency on zeroth-order optimization, EAs can even outperform RLs on some tasks. In order to solve multi-agent problems by EA, a value decomposition method is used to decompose the team reward. Our method is parallel on multiple cores, which can speed up our algorithm significantly. We test our algorithm on two benchmarking environments, and the experiment results show that our algorithm is better than traditional RL and other representative gradient-free methods.

Keywords: Multi-agent problems · Evolutionary algorithm · Value decomposition · Reinforcement learning

1 Introduction

Cooperative and competitive behavior is a common intelligent phenomenon that has been discovered in many domains, such as ant colony [1] and human social behavior [2]. There is a lot of research inspired by such phenomenon [3, 4]. Nowadays, people are becoming more interested in the research of how these behaviors emerge, and some works try to reproduce such phenomena through algorithms directly [5, 6]. This type of research problem can be formally defined as multi-agent tasks. Research on multi-agent problems can help us better understand our social behavior, design better traffic controlling system and so on. In this paper, we focus on cooperative behavior of multi-agent problems.

Recently, RL algorithms have made significant progress on single-agent problems [7, 8]. However, these traditional RL algorithms are not very effective for multi-agent

© Springer Nature Switzerland AG 2020
Y. Tan et al. (Eds.): ICSI 2020, LNCS 12145, pp. 616–627, 2020.
https://doi.org/10.1007/978-3-030-53956-6_57

problems, because the multi-agent problem is much more complicated than the single-agent problem. First, the environments of most single-agent problems are stationary. But, in the multi-agent problem setting, the policy of each agent changes over time, the environment would be non-stationary for an agent if it regards other agents as a part of the environment [9]. However, the stationary environment is one of prerequisites for traditional RL convergence [19]. So, the multi-agent problem is non-trivial to be solved by traditional RL algorithms.

Very recently, some research shows that Evolutionary Algorithms (EAs), also makes a competitive performance on single-agent problems [11, 12]. The performance of EA even outperforms RL in several single-agent control tasks. Compared to RL, EA is simple and easier to implement. Also, because EA is a gradient-free method, it is known as a better solution for non-convex optimization problems whose gradient is difficult to obtain. What is more, EA has better parallelization capability. EA is easier to be scaled on multi-core computers compare to some traditional RLs [22].

However, there are some difficulties for traditional EA to solve multi-agent problems. In the multi-agent environment, agents often only receive a shared reward of the whole team [13]. For example, a group of football players receives a reward only after they lost or win that match. If we directly use the team reward to optimize the independent policy through EA, it would be difficult for agents to learn proper cooperative behaviors.

In this paper, we propose an approach, named Parallel Evolution Strategies with Value Decomposition (PES-VD), for cooperative multi-agent problems. PES-VD is a hybrid method, combining with EA and RL. First, we extended the Parallelized Evolution Strategies [11] and designed a variant named Parallelized Evolution Strategies for direct policy search. Second, we take advantage of RL and developed a value decomposition approach to estimate fitness for policy evaluation. Third, in order to improve the efficiency of our approach, we parallel our algorithm in multiple cores.

2   Related Work

In recent years, several significant progresses have been made in the field of multi-agent problems. Multi-agent reinforcement learning [9, 10] is one of the most popular methods for multi-agent problems.

Similar to the traditional RL, there are two types of multi-agent reinforcement learning: value-based and policy-based. The first type of multi-agent reinforcement learning is always used for solving the multi-agent problem with discrete action-space. One of the most commonly applied methods for multi-agent problems is Independent Q-learning (IQL) [14]. IQL is extended directly from Q-learning, and train each agent through a separated Q-learning. However, this method does not work well for multi-agent problems. Because of the restriction of the tabular manner, IQL only could be used for low-dimension problems. Tampuu et al. replace the tabular manner by deep neural network [15]. With deep neural network, the approach has better generalization ability. Benefits from the decentralized training procedure, these approaches are easy to scale. But these methods are also unstable because of the decentralized training in the non-stationary environment where agents learn simultaneously.

In order to reduce the effect of the non-stationary in the environment, a set of works adopt centralized training and decentralized execution manners. Value Decomposition

Network (VDN) [16] acquires the idea from independent deep Q-learning. During the centralized training process, VDN sum up the Q-value of each agent for estimating a team reward. QMIX [17] is another value-based approach, which estimates total Q-value through a monotonic function of each agent's Q-value. It shows that monotonic function can guarantee consistency between centralized and decentralized policies. However, these value-based methods are not good solutions for multi-agent problems with continue or high-dimensional action space.

Policy-based RL approach is another type of algorithms for multi-agent problems. Counterfactual Multi-Agent Policy Gradients (COMA) [18] is based on the framework of actor-critic reinforcement learning. It needs to train a fully centralized critic in COMA, which will be impractical as the number of agents increasing. Multi-Agent Deep Deterministic Policy Gradient (MADDPG) [19] achieves great performance in a set of simple multi-agent problem environments. Although MADDPG only needs the combination of observations and actions of all agents as training data, the dimension of input space still will grow dramatically as the number of agents increasing.

Evolutionary algorithm (EA) as a type of gradient-free approaches also shows promising performance in agent controlling problems. From the perspective of RL, EAs also can be considered as policy-based algorithms [26]. NeuroEvolution of Augmenting Topologies (NEAT) [20] evolves both the structure and parameters of a neural network. But NEAT is a time-consuming approach, and it is not suitable for optimizing deep neural network. In recent years, researchers also adopt Random Search [21], Evolution Strategies [11] and Genetic Algorithm [12] for optimizing parameters of neural network. Benefit from the rapid development of parallelization technology, these traditional algorithms can gain competitive performance as state-of-the-art RL in some challenging single-agent problem. However, it is difficult for EA to be deployed in multi-agent problems directly, especially for the tasks which only provide a shared team reword. Agents might unable to learn proper behaviors by EA if we directly use the team reward as fitness.

3   Problem Description

Generally, the multi-agent problem can be formalized as a Markov Game [10] with a tuple $G = \{S, U, O, P, r, N, \gamma, T\}$. It defines an environment with a global state S, where there are N agents. Each agent $i \in \{1, \ldots N\}$ has its observations O_i and actions A_i. The state of the environment is initialized randomly by a distribution unavailable to all agents $\rho : S \rightarrow [0, 1]$. At each time step, agents carry out actions based on their observations. Typically, these actions are chosen through a policy $\pi_i : O_i \times A_i \rightarrow [0, 1]$, and form a joint action $U = A_1 \times \ldots \times A_N$. Then, the environment turns into a new state s' according to a transition function $P(s'|s, \boldsymbol{a}) : S \times U \times S \rightarrow [0, 1]$. For agent i, it receives new observations $o_i : S \rightarrow O_i$ and a reward $r_i : S \times U \rightarrow \mathbb{R}$ in this new environment state. γ is the reward discount factor and the time horizon T can be a finite or infinite.

In this paper, we consider the cooperation setting. All agents receive a shared team reward r from the environment with discrete time-space and partial observation. Each episode has finite time steps T. Agents choose actions through their deterministic policies

π. So in this cooperation Markov Game setting, the goal of the task is to maximize the expectation of team rewards (1).

$$\max_{\pi} R(\pi) = \mathbb{E}\left(\sum_{t=0}^{T} r\left(o^t, a^t\right)\right) \tag{1}$$

4 Proposed Method

Our method consists of two parts, value decomposition and policies. The value decomposition network can be considered as a coach for guiding the training of agents and is only used while training. A variant named Parallelized Evolution Strategies is designed for the training of independent policies. The overview of our algorithm is shown in Fig. 1. Our method is implemented in parallel. Workers are used to evaluate the policies and calculate the gradient of value decomposition network. Then, the master process collects data from workers to update policies and value decomposition network.

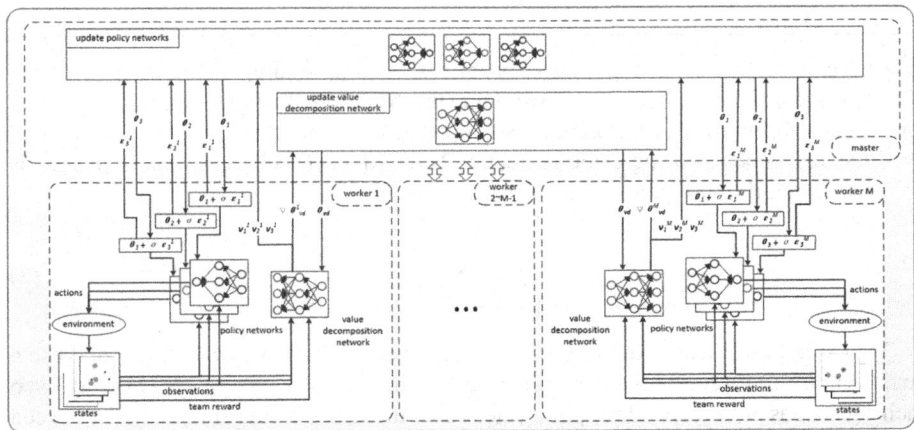

Fig. 1. The overview of our algorithm

Value decomposition network and policy networks learn simultaneously during the training process, while only policy networks are required during execution. Agents choose actions through their policies independently and interact with the environment. The input data of the policy network is the partial observation of the related agent. Value decomposition estimates fitness for the policies. The input data of the value decomposition network consists of whole observations and the team reward.

4.1 Parallelized Evolution Strategies

We employ an artificial neural network which is parameterized by θ to represents the policy of one agent. Different from gradient-based methods for neural network training, we train these policies through Evolution Strategies. Algorithm 1 illustrates the detail of the variant Parallelized Evolution Strategies used in our algorithm. M workers are used to evaluate the policies in multiple processes, and a master collects the data from workers to update policies.

Algorithm 1 A Variant Parallelized Evolution Strategies

1:   **Input:** learning rate α_p, noise standard deviation σ, initial policy parameters $\theta_1^0, \theta_2^0, ..., \theta_N^0$
2:   **Initialize:** M workers with known random seeds, and initial parameters $\theta_1^0, \theta_2^0, ..., \theta_N^0$
3:   **for** generation $g = 0, 1, 2, ...$ **do**
4:     **for** each worker $j = 1, ..., M$ **do**
5:       **for** each agent $i = 1, ..., N$ **do**
6:         Sample $\epsilon_i^j \sim \mathcal{N}(0, I)$
7:         Compute return $f_i^j = f(\theta_g^j + \sigma \epsilon_g^j)$
8:       **end for**
9:       Send scalar returns f_i to the master
10:     **end for**
11:     Master reconstruct all perturbation ϵ_i^j for $j = 1, ..., M$ and $i = 1, ..., N$ using know random seeds
12:     Set $\theta_i^{g+1} \leftarrow \theta_i^g + \alpha_p \, 1/n\sigma \sum_j^M f_i^j \epsilon_i^j$ for $i = 1, ..., N$
13:     Synchronize θ_i^{g+1} with workers for $i = 1, ..., N$
14:   **end for**

PES can work well on single-agent problems, even if we simply sum up the rewards of an episode as fitness 11. However, we found this fitness evaluation manner is not suited for cooperative multi-agent problems. So, a predicted state value v_i which is estimated by value decomposition (describe at Sect. 4.2) based on the observations of agent i is used for calculating the fitness f_i of a T steps episode (2).

$$f_i = \sum_{t=1}^{T} v_i^t \tag{2}$$

We extend our method directly from Parallelized Evolutionary Strategies and use a random noise to represent the variance added to the network parameters [11]. So, even each agent has its independent policy network, the overall data transmitted between processes is still acceptable.

4.2 Value Decomposition Network

For cooperative multi-agent problems, we found EA always does not work well if we simply regard the team reward as its fitness, because the team reward cannot effectively reflect the contribution of each agent for the whole group. For this reason, we developed a value decomposition network, for evaluating the proper contribution of each agent during the training process.

For the value decomposition network, each value network is parameterized by θ_i^v. At each step, value decomposition takes the observations of all agents as input data for calculating a join value v^t and individual values v_i of each agent. Taking all observations as input can significantly alleviate the effect of non-stationary problems in the multi-agent environment [19]. Inspired by [16], we also assume that the joint value function can be decomposed into value function across agents. So, we have the Eq. (3), and the team reward received from the environment can be used for the training of value decomposition network directly.

$$v^t \approx \sum_{i=1}^{N} v_i \qquad (3)$$

We adopt Temporal Differences (TD) error as a loss function for the network updating (4).

$$TD = r^t + \lambda v\left(o^{t+1}; \boldsymbol{\theta}^v\right) - v\left(o^t; \boldsymbol{\theta}^v\right) \qquad (4)$$

Because $Q\left(o^t, a^t\right) = \mathbb{E}\left(r^t + \lambda v\left(o^{t+1}; \boldsymbol{\theta}^v\right)\right)$ is not directly equal to $v\left(o^t; \boldsymbol{\theta}^v\right)$, loss function (4) might cannot accurately estimate the actual loss. However, the experiments from Asynchronous Advantage Actor-Critic (A3C) [22] show that this estimation manner can reduce the complexity of the neural network architecture and is more conducive to obtaining stable results.

Different from the critic network in A3C, we implement a separate network for estimating the target state value $v\left(o^{t+1}; \boldsymbol{\theta}^{v'}\right)$ similar to DQN [8]. The experiment results (Sect. 5.3) show that the separate network can significantly improve the efficiency and stability of our algorithm.

4.3 Parallelization

Our algorithm consists of two parts: policies and value decomposition. In order to accelerate the training efficiency and better use computer resources, we implement the policies and the value decomposition algorithm in parallel.

The parallelization of the policy has been introduced in Sect. 4.1. The parallel realization of the value decomposition is inspected by the idea of Parallel Reinforcement Learning in [22]. However, instead of running in multiple threads, we implement our algorithm in multiple cores. Although it will cost more communication resources, running in multiple cores can have better use of CPU resources [22].

Figure 2 illustrates the working flow of the value decomposition network in multiple processes.

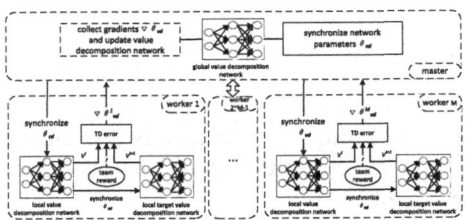

Fig. 2. Parallelization structure of value decomposition network

The master process maintains a global value decomposition network parameterized by θ_{vd} and each worker process has a local value decomposition network parameterized by θ_{vd}^j and a local target value decomposition network. The local value decomposition initializes its parameters from global value decomposition at the beginning. Then, at each generation of PES, the local value decomposition network calculates its gradients and uploads them to the master. Master updates the global value decomposition parameters based on the Eq. (5) and then synchronizes them to the local value decomposition at the beginning of the next generation.

$$\theta_{vd} \leftarrow \theta_{vd} + \alpha_{vd} \sum_{j}^{M} \partial(TD)/\partial\theta_{vd}^j \tag{5}$$

For the local target value decomposition network, we update its parameters every $\beta > 1$ generations. The training process will be more stable and efficient by using a separate network for estimating the target value [8].

5   Experiment Results

We compare our algorithm with both gradient-based and gradient-free methods in two different multi-agent environments: Multi-Agent Particle Environment (MAPE) [23] and StarCraft Multi-Agent Challenge (SMAC) [13]. For gradient-based methods, we compare with REINFORCE [24], Actor-Critic [25], DQN [8], VDN [16]. Particularly, VDN is a state-of-the-art value-based approach for multi-agent problems. For gradient-free methods, we also compare our method with Random Search (RS) [21] and Evolution Strategies (ES) [11].

We adopt the same network architecture for our algorithm in those two environments. For the Policy network, we use two tanh MLP with 256 units per layer. At each time step, each Policy network takes observations of the related agent as input and outputs actions.

The value network of value decomposition also has two hidden layers. The first layer is a MLP with 256 units, and the second layer is a LSTM with 256 units. The value network takes observations of the related agent as input and outputs a state value. The Mixer layer of value decomposition sums up the values output by each value network. We share the parameters of each value network, which can improve the convergence efficiency of the network in these cooperative multi-agent problems [16]. We run our algorithm on a server with 72 CPU cores.

5.1   Experiment on MAPE

Multi-Agent Particle Environment (MAPE) is a 2D simple world with N agents and L landmarks. Action-space is continuous and time is discrete in this environment. At each time step, agents carry out a discrete action. We evaluated our algorithm in the Cooperative Navigation task of MAPE

We compare our algorithm with RS, ES, REINFORCE, Actor-Critic, DQN, VDN in this environment. Each algorithm that we evaluate in this environment had been trained to converge. The max episode steps are 25 in this task.

We evaluate 100 episodes for each method and use the average distance from landmarks (Dist.), the number of collisions (Collisions), and the number of occupied landmarks (Occupied Landmarks) for comparison.

It can be seen from the results in Table 1 that both gradient-based methods (REINFORCE, Actor-Critic, DQN, and VDN) and gradient-free methods (RS and ES) cannot solve the Cooperative Navigation task properly. Those approaches only consider how to maximize the expected reward of the agent itself and ignore the whole team reward. Under this mechanism, agents would lose sign of which behaviors are more beneficial for their team.

Table 1. The results of cooperative navigation task

Algorithm	Dist.	Collisions	Occupied landmarks
RS	1.92	25.52	0.04
ES	1.37	26.69	0.11
REINFORCE	8.01	25.21	0.01
Actor-critic	1.36	25.73	0.13
DQN	1.56	26.31	0.09
VDN	2.21	25.12	0.5
CAES	0.31	27.11	1.6

However, for this task, we found our method causes more collisions than other approaches among agents while navigation. Because the Evolutionary Algorithm is more concerned about long-term rewards and ignores some short-term conditions. What is more, as agents approaching the landmarks simultaneously, it will be more prone to collisions between agents.

5.2 Experiment on SMAC

The StarCraft Multi-Agent Challenge (SMAC), focuses on micromanagement challenges where units are controlled by separated agents. The observations of this environment for each agent are partial. Agents only receive the information around them at a certain distance. There are two groups of units that fight with each other at the tasks of SMAC. One group is controlled by training agents, and the other is controlled by pre-designed rules. The goal of each group is to destroy the opposed one. Agents will receive positive collective rewards depending on how much harm they have made to the opposed group.

We test our algorithm in 3s_vs_4z and 2c_vs_64zg tasks of SMAC. The 3s_vs_4z and 2c_vs_64zg tasks both are homogeneous and asymmetric type missions. It evaluates kiting ability in the 3s_vs_4z task with 3 Stalker ally units and 4 Zealot enemy units. Besides, the 2c_vs_64zg task is a harder one which needs more positioning strategy for agents to win the competition. There are 2 Colossi allay units and 64 Zergling enemy units in the 2c_vs_64zg task. We compare our algorithm with gradient-free methods (RS, ES) in these two tasks.

We train these three algorithms for 1500 generations and evaluate the average episode team reward received at each generation.

As the results shown in Fig. 3 and Fig. 4, in these two SMAC tasks, our method can receive higher average episode rewards than RS and ES. We also found that the performances of RS and ES do not change too much even if been trained longer. On the contrary, our method has the ability to learn different cooperation strategies in different environments.

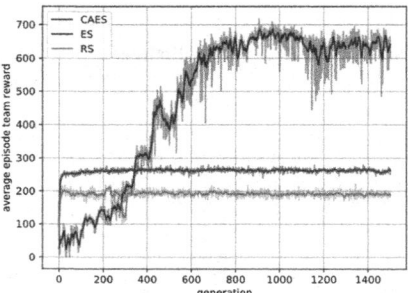

Fig. 3. Results in the 3s_vs_4z task

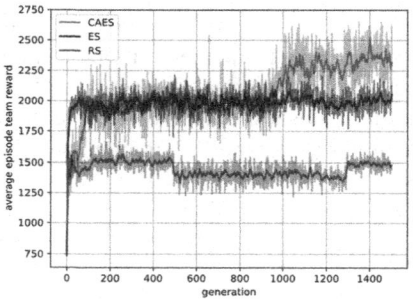

Fig. 4. Results in the 2c_vs_64zg task

5.3 Separate Network Ablation Experiment

Although A3C does not adopt a separate network for target value prediction, we found using a separate network can improve convergent efficiency and stability for our algorithm. Actually, the complex of our algorithm does not change too much while parallels in multiple processes with a separate network.

We both test our original algorithm and the one without a separate network in the Cooperative Navigation task of MAPE. The results are shown in Fig. 5.

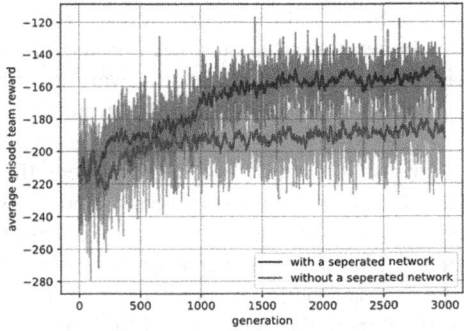

Fig. 5. Results of without a separated network and with a separated network in Cooperative Navigation task

The results show the average episode team rewards received by agents within 3000 generations of training. The agent trained by the algorithm with a separate network can reach a higher reward faster. However, without separate network one is less efficient, and the episode reward has not been enhanced much even if it has been trained for 6000 generations.

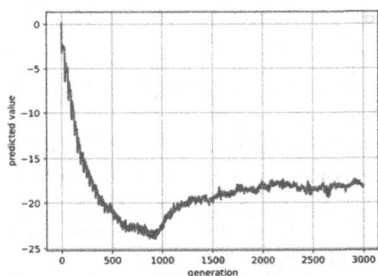

Fig. 6. Predicted fitness estimated by value decomposition

6 Conclusion and Future Work

Our approach is based on Evolutionary Algorithm which is used for the training of the policy networks. A value decomposition network is adopted for decomposing team reward. Policy networks and value decomposition network are trained simultaneously during the learning process. While only policy networks are needed in the execution phase. We test our algorithm in two different environments and compare it with REINFORCE, Actor-critic, DQN, VDN, RS, ES.

In both environments, our method achieves promising results. For the Cooperative Navigation task in MAPE, CAES is much better than both traditional RLs and gradient-free approaches.

For the other two tasks in SMAC, the experiment results also show that our method is applicable for different cooperative strategies. EA is considered to be not suitable for Multi-Agent problems if it directly using the team reward as fitness. There is a great improvement for EA by using the value decomposition network to predict fitness in Multi-Agent problems.

We also found that, during the training process, the prediction ability of the value decomposition network improves over time. As the predicted fitness estimated by value decomposition in the Cooperative Navigation task shown in Fig. 6, the output of value decomposition is not stable before the 600th generation where the predicted fitness decreases. This means the fitness function of policy also changes gradually. So, it can be seen as a dynamic problem from the perspective of optimization. We should design an algorithm which more suitable for this dynamic problem in our future work.

Acknowledgments. This work is partially supported by National Key R&D Program of China under the Grant No. 2017YFC0804003, National Science Foundation of China under grant number 61761136008, Shenzhen Peacock Plan under Grant No. KQTD2016112514355531, Program for Guangdong Introducing Innovative and Entrepreneurial Teams under grant number 2017ZT07X386, the Science and Technology Innovation Committee Foundation of Shenzhen under the Grant No. ZDSYS201703031748284, and the Guangdong Provincial Key Laboratory under the Grant No. 2020B121201001.

References

1. Oi, D.H., Pereira, R.M.: Ant behavior and microbial pathogens (Hymenoptera: Formicidae). Florida Entomol. **76**, 63–74 (1993)
2. Homans, G.C.: Social behavior: Its elementary forms (1974)
3. Dorigo, M.: Optimization, learning and natural algorithms. Ph.D. thesis, Politecnico di Milano (1992)
4. Shi, Y.: Particle swarm optimization: developments, applications and resources. In: Proceedings of the 2001 Congress on Evolutionary Computation (IEEE Cat. No. 01TH8546), vol. 1, pp. 81–86. IEEE (2001)
5. Rubenstein, M., Cornejo, A., Nagpal, R.: Programmable self-assembly in a thousand-robot swarm. Science **345**(6198), 795–799 (2014)
6. Zheng, L., et al.: MAgent: a many-agent reinforcement learning platform for artificial collective intelligence. In: Thirty-Second AAAI Conference on Artificial Intelligence (2018)
7. Singh, S., Okun, A., Jackson, A.: Artificial intelligence: learning to play Go from scratch. Nature **550**(7676), 336 (2017)
8. Mnih, V., et al.: Human-level control through deep reinforcement learning. Nature **518**(7540), 529 (2015)
9. Tuyls, K., Weiss, G.: Multiagent learning: basics, challenges, and prospects. AI Mag. **33**(3), 41 (2012)
10. Littman, M.L.: Markov games as a framework for multi-agent reinforcement learning. In: Machine Learning Proceedings, pp. 157–163. Morgan Kaufmann (1994)
11. Salimans, T., Ho, J., Chen, X., Sidor, S., Sutskever, I.: Evolution strategies as a scalable alternative to reinforcement learning. arXiv preprint arXiv:1703.03864 (2017)
12. Such, F.P., Madhavan, V., Conti, E., Lehman, J., Stanley, K.O., Clune, J.: Deep neuroevolution: genetic algorithms are a competitive alternative for training deep neural networks for reinforcement learning. arXiv preprint arXiv:1712.06567 (2017)

13. Samvelyan, M., et al.: The StarCraft multi-agent challenge. In: Proceedings of the 18th International Conference on Autonomous Agents and MultiAgent Systems, pp. 2186–2188. International Foundation for Autonomous Agents and Multiagent Systems (2019)
14. Tan, M.: Multi-agent reinforcement learning: Independent vs. cooperative agents. In: Proceedings of the Tenth International Conference on Machine Learning, pp. 330–337 (1993)
15. Tampuu, A., et al.: Multiagent cooperation and competition with deep reinforcement learning. PLoS ONE 12(4), e0172395 (2017)
16. Sunehag, P., et al.: Value-decomposition networks for cooperative multi-agent learning. arXiv preprint arXiv:1706.05296 (2017)
17. Rashid, T., et al.: QMIX: monotonic value function factorisation for deep multi-agent reinforcement learning. arXiv preprint arXiv:1803.11485 (2018)
18. Foerster, J.N., Farquhar, G., Afouras, T., Nardelli, N., Whiteson, S.: Counterfactual multi-agent policy gradients. In: Thirty-Second AAAI Conference on Artificial Intelligence (2018)
19. Lowe, R., Wu, Y., Tamar, A., Harb, J., Abbeel, O.P., Mordatch, I.: Multi-agent actor-critic for mixed cooperative-competitive environments. In: Advances in Neural Information Processing Systems, pp. 6379–6390 (2017)
20. Stanley, K.O., Miikkulainen, R.: Evolving neural networks through augmenting topologies. Evol. Comput. 10(2), 99–127 (2002)
21. Mania, H., Guy, A., Recht, B.: Simple random search of static linear policies is competitive for reinforcement learning. In: Advances in Neural Information Processing Systems, pp. 1800–1809 (2018)
22. Mnih, V., et al.: Asynchronous methods for deep reinforcement learning. In: International Conference on Machine Learning, pp. 1928–1937 (2016)
23. Mordatch, I., Abbeel, P.: Emergence of grounded compositional language in multi-agent populations. In: Thirty-Second AAAI Conference on Artificial Intelligence (2018)
24. Williams, R.J.: Simple statistical gradient-following algorithms for connectionist reinforcement learning. Mach. Learn. 8(3–4), 229–256 (1992). https://doi.org/10.1007/BF00992696
25. Konda, V.R., Tsitsiklis, J.N.: Actor-critic algorithms. In: Advances in Neural Information Processing Systems, pp. 1008–1014 (2000)
26. Arulkumaran, K., Deisenroth, M.P., Brundage, M., Bharath, A.A.: A brief survey of deep reinforcement learning. arXiv preprint arXiv:1708.05866 (2017)

O-Flocking: Optimized Flocking Model on Autonomous Navigation for Robotic Swarm

Li Ma[1], Weidong Bao[1]([✉]), Xiaomin Zhu[1], Meng Wu[1], Yuan Wang[1],
Yunxiang Ling[2], and Wen Zhou[1]

[1] College of Systems Engineering, National University of Defense Technology,
Changsha 410073, China
`18874857546@163.com`, `wy1020395067@hotmail.com`
`{wdbao,xmzhu,wumeng15,zhouwen}@nudt.edu.cn`
[2] Officers College of PAP, Chengdu, China
`2923821396@qq.com`

Abstract. Flocking model has been widely used in robotic swarm control. However, the traditional model still has some problems such as manually adjusted parameters, poor stability and low adaptability when dealing with autonomous navigation tasks in large-scale groups and complex environments. Therefore, it is an important and meaningful research problem to automatically generate Optimized Flocking model (O-flocking) with better performance and portability. To solve this problem, we design Comprehensive Flocking (C-flocking) model which can meet the requirements of formation keeping, collision avoidance of convex and non-convex obstacles and directional movement. At the same time, Genetic Optimization Framework for Flocking Model (GF) is proposed. The important parameters of C-flocking model are extracted as seeds to initialize the population, and the offspring are generated through operations such as crossover and mutation. The offspring model is input into the experimental scene of autonomous navigation for robotic swarms, and the comprehensive fitness function value is obtained. The model with smallest value is selected as the new seed to continue evolution repeatedly, which finally generates the O-flocking model. The extended simulation experiments are carried out in more complex scenes, and the O-flocking and C-flocking are compared. Simulation results show that the O-flocking model can be migrated and applied to large-scale and complex scenes, and its performance is better than that of C-flocking model in most aspects.

Keywords: Robotic swarms · Flocking model · Multi-agent systems

1 Introduction

Robotic swarm system has been increasingly used in complex tasks, such as search and rescue [1], map drawing [2], target tracking [3], etc., which aims at

© Springer Nature Switzerland AG 2020
Y. Tan et al. (Eds.): ICSI 2020, LNCS 12145, pp. 628–639, 2020.
https://doi.org/10.1007/978-3-030-53956-6_58

keeping human beings away from the boring, harsh and dangerous environment. The simple local interaction among individuals in the system produces some new features and phenomena observed at the system level [4]. These laws are very similar to their biological counterparts, such as fish [5], bird [6], ant [7] and cell [8]. Flocking is one of the typical collective forms. This form is robust and flexible for the agents who join and exit, especially when there are obstacles, dangers, new tasks and other emergencies. Although flocking has many advantages, it still faces the problem of low performance caused by large scale, dynamic environment and other reasons. This phenomenon is more obvious in military projects, such as GREMLINS [9] and LOCUST [10], because of the worst working environment for large-scale UAVs which is small, low-cost and semi-autonomous.

Traditional flocking model is mainly designed according to the three principles of Reynolds: short-distance repulsion, middle-distance alignment and long-distance attraction [11]. Some researchers considered obstacle avoidance problems on flocking model. Wang et al. [12] proposed an improved fast flocking algorithm with obstacle avoidance for multi-agent dynamic systems based on Olfati-Sabers algorithm. Li et al. [13] studied the flocking problem of multi-agent systems with obstacle avoidance, in the situation when only a fraction of the agents have information on the obstacles. Vrohidis et al. [14] considered a networked multi-robot system operating in an obstacle populated planar workspace under a single leader-multiple followers architecture. Besides, previous works applied learning methods or heuristic algorithms on flocking model. The reinforcement learning (RL) method can adjust the movement strategy in time by exploring-using ideas, but its performance is not stable enough [15,16]. Vásárhelyi et al. [17] considered the problems faced by the real self-organizing UAV cluster system and optimized the flocking model using evolutionary algorithm. Previous works improve the flocking model in several aspects, but it is still a challenge to automatically obtain a stable, scalable and portable flocking model for robotic swarm. The problems to be solved mainly include:

- Harsh environment. In the actual environment, there may be different kinds of obstacles, including convex and non-convex ones. The traditional flocking model is difficult to deal with them easily.
- Limited scale. Increasing scale of robotic swarm will bring new problems, such as frequent interactions, more conflicts and exceptions.
- Parameter adjustment is difficult. Many parameters need to be set when designing the system model. The performance of group algorithm depends not only on expert experience, but also on scientific methods. Especially when there is correlation between parameters, it is difficult to get the optimal model quickly [11].

Previous work has not solved these problems comprehensively. In order to achieve better performance of robotic swarm in complex environment, C-flocking model is designed and O-flocking model is generated by GF framework. The main contributions of this paper are as follows:

- We design the C-flocking model, which adds new obstacle avoidance strategies and directional movement strategy to the Reynolds' flocking model [19].

- We propose the Genetic Optimization Framework for Flocking Model (GF). The O-flocking model is obtained by this framework.
- O-flocking model can be transferred from simple scene model to complex scene, from small-scale group to large-scale group. Through comparative analysis with C-flocking model, it is found that the comprehensive performance of O-flocking model is the best.

The rest of this paper is organized as follows: Sect. 2 analyzes the GF framework, where the C-flocking model, fitness function, and GF algorithm are introduced. Section 3 analyzes the experimental results. Summary and future work are introduced in Sect. 4.

2   Genetic Optimization Framework for Flocking Model

Through the analysis of previous researches, we find that it is necessary to automatically generate an optimized flocking model. So we propose GF framework. The input is C-flocking model and the output is O-flocking model, which meets the requirements of reliability, scalability and portability. As shown in Fig. 1, in GF architecture, it is generally divided into robot (agent) layer and environment layer, among which robot (agent) is divided into three layers, including sensor layer, decision layer and action layer, which support basic autonomous navigation functions. Through the rule generalization speed update formula described by the weight parameter, the weight parameter develops through the interaction with the environment. Environment is divided into two layers: evaluation layer and evolution layer. The former provides fitness function for the latter.

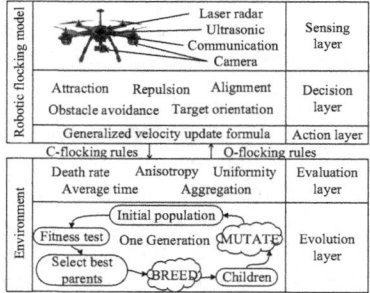

Fig. 1. Genetic optimization framework for flocking model

2.1   C-Flocking Model for Robotic Swarm

In this section, we extend Reynold's flocking model to C-flocking model, which simultaneously consider flocking-pattern maintenance, obstacle avoidance, and directional movements in its velocity updating formula.

We assume that each agent of flocking moves through a square-shaped arena with a side length of L^{arena}, where convex and nonconvex obstacles appear. They need to pass through the arena quickly without death. If they hit each other or obstacles (including the walls), they disappear, which represents being dead in our simulation. As shown in Fig. 2, a robot agent i has three detection areas: exclusion area, alignment area, and attraction area. Among them, the exclusion zone is the circular zone zor_{rep} with R_0 as radius, the alignment zone zor_{ali} is the ring zone between R_0 and R_1, the attraction zone zor_{att} is the ring zone between R_1 and R_2. The arrow of the agent represents its speed direction, while the speed direction of other agents in different areas of the agent i is roughly affected as shown in Fig. 2(a).

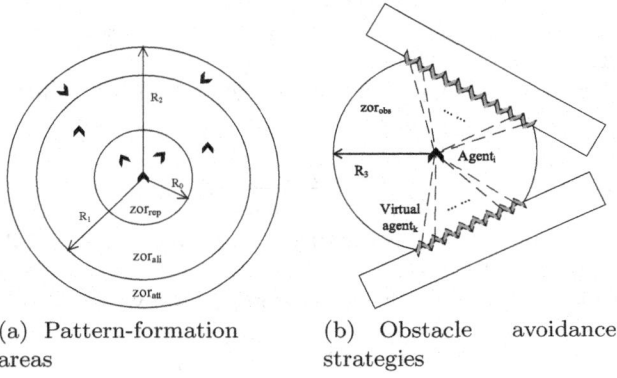

(a) Pattern-formation areas

(b) Obstacle avoidance strategies

Fig. 2. C-flocking model for robotic swarm

If the distance between agents is under r_0^{rep}, agents will move in the opposite direction of each other's connection:

$$\Delta v_i^{rep} = \sum_{j \neq i} (R_0 - r_{ij}) \cdot \frac{p_i - p_j}{r_{ij}}. \tag{1}$$

where $r_{ij} = |p_i - p_j|$ is the distance between agents i and j. p_i and p_j represent the position of agent i and j, respectively.

For pairwise alignment, we define the change of velocity relating to the difference of the velocity vectors of nearby agents [19].

$$\Delta v_i^{ali} = \frac{1}{N_{ali}} \sum_{j \neq i} \frac{v_j}{|v_j|}. \tag{2}$$

In Eq. (2), v_j is the velocity vector of agent j. N_{ali} is the number of agents in the area of alignment.

And for Long-range attraction, we define the term as follows:

$$\Delta v_i^{att} = \sum_{j \neq i} \frac{1}{(R_2 - r_{ij})} \cdot \frac{p_j - p_i}{r_{ij}}. \tag{3}$$

In Eq. (3), $r_{att} = |p_i - p_j|$ is the distance between agents i and j. p_i and p_j represent the position of agent i and j.

For obstacle avoidance, we virtualize the surface of the obstacle towards robotic agent i into a series of robotic agents arranged as shown in Fig. 2(b). Each one of them will influence the velocity of robotic agent i. We define the change of velocity influenced by obstacles as follows:

$$\Delta v_i^{obs} = \sum_{k}^{M} (R_3 - r_{ik}) \frac{p_i - p_k}{r_{ik}}, \tag{4}$$

where $R_3 (R_3 > R_2 > R_1 > R_0)$ is the maximum range of obstacle detection for robotic agent i, and $r_{ik} = |p_i - p_k|$ is the distance between agent i and virtual agent k. M is the number of the virtual agents.

For target orientation, we define the change of velocity influenced by target as follows:

$$\Delta v_i^{tar} = \frac{p_{tar} - p_i}{r_{itar}}. \tag{5}$$

In Eq. (5), $r_{itar} = |r_i - r_{t}ar|$ is the distance between agents i and target. p_{tar} represents the position of target.

We take the sum of all delta velocity proposed above:

$$v_i^{total} (t + \Delta t) = v_i (t) + \Delta v_i. \tag{6}$$

$$\Delta v_i = a\Delta v_i^{rep} + b\Delta v_i^{ali} + c\Delta v_i^{att} + d\Delta v_i^{obs} + e\Delta v_i^{tar}. \tag{7}$$

In Eq. (7), we define the weight parameters $a, b, c, d, e \in (0, 1)$, which is used to flexibly handle the generalization formula.

If we consider the possible combinations of all constraints (each constraint can have two choices of Boolean values 0 and 1, which respectively represent the existence of the class constraint and the absence of the class constraint), then we can have a total of 2^5 rules. Each rule should be designed according to expert experience. Through reference, design, analysis, and selection, we propose four main rules that can represent the main features of 2^5 rules, which basically guarantees the performance of the flocking behavior of the robot cluster.

$$\Delta v_i^{C-flocking} = \begin{cases} \Delta v_i^{ali} + \Delta v_i^{att} + \Delta v_i^{tar}, & if \, zor_{rep} = \emptyset \cap zor_{obs} = \emptyset \\ \Delta v_i^{obs}, & if \, zor_{rep} = \emptyset \cap zor_{obs} \neq \emptyset \\ \Delta v_i^{rep} + \Delta v_i^{obs}, & if \, zor_{rep} \neq \emptyset \cap zor_{obs} \neq \emptyset \\ \Delta v_i^{rep}, & if \, zor_{rep} \neq \emptyset \cap zor_{obs} = \emptyset \end{cases} \tag{8}$$

Tunning C-flocking model above means that we optimize the weight coefficient in the velocity Eq. (9). It is obvious that the parameter space is 20-dimensional, so manual adjustment of parameters will become very time-consuming.

2.2   The Genetic Algorithm for Model Evolution

Therefore, we propose genetic-flocking algorithm (GF) as the method for parameter tuning of flocking model. The specific operation is shown in Fig. 3:

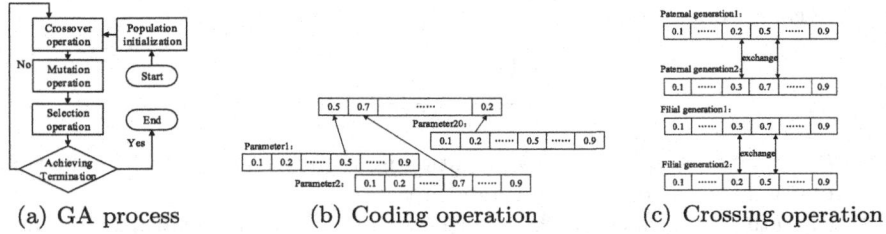

(a) GA process   (b) Coding operation   (c) Crossing operation

Fig. 3. GA process and its application on flocking model

1) Coding: The coding in this paper is based on natural number coding. Each chromosome has 20 DNA bits representing 20 parameters that require Parameter Tuning. The natural number coding is used for each DNA bit. The values are 0.1, 0.2, 0.3,.... 1. The specific encoding method is shown in the following figure:

2) Population Initialization: The method of population initialization adopts complete initialization. For each DNA bit in a chromosome, a value of 0.1 to 0.9 is generated and assigned to the chromosome referring to the C-flocking .

3) Cross-operation: This operation randomly selects two chromosomes in the population and randomly selects an equal length DNA segment on the two chromosomes for the exchange operation. The specific operation is as follows:

4) Mutation operation: Random mutation strategy is used in mutation operation. The strategy first chooses a random DNA site in a chromosome and randomly changes the value of the DNA site to another value. The value ranges from 0.1, 0.2, 0.3,... 1. The coefficient of variation was 0.5.

5) Selection Operations: Selection is performed in all the parents, offspring and mutants of the generation, and the individuals with the best evaluation results are selected to form the next generation's father.

In the algorithm, the C-flocking's rules R^{exp} are represented as: $\{R_0^1, R_0^2, R_0^3, R_0^4\}$, and $R_0^i = \{a_0^i, b_0^i, c_0^i, d_0^i, e_0^i\}, i = 1, 2, 3, 4$.

The outputs of GF algorithm are also a set of optimized rules: $R^{opt} = \{R_{opt}^1, R_{opt}^2, R_{opt}^3, R_{opt}^4\}$, and $R_{opt}^i = \{a_{opt}^i, b_{opt}^i, c_{opt}^i, d_{opt}^i, e_{opt}^i\}, i = 1, 2, 3, 4$.

2.3 Fitness Function for Evaluation

In the GF algorithm, we propose fitness function, consisting of several evaluation indexes, to select the model with the best performance.

Average time is defined as the average time taken since the beginning of the navigation until the robotic swarm reaches the target area. Accordingly, we compute the Average time

$$\tau = \frac{\sum\limits_{j} \left(T_j^{arrive} - T_j^{start} \right)}{N}, \tag{9}$$

where T_j^{start} is the time when the navigation is triggered, and T_j^{arrive} is the time when robotic agent j reaches the target area.

Death rate is described as the percentage of the robotic swarm being dead during the process of the navigation from the start area to the target area.

$$r^{death} = \frac{N_{death}}{N_{total}}, \tag{10}$$

where N_{death} represents the number of the dead agent, and N_{total} represents the number of the total agents in the robotic swarm.

The centroid formula is

$$r_\sigma = \frac{\sum m_j r_j}{M}, \tag{11}$$

but the "quality" (homogeneity) of each agent is certain. Considering that the centroid is expressed by the average coordinate directly, then the average value of the relative distance between each step's all points and the "centroid" is calculated, the aggregation and stability are analyzed, and these data are recorded, which can be used to analyze the changing rule of the two values in the whole process. Since our time is discrete, we can use discrete output to the aggregation formula of evolutionary algorithm:

$$\bar{\gamma} = \frac{\sum\limits_{t} \sum\limits_{j} \sqrt{\left(p_j^x - r_t^x \right)^2 + \left(p_j^y - r_t^y \right)^2}}{NT}, \tag{12}$$

where p_j^x and p_j^y are the abscissa and ordinate of the position of agent j, respectively. r_t^x and r_t^y are the abscissa and ordinate of the position of the swarm's centroid at time t. T is the total time of the whole navigation process, while N is the agent number of the whole swarm.

We define the Uniformity of the robotic swarm as the variance of the γ_t sequence, which describes whether the flock structure of this swarm is stable.

$$s_\gamma^2 = \frac{\sum_{t=0}^{T} \left(\gamma_t - \bar{\gamma} \right)^2}{T}, \tag{13}$$

$$\gamma_t = \frac{\sum\limits_{j} \sqrt{\left(p_j^x - r_t^x \right)^2 + \left(p_j^y - r_t^y \right)^2}}{N}. \tag{14}$$

We define anisotropic index to describe the variation of population velocity direction. Specifically, it needs to calculate the average angle of each individual velocity direction and flock velocity direction at a certain time, and then calculate the average value of the whole process, which is the index of anisotropic index. The variance of the average angle of the whole process represents the variation range of anisotropic index, and the formula of anisotropy is as follows:

$$s_\delta^2 = \frac{\sum\limits_t \sum\limits_j \left(\theta_j^t - \delta^t\right)^2}{NT}, \tag{15}$$

$$\delta^t = \frac{\sum\limits_j \theta_j}{N}. \tag{16}$$

In order to evaluate performance of models comprehensively, we firstly normalize the order parameters proposed above, and then define the global fitness function by the transfer function F(x).

$$F(x) = \frac{x - x_{\min}}{x_{\max} - x_{\min}}. \tag{17}$$

With the following transfer function, we can construct a single objective fitness function that considering all necessary requirements. This function F can be used in the selection process of the GF algorithm.

$$F = F(\tau) \cdot F(\bar{\gamma}) \cdot F(s_\gamma^2) \cdot F(s_\delta^2). \tag{18}$$

3   Experiment Analysis

To reveal the performance improvements of O-flocking, we compare it with C-flocking from the aspect of the following six metrics in Table 1 including the order parameters and fitness function proposed above:

Fitness function is the product of aggregation, anisotropy, average time, and uniformity. As a comprehensive evaluation index, fitness function plays an important role in our experiments. Besides, death rate is the basic constraint that must be considered when optimizing weight parameters of velocity formula, and it is also an evaluation index of the performance of each model. Experiments are performed on the computer with i7 processor, 8g memory and independent graphics card. The code for the related work has been put in [20]. The exact values of key parameters in our platform are as follows:

To find the performances differences, we apply C-flocking and O-flocking model in navigation experiment with three basic environmental elements including tunnel obstacle, non-convex obstacle and convex obstacle. As shown in Fig. 4, the C-flocking can complish the task basically, but they perform not good for their uniformity and stability. Meanwhile, our O-flocking model performs obviously better.

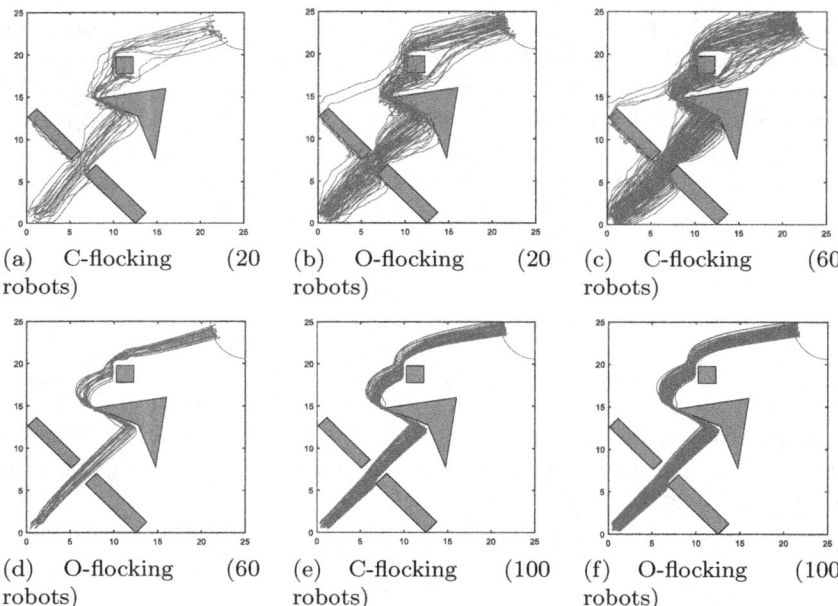

(a) C-flocking (20 robots) (b) O-flocking (20 robots) (c) C-flocking (60 robots)

(d) O-flocking (60 robots) (e) C-flocking (100 robots) (f) O-flocking (100 robots)

Fig. 4. C-flocking and O-flocking traces of the robotic swarm in autonomous navigation in complex environment (We tested 3 groups of experiments using 20, 60 and 100 robotic agents for simulation.)

$$\Delta v_i^{O-flocking} =$$

$$\begin{cases} \Delta v_i^{rep} + 0.7\Delta v_i^{ali} + 0.3\Delta v_i^{att} + 7\Delta v_i^{obs} + 0.4\Delta v_i^{tar}, & if\, zor_{rep} = \emptyset \cap zor_{obs} = \emptyset \\ 0.8\Delta v_i^{rep} + 0.4\Delta v_i^{ali} + 0.6\Delta v_i^{att} + 2\Delta v_i^{obs} + 0.9\Delta v_i^{tar}, & if\, zor_{rep} = \emptyset \cap zor_{obs} \neq \emptyset \\ 0.1\Delta v_i^{rep} + 0.9\Delta v_i^{ali} + 0.3\Delta v_i^{att} + \Delta v_i^{obs} + 0.2\Delta v_i^{tar}, & if\, zor_{rep} \neq \emptyset \cap zor_{obs} \neq \emptyset \\ 0.5\Delta v_i^{rep} + 0.7\Delta v_i^{ali} + 0.4\Delta v_i^{att} + \Delta v_i^{obs} + 0.8\Delta v_i^{tar}, & if\, zor_{rep} \neq \emptyset \cap zor_{obs} = \emptyset \end{cases}$$
(19)

Equation (19) is the velocity updating formula of O-flocking. From analyzing the meaning of the velocity formula of C-flocking and O-flocking, we can analyze the following conclusions:

- Whether obstacles are detected or not, we need to ensure that the obstacle avoidance coefficient in the formula keeps a larger value, which also proves that the obstacle avoidance strategy plays an important role in the completion of the whole task.
- In any case, it is important to ensure that all factors are taken into account at the same time, which is reflected in the formula without taking zero as the value of parameters.
- The parameters of the velocity formula are related to the order parameters of the fitness function. The alignment, attraction and the target orientation parameters (b, c, and e) are always kept at a higher value. Through analysis,

it is found that this is related to the fitness function we set up. The time is related to the target orientation coefficient. Also, the aggregation, anisotropy and uniformity are all related to the alignment and attraction coefficients. We set the threshold (0.2) of the swarm death rate as the constraints, which is mainly related to obstacle avoidance parameters (d), so the repulsion parameters (a) has little influence on the whole system. So it seems that the regulations of a are contrary to common sense. For example, when there is an individual in the repulsion area, the repulsion coefficient a is smaller.

Figure 4 shows directly that O-flocking performs better than C-flocking in uniformity and stability. Figure 4(a) and Fig. 4(b) represent the performance of these two model with 20 robotic agents, Fig. 4(c) and Fig. 4(d) with 60 robots, Fig. 4(e) and Fig. 4(f) with 100 robots. Obviously, with the increasing quantity, the performance of C-flocking is obviously getting worse and worse, while O-flocking is getting better and better.

Table 1. Comparisons between C-flocking & O-flocking with 20, 60 and 100 robots

Evaluation	$F(\bar{\gamma})$		$F(s_s^2)$		$F(\tau)$		$F(s_\gamma^2)$		$F(r^{death})$		F	
Algorithm	C–f	O–f	C–f	O–f	C–f	O–f	C–f	O–f	C–f	O–f	C–f	O–f
Num-20	0.85	0.47	38.69	5.31	130.05	84.50	0.29	0.01	0.35	0.00	6.11	0.01
Num-60	0.86	0.43	42.82	4.69	128.7	83.92	0.32	0.04	0.33	0.00	7.61	0.037
Num-100	1.17	0.46	50.15	4.99	115.80	84.25	0.21	0.03	2.74	0.00	92.82	0.03

Specific performance indicators are shown in Table 1. C–f represents the C-flocking model, while O–f represents the O-flocking model. We record the values of each evaluation index of the two models in three situations of the number and scale of robots. Generally, all the indicators of O-flocking model perform better (the smaller, the better). Specifically, aggregation of O-flocking is 56% lower than that of C-flocking while the reduction of other indicators (anisotropy, average time, uniformity, death rate, and fitness function) are 88.61%, 32.55%, 89.69%, 100%, and 99.92%, respectively.

Figure 5 shows the change of uniformity in the whole time step. The total time step of each group of experiments is not the same, but it can be seen from the figure that the data of each group of O-flocking are stable between 0 and 1, which means that the stability and tightness of the cluster are very good during the whole cruise. When C-flocking passes through obstacles, it can be seen that there will be large fluctuations near step 31 and step 71. Such fluctuations represent the situation of low cluster tightness and stability when cluster passes through narrow and non-convex obstacles, and the formation is not well maintained. At the same time, it can be seen that O-flocking has completed the whole task in about 84 s, while C-flocking has not completed the whole task.

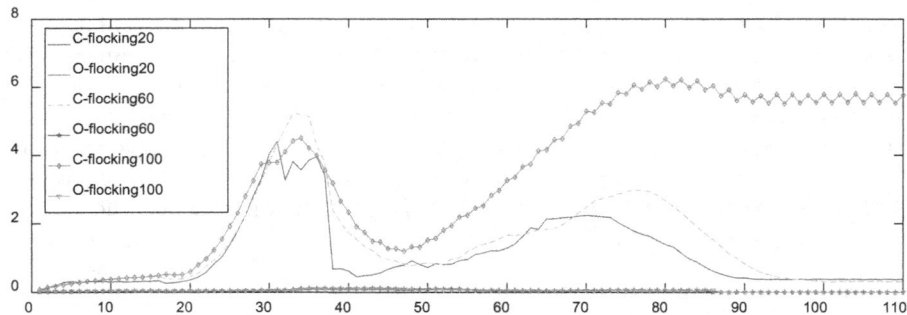

Fig. 5. The uniformity of the robotic swarm with each experiment changes through time.

4   Conclusions and Future Work

We presented in this paper an optimized flocking model for robotic swarm in autonomous navigation, that is O-flocking. This model is obtained through GF framework proposed by us, which is the combination of the genetic algorithm and robotic flocking model. This work comprehensively addresses the reliability, adaptivity and scalability of the robotic swarm during completing the navigation tasks. Also, we provide a simple way of thinking for robot researchers or users to solve problems. Only by building a simple model for a specific task and environment and abstracting the speed formula of the robot, we can quickly get a solution with superior performance. This greatly reduces the workload of manual parameter adjustment and improves the efficiency of task completion.

Our future works are as follows: First, we will extend our experiment to the real-world systems such as unmanned aerial systems and unmanned ground systems. Second, we will take more uncertainties of sceneries into the model to verify the correctness of our model, such as adding the moving obstacle, the irregular barriers, and even fluid barriers. Third, we consider allowing the system to evolve new rules on its own in an incomplete information environment, which is more in line with the actual scenario.

Acknowledgments. This work was supported by the National Natural Science Foundation of China 61872378, Research and Innovation Project for Graduate Students in Hunan Province CX2018B021, and the Scientific Research Project of National University of Defense Technology through grant ZK19-03.

References

1. Murphy, R.R., et al.: Search and rescue robotics. In: Siciliano, B., Khatib, O. (eds.) Springer Handbook of Robotics, pp. 1151–1173. Springer, Heidelberg (2008). https://doi.org/10.1007/978-3-540-30301-5_51
2. Dirafzoon, A., Lobaton, E.: Topological mapping of unknown environments using an unlocalized robotic swarm. In: IEEE/RSJ International Conference on Intelligent Robots & Systems. IEEE (2014)

3. Parker, L.E.: Multiple Mobile Robot Systems. In: Siciliano, B., Khatib, O. (eds.) Springer Handbook of Robotics, pp. 921–941. Springer, Heidelberg (2008). https://doi.org/10.1007/978-3-540-30301-5_41
4. Brown, D.S., Kerman, S.C., Goodrich, M.A.: Human-swarm interactions based on managing attractors. In: Proceedings of the 2014 ACM/IEEE International Conference on Human-Robot Interaction - HRI 2014, 3–6 March 2014, pp. 90–97. ACM Press, Bielefeld (2014)
5. Krause, J., Hoare, D., Krause, S., Hemelrijk, C.K., Rubenstein, D.I.: Leadership in fish shoals. Fish Fish. **1**(1), 82–89 (2015)
6. Nagy, M., Ákos, Z., Biro, D., Vicsek, T.: Hierarchical group dynamics in pigeon flocks. Nature **464**(7290), 890–893 (2010)
7. Feinerman, O., Pinkoviezky, I., Gelblum, A., Fonio, E., Gov, N.S.: The physics of cooperative transport in groups of ants. Nat. Phys. **14**(7), 683–693 (2018)
8. Cheung, K.J., Gabrielson, E., Werb, Z., et al.: Collective invasion in breast cancer requires a conserved basal epithelial program. Cell **155**(7), 1639–1651 (2013)
9. Husseini, T.: Gremlins are coming: DARPA enters Phase III of its UAV programme (2018). https://www.army-technology.com/features/gremlins-darpa-uav-programme/
10. Raytheon gets $29m for work on US Navy LOCUST UAV prototype. https://navaltoday.com/2018/06/28/raytheon-wins-contract-for-locus-inp/
11. Eversham, J., Ruiz, V.F.: Parameter analysis of reynolds flocking model. In: 2010 IEEE 9th International Conference on Cybernetic Intelligent Systems. IEEE (2010)
12. Wang, J., Xin, M.: Flocking of multi-agent system using a unified optimal control approach. J. Dyn. Syst. Meas. Control **135**(6), 061005 (2013)
13. Li, J., Zhang, W., Su, H., Yang, Y.: Flocking of partially-informed multi-agent systems avoiding obstacles with arbitrary shape. Auton. Agents Multi-Agent Syst. **29**(5), 943–972 (2014). https://doi.org/10.1007/s10458-014-9272-2
14. Vrohidis, C., Vlantis, P., Bechlioulis, C.P., Kyriakopoulos, K.J.: Reconfigurable multi-robot coordination with guaranteed convergence in obstacle cluttered environments under local communication. Auton. Robots **42**(4), 853–873 (2017). https://doi.org/10.1007/s10514-017-9660-y
15. Ueyama, A., Isokawa, T., Nishimura, H., Matsui, N.: A comparison of grouping behaviors on rule-based and learning-based multi-agent systems. In: Suzuki, Y., Hagiya, M. (eds.) Recent Advances in Natural Computing. MI, vol. 14, pp. 27–40. Springer, Tokyo (2016). https://doi.org/10.1007/978-4-431-55429-5_3
16. Morihiro, K., Matsui, N., Isokawa, T., Nishimura, H.: Reinforcement learning scheme for grouping and characterization of multi-agent network. In: Setchi, R., Jordanov, I., Howlett, R.J., Jain, L.C. (eds.) KES 2010. LNCS (LNAI), vol. 6278, pp. 592–601. Springer, Heidelberg (2010). https://doi.org/10.1007/978-3-642-15393-8_66
17. Vásárhelyi, G., Virágh, C., et al.: Optimized flocking of autonomous drones in confined environments. Sci. Robot. **3**(20), eaat3536 (2018)
18. Guilherme Henrique Polo Goncalves: simulando movimento de bando de passáros em javascript, Github (2010). https://github.com/gpolo/birdflocking/blob/master/doc/artigo.pdf
19. Braga, R.G., da Silva, R.C., Ramos, A.C.B., Mora-Camino, F.: Collision avoidance based on reynolds rules: a case study using quadrotors. In: Latifi, S. (ed.) Information Technology - New Generations. AISC, vol. 558, pp. 773–780. Springer, Cham (2018). https://doi.org/10.1007/978-3-319-54978-1_96
20. https://github.com/Downloadmarktown/Flocking-experiment-platform

A Multi-agent Ant Colony Optimization Algorithm for Effective Vehicular Traffic Management

Saju Sankar S[1]([✉]) and Vinod Chandra S S[2]

[1] Department of Computer Engineering, Government Polytechnic College, Punalur, India
tkmce@rediffmail.com
[2] Computer Center, University of Kerala, Thiruvananthapuram, India
vinod@keralauniversity.ac.in

Abstract. An intelligent agent refers to an autonomous entity directing its activity towards achieving goals, acting upon an environment using data obtained with the help of a sensory mechanism. Intelligent agent software is a software system that performs tasks independently on behalf of a user in a networking environment based on user interface and past experiences. By the design of an intelligent sensing software program we can regulate the flow of traffic in a transportation infrastructure network. The problems leading to inefficiencies like loss of time, decrease in safety of vehicles and pedestrians, massive pollution, high wastage of fuel energy, degradation in the quality of life can be achieved by the optimized design. Ant Colony Optimization (ACO) has proven to be a very powerful optimization model for combinatorial optimization problems. The algorithm has the objective of regulating high real time traffic enabling every vehicle in the network with increased efficiency to minimize factors like time delay and traffic congestion.

Keywords: Ant colony optimization · Traffic control · Ant system · Pheromone

1 Introduction

Vehicle traffic control and monitoring systems are receiving much attention since several years because of large volume of traffic flows resulting in problems relating to ecology, economy and safety. Numerous vehicle control simulation techniques are adopted locally by means of bidirectional communication systems. This results in reduction of traffic blocks in various junctions by slowing down or accelerating the time delay factor. Genetic algorithms are adopted for the smooth passage of vehicular traffic as well as for emergency vehicles. The parameters of distance, speed and time are adjusted to the system needs. Currently no intelligence or optimization is adopted for the above scenario [1].

Intelligent agents are created using web technology techniques, maintaining a suitable database for past memory and by the use of appropriate programming languages thereby allowing the flow of traffic in modern developed and developing nations. Intelligent control methods have proven to be more advantageous than the currently used signal

Y. Tan et al. (Eds.): ICSI 2020, LNCS 12145, pp. 640–647, 2020.
https://doi.org/10.1007/978-3-030-53956-6_59

control methodology. To reduce the traffic congestion in cities, Intelligent Transportation Systems (ITS) has been adopted in developed countries.

Jinjian et al. studied the traffic control problem in an intersection traffic point by avoiding traffic lights [2]. The method assumes that all vehicles receive two-way communication from a cooperative control structure such that all vehicles are in communication zone. All safety constraints are applied in the above process. The Artificial Bee Colony (ABC) optimization algorithm is adopted with dynamic programming methods. Risikat et al. proposed an adaptive dynamic scheduling algorithm based on ABC for controlled vehicle traffic [3]. The model minimized the average waiting time at the intersection and leads to reduced vehicle queues. The Artificial Bee Colony (ABC) algorithm is a population based meta-heuristic optimization which was inspired by the fore aging behavior of the honey bee swarm [4]. The ABC algorithm is employed to determine the appropriate green light duration for each of the roads forming a four-way intersection.

D Alves et al. introduced a static traffic prediction model which is based on Ant Dispersion Routing algorithm (ADR) and it is designed to reduce the travelling time and for improving the efficiency of the traffic system [5]. The process does not consider dynamic factors such as network pruning and flow optimization. Rutgar et al. [6] proposed an Ant Colony Optimization [ACO] algorithm for extracting solutions to problems related to distributed structures. The congestion is avoided by way of intelligent systems and future estimations.

Soner et al. explained an ACO based algorithm (ACROSES and ACOTRANS) for a group of signalized junctions by means of a software tool TRANSYT-F [7]. It uses Performance Index as the metric and the results shows better compared to genetic and hill climbing algorithms. Jayachithra et al. [8] proposed an ACO algorithm based on Vehicle Ad Hoc Network (VANET) for finding the less and highly congested paths and thereby reducing the total travelling time in the network. It uses ACO protocols AODV, DSDV and DSR which results in parameters like throughput and end to end delay. David et al. applied the ACO technique to reduce the user waiting time at traffic intersections by implementing a rank based ant system and the control signals are monitored by heuristic information [9].

In this paper, we propose an ant colony optimization based traffic management, with a quality software intensive system which works on the principle of depositing pheromones en route. The intensity of pheromone deposit and updating features are the main principle of Ant Colony Optimization (ACO) used in traffic management. ACO outperforms all the other optimization techniques like ABC used in traffic control and management by way of intelligent ant systems.

2   ACO Based Traffic Management System

ACO is a probabilistic technique which searches for optimal path. The behavior of ants is seeking a shortest path between their colony and source of food. It is a Meta heuristic optimization. The path is discovered by pheromone deposits when the ants move at random. More pheromone deposit on a path increases the probability of the path being followed. The path is selected based on the maximum pheromone deposit from start node and the path is analyzed for optimality.

ACO shows great performance in network routing and traffic scheduling. In the ant colony system algorithm, the original ant system was modified in three aspects i) the selection of path is biased towards the path with a large volume of pheromone ii) while building a solution, ants change the pheromone level of the edges they are selecting by applying a local pheromone updating rule iii) at the end of each iteration, only the best ant is allowed to update the pheromone value by applying a modified global pheromone updating rule.

2.1 ACO Algorithm for Traffic Management

The ACO algorithm is an agent based algorithm which gives optimized path in a large network [10]. In this study we have derived Procedure for dynamic pheromone update and detection quality of agent based computational technique that gives an optimal solution. The procedure that uses ant colony agent based computation is,

Input:
Set of ants $A = a_1, a_2 \ldots, a_n$.
Set of paths $P = p_1, p_2, \ldots p_m$.
A_n = vehicle incoming to the queue in each path.
q = queue length, d = decay factor, p = pheromone intensity value.
t = time delay, initially set to 1 min.
Output:

Time period 't' when the queue is maximum.

Method:

1. Initialize pheromone trails in each path, initially set to zero.
2. Arrival of ants in each path (p_1 to p_m).
3. Case 1: Cross junction

    a. All left paths are always open except pedestrian crossings.
    b. For paths 1 to m, generate ant movements marked by pheromone deposit.
    c. Update pheromone value in all paths.

    $$\tau_{ij} = (1 - \rho)\tau_{ij} + \Delta\tau_{ij}$$

    d. Generation of traffic movement based on pheromone value.
    e. On movement, pheromone value evaporation.
    f. Fixing priority path based on probability.

    $$P_{ij}^k(t) = \begin{cases} \dfrac{[\tau_{ij}(t)]^\alpha * [\eta_{ij}]^\beta}{\sum_{l \in \mathcal{N}_i^k} [\tau_{il}(t)]^\alpha * [\eta_{il}]^\beta}, & j \in \mathcal{N}_i^k \\ 0, & j \notin \mathcal{N}_i^k \end{cases}$$

    g. Repeat until threshold value of pheromone intensity is reached.
    h. Go to step 3, until all paths are optimized in a round robin manner.

4. Case 2: repeat step 3 for "Y" junction and "T" junction.
5. Calculation of waiting time for all three intersection methods.
6. End.

2.2 ACO Based Traffic Control Model

ACO is an algorithm based on the behavior of the real ants in finding the shortest path from a source to the food. Ant colony is used to determine the optimal path from source to destination. Routing is the act of moving information across a network from a source to destination. Ants deposit a certain amount of pheromone on its path. It is similar to common memory [11].

The artificial ants simulated as vehicles are driven by a probability rule to sequentially choose the solution components that make use of pheromone deposit intensities and heuristic information. Once an ant has constructed a solution, the ant evaluates the full solution to be used by the algorithm's next step in determining how much pheromone to deposit. The probability rule guides ant movement through a local decision policy that essentially depends on pheromone deposit, decay/evaporation information and heuristic information [12].

ACO can be applied to optimize traffic network problems. In this problem the vehicles are simulated as artificial ants from the source along the traffic network. The routes are estimated by the amount of pheromone deposits along the designated path. The entire path is monitored by the usage of image sensors and pheromone sensors [13]. While entering a cross junction, whether it is 4 way or 3 way, all the left free paths are open irrespective of the pheromone deposit.

In the case of all other path ways, the permission is based on the maximum queue length of the traffic. The queue length is estimated by the pheromone sensors for estimating which path has the highest pheromone deposit value. Ants simulated as vehicles are assigned weights depending upon the type – heavy, medium, light. They are assumed pheromone intensity weights as 2, 1 and 0.5. All the pheromone updates or scheduled information are stored in a database server for future predictions. The possible permissible paths of the vehicles are simulated in a graphical way whether they are in a 4-way junction or 3 way junctions (Y or T).

As soon as the most prioritized lane of vehicles passes the cross junction, the pheromone values for that vehicles are updated as zero or the decay factor for that lane is zero. The next path with highest pheromone deposit will be the next one who gets signaling. The process will continue in a round robin fashion until all the paths will be exhausted one after the other.

3   Results and Discussion

We have obtained data for testing the ACO algorithm from various government organizations like National Transportation Planning and Research Centre (NATPAC) and Center for Development for Advanced Computing (CDAC). The received data contained collection of Traffic Census on National Highways in the states of Kerala, Tamil Nadu, and Karnataka which involves around 300 major junctions. The simulation parameters are type of vehicle, count of incoming vehicles, volume of pheromone deposit, decay/evaporation factor, priority, waiting time in each queue and the average waiting time. The analysis of data gives a measure of the average waiting time of each vehicle obtained by the ACO optimization.

The following assumptions were made in our proposed method.

1. There are three separate queues in each direction.
2. Vehicles will be stationed as per choice of direction in each queue.
3. Measurement of pheromone deposit is read by way of intelligent sensors.
4. The data obtained from sensors are collected in a server for immediate processing and follow up of permission for traffic control.
5. Pedestrian crossing is also considered.

ACO optimization imparted in the simulation.

1. If the pheromone deposit intensity is equal, then there is no need of optimizing.

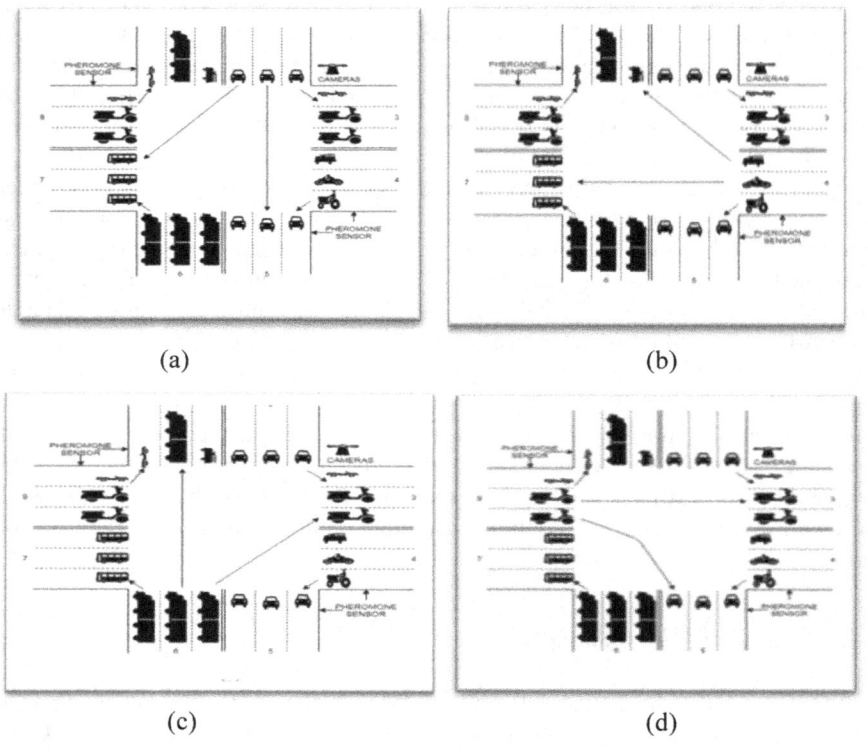

(a) (b) (c) (d)

Fig. 1. (a) shows the permissible path ways from lane 2 to other routes. (b) shows the permissible pathways from lane 4 to all other routes. (c) the permissible path ways from lane 6 to other routes. (d) shows the permissible pathways from lane 8 to all other routes.

2. Usually all paths are given a time duration of one minute.
3. If the pheromone intensity is varied considerably or unequal in one or more paths, then optimization is done by having the less pheromone path's passage time is deducted and assigned to the needy paths thereby optimizing time.
4. When there are pedestrians, then all the four paths are optimized.
5. When a priority vehicle arrives, then the path's pheromone value is reset and the current priority vehicle is set the maximum value and reset the path to the old value.

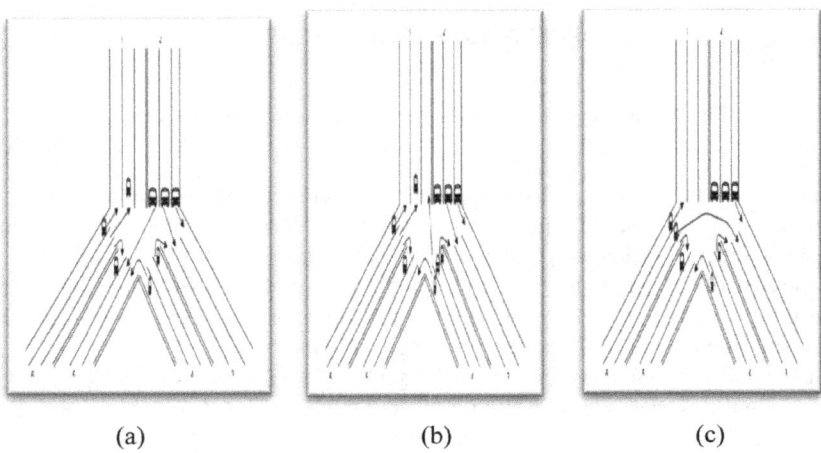

(a)   (b)   (c)

Fig. 2. (a) shows the permissible path ways from lane 2 to other routes, (b) shows the permissible pathways from lane 4 to all other routes. (c) shows the permissible pathways from lane 6 to all other routes.

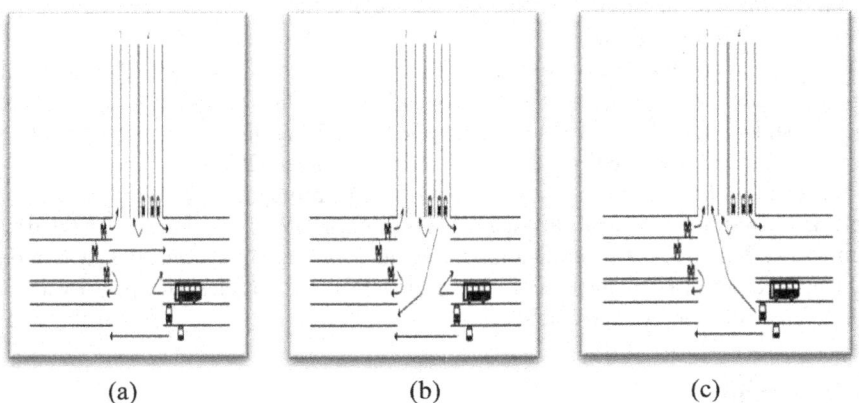

(a)   (b)   (c)

Fig. 3. (a) shows the permissible path ways from lane 2 to other routes, (b) shows the permissible pathways from lane 4 to all other routes and (c) shows the permissible pathways from lane 6 to all other routes.

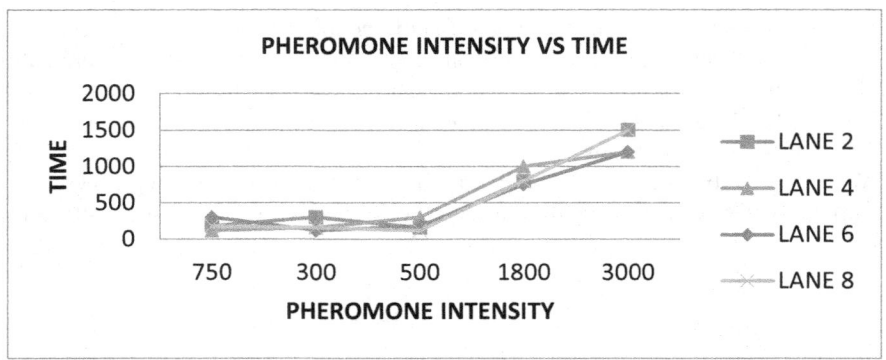

Fig. 4. Graph showing the time delay for each of the four lanes.

Figure 1(a) through Fig. 1(d) illustrate the adopted method of measuring the pheromone intensity in a cross junction for each of the lanes 2, 4, 6, 8 and their priority fixing mechanism. The lanes 1, 3, 5, 7 are for outgoing traffic only.

In the case of 'Y' junction, Fig. 2(a) through Fig. 2(c) illustrates the adopted method of measuring the pheromone intensity for each of the lanes 2, 4, 6 and the priority fixing mechanism. The lanes 1, 3, 5 are for outgoing traffic only.

In the case of 'T' junction, Fig. 3(a) through Fig. 3(c) illustrates the adopted method of measuring the pheromone intensity for each of the lanes 2, 4, 6 and the priority fixing mechanism. The lanes 1, 3, 5 are for outgoing traffic only

Traffic management being a real time application, the simulation was done on an intelligent software system implementing the features of the ant system. All the vehicle movements are represented by a graph connecting all the lanes in different directions. There will be a threshold sealing of pheromone deposit in a single lane to avoid priority assignment only for a single lane so that all lined vehicles will be permitted to pass through in a random fashion.

A graphical analysis was conducted for the ACO optimization. The graph has pheromone deposit intensity in the X-axis and time delay in seconds as the Y-axis. It clearly shows how the time stamp is mapped with pheromone deposit intensity for unequal traffic and how the time slice is effectively utilized (Fig. 4).

The results clearly emphasize that ACO based optimization reduced the waiting time delay to a minimum in all the lanes of all directions. While comparing to the traffic optimization done by ABC optimization model and routing algorithms, the ACO model produced better traffic management for varying flow of vehicles and priority is also implemented for emergency vehicles.

4   Conclusion

In our model, we concluded through our research and simulation, ACO techniques are highly suitable for effectively controlling huge traffic in cities due to its dynamic nature of traffic management. This is efficient because ant works as intelligent agents and the pheromone deposit is mapped with movements. The algorithm also prioritizes emergency vehicles in a traffic junction. The decay or evaporation of pheromone is also taken into consideration for scheduling traffic. Usage of intelligent sensors and by the dynamic nature of the software made the management of traffic outperforming all the other optimized techniques. The model can be applied to a chain of interconnected junctions thereby minimizing the traffic congestion in a large network.

Acknowledgement. Authors would like to thank National Transportation Planning and Research Centre (NATPAC), who provided us real time data of most of the cities in India needed for the simulation, experimental activities and their routing problems.

References

1. Kelly, M., Di Marzo Serugendo, G.: A decentralised car traffic control system simulation using local message propagation optimised with a genetic algorithm. In: Brueckner, S.A., Hassas, S., Jelasity, M., Yamins, D. (eds.) ESOA 2006. LNCS (LNAI), vol. 4335, pp. 192–210. Springer, Heidelberg (2007). https://doi.org/10.1007/978-3-540-69868-5_13
2. Li, J., et al.: Cooperative traffic control based on the artificial bee colony. J. Eng. Res. Appl. **6**(12(Part-I)), 46–55 (2016)
3. Adebiyi, R.F.O., et al.: Management of vehicular traffic system using artificial bee colony algorithm. Int. J. Image Graph. Sig. Process. **9**(11), 18–28 (2017)
4. Saritha, R., Vinod Chandra, S.S.: Multi modal foraging by honey bees toward optimizing profits at multiple colonies. IEEE Intell. Syst. **34**(1), 14–22 (2018)
5. Alves, D., et al.: Ant colony optimization for traffic dispersion routing. In: Proceedings of the 13th International IEEE Conference on Intelligent Transportation systems (ITSC), Portugal (2010)
6. Claes, R., Holvoet, T.: Cooperative ant colony optimization in traffic route calculations. In: Demazeau, Y., Müller, J., Rodríguez, J., Pérez, J. (eds.) Advances on Practical Applications of Agents and Multi-Agent Systems. AINSC, vol. 155, pp. 23–34. Springer, Heidelberg (2012). https://doi.org/10.1007/978-3-642-28786-2_3
7. Haldenbilen, S., et al.: An Ant Colony Optimization Algorithm for Area Traffic Control. INTECH (2013)
8. Jayachithra, N., et al.: Shortest path using ant colony optimization in VANET. Int. J. Eng. Res. Technol. (IJERT), RTICCT (2017)
9. Renfrew, D., et al.: Traffic Signal Optimization using Ant Colony algorithm. In: The International Joint Conference on Neural Networks (IJCNN), Australia (2012)
10. Vinod Chandra, S.S.: Smell detection agent based optimization algorithm. J. Inst. Eng. (India) Ser. B **97**, 431–436 (2016). https://doi.org/10.1007/s40031-014-0182-0
11. Vijayalaxmi, et al.: Ant colony optimization technique in network routing problem – a simulation study. In: International Conference on Innovations in engineering and Technology, ICIET 2013, Bangkok, Thailand, 25–26 December 2013 (2013)
12. Karova, M., et al.: Ant colony optimization algorithm for traffic flow estimation. In: International Conference on Computer Systems and Technologies – CompSysTech 2017, Ruse, Bulgaria (2017)
13. Kumar, D., et al.: Improvement in traffic light system with ant colony optimization technique. Int. J. Eng. Res. Appl. **3**(6), 1744–1749 (2013). ISSN 2248-9622

Other Applications

Site Selection of the Colombian Antarctic Research Station Based on Fuzzy-Topsis Algorithm

Jairo R. Coronado-Hernández[1]([✉]), Wilson A. Rios-Angulo[2], Camilo Segovia[2], Diana Urrego-Niño[2], and Alfonso R. Romero-Conrado[1]

[1] Researcher, Barranquilla, Colombia
jcoronad18@cuc.edu.co
[2] Armada Nacional de Colombia, Bogotá, Colombia

Abstract. By 2025 the Republic of Colombia aims to be an advisory member of the Antarctic Treaty System (ATS) and the installation of a scientific station is necessary to upscale the scientific capabilities. The aim of this paper is showing the results of the implementation of a Fuzzy TOPSIS algorithm for site selection of the Colombian Antarctic Scientific Station. A three-phase methodology was proposed, and the obtained results allowed to identify the optimum location for the station, considering key success factors and regulatory constraints.

Keywords: Site selection · Fuzzy TOPSIS · Antarctic station

1 Introduction

By 2025 the Republic of Colombia aims to be an advisory member of the Antarctic Treaty System (ATS). The location of a temporary scientific base in Antarctica before 2025 is one of the goals for the Colombian Antarctic Program agenda 2014-2035, looking for the exploration and exploitation of the Antarctic continent, as a space for geopolitical and scientific advances.

The objective of this project is to determine the optimal location of a temporary Colombian scientific base in the Antarctic that minimizes the total costs of the scientific operation subject to geographic and geopolitical restrictions. To determine the optimum location, a Fuzzy Topsis Algorithm was implemented.

Zadeh [1] implemented the concept of fuzzy sets theory to express the linguistic terms used in decision-making to alleviate the difficulty of operational management. Hwang and Yoon [2] first suggested the TOPSIS method, a linear weighting technique.

Different applications of this method have appeared in scientific literatures since then, but it has not been applied to optimization in Antarctic logistics [3–30].

In [31] was determinate a Site selection of the Turkish Antarctic Research station using Analytic Hierarchy Process. In [32] was determinate the sites for new a new

---

The original version of this chapter was revised: two modifications have been made. The correction to this chapter is available at https://doi.org/10.1007/978-3-030-53956-6_64

© Springer Nature Switzerland AG 2020, corrected publication 2020
Y. Tan et al. (Eds.): ICSI 2020, LNCS 12145, pp. 651–660, 2020.
https://doi.org/10.1007/978-3-030-53956-6_60

Antarctic Chinese research station using geographical information systems (GIS) and the fuzzy analytical hierarchy process (FAHP).

This paper is organized as follows: Sect. 2 shows the methodology stages that include data collection and the algorithm implementation. Section 3 shows the obtained results from the Fuzzy Topsis Methodology, and finally, Sect. 4 contains the main conclusions and main research opportunities.

2 Methodology

The proposed methodology is composed of three phases and aims the selection of the best site selection for the Colombian Antarctic Scientific Station Almirante Padilla (EACAP, for its acronym in Spanish).

2.1 Set of Alternate Locations and Key Factors for Location

Stage 1 aims the selection of a set of alternate locations for the EACAP, using geographic information systems (GIS). Ten alternate locations were selected, considering the research interests and their logistics capabilities.

Every alternate location complied with a set of requirements: proximity to other scientific stations, water supply (from glaciers), proximity to an airstrip, a sheltered bay, the existence of ship anchoring areas, some meteorological conditions, geopolitical restrictions within the Madrid protocol, and Antarctic Specially Protected Areas (ASPA).

2.2 Antarctic Expeditions and Fieldwork

Fieldwork in stage 2 consisted of two Antarctic expeditions: IV and V Colombian Expedition to Antarctica. The first in austral summer of 2017–2018, and the second expedition in 2018–2019, both with an approximate budget of 3.5 million dollars.

The expeditions included a schedule for visiting all alternate locations selected in stage 1. Soil composition analysis, drone mapping, and topographic studies were performed in every location. Also, wind sensors and wavemeters were installed in order to measure meteorological conditions. In this stage, every location was verified according to the protocol of Antarctic Specially Protected Areas (ASPA).

2.3 Fuzzy TOPSIS Algorithm for Site Selection

A multicriteria decision-making algorithm based on Fuzzy TOPSIS was implemented for the problem of site selection of the Colombian EACAP.

Step 0. Find the evaluation data. A group of scientists, expeditionaries, and military members with Antarctic expeditions experience were asked to judge and rank the selected weights and importances of criteria. A questionnaire (based on linguistics terms and triangular fuzzy numbers) was offered. Every participant assessed all alternate locations, establishing the importance of the criteria, the fulfillment of requirements, and the key success factors.

Step 1. Obtaining evaluation data from qualitative criteria. The evaluation data of qualitative criteria are given by experts in the form of fuzzy linguistic values that correspond to fuzzy numbers. The linguistic variable evaluation matrixes are transformed as fuzzy number matrixes, as shown below. The linguistic variable evaluation matrixes were transformed as fuzzy number matrixes, as $\tilde{x}_{i,j} = \left(\tilde{a}_{i,j}, \tilde{b}_{i,j}, \tilde{c}_{i,j} \right)$ and $\tilde{w}_j^k = \left(\tilde{w}_{j1}^k, \tilde{w}_{j2}^k, \tilde{w}_{j3}^k \right)$.

Step 2. The weighted fuzzy array was calculated from the aggregate decision variable $\tilde{x}_{i,j}$.

$$\tilde{x}_{i,j} = \left(a_{i,j}, b_{i,j}, c_{i,j} \right), \text{ where } a_{ij} = \min_k \left\{ a_{ij}^k \right\}, \quad b_{ij} = \frac{1}{K} \sum_{k=1}^{K} b_{ij}^k, \quad c_{ij} = \max_k \left\{ c_{ij}^k \right\}.$$

In the same way, the weighted fuzzy array $\tilde{w}_j$ was calculated from the linguistic terms:

$$\tilde{w}_j = \left(w_{j1}, w_{j2}, w_{j3} \right),$$

where $w_{j1} = \min_k \{ w_{jk1} \}$, $w_{j2} = \frac{1}{K} \sum_{k=1}^{K} w_{jk2}$, $w_{jk3} = \max_k \{ w_{jk3} \}$. And the aggregate decision matrix $\tilde{D}$ was obtained:

$$\tilde{D} = \begin{pmatrix} \tilde{x}_{11} & \tilde{x}_{12} & \cdots & \tilde{x}_{1n} \\ \tilde{x}_{21} & \tilde{x}_{22} & \cdots & \tilde{x}_{2n} \\ \cdots & \cdots & \tilde{x}_{ij} & \cdots \\ \tilde{x}_{m1} & \tilde{x}_{m2} & \cdots & \tilde{x}_{mn} \end{pmatrix} \text{ and } \tilde{W} = (\tilde{w}_1, \tilde{w}_2, \ldots, \tilde{w}_n)$$

Step 3. Normalized Decision matrix is calculated as $\tilde{R} = \left[\tilde{r}_{ij} \right]_{m \times n} \forall i = 1, 2, \ldots, m; \forall j = 1, 2, \ldots, n.$ where every element $\tilde{R}$ is calculated depending on the type of criteria.

$$\tilde{r}_{ij} = \begin{cases} \left(\dfrac{a_{ij}}{c_j^*}, \dfrac{b_{ij}}{c_j^*}, \dfrac{c_{ij}}{c_j^*} \right) \text{ and } c_j^* = \max_i \{ c_{ij} \} \text{ if the benefit criteria} \\ \left(\dfrac{a_j^-}{c_{ij}}, \dfrac{a_j^-}{b_{ij}}, \dfrac{a_j^-}{a_{ij}} \right) \text{ and } a_j^- = \min_i \{ a_{ij} \} \text{ if the cost criteria} \end{cases}$$

Step 4. Normalized weighted matrix is calculated as $\tilde{V} = \left[\tilde{v}_{ij} \right]_{m \times n} \forall i = 1, 2, \ldots, m; \forall j = 1, 2, \ldots, n$ where $\tilde{v}_{ij} = r_{ij}(\cdot) \tilde{w}_j$.

Step 5. The fuzzy positive ideal solution (FPIS) is calculated as $A^* = \left(\tilde{v}_1^*, \tilde{v}_2^*, \ldots, \tilde{v}_n^* \right)$ where

$$\tilde{v}_j^* = \max_i \{ v_{ij3} \} \ \forall i = 1, 2, \ldots, m; \ \forall j = 1, 2, \ldots, n$$

And the negative ideal solution is calculated (NPIS) as $A^- = \left(\tilde{v}_1^-, \tilde{v}_2^-, \ldots, \tilde{v}_n^- \right)$ where

$$\tilde{v}_j^- = \min_i \{ v_{ij1} \} \ \forall i = 1, 2, \ldots, m; \ \forall j = 1, 2, \ldots, n.$$

Step 6. Distances from every alternate to every solution FPIS and FNIS were calculated as

$$d_i^* = \sum_{j=1}^{n} d_v \left(\tilde{v}_{ij}, \tilde{v}_j^* \right), \ \forall i = 1, 2, \ldots, m \text{ and } d_i^- = \sum_{j=1}^{n} d_v \left(\tilde{v}_{ij}, \tilde{v}_j^- \right), \ \forall i = 1, 2, \ldots, m$$

The distance of each alternate from FPIS and FNIS are calculated with Euclidean distance formula.

$$d_v\left(\tilde{a},\tilde{b}\right) = \sqrt{\frac{1}{3}\left[(a_1 - b_1)^2 + (a_2 - b_2)^2 + (a_3 - b_3)^2\right]}$$

Step 7. The closeness coefficient of each alternate is calculated in order to ranking the alternates, the closest to FPIS and the farthest to FNIS.

$$CC_i = \frac{d_i^-}{d_i^- + d_i^*}, \forall i = 1, 2, \ldots, m$$

By comparing values CC_i, the ranking of alternates is determined.

3   Results

3.1   Set of Alternate Locations and Key Factors for Location

One of objectives of Colombia during continuous polar expeditions is determining the optimum location for the settlement of a future Colombian Antarctic Scientific Station.

A set of key success factors was defined by the group of experts: 1) Accessibility, 2) Object of study, 3) Proximity to other stations, 4) Proximity to water resources, and 5) Personnel Safety.

According to these factors, a set of coordinates was defined, as shown in Fig. 1.

ALTERNATE LOCATION	LATITUDE	LONGITUDE
Alternate Location 1	62°40'9.58"S	60°24'6.25"W
Alternate Location 2	62°39'37.59"S	60°22'22.57"W
Alternate Location 3	62°38'48.32"S	60°22'23.79"W
Alternate Location 4	62°39'4.00"S	60°36'9.78"W
Alternate Location 5	62°37'4.94"S	60°19'37.50"W
Alternate Location 6	62°26'49.56"S	59°43'35.45"W
Alternate Location 7	62°12'35.10"S	58°47'55.70"O
Alternate Location 8	62°05'32"S	58°29'50"W
Alternate Location 9	62°04'31"S	58°18'00"W
Alternate Location 10	62°09'47"S	58°27'34"W

Fig. 1.   Set of alternate locations for Colombian Antarctic Scientific Station.

3.2   Antarctic Expeditions and Field Work

The field work was carried out on board of the "ARC 20 de Julio", an offshore patrol vessel OPV80, made in Colombia [33]. The coordinates of the alternate locations were visited within the schedule of the IV and V Colombian Expeditions to Antarctica. These visits aimed obtaining information from each location based on the key success factors.

This step is illustrated with the exploration at the location that corresponds to Livistong Island with coordinates 62°38'48.32"S, 60°22'23.79"W which is close to the Juan

Carlos I base in Spain and the St. Kliment Ohridski of Bulgary. At this geographical point, a series of beaches with appropriate dimensions and a predominantly rocky composition were identified. The depth of its waters was optimal for access by ships, as well as the approach to the beaches in smaller boats. This point has a chain of mountains in the background and surrounding the bay which are a natural barrier to winds. It has no restrictions due to protected areas and in the upper part of the mountain there are water reservoirs which are used by Bulgaria. Stable rocky material was found in order to support buildings. A first exploration is carried out with a helicopter and then mapped with the drone to identify water sources, accesses and morphology (Fig. 2).

Fig. 2. Drone mapping image, Morphology, and meteorological conditions for the alternate locations.

3.3 Fuzzy TOPSIS Algorithm for Site Selection

The preliminary results from the Fuzzy TOPSIS algorithm for the location of the Colombian Antarctic scientific station are shown below.

According preliminary studies in stage 2, the results from the Fuzzy TOPSIS algorithm for the location of the Colombian Antarctic scientific station were obtained considering 10 alternate locations, 5 criteria, and a group conformed by 7 expert decision-makers.

Step 0: A questionnaire was prepared and based on the information collected at each alternate location during the field work of the expeditions, the linguistic assessment of each expert is constructed based on the assessment criteria (key success factors) and the assessment of each alternative based on to each criterion by each expert.

Step 1: A transduction of the linguistic matrix is made to Fuzzy numbers using the scale in the Table 1.

Table 1. The scale of fuzzy numbers

Fuzzy numbers			Alternative assessment	QA weights
1	1	3	Very Poor (VP)	Very Low (VL)
1	3	5	Poor (P)	Low (L)
3	5	7	Fair (F)	Medium (M)
5	7	9	Good (G)	High (H)

The resulting matrix of 5 × 70 triangular numbers contains 1050 elements.

Step 2: The aggregate decision variable matrix and the weighted fuzzy array was calculated in Table 2 and Table 3. The normalized decision variable matrix is shown in Table 4.

Table 2. The aggregate decision variable matrix

D D	A1			A2			A3			A4			A5			A6			A7			A8			A9			A10		
C1	3,00	6,14	9,00	3,00	6,52	9,00	5,00	7,14	9,00	1,00	4,71	9,00	1,00	4,71	9,00	1,00	5,19	9,00	3,00	6,14	9,00	1,00	5,57	9,00	1,00	6,71	9,00	1,00	5,38	9,00
C2	1,00	2,43	9,00	3,00	5,76	9,00	5,00	6,67	9,00	1,00	5,29	9,00	3,00	5,29	9,00	1,00	5,19	9,00	3,00	6,14	9,00	3,00	5,76	9,00	1,00	5,76	9,00	1,00	5,38	9,00
C3	1,00	5,48	9,00	1,00	5,76	9,00	7,00	7,05	9,00	1,00	5,86	9,00	1,00	5,86	9,00	1,00	6,05	9,00	5,00	7,19	9,00	1,00	4,81	9,00	1,00	5,29	9,00	1,00	6,43	9,00
C4	3,00	5,29	9,00	1,00	2,62	9,00	5,00	5,00	9,00	3,00	5,29	9,00	1,00	5,29	9,00	1,00	6,33	9,00	3,00	5,29	9,00	1,00	5,29	9,00	1,00	5,57	9,00	3,00	5,29	9,00
C5	1,00	5,38	9,00	1,00	6,43	9,00	3,00	7,14	9,00	3,00	5,48	9,00	1,00	5,48	9,00	1,00	5,67	9,00	1,00	5,76	9,00	1,00	5,48	9,00	1,00	6,43	9,00	1,00	5,48	9,00

Table 3. The weighted fuzzy array

Wj			
C1	7,00	8,33	9,00
C2	3,00	7,10	9,00
C3	1,00	5,00	9,00
C4	1,00	5,57	9,00
C5	3,00	6,71	9,00

Table 4. The normalized decision variable matrix

Rij	A1			A2			A3			A4			A5			A6			A7			A8			A9			A10		
C1	0,33	0,68	1,00	0,33	0,72	1,00	0,56	0,79	1,00	0,11	0,52	1,00	0,11	0,52	1,00	0,11	0,58	1,00	0,33	0,68	1,00	0,11	0,62	1,00	0,11	0,75	1,00	0,11	0,60	1,00
C2	0,11	0,27	1,00	0,33	0,64	1,00	0,56	0,74	1,00	0,11	0,59	1,00	0,33	0,59	1,00	0,11	0,58	1,00	0,33	0,68	1,00	0,33	0,64	1,00	0,11	0,64	1,00	0,11	0,60	1,00
C3	0,11	0,61	1,00	0,11	0,64	1,00	0,78	0,78	1,00	0,11	0,65	1,00	0,11	0,65	1,00	0,11	0,67	1,00	0,56	0,80	1,00	0,11	0,53	1,00	0,11	0,59	1,00	0,11	0,71	1,00
C4	0,33	0,59	1,00	0,11	0,29	1,00	0,56	0,56	1,00	0,33	0,59	1,00	0,11	0,59	1,00	0,11	0,70	1,00	0,33	0,59	1,00	0,11	0,59	1,00	0,11	0,62	1,00	0,33	0,59	1,00
C5	0,11	0,60	1,00	0,11	0,71	1,00	0,33	0,79	1,00	0,33	0,61	1,00	0,11	0,61	1,00	0,11	0,63	1,00	0,11	0,64	1,00	0,11	0,61	1,00	0,11	0,71	1,00	0,11	0,61	1,00

Step 3: Normalized weighted matrix is shown in Table 5.
Step 4: Calculations of FPIS and FNIS are shown in Tables 6 and 7.

Table 5. The normalized weighted matrix

V	A1			A2			A3			A4			A5			A6			A7			A8			A9			A10		
C1	2,33	5,69	9,00	2,33	6,04	9,00	3,89	6,61	9,00	0,78	4,37	9,00	0,78	4,37	9,00	0,78	4,81	9,00	2,33	5,69	9,00	0,78	5,16	9,00	0,78	6,22	9,00	0,78	4,98	9,00
C2	0,33	1,91	9,00	1,00	4,54	9,00	1,67	5,26	9,00	0,33	4,17	9,00	1,00	4,17	9,00	0,33	4,09	9,00	1,00	4,84	9,00	1,00	4,54	9,00	0,33	4,54	9,00	0,33	4,24	9,00
C3	0,11	3,04	9,00	0,11	3,20	9,00	0,78	3,92	9,00	0,11	3,25	9,00	0,11	3,25	9,00	0,11	3,36	9,00	0,56	3,99	9,00	0,11	2,67	9,00	0,11	2,94	9,00	0,11	3,57	9,00
C4	0,33	3,27	9,00	0,11	1,62	9,00	0,56	3,10	9,00	0,33	3,27	9,00	0,11	3,27	9,00	0,11	3,92	9,00	0,33	3,27	9,00	0,11	3,27	9,00	0,11	3,45	9,00	0,33	3,27	9,00
C5	0,33	4,01	9,00	0,33	4,80	9,00	1,00	5,33	9,00	1,00	4,09	9,00	0,33	4,09	9,00	0,33	4,23	9,00	0,33	4,30	9,00	0,33	4,09	9,00	0,33	4,80	9,00	0,33	4,09	9,00

Table 6. Calculations of FPIS

A*	FPIS		
C1	9,00	9,00	9,00
C2	9,00	9,00	9,00
C3	9,00	9,00	9,00
C4	9,00	9,00	9,00
C5	9,00	9,00	9,00

Table 7. Calculations of FNIS

A-	FNIS		
C1	0,78	0,78	0,78
C2	0,33	0,33	0,33
C3	0,11	0,11	0,11
C4	0,11	0,11	0,11
C5	0,33	0,33	0,33

Table 8. Euclidean Distances from every alternate to every solution FPIS

FPIS	A1	A2	A3	A4	A5	A6	A7	A8	A9	A10
C1	4,30	4,21	3,26	5,45	5,45	5,33	4,30	5,24	5,01	5,28
C2	6,46	5,29	4,75	5,73	5,40	5,75	5,21	5,29	5,63	5,71
C3	6,18	6,13	5,58	6,11	6,11	6,08	5,67	6,30	6,21	6,01
C4	6,00	6,67	5,95	6,00	6,11	5,91	6,00	6,11	6,05	6,00
C5	5,77	5,56	5,08	5,42	5,75	5,71	5,69	5,75	5,56	5,75
d	28,71	27,86	24,62	28,71	28,81	28,78	26,86	28,68	28,46	28,76

Step 5: Euclidean Distances from every alternate to every solution FPIS and FNIS were calculated as shown in Tables 8 and 9.

Step 6: The closeness coefficients were ranked as shown in Table 10.

Table 9. Euclidean Distances from every alternate to every solution FNIS

FPIS	A1	A2	A3	A4	A5	A6	A7	A8	A9	A10
C1	4,30	4,21	3,26	5,45	5,45	5,33	4,30	5,24	5,01	5,28
C2	6,46	5,29	4,75	5,73	5,40	5,75	5,21	5,29	5,63	5,71
C3	6,18	6,13	5,58	6,11	6,11	6,08	5,67	6,30	6,21	6,01
C4	6,00	6,67	5,95	6,00	6,11	5,91	6,00	6,11	6,05	6,00
C5	5,77	5,56	5,08	5,42	5,75	5,71	5,69	5,75	5,56	5,75
d	28,71	27,86	24,62	28,71	28,81	28,78	26,86	28,68	28,46	28,76

Table 10. The ranked closeness coefficients

Alternate location	CC(i)
A3	0,53823908
A7	0,5087023
A2	0,4972285
A9	0,49365632
A8	0,48667472
A6	0,48655725
A10	0,48636965
A4	0,48474844
A1	0,48443983
A5	0,48381333

These results allow to identify an optimum location for the Colombian Antarctic Scientific Station. According to the rank, the alternate location 3 is the best site to locate the Colombian Antarctic Station.

4 Conclusions

A Fuzzy Topsis algorithm was implement for selecting the optimum location for the Colombian Antarctic Scientific Station.

Future research opportunities include the application of alternate solution methods based on multicriteria approaches in order to validate the selected location.

Also, studies on simulations on direct and inverse logistics of the station will be performed in order to decide the final location.

Acknowledgments. The work described in this paper has been supported by the project "PLANEAMIENTO POR CAPACIDADES PARA EL ESTABLECIMIENTO DE UNA BASE TEMPORAL EN LA ANTÁRTICA COMO SOPORTE LOGÍSTICO A LAS OPERACIONES

CIENTÍFICAS - 65028" under the auspices of the Armada Nacional de Colombia and Ministry of Science, Technology and Innovation (MinCiencias).

References

1. Zadeh, L.A.: Fuzzy sets. Inf. Control **8**, 338–353 (1965)
2. Hwang, C.-L., Yoon, K.: Multiple Attribute Decision Making. Springer, Heidelberg (1981). https://doi.org/10.1007/978-3-642-48318-9
3. Sindhu, S., Nehra, V., Luthra, S.: Investigation of feasibility study of solar farms deployment using hybrid AHP-TOPSIS analysis: case study of India. Renew. Sustain. Energy Rev. **73**, 496–511 (2017)
4. Perera, A.T.D., Nik, V.M., Mauree, D., Scartezzini, J.-L.: An integrated approach to design site specific distributed electrical hubs combining optimization, multi-criterion assessment and decision making. Energy **134**, 103–120 (2017)
5. Zamri, N., Ahmad, F., Rose, A.N.M., Makhtar, M.: A fuzzy TOPSIS with Z-numbers approach for evaluation on accident at the construction site. In: Herawan, T., Ghazali, R., Nawi, N.M., Deris, M.M. (eds.) SCDM 2016. AISC, vol. 549, pp. 41–50. Springer, Cham (2017). https://doi.org/10.1007/978-3-319-51281-5_5
6. Bostanci, B., Bakir, N.Y., Doğan, U., Göngör, M.K.: Research on GIS-aided housing satisfaction using fuzzy decision-making techniques—Bulanik karar verme teknikleri ile CBS destekli konut memnuniyeti araştirmasi. J. Fac. Eng. Archit. Gazi Univ. **32**, 1193–1207 (2017)
7. Pahari, S., Ghosh, D., Pal, A.: An online review-based hotel selection process using intuitionistic fuzzy TOPSIS method. In: Pattnaik, P.K., Rautaray, S.S., Das, H., Nayak, J. (eds.) Progress in Computing, Analytics and Networking. AISC, vol. 710, pp. 203–214. Springer, Singapore (2018). https://doi.org/10.1007/978-981-10-7871-2_20
8. Wang, C.-N., Nguyen, V.T., Thai, H.T.N., Duong, D.H.: Multi-criteria decision making (MCDM) approaches for solar power plant location selection in Viet Nam. Energies **11**, 1504 (2018)
9. Hanine, M., Boutkhoum, O., Tikniouine, A., Agouti, T.: An application of OLAP/GIS-Fuzzy AHP-TOPSIS methodology for decision making: location selection for landfill of industrial wastes as a case study. KSCE J. Civ. Eng. **21**, 2074–2084 (2017)
10. Polat, G., Eray, E., Bingol, B.N.: An integrated fuzzy MCGDM approach for supplier selection problem. J. Civ. Eng. Manag. **23**, 926–942 (2017)
11. Deveci, M., Canıtez, F., Gökaşar, I.: WASPAS and TOPSIS based interval type-2 fuzzy MCDM method for a selection of a car sharing station. Sustain. Cities Soc. **41**, 777–791 (2018)
12. Trivedi, A., Singh, A.: Prioritizing emergency shelter areas using hybrid multi-criteria decision approach: a case study. J. Multi-Criteria Decis. Anal. **24**, 133–145 (2017)
13. Daneshvar Rouyendegh, B., Yildizbasi, A., Arikan, Ü.Z.B.: Using intuitionistic fuzzy TOPSIS in site selection of wind power plants in Turkey. Adv. Fuzzy Syst. **2018**, 14 (2018)
14. Darani, S.K., Eslami, A.A., Jabbari, M., Asefi, H.: Parking lot site selection using a fuzzy AHP-TOPSIS framework in Tuyserkan, Iran. J. Urban Plan. Dev. **144** (2018)
15. Noori, A., Bonakdari, H., Morovati, K., Gharabaghi, B.: The optimal dam site selection using a group decision-making method through fuzzy TOPSIS model. Environ. Syst. Decis. **38**, 471–488 (2018)
16. Kutlu Gündoğdu, F., Kahraman, C.: A novel VIKOR method using spherical fuzzy sets and its application to warehouse site selection. J. Intell. Fuzzy Syst. **37**, 1197–1211 (2019)
17. Erbaş, M., Kabak, M., Özceylan, E., Çetinkaya, C.: Optimal siting of electric vehicle charging stations: a GIS-based fuzzy Multi-Criteria Decision Analysis. Energy **163**, 1017–1031 (2018)

18. Wang, C.-N., Huang, Y.-F., Chai, Y.-C., Nguyen, V.T.: A Multi-Criteria Decision Making (MCDM) for renewable energy plants location selection in Vietnam under a fuzzy environment. Appl. Sci. **8**, 2069 (2018)
19. Mayaki, E.A., Adedipe, O., Lawal, S.A.: Multi-criteria evaluation of the appropriate offshore wind farm location in Nigeria. In: IOP Conference Series: Materials Science and Engineering (2018)
20. Drakaki, M., Gören, H.G., Tzionas, P.: Comparison of fuzzy multi criteria decision making approaches in an intelligent multi-agent system for refugee siting. In: Świątek, J., Borzemski, L., Wilimowska, Z. (eds.) ISAT 2018. AISC, vol. 853, pp. 361–370. Springer, Cham (2019). https://doi.org/10.1007/978-3-319-99996-8_33
21. Bakhtavar, E., Yousefi, S., Jafarpour, A.: Evaluation of shaft locations in underground mines: Fuzzy multiobjective optimization by ratio analysis with fuzzy cognitive map weights. J. South. Afr. Inst. Min. Metall. **119**, 855–864 (2019)
22. Seker, S., Aydin, N.: Hydrogen production facility location selection for Black Sea using entropy based TOPSIS under IVPF environment. Int. J. Hydrogen Energy **45**, 15855–15868 (2020)
23. Liang, X., Zhang, R., Liu, C.: Location analysis of regional disaster relief material reserve center: a case study in Sichuan Province, China. In: IEEE International Conference on Industrial Engineering and Engineering Management, pp. 1588–1592 (2019)
24. Mohsin, M., Zhang, J., Saidur, R., Sun, H., Sait, S.M.: Economic assessment and ranking of wind power potential using fuzzy-TOPSIS approach. Environ. Sci. Pollut. Res. **26**, 22494–22511 (2019)
25. Wang, B., Xie, H.-L., Ren, H.-Y., Li, X., Chen, L., Wu, B.-C.: Application of AHP, TOPSIS, and TFNs to plant selection for phytoremediation of petroleum-contaminated soils in shale gas and oil fields. J. Clean. Prod. **233**, 13–22 (2019)
26. Yildiz, A., Ayyildiz, E., Taskin Gumus, A., Ozkan, C.: A modified balanced scorecard based hybrid pythagorean fuzzy AHP-topsis methodology for ATM site selection problem. Int. J. Inf. Technol. Decis. Mak. **19**, 365–384 (2020)
27. Erdin, C., Akbaş, H.E.: A comparative analysis of fuzzy TOPSIS and geographic information systems (GIS) for the location selection of shopping malls: a case study from Turkey. Sustainability **11**, 3837 (2019)
28. Ortiz-Barrios, M., Nugent, C., Cleland, I., Donnelly, M., Verikas, A.: Selecting the most suitable classification algorithm for supporting assistive technology adoption for people with dementia: a multicriteria framework. J. Multi-Criteria Decis. Anal. **27**, 20–38 (2019)
29. León, O.P.: Logística Urbana desde la perspectiva del Agente Generador de Viajes. INGE CUC **15**, 45–62 (2019)
30. Restrepo, J.E., Neira Rodado, D., Viloria Silva, A.: Multicriteria strategic approach for the selection of concrete suppliers in a construction company in Colombia. In: Saeed, K., Dvorský, J. (eds.) CISIM 2020. LNCS, vol. 12133, pp. 184–194. Springer, Cham (2020). https://doi.org/10.1007/978-3-030-47679-3_16
31. Yavaşoğlu, H.H., et al.: Site selection of the turkish antarctic research station using analytic hierarchy process. Polar Sci. **22**, 1–12 (2019)
32. Pang, X., Liu, H., Zhao, X.: Selecting suitable sites for an Antarctic research station: a case for a new Chinese research station. Antarct. Sci. **26**, 479–490 (2014)
33. Correa, M.: ¿A qué volvemos a la Antártida?. https://www.elcolombiano.com/colombia/exp edicion-a-la-antartida-que-es-LK7862836

Newtonian Heating Effects of Oldroyd-B Liquid Flow with Cross-Diffusion and Second Order Slip

K. Loganathan[1]([✉]), K. Tamilvanan[2], Amelec Viloria[3,4], Noel Varela[3], and Omar Bonerge Pineda Lezama[5]

[1] Department of Mathematics, Faculty of Engineering,
Karpagam Academy of Higher Education, Coimbatore 641021, Tamilnadu, India
loganathankaruppusamy304@gmail.com
[2] Department of Mathematics, Government Arts College for Men,
Krishnagiri 635001, Tamilnadu, India
[3] Universidad de la Costa, Barranquilla, Colombia
[4] Universidad Peruana de Ciencias Aplicadas, Lima, Peru
[5] Universidad Tecnológica Centroamericana (UNITEC), San Pedro Sula, Honduras

Abstract. The current study highlights the Newtonian heating and second-order slip velocity with cross-diffusion effects on Oldroyd-B liquid flow. The modified Fourier heat flux is included in the energy equation system. The present problem is modeled with the physical governing system. The complexity of the governing system was reduced to a nonlinear ordinary system with the help of suitable transformations. A homotopy algorithm was used to validate the nonlinear system. This algorithm was solved via MATHEMATICA software. Their substantial aspects are further studied and reported in detail. We noticed that the influence of slip velocity order two is lower than the slip velocity order one.

Keywords: Oldroyd-B liquid · Second order slip · Cross diffusion effects · Convective heating · Cattaneo-Christov heat flux

1 Introduction

Heat transport through non-Newtonian fluids is the significant study in recent times because of its industrial and engineering applications. Oldroyd-B fluid is one of the types of non-Newtonian fluids. This fluid contains viscoelastic behaviour. Loganathan et al. [1] exposed the 2nd-order slip phenomena of Oldroyd-B fluid flow with cross diffusion impacts. Hayat et al. [2] performed the modified heat flux impacts with multiple chemical reactions on Oldroyd-B liquid flow. Eswaramoorthi et al. [3] studied the influence of cross-diffusion on viscoelastic liquid induced by an unsteady stretchy sheet. Elanchezhian et al. [4] examined the important facts of swimming motile microorganisms with stratification effects on Oldroyd-B fluid flow. Loganathan and Rajan [5] explored the entropy effects of Williamson nanoliquid caused by a stretchy plate with partial

© Springer Nature Switzerland AG 2020
Y. Tan et al. (Eds.): ICSI 2020, LNCS 12145, pp. 661–668, 2020.
https://doi.org/10.1007/978-3-030-53956-6_61

slip and convective surface conditions. The innovative research articles on non-Newtonian fluid flow with different geometry's and situations are studied in ref's [6–10].

As far as our survey report the Newtonian heating effects along with slip order two on Oldroyd-B liquid flow is not examined yet. The present study incorporates the cross diffusion and modified Fourier heat flux into the problem. The eminent homotopy technique [11–13] is employed for computing the ODE system and the results are reported via graphs.

2   Modeling

We have constructed the Oldroyd-B liquid flow subjected to below stated aspects:

1. Incompressible flow
2. Second-order velocity slip
3. Magnetic field
4. Binary chemical reaction
5. Stretching plate with linear velocity.
6. Cross-diffusion effects
7. Modified Fourier heat flux

Figure 1 represents graphical illustration of physical problem. The governing equations are stated below:

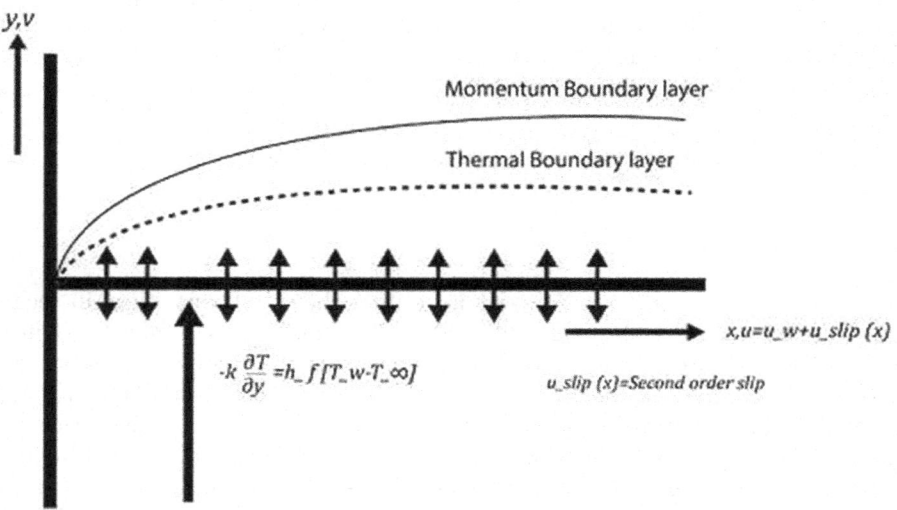

Fig. 1. Schematic diagram

$$\frac{\partial u}{\partial x} + \frac{\partial v}{\partial y} = 0, \tag{1}$$

$$\frac{\partial u}{\partial x}u + \frac{\partial u}{\partial y}v + A_1\left(u^2\frac{\partial^2 u}{\partial x^2} + v^2\frac{\partial^2 u}{\partial y^2} + 2uv\frac{\partial^2 u}{\partial x\partial y}\right) = \mu\frac{\partial^2 u}{\partial y^2}$$

$$-\mu A_2 v\frac{\partial^3 u}{\partial y^3} - \frac{\partial u}{\partial x}\frac{\partial^2 u}{\partial y^2} - \frac{\partial u}{\partial y}\frac{\partial^2 v}{\partial y^2} + \left(u\frac{\partial^3 u}{\partial x\partial y^2}\right) - \frac{\sigma B_0^2}{\rho}\left(u + A_1 v\frac{\partial u}{\partial y}\right), \tag{2}$$

$$\frac{\partial T}{\partial x}u + \frac{\partial T}{\partial y}v = \frac{k}{\rho c_p}\frac{\partial^2 T}{\partial y^2} - \frac{1}{\rho c_p}\frac{\partial q_r}{\partial y} + \frac{D_m k_T}{c_s c_p}\frac{\partial^2 C}{\partial y^2} \tag{3}$$

$$\frac{\partial C}{\partial x}u + \frac{\partial C}{\partial y}v = D_m\frac{\partial^2 C}{\partial y^2} + \frac{D_m k_T}{T_m}\frac{\partial^2 T}{\partial y^2} - k_m(C - C_\infty) \tag{4}$$

The boundary points are

$$u = u_w + u_{slip} = ax + \lambda_1\frac{\partial u}{\partial y} + \lambda_2\frac{\partial^2 u}{\partial y^2}, \quad v = 0,$$

$$-k\frac{\partial T}{\partial y} = h_f T, \quad C = C_w \quad \text{at } y = 0, \tag{5}$$

$$u(\to 0), \quad v(\to 0), \quad T(\to T_\infty), \quad C(\to C_\infty) \quad \text{as } y(\to \infty), \tag{6}$$

where A_1 (= relaxation time), A_2 (= retardation time), B_0 (= constant magnetic field), a (= stretching rate), c_p (= specific heat), c_∞ (= ambient concentration), c_w (= fluid wall concentration), D_m (= diffusion coefficient), k (= thermal conductivity), T_∞ (= ambient temperature), T_w (= convective surface temperature), u, v (= Velocity components), u_w (= velocity of the sheet), λ_1 (= first order slip velocity factor), λ_2 (= second order slip velocity factor), μ (= kinematic viscosity), ρ (= density), σ (= electrical conductivity), γ (= dimensionless thermal relaxation time). The energy equation updated with Cattaneo-Christov heat flux is defined as:

$$u\frac{\partial T}{\partial x} + v\frac{\partial T}{\partial y} + 2uv\frac{\partial T^2}{\partial x\partial y} + \lambda\left(u^2\frac{\partial^2 T}{\partial x^2} + v^2\frac{\partial^2 T}{\partial y^2} + \left(u\frac{\partial u}{\partial x} + v\frac{\partial u}{\partial y}\right)\frac{\partial T}{\partial x}\right.$$

$$\left. + \left(u\frac{\partial v}{\partial x} + v\frac{\partial v}{\partial y}\right)\frac{\partial T}{\partial y}\right) = \frac{k}{\rho c_p}\frac{\partial^2 T}{\partial y^2} - \frac{1}{\rho c_p}\frac{\partial q_r}{\partial y} + \frac{D_m k_T}{c_s c_p}\frac{\partial^2 C}{\partial y^2} \tag{7}$$

The transformations are

$$\psi = \sqrt{a\mu}xf(\eta), u = \frac{\partial\psi}{\partial y}, v = -\frac{\partial\psi}{\partial x}, \eta = \sqrt{\frac{a}{\mu}}y$$

$$v = -\sqrt{a\mu}f(\eta), \quad u = axf'(\eta), \quad \phi(\eta) = \frac{C - C_\infty}{C_w - C_\infty}, \theta(\eta) = \frac{T - T_\infty}{T_w - T_\infty}, \tag{8}$$

From the above transformations we derive the ODE system as follows,

$$f''' + \beta \left(f''^2 - f f^{iv} \right) + f f'' - f'^2 + \alpha \left(2 f f' f'' - f^2 f''' \right) - M \left(f' - \alpha f f'' \right) = 0 \quad (9)$$

$$f\theta' - \gamma \left(f^2 \theta'' + f f' \theta' \right) + \frac{1}{Pr}(1 + \frac{4}{3}Rd)\theta'' + D_f \phi'' = 0 \quad (10)$$

$$\frac{1}{Sc}\phi'' + f\phi' - Cr\phi + Sr\theta'' = 0 \quad (11)$$

with boundary points

$$f(0) = 0, \ f'(0) = 1 + \epsilon_1 f''(0) + \epsilon_2 f'''(0), \ \theta'(0) = -Nw(1 + \theta(0)), \ \phi(0) = 1$$
$$f'(\infty) = 0, \ \theta(\infty) = 0, \ \phi(\infty) = 0, \quad (12)$$

The variables are defined as:
$\epsilon_1 =$ (first order velocity constant) $= \lambda_1 \sqrt{a/\mu}$; $\epsilon_2 =$ (second order velocity constant) $= \lambda_2 \frac{a}{\mu} \frac{h_f}{k} \sqrt{\mu/a}$; $\alpha =$ (relaxation time constant) $= A_1 a$; $\beta =$ (retardation time constant) $= A_2 a$; M = (magnetic field constant) $= \frac{\sigma B_0^2}{\rho a}$; $Pr =$ (Prandtl number) $= \frac{\rho C_p}{k}$; $Rd =$ (radiation constant) $= \frac{4\sigma^* T_\infty^3}{k k^*}$; $\gamma = \lambda a$; $D_f =$ (Dufour number) $= \frac{D_m k_T}{\mu c_s c_p} \frac{c_w - c_\infty}{T_w - T_\infty}$; $Cr =$ (chemical reaction constant) $= \frac{k_m}{a}$; $Sc =$ (Schmidt number) $= \frac{\mu}{D_m}$; $Sr =$ (Soret number) $= \frac{D_m k_T}{\mu T_m} \frac{T_w - T_\infty}{c_w - c_\infty}$.

3   Solution Methodology

We using the homotopy technique for validate the convergence of the nonlinear systems. The basic guesses and linear operators are defined as:

$$f_0 = \eta e^{-\eta} + \frac{3\epsilon_2 - 2\epsilon_1}{\epsilon_2 - 1 - \epsilon_1} * e^{-\eta} - \frac{3\epsilon_2 - 2\epsilon_1}{\epsilon_2 - 1 - \epsilon_1}, \quad \phi_0 = e^{-\eta}, \quad \theta_0 = \frac{Nw * e^{-\eta}}{1 - Nw}$$
$$L_f = f'(f'' - 1), \qquad L_\phi = (\phi'') - (\phi), L_\theta = (\theta'') - (\theta).$$

which satisfies the property

$$L_f \left[D_1 + D_2 e^\eta + D_3 e^{-\eta} \right] = 0, \quad L_\phi \left[D_6 e^\eta + D_7 e^{-\eta} \right] = 0, \quad L_\theta \left[D_4 e^\eta + D_5 e^{-\eta} \right] = 0,$$

where $D_k(k = 1 - -7)$ are constants. The special solutions are

$$f_m(\eta) = f_m^*(\eta) + D_1 + D_2 e^\eta + D_3 e^{-\eta}$$
$$\phi_m(\eta) = \phi_m^*(\eta) + D_6 e^\eta + D_7 e^{-\eta}$$
$$\theta_m(\eta) = \theta_m^*(\eta) + D_4 e^\eta + D_5 e^{-\eta}.$$

In Fig. 2 the straight lines are named as h-curves. The permissible range of h_f, h_θ & h_ϕ are $-1.7 \le h_f \le -0.6, -1.2 \le h_\theta \le -0.2, -1.2 \le h_\phi \le -0.2$, respectively. Order of convergent series is depicted in Table 1. Table 2 depicts $f''(0)$ in the special case $M = \beta = 0$. It is noted that the $f''(0)$ values are well matched with the previous reports [14–16].

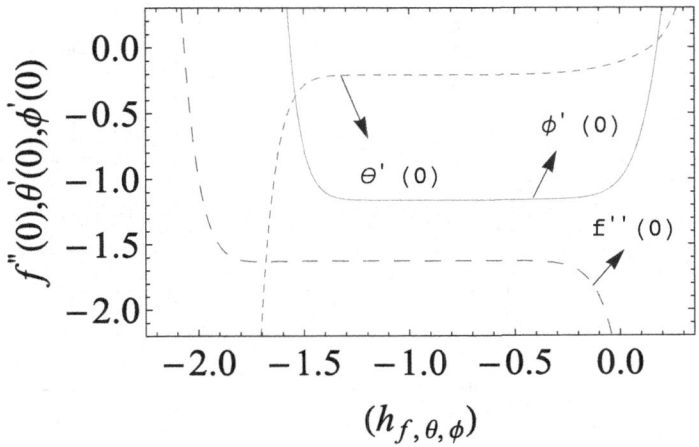

Fig. 2. h-curves for h_f, h_θ, h_ϕ

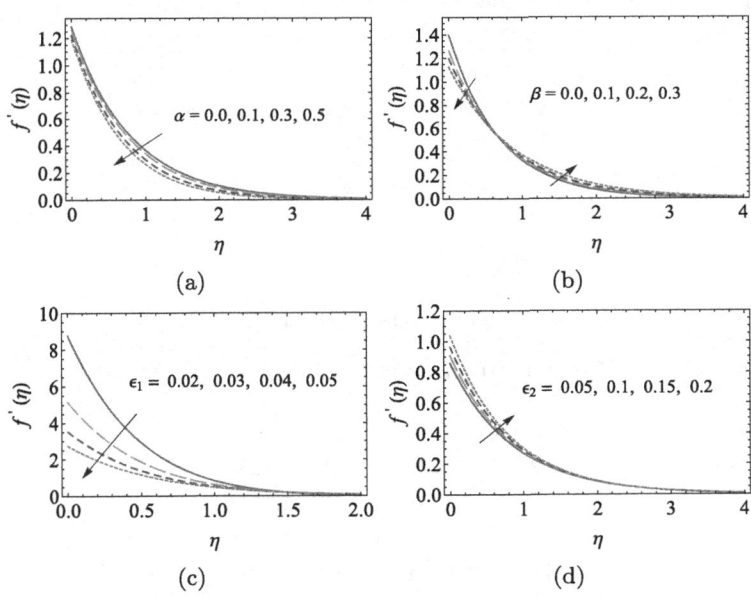

(a)

(b)

(c)

(d)

Fig. 3. $f'(\eta)$ for various range of parameters $(\alpha, \beta, \epsilon_1, \epsilon_2)$.

4   Results and Discussion

Physical Characteristics of rising parameters versus, Concentration $\phi(\eta)$, velocity $f(\eta)$ and temperature $\theta(\eta)$ are investigated in Figs. 3, 4 and 5. Figure 3 depicted the velocity distribution $f(\eta)$ for different range of α, β, ϵ_1, ϵ_2. It is noted that the velocity reduces for β and ϵ_1, while it increases for α and ϵ_2. The temperature

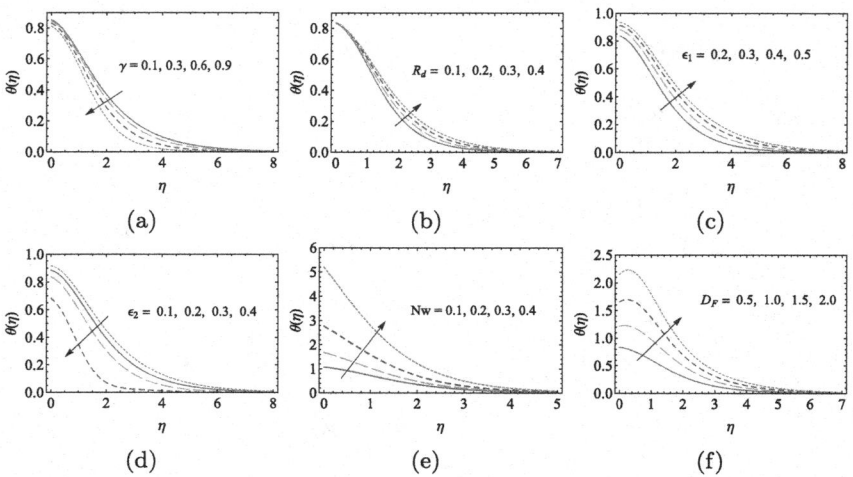

Fig. 4. $\theta(\eta)$ for various range of parameters (γ, R_d, ϵ_1, ϵ_2, Nw and D_F).

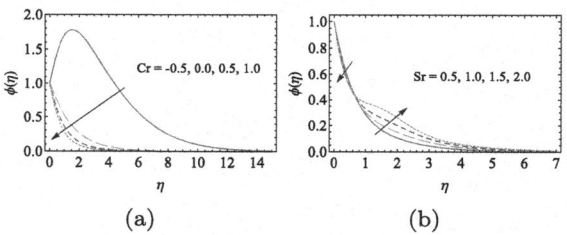

Fig. 5. $\phi(\eta)$ for various range of parameters (Cr and Sr).

Table 1. Approximations for convergence

Order	$-f''(0)$	$-\theta'(0)$	$-\phi'(0)$
2	1.8126	0.1532	1.1289
7	1.6331	0.1979	1.1558
12	1.6273	0.2059	1.1606
17	1.6274	0.2068	1.1616
22	1.6274	0.2068	1.1616
27	1.6274	0.2068	1.1616
35	1.6274	0.2068	1.1616

distribution $\theta(\eta)$ for different range of γ, R_d, ϵ_1, ϵ_2, Nw and D_F are sketched in Fig. 4. Thermal boundary layer decays with increasing the γ and ϵ_2 values. Larger values of R_d, ϵ_1 and D_F boosts the temperature distribution $\theta(\eta)$. Figure 5

Table 2. Validation of $f''(0)$ in the specific case for various α when $\beta = M = 0$

α	Ref. [14]	Ref. [15]	Ref. [16]	Present
0.0	1.000	0.9999963	1.00000	1.00000
0.2	1.0549	1.051949	1.05189	1.05189
0.4	1.10084	1.101851	1.10190	1.10190
0.6	1.0015016	1.150162	1.15014	1.15014
0.8	1.19872	1.196693	1.19671	1.19671

shows the influence on $\phi(\eta)$ for various values of Cr and Sr. These parameters shows the opposite effect in $\phi(\eta)$.

5   Conclusion

The salient outcomes the flow problem is given below:

1. Retardation time parameter (β) is inversely proportional to the relaxation time parameter (α) is in velocity profile.
2. Thermal boundary layer enhances due to increasing the R_d, Nw, D_F whereas it decays for higher ϵ_1 and γ.
3. Higher Soret number values enhance the solutal boundary thickness.

References

1. Loganathan, K., Sivasankaran, S., Bhuvaneshwari, M., Rajan, S.: Second-order slip, cross- diffusion and chemical reaction effects on magneto-convection of Oldroyd-B liquid using Cattaneo-Christov heat flux with convective heating. J. Therm. Anal. Calorim. **136**, 401–409 (2019). https://doi.org/10.1007/s10973-018-7912-5
2. Hayat, T., Imtiaz, M., Alsaedi, A., Almezal, S.: On Cattaneo-Christov heat flux in MHD flow of Oldroyd-B fluid with homogeneous-heterogeneous reactions. J. Magn. Mater. **401**(1), 296–303 (2016)
3. Eswaramoorthi, S., Sivasankaran, S., Bhuvaneswari, M., Rajan, S.: Soret and Dufour effects on viscoelastic boundary layer flow over a stretchy surface with convective boundary condition with radiation and chemical reaction. Sci. Iran B. **23**(6), 2575–2586 (2016)
4. Elanchezhian, E., Nirmalkumar, R., Balamurugan, M., Mohana, K., Prabu, K.M.: Amelec Viloria: heat and mass transmission of an Oldroyd-B nanofluid flow through a stratified medium with swimming of motile gyrotactic microorganisms and nanoparticles. J. Therm. Anal. Calorim. (2020). https://doi.org/10.1007/s10973-020-09847-w
5. Loganathan, K., Rajan, S.: An entropy approach of Williamson nanofluid flow with Joule heating and zero nanoparticle mass flux. J. Therm. Anal. Calorim. (2020). https://doi.org/10.1007/s10973-020-09414-3

6. Bhuvaneswari, M., Eswaramoorthi, S., Sivasankaran, S., Hussein, A.K.: Cross-diffusion effects on MHD mixed convection over a stretching surface in a porous medium with chemical reaction and convective condition. Eng. Trans. **67**(1), 3–19 (2019)

7. Loganathan, K., Sivasankaran, S., Bhuvaneswari, M., Rajan, S.: Dufour and Soret effects on MHD convection of Oldroyd-B liquid over stretching surface with chemical reaction and radiation using Cattaneo-Christov heat flux. IOP: Mater. Sci. Eng. **390**, 012077 (2018)

8. Bhuvaneswari, M., Eswaramoorthi, S., Sivasankaran, S., Rajan, S., Saleh Alshomrani, A.: Effects of viscous dissipation and convective heating on convection flow of a second-grade liquid over a stretching surface: an analytical and numerical study. Sci. Iran. B **26**(3), 1350–1357 (2019)

9. Muhammad, T., Alamri, S.Z., Waqas, H., et al.: Bioconvection flow of magnetized Carreau nanofluid under the influence of slip over a wedge with motile microorganisms. J. Therm. Anal. Calorim. (2020). https://doi.org/10.1007/s10973-020-09580-4

10. Abbasbandy, S., Hayat, T., Alsaedi, A., Rashidi, M.M.: Numerical and analytical solutions for Falkner-Skan flow of MHD Oldroyd-B fluid. Int. J. Numer. Methods Heat Fluid Flow **24**, 390–401 (2014)

11. Liao, S., Tan, Y.A.: General approach to obtain series solutions of nonlinear differential. Stud. Appl. Math. **119**(4), 297–354 (2007)

12. Liao, S.J.: An explicit, totally analytic approximation of Blasius viscous flow problems. Int. J. Non-Linear Mech. **34**, 759–778 (1999)

13. Loganathan, K., Mohana, K., Mohanraj, M., Sakthivel, P., Rajan, S., Impact of 3rd-grade nanofluid flow across a convective surface in the presence of inclined Lorentz force: an approach to entropy optimization. J. Therm. Anal. Calorim. (2020). https://doi.org/10.1007/s10973-020-09751-3

14. Sadeghy, K., Hajibeygi, H., Taghavi, S.M.: Stagnation-point flow of upper-convected Maxwell fluids. Int. J. Non-linear Mech. **41**, 1242 (2006)

15. Mukhopadhyay, S.: Heat transfer analysis of the unsteady flow of a Maxwell fluid over a stretching surface in the presence of a heat source/sink. Chin. Phys. Lett. **29**, 054703 (2012)

16. Abbasi, F.M., Mustafa, M., Shehzad, S.A., Alhuthali, M.S., Hayat, T.: Analytical study of Cattaneo-Christov heat flux model for a boundary layer flow of Oldroyd-B fluid. Chin. Phys. B. **25**(1), 014701 (2016)

Econometric Algorithms Applied to the Incidence of Income on Satisfaction with Quality of Life in Latin American Capitals

Carolina Henao-Rodríguez[1], Mercedes Gaitán-Angulo[2,4],
Jenny Paola Lis-Gutiérrez[3,4(✉)], and Leonor Mojica Sánchez[5]

[1] Unipanamericana Fundación Universitaria, Bogotá, Colombia
lchenaor@unipanamericana.edu.co
[2] Corporación Universitaria Empresarial de Salamanca, Barranquilla, Colombia
m_gaitan689@cues.edu.co
[3] Universidad de la Costa, Barranquilla, Colombia
jlis@cuc.edu.co
[4] Universidad de Granada, Melilla, Spain
{e.mercedesgaitan,e.jennypaolalis}@go.ugr.es
[5] Corporación Universitaria del Meta, Villavicencio, Colombia
leonor.mojica@unimeta.edu.co

Abstract. The purpose of this research is to determine the incidence of income on the satisfaction of quality of life in Latin American capitals. The data was taken from the CAF Survey in 2017 (ECAF), made by Development Bank of Latin America. To do this, an econometric model was constructed which represents the relationship between the studied variables. Among the main findings, it was identified that, except for Mexico City, in all the analyzed cities a deteriorated state of health reduces the probability that the individual feels satisfied with his or her life. Therefore, health is a crucial element to increase the citizens' perception of the quality of life in Latin American cities.

Keywords: Income · Life satisfaction · Quality of life · Econometric studies · Latin America

1 Introduction

In countries, the economic development and quality of life level are not only related to income, since in addition to per capita income other factors largely affect the socioeconomic development in a country [1]. Quality of life is an indicator that, in addition to being dependent on many factors, presents the essential features that make this a complex indicator. In a first instance, apparently, the economic development of a country would guarantee a growing trend in the standard of living of its citizens. In practice, the observed facts do not confirm this hypothesis: a substantial number of countries above the average in economic growth present state regulations that do not fully guarantee

© Springer Nature Switzerland AG 2020
Y. Tan et al. (Eds.): ICSI 2020, LNCS 12145, pp. 669–677, 2020.
https://doi.org/10.1007/978-3-030-53956-6_62

human rights, in addition to production systems that are highly harmful to the natural environment. [2].

In Latin American countries there are problems associated with inequality and economic growth that is concentrated in a few sectors and territories [3], which impedes a better quality of life for its inhabitants. It is therefore of great importance that Latin American countries develop effective public policies that improve the living conditions of their inhabitants so that their welfare receives a significant positive impact. For an adequate understanding, inequality should be studied from its structure to facilitate a holistic approach that allows observing it from different perspectives: the spatial concentration of resources, assets and opportunities and differences in quality of life and well-being among the different territories [4].

From the above reflection, it is essential to achieve a comparative analysis of the influence of income on satisfaction and quality of life in Latin America, considering the particularities of the environment, and relying on econometric techniques that allow establishing causal relationships in a quantitative way.

2 State of the Art

The role of the state in improving the quality of life and economic growth is a hot topic at present. [5] stated that, at present, a fundamental task is the definition of the role that the government of a country should play in its economic development. When, in a country it is found that the information is not correct, adequate or sufficient, as well as there are imperfect markets, it is possible that its legislation and government systems have tools that allow them to promote better standards of living. [6].

Complexity greatly limits the study of indicators of quality of life and well-being, as shown by the few interdisciplinary studies that have been published about the use of indicators. In addition, the indicators of quality of life, well-being and sustainability have weak theoretical support, future research must be centered on find key indicators, which are fundamental when trying to interpretate and contextualize the complex dynamics under study [7]. Among the most recent studies about quality of life we can find the work of [8] who studied the Organization for Economic Cooperation and Development countries and found that developed countries have as a characteristic attribute a decelerated economic growth, since the growth rate of their GDP has increased between 2 and 3 times in the last 50 years. In agreement with the Easterlin paradox, long term dynamics of the GPD in developed countries show that richer persons don't present a higher life quality satisfaction. Furthermore, studies on that dynamics found and statistically irrelevant correlation between the rate of change in GPD and life satisfaction.

[9] used the self-reported happiness of American citizens between 1976 and 2006 found strong evidence to affirm that the perception of happiness increased when the state government made more investment in the supply of public goods. [10] studied the dispersion and growth of immigrant in the United States for 366 metropolitan in 2010. They examined how immigration has influenced four dimensions of quality of life: economic well-being, social welfare, healthy living and urban mobility. The authors found that the concentration of immigrants tends to have negative effects on the quality of urban life, but these effects dissipate when considering the diversity of immigrants.

[11] examined the different levels of health and social security services in rural and urban areas of China and India, with representative data at the national level of individuals 50 years of age or older, between 2008 and 2010 in China and 2007 and 2008 in India.

3 Methodology

3.1 Data

The data was taken from the CAF Survey in 2017 [12], made by the Development Bank of Latin America, taking as a sample individuals in households and conducted annually since 2008 in the main cities of Latin America. The survey collects demographic and socioeconomic information from the individuals in the sample, and records information about a set of characteristics at the household level. The survey contains general modules that allow estimates on access, quality, spending and satisfaction in urban transport services, security, garbage collection, water and sanitation, electricity and housing. The universe under study was the urban population between 20 and 60 years old, residents in the cities included in the sample, these were Buenos Aires, Bogota, La Paz, Lima, Mexico City, Montevideo, Panama City, Quito, São Paulo and Santiago.

To guarantee a balanced sample that would allow the study population to be represented, sex and age quotas were used, and 12 demographic groups were used, so that the distribution of the sample between groups did not differ statistically from the population distribution in each city. The data from the ECAF were collected using a stratified, multistage cluster sampling design. In addition, the 2017 ECAF includes multiple imputations to alleviate the problem of lost/un-reported information on personal income.

3.2 Variables

The endogenous variable is the answer to the question (P3): how satisfied are you with your life? On a scale of 1 to 10, 1 is "Not satisfied" and 10 is "Totally satisfied".

The exogenous variables are (i) level of income, (ii) subsidies received from the government, (iii) marital status, (iv) health and (v) education. Next, each of these variables is explained.

Logingre: logarithm of the monthly income level. Because the income variable was imputed, the logarithmic transformation was performed on all its versions. The most efficient way is using the command.
P48_1: If in the last three months the individual received subsidies, social plans or social assistance from the government
P4: Marital status (single (2), separated (3), widow (4) and living/united freely (5))
P41: Appreciation by the individual about his health (very good (2), good (3), regular (4), bad (5))
P49: Employment status: (owner or partner of a business of its own (2), employed in a private sector company or institution (3), employed in a public sector institution or company (4), worker of a cooperative (5); worker of domestic service in private households (6), unpaid family worker (7).)

P101_1: Level of education (without instruction (1), preschool (2), basic/incomplete primary (3), basic/complete primary (4), secondary/diversified media and professional/incomplete high school (5), secondary/diversified media and professional/complete high school (6), incomplete university/tertiary non-university (7), full university/tertiary non-university (8), incomplete university (9), full university (10), specialization/master/doctorate (11).

3.3 Model

The dependent variable that is the answer to: on a scale of 1 to 10 where 1 is "Not at all satisfied" and 10 is "Totally satisfied", how satisfied are you with the life you lead? which is a discrete ordinal variable. In the ordinal family, the answer Y assumes one of the k single values. Actual values are irrelevant, except that it is assumed that the highest values correspond to "higher" results. Without loss of generality, it is assumed that Y assumes the values $1;\ldots; k$. The ordinal family with k results has cutoff points $k_0; k_1;\ldots,$ k_k, where $k_0 = -\infty$, $k_y < k_{y+1}$ $yk_k = \infty$. The coefficients were estimated using the maximum likelihood as described in this parameterization. No constant appears, because the effect is absorbed at the cut points. The probability of a given observation for ordered logit is:

$$P_{ij} = \Pr\left(y_j = i\right) = \Pr = (\kappa_i - 1 < x_j\beta + u \leq \kappa_i)$$
$$= (1/(1 + \exp(-\kappa_i + x_j\beta)) - (1/(1 + \exp(-\kappa_{i-1} + x_j\beta)) \tag{1}$$

The imputed values were obtained from the models chain

$$Y1^{(t+1)} \sim g(Y_1|Y_2^{(t)}, \ldots, Yk^{(t)}, Z; \varphi 1) \tag{2}$$

$$Y2^{(t+1)} \sim g(Y_2|Y_1^{(t+1)}, Y3^{(t)}, \ldots, Yk^{(t)}, Z; \varphi 2) \tag{3}$$

$$Yk^{(t+1)} \sim g(Yk|Y1^{(t+1)}, Y2^{(t+1)}, \ldots, Y_{k-1}^{(t+1)}, Z; \varphi k) \tag{4}$$

By iterating $t = 0, 1, \ldots, T$ times until obtain convergence at $t = T$; φj, $j = 1, \ldots, k$ represents the model parámeter g for the variable Yj [13].

4   Results

An estimate was made for each country except Venezuela due to the highly irregular alterations on its official exchange rate which produce skewness in the estimate. Each output is the result of adding 11 ordinal regressions, equivalent to analyzing 11 databases, the original and the 10 bases formed by each imputation and the variables derived from them, and then add these regressions, as shown below. The F test showed in all the models that it can not be rejected that the models are statistically significant, with a level of significance of 1%. The auxiliary parameters are not specified in this document, since they are the cut-off points, as shown below (Table 1).

Table 1. Variables statistically significant

City	Observations	***p < 0.01	**p < 0.05	*p < 0.1
Buenos Aires (Argentina)	662	2.p4, −1.050*** (0.233); 3.p4, −1.596*** (0.297); 3.p41, −0.666*** (0.256); 4.p41, −1.515*** (0.396)	4.p4, −1.565**, (0.790); 5.p4, 0.483** (0.225); 5.p4, −1.989** (0.782)	2.p41, −0.501* (0.290)
La Paz (Bolivia)	707	3.p4, 1-1.340*** (0.449); 4.p41, −1.911*** (0.431); 5.p41, −3.229*** (0.645); 5.p49, 0.830*** (0.218)	2.p41, −1.211** (0.488);	logingre 0.266* (0.146); 4.p4 −0.885* (0.485)
São Paulo (Brazil)	504	3.p41, −0.926*** (0.274); 4.p41, −1.407*** (0.291); 5.p41, −1.994*** (0.610); 6.p49, 1.266** (0.444); 5.p101_1, −2.659*** (0.997)	2.p49, −0.844** (0.418); 3.p101_1, −2.388** (0.965); 6.p101_1, −2.114** (0.949); 7.p101_1, −2.186** (1.017); 8.p101_1, −2.565** (0.991); 9.p101_1, −2.594** (1.002); 10.p101_1, − 1.838** (0.929)	1.p101_1, −2.143* (1.218); 4.p101_1, −1.853* (0.999); 11.p101_1, −2.577* (1.490)
Santiago (Chile)	601	4.p41, −1.731*** (0.324); 5.p41, −2.418*** (0.877)	3.p41, −0.664** (0.275); 4.p101_1, −2.552** (1.061); 5.p101_1, −2.361** (1.078); 6.p101_1, −2.385** (1.038); 7.p101_1, −2.694** (1.062); 8.p101_1, −2.683** (1.068); 9.p101_1, −2.643** (1.138); 10.p101_1, −2.146** (1.072)	11.p101_1, −2.015* (1.107)
Bogota (Colombia)	655	3.p41, −0.890*** (0.198); 4.p41, −1.116*** (0.319)	3.p4, −0.557** (0.248)	2.p41, −0.385* (0.224)
Quito (Ecuador)	636	2.p41, −1.071*** (0.332); 3.p41, −1.307*** (0.307); 4.p41, −1.521*** (0.334)	5.p4,0.595** (0.255); p48_1,1.036** (0.435); 5.p41, −1.718** (0.803)	4.p101_1, −1.264* (0.742)
Mexico City (México)	486	5.p4, 1.003*** (0.329)	4.p4,1.432** (0.649)	p48_1, −0.485* (0.246)
Panama City (Panamá)	342	4.p41, −1.183*** (0.398); 3.p101_1,6.822*** (1.354); 4.p101_1,6.574*** (1.093); 5.p101_1, 5.183*** (1.075); 6.p101_1,5.641*** (1.053); 7.p101_1,4.853*** (1.018); 8.p101_1,5.259*** (1.042); 9.p101_1,5.475*** (1.051); 10.p101_1,5.833*** (0.992); 11.p101_1,4.146*** (1.071)	p48_1, −0.586** (0.282)	logingre, 0.357* (0.187)
Lima (Peru)	557			logingre, 0.216* (0.126)
Montevideo (Uruguay)	651	3.p41, −0.887*** (0.221); 4.p41, −1.420*** (0.302); 4.p101_1,1.208*** (0.356); 5.p101_1,1.149*** (0.245); 6.p101_1,1.367*** (0.339); 7.p101_1,1.752*** (0.375); 8.p101_1,1.311*** (0.383); 9.p101_1,1.459*** (0.348); 10.p101_1,1.337*** (0.335); 11.p101_1,1.213*** (0.428).	2.p4, −0.366** (0.174); 3.p4, −0.617** (0.255); 5.p41, −1.847** (0.900); 2.p101_1, −2.640** (1.202); 3.p101_1, 1.353** (0.624)	

The empirical evidence showed that La Paz, Lima and Panama City are the only cities that presented a growing and significant association between the satisfaction that the individual reported with his life and income, therefore, for these countries the probability of an increase in The perception of satisfaction with their quality of life increases with income.

The coefficient corresponding to logingre shows a value with a higher value in the case of Panama City. We proceeded to test if the estimated difference is significant. For this purpose, the conversion of the currency of Bolivia and Peru to USD was made at the time of collection according to the official exchange rates. An estimate was made where the only exogenous variable was the logarithm of the income in dollars. To compare these countries, we then proceeded to estimate the difference between the parameters using the standard errors and data from the estimation of the previous model.

```
Multiple-imputation estimates Imputations = 10
Survey: Ordered logistic regression Number of obs = 1,623

Number of strata = 16 Population size = 4,638,423
Number of PSUs = 509
 Average RVI = 0.0129
 Largest FMI = 0.0648
 Complete DF = 493
DF adjustment: Small sample DF: min = 380.78
 avg = 399.91
 max = 454.75
Model F test: Equal FMI F( 5, 484.0) = 34.26
Within VCE type: Linearized Prob > F = 0.0000

-------------------------------------------------------------------------
p3 | Coef. Std. Err. t P>|t| [95% Conf. Interval]
-----------------+-------------------------------------------------------
pais |
Panamá | 2.179527 1.271468 1.71 0.087 -.3191543 4.678209
Perú | 1.023309 1.019053 1.00 0.316 -.9800239 3.026642
 |
pais#c.loging_usd |
Bolivia | .4136857 .1401791 2.95 0.003 .1380637 .6893077
Panamá | .2837042 .1463086 1.94 0.053 -.0038231 .5712315
Perú | .3053094 .1003372 3.04 0.003 .1080269 .5025919
-----------------+-------------------------------------------------------
/cut1 | -2.044947 .8642135 -2.37 0.018 -3.743841 -.3460522
/cut2 | -1.322942 .8375296 -1.58 0.115 -2.969483 .3235987
/cut3 | -.7519919 .8295073 -0.91 0.365 -2.382798 .8788141
/cut4 | -.182877 .8169945 -0.22 0.823 -1.789142 1.423388
/cut5 | 1.124355 .8106418 1.39 0.166 -.4694642 2.718173
/cut6 | 1.914093 .8115732 2.36 0.019 .3184374 3.509749
/cut7 | 2.754236 .8162825 3.37 0.001 1.149334 4.359139
/cut8 | 3.978042 .8234714 4.83 0.000 2.359024 5.59706
/cut9 | 4.796177 .8276484 5.79 0.000 3.16896 6.423394
-------------------------------------------------------------------------

Transformations Average RVI = 0.0394
 Largest FMI = 0.0383
 Complete DF = 493
DF adjustment: Small sample DF: min = 439.34
 avg = 439.34

Within VCE type: Linearized max = 439.34

--------------------------------------------------------------------------
p3 | Coef. Std. Err. t P>|t| [95% Conf. Interval]
-------------+------------------------------------------------------------
diff | -.4352909 .2233512 -1.95 0.052 -.8742605 .0036787
--------------------------------------------------------------------------

diff: _b[8.pais#c.loging_usd] - _b[2.pais#c.loging_usd] - _b[9.pais#c.loging_usd]

(1) diff = 0

F(1, 439.3) = 3.80
Prob > F = 0.0519
```

The joint tests of transformed coefficients (the differences) showed that the difference observed is not statistically significant at a level of significance of 5%.

5   Discussion

The empirical evidence showed that for all the cities analyzed, except for Mexico City, a more deteriorated state of health reduces the probability that the individual feels satisfied with his or her life. Therefore, health is a crucial element to increase the quality of life of citizens. In this context, economic development is often not a linear process of economic growth, so social security is a mechanism that is necessary in a market economy to rise the quality of life of the habitants. In this context, the government must create and maintain a social security net, including access to basic health services, since living standards cover more than the variables captured in GDP statistics [11].

In Buenos Aires, marital status is a significant variable, where "separate" is the marital status that decreases the likelihood that the individual feels satisfied with their life and "lives with a partner" is the marital status that decreases less the probability of increasing the perception of the quality of life. The education, the profession, the level of income and the subsidies received by the citizens in the last three months were not significant.

The results obtained showed that in La Paz there is a positive and significant relationship between the probability that an individual feels satisfied with his life and the level of income. Widowhood is the marital status that decreases the likelihood of satisfaction with the quality of life. The workers of a cooperative are more likely to increase the perception of satisfaction with their life. The educational level and subsidies, social plans or government social assistance received in the last three months were not significant in the estimation.

In São Paulo, the estimations showed that single people are more likely to feel satisfied with their lives. Working in domestic service presented a positive relationship with the probability of satisfaction with the life that leads, this may be due to the fact that in other professions higher levels of stress can be managed. However, this issue should be addressed by new studies that empirically validate the previous statement. Education on the other hand, presented a significant and negative relationship with the satisfaction that individuals reported with their lives. The level of income and subsidies received by citizens in the last three months were not significant.

The data studied for Santiago de Chile showed that divorced people are less likely to feel satisfied with their lives. Education presented a significant and negative relationship with the satisfaction that individuals reported with their lives, as was observed for the estimates made for São Paulo. The level of income, the employment situation and the subsidies received by the citizens in the last three months were not significant in the proposed models.

The empirical evidence for Bogotá showed that, as evidenced in Santiago de Chile, divorced persons are less likely to feel satisfied with their lives. The level of income, the employment situation and the subsidies received by the citizens in the last three months were not significant.

For Quito it was possible to conclude that the subsidies received by the citizens in the last three months increase the probability of satisfaction with the quality of life. People who have a complete primary school level are less likely to have greater life satisfaction [14]. Finally, the income level and the employment situation were not significant in the estimates.

In contrast to what was evidenced in Quito, in Mexico City it was evident that the subsidies received by the citizens in the last three months decrease the probability of satisfaction with the quality of life increase. Widowed people who live with a partner are more likely to increase their satisfaction with their lives. Variables such as income level, health, education and employment situation were not significant.

The estimate made for Panama City showed that there is a positive and significant relationship between the probability that an individual feels satisfied with their life and the level of income. Subsidies, social plans or government social assistance received in the last three months reduce the probability of satisfaction with the quality of life. Marital status and profession were not significant. Finally, the educational level presents a positive and significant relationship with the probability of feeling satisfied with their life, as compared to what was found in Santiago de Chile and São Paulo.

In Lima there is a positive and significant relationship between the level of income and the probability that an individual feels satisfied with their life, as well as the performance of unpaid family work. Divorce is the marital status that decreases the likelihood of satisfaction with the quality of life. The educational level and subsidies, social plans or government social assistance received in the last three months were not significant.

The study conducted for Montevideo showed that single and separate are the civil states that are significant and diminish the probability that the individual feels satisfied with their life. The income level, job performance and subsidies, social plans or government social assistance received in the last three months were not significant. Finally, the educational level have a positive and significant relationship with the likelihood of feeling satisfied with their lives, except for people who have pre-school studies that have a negative relationship with the probability that the individual reports greater satisfaction with their current life.

References

1. Chisadza, C., Bittencourt, M.: Economic development and democracy: the modernization hypothesis in sub-Saharan Africa. Soc. Sci. J. **56**(2), 243–254 (2019). https://www.sciencedi rect.com/science/article/pii/S0362331918301484
2. Hajduová, Z., Andrejovský, P., Beslerová, S.: Development of quality of life economic indicators with regard to the environment. Procedia – Soc. Behav. Sci. **110**(24), 747–754 (2014). https://www.sciencedirect.com/science/article/pii/S1877042813055596
3. Economic Commission for Latin America and the Caribbean: La ineficiencia de la desigualdad (LC/SES.37/3-P): Santiago de Chile: CEPAL (2018). https://www.cepal.org/es/publicaci ones/43442-la-ineficiencia-la-desigualdad
4. Economic Commission for Latin America and the Caribbean: Desarrollo territorial en América Latina y el Caribe: desafíos para la implementación de la agenda 2030 para el desarrollo sostenible (LC/MDCRP.27/3). Santiago de Chile: CEPAL (2018). https://www.cepal.org/es/publicaciones/43972-desarrollo-territorial-america-latina-caribe-desafios-la-implementacion-la
5. Stiglitz, J.E.: The role of government in economic development. In: Annual World Bank Conference on Development Economics, pp. 11–23. World Bank, Washington D.C. (1997)
6. Urzúa, M.A., Caqueo-Urízar, A.: Calidad de vida: Una revisión teórica del concepto. Terapia psicológica **30**(1), 61–71 (2012)
7. Pissourios, I.: An interdisciplinary study on indicators: a comparative review of quality-of-life, macroeconomic, environmental, welfare and sustainability indicators. Ecol. Ind. **34**, 420–427 (2013). https://doi.org/10.1016/j.ecolind.2013.06.008
8. Juknys, R., Liobikienė, G., Dagiliūtė, R.: Deceleration of economic growth - the main course seeking sustainability in developed countries. J. Clean. Prod. **192**(10), 1–8 (2018)

9. Flavin, P.: State government public goods spending and citizens' quality of life. Soc. Sci. Res. **78**, 28–40 (2019). https://www.sciencedirect.com/science/article/pii/S0049089X18302801

10. Wallace, M., Wu, Q.: Immigration and the quality of life in U.S. metropolitan areas. Soc. Sci. J. **56**, 443–457 (2018). https://doi.org/10.1016/j.soscij.2018.09.016. https://www.scienc edirect.com/science/article/pii/S0362331918301411

11. Hu, S., Das, D.: Quality of life among older adults in China and India: does productive engagement help? Soc. Sci. Med. **229**, 144–153 (2019). https://www.sciencedirect.com/sci ence/article/pii/S0277953618303368

12. CAF – Banco de Desarrollo de América Latina. Encuesta anual a individuos en hogares Trayectorias laborales y productivas en América Latina 2017. CAF, Caracas (2017). http:// scioteca.caf.com/handle/123456789/1400

13. Molina, E.: Imputación múltiple de ingresos individuales y familiares en la encuesta CAF 2017. Presentación, Métodos y Ejemplos. CAF, Caracas (2018)

14. Lis-Gutiérrez, J.P., Reyna-Niño, H.E., Gaitán-Angulo, M., Viloria, A., Abril, J.E.S.: Hierarchical ascending classification: an application to contraband apprehensions in Colombia (2015–2016). In: Tan, Y., Shi, Y., Tang, Q. (eds.) Data Mining and Big Data. Lecture Notes in Computer Science, vol. 10943, pp. 168–178. Springer, Cham (2018). https://doi.org/10. 1007/978-3-319-93803-5_16

Analytical Study of Radiative Casson Nanoliquid Flow with Heat Absorption

K. Loganathan[1]([✉]), K. Tamilvanan[2], Amelec Viloria[3,4], Noel Varela[4], and Omar Bonerge Pineda Lezama[5]

[1] Department Mathematics, Faculty of Engineering,
Karpagam Academy of Higher Education, Coimbatore 641021, Tamilnadu, India
loganathankaruppusamy304@gmail.com
[2] Department of Mathematics, Government Arts College for Men,
Krishnagiri 635001, Tamilnadu, India
[3] Universidad de la Costa, Barranquilla, Colombia
[4] Universidad Peruana de Ciencias Aplicadas, Lima, Peru
[5] Universidad Tecnolgica Centroamericana (UNITEC), San Pedro Sula, Honduras

Abstract. The divergence of thermally radiative MHD flow of a Casson nanofluid over a stretching paper alongside heat absorption. The governing non linear equations are remodeled into a nonlinear ODE's. The HAM is adopted to find the series solution. The changes of pertinent parameters are analyzed with diagrams and tables. The fluid velocity is controlled by suction and it develops with injection. The local Nusselt number rapidly suppresses with increasing the magnetic field parameter in heat generation case.

Keywords: Casson nanoliquid · Heat absorption · Magnetic field · Thermal radiation

1 Introduction

Most of the engineering and industrial processes depend on heat transfer mechanism, because they have cooling and heating processes. In general, the ordinary fluids are transfer less amount heat because they owing poor thermal conductivity. Various researchers are tried to increase the fluid thermal conductivity in different ways. One of the simplest method is nanosized particles are suspended into an ordinary fluids to raise the fluid thermal conductivity. Applications of nanofluids are investigated by many authors for both the nanofluids with Newtonian or non-Newtonian base with different geometrical shapes. One of the base fluid is Casson fluid and which posses yield stress. After applying the shear stress, Casson fluid performs as a solid when low shear stress and it moves when higher shear stress compared to the yield stress. Example of these fluids are soup, blood, jelly, tomato sauce, etc. Some important studies in this directions are [1–10].

© Springer Nature Switzerland AG 2020
Y. Tan et al. (Eds.): ICSI 2020, LNCS 12145, pp. 678–685, 2020.
https://doi.org/10.1007/978-3-030-53956-6_63

2 Governing Equations

The flow system is modeled with

1. Incompressible flow
2. Casson nanoliquid
3. thermal radiation
4. Magnetic field
5. Buongiorno nanofluid model
6. Stretching sheet with linear velocity.
7. heat absorption

$$\frac{\partial u}{\partial x} + \frac{\partial v}{\partial y} = 0 \tag{1}$$

$$u\frac{\partial u}{\partial x} + v\frac{\partial u}{\partial y} = v\left(1 + \frac{1}{\beta}\right)\frac{\partial^2 u}{\partial y^2} - \left(\frac{\sigma B_n^2}{\rho}\right) \tag{2}$$

$$u\frac{\partial T}{\partial x} + v\frac{\partial T}{\partial y} = \alpha_T \frac{\partial^2 T}{\partial y^2} - \frac{16\sigma_s T_\infty^2}{3k_e \rho C_p} + \frac{\rho^* C_p^*}{\rho C_p}\left[D_B \frac{\partial C}{\partial y}\frac{\partial T}{\partial y} + \frac{D_T}{T_\infty}\frac{\partial T}{\partial y}^2\right]$$

$$+ \frac{Q}{\rho C_p}(T - T_\infty) \tag{3}$$

$$u\frac{\partial C}{\partial x} + v\frac{\partial C}{\partial y} = D_B \frac{\partial^2 C}{\partial y^2} + \frac{D_T}{T_\infty}\frac{\partial^2 T}{\partial y^2} \tag{4}$$

The boundary points of the above system are:

$$u = u_w(x) = ax, \ v = v_w, \ at \ y = 0 \tag{5}$$

$$u \to 0, \ v \to 0, \ T \to T_\infty, \ C \to C_\infty, \ at \ y \to \infty \tag{6}$$

where β (=Casson fluid parameter), σ (=electrical conductivity), ρ (=density of fluid), α_T (=thermal diffusivity), C_p (=specific heat), D_B(= Brownian diffusion), D_T (+ thermophoretic diffusion coefficient), Q (=heat absorption/generation coefficient).

Consider the transformations:

$$\eta = \sqrt{\frac{a}{\nu}}y, \ v = -\sqrt{a\nu}f(\eta), \ u = axf'(\eta), \ \theta = \frac{T - T_\infty}{T_w - T_\infty}; \ \theta = \frac{C - C_\infty}{C_w - C_\infty} \tag{7}$$

The following ODEs are retreived from the governing system using above transformations,

$$\left(1 + \frac{1}{\beta}\right)f'''(\eta) + f''(\eta)f(\eta) - f'^2(\eta) - Mf'(\eta) = 0 \tag{8}$$

$$\left(1 + \frac{4}{3}Rd\right)\theta''(\eta) + Pr\theta'(\eta)f(\eta) + PrNb\theta'(\eta)\phi'(\eta) + PrNt\theta'^2(\eta)$$

$$+ PrHg\theta = 0 \tag{9}$$

$$\phi''(\eta) + Sc(f\phi') + \frac{Nt}{Nb}\theta''(\eta) = 0 \tag{10}$$

The boundary points of f, θ, ϕ becomes

$$f(0) = f_w, f'(0) = 1, f'(\infty) = 0, \theta(\infty) = 0, \phi(\infty) = 0 \tag{11}$$

where $M = \frac{\sigma B_n^2}{\rho}$ [=magnetic field parameter], $Pr = \nu/\alpha_T$ [=Prandtl number], $Nb = (\frac{\rho^* c_p^*}{\rho c_p} D_B(C_W - C_\infty))/\nu$ [=Brownian motion] parameter, $Nt = (\frac{\rho^* c_p^*}{\rho c_p} D_T(T_W - T_\infty))/(\nu T_\infty)$ [=thermophoresis parameter], $Hg = Q/\rho c_p a$ [=heat generation/absorption parameter], $Sc = \frac{\nu}{D_B}$ [= Schmidt number], $Rd = \frac{4}{3}\frac{\sigma_s T_\infty^3}{k_e \rho c_p \alpha_T}$ [=radiation parameter].

The surface drag force and heat transfer rate can be defined as:

$$\frac{1}{2} C_f \sqrt{Re} = f''(0)\left(1 + \frac{1}{\beta}\right) \text{ and } \frac{Nu}{\sqrt{Re}} = -\theta'(0)\left(1 + \frac{4}{3}Rd\right)$$

Table 1. Order of approximations

Order	$-F_{\eta\eta}(0)$	$-\theta_\eta(0)$	$-\phi_\eta(0)$
1	-1.875	-0.229472	-0.825641
5	-2.07069	-0.235657	-0.631038
10	-2.07751	-0.234869	-0.61575
15	-2.07737	-0.235076	-0.621188
20	-2.07737	-0.235057	-0.620607
25	-2.07737	-0.235014	-0.620104
30	-2.07737	-0.235064	-0.620437
35	-2.07737	-0.235032	-0.620348
40	-2.07737	-0.235041	-0.620326

3   Results and Discussion

The present nonlinear system was solve through HAM technique. The HAM was computed via MATHEMATICA software. Figure 1 sketched for the convergent solutions of the current study. Appoximation orders of HAM is shown in Table 1. The examinations are complete for various range of the relevant parameters intricate in this study. It is clear from Fig. 2 the velocity profile enhances for magnetic parameter (M) whereas it reduces for suction/ injection parameter

Table 2. The surface drag force and heat transfer rate values of β, F_w, M, Nb, Nt, Rd, Hg

β	F_w	M	Nb	Nt	Rd	Hg	$\frac{1}{2}C_f\sqrt{Re}$	$\frac{Nu}{\sqrt{Re}}$
0.3	0.2	0.3	-0.2	0.1	0.2	0.2	-2.23314	-0.329693
0.1							-1.96458	-o.329552
1.5							-1.81318	-0.328395
0.1							-1.75965	-0.327874
0.5	0.2	0.3	0.1	0.1	0.3	-0.2	-1.74059	-0.275054
		-0.5					-1.83052	-0.312842
		0.5					-1.92547	-0.354811
		0.1					-1.97484	-0.400887
0.5	0.2	0.3	0.1	0.1	0.3	-0.2	-1.83493	-0.640482
			0				-1.91934	-0.633721
			0.5				-2.15183	-0.633721
			0.1				-2.22367	-0.615345
				0			-1.87965	-0.621188
				2			-1.81318	-0.610898
				0.1			-1.75965	-0.602256
0.5	0.2	0.3	0.1	0.1	0.3	-0.2	-0.329107	-0.791791
					0		-0.328067	-0.621188
					2		-0.327535	-0.451693
					0.1		-0.326996	-0.28316
0.5	0.2	0.3	0.1	0.1	0.3	-0.2	-0.434391	-0.607522
	0						-0.45963	-0.636994
	2						-0.64889	-0.639523
	0.1						-0.67117	-0.64451
0.5	0.2	0.3	0.1	0.1	0.3	-0.2	-0.340084	-0.616351
						-0.5	-0.333235	-0.627037
						0.5	-0.329107	-0.634088
						0.1	-0.271261	-0.65124

(f_w). In Fig. 3 temperature $(\theta(\eta))$ increases for the radiation (Rd), Brownian constant (Nb), heat absorption constant (Hg), thermophoresis constant (Nt) and Casson parameter (β) and it decays for suction/injection parameter (f_w) and Prandtl number (Pr). The concentration $(\phi(\eta))$ rises with higher (β) and Nt but it diminishes with upsurge in (f_w) and Sc (see Fig. 4) (Table 2).

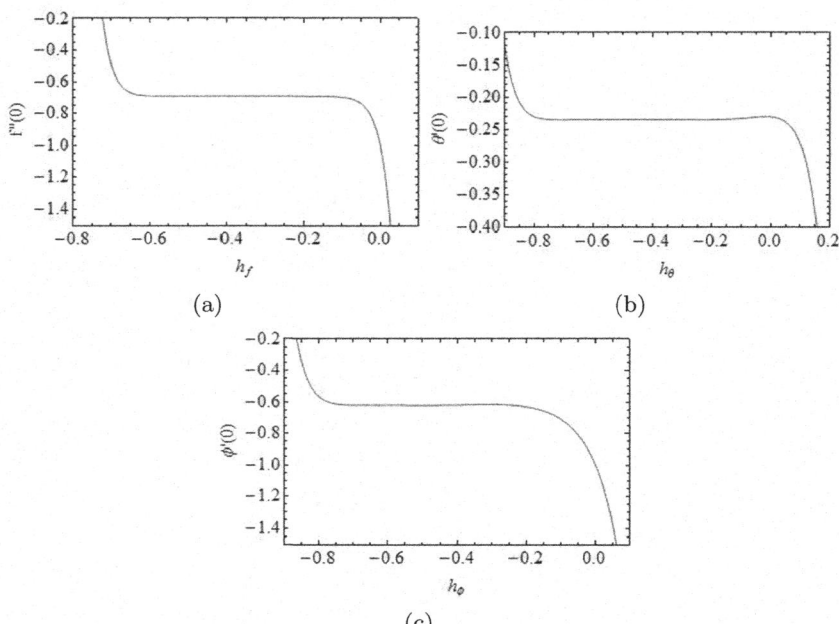

Fig. 1. h-curves for $h_{f,\theta,\phi}$

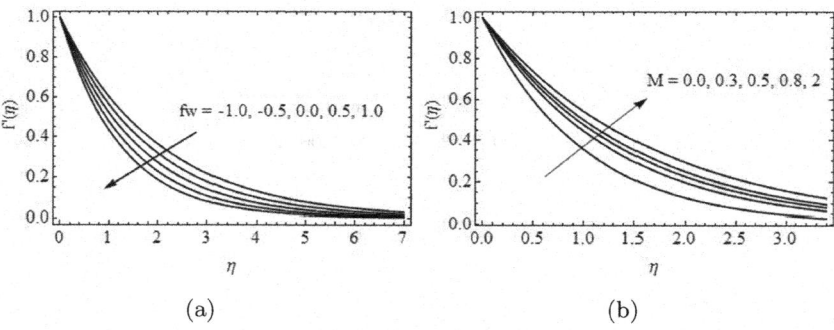

Fig. 2. Influence of f_w and M on velocity

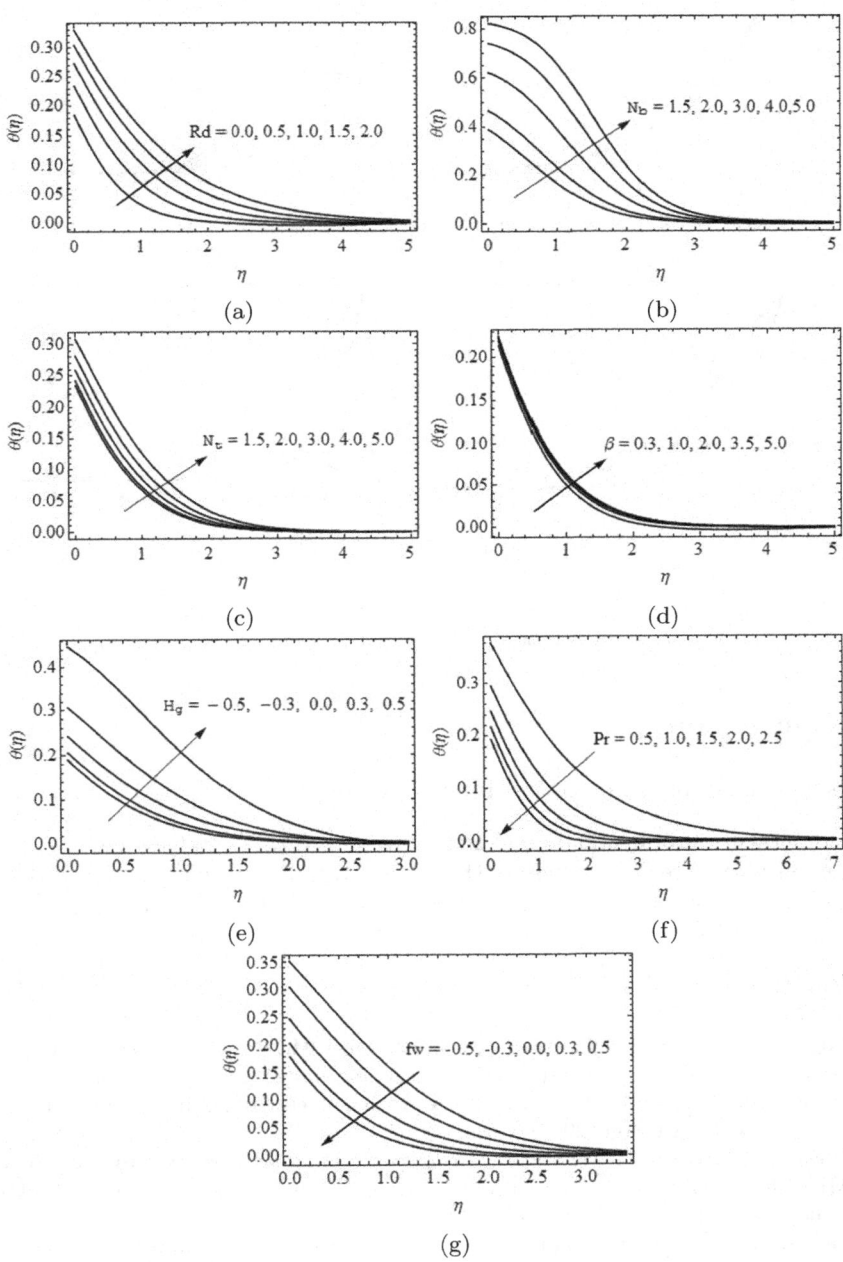

Fig. 3. Influence of Rd, Nb, Nt, β, Hg, Pr and f_w on temperature

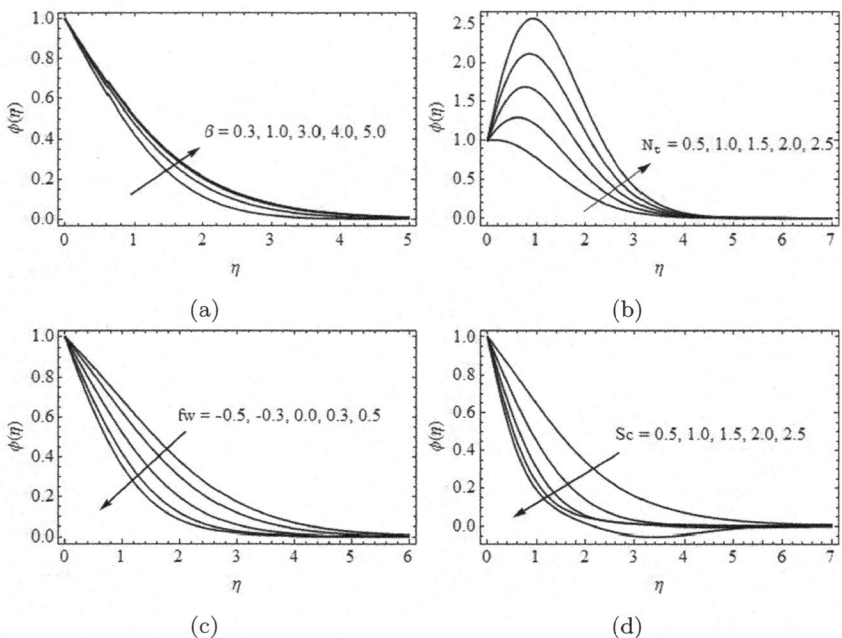

Fig. 4. Influence of β, Nb, f_w and Sc on concentration

4   Conclusion

The key features of the present study is given below:

– Temperature profile enhances while increasing Rd, Nb, Nt, and Hg.
– Casson parameter (β) enhances the concentration and temperature profiles.
– Higher range of Prandtl number (Pr) deduce the thermal boundary.

References

1. Loganathan, K., Sivasankaran, S., Bhuvaneshwari, M., Rajan, S.: Second-order slip, cross- diffusion and chemical reaction effects on magneto-convection of Oldroyd-B liquid using Cattaneo-Christov heat flux with convective heating. J. Therm. Anal. Calorim. **136**, 401–409 (2019)
2. Hayat, T., Imtiaz, M., Alsaedi, A., Almezal, S.: On Cattaneo-Christov heat flux in MHD flow of Oldroyd-B fluid with homogeneous-heterogeneous reactions. J. Magn. Mater. **401**(1), 296–303 (2016)
3. Eswaramoorthi, S., Sivasankaran, S., Bhuvaneswari, M., Rajan, S.: Soret and Dufour effects on viscoelastic boundary layer flow over a stretchy surface with convective boundary condition with radiation and chemical reaction. Sci. Iran B. **23**(6), 2575–2586 (2016)

4. Elanchezhian, E., Nirmalkumar, R., Balamurugan, M., Mohana, K., Prabu, K.M.: Amelec Viloria: Heat and mass transmission of an Oldroyd-B nanofluid flow through a stratified medium with swimming of motile gyrotactic microorganisms and nanoparticles. J. Therm. Anal. Calorim. (2020). https://doi.org/10.1007/s10973-020-09847-w
5. Loganathan, K., Rajan, S.: An entropy approach of Williamson nanofluid flow with Joule heating and zero nanoparticle mass flux. J. Therm. Anal. Calorim. (2020). https://doi.org/10.1007/s10973-020-09414-3
6. Bhuvaneswari, M., Eswaramoorthi, S., Sivasankaran, S., Hussein, A.K.: Cross-diffusion effects on MHD mixed convection over a stretching surface in a porous medium with chemical reaction and convective condition. Eng. Trans. **67**(1), 3–19 (2019)
7. Loganathan, K., Sivasankaran, S., Bhuvaneswari, M., Rajan S.: Dufour and Soret effects on MHD convection of Oldroyd-B liquid over stretching surface with chemical reaction and radiation using Cattaneo-Christov heat flux. IOP: Mater. Sci. Eng. **390**, 012077 (2018)
8. Bhuvaneswari, M., Eswaramoorthi, S., Sivasankaran, S., Rajan, S., Saleh Alshomrani, A.: Effects of viscous dissipation and convective heating on convection flow of a second-grade liquid over a stretching surface: an analytical and numerical study. Scientia Iranica B **26**(3), 1350–1357 (2019)
9. Loganathan, K., Mohana, K., Mohanraj, M., Sakthivel, P., Rajan, S.: Impact of 3rd-grade nanofluid flow across a convective surface in the presence of inclined Lorentz force: an approach to entropy optimization. J. Therm. Anal. Calorim. (2020). https://doi.org/10.1007/s10973-020-09751-3
10. Abbasbandy, S., Hayat, T., Alsaedi, A., Rashidi, M.M.: Numerical and analytical solutions for Falkner-Skan flow of MHD Oldroyd-B fluid. Int. J. Numer. Methods Heat Fluid Flow **24**, 390–401 (2014)

Correction to: Advances in Swarm Intelligence

Ying Tan⑩, Yuhui Shi, and Milan Tuba

Correction to:
Y. Tan et al. (Eds.): *Advances in Swarm Intelligence*,
LNCS 12145, https://doi.org/10.1007/978-3-030-53956-6

In the version of the paper 60 that was originally published the affiliation of Jairo R. Coronado and Alfonso Romero has been changed from "Universidad de la Costa" to "Researcher" because this paper was made within the framework of a project of the Colombian Navy.

Further the following acknowledgments has been placed at end of the paper: The work described in this paper has been supported by the project "PLANEAMIENTO POR CAPACIDADES PARA EL ESTABLECIMIENTO DE UNA BASE TEMPORAL EN LA ANTÁRTICA COMO SOPORTE LOGÍSTICO A LAS OPERACIONES CIENTÍFICAS - 65028" under the auspices of the Armada Nacional de Colombia and Ministry of Science, Technology and Innovation (MinCiencias).

The original version of the chapter 27 was revised. The author name "Yingshi Tan" is updated to "Yingsi Tan".

The updated version of these chapters can be found at
https://doi.org/10.1007/978-3-030-53956-6_27
https://doi.org/10.1007/978-3-030-53956-6_60

Author Index

Printed in the United States
By Bookmasters